THE POWER OF THEN

Revealing Egypt's Lost Wisdom
Revised and Updated

THE POWER OF THEN: REVEALING EGYPT'S LOST WISDOM
Revised and Updated
HOWDIE MICKOSKI

Cataloging in Publication Data:
ISBN
978-82-691266-0-0
Published originally by Tehuti Press

THE POWER OF THEN

Revealing Egypt's Lost Wisdom
Revised and Updated

BY
HOWDIE MICKOSKI

TABLE OF CONTENTS

VOLUME 1-The Spiritual Volume

My reason for the research, investigation and writing of the three volumes of this book..

Original Appendix has been omitted

Back Matter

Photo Credits

Bibliography

About the Author

ACKNOWLEDGEMENTS

I wish to thank the following writers who inspired me on this quest: John Anthony West (especially his book *Serpent in the Sky*), Graham Hancock, Roy Norvill (whose book *Hermes Unveiled* provided the initial wisdom to understanding fairy tales), RA Schwaller de Lubicz, Carlos Castaneda, Muata Ashby, Theun Mares, Victor Sanchez and Peter Tompkins.

To my original editor Dawn Lasby and publishing consultants Gwen Gades and Lisa Yargeau, for their work to correct my most glaring errors. Others have reviewed the book after revision. Guro Dalsegg of Dalsgren Design who redesigned the cover.

Thank you to the office of Zahi Hawass at the Supreme Council for Antiquities in Cairo and to Kamel Wahid at Sakkara for their permissions to enter the closed Pyramid of Unas. A special thanks to all of my friends over the last ten years who may not have understood the 'strange' behavior, long hours of research or the meditations…this was one of the results. Of course to all of my teachers: Byung Chool Park,, Bruce Starlight, Dennis Mckay, Clayton Bunn, and Sahu Omri for their kindness and wisdom.

I am Canadian by birth, and as such write using Canadian, not American English. Hence words such as favour or honour appear spelled as such within my text.

Thank you for reading...

REVISIONS
2018

In January 2018 I began to revise this text. In the twelve years since this book was first completed (2005) I had come across some new information that I felt had to be shared. Most chapters were left as they were originally, but a few such as the chapter on Pyramids have had much revised.

In one sense I could have revised so much more in the book. When I wrote it, while I considered there to be a legacy of an much more ancient culture- I still felt that Old Kingdom Egypt did much of the spectacular building that is found at the Northern Pyramid sites, and retained much of the amazing knowledge. I am not so sure of that anymore. Of course they were more advanced than us today in the understanding of how to interact with nature, and with the energetic world around us. But further research is now indicating to me that the most tremendous things still seen on the sties were set in place in the far ancient past. These include not only almost all of the large pyramids, but also including amazing cut, carved and laid giant blocks on the sites. When I compare it with what is clearly Old Kingdom Egyptian building, the two types of techniques do not match. One is perfect and may not be able to be done today even with advanced lasers, while the other is basically just pile and support. This is also found with statues, temples and the like. It is forcing me to revise everything that I have believed. Some of that has made it into parts of the book- especially the revised Pyramid chapter.

I could have revised this in even greater detail based on more updated historical research I am currently involved in. Book like this can be forever. The point is that there comes a time when it must be as it is, and allow future projects and articles to take things another step farther. Stop by my website to see what is currently being studied and written.

ODE TO TEHUTI

Of the event it is tough to talk,
When you appeared upon the rock.
I had meditated long and hard,
Your appearance caught me way off guard.
What words to speak, yell or sing,
When I first caught glimpse of your outstretched wings.
You looked at me, I was in awe,
The one who invented the sacred law.
I felt my limbs go quickly numb,
Would you impart your divine wisdom.
But you simply looked at me for a time,
Then turned quickly on a dime.
Within my eyes welled up a tear,
Overcome with joy of an event so dear.
Initiation, what can I do,
Sacred ibis, I will always follow you.

HM July 1999

Exit from Valley Temple to Khafre causeway next to the Sphinx

THE POWER OF THEN

Volume 1: Egyptian Secrets

"I have written (this book) not for my own pleasure, but for your advantage, that by pointing to the foundation of truth I might lead you back from the pathless wilderness onto the right way." The Golden Tract[1]

"Making friends with Set, we cause the clothing of his face to fall down and reveal the hidden things." Ancient Egyptian Book of the Dead, Chapter 125

---

[1] Anonymous "The Golden Tract" found in Waite, AE *The Hermetic Museum* (Samuel Weiser reprint 1990) p.7

INTRODUCTION

1: Looking directly at the front of the Sphinx through the blocks of the Sphinx Temple. Pyramid of Khafre is behind

This book has taken me twelve years to complete. It contains elements of Hermeticism, Qi Gong, Alchemy, Shamanism, Yoga, archaeological fieldwork done at ancient sites and the study of ancient texts. This is a book developed from personal experience. I have written it with the hope that you too will decide to re-examine what our ancient ancestors had to say about the reality we experience. The current truths that are so greatly defended by archaeologists, historians, scientists and religious organizations are now open to question. The answers that are coming back is that the current truths are not truths at all.

"This is a journey of knowledge. Speed towards this knowledge…"
Hermetic Wisdom[2]

Looking for where we are, and who we are, was the main focus of the Ancient Egyptian mystery temples. Since this wisdom existed all over the world, it will be explored in more locations than just Egypt. To exclude one religion or philosophy in favour of another will always lead to ignorance. Egypt was the center of the earth circle where this wisdom was dispersed and became the inspiration for other wisdom systems such as Hindu, Taoist, Maya or Greek. Yet few understand that the source was Ancient Egypt. This book will unlock some of the hidden symbols "created" in order to pass on wisdom. Once understood, the Hermetic Wisdom can be found in ancient sites and religious texts all over the world.

---

[2] Freke, Timothy and Gandy, Peter Hermetica (Piatkus 1997) p.146

"If anyone wishes to apply himself to the various branches of divine knowledge, or to the examination of metaphysics, he will find that the whole world owes this kind of learning to Egypt."

Ammianus Marcellinus, Roman Historian[3]

A point of view is not really the truth, rather it is a conglomerate of beliefs, opinions and ideas that have been conditioned upon us by the rest of the world. It started with our parents and teachers, then from our friends, and finally from books, TV and society. When a majority of people share the same point of view it becomes a "great truth" and no other points of view are considered. This includes not only what clothes we should wear, but what our beliefs of history should be. Just because everyone else believes something does not make it the truth. The first thing that I challenge all of my readers to do is to think. It is easy to just follow along with the crowd, yet where does that lead you? The slaughterhouse if you are a cow! Most humans have allowed themselves to become ordinary, because of ordinary thinking. Historians have now found that Washington's winter at Valley Forge was not that difficult, he just lied to Congress to get more money for the army. The pyramid fields at Giza have been shown not to be tombs, but magnificent places of realization. Other historical sites have been found to push civilization back 50,000 years. Yet such things are either ridiculed or covered up to keep the present "truths." None finds its way into school and university texts, which continue the standard points of view. Thankfully, many people are waking up to the fact that just because a book or scholar tells them something, they do not have to believe it. As Gandhi said, "even in a minority of one, the truth is still the truth."

Few today would dare say that the people of the ancient past had more wisdom and knowledge than we do today. Even though they could build pyramids or raise 400-ton blocks of stone (things impossible today) they are still considered inferior to us. The problem is that we have been taught that humans have progressed. Each year humans become more evolved and civilized. The proof is the technological inventions that "we" have. We are more advanced than people in the 4th century because we have washing machines, cars, cd players and telephones. We also have nuclear weapons, genetic food, pollution, and polluted air and water but no one mentions these to show "our" evolution. Our modern belief of civilization is rooted in self-importance and arrogance (look how good I am compared to those idiots from the past). Those who do claim great ancient wisdom existed, usually look for proof from technology. Whether an ancient civilization had light bulbs, magnifying glasses or even airplanes is not really a sign of advancement. It is

---

[3] Baigent, Michael and Leigh, Richard Elixir and the Stone (Penguin 1997) p.17

only a sign to those who follow the point of view that technology is the sign of evolved humanity. A truly advanced society may have invented hairspray, but realized its offshoots would damage the ozone layer. Instead of finding new ways to kill people, they may have tried to find more ways to love people. If a culture did not need eyeglasses because they could heal any eye problems are they more or less advanced because glasses are not discovered at their sites?

The ancient world was a world of harmony with the earth, realizing that she is our mother and without her we would all die. There was no reason to invent anything, no mater how helpful to humans, if it caused damage to the plants, animals, water or the air. We in our so-called advancement have been able to invent technological conveniences, but at the price of the co-existence of the planet. What good is a car or oven or TV if there is no fresh water to drink? The ancients did have a powerful technology, wisdom. This wisdom was the understanding of the secrets of Creation, and of the illusion of this reality, so each one of us could have the power to gain the knowledge of exactly who we are, why we are here, what life really is. It was a way of learning that how to live was more important than possessions and self-importance. Recently many are beginning to believe that perhaps the ancients did live in a better way, and that the past is not just a benchmark to measure how great we are now, but perhaps the very way that we need to return to.

2: Hypostyle Hall, Temple of Khonsu, Karnak

Everything the Egyptians did was part of a whole. Nothing should be viewed separately, the opposite of world thinking today. They understood that everything was in some way reflective of Creation. They had little need to write books about what they thought about Creation or the universe. Every piece of artwork, every temple, every hieroglyph is designed to offer instant information about the whole. Everything from the system of measure, to the way the myths were organized - had a grand purpose. They were the originators of what became the Platonic idea of body, mind, and spirit acting as a whole. They saw everything in this way. They understood that all of our cells make up a whole called our body. If a group of cells are sick, we as a whole are sick. Science today teaches us all this, but that is where science stops. Our world sees only how things are connected to us, not how we are connected to the rest.

We are not taught that all humans are a part of humanity (as each cell is a part of us), humanity part of the earth, earth part of the solar system, solar system part of the galaxy etc. Thus the ancients took the time to understand things on a grander scale. How would each individual's actions affect humanity, earth and the solar system? Few think that their seemingly insignificant actions could affect the entire galaxy. But they can. Your anklebone has a key function for your whole being, if it didn't work properly or is injured, you can't walk. Yet how many wonder what the earth's function is for our solar system. If the earth does not function right, the solar system will get sick. If all humanity is not doing its function, the earth will be sick. We don't ask our anklebone to smell, but few ponder what the human role is to maintaining the harmony of the whole. That is what the priests of Egypt undertook. Understanding the whole, and everything's place in it, then to teach it to the rest of the world. The transformation of all of human society one individual at a time. Many of the illnesses that modern humans are experiencing is a direct correlation to the fact that we are causing the universe to be out of balance.

"Words (books) lead us to the doorway of truth, but only by contemplating their meaning can we pass through."

Hermetic Wisdom[4]

The best way to learn and grow is through personal experience. Books and texts are only information understood by the conscious mind. It must be lived to become part of the heart, the way to inner knowing. Please do not take my words as the truth. Read with an inquiring mind, look up my sources, and ask questions. Let personal experience be your proof. Try to put your preconceived ideas aside while you read and see where you are led. Let my

---

[4] Freke Hermetica p.143

4

words be the facilitation to inspiring your inner knowing; but also do not trust them unquestioningly.

This is a special time. Ancient wisdom texts like the Tao Te Ching, Bhagavad-Gita, or New Testament are available in virtually every language in the world. Just one hundred years ago this was not the case. As such no one really looked to connect ancient religious teachings to what was found in Egyptian tombs. The heart of any mystical path was to help the initiate find answers. They show that there is no real need for churches or places of worship, because you are all that is truly needed. You have everything you need, and the place you now find yourself is as good as any other. You need only the deep commitment to know. And not stop until you do.

The last chapter is on the upcoming world age. I have written it as a warning to all of my readers. Great changes are coming, and those changes will be affected and influenced by the way each one of us is living our lives. I write it as a call to action that the changes are not that far away. Work on yourself must begin immediately. The ancient traditions and knowledge have become available to the average person in a depth unknown in modern human history. I urge you to take full advantage of it. Learning the Ancient Egyptian Wisdom will help to unlock an entirely new world. There is no one right path, but several, however they are interconnected and similar. I can only hope that this book will be a small tool to help you on your quest.

"We will not seek to follow in the footsteps of masters of old, we will seek what they sought."

Matsuo-Basho[5]

Each volume of this text is designed to move one step deeper into the three-fold Hermetic wisdom. Volume 1 is foundation of the symbolic nature of Hermetic writing, artwork, temple design and spiritual beliefs. The second volume is the Hermetic gateways presented in ancient mythology, fairy tales and structures as teachings of personal practice of looking within and without. The third volume might be classified as unspiritual, with the presentation of Absolute Reality, no-self, a parasite mind, and control of perception in an artificial holographic dreamworld. So I offer this work as a challenge to my readers, who wish to walk through each volume to a deeper part of Ancient Egyptian mystery teachings.

It is important to realize that what anyone has to say about Ancient Civilization is a theory. That includes me, other writers and the archaeologists. We were not there to see it with our own eyes first hand, and must piece

---

[5] Schneider, Michael A Beginner's Guide to Constructing the Universe (Harper 1995) p.216

together the past from small fragments of temples, pyramids, statues, books and whatnot that remain. My entire book might be seen as a possible look at the past, but as I already said, certain facts (stones are Abu Sir or Giza seem to be machine drilled) are there for all to see who goes- what it means is up for interpretation from each individual point of view. Look, read, think and come up with your own conclusions about all of this.

Remember the wisdom is not out there, or even in this book. The wisdom is within you. Let this book be a method of self-discovery to unlock the secrets of the universe which lie inside you, unused and forgotten. Some will want to travel on the path farther than others. It is all about the effort you put in, and the way you put the teachings into practice in your life. This book will provide a background on Egyptian mythology and religion that may help you to unlock Egypt's hidden Hermetic truths.

Good luck, and blessings all around.

Howdie Mickoski

CHAPTER 1
MYSTERY SCHOOLS

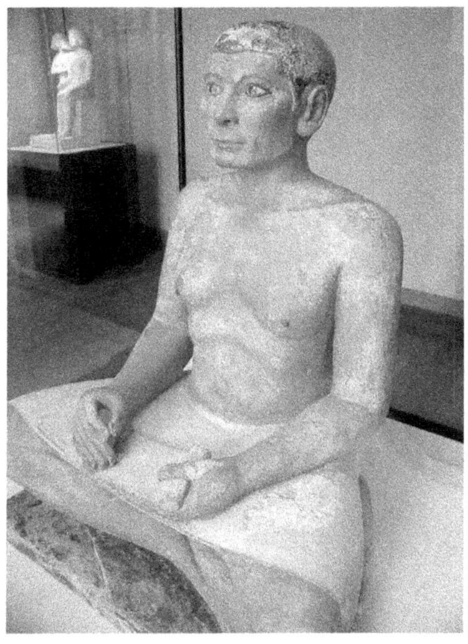

3: Statue of a scribe found at Sakkara, now in Louvre in Paris

To begin to understand the ancient wisdom concepts, a look at the system itself must be undertaken.

Name of Egypt

"Give not that which is holy unto the dogs, neither cast ye your pearls before swine, lest they trample them under their feet." Matthew 7:6

Egypt is an English word derived from the Greek "Aegyptus." This was a corruption of the word Hi-Gi-Ptos, a Greek translation of the Egyptian word Het-Ka-Ptah (the Place of the Ka of Ptah) today known as Memphis. The Egyptians themselves used the word KMT frequently. Without written vowels in the Egyptian language, modern Egyptologists add an e between the letters for easier modern reading. Kemet meant the 'black land,' a place of the fertile Nile Valley that allowed plants to grow. Black is also the first stage (Nigredo) of the alchemic process of transformation, which can create a shining gold. The word alchemy descended from Kemet with the Arabic article Al added. The Egyptians also used the word Ta-Meri (Beloved Earth, or Magnetic Earth) to refer to Egypt. The land acted like a magnet of love (mer) to bring down the powers of the Neteru (gods) to Ta (earth).[6]

Ancient people believed Egypt was a very special place. The Corpus Hermeticum claimed Egypt was an "image of heaven…our land is the temple of the entire cosmos." The Egyptians saw their country as the whole world. This is similar to Maya villages in 1970's Guatemala who saw no real reason to leave their geographical area, because it was (or contained) the entire universe.

---

[6] Naydler, Jeremy Temple of the Cosmos (Inner Traditions 1996) p.3; Schwaller de Lubicz, Isha Her Bak (Hodder and Stoughtan) pp.305-6

The Hermetic axiom is that a human is a microcosm of the macrocosm, thus a human (or in fact any object in the world) contains the entire universe within them. There are special places on earth, like the Hopi believe of Hotevilla, that allow this connection to be more easily seen. The Hopi claim that if it happens in Hotevilla it is happening somewhere in the world. If the government begins to dump garbage in this village it is happening to the earth; clean up the garbage and the same will be happening to the earth.

Egypt was seen as the place where the wisdom of the cosmos could be best expressed. Perhaps it will be found that the earth's energy grid system (similar to the meridians that run in the human body) have a greater focus in Egypt (as ours do at our particular organs). Egypt could have been the symbolic heart of the entire earth. The Egyptians believed they had an obligation, not just to other Egyptians but also to the entire created universe, to keep the land and people of Egypt in Maat (cosmic order, truth, and harmony). Just as the Egyptians would see every person, place or thing as a marvel of creation, the ancient mysteries would want us to begin our study with the person, place or thing we have the most access to…ourself. All great teachers from Lao-Tzu to Socrates to Ficino have urged us to "know thyself," because within us is the explanation of everything.

History

4: King's List, Hallway of Temple of Seti I at Abydos

Modern Egyptologists give a complete chronology of Egypt in their history books (and can be referenced in appendix 1). All that is really needed to

8

be known is that periods of time are grouped together to form Dynasties, which are further broken down by the Pharaohs that ruled. This information comes mostly from the Tablet of Karnak, Hallway of Abydos, Tablet of Sakkara, Papyrus of Turin and chronology of Mantheo. The oldest dynasty is known as, no surprise, the Old Kingdom, followed by the Middle and New Kingdoms. Modern archaeologists claim that Egypt was a country of uncivilized savages until around 3100BC when a highly advanced civilization was formed under the unification of the first Pharaoh, Menes, shown on the Narmer Tablet with odd long necked animals and dinosaurs being roped together. They do not explain how civilization, writing, or pyramid building appears from uncivilized savages all of a sudden. The Egyptian writings themselves claim that their civilization dates back over 20,000 years to when the Neteru (gods) walked the earth in human form. This period was known as Zep (First) Tepi (Time). The First Time began after the water receded and light was given to civilization. Some believe this period refers to the time following the primeval ocean of Nun (see creation myths) or the period after the flooding of the last ice age around 10,500 BC. The period of Zep Tepi remained until the final god, Horus, ruled the earth. At the end of his reign he turned over his rule to humans knows as the Shem-Shu-Hor (Followers of Horus). Only recently did human Pharaohs become Kings.[7] With current archaeological questioning of sites like Giza in Egypt or Tiahuanaco in Bolivia, these ancient dates may in fact be correct.

The Followers of Horus or "Those who know the Secrets of Horus," were in fact the high priests of Egypt. Each priest was seen to be a Horus who was battling Set within themselves. Thus they were following the myth of Horus, his path to Light and wisdom. They lived from the heart and could be trusted to run Egypt in the proper manner for every citizen. The Egyptian viewed the First Time as a 'Golden Age,' a time before "strife, rage or uproar." Egyptologists view this First Time as a myth. The Ancient Egyptians themselves gave actual figures for the length of the First Time, and not only do they not fit into the confines of the modern dates for Egyptian civilization, they do not fit into the confines of dates for human civilization! The Turin Papyrus puts the rule of the gods at 23,200 years, and the Shem-Shu-Hor at 13,420 for a total of 36,620 years; Diodorus Siculus listed the years for the gods as 33,000; Mantheo from the 3rd century BC arrived at a figure of non-human rule at 24,925 years and human kings for 12,000 years. All of these dates were far beyond the Biblical date given for the creation of the earth (4004 BC), and early scholars of the 19th century changed the dates to fit the timeframe of the Bible. The other scholars at the time were Evolutionists who needed to prove the advancement of humanity. One group was looking to rewrite history, and

---

[7] Hancock, Graham Fingerprints of the Gods (Doubleday 1995) p.403; Hancock, Graham and Bauval, Robert Message of the Sphinx: Keeper of the Genesis (Doubleday 1996) p.140

the other only looking for signs that those in the past were inferior. Any evidence of great wisdom or a very old civilization was often ignored.

It must be noted that Mantheo's numbers add up to 36,525, which is (with a change of decimal point) 365.25, the equivalent of the Sothic Year (our calendar). While history is included within myth, we must be careful not to take any myth or religious writing at face value. A myth is trying to explain key facts of the forces of the universe. The historical fact is less important than the message that the myth is trying to explain. Mantheo for example may be saying that gods and humans ruled the earth for a complete circuit, perhaps a precessional age which lasts 25, 920 years.

Even if one accepts the current chronological timeline, it also leads to some problems. Egypt was a far different place in 3000 BC than it was in 1200 BC, much as the United States was very different in 1500 AD than in 2015 AD. In Egypt's earliest stages the concept of Maat (order) was most established. It was a time when the wisdom priests and the ancient texts held the greatest sway in every aspect of Egyptian life. The process of spiritual awakening was taught more openly to the people, and in fact it seems there were rather few Neteru (gods) in the teachings similar to early forms of Taoism, Buddhism and Gnosticm. As time advanced more deities were added to the pantheon of gods (see chapter 3 Neteru) which allowed certain teachings to be explained more completely and also the opportunity for groups to take advantage of the population due to confusion (see mummification).[8] Most of what is written about the Old Kingdom (the earliest periods of Egyptian history) has ideas superimposed on the period from the New Kingdom.

For some unknown reason the period of peace, harmony, and great building that defined the Old Kingdom came to a sudden end over 4,000 years ago. Modern archaeologists usually claim the country was overrun by invaders, but have no explanation as to exactly who these invaders were, how long they stayed, or what the results were. They seem to think that Egyptian society, ideas and temple practices were exactly the same after these 'invasions.' It was not. It was during these periods of calamity that many of the orders of priests left Egypt and took their knowledge with them. Around 1500 BC as Egyptian wisdom was beginning to decline came the growth of the Mexican Maya, Taoism, Buddhism, Hinduism, Hermeticism, and the Old Testament. The Egyptian priests begin to leave to help keep the ancient wisdom alive, thus the reason to study other ancient cultures for they are markers of the Egyptian influence. There are reports that the priests went to places that they have not been credited such as the Grand Canyon in Arizona, and Rocky Mountains outside of Canmore, Alberta. Egyptian tombs were found in the Grand Canyon in 1909, then quickly covered up by the authorities, though the "find" did make the front page of the Phoenix Gazette in April, until they were "forced" to print

---

[8] Ashby, Muata Egyptian Yoga (Cruzian Mystic Books 1997) p.53

10

a retraction. Other such Egyptian sites are waiting to be found all over the world. However many priests did stay, even though living the old ways of Maat and wisdom were becoming increasingly more difficult. As the decline began so too did the wisdom become misunderstood or used for personal gain and profit by a new group of priests not initiated in the old ways. The hieroglyphs stopped being used, mummification practices changed. This led to the way for the country to be taken over by the Greeks.

Greeks

"The names of all the gods came to Greece from Egypt...for the names of all the gods have been known in Egypt from the beginning of time." Herodotus

By 500 BC Egypt was in a great decline and was soon invaded by the Greeks and Alexander the Great. The Greeks had previously been forbidden in most cases from gaining access to the Mystery Temples, but with victory came the spoils. They forced their way in. The temple libraries of secret books were confiscated and taken to set up the new Greek library built at Alexandria. These Greek wisdom seekers, exemplified by Aristotle, came to the temples and demanded knowledge. Some temples at the time were run by a new group of priests who didn't have all the mystical information, but didn't mind selling what they knew. Few priests remained with all of the old connections to Gnosis. Since all the knowledge was passed on orally, and no Greek could read the hieroglyphs, the old Egyptian priests had an out. They could pass on some of the wisdom (hoping the Greeks would transform), but not all the wisdom.

Plato wrote that the Egyptians referred to the Greeks as "children" in the ways of spirituality and religion, for they had only learned what the Egyptian sages decided to tell them. The Corpus Hermeticum warned to not let the Egyptian letters be changed into the Greek characters where they would lose all of their power. That is not to say that all the Greeks were excluded. A few showed to be of such high moral character and intelligence that they were taught the full system with the hope that they could pass it on correctly. Solon was trained at Heliopolis where he learned the tales of Atlantis. Socrates, Plato, Homer and Pythagoras were all initiated into the Egyptian mysteries.[9]

Greece was not the source of the arts, sciences or math that it has always been believed to be. The Greeks were merely the first to place it in books or use it for profit. Most Greeks focused on the exoteric (outer) intellectual knowledge of the conscious mind to explain the universe, ignoring the esoteric (inner) wisdom of the heart. Two distinct schools began in Greece. The Aristotle tradition, derived from Babylon and partial Egyptian knowledge

---

[9] Ozaniec, Nvaomi The Elements of Egyptian Wisdom (Element 1994) p.4; Hall, Manly Freemasonry of the Ancient Egyptians (Philosopher's Press 1937) p.57

was the way of science, the physical realm, desires, possessions and valuing your worth based on what you had or how you looked. The other school was of Plato and Pythagoras, who were trained in the Egyptian teachings of Gnosis (divine knowledge) and truth.

The few priests in Egypt connected to Gnosis realized that their civilization was at an end, and a new world age was coming. Many of the current surviving temples in Egypt were built during the Greek (known as Ptolemaic) period. They were built over older temples on the same location. While these temples such as Edfu or Dendera are wonderful for us as they give us some sense of what completed Ancient Egyptian temples were actually like, they also offer us interesting hidden information as to what was occurring at the time of their construction. The reliefs here are often depicted very differently than in older temples, with the gods more humanized, and with a greater focus on the physical world. At Esna the depictions look "fleshy, human, old and fat," not the way all-powerful Egyptian Neteru would ever be depicted unless this was showing that their "time was up...It is a perfect artistic impression of the state of Egypt during the building of these temples."[10] It is said that the Egyptian priests were passing on information that the great period of spiritual teaching in Egypt, and of living from the heart was coming to an end for a new period (cycle) was beginning with a focus on the material world and the physical body. The earth was entering this phase that became Swiss bank accounts, face lifts, oil drilling in the rainforest, infomercials, the relation of every emotion to sex, and the forgetting that only God exists. These reliefs were the warning of what was coming.

The Christian religion originated in opposition to a group from Egypt later called the Gnostics, Egyptian Hermeticists who began a new series of teachings (based on the myth of Osiris, Isis and Horus). The opposing group took a more literal belief to these myths, which evolved into the New Testament. The Christian religion was able to take hold in Egypt so rapidly because the population was easily able to recognize that it was just another form of their previous Egyptian Neteru (gods). Even when the Gnostics were eliminated, Christianity still had two opposing views of the meaning in the holy scriptures.

A great division was to happen between the Western Catholic Church, based in Rome, and the Eastern based in Constantinople. The Church of Rome wanted to use religion to control their empire, and eschewed the Gnostic teachings of Jesus as an allegory which when understood would lead the aspirant into personal Gnosis (divine knowing) and Oneness with God. They chose instead the literal translation of the texts and broke with Constantinople.

---

[10] Schwaller Sacred p.19; West, John Anthony Traveler's Key to Ancient Egypt (Quest 1985) pp.298, 436

The Roman Catholic Church forbid worship in Egyptian temples and many were destroyed, the great library at Alexandria burnt claiming the books were of the devil. Book burning began all across the Middle East, it is for this reason the now famous Nag Hammadi Gnostic Text, found in 1945, was hidden in the caves. The Roman Church realized that to institute their new teachings, they needed all of the old documents that showed its true origin to be eliminated. Thus the Gnostic, Hermetic, Greek and especially the Egyptian works had to be burnt, as well as the people who taught it. A few isolated priests kept teaching at the temple of Isis at Philae in southern Egypt until the 6th century when Justinian had the last people who could properly read and write the hieroglyphs burnt alive. In 640 AD the books of Alexandria that survived the previous burnings were destroyed by the new conquerors, the Islamic Arabs, who used the books unholy to the Koran to fuel their steam baths.[11]

When all of the destruction was finished in Egypt, the Dark Ages spread across much of the world. True wisdom and knowledge were almost lost. Thankfully there were groups: Gnostic Christians, Hermeticists, Islamic Sufi's, Native Indians, Mexicans, Australian Aboriginals and Africans kept the wisdom alive in spite of the most vile treatment. The wise men and women understood that the passing on of the wisdom was even more important than their life. People today still live hidden with the understanding that this wisdom must be kept alive, as the future of every human, plant, animal and object on the earth depends on it. This wisdom originated in the Egyptian temples through a teaching system known as the mysteries.

Mystery Schools

"Our soul has to be at the moment of death as it is during the mysteries, free from any blemish, passion, envy or anger." Porphyry 3rd century AD[12]

The system of teaching the wisdom became known as the Mystery Schools. It was a secret order, with oral teachings, vows of secrecy and the forbidding of students to write what they had learned. Mystery comes from the Greek word Myein (to close) referring to the lips and the eyes. We must see the mysteries not with the outer eyes, but must close them to use our inner eyes. Our mouth must also remain closed for the experiences of the mystic are impossible to put into words. The need for secrecy in the teachings is not out of

---

[11] Tompkins, Peter Mysteries of the Great Pyramid (Harper and Row 1972) p.4; Chaney, Farlyne and Messick, William Kundalini and the Third Eye (Astara 1980) p.12; Fowden, Garth The Egyptian Hermes (Princeton 1986) p.183
[12] Freke, Timothy The Complete Guide to World Mysticism (Piatkus 1997) p.6

a sense of exclusion, that many scholars today believe, but because the experience cannot be explained. The mystery schools were about teaching the steps necessary for the student to have similar mystical experiences that they too could never properly explain.[13]

It has been written that those who became proficient in the mysteries could read the future, heal with herbs, stones and music, could levitate, and even make themselves invisible. Anyone who has met a Native shaman or an Asian master knows this is all possible. Yet unlike today when most would want to learn these practices to gain the powers, the real reason for studying the mysteries was to gain access to the light of the soul and allow us to merge with Neter (God). The powers were just things that came along the way. If one was simply after the powers, they were usually not taught anything by the mystery teachers.

There were two sets of schools in Egypt. The first education was for the social needs of the people (what our modern elementary schools are supposed to be). The other schooling was the part of the Temple. The average citizen had little interest in learning mysticism and spiritual matters (as is still the case today). They lived a life according to the idea of immediate results: reward, punishment. Those who were admitted into the mysteries showed a desire to learn, a willingness to understand the cosmos and themselves, and most importantly they were willing to make these new teachings and understandings the complete basis of their life. As they progressed they became judges, governors, and architects that helped to run the country.

Women and men were both equally included in the mysteries, as the priests understood the Oneness of the universe. The concept of male or female has only a meaning in the physical world of duality, yet they taught the importance of a male to learn masculinity and a female to learn femininity. Usually female priests were initiated in the mysteries of a feminine Neteru like Isis, Hathor or Sekhemet, but not necessarily. There were male priests of Isis and female priests of Osiris. It is important to know that no one was ever refused admittance to the mysteries, but the aspirant may have to spend years of personal work and effort before they were admitted. They had to show the willingness, effort and moral character in every aspect of their day-to-day life to be allowed in. Even today most try to learn spiritual matters as concepts and ideas that can be added to their current life to make it better. They do not understand that to truly advance in the mysteries, one's entire life, beliefs, and thinking will all have to be left behind. Only when the closet is empty can new clothes be brought in. Eliminating a shirt or two really makes no difference. All the old has to go to make room for the unbelievable new. One must "die" to their old self, or their spiritual work will have little effect and cause little change.

---

[13] Ozaniec 217

14

The aspirant was closely watched, for to acquire wisdom was great power. Great tests were included in the teachings to see how the students would respond. Many students had their teachings stopped if they were found to be using the wisdom for improper uses. The initial part of the teachings was to learn about nature, and how the world interacts. A great deal of time would be spent learning to pay attention to the wisdom that surrounds us every day. Purifications would take place, as would healing to assist the body and soul to open to the new vibrations and energies they would be encountering. Living the teachings in one's life became imperative for it was no sense going through the difficulties of purification if the next week one was going to go back to the same improper living patterns.

The mystery teachings are the very foundation of our Western culture. Everything from theater, to sports, to music, to art all had their basis in the Mystery temples. Books were available for students, but they were always written in symbol. Learning the mysteries is a personal experience, thus simply reading it from a book takes away the student's own learning. To decipher and understand the symbol yourself was to gain personal wisdom of the mystery. There is an alchemic saying, "burn your books and whiten your latten." The line refers to the idea that books are powerful learning tools along the way, but at some point we must decide that we are truly living and experiencing the knowledge thus we have no need for the books or notes of paper anymore. We must take a leap of faith and rid ourselves of them and have faith that we have indeed learned what we tried to learn.

The temples were more than just teaching centers for the priests. While these priests often went into society to help keep Egypt in harmony, parts of the temple were open to the average person. The inner parts of the temple (where the god resided) were strictly off limits except to the highest of the initiated. However, the temples often put on theater plays for the population that would help bring the teachings of myth to life. Many temples included healing areas (first hospitals) where those sick or unsure could come for help from priests who studied the healing arts. The troubled could also sleep the night in special dream areas, where the Neteru (god) of the temple would pass on information to them in the dream state.

Mystic

Those who follow the mystery tradition are called mystics. A mystic is one who searches for the answers to such questions as who am I, what am I, what is God, or what is the universe? They seek out these answers through acquired knowledge, personal experience, and altered states of consciousness where they attempt to reach the truths beyond the physical world. The experience of mysticism is beyond words. It can never be explained, but the explanations entice others to follow a similar path and experience similar beauty. Mysticism is not religion, yet at the heart of all religion is mysticism. It is not concerned with beliefs, doctrines or rules, but to find answers to life's deepest questions. Any event can suddenly create a mystical revelation: a car crash, love affair, foreign travel, luck or misfortune, illness, sex or war... anything that frees someone for a moment from the ego and opens us to our own soul.[14] Mystics will use specific exercises like mediation, prayer, or dreaming to help them to lock into these moments. In the beginning these mystical periods will be brief glimpses, yet each one is so full of intense feeling and love that attaining this state becomes their focus. They then return to the physical to try and make some sense of what transpired, which is most often seen as a gift or miracle. The longer one spends in these places of joy and wonder, the longer one will want to be there the next time.

Of course this is just one part of a truth seeker- the mystical side. It is the one that gets the most attention, because it is the most "nice." The other side of the seeker is to go into the darkness. To explore the depth of their subconscious mind, their egoic masks and walls, the entire system of why we think and act as we do- and why most of it is so destructive- for self and others. The Mystery schools were about both parts. The expansive looks of unity, harmony, and power- and the inner egoic subconscious and its exterior influences that is the blocking wall to the natural functioning of the human species.

Most mystics are usually not well accepted by the rest of modern society: Jesus, Pythagoras and Socrates were all killed by the reigning order. Regular society has developed a series of beliefs, rules and guidelines (even religion) that keep the average person in slavery. The mystic has managed to go beyond beliefs and opinions, for they have experienced something much greater than self. The mystic has found that all religions are at their heart the same, thus there is no need to argue which is better as they are all equal. At the same time they see religion as unimportant, only truth is important and truth can be found with, or without, religion.

Priests

---

[14] Freke World Mysticism pp.14, 119

5: *Scenes of priests in procession with the figure of temple Neteru- still showing original paint, Medinet Habu*

There were many levels and titles depending on a priest's advancement and particular function (see *Sacred Tradition in Ancient Egypt* by Rosemary Clark for numerous titles for priests). Other than the highest priests of the temple, who would almost never leave, the rest of the priests were only there for certain periods of the year. They would come to the temple for three months a year for intense training and purification. For the other nine months they would be back in Egyptian society. The reason was twofold. Firstly their new higher knowledge and wisdom were needed to help run the society. The second reason was they needed to be outside of the calm temple environment to put their teachings to the test. It is like someone who today only studies on a mountaintop, where it is easier to find inner peace. At times they would have to return to the center of the city to see if they could keep their level of peace and inner wisdom. It is a main reason why the average person was not allowed into the temple itself, for it needed to be a sanctuary where the students could learn and mediate in peace and calmness…they would get enough challenge during their nine months in the community.

A good depiction of how the Egyptian mystery temples ran society in Egypt's early days was described in the books *Secrets of the Talking Jaguar* and *Honey in the Heart* by Martin Prechtel. He described the tribal life of the Mayan villages that existed until the 1970's until obliterated by government intrusion, Christian missionaries and big business. In the villages were two sets of government. The first was the individual shamans, the healers who worked with the villagers when they became sick or needed help. Each Egyptian village and city would have their own trained shamans. The second was a hierarchy of officials who ran the village, of which the shamans could be a part. They handled the initiations, the rituals to appease the gods and looked after the village's welfare. This ruling hierarchy in Egypt was the temple elite. To become a part of the Maya village hierarchy, one first had to show great moral character, knowledge and often obtaining wealth and property.

When a person was finally accepted as one of the village hierarchy, they had to give away all of their money and property. The idea was to show the entire community that they were beyond self-importance and personal gain. The gain of the whole community was all that was now important. This attitude angered the Christians and businesspeople who believed one should be acquiring more money and more power, not giving any of it away. Whatever the hierarchy actually needed, the temple provided. You see, if one in a place of running something like a village (or country) is doing it for personal gain, power, and wealth (like all modern politicians) then they can be bribed. People and groups can offer property, wealth or positions if the politicians just agree to what they want. Without the need for these things anymore the only decision made by leaders would be the one that benefits the entire community. The poorest to the richest villager would have just as much say and importance in any decision made by the hierarchy.

"When power is placed in the hands of men who are themselves not dominated by a superior force, its road will inevitably lead to evil." RA Schwaller de Lubicz[15]

As the priests learned the mysteries they were also learning to lose their own self-importance. As our desires for things and money lessen, we can open our hearts to helping all, which in Egypt meant living Maat (cosmic harmony). An individual would submit to symbolic death and rebirth, and emerge with a new identity and often a new name. Such rituals were conducted under astrologically prosperous circumstances and could even correct supposed difficulties in one's horoscope. The priests were said to be in extraordinary health (as are older shamans and oriental masters). "They spent their lives in good health and were energetic enough for all normal activities. For their duties they incurred in maintaining the cult of the gods were very onerous, and their labours surpassed the capacity of men of average strength. They divided the night for observation of the heavens, sometimes also for divine ritual. The daytime was for the adoration of the gods to whom they sang hymns 3-4 times a day. The rest of their time was spent in the study, and they were constantly searching for and discovering something new, caring nothing for reward for

---

[15] Schwaller Sacred p.151

18

they had freed themselves from that bad master, luxury. This hard and increasing labour attests their endurance and their absence of desire attests to their self-control."[16]

The highest ranking priests wore a leopard skin (as was similar with the Maya) and shaved their head. They were in charge of teaching the adepts and taking care of the statue of the temple Neteru (god) that was kept in the Holy of Holies or Inner Sanctuary. They would be a being who had broken through all the walls and masks to find Ultimate Answers. One would be a seer (or a Beholder in the Eleusian Mysteries) who could "see" the true reality beyond the dream of this physical world.

Grades

There were different grades for the teachings, as still exist in our school system. One began by learning the lesser mysteries (mostly concerning nature and our connection with it) before they could advance to the greater mysteries. There was no time limit, the length of time needed at each level was as long as it took, not to just intellectually learn the teachings but to be living them. As a modern shaman would say, knowledge becomes wisdom when it becomes a part of them. It is no longer in a book, it is in their bones and blood because they have lived the teaching in their life. No longer is it an idea, but it is an experience. "Many devotees are so busy reading and researching that they never settle into serious inner exploration."[17] Without experiences all the teachings and knowledge in the world is useless. It was through their daily work that the teachings would gain a new meaning for them, not in their head but in their heart. They were becoming the teaching.

The initial students learned about awakening their consciousness (what the Buddhist would call mindfulness, or a shaman, awareness). They were expected to observe, take responsibility for their actions, and gain an understanding of their entire life through the process of recapitulation. They would begin to experience spirit on an even greater level, how it would speak to them in the sound of a bird, the rays of the sun, or the coolness of the wind. It was only with these initial teachings solidly under their belt were they ready to go further. The students were expected at the initial stages to live by particular codes of conduct. One of these is the famous ten virtues: control of thought, control of action, devotion of purpose, faith in your master, being free from resentment under experience of persecution, evidence of a mission in life, confidence in one's ability to learn and to act with wisdom, confidence to learn right from wrong, confidence to learn the real from the unreal, faith to accept

---

[16] Fowden pp.54-55
[17] Cheney 60

the truth, readiness for initiation "when the student is ready, the master will appear."[18]

For the lower priests chastity was not compulsory, many had a wife and children. The teachings did not try to stop sex but teach students the proper way (tantra) so as to not lose the powerful sexual energy. In fact it was not just the leakage of sexual energy that the initiates were taught how to contain, but all the ways that we leak out our vital energy from our bodies. The Corpus Hermeticum claimed how disappointing a man's life is if he does not have children. Many have taken this to mean all Hermetic priests were expected to marry. However this passage is symbolic. As one advances to very high stages of teaching, they are at a level where to their students they are a father or mother; while the students are sons and daughters. These are the children that are truly expected. The meaning of the statement is that if one becomes an adult (full of the mystery wisdom) and does not have children (students to pass on the teaching) their life will be disappointing for the wisdom would stop with them. The Egyptian word Sebai meant "Illuminator of the mysteries." The teachers understood that they were just the facilitator. The teachings were the real key.

Only in the final stages of training would the students learn healing, as opposed to the new age way today were people take a weekend course and then begin 'healing' people. The ancients understood that all of us are suffering from very deep physical and emotional wounding. It is impossible to truly be able to heal another until we have worked on ourself. Thus the steps were focused on the healing of the individual student, and not on giving them knowledge to heal others. If we are spending our time trying to heal others when we should be spending time on ourself, we will become stuck at the place we are at. However once the required difficult work of cleansing was complete, the priest was expected to use their skills to help others. They had made themselves whole and were now able to allow the voice of spirit they had cultivated in their early training to step in and fill them with the wisdom of how to proceed with each individual patient. The greater mysteries would also teach the Books of Tehuti (Thoth), the sciences of hieroglyphic writing, symbolic artwork, architecture, sacred number and geometry, the deeper meanings of the myths, and the truth about what happens before birth and after death.

Initiations
"The rites of the mystery schools are called initiations...we have gained the understanding not only to live happily, but also to die with better hope." Cicero, Roman initiate[19]

---

[18] James, George Stolen Legacy (Julian Richardson 1998) pp.30-31; Ashby, Muata Egyptian Proverbs (Cruzian 1997) p.33
[19] Freke World Mysticism p.66

It was assumed much of the teaching came through the process known as initiations. Actually an initiation is either a marker point for one to gain a new level (like a birthday or a wedding) or is in fact a test to see what you have learned. There have been many books written on the Egyptian initiations, such as in Manly Hall's Freemasonry of the Ancient Egyptians. The real understanding of what is an initiation and how it was performed are not that well understood today.

Certain initiations were performed along the way, such as the choosing of a new name. Native Indian cultures often still wait years before naming a child, until the child's gifts and personality has developed. Often such a ceremony follows the young adult's vision quest. Today most everyone takes the exact name they were given at birth, without ever questioning what that name means or how it affects them. Women even change their name to that of their husband, in effect becoming his property. In the mysteries the students would learn the power of words and sound and would begin to search for a name that exemplified the specific energies they wanted in their life. Think how many times a day your name is spoken, and each time it is creating a certain energy. This name change is also symbolic as to show our inner us that we are no longer the person we were before.

Initiations were designed to find ways to help lift the Veil of Isis, the covering over our true sight. The teachings are not a bunch of books to be read, or an accumulation of information, but is an awakening of an inner connection to Gnosis (divine wisdom of everything). The initiation does not give us great powers like people think, instead they open us to our own inner power and our soul. We have some deeper connection to the world around us, and at the same time seem farther away from everything. Each initiation helps bit by bit to free up our energy so we can connect to this source of Gnosis. The ancient initiations were very hard, often with death as a possible result. Initiation is always a one to one experience between the initiate and the power, energy or god they are attempting to understand. The difficult initiations that make their way into books were used in order to shock or scare the initiate into using all of their personal power gained within the training. The initiate does not realize until later that no challenge (including any initiation) is given to us if those spirit forces do not deem us to have the necessary power to be able to deal with it properly. Thus putting an initiate under the most severe consequences will force them to learn fast how to channel all the power and knowledge they have gained to this point, or perhaps die. Should they fail and remain alive, the initiation process will have revealed another part of their own beliefs that held them back. They will then have a first hand experience on what to work with.[20]

---

[20] Ashby, Muata Initiation into Egyptian Yoga (Cruzian 2001) p.14; Matthews, Caitlin and John The Western Way (Arkana 1986) vol.2 pp.31, 35, 37

Part of the reason for the hard initiation is the fact that teaching was done in a very serene and peaceful environment (the temple), but real tests had to be given to see how the initiate would respond. Today the need for such terrifying initiations are rare, as most are now training not in serene silence but in a modern world that is fraught with difficulty. Modern initiations will often be soft, and have a touch of nature. The idea of any initiation is to shake us up to a higher state of consciousness and knowing. One initiation I had occurred when the ibis bird of Tehuti, which does not live for thousands of miles from where I resided, appeared one night in nature while in a state of mediation. This experience touched my heart in ways that cannot possibly be explained.

The ritual death was an important part of the ancient initiations. If we cannot become friends with our death, we will never have a life. Most today live with a fear of death or the belief that death is a long way off. They have lots of time to tell people they love them, or to work hard and acquire wealth. Yet in truth we could die in the next five minutes, thus the teachings of the ritual death are to learn the understanding that death is nothing to be feared. They focus on the immortality of the soul, and understand the lack of time in this body so the focus is on the present moment. Another ritual death had people buried to the head in the ground overnight, or forced to spend it in their own grave. They would help let go of the grip of the conscious mind and ego on our being. Actually a ritual death is a full life recapitulation, where one has fully relived every second of their life to regain their lost energy and let go of their previous false identity. This is called the "little death."

Similar to ritual death were a series of exercises for the initiates to have out of body experiences to again reach the understanding we are more than just our body and mind. Some compared the ritual death to the mystical period known as the Dark Night of the Soul, where the mystic must encounter all of their fears and impure parts. Yet only by having this challenge can we examine our faults, and use our own power to overcome them and advance to greater heights.

"There is no way to understand the practices except by living them." Muata Ashby[21]

Drama/Sports/Games

Even today stage productions, movies and television shows can bring out great emotion. Shakespeare kept alive many aspects of the ancient mystery tradition when he revived plays during the Renaissance. In Egypt plays were used as a way to portray myths that would be better remembered by the initiates. In time the initiate themselves would also get to play a part in the play

---

[21] Ashby Initiation p.14

to help connect better with the god in the myth. The Greek word Catharsis means purification, and the plays were ways people could dig deep into their inner ailments which created a cleansing. Most of the theaters built during the Renaissance were constructed using sacred geometry. Thus the very place the play was being performed would allow the catharsis to happen. Our word personality comes from the Greek word 'persona' meaning a mask used during the ritual dramas. They were explaining that our personality is no more than a mask that hides our true being or true self. One must learn how to rid of the mask in order to let our true being shine through.[22]

Sports are also a great way to connect with our true being and the wonders of the universe. Each temple included some sort of facility for sports. Just as the Maya ballgame was originally a teaching ground for awakening not the game of sacrifice it became for the Aztec, so too were sports used to teach higher wisdom. When participating in sports there is no time to think as a tennis ball is coming, football is thrown, or puck is shot. We cannot take time to predict, only react. This reaction is a connection to a deeper instinctual part of ourselves, that if done properly can help us to tap into this instinct when not involved in the activity. Sports help to teach patience, living in the moment, and open us to higher states of consciousness. Most long time athletes can remind themselves of a time when everything seemed perfect, or time slowed down while they were still moving at normal speed. They were in some way tapping into a power beyond their normal awareness.

True sport is not the way it has become. Today we, or as part of a team, take on an opponent that is seen as the enemy. This enemy must be defeated which will lead to conflict. Since the greatest joy is believed to come from winning, what happens when we don't win? We feel sad. True sport is meant for each of us to participate to the best of our ability, to use the experience for joy and comradeship that we take with us when it is finished. When in this state of peace and detachment one can use the activity to reach deeper states of being. The mystics of India see all life as a game or sport that they call Leela. With this understanding there is no need to win, or to be better than anyone else, just to do your best and enjoy the experience.

On the walls of Egyptian temples many sports are depicted including: boxing, wrestling, bat/ball games and stick fighting. These sports when performed in the African way (as with dance) were exercise, martial arts, and ways to open consciousness. The actual competition was not as important compared to what each of the participants was learning from it. Sometimes sporting competitions would be held for the public, but usually opponents were delegated with being either Set or Horus. Of course Horus would always win, thus these competitions were more set up along the lines of a ritual play to use

---

[22] Freke World Mysticism pp.68, 71; Baigent, Michael Elixir and the Stone (Penguin 1998) p. 229

23

the skill of the participants to help teach a lesson. The best modern example of this I can give is the Harlem Globetrotters. They produce an event in which one side will always wind up winning (portraying the myth of good over evil) will showcase magnificent athletic skill in an environment that allowed the skill to occur. The Globetrotters also use humour and laughter so the entire audience goes home entertained and happy. This is the Egyptian way, with the crowd not choosing sides but simply entertained by the skills while laughing and receiving lessons. The players would be free of intense competition to allow altered states of consciousness that would lead to a greater display of skill.

While there were many games in Egypt, the most famous was Senet, played on a board that symbolized the passage of the dead through the underworld. The object was to move pieces around a board of thirty squares (called houses) while avoiding hazardous squares and finding positive helping squares (similar to modern snakes and ladders). This game was often shown in chapter 17 of the Book of the Dead. The person is rarely shown playing an opponent, thus represents the meditative focus that the game demands. It is shown played in a hall or room, which is representative of our inner mind where we will play out the game symbolically. Its inclusion in such a work shows that Senet was far more than just a game, but was used as a teaching instruction of the mysteries.

Though few realize it, the game of chess is a powerful teaching tool of mysticism. The board is a square, which symbolizes the number four and the earth. It contains 64 squares, the same number of hexagrams in the I Ching or parts of human DNA. The alternating white and black squares can be seen as the yin and yang that constantly mesh together upon the board (earth). The pieces used become the energies of the universe, while the rules imposed on play are the laws of nature. The pieces allow for action or the movement of energy within the world. Each of the pieces, and their relationship to each other, are some aspect of ourselves.

We each have a male part and a female part, symbolized in chess by the king and the queen. The king, while the most important piece on the board for the entire game revolves around it, is rarely used and hidden or protected most of the time. This king symbolized our true essence that we mostly hide or keep protected in some way. Just like our soul, the king can never be captured or taken for the game ends when it can no longer move. Our soul will likewise end our game of life when it (our body) can no longer move. It also symbolizes the conscious mind, often depicted by alchemists as the ego king. The game ends with a check-mate, or shah-mata (the king is dead) in Persian. The queen meanwhile is the most powerful piece on the board. She can move unlimited squares in eight directions (the number of Tehuti and wisdom). The bishop must spend the entire game on a set of squares, white for intellect (mind) and black for the heart. The knight moves in what few notice as right angled triangles, while all of its moves could form an octagon. It represents the initiate who moves ahead by jumps using the power of sacred wisdom. The rook only moves in straight lines and is our ability to act in the physical world. The pawn is us. It attempts to cross the entire board (seven squares) which is actually the seven chakras we are trying to master. The pawn can only move one step at a time, or two in case of a first move perhaps signifying past life wisdom. It can never move backwards, explaining that we can only go forward on the path. The pawn has a very hard time as so many of the other pieces (energies) are waiting to stop us at our current place. If the pawn can reach the end, the 7th chakra, it becomes free to choose what it wants to be.[23]

Pharaoh/Male-Female

The mystery temples actually ran the country of Egypt. In the Old Kingdom, Pharaohs were not sons of previous Pharaohs as became the case in later periods. The Pharaoh was originally a high priest of the mystery traditions. When the previous Pharaoh died, the high priests would gather (likely at Heliopolis) to elect a new King. This King would be deemed to be of the highest moral standing and have learned the secrets of the universe. Thus the Pharaoh reached a state of purity and knowledge that allowed them to take on a role that would for the rest of their lives require them to fulfill specific ritual on a daily basis that would keep Egypt, and in fact the earth, living with Maat (harmony). The Pharaoh represented every Egyptian person and he performed each aspect of his life for the benefit of every Egyptian. Some handled this task better than others, and if the choice was found to be a poor one, a change would be made.

Just because a high priest was elected to be King did not necessarily mean this would come to pass. The rulership of Egypt went through the female bloodline of the previous King. The newly elected Pharaoh would have to marry the daughter of the previous one. The daughter had complete control of the situation, for she herself would be trained as a high priestess. All of her qualities of intuition and prophecy would be required. She could either accept or reject the elected choice of the priests. If she rejected, an entire new election was needed. The word Pharaoh comes from the word Per-Ah, which is the female word for seat. It is the seat Hathor gives for Horus to rest, or the throne Isis has that Osiris can become king by sitting in. The word means the seat of power (which is the female) not the male who sits in that seat. This system of rulership was based on a male-female balance to the rule of Egypt (only by balance could Maat be sustained). As the age of Aries came into being around 2000BC, new ideas based on male energy dominance and worship of only the sun (male) took over while the female energies (moon) were excluded. It is why

____

[23] Schneider Michael A Beginners Guide to Constructing the Universe (Harper 1995) pp.292-94

God began to be seen as a male and called the Father, for they were in effect worshiping only the male energy. As this took over Egypt, the kingship began to be controlled and passed on from father to son. It was symbolic of the exclusion of the feminine all over the world. Yet at its heart, the Egyptian mystery tradition and rulership in its glory years was one of complete balance.

The goal of the teachings was to combine our male and female parts into one. Just as a male and female must come together to create a new life form, so too must we internally to create a new consciousness. The combination is still understood in Oriental medicine where different channels and organs are Yin or Yang (male or female). Different ailments will require different remedies. In Egypt these teachings were expressed with the Eye of Horus where the right male eye of the sun was combined with the left feminine eye of Tehuti.

Purification

6: Scene of purification with flowing water while holding a lotus flower, Leiden Museum

The ideas of purification were very important in the mystery tradition. To purify means one first removes from our personal temple all of the impure things we have added to it from food, drink and the environment. Next one cleans the emotional impurities formed from our own mind. Finally we begin to purify our higher subtle bodies, our DNA (what was given to us from our parents), until we can reach our perfected soul. It is a hard concept to get across to students that everyone of us comes into the earth perfect, and is in fact still perfect. All of those parts of us that make us perfect never go away. The problem is that as we grow up we add all sorts of things that are not ours. We must think of ourselves as a garden that starts out with the perfect array of flowers, soil, insects etc. With time, flowers we don't need for our journey, weeds and other plants and animals are given to us. Thus we must remove all of the things that were not there in the first place. This is the essence of purification, the removing of all that we have acquired that takes us away from our true essence.

Every ancient Egyptian temple had a sacred lake where the holy waters were used in purification ceremonies and the first baptisms were performed. Fasting was also a means of helping to purify the body and remove the toxins acquired. There were many ways to provide health, balance and inner power including specific energy extraction, cupping, massage, hands on healing, journeying, fire, sound, herbs and stones that would provide health, balance and inner power. Egyptian purifications were often shown in reliefs with two gods, usually Tehuti (wisdom) and Horus (that which overcomes opposition) pouring streams of water or ankhs over the head the individual. This symbolized the entire process of the ritual purification, but when the ankh, uas or djed were shown it symbolized more than just a physical purification.

No one else can do the work for us. All a helper can do is help us become aware of these parts in us so that we can deal with them face to face. It can be as simple as dealing with the fact we like to smoke cigarettes, to as heavy as beliefs acquired from a traumatic childhood incident. We are the ones who face the cleaning process, the purification is just a means to take the block out of its trapped state and put it right in front of our face to deal with. As our inner world changes so to will the outer.

CHAPTER 2
EGYPTIAN RELIGION

7: Osiris statues from the Rameseum

"Few people can be so misunderstood as the Ancient Egyptians. They are too often dismissed as oppressive taskmasters, cruelly lashing gangs of slaves into building useless uninspired monuments to their megalomania, or as a nation of undertakers pre-occupied with the perception of death and burial, worshiping a bizarre collection of gods and beasts, writing mumbo-jumbo in a hopelessly complex and quite unintelligible script...yet for 3,000 years they made incredible achievements in the arts, sciences, technology, politics, religion, philosophy, fine sculpture, painting, literature, scientific observation, religion and medicine."[24]

The above quote seems to sum up the average person's complex understanding of Egypt, yet very little of it is true. For the most part there were no slaves used in Egypt, and only in the last stages of the decline when the

---

[24] Schneider Michael A Beginners Guide to Constructing the Universe (Harper 1995) pp.292-94

28

control of the country was no longer in the hands of the temple. We are told again and again that the Egyptians were far behind us in technology, knowledge and religion but no one can explain how they created the monuments that still stand. The modern world is told that the Egyptians worshiped a great number of gods. While this is partially true they, like all ancient cultures, believed in only one God. A system of gods was created as a teaching tool, as will be explained in chapter three. Beyond all this, especially due to the mummies in museums, the average person thinks that the Egyptian society was one that was obsessed with death. In fact it was the opposite, this was a culture obsessed with life. The Egyptians tried to live life to the fullest, learning its truths, living with the wonder of spirit all around, seeing all nature as a divine gift that we must work with and thank. By doing so they could use their time in a body on the earth as a great gift of the spirit.

Religion/Yoga

"Egypt's entire civilization was based upon religion..."

John Anthony West[25]

8: Statue of Idu in a tomb on the Giza Plateau, looking similar to a figure of Buddha, rising from the earth.

Religion is a very strange thing. "All religion is an attempt to explain the unexplained fact that creation does somehow exist because the senses perceive it, but it is beyond the grasp of the human mind to comprehend." Religion was formed originally as steps for the average person to gain experiential wisdom of the cosmos. Every religion at its core holds the tenants of love and tolerance for others. In time, those who are at the top of a hierarchy use their position of knowledge to gain control over those without it, and in a short few generations the understandings that the religion is attempting to teach can be all but forgotten. People are taught their religion is the only right one, and that all others are wrong. In the ancient tradition, and in the few native societies where

---

[25] West, John Anthony Serpent in the Sky (Theosophical 1993)

the modern world has not fully driven them out, everything in life was spirit. In our world today people go to church on Sunday for three hours, and spend the rest of the week doing their normal life. The ancients understood spirit was always present and always communicating with us, thus there was no need to go to a place of worship because the same amount of spirit could be found in a leaf as in a church. They knew a rock was more than a rock, or the bird that flew by to be more than just a bird. They also did not worship three hours a week, but worshiped constantly. When they washed clothes, tended gardens, ate dinner, or built a house…it was religion.

If one wants to truly understand the Egyptian monuments, tombs, texts, religion, or even day-to-day life, it is important that we not try to understand them from a modern point of view. To truly understand any pyramid, temple or papyrus, we need to live, think and act like an ancient Egyptian. Just as the only way to understand the life of an NFL linebacker is to be one, one must live like an Egyptian to understand the Egyptian wisdom. Since at its heart the true leaders of their society were the mystical priesthood, one must begin to live like a mystic. Hearing the ideas of an Egyptian monument from a Native Indian elder is preferable to listening to them from an archaeologist, for the Native is living a life closer to that of the actual people who constructed it.

The word religion comes from the Latin word religare (to bind back). The word Yoga actually means to yoke, also to bind back. This binding back is a union. Thus the actual meaning of the two words is to return back in union with the source of Creation (Oneness, God, Supreme Being). Understanding the deeper meanings of yoga will help one to understand what religion is supposed to entail. The average person in the west believes yoga to be a series of body postures and breathing which help to enhance physical health, promote relaxation and strengthen the body. While this form of Yoga, called Hatha (designed to connect the Ha (sun, yang) and Tha (moon, yin) meridians of the body), does have these benefits it is not the true purpose of yoga. Just as mediation is not really supposed to be done to relax, or Tai Chi to feel better, yoga (if done correctly) is meant to provide the steps of inner purification that leads to knowledge and wisdom. Religion is meant to be exercises and practiced- something most Western religions are lacking currently.

Just as there are different forms of Qi Gong in China or shamanic exercises in differing Indian tribes, no one form of Yoga is seen to be superior to any other. Each form of Yoga should be seen as a starting point. It is the main focus of your efforts based on a personal choice, but every student will realize in time that they well likely study all of the Yoga disciplines as they continue. For example one may begin with the yoga of wisdom and knowledge by reading ancient texts while also doing Hatha Yoga or Qi Gong to increase their health. Quickly they will learn new teachings and ways to live that need to be put into outer practice (yoga of right action), while mediating at night (Raja yoga). This can relate to the four shamanic techniques of recapitulation, erasing personal history, not-doing and dreaming while performing specific movement exercises. As a shaman realizes that to only do one of the techniques will lead to an imbalance, a student begins with one form of Yoga but then moves on to the other techniques simultaneously. So should be true for the student of religion.

Whatever religion you have chosen as your main focus, or likely had chosen for you by your parents, it is still just a form yoga/religion. As long as it brings you joy to practice it, use it as your starting point. But the true student will quickly learn that if they only focus on one religion, as with one technique, they will get out of balance. A Hindu would use this religion as the base, but add Christianity, Buddhism and Tantric Yoga for example. When this occurs not only is the student obtaining the wisdom of the various paths (for each path takes us to the same place just by different methods), but also we are giving ourselves more tools to use in our life. We will also gain an acceptance and understanding of all the religions because we are no longer locked into our system of one is right and the others are wrong.

Central Themes

"The religious rites and ceremonies of Egypt...were never built upon mere fable and superstition, but founded with a view to promote the morality and happiness of those who observe them." Plutarch[26]

A basic background of Egyptian religious beliefs is actually a hard thing. The temple priests of the mystery schools lived in a very different manner from the average population who were given a lesser form of the wisdom for their daily lives. The Egyptian teachings first taught that we are more than a physical body. The true part of us is not something that dies but is everlasting and eternal and not only comes from God, but is God. This has caused an error for people who believed themselves to be God and led them to self-importance and superiority. They did not understand that a rock, mat, table, or air molecule is also God. Thus we are no better or worse than anything else, because at heart we are all the same. This understanding will take one from a sense of superiority to a sense of humility. We are equal to everything. The idea that we are separate and different from everything else is the basis of the concept of Maya (the illusion of reality). By believing things to be separate we gain desires (the need of a certain object to be happy), fears (that something will happen to us) or anger (that something did not do what we wanted it to). Thus the religious practices of the Egyptian worked to take one away from

---

[26] Clark, Rosemary Sacred Tradition in Ancient Egypt (Llewellyn 1999) p.4

emotions, caused by the motion of the mind, to feeling which is the direct experience of the heart.

Meditation would be a part of any religious experience in Egypt, but likely would not be as important for students as is needed today. The Egyptians would spend less time rushing around, doing countless things or thinking about things because spirit was always around and trying to talk to them. Rushing and making deadlines would only take them away from noticing the messages of the gods. It became important from childhood to pay close attention to nature. By observing how plants grow, or animals act provided not only insights into the workings of the universe, but also ourselves. The Egyptians noticed co-incidence and synchronistic events constantly occurring. It is our job as humans to slow down and notice them.

The central theme of New Egyptian religion was reincarnation, and what happens to the soul after death. They saw life on earth as an opportunity to experience, grow and return to the Source therefore having no need for another human incarnation. This coincides with the Eastern ideas of Karma, called Meskhenet in Egypt. The process of karmic rebirth or the reliving of specific events was always thought of a wheel, referred to as the "grievous wheel," "wheel of necessity" or "wheel of karma," never ending or ceasing. The ancients saw this wheel as representing the stars of the zodiac, whose cycles foretell the fate that lies for each one of us. The path of the mystic is to escape the wheel through gaining wisdom in order to no longer be bound by the astrological fate of the time of our birth. All of our true essence, wisdom and love is found in the heart, which holds the answers, knows our destiny, and only acts out of love and compassion. It is why it was the heart that was balanced against the feather of Maat. Maat is harmony, order, or acting in the purest sense of the word.

I mentioned that this would be the basic teaching found in the New Kingdom, but it can not be sure if the same ideas were held to in the Old Kingdom (pyramid building Egypt). As I mention later in this book, to our farthest ancient ancestors they may have seen what became known as the "wheel of karma," not as cyclic rebirth but perhaps as a recurring time loop.

The heart is our true mind, but we were given another mind that is found in our head. This mind is not ours. It is a mind that lives in fear, anger, self-importance, ego, I, and personality. Humans gain this other mind while still children and includes the beliefs, opinions, behaviour and judgments of others. Babies have none of these things. This conscious mind then creates an entire illusionary world out of itself that we believe to be real. The religious system in Egypt was a system designed to try to stop this conscious mind from being implanted in children in the first place, or to teach the steps we must do to purify and lose this mind to return to the heart.

They compared our waking state with that of being asleep, thus the calls of every religion to awaken. Just as we wake from dreams to say they were not real, the ancient masters also claim that this waking state is also unreal and that we need to learn to awaken from it to a higher state of consciousness. Then we can look back and say, "oh it was only life." Paradoxically that means our dream world is just as real as the one we live during waking.

Interestingly modern religions seem to have a greater teaching about hell than paradise. As anyone knows whatever the mind focuses on will move us in that way. If we are always told about hell, guess where we will wind up? Yet if we forget about hell, focus on paradise and love, guess where we will wind up? This is the Egyptian way, live less from fear and more from actually living life as full and completely as possible. At its essence a true religion will not teach us to believe in a saviour, or even God. They teach how to believe in ourself, to love ourself and to accept ourself just the way we are. How could we ever love or accept someone else if we cannot first do so with ourself? That is the most important thing any religion can teach us. The Egyptian system wanted us to continue our journey until we could live everlasting life as a star in the sky. Most take this as a literal meaning, yet the concept of becoming a star is the process of learning the true parts of the self.

Body/Soul/Spirit

9:Horus as the falcon outside of the second pylon, Edfu

The human being was seen as a microcosm of the macrocosm. This means that everything that is found in the entire created universe can be found in every human. Each one of our atoms for example, looks like a mini version of our solar system. It is possible that each individual cell may be its own solar system. The ancients realized that one did not need to travel to the far reaches of outer space to understand the universe, each one of us had the best laboratory available twenty-four hours a day. The first component of any teaching was for the student to "know thyself." If one wants to understand the relation of the planets to one another (the golden section) then realize that our body contains the same golden section in its makeup. The entire structure of the body, and parts that make up the spirit and soul had to be understood. Because it represented the whole universe, the body was seen as a temple that needed to be looked after. To understand the entire package the Egyptians broke down a human into several parts.

Khat

The Khat in Egypt was the physical body. The word is connected with the idea of something which is liable to decay, while the other "bodies" mentioned do not decay. Thus the Khat is the only part of us that will destruct, while the other parts of us have a longer lasting quality. A partially reversed word Akh means the glorious everlasting light. The Egyptian language used opposites as a teaching tool to help students recognise opposite concepts.

The body was understood not only physically, but symbolically and spiritually. The body is what allowed us to interact with the physical world, and was part of the understanding of "know thyself." The mouth for example had special properties and represented the connection between the physical and psychic realms. The mouth was regarded as the entry and exit points of life. Ceremonies to animate a statue concentrated on the mouth to open. When a baby is born it makes its first announcement to the world by crying. At death we wonder what a person's last words are. It is because the mouth holds the properties of sound. Words occur from the mouth, the word created the universe. If the mouth were not opened then no sound could emanate and nothing could be created. This opening of the mouth ceremony used an object called an adze, thought to symbolize the constellation of the big dipper. It was made of iron, called B'ja (Divine Metal) in the Pyramid Texts. Iron was connected to the stars and gods, since the source of this metal was from fallen meteors. By opening the mouth with iron, the King is performing the same actions that Osiris used to create an immortal life in the Duat and sit upon the iron throne. Actually the Opening of the Mouth ceremony was a ritual initiation for the living that involved the use of sexual energy as Tantra Yoga. This will be explained in future books.

The eye was also opened during the mouth ceremony, as the eyes were key representations of one's descent into the realm of the psychic. It is our two eyes that give us the main sense perceptions of this world around us. A new Eye of Horus (combined our two eyes into one) is needed to be created in order to see past this world of illusion and duality. This combining of male and female eyes will be explained in the section on Horus. The belly symbolized our personal power. All breath work in Oriental teachings is brought to this location, known as the Dan Tien, in order to charge our battery with Qi energy. Those with tremendous power, like the Buddha, were often depicted in statues with big bellies. This does not mean they were fat, but is a symbol for the strength of inner power stored in the lower alchemic furnace.

Ren

The Ren is a person's (or object's) name. While a name is something that distinguishes one person from another, it has a far deeper meaning. The name anything uses will determine the energy that surrounds it. This is a key reason for the use of naming rituals in ancient societies, for each person will need the correct name (thus correct energies) to reflect the type of life they wish to lead. The name we use will determine our fate. Ask anyone (especially married women) how different their life has become with a name change.

The Egyptians would claim that the choice of name was one of the most important that a person will make. With new growth or occupation the old name may become a burden. Priests often suggested at different stages of life we need a new name. The Maya and Aztecs named their children for the day they were born like 4 Reed, the equivalent of naming a child September 16. This gave the family 5-10 years to watch the child's progress to find a name that would suit them, as opposed to how Westerners chose a name before they even see any of the personality of the child. Wallace Black Elk laughed at how white anthropologists believed Indian women named their children after the very first object that they saw after birth: buffalo, horse or butterfly. If that tradition were correct, would there not be Indian children today named Television or Budweiser? In Egypt, the Ren is considered to be one's for a lifetime and is found encircled by a "rope of light" or life force called a cartouche. This was associated with the eternity symbol of the shen.[27]

Every Egyptian would have at least two names in a lifetime. The little name was the ability to distinguish a person from another and would be made public. To allow one's name to be wounded was the equivalent as harming the physical body. Many today would agree who have had their names destroyed in newspaper tabloids. Everything, including humans, had a big name or true name. To know something's true name was considered to have power over it, thus the need to keep our real name secret. This is shown by Isis learning the secret (true) name of RA to gain his power, or in the statement in the Book of the Dead, " I know you, I know your name." The Egyptians claim the world was brought about by the word. Nothing actually exits until it is named. Shamans believe that each thing makes a specific sound, and this sound is the Word that created it. In the Old Testament Adam named all the creatures of the earth, thus knowing their true sounds.[28] Even the Neteru (gods) have a real name. To know the real name of a human being was power, of an element of nature great power, of a Neteru the power over that aspect of the Supreme. This is why the names of the Neteru needed to be hid to stop unchecked access to the proper name.

Sa/Sekhem

These two words are related to concepts of Oriental mysticism. The Sa was the fluid life force that filled the universe and animated all life. The Sa could be seen as relating to Qi (pronounced chee) or Prana, the energy that we bring into our being through food, water, breath and absorption that actually

---

[27] Lamy, p.19; West Key p.65; Ashby Egyptian p.89; Crowley, Brian Words of Power (Llewellyn 192) p.111; Black Elk, Wallace Black Elk: the Sacred Way of the Lakota (Harper Collins 1990) p.157

[28] Crowley pp.4, 6, 111; Isha p.xiv; Berendt Joachim-Ernst The World is Sound (Destiny 1987) p.35; Faulkner, RO Book of the Dead (Chronicle 1998) p.151

allows us to live. The Sekhem is translated by Egyptologists as "power or "form." This word is actually the Egyptian word for personal power, which is our energy storehouse. Anything we do, any good or bad luck, comes as a direct result of our personal power. With more Sekhem we could function in the realms beyond the physical. Sekhem is also associated with Kundalini, the coiled serpent that lies in our pelvis. By cleansing our chakra system (the energy centers that spin universal Sekhem and Sa in and out of our being) the kundalini can rise. Many Egyptian texts refer to phrases like "Master the Fire of the Back." When the kundalini serpent can rise up the spine, it purifies our lower energies allowing us to connect to the higher vibrations of spirit. Some suggest that all purifications, meditations and exercises are actually designed to increase our personal power, which will release more of the kundalini fire and lead on its own to our enlightenment.

Ba

The BA is a very complex concept. It is usually translated as soul, magnet, or the astral body, but this not correct. In fact our "soul" is just God, thus any other part or principle must also be an aspect of this Oneness. The BA is depicted as a migratory bird (a jabiru or stork) accompanied by a pot with a flame (incense) burning. The stork, the symbol for the delivery of a new baby, is known to have a great homing instinct suggesting the BA bird is what brings the soul to the new child. The more common way to depict the BA was as a human headed falcon with the face of the person it represented. The BA is often shown flying near the deceased, coming back to visit and converse with the dead body. It seemed important for the BA to see the physical body as a lifeless corpse. It could take any shape or form, and could easily pass into the world of the afterlife. This concept has come from a Western idea of the afterlife not an Egyptian one. The BA is a controlling influence. A small statue of the Pharaoh Khafre has a Horus falcon BA behind it to show that it is the BA that controls the body, as we sit behind the wheel of a car. The question has to be asked, does the soul actually drive our body or is it something else? All individual BA's are part of the one Universal BA. While the Neteru have a BA on the physical plane, all other creatures on earth have their BA on the spiritual plane. The BA keeps the elements together in the physical body and when the BA has no more use for it, it will leave to find another body (physical or spiritual) to incarnate.[29]

In fact the BA is our limited individual self, not the All. Since this world is an illusion, and the BA is what is guiding the physical body means it can not be our soul, for our soul only wants to link us back to God. Thus the BA is what we identify with, the part of us that believes us to be an individual.

---

[29] Naydler pp.20, 201-04; lamy p.25; Budge, EA Wallis The Egyptian Book of the Dead (Dover 1967) p.63; West Key p.64; Lamy p.25; Ashby Egyptian pp.88 91

That is why it is shown to be flying away in tomb paintings. The tomb paintings were not created to show the after death process per say, but as a metaphor for what the initiates needed to do to bring about their symbolic death to the world of illusion. It is not the soul that is flying away, for in fact there is nowhere for the soul to fly away to. Our soul is here (beyond time and space) and will always be so. But to understand this, our connection to the part of us that makes us an individual must leave us (fly away) in which we can then open up to our true self. It is important to show that the symbol used for the BA is either the hawk (Horus) or stork (connected to Tehuti). The symbols show that it is through the teachings of these two Neteru that we can overcome the effects of the BA, allow it to fly away, and leave us living from our higher self. This is the true message of the texts.

Ka

Egyptologists describe the KA as the source of vital energy. However, the Sekhem and SA is our personal power and QI so the KA must be something else. The KA is usually translated as double or mirror. The KA is often shown standing beside the physical body and newborn children were sometimes painted with their KA double. It is translated as a double because it is often shown together with the physical body, and is able to separate and travel at will. To some that reminds them of the etheric body that you "step into" during an out of body experience, you actually believe that you are in your physical body, you may even be wearing the same clothes. That is until you see your physical body asleep, or place your arm through a wall. Thus the etheric body simulates the physical, but is composed of "finer" material. Statues, texts and offerings are dedicated to the KA. The KA of someone would reside in their painting or statue. Modern natives refuse to allow photographs to be taken of them, believing that a small piece of their essence would be taken and put in the photo. On the other hand, to have a photograph or statue of someone means one has a direct connection for a small piece of their energy is present. There are a number of different KA's.[30] The fact that there is more than one type of KA gives a clue to the meaning of the concept.

The KA is linked to the ancestors that were said to control the flow of energy to the physical realm. The tomb was a vital interchange between the dead and living for the dead become the directors of KA energy. It is depicted by a pair of outstretched arms, the same gesture as made by Shu who splits heaven and earth apart. It is this split of Geb and Nut that creates the illusion of duality in the physical world. The physical body was the Khat and is made up with the word KA showing a connection between the KA and the body. To keep the KA associated with the physical world of illusion will keep the higher self (our true soul) in a state unable to merge with the One.

---

[30] Naydler p.190; Lamy pp.7,26

In Egypt the process of impregnating a female is called Bka. The creation of a new human needs both the BA and the KA. To create a transformed human the initiate also needs to unite the BA and KA, but in a different way. Instead of impregnating a female with sperm, we must impregnate our being with knowledge and wisdom. This is the famed Virgin Birth that actually happens within us. The KA is a representation of one's thoughts, beliefs, and physical experiences. These are in fact the things that we must first love, accept then transform. Upon death it is claimed that if the KA and BA cannot be united, the KA will break up into its component parts and will return again to reincarnate. If it is the KA breaking into parts that causes us to reincarnate, then the KA must be the parts of the energy body, which are actually the fine components of the conscious mind. Think of hating someone and we create an etheric block in our energy body that will stick there until we remove it. A block strong enough could move down to be an illness in the physical body. That is the true meaning of the idea of the double, it is the double form of the thoughts of the mind itself.

The KA would also represent the part of us that goes into each object we come into contact with. It is how psychics perform the art of psychometry. They pick up our left over residue on an object that we held, which is really a small piece of our KA. The more attached to the object, the more of our KA will be within it. The KA is the part of our consciousness that remains on the earth, connected to the places where the physical body lived and the objects it possessed. The KA includes all the genetic material of our parents and ancestors, for their thoughts and beliefs are part of our makeup in the physical body. If your father was an alcoholic, you may not drink but you will still have the genetics of alcoholism. This is the reason for the importance of remembering the ancestors as they are infusing us with some of the positive traits we are taking with us, and also some of our challenges. This is the meaning of the ancestors living on inside of us, for often we are fighting the same battles they did not have the personal power to overcome. We need to pay homage to them, for when we fight similar battles they are in a sense having the opportunity to overcome their challenge through us. They can infuse us with some of their power and perhaps together the ancestor and us can overcome a challenge that is beyond our strength as an individual.

At death it is claimed we must unite all of our KA's together. This is similar to the shamanic techniques of soul retrieval and recapitulation that claims every interaction has caused a trading of energy. The more emotional the interaction, the greater the energy exchanged. One must call back all of our energy body to fullness and release the parts of KA's we have accumulated. Upon death we all go through a recapitulation process (life flashing before our eyes) to regain these parts, and understand the truth of our lives. That is why a mystic wants to do this before death, so as to have all their energy body back while alive. Through the recap they would also learn what actions provided a loss of their KA (actions based on self-importance or emotion) and see certain interactions that did not diminish the KA (based on love and compassion). This process of understanding the KA while alive would also allow one to change the habits and routines of their life to make it one of love, harmony and kindness. They could see that any parts of the KA not united would attract (magnet symbolism) them to return to the earth to relive that experience.

This idea also relates to the misunderstood need of the ancients at death to be buried with all of their personal objects. As long as we have an object, and are attached to it in some way, it in effect has a part of us. This is the true meaning of the oriental teaching to not have any attachments to the physical world, for every object you have has a part of you in it, thus you are not whole. They understood that we need objects to help us function in the daily world, so the key was to have as few of them as possible to not allow too much of our KA to be used (see more in mummification). When archaeologists find few objects buried with a body (as opposed to great burials in more recent times) they assume the older burials were of very poor people. In fact they could have been the richest and wisest people from understanding that each object would have some of their KA, so they lived with only the barest of necessities. At death every object would have to be buried with the physical body so that the KA could be extracted by the deceased. If one lived this life of non-attachment they would have few objects buried with them. Less material objects in a burial does not necessarily show a less advanced civilization, but perhaps a more advanced one. The food in the tomb may be the last bits of food in a person's home before death, since this food "acquired" the KA and also needed also to be buried with the body.

Khaibut

The Khaibut is translated as the shadow by Egyptologists and is associated with the BA. In modern psychological language the shadow is the inner, negative parts of ourself which we refuse to acknowledge. Some who have this notion refer to the Khaibut as a ghost or an object that intercepts the light. They claim it is our negative parts which, if not eliminated, will trap the BA forever in the physical. Yet we have already seen that the BA is not the soul. Muata Ashby views the shadow as the reflection of God, just as shamans see the objects of this world as a shadow of their real essence which lies unseen in another dimension. Another example is the shadows on the cave in Plato's Republic. The shadow is a projection of that which is real, of truth, but not the real or truth directly. To believe so is to be caught in the illusion. God creates and continues to create out of God's own self, thus would perceive the universe as nothing but its own shadow.[31] As our true essence is but a part of God, and

---

[31] Ashby Egyptian p.60

the BA is what really keeps us from God, the BA must be a shadow…of the shadow. By spending time viewing the shadow of an object we can gain a better understanding than viewing the object itself. A shadow occurs because an object blocks the light, so the shadow of the object must provide clues as to what is actually blocking the light (God) and what that Light really is.

Ab

"My heart, the mother of my coming into being." Book of the Dead, chapter 30

The AB is the heart, the seat of our true mind as opposed to the conscious mind that attracts the KA and BA. The head creates emotions (fear, anger, jealousy), while the heart creates only feelings (love, peace, joy, and Gnosis). Thus the heart not the head is really the place of knowledge, the place of true memories, and is the place of Meskhenet (karma) for it knows the true thoughts and actions we undertook. It is why this part of the body was weighed (judged) in the hall of the Double Maat, (see Hall of Maat).

The heart is in fact the connection source to our higher self (our soul). To learn to listen to the heart means to follow the guidance of intuition which knows what life we are supposed to be living, and how we are to be living it. It may want us to move to other parts of the world, divorce our spouse, and take up professions which the rest of our friends see as not a good way to make a living. The mind only wants, while the heart only wants to give. Do not put too much stock in what your friends or society says. You have likely been listening to their ideas and opinions for a long time, which is why you are in the unhappy state you find yourself in and looking for new options.

Shamans teach that our most important choice in life is to follow a path with heart, the path that brings joy to our soul. It is the path or way our soul intended us to live. It may not be any easier than living a normal life like everyone else, but it will be one filled with the joys and warmth of living the destiny that your very soul aspired for you upon creation. AB spelled backwards is BA. We have already found that we must release the BA's grips upon us, or turn the BA around, to go from individuality to connection at the heart level. The BA turned around is AB. The Egyptians have again symbolically told us what we need to do, connect less with the BA (our individual self) and more to the AB (heart connection to everything).

Khu

The Khu is a higher spiritual component of a human, a shining or luminous part that is immortal. It is a special energy that connects through our heart for our best interest. Khu's were said to be celestial beings living with the gods, and relates to the idea of a guardian angel or spirit guide. When one has purified themselves enough to enter the world of the Khu, they have reached the level beyond having a human being for their main teacher. They are now the direct student of a Neteru or spirit guide. The human teacher of the mysteries will still assist the student, but they must now be second in the teaching ladder.[32] The teacher has done their job, to instruct the mystery student how to overcome and unite key parts of themselves and greatly reduce the hold of the conscious mind (thus live more from the heart). This state of the luminous Khu is not necessarily permanent, but like the state of mystical awareness must be constantly aspired to. When I first reached a mild state of Khu, it lasted until I began to regain my old impure ways of being. The state itself took a long time to even regain a glimpse of, thus when one attains the Khu it is recommended they put forth all of their personal power to keep this most direct line to the ancient wisdom. Actually the Khu is not the light itself that we seek, but the means to gain that light.

Akh

10: The akh from a wall in Edfu

The Akh is the place of shining or illumination. Its glyph is the crested ibis, the same as the symbol for Tehuti. The ibis has green plumage with glittering specs that seem to shine. Thus this shining light represented here, must be related to the Gnosis of Tehuti. The Akh is sometimes used to refer to the third eye. This light we seek is also the light from which we originated, but we must get here to fully understand this concept. By adding the letter N we get the word Ankh, the symbol of everlasting life- thus the radiant Akh is a key to everlasting life. The Akh is also the opposite of the physical body Khat or Kha. Since the physical body perishes, the Akh must be immortal. The pyramid texts refer to the Akh being for heaven (above) and the Khat for the earth (below). The Akhu were a special group referred to as "shinning ones", as were The Followers of Horus. In the Liturgy of Funerary Offerings it claims, "become an Akh, and arrive at the Sekhem.

---

[32] West Key p.65; Ashby Egyptian p.89; Masters, Robert The Goddess Sekhmet (Amity House 1988) p.28

Lucie Lamy relates information of an Igluik Eskimo shamanic initiation that ends with the angakoq (similar to the word Akh), meaning lightening or illumination. It is a luminous fire (light) which enables the shaman to see with both eyes (literally and metaphorically). Now even with closed eyes they can see through darkness and perceive things hidden from others.[33] Seeing allows one to go past the physical world to see what something 'really' is. Not every person we pass on the street is a human, not every tree a tree, not every empty space an empty space. Only by the illumination of our third eye (the Eye of Horus) are we able to pass through the shadow world to see what is real. It would allow us to be in a complete state of Gnosis where we can gain an understanding of all things. It is our goal to become a shining one, a star of light emanating in the universe in order to connect to our true inner core, which is that star of light that we seek. The Egyptian religion called for the Pharaoh, who represented the potential journey of every Egyptian, to become a star. Yet the star is not out there in the sky, the star of light is already inside of us; we just need to find it again.

Sahu

Sahus are said to be "free and noble," thus is the place of the soul. The final stage is when the Akh is formed within us and we understand how to be released from the physical body, and gain a new awareness of our spiritual bodies. To attain this stage one must get all of their members, representing the parts or fragments of the self. Some say this is the stage where Osiris was reanimated. The Pyramid texts claim, "I have passed through the Duat, I have seen my father Osiris. I have become a Sahu. I have become equipped…Thou hast received thy Sahu, not shall be fettered thy foot in heaven, not shalt thou be turned back upon earth."[34] The Pyramid Texts claim a Sahu is a spiritually perfected being, an enlightened one who no longer needs to reincarnate on earth. One needs to reach the state of Akh (seeing, or illumination) so as to break the hold of the illusion and gain the Gnosis that can only be given by the Creator itself.

---

[33] Lamy p.24
[34] Naydler pp.210, 214; Budge p.lx; Ashby Egyptian p.89; Clark p.314

CHAPTER 3
WHAT ARE NETERU?

11: Detailed Hieroglyph for Neter, from Leiden Museum

Neter

An in depth look into Ancient Egypt must begin with the Neteru. Egyptologists translate the Neteru as gods or goddesses but this is far from the truth. No matter what the books, Egyptologists, or documentaries continue to mass market, Egypt believed in only One God who according to A.E. Wallis Budge was "self-evident, immortal, invisible, external, omnipotent, almighty, the maker of the heaven and the underworld, the creator of all things."[35]

The Ancient Egyptians used the name Neter to describe this concept, known as Brahma to Hindus, Hunab Ku to the Maya, Tao to Taoists, and Great Spirit to Native Indians. All religions have always held the belief of one God. The symbol for Neter has been translated as an axe. It is claimed that the mightiest man in prehistoric days had the best weapon, thus the mightiest axe became the symbol for the mightiest thing, God. The symbol is most likely a flag, which appeared at even the earliest temples. Neter, or God, as the creator of the universe was symbolized by the wind. It is an unseen force on the earth, but as with a hurricane, holds tremendous power. This unseen God can in fact be seen, through the moving flag. Thus the flag symbolizes that just as the wind can be noticed from the movement of the flag, so to can God be seen through the movements of material objects of the earth.

An Ancient Egyptian text provides this description of Neter (referred to as God in this translation by Dr. Brugsch), "God is one and alone, and none other existeth with Him. God is the one, the one who hath made things. God is

---

[35] Budge, EA Wallis Egyptian Ideas of the Future Life (Putnam 1899) p.1

spirit, the spirit of spirits, the great spirit of Egypt…He existed when nothing else existed, and what existeth He created after coming into being…God is hidden and no man can know His form. No man hath been able to seek out His likeness, He is hidden to gods and men…His name remaineth hidden…He is the King of Truth. He gives life to man…God is the father and the mother…He produceth, but was never produced…He createth but was never created…When He hath spoken, it cometh to pass and endureth for ever…God knoweth him that acknowledge Him. He rewards him that serveth Him, and He protecteth him that follows Him."[36]

The translation provides some excellent ideas on the Egyptian ideas of the Creator, however Brugsch has added his own personal religious beliefs into the translation by using the word Him to describe Neter. In the text Neter was referred to as "father and mother." Thus Neter is not a male creator, but a perfect combination of both male and female energies which is the heart of any mystical teachings. The idea of a male God is a 'modern' revelation imposed by a male dominated society who wished to suppress feminine energy and place women into subservience. Our goal as mystical humans is to obtain a perfect blending of male (right eye) and female (left eye) energies. To have too much of one will make you unbalanced, thus unlike the perfect balance of the Creator.

It is also interesting that the Egyptian passage claims, "No man can know His form, or name." The Hermetica also explains, "There is nothing that He is not, for He is also all that is, and this is why He is all names…and why He has no name, because He is Father of them all…He is One not two. He is All not many. The All is not many separate things, but the Oneness that subsumes the parts."[37] When one understands that all that exists is God, you come to a very important place. When you see a tree, or a person, or a desk, you are seeing them but also the Creator Spirit at the same time. When you say staple, table or banana you are also saying the Creator. Thus the Creator can be found in everything, and since we (like the other objects) spring from the same source, we too must only be Neter. To injure someone actually means we are injuring ourselves because we are the only thing that exists. The alchemist refers to this concept by stating that everything on earth is just the One Thing (all is the same) which comes from the One Mind (God) yet this One Mind and One Thing are the same. It was important to show reverence and respect, for God is part of every second of our lives.

Neteru

The best way that Neter can be experienced is through its creations. The most powerful of these are called the Neteru. This brings my faithful reader back to the concept suggested in the previous section, if God cannot be named

---

[36] Budge Book p.93
[37] Copenhaver Heremtica (Cambridge U 1982) p.20, Corpus Hermeticum Book 5

why use a name of Neter? In English we use the term God to refer to the Almighty, but use the term gods to refer false deities of cultures not as advanced as ours. Thus God and gods are really not related and are opposites of each other, but at the core this is like saying that cat and cats are not related. Today through the misguided teachings of modern religion, we have lost the true connection that the word God and gods are supposed to have. The Egyptians named the almighty Neter and what came from it, Neteru, to show a connection. What we perceive, Neteru, is actually part of Neter. The Bible itself uses many words that are all lumped together in modern translations as God, including the plural Elohim (gods).

The symbolism for Neter is a single flag, explaining the Creator is One and alone. It is the undefined Monad. The symbol for Neteru is three flags. As will be further explained in the chapter on sacred number, the Neteru must manifest in the plural. When duality, two, is present there is nothing. A male and female can be in the same room for eternity and nothing will happen until a third force, love or lust, enters to combine the opposites. From this combining of opposites create the many. In fact when one says they have three of anything, they in fact have an unlimited number. Another name for this All was the Nebertcher, meaning All-powerful and was defined as a trinity of the Neteru Amun-Ra-Ptah.

The creation of a pantheon of "gods" is not the work of some unknowing savages who do not understand the universe. It is modern humans that may be the unknowing ones. When one does not see equality in all things and all forms, this leads to battles of my God versus your untrue God. By acknowledging many different gods it allows a person to follow many different paths, understanding that each is just a way back to the All. No one God would be seen as better or worse, just an individual's choice. Teaching texts, like the Instructions of Ptah-Hotep, often left blank spaces for the student to write in the name of their particular Neter. Again the idea that no student's deity was better than anyone else's, all were equal just simply a matter of preference as one who likes chocolate to vanilla ice cream. They are both just ice cream. Why can't we do that today with religion?

In China a myth claims that Empress Wu asked sage Fa Tsang to show the relationship between Oneness and the apparent multiplicity of life. In a room he placed eight mirrors at the compass points and one on the floor and ceiling. A candle was supported in the center of the room, and when the Empress entered it was lit. The room was filled with the splendour of the reflected light. "You see your majesty, the candle is the One consciousness of God and the reflections are the many individual consciousness of His creation." Thus the source and the reflection are the same light.[38] The candle is Neter, the

---

reflections are us, while the streams (fibers) of light that bind the two are Neteru.

How is this concept of Neteru helpful to the initiate of the mysteries? The Creator, when manifesting in Creation, does so in many different forms or qualities. These aspects, such as love, wisdom, healing, writing, anger, fish, birds are all part of the perfect All, but some parts will have greater strength or intensity than other aspects. The Hermetica stressed that God is One and the Creator of all things. The powers that bind this structure together are called energies. These energies operate all bodies, whether immortal or mortal, animate or inanimate. They are what cause growth, decay and sensation and were the origins of the arts, sciences and every other human activity.

However it becomes hard for a seemingly imperfect being (us) to learn and understand something that is All-perfect. It is what makes modern religions a very difficult chore to fully understand. In Egypt each of these individual aspects or energies of the All-perfect Creator, were expressed by the Neteru. Jeremy Naydler calls a Neteru "not a god, but a divine principle," while E.A. Wallis Budge says, "Neteru refers to the great cosmic power…and are nothing more, nor less, than forms, manifestations, phases or attributes of the One God." The One God, which cannot be represented in its true form, can be better represented through its attributes and functions. The Hermetica explains that we "speak, hear, touch, taste, walk, breathe, think…it is not a different you who does these things, but one being who does them all."[39]

Each of the Neteru were given a name such as Osiris, Isis or Atum that were actually carefully chosen to reflect specific energies, vibration and number. The word Neteru, through Greek and Latin, became the English word nature. Thus the Neteru, the attributes of God, are seen in nature around us. This is why studying nature is such an important starting point for those following the mysteries. When one understands that every part of nature is in fact a Neteru, they realize that God is involved directly in each second in our life and can be communicated with through every part of nature. We know Ptah can communicate with us through every rock, Ra through every ray of sunshine. This would keep the student in a state of awareness, looking for omens that would be speaking directly to our heart, helping us open the feelings of love and increase our connection with God. We have 360 Neteru, aspects within us, yet most today use only five. Thus the other 355 are dormant, yet as we access a new Neteru within a sense of life comes from within. An ancient site or temple was designed to help open us to these inner Neteru.

Each temple in Egypt was designed to completely express one of the Neteru. Instead of having to understand this All-perfect being immediately, we can learn one aspect at a time. Love can be studied at the temple of Hathor, inner knowing from Tehuti, or physical matter from Ptah. Once one has traveled through all the temples they will have gained an understanding of all

---

[39] Naydler p.154; Budge Book p.83; Budge Future Life p.29; Copenhaver p.42

the parts, just as one learns the parts of an car engine separately. Lao-Tzu wrote, "Truly to know the mother, is to know her children." This is a perfect example. Learn one aspect like Horus. Then learn Isis. By the time you have fully understood all of the different aspects, you will understand the whole.

Symbolism

"The mysteries and symbols are only obscure and unintelligible to the uninformed." Plutarch[40]
"Without the help of symbol, no ancient scripture can ever be correctly understood." Blavatsky[41]

12: Wall relief from a tomb in Sakkara showing the Mer, symbol for love from the tool for planting.

To understand a Neteru one may begin with myths and stories, but the stories alone do not provide enough information. The ancient myths were written using the technique of symbolism. A painting of a Neteru could tell you as much, if not more, than an entire story. The symbols: dress, crown,

---

[40] Ozaniec p.84
[41] Chaney p.83

equipment, colour, position, size and gestures will provide a wealth of information about the energy the Neteru represents. This is why pictures were often included with a text or added to tomb walls because they provide extra symbolic information to compliment the text. The entire written language of the Egyptians were actually symbolic letters. Words are but a bunch of facts (information) that gets stored in our head, but a symbol is understood without words with the heart. Symbols take us to Gnosis

The symbols in Egypt were carefully chosen and were very important. Information (no matter how excellent) is useless unless it can be transferred into easy understanding for the recipient. "Thus the use of symbols [turns out] to be the exact opposite of what it is believed to be. Symbols are direct and exact, it is language (especially modern language) that is misleading and hard to understand."[42] Today symbols are still used by advertisers and the media effectively. Our whole world today is influenced by symbol except we do not even realize it. Ask what is the symbol of McDonald's, a crosswalk or the Montreal Canadiens and most will know the answer. In fact we do not even need to say McDonald's or Montreal Canadiens, the symbol is enough.

In order to use a symbol most effectively, that symbol must be studied from several different angles for a long period of time. It "involved careful considered choice, and a deep understanding, based on meticulous observation of the nature of the chosen symbol." While modern Western writing is just a series of scratches upon paper that reveals a fixed concept for our conscious mind, the ancient symbol allowed what was depicted to reach our own places of meaning and knowledge. Each of the Egyptian paintings, books or architecture was designed to have different meanings that could not be understood by our rational mind. In fact, the very use of our modern language itself with a fixed word for a fixed concept actually makes it harder for any of us to reach our heart. The conscious mind wants to fix values for everything from "this is a table," to "this is Bill who never eats peas." In hieroglyphic symbolism a table could mean a table, or stability, or wood, or offerings. As our language becomes less fixed, we ourselves will become less fixed in what we believe is real in the world.

A word can become a different meaning as time goes on. In the 1920's rubbers were things you wore on your feet, now they are the slang for condoms. A symbol by contrast does not lose its power to express truth, for the truth always exists in our heart. The more symbols that can be added to one's life, the greater chance for heart connection. The human heart (our true mind) understands things by actually making a mental picture of it, and then our rational mind takes that mental picture and adds associations and thoughts. When the word "door" is seen in this sentence, our true mind actually gets a mental picture of a door. We don't see the letters d-o-o-r. Thus a symbolic picture will actually translate information to our true mind far more quickly

---

[42] West Serpent p.130

than words. Only a quick look at a US flag, grim reaper or dollar sign in a cartoon may be enough to pass on a wealth of information. Think of a business meeting with graphs and charts to explain vast amounts of material in a short space or the statement "a picture is worth a thousand words."

13: Owl hieroglyph, relief in British Museum

A more complex example is the Egyptian glyph of the owl. In modern translations the owl is shown to depict the letter M. When shown alone in a text the usual translation of M is 'in, into, from, at, as or with.' This may in fact be true but it is definitely missing a key component of the information. The owl is well known for its ability to see at night. Egyptian hieroglyphs use close to fifty birds, but only the owl is shown looking towards the reader. This holds significance that few ponder. It could just as easily be drawn like the others, from the side, but it is not. The owl is turning to look at us. Thus the glyph must include the ideas of looking, penetrating, seeing beyond darkness. This is but a small example of one glyph, one idea that needs to be fully examined.

Another example comes when experts claim that the Egyptians often depicted their daily activities, like hunting or fishing, in art. Ancient Egyptians did not really care about day to day affairs, and certainly would not waste valuable time making pictures of it. They are symbol, of events to which the initiates could relate. To hunt a bull is to hunt the inner sexual desires of the body. To throw a net around birds is to grab hold of the conscious thoughts, which can disrupt our attempt of hotep (inner peace). A glyph painted in green will have a completely different meaning to a glyph painted in red. It is not because the painter ran out of the colour so decided to use another, the explanation of Egyptologists. The glyph's colour, sound the words make, and the symbol used to carry the sound are but some of the things one needs to lean in order to fully open to the wisdom of Egypt.

To truly work with the symbols requires one to understand nature around them. If the hieroglyph of a door bolt is to be understood one needs to spend time studying a door bolt, how it operates and what it does. If a lotus is drawn one needs to spend time with the lotus and watch how it opens in the light and closes at night. As you begin to try and understand the symbols, you may begin to look at things differently. The coffee table in the living room could become a symbol. It could show tiredness as one rests their feet upon it at the end of the day, or stability as things are placed upon it. Working with the symbolic ideas behind hieroglyphs will change your entire life. It forces us to spend more time focusing on the world around us, and to see the many aspects of that world beyond what we normally think. Symbols help to open us to more of the potential of the universe. Egyptian priests spent tremendous time and effort to choose the correct symbol to explain a key concept and help with an individual's quest for the mystical.

The Hermetic wisdom was transmitted in pictures and symbols because images could be sealed and kept pure. Thus the idea that anything Hermetically sealed is air tight. While words can be mistaken, like the rubbers, the Hermetic symbolism only explains the truth. The Hermetic truths were said to contain 72 layers, and this is why the modern word for word translation of hieroglyphic text is so incomplete. This is but one of the 72 layers of symbolic wisdom, while 71 other layers are left hidden for the wisdom of the heart. A problem with symbols is that the conscious mind will try and step in to do what it does with everything else in the world it perceives, fix it to one and only one value. The symbol is a table, and can only be a table. As long as we question the reality of the world around us, the conscious mind knows we can also start to question its reality. So instead of allowing the heart to register the symbol and find ways to develop that particular quality in ourself, it may cause us to believe that the power is in a statue, or a painting, or some other person who is 'better than us.' Horus or Christ are not real beings or in the pages of some book, but are within all of us.

Egyptian Animal Symbols

"It is the unexplainable force of symbols which give awareness of divine things." Iamblichus[43]

I would now like to examine a few of the Egyptian symbols in order to give my readers a start on a new examination of all Egyptian painting, texts and reliefs. Animals were one of the main symbols used and this had led "experts" to believe that the Egyptians followed cults of animal worship, and that temples of different animal gods fought each other for supremacy in the country. There was NO animal worship in Egypt. The animal-headed Neteru were symbolic expressions of a deep spiritual understanding. Usually the Neteru were shown with a human body, and a specific animal head. The Greeks portrayed all of their gods in human form, but in Egypt the Neteru were not brought down to Earth to become human, rather they were attempting to explain that it is humans "who must be raised to become gods." That being said, some Neteru

---

[43] Lamy 24

are only depicted in human form, for example Amun, Atum, Ptah, and Maat. In human form they represent the forces of the creation that sustain the universe. These energies are so powerful and important that no animal could possibly convey their meaning. Usually they are shown as having no navel, thus they are not connected to the energies of creation; they are the energies of creation.

Some Neteru were shown purely in animal form, and these operate only upon the physical sphere on Earth (birth, death, and decay). If they are shown in human form with an animal head, they symbolize energy within the human sphere that is connected beyond the physical world (wisdom, strength, instinct). During the myth of Horus and Set, the human depicted Neteru could not make a judgment on who should rule because they are aspects that represent the harmony of creation. Only Thoth (combined human and animal attributes) could become a judge because he had attributes that went beyond the fixed values of the creation that could operate on the physical sphere.[44] Their headgear related to spiritual creative power, while what were held in their hands were the principles that could be used in the human sphere. Thus the priest would have to know not only which specific Neteru was needed for specific rituals, but also which form of the Neteru was required.

Animals were used to explain a specific idea, and are still used today when someone says they are as "sly as a fox," or "slow as a tortoise." This is another reason nature was so vital. The idea that the fox represented slyness, the dog loyalty, or a vulture motherhood would never be specifically explained to the student. These are things they would have to observe themselves. Nearly every great ancient site from Mexico to Egypt to Cambodia used the serpent symbolism. Today the serpent has gathered a very sinister meaning, due to its symbolic description in the Bible. The serpent can carry a sinister meaning, but it also carries a very positive one as well. The serpent is actually the symbolic depiction of the two forces that exists in the human etheric body. Many are aware of what the Asian teachings call kundalini, the sleeping serpent that lies coiled at the base of the spine. As explained this serpent must be awakened to rise through the energy centers (chakras) to reach enlightenment. However almost no texts today tell of the second serpent that lies within our being. While the kundalini serpent tries to take us upward, this other serpent tries to bring us back down to the physical.

Kundalini and Chakras

The modern teachings of kundalini today come from Asia. However, all ancient mystery traditions understood these great forces. The chakras are invisible locations of the body that spin energy in and out of our being. While there are hundreds of points, seven centers are key areas. They travel up the spine from the pelvis to the head. These seven centers are acknowledge in myth

---

[44] Schwaller Sacred p.142; West Serpent 133

as seven: headed snakes, steps to heaven, gates of the underworld, liberal arts, dwarves, seals, swords etc. Each major chakra relates to one of the bodies of our being: physical, emotional, spiritual etc. Should one obtain the place of purified chakras it will lead to a state of health, love and peace. They could miraculously heal, and gain the seeing powers listed above. These were typified in medieval paintings as a person with halo surrounding them, showing the flow of energy through the head after the purifications.

As each chakra is purified, so to is a part of our being. It is an important teaching of the ancients that one must first work on their lower four bodies (chakras) signified by the four Sons of Horus in Egypt, before working on the higher centers Too many begin work of the upper chakras without first producing a vehicle that can handle the higher energies that it can create. It is the equivalent of plugging a 110 volt body into a 220 volt socket. We would fry ourselves. Thus to try to gain psychic powers (fifth and sixth chakras) without the lower work done, leads to the inability to use the power properly even if obtained. In fact, if the work is done in proper sequence, conditions one day will occur naturally to obtain these powers without even striving to obtain them. They are the gifts of the process and not the goal.

We all have our own personal life force, called kundalini. It is depicted as a sleeping, coiled serpent that lives at the base of the spine. The spine and upper energy centers were symbolized in Egypt by the djed pillar of Osiris. When the serpent force is aroused, either by spiritual growth or personal life training, it will rise up one of three channels. There is a male and female channel along with the central spine, and the serpent is symbolized winding its way up. This is symbolized by the caduceus held by Tehuti in the tomb of Seti I, and by his heir Hermes Trismegistus. The caduceus, now used as a symbol for the modern medical profession, depicts the three channels by which this serpent energy can flow.

The inner spiritual force is shown sleeping because it lies dormant from our lack of development. As it rises trying to reach the head, it will reach blocks we have created in our being. Since it rises from the spine, it will begin with the lowest ones first. This can lead to tremendous pain and torture while it cleans as it tries to rise, especially in cases where the person does not know that it is raising kundalini. Many illnesses or strange experiences are the result of an unknown release. Thus the need to assist the purification process as much as possible, to not waste the energy of the kundalini to face issues we can do ourself.

The downward turning serpent is related to the conscious mind. As anyone who had first tried to mediate will tell you, it is very hard to stop the mind from moving. This was symbolized as the serpent Apop, which is the constant moving and wiggling thoughts of our mind. This lower snake will always be shown with its belly on the ground (where it is keeping us) or having a great number of undulations (the moving thoughts of the mind). The kundalini serpent can defeat Apop and take us up to the height of our being, the third Eye of Horus and the ability to embrace the Light. The upward moving serpent can be shown standing upright or with wings in the sky. The ancients understood snakes do not fly, but just like in Mexico (with Quetzalcoatl, the feathered serpent) they are symbolizing that the kundalini serpent will give us the power to no longer crawl on the earth but gain the wings of freedom (associated with Horus) to rise to the heavens and connect with God.

Statues

14: Minkaure Statue, Cairo Museum

Every temple included great numbers of various statues. The most important were very small by comparison to some of the larger ones found in the rest of the temple. They were kept in the farthest room from the temple entrance, and represented not only that big things come in small packages, but also the distance to travel from the entrance represented the distance one had to travel on the spiritual path. Only the highest of priests had access to this room. While this statue was the most direct link, all statues were considered the earthly residences of the Neteru. Each statue of Isis gave a person the chance to connect directly with the energy of Isis, for the statue actually held some of the energy of the particular deity. When visiting the Oriental room at the Glenbow Museum in Calgary, I am always drawn to a few Buddhist statues. Some of them are still alive with the energy of the Buddha that can be felt and seen when one changes their state of awareness. The main temple statues were well looked after, bathed, clothed and fed on a daily basis. It was not that the statue was revered, but the cosmic principles the statue represented. One does not need a statue or picture of any kind to connect with Christ, Buddha or Osiris, yet until we are fully aware of this fact and of the ways to do so, the statue which has the specific energy of the deity concentrated in it could help us begin the process.

In the west many are still frightened from a line in Exodus, "thou shall not make yourself a carved image or any likeness in heaven or earth; you shall not bow down or serve them for I Yahweh am a jealous God."[45] While this

---

[45] Naydler p.132; Exodus 20,4-5

quote holds power on the human mind, one must wonder if it should. The mystic knows that all that exists is God, thus how could the All possibly be jealous with anything? It is our conscious mind that gets jealous. It is key that any image made by the ancients is really just an outer symbol which is only able to help the heart when it is ready to transcend the symbol itself. This is why there are many statues in India, Mexico and Egypt. Each symbol or myth carries a different aspect or view of the divine, which helps the aspirant better understand the nature of the divine. If one does not understand that the image is helping them to connect with a part of God, but instead worships the statue as an actual divine thing then they have gone beyond the power of the statue.

The Egyptians made statues not as pieces of artwork, but were carefully created to draw in the specific energies of that which they were calling on. The type of stone used, its exact mathematical measurements, or the exact timing when making it were all key factors during its creation. The Renaissance Hermeticists knew of the Egyptian wisdom when it came to statues. Marsiglio Ficino wrote about making the particular image of Scorpio when the moon is in Scorpio, "as was done in Egypt…so that the spirits of the stars are enclosed in them." They used the symbols to reach the power of God. The Western religions in time began to teach that the world of spirit cannot be reached in the physical (or otherwise everyone could do it and have no need for them), thus soon physical objects began to be seen as stuff to be possessed. An idol is a physical object, but the Egyptians understood that nothing was just a physical object, the gods could speak to them through any object or force of nature.[46]

15: Sekhemet statue, Cairo Museum

The beauty of artwork, reliefs, temples or books were all a spark for humans to understand the beauty involved in creation. When a statue was finished it was then charged with the specific energy of the Neteru it was made for. Charging is similar to the idea of charging a battery today, to infuse something with power that has the space to hold it. One of the first statues I personally charged was a statue of Horus. During it I felt as if I was growing, while the statue began to glow a brilliant blue (the colour of Horus). The falcon statue seemed to come to life, with eyes that glowed and followed my rise within

---

[46] Ficino, Marsiglio Book of Life p.152; Naydler p.134

the room. While it never actually flew, it would not have surprised me if it actually did. After this the statue is charged, it can be used to reach Horus directly. During an Egyptian exhibit at the Glenbow, I provided tours for many mystical groups and individuals. Unfortunately most of the exhibit was only replicas. Most would not understand the need for the actual Egyptian pieces, for usually the replicas are in much better "shape" than the original. However all ancient statues were charged, thus they hold power. The modern replicas, no matter how nice looking, are just pieces of art. An example of this was one of the few actual pieces, a statue of the Neteru Sekhemet. She was a goddess of healing and I directed an individual with a very bad back to touch the statue. Within a few moments the pain in her back was gone. I repeated this healing work with a few others who needed help. This is the power of a true statue; for they are beyond just a symbol they are the energy of the universe itself that can be tapped into through the charged piece.

"Once it is grasped that the Neteru are interwoven with states of consciousness, the religion of Ancient Egypt assumes something of its original power. The Book Of the Dead and other texts are not the products of some wishful fantasy about life after death, but are guides to the unfolding and ever more refined elevated levels of spiritual awareness."[47] When you are finally able to understand the myth, bridged with the symbolism of nature, along with sacred number/geometry (discussed in the knowledge section) - you will fully begin to understand what the individual Neteru represented, what their energies were, and more importantly, when performing healing or transformation you will know what Neteru is needed for success.

Illusion
" All things on earth are unreal..." Hermetic wisdom

The Hindus refer to the world around us as Maya, meaning illusion. To the Egyptians this was called the Veil of Isis, something draped over our eyes to obscure truth. The world we experience every day is thought of as a dual world (up-down, good-bad, male-female) but in reality there is only One. To the alchemist this would be described as every object is but the One Thing, all created by One Mind, and the One Mind and the One Thing are the same. Most people do not live in a world of Oneness but rather a world of separateness, believing they are this body, but not that person, or rock, or tree, or stream. Buddhists teach that we suffer because we believe that we are our body. Gurdjieff and eastern mystics often explained that we are in a prison and we are asleep. We have created the prison (our mind) and our first step is to be aware of this fact. They claim that we are asleep during the day, just as we sleep at night. When we wake in the morning most ignore our night experiences saying

---

[47] Naydler p.27

they were just a dream. With awakening it is claimed that one day we will wake from our daily consciousness and say "oh it was just life." By this token, our waking life is as unreal as the dream world, and paradoxically then the dream world must be as real as this world. This life is really a dream, but instead of waking up from the dream, we want to wake up IN the dream.

Even the world of science is now not so sure of the reality of things. All of what we experience comes from the work of our senses. Yet our senses are just electro-magnetic impulses that are registered in our brain. Thus the world of science now claims that the world is not really out there, but made up in our own brains. Another scientific problem has to do with the makeup of matter. Anything in our physical world, including you, is really made up of very few atoms and molecules, made up of empty space. It is claimed that if "a human being were compressed to the parts that were actually matter, they would be invisible to the human eye." Some say that 'empty space' is made up of more matter (atoms and molecules) than the things we believe to be solid. Thus the Zen teaching of "matter is void, and void is matter."[48] One of my teachers claims that everything you believe about the world is actually the opposite.

Of course a mystic or enlightened being is not really interested what science has to say at all, they are concerned with their personal experience which tells them that the world is not that solid. Some compare it to the 1999 movie *the Matrix*, while Graham Hancock claims eastern mystics call it a "sinister virtual reality game…a mass hallucination designed to distract souls from awakening."[49] The big problem with the hallucination is that we are a part of it, not just affected by it.

However this world also exists. Life is not the illusion, but rather it is our perception of it that is the illusion. Any illusion by definition is something that is mistaken for something else. There is definitely something being perceived, but just because mind replies back chair or mountain, and out there, is not actually correct. Our conscious mind tells us what is real, and not to question its perception. No one ever contemplates if what the conscious mind is telling us is in fact correct. Actually we rarely even have the chance to do so, for our own conscious mind quickly uses words to explain these perceptions to us and others. Not only have we believed the illusion; we have become it.

Carlos Castaneda would describe that we experience the world through our assemblage point. This point registers certain energy streams out of the many that exist in the universe, based on the point's location, which we usually keep in the same place. The few filaments that the point registers is what we use to make up the world. If we move the point, we will register new filaments, thus perceive a completely different world, as happens when we dream. In fact potentially millions of 'worlds' exist simultaneously, but we only experience the same one during waking consciousness. He says this is because we have

---

⁴⁸ Berendt pp.104-06
⁴⁹ Hancock, Graham Heaven's Mirror (Doubleday Canada 1998) p.157

allowed the point to become fixed at a particular place, the same place that most other humans are fixed. Children's points are not fixed but can move easily which allow them to experience many different worlds. Those imaginary friends are only imaginary to adults; the child may have tapped into another world. In time adults and teachers will fix the child's point, at the same place as their own, by rewarding when the child sees or experiences the same world as the adult, or punishing them when they do not. Soon the child will gain the same fixed point as everyone else, so we all experience the same world in roughly the same way. While this reality exists, there are many other worlds and realities that exist on top or with this one. He would claim to not get too focused on this world as it is only here because we make it be here, by fixing our assemblage point. Our habits and patterns (created by the conscious mind) is what will over time keep the point fixed, thus the need to begin breaking our patterns and habits. However to break those habits would mean we would potentially no longer believe everything we currently believe.[50]

What creates all of this illusion is really our conscious mind. That is why all the true teachings in the ancient wisdom are designed around eliminating its hold on us. Our personality, beliefs and thoughts make up the world. As long as you think, "it is a tree," it will always be a tree. When one begins to question that perhaps it may not be a tree, the object (energy) is freed to be something else. We make our world by repeating it to ourselves over and over. Without these thoughts, our conscious mind can no longer force the energy streams to be perceived in the way our thoughts want it to. With enough time and effort, the world may one day stop. The limitations we have always thought ourselves to have, and the world we have always believed to be solid and real, just goes away. I can safely say that nothing can prepare you for the first glimpse of that moment, as it can only be experienced. It is only then that the idea of the world is an illusion really hits home. That being said, when one understands the world is an illusion and they choose at this moment to be in this particular one - they do so to the best of their ability yet still understanding its true nature.

By performing enough personal work, one can gain the shamanic technique of "seeing." Seeing is not done with the eyes, but with the Egyptian Eye of Horus. When Horus can finally defeat Set, representing the inner forces of the conscious mind that tie us to this world and create disorder and hate and unhappiness, the Eye will open. This Eye allows us to perceive not just with our normal eyes, but with our entire being and experience the reality of the universe as it is. This is the goal of all ancient traditions, to "see" the universe as it is not as our conscious mind makes us believe that it is. It is the core of the teachings of Tehuti/Hermes.

---

[50] Books of Carlos Castaneda.

CHAPTER 4
EGYPTIAN PYRAMIDS

145: Looking up the south-west corner of the Great Pyramid

The Egyptian pyramids at Giza are the last surviving member of the seven ancient wonders of the world. The standard story is that pyramids were built as tombs for pharaohs; first at Sakkara, improved on at Daschur, then perfected at Giza- before dropping back to building the original crappy versions again at Sakkara and Abu Sir and other locations. The pyramid building story concludes with the belief that these "tombs" were getting too easy for grave robbers to find, thus the entire process was scrapped and led to the building of new tombs at the Valley of the Kings near Luxor. While told over and over again in every school book, any examination of the tomb theory makes no sense. No original burial has ever been found in one of the original old pyramids, and only the Zozer pyramid at Sakkara even resembles the standard look of an Egyptian tomb. Tomb pyramids do appear in the workers village near the Valley of the Kings from the New Kingdom, but I think the "pyramids as tombs theory" had already been fed to the Egyptian population at that time, and has nothing to do with the original building intent of the giants to the north.

The story may have been created to keep the standard person away from inquiring into what these mountains of stone were for (as continues today). And as one digs more deeply into the standard pyramid story, one finds more holes than Swiss cheese.[51]

Pyramids are found all over the world: Mexico, Peru, North America, Europe, Asia (including some giants ones in China), Africa, as well as several found underwater (pre 8000BC flooding). If we could look under the Antarctic ice sheet, we likely would find them there as well. Standard dating places Egyptian Pyramid building between 2600-2000BC, during the period known as the Old Kingdom. There are no actual building records of course, so these dates are mostly archaeological speculation. In my understanding there were two phases of Egyptian pyramid building. The first came from the Pre-Egyptian, a time at least 10,000 BC and perhaps even older (when the world was supposedly inhabited by primitive cave men), and matches other huge stone monolithic construction found around the world. Not just amazing feats of construction, they were also produced with perfect mathematics, geometry, and proportional harmonies- all the while made with at times with 100 ton stones shaped and carved perfectly. A second Egyptian pyramid building phase did occur after 3000BC, but these pyramids were attempted copies of the giants that had been there for thousands of years. Without recognizing this time dilemma it can be easy to get lost in the wilderness of understanding Egyptian pyramids.

Each individual pyramid also included a temple near a body of water or Nile, a long covered causeway (like a giant hallway of wall paintings to make a long meditative trip in), a second temple on the (usually) east face of the pyramid, then a short passageway to the pyramid entrance. Most had their entrance in the north face, thus be walking in to the south- the direction of dreaming and power, into a stone structure that often contained many chambers and passages. Any pyramid built was not just an object all on its own. Usually it was meant to connect with other pyramids and temples within the same location. Most pyramid sites also include an entire underground labyrinth of tunnels, chambers, temples and perhaps even underground pyramids. We will come to all that in time.

The word pyramid comes from the Greek words 'pyro' (fire) and 'amid' (being at the center). Thus the Greeks saw the pyramids to be the center of the great fire. It is not the sun's fire they were talking about here, but

---

[51] For some odd reason most of the footnotes for this chapter disappeared on revision. However the main source texts for this was *Secrets of The Great Pyramid* by Peter Tompkins, *Giza Power Plant* by Chistopher Dunn, and *The Pyramids and the Sphinx*, American University in Cairo Press

something else, and when one understands that something else, you, the mystery of pyramids begins to unfold.

Medium, Fayum and Daschur

146: Early morning photo of the Red Pyramid, Daschur

To better understand the Giza marvels, it is best to examine other pyramid sites first, as background. At Medium, in the Fayum Oasis south of Giza, is an odd "cone" remnant, a collapsed step pyramid due to poor building methods. It is said to have been built for the Pharaoh Sneferu. The problem is that he also has two other pyramids at Daschur. If tombs are burial places, why does someone need 2, or perhaps 3? The Medium pyramid has been closely studied because standard theory has this as the bridge between the first pyramid at Sakkara and the later masterpieces at Giza (via Daschur)- making Medium the "missing link" of pyramids. Its interior is similar to ones at Daschur, but as John Anthony West claimed in his *Traveler's Guide to Ancient Egypt,* many visitors feel a very unsettling atmosphere, which means to be aware when visiting. However we see that there were giant perfect stones at the interior, indicating the base was a much older structure, than what was built overtop. This concept, a very old middle with a much later addition over it is critical to begin to see pyramids in their origin.

At El Lahun and Harawa the pyramids are mostly made of mud brick. Any mud brick pyramid is from a much later building time, when workers were no longer proficient with stone. At Harawa, the inner chamber of this pyramid is similar to a mini- king's chamber at Giza. This pyramid is odd due to the fact it is one of the few pyramids to not have its entrance at the north (but here from the south.) Most claim that the temple in front of this pyramid was what Herodotus called the Labyrinth in his writing, a 60,000 square meter space with 3000 rooms on two levels, connected by a maze of winding corridors. But new ground penetration radar in 2017 revealed a giant underground area, perhaps hundreds of football fields in size, that my in fact be the labyrinth spoken of. Of note, close to Harawa is an area known as the "Valley of the Whales," where numerous whale and mammal skeletons have been found from when the area was a tropical sea. The main modern labyrinth myth comes from the island of Crete, where upon the walls of Knossos are numerous paintings of whales.

Traveling north we come to the site that contains two of the four largest pyramids in Egypt. Even though the pyramids are huge it gets rather few visitors due to its long drive from Cairo, thus most tour guides and taxi drivers don't want to visit. But don't miss it. The largest pyramid at Daschur is the Red Pyramid (so named for the red colour of the building stone) and is 341 Ft by 721 FT, second only to the Great Pyramid at Giza in overall size. Following a long climb up to the entrance, and down the descending passage into the interior- one comes to the first of three similar chambers. Each has a vaulted ceiling which produce some amazing acoustics. Pyramids are pieces of music set in stone and will have a "vibrational" effect on anyone who enters, and will be more discussed in detail at Giza. There is also a unique carved out area, which may in fact be an original monolithic structure that the pyramid was later built overtop of.

Illustration 1: 147 Bent Pyramid of Daschur

Daschur is most famous for its "Bent" pyramid, claimed by archaeologists to be a building mistake. The two large pyramids here (Bent and Red) are said to be for the Pharaoh Sneferu- the Pharaoh that needed many tombs. Why? Put half his body in one and half in the other? Remember no original burial has been found in an Old Kingdom pyramid and they are devoid of all tomb art and leavings. The trick is to see that pyramids were not named after a pharaoh buried there, but after a god (whom a later pharaoh may have taken the name of as say in the case of Seti 1 or Thutmosis III). The name Sneferu, when translated from Egyptian hieroglyphs, means Double Harmony, and thus may be related to an aspect of the goddess Maat (Double Cosmic Harmony). Thus a site built for the "Double Neteru" would need "double" the pyramids. Once you get that pyramids were built for Neters not Pharaohs, things will open up. The Bent Pyramid, thought of as the mistake due to its two different angles (53 and 43 degrees) that change half way up. Seeing pyramids as music in stone, you will understand that this pyramid's final shape was not due to a mistake, but was designed that way. Its upper angle is 43 degrees, the same slope as the Red Pyramid beside, likely meaning the two resonate together in some way as a harmonic over and under-tone. This dual aspect continues in the interior, where there are TWO entrances. The usual one in the north and another in the west. The name Sneferu "Dual Harmony" may also relate that these two pyramids operate together musically to lift the veil of the inharmonious matrix that traps the fictional self. Also note the amazing block placement in the Bent Pyramid, where stones which no longer have support stones below it, are still able to almost hang in the air, as they were fitted together like Lego.

Surrounding are a few inferior Middle Kingdom pyramids, now near ruins, but we get very unique names. Two of these pyramids are known as the White Pyramid and the Black Pyramid. That makes the 3 main hermetic colours, and I would not be surprised if there was another known as the yellow pyramid somewhere nearby. Note that the copies are near the Nile, while the old large ones are built much farther away in the desert. But all around is evidence of ancient lakes, canals and docks. Where did all the water come from? In 2500BC when they were supposed to be built, the place was like it is today, a desert, and if you wanted water you would have followed the Middle Kingdom idea and built pyramids close to the Nile. Added to this anomaly is the fact Steven Mehler realized that the ground slopes west to east (towards the Nile) which would have made bringing in water from the river an even a greater challenge. However some 7-10,000 years ago there was a combination of a wetter climate in the area, as well as what he believed to be and called the Ur Nil (an older Nile that flowed in the middle of the now dry in the Sahara) which is where water was likely was brought from, following gravity, to the site. This is important as to date the site to the time the old Nile was flowing pushes the building dates back at least to 7,000 BC.

148: Corbeled ceiling interior of the Red Pyramid at Daschur

Sakkara

149:Zozer's Step Pyramid and courtyard, Sakkara

Sakkara is the largest site under excavation in Egypt, having hundreds of temples, courtyards, and pyramids. It is the one site in Egypt that I recommend visitors do some preparation for the night previous. While a huge site with lots to explore, it is known mostly for the step pyramid of Zozer, considered the first pyramid built in Egypt. It is also known for secondary pyramids that contain the famous Pyramid Texts, the earliest known religious and mystical writings in history (my translation in chapter 24), and for an underground chamber of large stone boxes known as the Serapeum.

The step pyramid complex is so "un" Egyptian looking that right away I had the feeling that it was not Egyptian at all but something else. Before even getting inside the step pyramid area, one is confronted by a giant enclosure wall that is a marvelous piece of art (most of what you see is restoration), that was copied to make Universities in the American Southwest. The entrance to the temple proper is though a "forest" of 40 palm columns, each made to look like groups of 17 or 19 rolls of papyrus reeds bunched together. 17 and 19 are key numbers in Egyptian art. The columns themselves are very unique for Egypt, as they are not free-standing, but are attached to the surrounding masonry. John West has commented that as one moves farther through the columns, the space between narrows "exaggerating the illusion of distance," which is similar to shortening the space of the strings as one moves up a guitar neck. This lead in area could be one long guitar made in stone.

150:One of the very unique "attached" columns near the Step Pyramid, Sakkara

Exiting the "guitar" one comes to a gigantic courtyard, that included two giant B's of stone in the center. It is claimed that this was the area that the famous heb-sed festival was held, where the pharaoh was required to run a special race every 30 years to prove his physical fitness to still be the king. Yet, as described by Jeremy Naydler in his book *Shamanic Wisdom in the Pyramid Texts*, this race was not about physical prowess, but was a journey of initiation and awakening. The floor of the Sakkara courtyard area was made of pure alabaster, special resonator of energies. That is reminder that everywhere you go in Egypt, pay attention to stone- not just upright and standing, but what was used to make the floor. It is all connected.

At the end of the courtyard is the Step Pyramid. Recently it has been found that there never was a cover of white Tura limestone as on other pyramids, but instead was covered with mud brick painted white to look like tura limestone. Why make a pyramid to look like "something" if this is the first. There would be nothing for it to look like. This shows that this could not be the first pyramid built, but the first attempted copy of something already existing. This was the beginning to simulate the great structures at Giza and Daschur with no real idea of how to do it. More unique with this pyramid is also the fact that the interior passageways and chambers, which were originally part of a prior mastaba, has wall carvings, pottery and jars left, star covered ceiling, blue fience on the walls. It is definitely a tomb that later had a step pyramid built overtop of it. But none of the supposed later built pyramids had anything that looked like a New Kingdom burial chamber. If this was the first this design it should have been continued. The name Zozer also does not appear for 1000 years after this was supposedly built. Carvings from the date of construction say the pyramid was built for Horus-Neter Khet, which many claim was the name of the Pharaoh Zozer at the time. Again Zozer might be a Pharaoh from a far later period wanting to associate with the pyramid temple of a Neter, in this case, Horus-Neter Khet.

The layout of the site however was something that got my attention. It reminded me of the many Mayan sites in Mexico that I had been to, especially sites along the Ruuta Puuc. Near the enclosure wall is an area called the heb-sed court, which looked almost exactly like a Mayan ball court, I even found round holes on top of the west wall that could have easily held the hoop or ring used in the famous Mexican game. I could even see in my mind's eye and early version of the Zozer step pyramid with a long staircase in front similar to pyramids in Mexico. Back when I made my first trip here in 2004 I felt there was a high possibility that this part of Sakkara was a Mayan site in Egypt, or an attempt to link the two cultures. It was a few years later I came across the book *Land of Osiris* by Stephen Mehler. In it he wrote of being given entrance into the newly excavated Temple of Maya, supposedly a 28th Dynasty figure, whose amazing statues of he and his wife Merit are on display in the Egyptian Museum in Leiden, Holland. These depictions in stone closely resemble how the Hindu goddess Maya (goddess of illusion) is depicted. While inside of this temple, Mehler photographed a very strange ceiling with what appeared to be Mayan hieroglyphs. This was later confirmed by a Mayan elder in Guatemala. So what are Mayan hieroglyphs doing inside an Egyptian temple, that also has the name Maya? This was a confirmation for me that my original views on this site were correct.

Sakkara is also known as the place where one can find the Pyramid Texts, usually viewed in the Pyramid of Teti. To really get the extent of the power of this hieroglyphic text you have to go to the pyramid where they were first carved, the Pyramid of Unas (now closed to the public but Zahi Hawass and Kamel Wahid of the Egyptian Antiquities Organization allowed my entrance. As of 2017 it seems they have re-opened the pyramid for tourists). To really experience the Pyramid Texts of Unas, you need to place yourself back into the ancient context. To do that properly you must begin not at the pyramid itself, but way back at the Valley Temple- that ruined structure near the ticket office about 1km away. From this temple you can walk the remains of the causeway to the Unas Pyramid. The small remnants give an impression of what the completed causeway must have been like. Along the causeway are numerous temples and shrines- a couple of them are extremely powerful, and again can find amazing alabaster and quartzite floors. The mortuary temple in front of the pyramid had a basalt floor.

After a long passage into the pyramid (the other pyramid texts pyramids have similar interiors) itself, one comes to three inner chambers. To the left is a room that looks like a giant E, with two stone pillars and no carvings. The central room is mainly square and here one finds the carved, blue painted pyramid texts, that begin on the entrance passageway. Touching them sent sparks of electricity through my arm, and I could feel the glyphs pulsing like a giant heartbeat. The texts continue into the chamber to the right, which includes a perfectly smooth sarcophagus box, different than the one in the Great Pyramid, but equally mesmerizing. Three walls have the inscribed texts, while the back wall, made of alabaster instead of limestone, has a series of graphic designs. This entire area and the texts themselves are fully examined in the Pyramid Texts chapter.

150A Userkaf Temple area

Another pyramid worth checking out is the Pyramid of Userkaf. While the pyramid itself is in ruin, and is closed for entrance- it is the temple that is to be seen. Here is a near close resemblance of what one can find at Abu Sir. Large basalt blocks make up the floor, with huge pieces of granite surround. You can get a good glimpse of impossible carving techniques as you can see huge holes sent deep into the granite stones (that can only have been make with some sort of specialized drill), as well as several deep cuts in the stone that one would only find today with laser saws. That this could have been made with copper tools as suggested in books is ludicrous. Recall as well that it was at Sakkara that the famous Schist Plates in the Cairo Museum were found. These plates seem to be the working gears of some type of machine, and are possibly part of unlocking the secret of how the Ancients could do what they did with the hardest of stone.

151:Statue of Meruka in a false door, in his "burial temple," Sakkara

Another key area not to miss at Sakkara are the private tombs, which are less burial areas and more temple complexes. Along the walls are carved spectacular painted reliefs that display symbolic scenes of daily life, used to explain some aspect of spiritual transformation. For sure do not miss the older tombs like Ti and Ptah-hotep for they have the most sacred geometry used in the relief making. The later tombs, like the famous Meruka, while still spectacular, one can notice a decline in the craftsmanship and carving. Most mastabas contain what are called false doors, the coolest maybe the red painted one in the mastaba of Mehu. These doors are said to be for the Ka of the deceased to enter and exit. I spent much time with the "doors" and found them to have a very magnetic pull, and by falling in you likely would fall into a crack in reality, or a crack in the bubble of self. Experiments with them showed to me this was the case. Castaneda mentioned that falling backwards was a way to cross over the parallel lines. You might say that was a hint.

Also at Sakkara is the area known as the Serapeum- usually closed- that was the burial place of the Apis bull of Ptah. And while one can find thousands of mummified bulls here, the real thing to note is the stone sarcophagus boxes, 80 to 100 tons each, likely needing to be carved in the very spot they now sit and unlikely to have been done with the supposed copper tools of the time. The boxes come from a period before the chamber was taken over for the bulls, and is said to be a pre-dynastic temple of healing and these "coffins" were part of the sound and dimensional journeying healing that took place here. This may be the main reason it is closed to the public, the more powerful a place the less they want people in it. Also note that beneath the desert surface is an entire underground world here, if you know where to look you can still find the entrances.

One last thing to think about is the name of the location itself, Sakkara. If you break this down, Sah is the Egyptian word for a star or a doorway. Ka the physical element of the person, and Ra the energy behind light or the sun.

Thus we have the star or doorway between the physical mind and the Light. Puts Sakkara in a new "light" don't you think?

Abu Sir-Abu Ghurab

150b Abu Sir main temple

Just north of Sakkara is another rarely visited site, but potentially important. Abu Sir,directly translated from Arabic means "place of sardines," which makes no sense. But the name does reveal something, if you look at the word as Ab-Busir. Ab is the Egyptian name for heart or center, while Usir is an abbreviation of Ausir (Osiris) thus is the "center or heart of Osiris." This in fact could have been the heart center of the entire pre-dynastic civilization. At Abu Sir are three still standing pyramids that give a similar (smaller) impression of Giza. The mortuary temples with them are models of geometry with basalt floors, granite blocks filled with drill holes and saw cuts. However, the pyramids are literally falling apart. Why if these are supposed to be the one's built right after Giza are they falling apart so badly? My feeling is that what is seen at Abu Sir is the rebuilding of the site by the Old Kingdom Egyptians, built overtop of the original. The pre-Old Kingdom stuff is under what is there now (or at anything's base if you look closely enough), save for a few key parts left in tact. Egypt was known for rebuilding on old sites, temples built one on top of the other, tapping the original power source below. A walk into the surrounding desert reveals tons of fragments showing this was once a giant site. Ancient tradition in the area claims that this may be not only the oldest site in Egypt but perhaps on the earth and is sometimes referred to as the "landing
70

spot," the place where the Neters first descended to the planet from the heavens. One place to point out is the huge mastaba of Ptah-Shep-ser, second only in size to Meruka's at Sakkara. Here there is a special area that had 20 stone pillars arranged in a square. In Castaneda terms this could be the 20 warriors of the nagual's party, arranged into the four directions. The 21st (nagual man and woman) is either the center spot or is the entire mastaba/temple itself. There should be a 22nd pillar as well, the 0 fool, and should be found here with more examination.

150c How exactly are perfect holes like this drilled in the ancient past with supposedly copper tools? Obviously this stone, and many others at Abu Sir, were in someway driled. The holes within are near perfectly smooth.

Just north is the sister site of Abu Ghurab. While there are no pyramids here, there are what are called "sun temples," giant obelisks placed on huge blocks of stone. The first three of these were supposedly built for the pharaoh Userkaf and have their temple dedicated to Neith, and very feminine like statues of Userkaf were found here. Even some Egyptologists are willing to suggest that Userkaf was Neith in form. There it is again. This site is not for pharaohs but for the neters. The most famous structure at Abu Guhrab is the Niussurre structure. Here is an alter made of five pieces of alabaster, set together as 4 hotep symbols around a center. The four directions around the center (Osiris- Absolute, the 4 DNA proteins around consciousness). This alter can be seen as a form of square medicine wheel. Further off in the courtyard are a series of square, perfectly cut (perhaps machine cut) pieces of fine alabaster with large circular holes drilled into the tops. They are referred to as basins, to hold water or blood from sacrifices. Typical thinking from those who see our ancients as primitive savages. Alabaster is a stone used for mental clarity and stopping the mind. What is interesting is that surrounding these basins are teeth-like grooves that lead to all sorts of speculation. They are pieces that should be examined very closely.

Just north of Abu Sir is the site of Zawiyat Al Abran, where there exist two pyramid remnants, that if complete that would have been as large as those on the Giza plateau. Apparently the site was built to take the use of a large power spot that exists close by. Originally that power spot had an Egyptian Temple over it, then a Coptic Church, now a mosque that is closely guarded and unable to be entered. Some suggest that this is the "central" pyramid site that all the others were built around, and this power spot might have been the main "power spot" for the entire Egyptian civilization. Another ruined Pre-Dynastic pyramid can be found at Abu Rawash is 7 Km north-east of the Giza, which still contains is underground passage make of gigantic blocks.

Giza

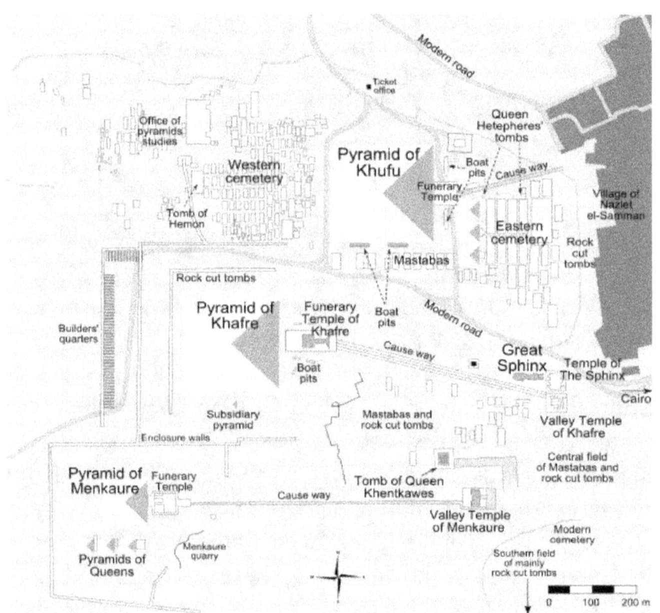

151 A: The site of Giza

The greatest known ancient site on the planet earth is said by Egyptologists to have been built around 2500 BC, with three large pyramids built as tombs for subsequent pharaohs: Khufu, Khafre and Menkaure. Together the stone used in these three pyramids is enough to build a 3 meter high, 1 meter thick wall entirely around France. In front of the Khafre pyramid is the famous Sphinx, said to be carved in the likeness of Khafre. Surrounding all of this is hundreds of mastaba tombs, similar to what is found at Sakkara. Though not spoken of, an entire underground city exists here, again complete with temple complexes and perhaps underground pyramids.

The Sphinx

152:Side view of the Sphinx, Giza

This amazing structure is 240 feet long, 66 feet high (the height of a six story building) and is 34 feet across. Carved directly out of the limestone, it has left a trench 18 feet wide and 25 feet deep. The blocks removed from the excavation were used to build the temples that sit in front and beside of it. The Sphinx is (now) the body of a lion with the head of a Pharaoh, but that may not have always been the case. The Sphinx faces due east (the rising sun and the equinox) yet I sort of feel sorry for it because now all day it must stare directly at a Kentucky Fried Chicken and a Pizza Hut. Modern archaeologists claim the Sphinx was carved in 2500 BC by the Pharaoh Khafre, as a guardian of the entire Giza plateau, and his own pyramid behind. They claim that the face on the Sphinx is of Khafre's face, supposedly matched by Mark Lehner with a couple of statues in the Cairo Museum. However many others, including senior New York Police forensic sketch artist Frank Domingo, claim the Sphinx face and the statue faces do not match.

At one time, a gigantic obelisk sat at the base of the Sphinx. Still standing on the spot is what is called the Sphinx Stela, erected in 1400 BC by 18th Dynasty Pharaoh Thutmosis IV who claimed the Sphinx came to him in a dream telling the young man to clear the area of sand, having been unattended for a long while. If he did so he would become the new Pharaoh. Taken the stela literally, if the Sphinx had been covered with sand, the area must have been left unattended for a long period of time. Looked at more symbolically this was around the period of time of the Second Hyksos (Sumerian alien) rule of Egypt, and what is translated as "sand" that Thutmosis was called to clear away from the Giza Plateau, may have in fact been the presence of the Sumerian archons. If he could clear these away, he could be the Pharaoh. Within two generations of Thumosis IV came the reign of Akhenaten- which could have been an outside response to to this attempt to "clear the sand."

The age of the Sphinx is a great controversy. The first archaeologists at Giza in the 1800's felt that the Sphinx was far older than the rest of the site, and it was only in the 20th century that Egyptologists changed this idea (due to finding the name Khafre in a small temple close to the sphinx). They claimed the Sphinx was built by Khafre due to association. They also used line 13 of the Sphinx Stela that hailed Khafre for his work in restoring the Sphinx, which Egyptologists claim is an error on the stela, that instead the inscription should have read he built it, not repaired it. Did the people who erected that monument really make a mistake? They were thousands of years closer to its construction than we are, shouldn't what they have to say carry a bit of weight on the subject, but to agree with their writing would throw the current dating of the the Giza plateau to the wind. The Sphinx Stela also claims, "Now a great magical power had existed in this place from the beginning of all time and it existed over all the reigns…And at this time the Sphinx-form of the most mighty Khepera came to this place and the greatest of souls, the holiest of the holy ones visited there." The sphinx based on the Stela is connected with Khepera, transformation from darkness to light. The sphinx also had the ancient name Sheshep-Ankh-Atum "The living image of Atum." Indeed the Sphinx's English name is a corruption, through Greek of Sheshep-Ankh, so it seems more likely the Sphinx is energetically connected to Khepera and Atum, not some pharaoh named Khafre.

Another stela, The Inventory Stela in the Cairo Museum, was found in 1821 in a small Isis temple just east of the Great Pyramid. The stela provides an inventory for the statues Khufu FOUND in the Isis Temple when he came to repair it. It also claims that Khufu (Khafre's father) saw the Sphinx. Thus the temple of Isis was already old at the site and needed repair, and if Khufu saw the Sphinx there is no way then that Khafre could be the builder. Isis is called Mistress of the Pyramid, there must have at least been one pyramid there for her to the Mistress of. If a pharaoh named Khufu did build a pyramid for himself, it would be one of the three smaller pyramids to the east of the great Pyramid, which is what I believe they are, smaller Old Kingdom copies of the giants beside. However instead of investigating anything that the stela has to say, Egyptologists simply ignore it claiming it is a fake or a mistake. Out of sight out of mind. They do rightly claim that the stela was written in 1020 BC, 1500 years after the pyramids were supposed to have been built, but that does not mean the information is not accurate for the Egyptians were well know for copying stelas once they began to show signs of wear and age. If this was all the Egyptologists had to dodge it would not be so bad, but they also have to dodge geology.

153:Photo of the Sphinx trench showing definite signs of water erosion, Giza

Modern symbolist author John Anthony West was the one who brought back the theories of RA Schwaller de Lubicz, who spent much of his life between 1930-50 studying symbolic aspects of Ancient Egypt, particularly the temple of Luxor. In one of Schwaller's books, West noticed that he casually mentions that the Sphinx was weathered by water not by sand or wind. West saw this sentence as monumental in significance. How could the Sphinx be weathered by water, the Sahara is a desert? With the help of paleo-geology, West was shown that the Sahara was not always a desert, and there was water present as late as 7000BC, while around 12,000 BC the region was a tropical paradise. West brought in Boston University geologist, Dr. Robert Schoch to examine the area. Schoch instantly recognized the erosion pattern was consistent with water, specifically rain water, evident as the water finds weak spots in the rock that it uses a channels. Wind or sand erosion has more of a blasting effect, which is not really seen in the sphinx area. Most of the stone that now covers the lower half of the sphinx is a very poorly done modern restoration that covers much of the underlying stone, and which began shortly after West and Schoch came up with their new theory, perhaps to hide the most damaging evidence. However it can still be easily seen in the trench areas itself. In fact an exploration of the entire Giza Plateau shows that only the Sphinx, Sphinx Temples and a few other structures show this water weathering. The rest are weathered by wind and sand. A prehistoric Sphinx would revolutionize not just Egyptian history, but human history. The main attack against an ancient Sphinx, is that there is not SUPPOSED to be any civilization at 10,000+ BC. (*Fingerprints of the Gods* is a good work for anyone wanting to read more detail on the dating and geologic evidence of the sphinx investigation).

A couple of other things to consider about the Sphinx. One is why is it carved in the shape of a lion? Some claim it is an equinox and presessional marker, as it faces the sunrise on the equinox. Yet during the period the sphinx was supposed to be built, 2500 BC, the sun rose in the constellation of Taurus (bull) and only around 12,000 BC did Leo the lion rise on the horizon. Another lion connection is that the Sphinx may originally have had a female lion head, that of the goddess Tefnut or Sekhmet. Also to keep in mind is that during the New Kingdom, two sphinxes were always placed at the doorways of temple as guardians. Called the Aker (one yesterday the other tomorrow) they guard time to allow only the present moment to enter between. Thus at Giza it should be odd that there is only one. It is possible that a second sphinx does exist, perhaps in the western part of the plateau or maybe even a mirror underground. The underground possibility comes from the many sources that say the Sphinx was the entry point to a series of temple complexes where priests were initiated. Lately more suggestions have been made that the original form was not a lion at all, but was a representation of the dog Anubis, in the form of Upuat, Opener of the Ways. And when one examines the remains, especially the back legs and tail, this is quite likely. For today we know the current head is not the original for it is too small in proportion to the body. Some have suggested a feminine face as the original, again others that this was in fact first a seated Anubis statue.

Also recognize that what you see now as the Sphinx, is something that has had much restoration work done, and it is hard to tell how far away from the original re-found by the French in 1700's it is. The modern cement masonry looks out of place. The hole that showed in a rare hot air balloon photo on the top of the Sphinx's head is gone (one of the many suggested entrances to the underground world below) and one can see today a circular cement like plug. There also appears to be structures very close to it in 1800's photographs that are no longer there.

Sphinx Temples

154: Some giant granite blocks in the Valley Temple. Notice the many joints to the stone in the center, reminiscent of Inca stonework in Cuzco Peru and difficult to accomplish, Giza

In front of the great Sphinx are two temples, referred to as the Sphinx and Valley Temples. The blocks for the temples were built from the same rock that was carved away from the Sphinx enclosure. The temples have a similar look to the Osireian at Abydos. A layer of granite was placed over the weaker limestone blocks to protect them. Some blocks in the Sphinx Temple are 200 tons and raised more than 40 feet of the ground. Today, only two land-based cranes on the Earth could lift and place the blocks, but the builders at Giza seemed to move them like they were Lego. The blocks could have been cut into smaller more movable pieces like at other temples, but the Giza builders chose not to do this, but do it the hard way.

155:Back chamber area of the Valley Temple with stone blocks arranged similar to the Osireion at Abydos, suggesting that both were built during the same period the Sphinx temple

Beside is what is known as the Valley Temple, where stones (some 50 tons) are placed together in a jigsaw fashion, similar to Cuzco in Peru, an amazing amount of work is needed to shape and place the stones for this result. The entrance to the Valley Temple is made of 6 layers of stone. Some of these layers have a curve to them, while others are straight. The doorway is at the exact point where the top 3 and bottom 3 divide. I saw this instantly as the 6 lines of the Chinese I Ching, divided into two 3-line tigrams. Solid or broken lines make up one of 64 possible tigrams of the Chinese Oracle. Here at Giza they run 0 for curved, - for straightness.

0 - - 0 - 0

This tigrams is #48 "The Well of Knowledge." and perhaps this temple is the actual personification of tigram 48 in stone. The interior of the temple is made of two rows of five pillars (the number of Horus) and they were placed over a floor of alabaster that allows fast energy movement.

153a Another example of near perfect craftsmanship outside the Sphinx Temple

Just outside of the Sphinx Temple is a great place to see some of the amazing stone work on the Giza plateau. Here large stone blocks are carved in C-cuts, to perfect smoothness, then layered with a perfectly smoothed top. To make such smooth giant C cuts into such stone is basically phenomenal, and for sure impossible with the supposed copper tools of the era, for their would be no way to make the roundness or smoothness without a very sophisticated type of tool work.

Matabas

156:Temple of Seshmenefer IV, Giza

Around the pyramid and the Sphinx area are the mastaba fields, often made from cyclopean blocks and are littered with false doors. I recommend spending time in these areas, rarely visited by tourists, thus you can have some time alone (rare on the Giza site). There are some shafts near the Khafre pyramid that run 70 feet down, that lead to some nice carvings and reliefs, though there is more than enough to see with the more accessible mastabas above ground. Perhaps my favourite mastaba on the plateau is the one of Seshmenefer IV, just a walk up from the Sphinx. It contains a purification pool, a recapitulation area below ground, and a two benches between a false door, and a still functioning ancient healing temple. A few others I suggest are Senegemid-Inti (some nice raised reliefs and an eight pillared room), Khenementi (a stair way connects the two sides with amazing false doors), Kapuniset Kai, Idu (where a Buddha like stature appears to be rising from the ground- photo chapter 2), and Imry.

The Pyramids

Giza currently has three large main pyramids, known with the names Khufu, Khafre and Menkaure. Subsequent are two sets of three small pyramids which are known as "Queen's Pyramids." There is also just the shaft left of a subsidiary pyramid beside the middle Khafre pyramid that is never discussed. There also appears to be evidence of at least two more giant pyramids that used to exist further out into the desert.

Around the plateau at least six small pyramids were said to have been built for the Pharaoh's queens or daughters. Yet when you examine these structures the blocks are crumbling and they don't appear well built. Why? If they were built at the exact same time as the giants beside they should show equal workmanship. That being said these small pyramids make for a nice trip inside, again rarely visited.

Bauval and Hancock were one of the first people to write that they felt that the three main pyramids on the site were meant to signify the belt stars of the constellation Orion. However, each set of three Queen's Pyramids might be telling something far more than this. The grouping by the Menkaure Pyramid, at the far south end of the site, are a match of the belt stars of Orion at its high point in the precessional cycle- some 25, 0000 years ago. The queen's pyramids by the Great Pyramid, are a match for how Orion's belt stars will look at the end of the precessional cycle, (sometime in the next few hundred years, perhaps 2012). This amazing layout, and a line that links these, may in fact be a key to helping to relate that the dates of 10,000 BC and 2012 AD were included in the building of the site.

To me however, I feel that the three main pyramids on the site are more directly related to the key myth of Egypt. The Great Pyramid represents Osiris, middle pyramid for Isis, and the third not only for Horus- but his ongoing challenge from Set. If there is anything that amazes me about the Giza Plateau is this fact, almost all the research, books and documentaries are all about the Great Pyramid. It gets probably 95% of all the attention, yet right beside it is a pyramid almost of equal size (though a bit less romantic inside), and then the Menkaure pyramid,while seemingly small beside the other two-is quite the amazing structure. What I present will also give more excess info on the Great Pyramid, simply because it has most of the research done. My goal is in the next few years to put out a small book ONLY on the other pyramids on the site. For now lets examine the pyramids.

Menkaure

157:The Menkaure pyramid behind its three "queen's" pyramids, Giza

This pyramid (215 feet high and 356 feet in length) is much smaller than the other two pyramids and many tend to ignore this one. It is still a powerful presence when viewed with the other two at your back. In 1837 Howard-Vyse entered and found and empty basalt box and some bones. The natural assumption was that these were the bones of Menkaure. Modern scientific tests showed that the bones do not date to the pyramid age, but to the Christian Age some 2000 years later. This shows the signs of an 'intrusive' burial. The upper tiers of the pyramid were originally cased in white Tura limestone, while the lower courses were in red granite from Aswan. This is the symbolism of white representing Horus and red representing Set, and the pyramid is meant to personify the battle between heart and mind. Look closely at some of the casing blocks. Parts of the outer pyramid have been completely smoothed flat, and then stop at a line running up the pyramid, where the remaining stones are rough and unfinished. This happens in two places. It is one of the oddities, why smooth the outer stone for a while and stop exactly at a line running top-bottom?

This pyramid has two entrances, though few know this. The second leads from the main room but stops part way into the pyramid, or at least is claimed to stop. I myself have not verified this second entrance does indeed stop at a wall as suggested.

Inside the structure are three chambers hacked out of the solid bedrock. In one chamber are six 'cells' similar to medieval monk's sleeping quarters. Egyptologists claim they are "magazines for storing objects that the dead king would require close to his body, but upon examination they were the perfect shape to be meditation spaces. I did this for an hour, and doing so led me to some very odd experiences as reality began to break. The main chamber has blocks fitted together in the style of the Valley Temple and Cuzco Peru. Huge monolithic blocks form the ceiling. To fit them together is a near impossibility. They seem to have had to be placed from below, but they require perhaps 100 men to lift them, and the chamber does not have that much space. So how could they have been raised and placed?

158 Giant Stone block in the Minkaure Temple

The outer temple is made again of giant limestone blocks, maybe 100-150 tons each, and show a depth of weathering not found the stone of the surrounding mastabas, supposedly built at the same period of time. This can be a great place to sit on the Giza Plateau, as this area tends to get some of the fewest visitors and from a few spots you can get great views of the Khafre Pyramid.

Pyramid of Khafre

159:Khafre pyramid, Giza

The middle pyramid is recognizable due to the fact that some of the original casing stones are still left at the top. This pyramid is 471 feet high with sides of 708 feet. While it is slightly smaller than the Great Pyramid, it appears to be the same height because it is built on higher ground. The base is built out of huge cyclopean blocks, some weighing as much as 200 tons. It is possible that there may have been an original old structure here before even the Pre-Egyptians started to build pyramids over top of it. I am comfortable saying that this is the oldest pyramid on the site.

You enter from the Northern face in a corridor that descends at 25 degrees 55, but most interesting is the fact that there is a second entrance (or the exit as I like to think of it). Within the pyramid is a room with almost the exact same dimensions as the King's Chamber of the Great Pyramid, only not built in Granite but limestone. The Khafre chamber equals the King's Chamber in length, but has a different width. Archaeologists claim this is a storeroom, but see no great oddity that it is the EXACT same length as the King's Chamber in the Great Pyramid. This is no co-incidence and in some way these two rooms in the two pyramids are linked. Another strange anomaly is that the man I call Russia's John West, Andrei Syklarov, showed that the original casing stones of this pyramid were painted, either a red or yellow colour. No explanation has been given for the need to paint the white limestone casing stones.

In the theory listed at the end of this chapter, in conversations between Scott Creighton and I, he noticed that the Khafre Pyramid is actually the exact center point of the circle the touches the key monuments of the plateau. Which could make the case that this is in fact the oldest pyramid, for they built the center first- to act as a proper radius marker point for keeping the rest of the site within the circular layout. Since this is for Isis "Mistress of the Pyramid," I would be expecting a more hidden wisdom to be built into the stonework than is found with the Great Pyramid beside.

160:Inside the main chamber of the Khafre Pyramid

Great Pyramid

161:Modern entrance of the Great Pyramid

The Great Pyramid is 482 feet high (over 40 stories in the air) and has a near square base of 755 feet. Some 3 million individual blocks of limestone and granite, weighing between 2-70 tons, were used to build the pyramid in 201 stepped tiers. "The Great Pyramid contains more masonry than all the medieval cathedrals and chapels built in England." While today we see only the 'interior' blocks, in its heyday 115,000 casing blocks of pure white limestone 8 feet wide, 12 feet long and 5 feet high were placed over the interior masonry. A few remaining casing stones survive at the bottom of the pyramid. They were cemented together so perfectly that the joints are nearly invisible, and what stones remain even a razor blade can not fit between them (see photo 168). They were joined so perfectly "that one would have said it to be a single slab from top to bottom," and would have glistened with the light of the sun, resembling a giant lighthouse. In the 13th and 14th century, Cairo was destroyed by earthquakes and the pyramid casings were torn down to help rebuild the city. The Grand Mosque was built entirely out of pyramid casings.

Another interesting feature, rarely noted, is that the sides of the structure are hollowed in, check when you are there. You will need the right time of day for the shadows to be cast properly for you to see it. As well, the blocks do not get smaller as one goes up the pyramid. At around the 35th course, the blocks actually get very large, which defies normal logic of letting the blocks get smaller as one builds upward. In fact, near the top are some massive stones. The Great Pyramid appears to be built on what seems to be a perfectly level piece of manufactured concrete. However this is not the case, because the pyramid itself is actually built overtop of a 30 foot hill. (see How Built). It is built to a standard that is incomparable in modern building practices, but it gets even more amazing upon looking at what was built inside.

The standard story is that the Great Pyramid was a giant tomb to house the body of the pharaoh Khufu (Cheops in Greek). A number of burial chambers were built, supposedly considered inadequate and a new one was built. The story says that the pyramid was un-entered for centuries until an Arab explorer in 820 AD, Al Mamun, came searching for treasure and rare manuscripts. He broke into the pyramid, and found it completely empty without even finding a pottery shard. I will examine this story in more detail later.

Mathematics and Core Features

The pyramid is almost perfectly aligned to the cardinal points (N/S/E/W), and is aligned to true north more perfectly than the Meridian Building of the Greenwich Observatory in London.

The Great Pyramid is a mathematical monument. To begin with, the slope is 50 degrees 51. This makes the Great Pyramid's height/base ratio a perfect π relationship. Some speculate pi was included to make the Great Pyramid a perfect representation of the Northern Hemisphere with a 1: 43,200 (a precessional number) the base the equator and the apex the pole, while the base is a 1/8th of a degree of latitude. If you divide half the perimeter by the height you get the Golden Section 1.618. The floor of the Kings Chamber is ten times pi, while without one of the smaller sides added- it is ten times golden section squared.

The Egyptian Royal Cubit used the build the pyramid was claimed in 1925 to be 0.5236 modern meters. Today most prefer not to give a measurement for the old cubit. But just to note that if you take pi 3.1416, and subtract the Golden Section squared 2.618, the result will be 0.5236. That is too amazing a co-incidence for the choice of the pyramid builders base measurements.

Yet the math gets even stranger. Make two circles, one around the outside of the GP, one around the inside edges. Subtract the length of the inner from the outer and the answer is 299, 79613. 299,792458 is the speed of light in million of meters per second. The exact latitude of the Great Pyramid is 29 d 58' 4528", works out to be 29.9792458 N. And more so I found that if you take the Khafre Pyramid and multiply 2 times the base (706 X2) by height, (471), the answer is 2.99787685775 ,again close to speed of light. This insistence on bringing the value for the speed of light I will reveal at the end of this chapter.

How about this from the French documentary "Revelation of the Pyramids" to get you thinking. Run a line on the earth from Easter Island through Giza, along a 100KM wide front you will hit, Nazca, Machu Picchu, Cuzco, Dogan lands, Siva Oasis, Giza, Petra, UR, Persepolis, and Ankhor Wat. The distance between Nazca to Giza, is the same as Teotihuacan to Giza. Giza to Easter island distance is 10,000 x phi. Ankhor to Giza distance multiplied by the golden section, is equal to the distance from Giza to Nazca. If you make this line an equator, the north pole would be where magnetic north is right now.

Name

Since Herodotus's writing, the Great Pyramid has been regarded as the tomb monument of the the very unpopular Pharaoh Khufu, who ruled for 50 years. Herodotus claims that 10,000 men were used to build it, and that they worked consistently for 20 years. His words read that it was a monument to Khufu, not a tomb as is reported. The actual body of Khufu was said to rest on an island under or near the pyramid, surrounded by water brought in from the Nile by an artificial duct.

Egyptologists point to a small number of quarry marks in a chamber discovered by Howard-Vyse in 1837 as proof the pyramid was Khufu's tomb. Howard-Vyse's expedition in Egypt was very costly in 1837, and was in potential danger of returning to England a broke failure. Davidson had previously located four chambers above the King's Chamber but nothing to be found in any one of them. Vyse found another chamber. In his personal diary, a through inspection was made the day of the discovery, but there is no mention in his diary of any hieroglyphic markings. The next day when he returned with witnesses, hieroglyphic marks suddenly appear.

There are some strange things regarding these markings. To begin with the angles of the glyphs appear to not be made at the quarry (as they are said to have be done) but by someone working in very cramped quarters. Howard-Vyse sent copies of the hieroglyphs to the British Museum and Samuel Birch who was their hieroglyphic expert for confirmation. Contrary to modern thought, Birch did not give a confirmation. He claimed that the symbols were strange, with symbols appearing from different eras. The style itself was one which did not appear in Egypt until some 1,000 years later, and some not until 26th Dynasty in 664BC.

Few hieroglyphic books existed in 1837. The best at the time was Materia Hieroglyphica by John Gardner Wilkinson. In 1837 Wilkinson had realized that his book had several mistakes and a revised copy was printed. His book had made errors like confusing the sign for KH with the sundisk representing RA. Some of the names found in the Vyse chamber do not say Khufu, they make the same mistake as the book, the name appearing is Rafu. No ancient could have possibly made a mistake like this. It would have been like a modern builder in Washington spelling the President's name wrong on a monument. To make matters worse, this was not a President, but a direct descendant of the Neteru. Such a mistake would have had the carver fearing instant death from Ra for making such a monumental mistake. This means the workmen either did not know who the Pharaoh of Egypt was, or it is a "shameful archaeological fraud." Interestingly, in 1837 the revised hieroglyphic book arrived in Cairo shortly after the discovery by Howard-Vyse. On the day of the book's arrival, Vyse made a trip to Cairo. The glyphs in the chamber that are spelled correctly seem to have been redone. Amazingly, this 'graffiti' is enough for Egyptologists to "accurately say that the Great Pyramid was built in Khufu's time."

The current dating of the pharaohs of Egypt comes form three sources: Tablet of Karnak, Wall of Abydos and the Tablet of Sakkara. They are all New Kingdom documents, not in order, and not complete. The only statue found of this supposed famous pharaoh Khufu is a small ivory figure, and was not found at Giza, but at Abydos. When the name is found inscribed somewhere it is either Khufu or Knhum-Khuf, and is connected at times with Thoth. William Fix felt that Khufu is not a person, but a deity. The pyramid itself might be named Khufu, but not after any pharaoh. It seems the name became a powerful charm in Ptolemaic Egypt and is found often, much like a Christian cross, as a sign of protection. Just because a cross is found on a church no one would think that Jesus built it, but this is the thinking of Pyramids in Egypt. The name Khufu connecting to Thoth is not surprising, as many ancient chroniclers stated that Thoth/Hermes was the real builder of the pyramids.

Inside the Pyramid

162:Ascending Passage of the Great Pyramid, Giza

When one enters the Great Pyramid today, you enter from the forced entrance. According to Strebo, the original entrance was a kind of hinged stone which could be raised, but was indistinguishable from the surrounding masonry when it lay flush. The original entrance can be seen about twenty courses up from the current one, and has a corbelled roof of several massive stones. As yet no one has properly explained the need for the giant roofing of the entrance. A passage leads downward at an angle of 26 degrees 17'. It is 350 feet in length, 3.6 feet wide and 3 feet 11' in height. Some of this passage is cut through the original rocky mound before the pyramid was put on top. The passage is perfectly straight, and the magnitude of workmanship on what is actually a tunnel is amazing. Eventually one comes to the lower chamber, some 600 feet below the pyramid in a claustrophobic atmosphere. Today visitors are not allowed into the lower chamber. According to the Egyptologists this was originally the burial place of the Pharaoh Khufu, but for some reason, the designers changed their mind and decided on a burial farther up in the pyramid. The workmen must have been happy after digging out 2000 tons of sold rock through a crowded passage, in no light, to be told to do it again.

Actually this lower chamber is part of the grand design. It is not here by some accident, and although it appears unfinished, it is cut and carved the way it was supposed to be. Some believe that there is a subterranean chamber beneath the lower chamber, and this place is likely off limits to tourists who might be able to notice exit passages into the Giza underground world. Some suggest that the lower chamber blocks were cut to represent flames, the original Egyptian central fire, the place of ordeal and initiation of the alchemical furnace. The Chinese say there are three burners in the body and this lower chamber may represent the dan tien, the queen's chamber the heart and the king's chamber the third eye (why most mystical experiences for people happen in the king's chamber).

Half way down the descending passage, another passage leads upwards into the heart of the pyramid, the supposed resting place of Khufu. This passage is almost exactly at the forced entrance, an oddity I will explain later. It is claimed that in order to protect Khufu, three large granite blocks were slid down the 129 foot length from the grand gallery to their current resting place to act as a plug. No one is quite sure how this was done, or where the workers who did it (as they would have been sealed into the pyramid) went to, but that gets explained by what is called the well shaft. You can still see two of the original plugs as you walk past. Modern builders claim that it "would be impossible to slide the slabs a matter of inches, let alone 100 feet." Many now feel that this passage must have been plugged while it was being built. Flinders Petrie felt that the plugs were cemented to the floor, thus could not have been slid down the passageway. No matter, the plugs did not stop intruders as Al Mamun's group simply tunneled around them. However, if the pyramid had other purposes instead of burial, it might make sense to plug it so that it could not again be 'used.' Another interesting observation is that no one has checked to see if the granite plugs concealed an east/west passage (from the sides), not the north/south (along the passageway) as is thought. Al Mamun tunneled around on the west side, but no one has of checked the east side.

As one continues up the ascending passage, the first room encountered is the Queen's Chamber. It was called this by the Arabs because it's roof is similar to the roofs used in Arabic female burials. The ascending passage here was 127 feet long and straight, then suddenly drops two feet. The Queen's Chamber, which has 15 foot high ceiling, and has a large niche cut into the east wall that so far no one has been able to explain. The chamber is also littered with salt crystals. Chris Dunn has claimed that what he has found in this chamber help him to present the theory that the pyramid was a power plant, using various chemicals to produce energy. While I do agree that the pyramid was producing energy, I disagree with Dunn's theory that chemicals of any kind were needed.

The well shaft occurs where the ascending passage and the grand gallery meet. It is a near vertical tunnel that has some sharp twisting turns. The shaft itself is less than three feet in diameter and eventually joins up with the descending corridor. A part of it was enlarged and is known as the grotto. The work done on the grotto is not as well done as the rest of the shaft, but it definitely feels part of the design. Cut into the solid bedrock, the grotto contains a large block of granite. Why? The shaft is claimed to have been built as an 'escape hatch' for the workmen who were to push the granite plugs in place, and used by the tomb robbers to steal the treasure (which of course there was no treasure). Why make the walls of a simple escape hatch to near standards, create the grotto and bring a giant granite boulder there? And if the plugs were never slid down, then why need the well shaft at all?

The Grand Gallery is something that no photograph can do any justice to. It is 153 feet long, 7 feet wide at the floor, and is 28 feet high. It looms as gigantic after being in the ascending passage. Even more interesting is that the walls are narrower at the top than at the bottom, making it a gigantic slit. There are 27 oblong slots cut vertically into the walls which make it a very strange place. Some feel that the Grand Gallery is actually a gigantic telescope (more on this later). The main question that someone must remind themselves is why build something so magnificent and difficult, inside a pyramid. If the main reason was to walk to the next level, stairs or a bigger passage would have been fine. There is a reason the Grand Gallery is there, but few look as to why.

163:King's Chamber, Great Pyramid, Giza

At the top of the Grand Gallery comes a step that leads to a small narrow passageway. Original photos of this step show it to have a v shape or cut at the top, as if liquid could have run down it. Today there is a modern repair done to the top to make the stone flat. Beyond is a passage is called the antechamber. At the EXACT point where the limestone blocks give way to the granite blocks is a small space large enough to stand up in. At eye level is something carved into the granite known as the "boss," a raised half circle that some have said is the key to understanding the entire pyramid. Others see it as a seal. I got the sense it might be a symbolic button that may in fact turn something on by being pushed. A little farther into the antechamber is a small raised area said to have been for large granite slabs to have been placed. But where are they, there is no trace of them, not even a fragment chip from being hacked through. If they were there every last remaining piece was chipped away or else they were vaporized. Continuing one one comes through a small doorway into the fabulous room known as the King's Chamber. Built of large interlocking granite blocks for the walls, 15 massive granite blocks for the floor, and 9 50-ton granite blocks for the ceiling, the place exudes otherworldliness. No treasure, body or object has been found in this room except for the large granite lidless box that is still there.

The chamber exhibits some very interesting mathematics. The first interesting feature is that the King's Chamber exists at a level where "the vertical section of the pyramid is halved, the area of the horizontal section is one-half the base, where the diagonal from corner to corner is equal to the length of the base, and where the width of the face is equal to ½ the diagonal of the base." The whole King's Chamber also works out the famed golden section (phi) perfectly, and the exact sothic solar year. So special is this room deemed to be that Hitler had an exact replica of it built and placed underneath Nuremberg Stadium, where he meditated prior to Nazi rallies. The room will simply amplify that which comes into it, thus it is not the chamber itself that is good or bad- but who or what comes into it.

164: The Northern shaft, King's Chamber

Within both the King's and Queen's Chambers are wall shafts that run diagonally into the rock. The ones from the King's Chamber reach the outside at the 103rd course. The Queen's Chamber shafts do not reach the outside. So far only the Great Pyramid has shown to have these type of shafts. The amazing thing about the shafts is that they were not drilled through the finished masonry as many expect, but they were constructed in a step-by-step manner as the pyramid rose. Thus they were built into the pyramid masonry. This is a very complex and sophisticated engineering job. The theory for years has been that these shafts were 'air vents,' so those inside would not suffocate. However a horizontal air vent would have been much easier to build if getting air was the only requirement of the shafts. To build them on an incline requires special shaped blocks with one face sloping upward for the floor, and other blocks in a u-shape for the walls and ceilings. Remember, all of this was done with the rest of the pyramid was being built up.

In 1964, Virginia Temple noticed the southern shaft of the King's Chamber pointed at Orion's belt during the period of 2500BC. This suggested that the shaft may have been more than an air vent, and had astronomical connections. Bauval and Hancock checked out the other shafts at 2500BC and got the following: King's Chamber south (Al Nitak- Orion), King's Chamber north (Alpha Draconius), Queen's Chamber south (Sirius), Queen's Chamber north (Ursa Minor, top star of big dipper). The man who put in the air conditioning in 1990's, Rudolph Gatenbrink, decided to use a robot to investigate the Queen's' Chamber air vents. He found one of the shafts led to a sealed solid limestone door with metal fittings. Zahi Hawass stopped any investigation. A few years later, on supposed "live television," Hawass tried to open the door himself in an obvious staged performance, and "found" another door behind it. My African teacher told me that the air shafts of the King's Chamber create the musical resonance F# (F sharp), from the air moving down these vents made to be a type of flute or trumpet. I can say that standing between them does create some type of energy within the body.

The most marvelous thing about the King's Chamber to me was the perfect amplification of sound in the chamber. Every sound uttered seems to have this beautiful reverberation. The black stone used may have been chosen to activate a person's pineal gland, thus lead to illumination and light within, combining light and sound in a specific way in the human body. After sitting in several power spots in the King's Chamber, I always take a nice walk to the sarcophagus box, a Greek word that means "eater of the flesh" a reference to the self that must be consumed. The granite coffer is cut from a solid block of granite that includes feldspar quartz and mica. It is a stone far harder than the granite walls of the chamber. The external volume is 2332.8 liters which is exactly twice the internal volume of 1166,4 liters. The north and south faces of the box are concave, near perfect craftsmanship. Some claim that even with modern tools this box would be almost impossible to duplicate. Because the box could fit a human body, it has long believed to be a sarcophagus by Egyptologists.

The stone for this box is fabled to have come as far away as America or even Atlantis. Biblical scholars claim the box in the King's Chamber would exactly accommodate the Ark of the Covenant. When Petrie had the coffer raised and struck , it provided a deep bell-like sound of "eerie beauty." When I sounded into the box, the harmonic melodies were amplified and returned. The box was also unlike anything I felt. Following a Hungarian woman, I also laid inside the box, and had my Egyptian mystical mantra sounds feel as if they were swirling around me in a circular wave of sound. Some also feel that the box was placed where it is now (at the far end of the chamber) rather than its old resting place in the chamber because too many people laying down in it had too many bizarre experiences. While in the King's Chamber I got to see superimposed on the walls a winged Isis, surrounded by Osiris, Hathor, Sekhmet and a Pharaoh. It was like they were applied to the stone in 4-dimensions, thus you could not see them while your consciousness was in the third dimension, normal reality. On my third visit inside, all of a sudden I smelled a waft of perfume, but then I noticed that no one had entered for the scent to be attributed to. I had the thought that I was smelling the scent of a lotus, and perhaps I was the only one smelling it.

Above the King's Chamber are a series of smaller chambers, said to be built when the ceiling started cracking, to add extra support in case of earthquake. Even more bizarre is that few realize that underneath the granite floor is a granite layer similar to an egg carton, while the blocks that make up the ceiling are smooth only on the bottom side, while rough on the top. In fact more work was done on the rough side than the smoothed side. I will try to explain these odd features later on, but I feel all of these factors help to make the chamber, and in fact the entire pyramid, a musical instrument that causes great "changes" in the DNA of any living object who enters.

How Built

166:Some of the large stone blocks in the lower courses of the Great Pyramid's construction.

The first question that one usually asks is how were these things built? The Japanese in the 1980's tried to build a small 35 foot high replica of the Great Pyramid using the 'ancient' techniques. When this project failed, they brought in modern equipment that also failed. This was a pyramid some 1/20th the size of Giza and was no match for modern equipment. Nova tried to build a 6 foot high pyramid and needed a front end loader and modern cutting equipment just to do that. Herodotus, who wrote in 500 BC at least some 2000 years after the pyramids are said to have been built, claimed that the Great Pyramid took 20 years to build. With an estimated 2.3 million blocks, 31 blocks per hour every day of the year would be needed to be quarried, moved and placed. At the same time shafts and chambers were built within the pyramid. And right beside are two other monster pyramids requiring similar effort to create.

So let us examine this project a little more closely with what we can see. The Egyptians first placed a permanent platform of fine polished limestone, and in some parts black basalt, on the ground. However the land was not made perfectly flat, actually a massive natural mound was left- likely to represent the primordial hill of creation, estimated to be some 30 feet high at the exact center of the pyramid. They built around and overtop of a gigantic hunk of rock. They could have removed this rock to begin with a perfectly flat surface, a far easier building project, but they did not. Time and time again the Egyptians do not do the easy thing, but the hardest thing. Therefore it must represent something that had to be part of the pyramid. Most likely it was the symbolic primeval mound, the first part of land that rose from the chaotic waters of Nun at the creation.

167:Part of the basalt temple floor on the east side of the Great Pyramid

The pyramid rises almost perfectly aligned to the cardinal directions. To do this properly it would need to be kept perfectly level, ie no twisting involved as it raised up. Proctor believes that this is the true use of the descending passage. In the time of Ancient Egypt the Pole Star was Alpha Draconius. In order to pinpoint it exactly you would need a slot at an angle of 26 degrees 17' (which is exactly the angle of the descending passage). One could use the pole star to guide the rise of the pyramid. Proctor says that the lower chamber could have been filled with water, which would reflect the pole star like a mirror in a modern telescope. By building the ascending passage at the same angle as the descending (which was done) they could reflect the pole star off the water in the pit to the ascending passage. This would keep the passage perfectly aligned and keep the pyramid perfectly level as it rose.

One hundred yards east of the Great Pyramid are what are known as trial shafts, cut into the bedrock. It is claimed that they were cut to let workers practice their skills before the pyramid was built. A descending and ascending passage were found. There is also an upward shaft where the two meet, perhaps in the pyramid design and hidden by the current plugs (again no one has checked if the plugs hide a passage above or below the plug). A grand gallery is also in this trial area, but there are no chambers, just shafts that lead to where the chambers would be. Why are these here and why practice cutting into bedrock, when much of the cutting in the pyramid itself would be through limestone blocks, a totally different task? Why are there no chambers just shafts? Thus they were not tests for the building skills of the workers, but tests of something else. Another suggestion is that they could have been a map.

It is usually suspected that thousands of slaves were used in forced work gangs in order to haul and carry the millions of stones into place, mostly because of what is written in the Old Testament. However, there is no evidence to suggest that people were compelled to take part in the massive enterprise against their will, if anything it is the opposite. The sheer quality of workmanship in the construction suggest a pride in the work. The more accepted theory is that the main work was conducted by the average population during the inundations of the Nile, when farmers could no longer tend to their farms (for they were underwater). During the other nine months, the priests, artisans and masons would remain to continue key aspects of the process. But that is an answer still based on the idea that hundreds of thousands of people were needed for the construction. While there is evidence of large encampments on the Giza Plateau, no one is actually sure how many people were used to build the pyramids, but there was definitely a lot of work on the surrounding tombs, mastabas and monuments. To me, these found camps, quarries and work sites have nothing to do with the building of the three main pyramids and sphinx area, but are associated with the builders of the rest of the site: smaller pyramids, mastabas and temples. These were the parts that were actually built in the Old Kingdom, as a way of connecting to what was already old and revered at the site, like wanting to build your house next to a famous monument. If the surrounding structures were built at the same time, by the same workers, they should show a similarity in workmanship. But they do not- the large structures show perfection in construction, while the others show to be shoddy copies.

The raising of the stone blocks is one of the most controversial areas. Some believe a giant system of levers was used. Yet one look at the Nova documentary shows that the crib/lever system would get very precarious as blocks were moved farther up the pyramid. The steps get very small as one gets up the structure, and levers are simple unsuitable in the confined steps up the pyramid. Some Egyptologists will still say that one large ramp was built to raise the blocks up an inclined plane. To build a long ramp, at a gradient of 1:10 would require a ramp 4,800 feet long. The ramp would then contain three times as much masonry as the pyramid itself, and would actually be a larger building project. Most archaeologists today believe that a spiral ramp was used which wound around the pyramid. However a spiral ramp would be unable to reach the top, due to overlap. It would have presented deadly turns, and would also have covered the whole pyramid thus making it tough for architects to check the alignment of the building process. The average side of the pyramid is not out less than 8 inches, and the corners are near perfect right angles. Also note that the block size does not diminish at the upper levels of the pyramid, some courses go back to large blocks. Again showing the most simple building practices were not followed here.

168: Casing stones placed together so perfectly that even my knife blade can not get between them.

Other theories have been put out there. These include water ramps connected to a system of locks to float the blocks up the slope. Another that priests had the ability to use sound or magnetics to levitate the rocks. Another theory by Joseph Davidovits claims that the rocks used are not actually rock, but a form of made cement. Davidovits wondered why the Grand Gallery displays high humidity. The bedrock of Giza is dry, yet the pyramid is full of moisture. The blocks themselves are a mystery. Some believe that the rock came from 20 sites all over the Nile valley, while others feel the rock was quarried right on the Giza Plateau. However, the bedrock of the Giza Plateau is made up of strata, and the pyramid blocks contain no strata. The casing blocks in the Great Pyramid are very hard as they contain large fossil shells, unlike the soft Tura limestone that is supposedly used and is now used in modern restoration projects. He also found air bubbles in some of the rocks, like are found when mixing clay. Another interesting tidbit is Edward Leedskalnin, who built Coral Castle of huge blocks of raised stone without cranes near Homestead Florida in the 1940's. He died in 1952 without telling anyone how he did it, but he did say that he claimed to know how the Egyptian pyramids were built and hinted it was due to magnets or an anti-gravity device.

Another aspect has to do with tools. Everything is said to have been cut and shaped with copper tools. Yet the casing blocks are too perfect to be done with hammer an chisels. There is evidence on the site of drilling and machining, and many of the statues found are impossible to make with out lasers. The area to the south of the pyramid, where the temple originally stood are granite blocks with obvious saw cuts, drill holes and curved surfaces. Impossible to make with the supposed tools of the time.

Why Built

169:"The Boss"

Most of the focus today from pyramid researchers is all about the how, how did they build and create the machined quality stone? As valuable as the question is, to me a far more important question is, why?

Egyptologists will tell you the reason nothing has ever found in the pyramid was due to tomb robbers who took everything. How? Prior to Al Mamun's entrance, the granite plugs were in place. So Egyptologists point to the well shaft as the entrance and escape route for thieves. The well shaft is only three feet in diameter, too small for over half of Tutankhamun's treasure. Therefore, the larger pieces should have been left behind. Other pieces, such as pottery or bowls were never of use to the tomb robbers and they always left them behind. But there was nothing found in the Great Pyramid. No large objects that did not fit through the shaft, no pottery, cloth, statues…nothing! To make the argument against a tomb even stronger is that the ascending passage that leads to the supposed burial place of the king is far too narrow for the sarcophagus box in the King's Chamber to pass through. Thus the box that now sits there had to be placed in the before the pyramid was completed, and the body in Egyptian burials were always brought in with the box they were to rest in.

Over the years there are many ideas as to what the pyramids were built for. Mendelssohn felt that Giza was built to give the nation a common religious task, Robert T Ballard believed that the pyramid could be used to survey and distribute all the land all along the Nile, others as giant geodetic markers. Some felt they were tall obelisks, whom shadows could be used a giant sundial to mark equinox and solstice. Others said that the grand gallery was a giant telescope, that produced the charts that Kepler and Galileo used in the Middle Ages for individual astrological readings. Another theory claims it chronicles a super nova (exploding star) 6,000 years ago, and the Grand Gallery was built to watch the event. However the telescope theory fails to answer why then the need to build two other giant pyramids along with it, that have no telescope looking galleries.

In the 1970's the term pyramid power appeared. It was found that the pyramid shape automatically dehydrated animals, kept milk fresh without refrigeration, kept razor blades sharp and could purify water. Thus it has some very interesting properties on objects. Those who have slept overnight in the King's Chamber have told of odd experiences. Napoleon, who was a freemason, appeared the next morning "pale and shaken" and told no one of his experiences, only that no one would believe him. Others who have stayed the night have claimed to have been besieged by spirits, Ancient Egyptians who after attempting to scare them, offered the secrets of Egyptian initiation and the secrets of the universe. Sitting inside a pyramid will provide incredible healing powers. I personally feel that any time inside of a pyramid is life changing, but any time spent alone in one is multiplied by a great degree. One minute alone is like one hour with others. I feel it alters the entire structure of the human DNA when inside. I have not slept overnight in one, but the effect might be truly mind-blowing.

The Arabic manuscript Akbar Ezzeman, as well as mystic Ammanias Marcellinus wrote that the pyramids were built to house ancient wisdom from before the flood. Masoodi wrote in 943AD "Surid...one of the kings of Egypt before the flood built two pyramids...300 years before the flood he dreamed that the earth was twisted around, stars fell from the sky and clashed together with noise and that all of mankind took refuge in great terror. After summoning his dream interpreters he ordered the positions of the stars examined. The stars foretold a great flood that would come from the constellation of Leo. When told Egypt would flourish again after the flood, he ordered the pyramids built to house the secrets of science, math, religion." Masoudi also refers to Automata, monstrous idols of stone and metal that are animated by spirits that protect the sacred areas and destroy anyone who violates the pyramid.[52]

Another theory is that the pyramid was a place for special initiations into the Mystery Schools. The initiates were said in time to be shown the laws and principles of the cosmos, and man's relation to it. They had to die to the old self, and be reborn in the King's Chamber, with the knowledge of immortality and experienced a second birth." For these rights to have been performed after the pyramids were built, there must have been a way to enter the pyramid in a yet undiscovered passageway. Some suggest that the Giza plateau was a key test was to see if one could tell the difference between what was real and what an illusion, and great challenges of endurance were given. Those who passed these tests became high priests in the temples. The layout of the pyramids are up for question. Bauval and Hancock believe that the the pyramids could be layed out to match the three stars of Orion's belt in they sky, while others say they resemble a golden spiral and other mathematical layouts. Other theories include that the pyramid passages record the history of the earth as found in the Bible, or that the pyramid geometry reflects the spiraling movement of consciousness from above to below, while another that Giza is the creation of the entire illusion of space-time reality, via a multi dimensional grid system.

The pyramids were designed to resonate in vibrational-musical harmony with something, perhaps the earth's vibrational frequency. The passages increase the movement of sound because you can hear the lower pit at the top of the grand gallery. The granite in the King's Chamber is 55% silicon quartz, making it an energy transmitter. But the quartz needs to be squeezed. All the ceiling beams are polished on 3 sides, but rough on top as mentioned. They tuned the rock by removing the exact amount from the top to make the pitch that they wanted. The entire chamber is freestanding, on the egg carton floor which allows it to vibrate at peak efficiency. Thus it is a giant musical instrument. The antechamber may have had slabs, but not to seal it off, but actually to act like a filter for sounds. Raise or lower depending on the vibration coming in.

The cracks in the ceiling of the King's Chamber are said to be from an earthquake, but if this is so, why is this the only place to show this? Above the chambers are a layer of black dust ecuvine (cast of shells of insects). There are no living insects in the pyramid so where did they come from? Decoding the Great Pyramid thinks the chamber was an energy generating device and that the Queen's Chamber brought in two differing types of chemicals for the reaction. An explosion in the Kings Chamber could have been enough heat to cook the insect shells in the limestone. Could the Egyptians themselves have blown up and or dismantled the pyramid at the end of their era to prevent its total power from falling into the hands of beings who could not use it for its original task?

---

[52] William Fix 52

The famous Toltec site at Teotihuacan was destroyed deliberately by a fire set by the inhabitants, so that too is a possibility here.

Secret Chambers

One of the things well known to insiders, but kept quiet from the public, is the large number of tunnels, chambers and passageways under the ground. There may be more beneath the surface than above. In the 1970's the Egyptian authorities did some tests at Giza. On the project was Dr. Jim Hurtak, who took video footage of a vast underground metropolis under Giza, with massive chambers with huge statues, underground waterways and lakes. They entered through a shaft found by Selim Hassan in the 1930's below the Khafre causeway, and it here twenty years later that Zahi Hawass "found" the tomb of Osiris. On my first trip to Egypt, one of the site guardians took me to this passage and gave me the chance to do down to this underground world. Just as I began to walk down the long ladder, he said to my Arabic friend, "Be careful, it is very dangerous down there, you can die." Ahh. Good way to start my first week in Egypt, and chose instead to not tempt fate, or the authorities.

Steven Mehler believes that below the surface was constructed special water rivers, and that temples and sites were built on top to harness the power of water (Asgat Nefer- harmony of water in Ancient Egyptian). Flowing water has a great vibration. Temples were built in such a way as to have flowing water run under the site to increase the harmonic vibration of the stones. Thus the stones give energy to the water, while the water gave energy to the stone.

170:Passageway in the ground between the Khufu and Khafre Pyramids, obscured by garbage.

There are many questions for me on the Giza site. In between the Great and Khafre Pyramids is an empty flat area that is mostly used now as a tour bus parking area. The rest of the site is built on, but not this area. Was things on that area removed, or if not, why was it left open? While walking around I saw a long shaft in the pavement, half concealed with garbage. This was all that remains of a satellite pyramid that once stood here. I took a bit of look down and got right to the level of the deepest garbage and shone my light past. Below I saw a rectangular stone chamber under the pavement, and shadows "moving or dancing" quickly. Right above that spot is a bunch of giant singular stones, perhaps a few remaining pieces of the pyramid. My guess is the shaft was blocked off, with garbage to not have people pay any attention to it, the way putting iron bars there would often generate curiosity of "why is that gated up?"

J Kinneman claimed he worked with Flinders Petrie on the site, and that together they found a south entrance to the pyramid and explored many new rooms and chambers within. David H Lewis in his 1976 book *Mysteries of the Great Pyramid,* said he also found rooms and sealed doors in a passage from the south. The south side of the pyramid now has the "goofy" solar boat museum, that to me may in fact cover an entrance, possibly confirmed with an odd conversation with a worker there on my first visit at the boat museum. Also along the south face are odd openings about 43 meters up, as if someone had attempted to blast through at this level. So far I have not been able to climb up and confirm what actually is on that south face.

About 70 feet along the north side of the pyramid, from the north east corner, is a 4X10 stone sunk into the foundation at an angle. The joints are very precise and is the only stone not at a right angle to the rest of the construction. It may cover an entrance. And along the NE corner is where Bob Brier and Japanese researchers found a small room in the edge of the pyramid. The space is carved out and is just about the height for a person to easily stand in. No one has adequately explained why it is there, or how many more there could be. Just a few months ago, November 2017, came the news that the Scan Pyramids group found a void within the pyramid, just up from the Grand Gallery,and possibly as large.

This next theory comes from Frenchmen Robert Houdin. He first became curious as to what happened to a large granite block that used to sit next to the sarcophagus by the wall. It can be seen in some photos of from the 1970's. It was said to be a blocking plug of the entrance that had been bored through and pushed into the chamber. For a while it covered over the hole made in the floor from deep excavation work. The stone is now gone after they sealed over the hole. No one has any idea where it may be. It has just seemed to have disappeared.

Supposedly this hole was dug at the time of Al Mamun's entrance. If so why did Al Mamun's men dig a hole into the floor at this exact spot,and only here. There shows no other digging (except for a small hole in far corner of the room). Houdin felt that all of this was odd to have the hold and this stone right next to a very odd looking block in the wall of the chamber right across from the box. It just looks out of place, like it was put there at some later time. Houdin believes that this stone hides a second entrance to the King's Chamber, and he wrote that he felt there were a whole series of corridors and rooms (what he believed to look similar to the corbelled roofs of Daschur). Most of his suggestions sit right where the Japanese-French team found the void. Needless to say his idea of a second complete chamber and passage system to the King's Chamber may have great merit.

Added to this was that a Japanese team from Waseda University in 1987 used radar in the Queen's Chamber and claimed to indicate a hidden corridor in the NW corner of the North wall, the same corner where there is an odd block in the Kings Chamber. What is the connection? No one publicly has done any checking on the matter, but I am very sure someone has indeed checked all this out.

In the King's Chamber, all the stone joints are tight except a corner of the west wall. Here the joints are larger and covered with re-laid mortar indicating the possibility of another passage. Egyptian authorities has refused exploration of these areas.

There is much talk, especially from the new age community following the writings of Edgar Cayce, around something he called the Hall of Records, an ancient room that contains all the wisdom of the universe- supposedly left by the old Atlantean civilization for those in the future. Many believe it exists beneath the Sphinx. Most think the Hall of Records will be a chamber which will have all sorts of books or scrolls. I find this to be totally false. To begin with, if they were attempting to preserve secrets, so that someone in the future could use them, they need to survive. The odds on the survival of paper for possibly thousands of years is very low. Even carved in stone leaves the possibility that those in the future will be unable to read the language. These texts are too important for paper or to be carved in walls. They will be accessed by using the mind, perhaps they are holographic. It may be a space to allow us to access the "dormant" parts of our DNA which is where the hall of records may be, inside of our own bodies, or perhaps encoded in the original 8 cells that still sit at the base of your spine (where kundalini energy rises from). This hall of records may be a space that opens within us something that plugs directly into the holographic nature of reality. They will not be able to be accessed by those who have not devoted a large portion of their life to raise their vibration.

As for guarded entrances in this area; my African teacher was in Egypt recently and attempted to go down a tunnel that had been found behind the Sphinx. A workman stopped him. In Egypt you can pretty much get anywhere by giving some money. Not here. While the workman's English was not excellent, he did make the point of someone who had gone down the tunnel had been badly burnt. Burnt in a tunnel? He said this was a special tunnel, one accessed by only those with a very high vibration, and someone who enters with a vibration too low will burn. Thus when wanting to go down tunnels or into secret areas at ancient sites, I recommend moving with extreme caution.

New Theories

A new theory, created by Scott Creighton, I first saw on the "AboveTopSecret" message board. To understand this fully requires following along with diagrams that he has made of the Giza Plateau, that can be found at this website...but I will do my best to provide an overview with only words here. Creighton claims that one of Giza's main reasons for being built, was to act as a precessional time marker. This general idea found its way into books in 1990's, but Creighton has taken things a step further by using more than just the three main pyramids- but examines the whole site. What Creighton claims is that the outer edges of the site (the north-east corner of the Great Pyramid, the northern Khufu Queen's pyramid, the western Menkaure Queen's Pyramid, and the back end of the Sphinx) all would link in a perfect geometric circle around the site. A line called the *Lehner Line*, named after Mark Lehner's discovery in 1980, runs diagonally perfect along the sides of the three main pyramids and the queen's pyramids, making it part of the original building design. At each end of this line are the two odd groups of small pyramids, claimed by Egyptologists to be for the Pharaoh's queens. Robert Bauval mentioned that the layout of the three main pyramids on the Giza plateau matched the layout of the three belt stars of Orion. Yet no one checked the layouts of the sets of Queen's pyramids, also in groups of three. I had felt on my first Egypt trip that they were in some way copies of the larger giants, but I too never examined exactly how. Interestingly, Creighton found that the far Southern group match the belt stars of Orion at its high point in the precessional cycle, while the Queen's set near the Great Pyramid, marks the low point. The Lehner line, to Creighton, actually is a connecting line between the two sets of Queen's Pyramids, that mark the high (12, 000 BC) and the low point (2,500 AD) of Orion. Thus the line becomes a precessional time marker between the two astronomical events.

If this line marks time that begins at one point and ends at another, flowing time can be marked along it. But how to know if the Ancient Egyptians tried to bring attention to certain dates on this timeline? Creighton felt that another intersecting line crossing it could be the way to obtain an exact date. He used the Sphinx as the marker to check, and found that drawing a line directly up to the Lehner Line, intersects the time line at exactly the half way point (3,900 BC). In conversation with Scott, I suggested that he also check the Sphinx causeway, which does not run at a 90 degree angle towards the pyramid, but instead runs off-center. It seemed to me that a line from the causeway would intersect the Lehner Line close to the start of the Maya calendar of around 3114 BC, which Creighton confirmed. On further examination he also noticed that the exact center of the entire Giza circle is at a point in the exact middle of the second/Khafre Pyramid. This links to my feelings that the middle pyramid is in fact the oldest on the site.

From the point of just outside of the paws of the Sphinx, Creighton used the spot of the Sphinx-Thutmosis stela, drew lines to the two outer edges of the circle (the Menkaure Queen's Pyramid, and the edge of the Great Pyramid). This first line intersected the Lehner Time-Line at 9,800 BC- which to him marks as the destruction of Atlantis. The time period around 10,000 BC was a moment of great earth change- the end of the last ice age leading to a great flood, last overturning of the earth poles, and many ancient sites all mathematically attempt to link in some way to around 10,000 BC. The second line drawn from the Sphinx, bisects the time line at a point about 2012 AD. The first intersection marker seemed to indicate a time of worldwide catastrophe, while the second marker might be marking the next great change, that lists as almost the exact end of the Mayan Calendar. Please view his diagrams and information to see the detail of his theory. While I am not in 100% agreement with him, I do feel that he is very close to unlocking a very important aspect about the layout of the entire Giza plateau and how, just like its Mexico sister site of Teotihuacan- relates not only to space, but to time.

A final theory I want to share comes from the article *Tunnel Vision* by Mark Foster and Ralph Ellis. It comes from their very unique conclusion, why is the "forced entrance" almost perfectly situated to run in a straight line to the Descending Passage and Ascending Passage. Basically if they were just digging by chance, they could not have gotten more lucky. So the question they had,was maybe it was not luck, but they knew what they were doing. And the tunnel was not made to get them in, but was made to get something out.

Their theory suggests that Al Mamun knew the entrance to the pyramid, as many others had and gone to the Descending Pit to find nothing. Somehow they noticed the plugs and decided to tunnel around them. Why them? Why did they know there was something beyond the plugs. The reason may lie in the trial shafts.

For the shafts may not have been for tests for the workers to dig, but might have in fact been a map left in the Giza bedrock, for someone to come along later and figure it out- because if you saw that iit was a replica of the pyramid descending passage, it would have clued in "there should be a passage here" where these blocked plugs were. So why need the exit tunnel? It must be because they had something that was heavy, and difficult to get up the descending passage or perhaps even too big for it. Their answer? The lid of the sarcophagus box. The fact the lid is gone is very interesting and no one has really explained where it is. The suggesting is that it was dug to walk it straight out, This tunnel has been greatly enlarged for tourists, but the original was not this high. They further suggest that the lid was taken out of the pyramid this way, and perhaps taken back to be a part of the famous black box of Mecca, which contains a special black stone of unknown origin. It is one of the best theories for the forced entrance and the missing box lid hat I have seen to date.

Another theory suggests that the passage around the plugs was not done at all by Al Muman in 820 AD,but had been dug much before. It seems such authors as Strabo and Pliny had long prior recorded about interior passages in the pyramid. So they were known long before Al Manun. This alternate theory suggests that the digging around the granite plugs was by the Old Kingdom Egyptians themselves, gaining access again to the already very ancient monument themselves. It is still one of the most confusing parts of the pyramid, who in fact dug these tunnels and exactly why?

170a Pyramid core blocks.

Examination

It is clear that pyramids are not the simple tombs that they have been described to be for the last 2000 years, but are instead marvels of construction designed to work not only with the natural vibrational harmony of the earth,- but also with the human DNA structure and perhaps the entire looping nature of this reality. It is no wonder why pyramids, not just in Egypt but all over the world, have fascinated everyone who has come across them. My suggestion is to get into as many of them as you can, and then prepare for them to work on deep levels of your DNA and egoic false self simply by being within their incredible harmonious construction.

A small clue that I can share with you is the world light. I can say that I have had experiences within Egyptian pyramids that involved light. I do not want to say here what that means, or what I mean by light, but I am sure that what I saw in those experiences are in fact a key element into understanding the core nature of these structures.

CHAPTER 5
EGYPTIAN TEXTS

16: Hieroglyphs, from internal wall, Edfu

Language

"The Gnosis of man[kind] still awaits decipherment in Egypt, it is hidden in her glyphs and symbols…but that Gnosis will never yield its secret to those who persist in interpreting the symbols of the language of the gods into those lower forms [modern languages], forms intended for children [uninitiated] and not for men [Hermetic initiates]." GRS MEAD[53]

We begin our esoteric journey with language itself. Many Mystery School teachers believe that the type of language used by a group of people will determine the way that group will think, act, even their moral outlook. RA Schwaller de Lubicz believed two forms of writing exist and they have their roots in the oldest 'known' civilizations on the planet. One is scientific/Aristotle, which evolved from Babylon and Sumeria but gained its

---

[53] Mead vol 3 p326

greatest use in Greece. They use a rapidly written cursive and are languages that separated the subject and object. This form is common to all Western languages. Aristotle claimed that only reason (intellect, logic, skepticism and the mind) could discover the nature of our reality.[54] Thus all knowledge to this group can be understood by the use of our thinking conscious mind. Our modern world is now dominated by scientific thinking.

The other is the Metaphysical/Pythagorean system that originated in Egypt and uses a form of picture writing. Western thinking has developed the concept that a piece of paper is not a chair, or a human is not a tree. This is the separation of things in an attempt to see what is different. The Eastern minds of Plato, Pythagoras and the Taoists claim, "What is one, is one. What is not-one is also one." Thus they are looking for what is similar and for a connection of all things, something that is lacking in our modern world. Those that follow the scientific way of looking for what is different will also develop the idea that we can control nature because it and us are different. Pythagoras claimed that true knowledge was based not on the mind, but on revelation from forces in the universe. When one had purified themselves enough, the Gnosis (divine knowing) could enter the true mind (heart).[55] The ancients taught that there is only One, the reason we see things as different is because we are caught up in the illusion of the world. The ancient ways teach us that we are nature, thus the need to get to know and love every part of it for it is just a part of ourselves. All of the techniques taught by the Aristotle school, using the mind to understand the world, would be avoided. This would include even the words used to explain their beliefs.

The Word
"We use not just words, but sounds full of efficiency, for that it's very quality of sound, the very power of the Egyptian names, have in themselves the bringing into act of what is said." Corpus Hermeticum[56]

Words were seen as vital in the ancient world. The Egyptian creation mythology of Hermopolis relates how Tehuti was able to create simply by the sound of his voice. "I am the Eternal, I am Ra…I am that which uttered the word, I am the word." In the Old Testament God said, "Let there be light, and there was light." St John's Gospel begins, "In the beginning was the word, and the word was with God, and the word was God." The Indian Upanishads say the world was created with the uttering of the primal sound. The Popul Vuh of the Maya claim there was only "immobility and silence in the darkness…then

---

[54] Berendt p.45; Baigent, Michael Ancient Traces (Penguin 1998) p.206
[55] Baigent p.203; Houston, Jean The Passion of Osiris and Isis (Ballentyne 1995) pp.116-17; Berendt p.44
[56] Corpus Hermeticum book 15

110

came the word." In Guatemala, two gods said a word and immediately the earth was created." The Nag Hammadi Gnostic text "Origin of the World" claims, "His thought was made complete by the word…and he created an androgynous being by means of the word." The Book of Mormon in Jacob 4:9 says, "For behold by the power of His word, man came upon the face of the earth."[57]

The word usually translated into English from the ancient texts as 'word' was actually "Logos", which was used to explain the combined power of words, speech and reason. Thus the word has a far greater meaning than simply the letters placed together to make a sound. Thinking something in the mind has power and bringing that forth using the mouth, combining the concept in the mind with the breath of life allowed for creation. Renaissance alchemist Henry Cornelius Agrippa wrote, "words carry not only the conception of the mind, but also the virtue of the speaker unto the hearers, that often they change not only the hearers but also other bodies and things that have not life, by the virtue of the speaker." To the ancients the word is actually the spoken ideas of the heart. Thus the words used in creation "Logos" are far different than the words used by the average person. Writing is seen as the last expression of the mind.[58]

Hebrew mystics understand that their alphabet are words of power, and their language is supposed to allow a connection to heaven. The Cabbala claims that speech is the medium of God's revelation, which makes language itself sacred and an object of mystical contemplation. The twenty-two letters of the Hebrew alphabet are considered component parts of a 'living language of universal light', and part of the building blocks of creation. Heaven and earth can be connected through words.

A name is a representation of a concept and a material thing. Plato taught that words held the power of the thing. To the ancient mind, nothing existed before the word. Nothing lived until it was named, and once named it could be known. What could not be named did not exist because it could not be known. In Genesis, Adam gave the first names to all things. The symbolic significance is that once you know the name of something you can call upon its true essence. In a sense you are able to become one with that thing. To know the true name of something meant one could parallel creation and call that thing into existence. This is the basis of the discipline often referred to as magic.[59]

The initiates in Egypt had to learn speak with "true sound of voice." When an Egyptian priest spoke, "he used sound like an artist creating a word picture of marvelous strength and influence." Every Egyptian (like us) was given a name or "ren." While a name distinguishes one person from another it also holds a far deeper concept. The name is often considered to be one's for a lifetime and can be found symbolically encircling a person by a "rope of light"

---

[57] Crowley 109, Houston 132
[58] Agrippa, Henry Cornelius *Three Books of Occult Magic* pp.208, 215
[59] Crowley 110, Agrippa 209

or "infinite thread of eternity" called a cartouche. The rope of light (or life force) circled the name; thus one's name was infused with energy and would be needed to be protected.[60]

Each of the Neteru (gods) has a specific name and if one could learn that true name they can come in contact with those energies. To know the real name of a Neteru opened the possibility of the power of the Supreme. Come into direct contact with the Neteru and everything can be created or destroyed. Of course these concepts of the incredible powerful use of words are for masters and high initiates who have learned many of the secrets of the universe. They can use their words as power, as they have learned what power is. To the average man or woman, words are a very different matter.

Knowledge and Words
"Those reading my books would find their organization very simple and clear when, on the contrary, it is unclear and keeps the meanings of its words concealed." Corpus Hermeticum[61]

Even with the incredible power that words can bring, they are not knowledge and truth. People usually only use words/language today to uphold their beliefs, patterns, and habits that allow them to keep their view of the world. A student of the mysteries knows that there are many views of the world, not just the one that someone believes, thus they will be very careful with the words they use or how they listen to the words of another. One must fully understand that words are not knowledge, but are used by the mystic as a symbol for what they have experienced (for the mystical experience can never be explained). Thus the paradox that words can lead to true knowledge, but are not the knowledge itself.[62] The best way to learn about Switzerland, is by traveling there, while a travel guide (book knowledge and words) can help to provide background and preparations for particular experiences, but only by going there personally can the true wisdom be gained.

In fact (imagine an author writing this) most words are useless. Yet they lead to truth. Those few who have been fortunate enough to train with a real master will understand the following example. During a recent visit, my teacher began to answer my very deep questions of the universe with the most bizarre responses: a 73-year-old man's hips and Oriental restaurants. When he was finished speaking and retired to his room, my African teacher replied, "did you get all that?" I looked perplexed. "He just answered every one of your questions." By focusing only on his words, what I believed he was telling me with my mind, I came away empty with nothing. I was reminded that, "it

---

[60] Ashby Egyptian p.89; Lamy p.19; West Key p.65; Crowley pp. 110-11
[61] Corpus Hermeticum book 16
[62] Mares, Theun Return of the Warriors (Lionheart 1995) pp.53-54

doesn't matter what he says, it's what you feel." With that insight I was fortunate to have a second conversation with my teacher that week. This time I ignored what he was saying and instead "listened with my heart." From a similar talk I now gained feeling, insight and wisdom because I was allowing his words to be a guide to my heart where the true knowledge resides.

A simpler example is when a person says, "I love you." Taking the words at face value could lead to many problems. It could mean the person loves you, but depending on the tone, physical expressions and body language they could in fact be telling us they hate us. That is the danger of words. It would be better off to look for the feeling, what that person is really trying to convey not the specific words they are using to convey it. Thus when I speak about the magical power of the word, I mean used by those who are trained not only in the power of words themselves, but also in the exact way to use those words to provide knowledge.

Confucius considered that "while words contain genuine meanings which reflect certain absolute truths in the universe, most people have lost contact with these truths and so use language to suit their own convenience. This led, he felt, to lax thinking, erroneous judgments, confused actions and finally to the wrong people acquiring political power."[63]

The idea in the modern world that words are just symbols is very hard for the average person to agree with. Words have become our lifeline. In our era they have become fixed things, a table is a table. Everything in our world is what it is, they have no inner space, no life and no wisdom. Of course never mind suggesting to someone that physical objects do not really exist at all. That idea could not even be pondered, for the language that is used is for absolutes, thus modern use of words can only take a person to one view of the world. A language made up of pictures, like hieroglyphs, does not have this problem for the sign is immediately understood as a symbol that can convey all sorts of ideas, not just one fixed view.

A mystic knows that words are part of the great mystery of the universe, a universe that is not static and constant but always changing, always unknown thus always a new experience. Those who follow true wisdom are able to use words to help find the hidden meaning in not only the universe but in themselves. For one to accept words as absolutes "is to walk straight into the trap of ignorance and boredom – something which is meaningless and a stupid waste of time and energy."[64]

The Japanese language sees no need for a subject and an object. They won't say "I see the mountain" but rather "mountain seeing." The act of seeing includes both aspects of the seer and what is seen. Languages like English add a lot of extra waste to our speech that could be used for other things. Roberto, a Brazilian shaman, taught me about the useless way people use words in

---

[63] Berendt 53
[64] Mares, Theun Return of the Warriors (Lionheart 1995) pp.53-54

English. A "deadline" is literally a line not to be crossed or face death. Every business in North America brings the energy of death to their employees when using this word. By saying "I don't buy it" to someone of non-western background would likely gain a response that they were not selling anything. The phrase "I was so happy I jumped up and down" is incorrect. Actually we jumped up; the force of gravity brought us down unless we jumped onto something in which case we could have jumped down. Again a picture language is not concerned with these problems.

Hermetic means "sealed" or "tight." The knowledge of Hermes was transmitted by pictures and symbols, for images could be "sealed in and made airtight." Words created by letters do not have this quality, "as they are fragile things which lost their energies and changed their meanings, and are essentially unsuitable for transmitting knowledge of secret things." Words can go wrong and provide the wrong message. A suggestion can be taken as criticism, a joke as an insult. Through a hieroglyphic symbol one gains the opportunity to become one with the picture they are working with.[65]

In truth the wisdom of Tehuti comes without words, and cannot be explained by words. Words are merely an attempt by our mystical side to explain the unexplainable. They are best seen as a doorway. The wisdom of Tehuti is Gnosis, the direct experience of wisdom. No one can tell you, no one needs to read it to you or explain it. You have an experience (which can include words of reading a book or hearing someone talk), but something inside without the need of words will respond with a feeling like, yes that is true (as I hope something in you will do after finishing this book). You could also get a revelation while just walking down the street.

However our modern world has been trained to think that if it can not be explained by words, it cannot be true. This is the exact opposite of true wisdom. "True knowledge cannot be turned into words. That knowledge was there for everyone. It was there to be felt, to be used, but not to be explained. Heightened awareness (altered consciousness) was an entrance, but even the entrance cannot be explained."[66]

I had an experience recently that I wish to share as a poem. "This afternoon I understood how poets could write six pages on a blade of grass. I placed a small stick in the ground to observe the shadow. As I observed the shadow I focused more upon the grass. Soon it became fuller and more alive. I could see the individual blades of grass that grow together in small clusters. The clusters gained an extra strength of colour and beauty. I could definitely feel a sense of love towards not just the grass, but each of the individual blades that I saw. Each blade seemed to sparkle, to offer its own light. What was amazing was the fullness of the strength of the colours and the depth of my

---

[65] Isha p.139; Gettings, Fred The Secret Lore of the Cat (Grafton Books 1989) p.6
[66] Castaneda, Carlos Power of Silence (Simon and Schuster 1987) p.85

114

personal feeling. As my focus returned to waking consciousness I saw the ground regain its 'normal' form. It was not full of bright beautiful grass, as I had just experienced. There were large patches of dirt, trampled down grass, and in fact few of the clusters I had observed. The sense of the grass being alive was gone. Yet in that previous moment, in that instant, all that existed in the whole universe was me and those blades of grass. Of course, in that moment, I myself could have been a blade of grass!"

How can you explain the feeling of seeing every blade of grass as an individual entity? The short poem I wrote on this experience is but a frail attempt at explaining the experience to someone else. However, once this wisdom is brought into our being, it cannot be lost. If it can be lost, then it is not true wisdom. Mystic Al-Ghazi learned this when all of his knowledge, kept as lecture notes were stolen and he replied, "knowledge that can be stolen is not worth having."[67]

Hieroglyphs

"Even though the writing has been interpreted by Egyptologists, they have little understanding of the thoughts and beliefs expressed in them, as modern English teachers have little understanding of the Hermetic philosophy enshrined in Shakespeare." John Anthony West[68]

The modern world *"should not be too confident of our translations realizing that beneath the surface we have lighted a small ray of knowledge."* Manly Hall[69]

In ancient society all over the world are found the strange picture writing known as hieroglyphs. The most famous are found in Egypt, but they are also found with the Mexican Maya, Asia, even in strange tablets discovered on Easter Island. While many today believe the hieroglyphs have been deciphered, this is not the case. Most modern scholars are only beginning to unlock the secrets of the hieroglyphs. The picture symbols are a link to the wisdom of the creation and were thought to be a divine gift from Tehuti, Neteru of wisdom.

The finding of the Rosetta Stone (a Greek tablet inscribed with Egyptian hieroglyphs) in 1799 allowed for the beginnings of understanding the Egyptian language. Yet even Jean Francois Champollion, who followed the work of Akerblad and Tomas Young and was able to match modern letters with the Egyptian pictures, did not believe that he had revealed all that hieroglyphs

---

[67] Speeth, Kathleen The Gurdjieff Work (Putnam 1989) p.93
[68] West, Serpent p vii
[69] Hall p15

conceal. He was looking for a second meaning to the glyphs, but he died before he could complete this new section of work. Subsequent scholars simply continued his original ideas.[70]

Prior to the glyphs being deciphered most scholars believed that any civilization that was able to produce such incredible architectural wonders as the Egyptians must have had a high degree of knowledge. However, when the texts first began to be deciphered and the language seemed incoherent and unintelligent, the Egyptians were described as stupid. It has only been recently that the concept of Ancient Egypt as an advanced civilization is being looked at seriously.

Hieroglyphs (picture symbols) are the oldest and most important form of writing. In time new writing styles appeared in Egypt: Other Egyptian languages used were: Hieratic (a quick representation of glyphs similar to our writing compared to printing), Demotic (developed from Hieratic and was more script-like), and Coptic (the language of the Egyptian Christians who used the Greek alphabet and added six Demotic characters for sounds specific to the Egyptian language). Even though these other systems were in use, the respect for the hieroglyphs never waned. Hieroglyph is actually a Greek word made up of two roots, "hieros" (holy) and "glyphos" (carvings) thus they were holy script. The Greeks knew the power of the ancient picture writing, even though they could not read it. The Egyptians themselves called the script medu-neter (words of God). In fact the Corpus Hermeticum, written in Greek, advised the readers to not let the script of Egypt be translated to other languages to produce "writing in the greatest distortion and unclarity."[71]

Egyptian hieroglyphs have an alphabet of 24-28 letter/phonetic signs, where one sign equals a sound like in our alphabet. Bilateral signs are pictures that represent two or more sounds. The language also contains over 1000 pictorial/syllabic signs in which one picture represents an entire word. The signs all produce consonants, there are no vowels in Egyptian writing thus the pictorial signs were very helpful. If for example you were given the English consonants B and D, it could read as bad, bed, bid, bead, bod or bud. To differentiate a picture of a bed would follow the letters BD. You still wouldn't know how the word sounds but you would still know what it represents. Sometimes the BD (phonetics) of the word would not be recorded and simply the bed (syllabic) would be provided.[72] A syllabic is only needed when the preceding pictures represent sounds. To simplify pronunciation matters, modern scholars have agreed to a certain way to pronounce the hieroglyphs usually by

---

[70] West *Key* pp.34, 36; West *Serpent* pp.10, 28; Tompkins p.53; Hall, p.14

[71] Budge, EA Wallis *Egyptian Language: Lessons in Hieroglyphs* (Dorsett Press reprint 1993) p.5; Gadalla, Moustafa *The Historical Deception* (Bastet Press 1996) p.38; Crowley p.109; *Corpus Hermeticum* 16:2

[72] Gadalla p.23

adding an E between the consonants. This is by no means accurate, but is simply a way for us to pronounce the words we are seeing. Those not trained in the ancient mysteries of Tehuti will have no idea what the actual sounds were.

As Egyptologists worked on more and more documents, papyrus and stone carvings, a conclusion has been made. Most of the written material is non-religious, containing state documents, taxes or personal letters. They are easy for the scholars to translate and understand. However the religious documents seem untranslatable into workable sentences or ideas. This in itself should be a clue. Texts can be easily deciphered and understood, but religious texts are difficult to translate. Why? It is definitely showing that the religious writings are either offering another kind of knowledge or are written in a way to conceal the knowledge from the average person who read only the other types of documents.[73] To truly begin to understand hieroglyphs, or any ideas of the ancient world one must have a background in the Mysteries and Hermeticism.

All sound is a particular vibrational frequency that can be expressed as a number. Everything material in the universe is actually a number. The teachings of sacred number and sacred geometry are imperative to the understanding of not just everything in the ancient world from architecture to language, but to all of nature itself. All language in the ancient world was linked with sacred number. Each letter or glyph provided a sound, which in turn could be represented by a number. The Hebrews used this method of the Cabbala when writing the original text of the Bible, as the book *Cipher of the Genesis* explained. Anyone not familiar with the Hebrew Cabbala number system will be unable to properly translate to most of the Old Testament's information. Since all modern renditions of the Old Testament, including most modern Hebrew texts, were translated without knowledge of sacred number they create versions far apart from the initial concepts and ideas of the writers.[74]

Egyptian hieroglyphs were very much ruled by the aspects of sacred sound and number. It can best be understood that words and letters are batteries that are stored with energy and can be brought into the physical world. The ancient field of understanding the numeric value of words was called gematria. It was related to music as sacred music is a component of sacred sound, number, geometry and harmonics.

Vowels

"In Egypt the priests when singing hymns of praise of the gods employ the 7 vowels, which they utter in due successions, and the sound of these letters is so euphorious that men listen to it in place of the flute and lyre."

Demetrius, Roman writer[75]

---

[73] West *Serpent* p.140

[74] James p.133; West *Serpent* p.135; see also Suares, Carlos *Cipher of the Genesis* (Shambhala Publishing 1970)

[75] Fowden p.118

17:Tools of the Egyptian Scribe, Leiden Museum

Why were there no vowels in the Egyptian writing? We know they existed in the spoken language. There was a key reason for their omission and it is completely misunderstood by the Egyptologists. Modern scholars view the same reason for the omission of vowels as for the different paint on glyphs. Scribes got sloppy, ran out of time, and attempted to make the job easier by omitting the least important parts if the writing. Actually the vowels are the MOST important part of the writing (hence the opposite of what most believe). Rudolph Steiner claimed that consonants represented the sound of the external, while the vowel represented the sound of the inner.[76]

When you have the vowels present, you have the true sound of the word. You will know all, for the sound itself is creation. Sound is vibration, vibration is number, and number is in direct connection to the energies of the universe. To know sound, especially the vowels, was to have true power. It was by use of the 'vowels' that the Egyptians could carry out their incredible healing and purification of the body, mind and spirit. The seven vowels are the sounds of the seven chakras of the Eastern traditions and the seven planets of the western alchemic tradition.

To control a word, to know its proper name, meant control of the thing. The word creates the power. Words are but symbols for wisdom, but in the hands of a trained master who can use those energies properly - they become

---

[76] Houston p.117

118

energy, not the doorway to it. Because of the power involved, the Egyptian masters needed to hide that power from those who were not trained to handle it. If you can learn how to manifest something, it is just as easy to make an apple to share as a nuclear missile to destroy. One's moral character, intelligence, and especially their heart would have to be closely watched as the training progressed to see if one would be able to handle the power with Maat (truth, order, harmony).

The Hermetic axiom "hide the secret in plain view" means that the information could not be completely hidden. Those who wish to follow the wisdom need to have some of it available to them at all times. The writings would give you the consonants H and T so you could understand mentally what was being written about, but it was up to you through personal study to determine the vowel to be inserted. Each vowel will provide a completely different sound, different vibration and therefore a different energy. It would become a personal journey of understanding the sound, word, symbol, number, and the stopping of the conscious mind to understand which vowel sound was indeed the correct vowel. Is the Egyptian word for Horus (HR) Heru, Hara, Hera, Hure or the many other possibilities? Only through personal work with all of the possible names could the doorway to what the symbol referred to be opened. Once known and used in personal mantra the growth of the pupil towards that energy and wisdom would be rapid. Many scribes would have learned the writing system, what glyphs to insert for texts they were writing but may never have known the actual vowels that 'lived' between their drawn consonants.

How powerful are the ancient vowel sounds? To the Hebrews the name Jehovah is not supposed to be spoken. The question is why? The Hebrews themselves have no satisfactory answer, and the few that know do not want to share the secret. The vowels may be the answer. By taking the vowel sounds in alphabetic order we have: ah, a, e, i, o, ooo, and u. By saying these seven vowels backwards quickly produces a sound similar to Jehovah. Perhaps the word was never to be spoken because the Hebrew name of God contains all of the vowel sounds.

The purpose of the hieroglyphs is to pass on a wealth of information, but not too much. At different stages of personal development we will be able to unlock different secrets of the hidden wisdom. We have to do the work, and then use our learned insights with the glyphs. This would protect the power of a word from falling into the wrong hands. The same wisdom that can heal can also destroy. To believe information was very powerful and place it in a secret code would make it nearly impossible to understand for those not willing to spend their lives to translate it. To accomplish such a task, a master (who already acquired the wisdom) could check the moral character of the apprentice and weed out those likely to use the power for actions against the harmony of the universe.

Wisdom Revealed

So how can one begin to read hieroglyphs? It will require a tremendous amount of effort. One must first work with symbol, sound and number. There is a final part of the puzzle that has only been mentioned briefly, which is meditation.

"Hieroglyphic text of Egypt, few of us will ever properly read. They demand the heightened state of consciousness that today some people experience after years of meditative practice."[77] When Japanese samurai write their texts, they are in a meditative state for potentially hours before they begin. Before I create copies of the Ancient Egyptian texts, I meditate. By mediation I am referring the ability to use any activity to shift the consciousness away from the material, physical world.

At the Cross-group of Palenque in Mexico, I was looking at the reliefs in the temple area. Today all that is seen are worn and eroded inscriptions. I wondered what the reliefs looked like before they were eroded and were full of colour. Following a short meditation, I began some Egyptian chanting. The relief seemed to grow to life, and become real. The figures became alive and colours began to appear. Things became much clearer and I took a photo. Even the photo reveals extra colour and shape. I did this for only fifteen minutes, but imagine if I had done it for five hours? Perhaps the entire relief would not only have appeared, but the actual meaning of the carvings would surface. This is a good example of the state required for Egyptian hieroglyphs.

With the right state of mind, correct sounds, patience and understanding, the insights can be revealed after hard work. My teacher, Sahu Omri, claims that if you follow these procedures, "The glyphs will jump out at you, perhaps even surround you as a hologram. You will not longer be reading them, you will be a part of them." It is quite a feeling to have an event like this happen to you, as occurred with some carved Egyptian glyphs.

The glyphs can be read like words in a book, but they have a deeper meaning. This is what the Corpus Hermeticum referred to when warning of the Egyptian script being translated into the Greek script. By learning the different disciplines suggested in this chapter you might be able with time to unlock the secret mysteries of the Egyptian hieroglyphs personally.

Pyramid Texts

While most are familiar with the Egyptian Text referred to as the Book of the Dead, it is a late comer by Egyptian standards. The oldest religious document in the world is the Pyramid Texts. They are found carved into the walls of small pyramids at Sakkara, the most famous for Unas, Pepi 1 and Teti.

---

[77] West *Serpent* p.85

The glyphs are coloured turquoise or green (thus relate to the heart chakra), and are written in vertical rows that do not include any drawings or pictures (as appear in later texts). The glyphs themselves are pure, meaning they include all of the information needed within them.

The texts are the teachings for the ancient Followers of Horus from nearby Heliopolis (Annu). Some in fact believe that the texts go far beyond just Egyptian wisdom but are in fact remnants of texts and ideas from a time long before Egypt. Wallis Budge even claims that the layout of the texts gives the impression that the scribes themselves did not fully understand what the glyphs were carving and, "the general impression is that the priests who drafted these copies made extracts from several compositions of different ages and having different contents." Some believe the Pyramid Texts are the Egyptian copies from their predecessors of Atlantis. A Book of the Dead is nearly impossible for the non-mystic to understand, but the information in the Pyramid Texts is a sheer mystery for modern translators. Passages make no sense, words and letters exist that translators have found in no other Egyptian text.[78]

"They weren't carved in stone as nonsense…no one will fully understand the meaning of the texts until translating them on an esoteric basis."[79] Many writers today are focusing only on astronomical information that they are finding in the text, but like any great Hermetic work there are some 72 layers of information. These scholars have found but another of the layers. There are some who believe that the Egyptians themselves were facing a similar problem. Some believe that the Pyramid Texts are a translation of works from other cultures to which even the Egyptians had trouble understanding. That could explain why signs and words exist only here, for the Egyptian translators had to come up with something to express ideas that they had not been introduced to. I believe that it is possible that the Pyramid Texts could be the conglomeration of all the religious traditions of the world at the time. The synthesis of all the world's knowledge might in fact be found on the walls of pyramids in Sakkara, and are detailed in full in Volume 3.

Coffin Texts

The Coffin Texts appeared late in the Old Kingdom, evolved out of the Pyramid Texts, and focused on Osiris and Horus. It describes how Hours, as the divine falcon, goes to the Duat to defeat Set and allow for the rebirth of Osiris. This is a book of the light of Horus and how it can be used to "reveal the mysteries" and allow the meeting of Osiris. It was the first time a distinct text that described a journey in the underworld was listed. From this text emerged the Book of Two Ways, which was the first to provide pictures (called vignettes) along with the hieroglyphs. It describes the two routes to the afterlife (water or land), which are separated by the island of fire. It provided a map to

---

[78] Budge *Book* p.12; Hancock *Fingerprints* p.400
[79] West *Serpent* pp.137, 140

the mansions of Tehuti and showed the way to Field of Hotep (peace). It also was the first text to describe the path of Ra through the twelve hours of the day and night of the Duat. These two texts became the forerunner to all Middle and New Kingdom funerary texts.

Middle/New Kingdom Books

When tomb building shifted to the Valley of the Kings a number of texts were placed on the walls made to look like great unrolled papyrus. Three texts are related: The Book of What is in the Duat, Book of Gates, and Book of Caverns. Each of these texts describes the journey of the Sun through the Duat during the twelve hours of the night. Along the way, the challenges or hindrances to this journey are listed. Of course we are Ra traveling in our own solar boat as we face the challenges and pitfalls on our own journey to light. The transformative nature of these works are symbolized by most ending with Khepera, who represents the inner light that comes from our darkness. Other texts of this period are the Book of Aker (or the earth), The Litany of Ra, The Book of the Divine Cow, the Book of Day and Night (appearing astronomically on the tomb ceiling) and the Book of the Dead.

During this period a new type of literature, called Wisdom texts, were found. These are teaching tools, written as father to son, in which moral or life behaviour was handed out (Dr. Phil would be impressed). These texts were listed as short series of lines, like small poems, that likely often rhymed to allow for easier memory. They were the basic tenants how to live one's daily life in order to find favour from the Neteru. One of the most famous is the Instructions of Ptah-hotep, while a famous story is that of Sinue.

Funerary books were found in the tombs of the average population. These included the Book of Opening the Mouth which was 28 ceremonies to keep one's human faculties (eating, senses, talking) in the afterlife in order to partake in the funerary feast that followed the entombment of the mummy. The Liturgy of Funerary Offerings is 114 ceremonies that involve presentation of food, drink, oils, clothing etc to the deceased, who is arriving in the afterlife with their functions restored. These texts were not true Egyptian teaching in its pure sense for they are attempting to keep a person's individuality and life in the next world. As mentioned in mummification, the Egyptian temples taught the need to awaken and experience the truth of the cosmos, not to want to continue this world of illusion again and again.

Another great text, the famous 42 Books of Tehuti, is often mentioned but it has not been found. The Hermetic literature is thought to be derived from these texts, including the Greek Corpus Hermeticum and the Emerald Tablet of alchemy. Clement of Alexandria listed what he believed were the titles of the 42 books that included hymns, astrology, geography, the building of temples, ritual, law and medicine. It is thought that these were the highest teaching that could be provided in book form in the temples. They were claimed to be written in strange symbols which could alter a person's consciousness to allow them to reach the abode of the gods. Some Legends claim that the symbols were infused into what are now called Tarot cards.[80]

Late in the Egyptian period, temple priests began to place the equivalent of card catalogues upon the walls of new built temples like found at the Temple of Horus at Edfu. No one today is quite sure what these texts actually were or what they specifically contained, or if any have actually been discovered. Many papyrus have been found from the Greek and Roman period that are less religious in nature but provide much knowledge and information. They include papyrus on medicine, temple building, sacred number, magic, protection etc.

Book of the Dead
(section originally appearing here has now moved to volume 3)

---

[80] Fowden pp.58-59; Schwaller *Sacred* p.7; Hauck p.19; see Mead vol 3 pp.222-25 for list from clement

CHAPTER 6
CREATION MYTHOLOGY

18: Tehuti the scribe, on a wall at Luxor Temple

Egyptian Creation Myths
"The whole of Egyptian civilization was organized upon myth." John Anthony West[81]

To most people in the modern world, mythology seems to have little significance, little more than the undeveloped state of mind of our ancient brothers and sisters. However, "myth is a deliberately chosen means for communicating knowledge." Myth is not children's stories, or made up ways to explain an unknown universe, they are the records of ancient knowledge and science.[82] When one begins to study ancient myth and religious texts, the first observation is the similarity of all the stories around the world. The similarity shows their root in some form of truth. The fact that historical events appear is usually just to help give it a frame of reference for the reader at the time. The historical fact is less important than what the myth is trying to tell us. Every part of the myth has key meaning, veiled in symbolism. There is a reason for that number of thieves, wives or days. From the understanding of the myths we can gain a deeper connection to our own wisdom that resides within our heart (for more information please read the chapter Fairy Tales).

"Egyptologists know everything about Egyptian religion, everything except its soul." Jean Capart, Belgian Egyptologist [83]

---

[81] West *Serpent* p.127

[82] West *Serpent* p.127

[83] West *Serpent* p.152

The creation of the universe is a very important part of the mythology (knowledge) of the Ancient Egyptians. Egypt had several different creation myths, but four are seen as holding major significance. Each of the four myths is named after the Egyptian city from which that myth was localized: The Ennead of Heliopolis, Ogdoad of Hermopolis, Ptah at Memphis, and a special myth at Luxor. While the four creation myths contain similarities, they are remarkably different from each other, containing different Neteru. Today if we take a copy of Snow White out of the library, we know that it will contain the same basic plot lines. There will be 7 dwarfs not 12 giraffes. The fact that an important event like the creation of the universe has completely different stories has led to odd interpretations. Egyptologists claim that each story was the basis of a completely different center of worship that were rivals of each other. Depending on the most dominant priests at any particular time, that particular creation myth would reign in Egypt. As Jeremy Naydler so eloquently writes, "These stories are not rivals, but rather each story articulates different aspects of the unfolding of spirit into matter."[84] Egyptian creation myths are not separate; they are interlocked. They each provide a different view, or focus, on the creation of the universe and earth. The Egyptians decided that rather than one long story encompassing all of the different elements, they broke it up into more manageable parts. No one myth is any more important than any other, but each is needed in order to have the complete information. Egyptian creation mythology is very deep and mystical. An important note is that as the creation myths are provided, I will also be including information of the individual Neteru.

1 Heliopolis

The first Creation myth comes from Annu (On or Heliopolis) and is known as the myth of the Ennead for the nine Neteru that are created from Atum-Ra. Lucie Lamy has shown that the myth of the nine may in fact help to explain the entire process of not only the solar system but also the creation and birth of human babies (see Number).

Nun/Nehebkau

The myth begins with the dark abysmal waters of Nun. Nun stretches everywhere, endlessly. Before there was an earth, time or the Neteru all there was Nun. The Pyramid Texts claim, "Nun exists before the sky existed, before the earth existed." Nun is usually portrayed as dark, formless, or inert. Nun is that from which the universe came, the potential for existence symbolized by

---

[84] Naydler p.34

the formless fluidity of water. This is the primordial ocean, without shape or definition. Before there was a yes/no, high/low, light/shadow, thus before the number two, there was only Nun. Nun represents the number one and the All. Just as the waves of an ocean are not separate from the water, so too is nothing separate from Nun. Nun would have no shape, just as water has no shape taking the form of that which contains it.[85]

Mystically Nun would be seen as the building block of all that exists. The first tenet of the Hermetic Kyballion is that "All is Mind." When forms began to appear from the primordial ocean, they came as a thought in the heart (mind) of Neter (God). This would be likened to a human dream state where in our mind we create different objects and characters, or create a dream out of a previous dream. We create the forms in our dream that we believe to be real, so too is Nun (God) having numerous dreams. Nothing is separate from the primordial ocean of Nun just as a wave is not separate from the Atlantic Ocean. It is a part of it. In the creation of matter, Nun uses the ocean and Cosmic Mind to create.[86] Nun is found at the beginning of all Egyptian creation myths and is the only true constant within them all. This primordial ocean is also a key component of most of the creation stories of modern religions. That being understood, the actual method that the creator uses is explained in the rest of the myth.

During this primordial condition there is sometimes shown a serpent of many coils. This is a manifestation of something out of the watery nothing. This serpent is called Nehebkau "provider of life energies" in the Pyramid Texts. The snake's coils symbolize the sleeping kundalini in us that awaits arousal by our spiritual work. As the kundalini serpent's coils are holding the energies needed for our transformation, so too would Nehebkau be seen as the potential energies for manifestation of all life.

Atum

---

[85] Naydler pp.32, 36; *Pyramid Text* 1040; Lamy p.9; Norville, Roy *Hermes Unveiled* (Ashgrove 1986) p.53

[86] Ashby, Muata *Properties of Matter* (Cruzian 1998) p.30

19: Atum as the cat cutting off Apop's head, Papyrus of Ani, British Museum

The Egyptians referred to the creative principle that could manifest within these energies as Atum, "the All and Nothing." Atum is the Neteru who can activate the energies inherent in Nun. Atum is not different from Nun or the serpent, but is a part of them both as only they exist. "The sky had not been created, the earth had not yet been created, the children of the earth and the reptile had not yet been fashioned...I Atum was one by myself...there existed no other who worked with me."[87] Prior to Atum there was no life or death, just inert blackness that in later times was associated with Osiris.

At the beginning Atum claimed in the Coffin Texts, "I was alone in the waters, in a state of inertness before I had found anywhere to stand or sit, before Heliopolis had been formed." Eventually Atum was found inside the coils of the serpent, thus in someway had to become separate from Nun and the serpent. It is claimed that Atum "projected" himself out of the waters of Nun. He was the original god of light, a figure that latter became associated with, then overtaken by Ra and Horus. Atum is sometimes shown freeing himself from the serpent's coils by changing into a cat or a mongoose in order to kill the serpent. A tree springs up outside of the serpent's coils. The world tree is an original symbol for the cross and the ankh. Everything that exists came from Atum, as Atum in some way came from Nun. Paradoxically since everything that exists comes from Atum, then each time something is created so too is

---

[87] Hancock *Fingerprints* p.382; Naydler pp.30, 37

Atum created. He is the combined act that not only brings himself into existence, but also everything else at the same time. While Atum is depicted as a male in the texts (showing that Atum creatively uses the male energy of action like one who plants a seed) he is actually a he/she, a blend of feminine and masculine parts (for everything that is created has these parts).[88]

Atum is also related to the ideas of world ages and precession (see Chapter World Age). In time a form of Atum, called Tem or Tum, began to symbolize the west and the setting sun. This end of the journey of the sun is also the beginning, for it will rise again the next day. In this form he can be depicted as an old man leaning on a stick, similar to Tarot Card Nine. He is associated with the scarab, primordial hill, Benben, and Ra. The way Atum creates will be described below.

Khepera

The principle of becoming or of transforming was known as Khepera, represented by a scarab beetle. Khepera represents the rising sun each morning, which is a reborn or transformed sun from the night before. The rise of Khepera (a form of Atum, young Horus), leads to the birth of Ra (sun). The scarab in order to give birth (transform) lays its eggs in a ball of dung, which it rolls about wherever it goes. Egyptologists claim the symbol of the scarab for Khepera is because it rolls this ball (which looks like the sun) during the day. In truth the symbol is representative of the alchemic transformative process. The light will be found in our own dung, our own ugly waste products. Rather than ignore them, Khepera wants us to explore, use and transform them to something wonderful. Just as the night sun is to be transformed into Ra each day, we too are tying to follow this teaching. It is the reason that in Egyptian texts like the Book of Caverns, Khepera is associated with the beginning and ending of the text. Our astral gold will be found in our own darkness. Most other ancient cultures used a butterfly instead of a scarab, as a larva worm transforms into a beautiful flying insect. Khepera is also symbolized as an amulet or a green beetle that is placed on the heart during the opening of the mouth ceremony. Khepera is also associated with Heru-Khuti, the Sphinx at Giza.

Primordial Hill/Phoenix/Benben

The becoming of Khepera by Atum was symbolized as either a primeval mound, a bennu bird (phoenix) or as a Benben stone. As a primordial hill, Atum was seen as the first land rising from the waters of the ocean. Egypt itself was often thought of as this land, and most every Egyptian temple had a raised platform in the center representing this first hill. Some texts claim that

---

[88] Lamy p.8-9; Naydler pp. 3, 32, 80

the primordial hill was the area of Giza where the Sphinx and Pyramids now rest. The rising of the primordial hill was also symbolically repeated each year as the land reappeared following the flooding of the Nile. The primordial hill is a representation of light out of the dark waters. This should not be confused with the rising sun, as the material universe had not been created. It could more be seen as the spark that will bring light. The hill is the energy behind what will become all matter, not the matter itself. From this hill papyrus or plant life sprang forth. All Hypostyle Halls in temples are representative of this first plant life that sprang forth from the hill, or the sense that the energy of the hill would be used to grow things. It is the papyrus swamp where Horus, Moses and Jesus were all raised in secrecy.[89]

This hill was often associated with the famed Benben Stone or the bennu bird (Phoenix) which was a bird of light that came down to a reed that washed on the shore of the hill. The bird brings light from the darkness and is another symbol of spiritual transformation. The Phoenix is the bird of rebirth and is said to live for 500 years at the end of which it cremates itself on a funeral pyre only to rise from its own ashes. In some texts the Phoenix comes to rest on the sacred Benben stone, a form of the primordial hill. This stone was believed to be an actual physical object and was claimed to hold the "hiddenness of the Duat (underworld)." Paintings and texts show the Benben as pyramid shaped. The Benben was a stone that fell to the earth from heaven, and was believed to be the first piece of solid matter created by Atum. The Benben stone was put on display atop the obelisk at Heliopolis and once a year a pilgrimage was made to it similar to the black meteorite stone at Mecca. The Egyptian word Ben is connected to flowing out, especially to male semen and is a reason many equate the obelisk as a phallic symbol.[90] Some suggest the physical object was a meteor, which in some way spawned life on earth. Or it could be a metaphor to show that the seeding of the earth came from outer space. All initiates in Egypt sought what the Bennu bird represented (light) as described in passages of the Book of the Dead. Atum at times was also claimed to have laid an egg which created Ra.

Ra

With the emergence of Atum in a number of forms, light is finally able to be created. This principle is symbolized by Ra. Often the three beings (Atum-Khepera-Ra) are merged into one deity; Khepera is the rising sun, Ra the noon sun and Atum the setting sun. They are separate, but the same. Ra is usually symbolized as the sun, but this is not entirely correct. Ra is not the sun but the principle behind which makes the sun shine. The sun itself is merely the

---

[89] Laviolete, Paul *Beyond the Big Bang* (Park St. 1995) p.103; West *Key* p.246

[90] Hancock *Heaven's* pp. 104, 106, 107, 109; *Pyramid Text* 1652; Lamy p.7; Laviolete p.104

eye of Ra or the sun disk Aten. The average Egyptian viewed the time of the day as morning, midday, evening and night according to the sun's journey across the sky. It was not just the sun, it was a spiritual object and represented the Supreme Being. The sun was believed each night to be swallowed by the goddess Nut, and reborn the next morning. The Egyptian priests knew that the sun was not actually swallowed for they understood the science of our solar system, but was used as a metaphor for internal transformation.[91]

Ra is light, that inner part of our being that could shine and bring us back to oneness with Atum and Nun. He shows that just as the sun is needed to sustain all life on earth, so too does the essence of God sustain the existence of everything in the universe. Because of the symbolic importance of this inner fire that is used to reach our True Self, Ra became a key part of daily prayer. In time, Ra's symbolic nature was lost and instead the sun itself began to be worshiped. The texts want us to connect with our own inner Ra, not the sun. The sun's energy is male energy, and this must be balanced with female energy. Modern religions were influenced by the later mistakes of Egypt/Sumeria and began to create religions based on the male energy of the sun, rather than the symbolic meaning of the energy behind the sun.

Ra can be depicted as a royal child resting on a lotus (which emerges each day from the swamp to open to the light), as a man with a solar disk on his head, or combined with the falcon Horus, showing the creator is but Horus, our own heart. In the ancient world the sun was often given the symbol of a circle with a dot in the center, which is a representative of the number one. Even at the stage in creation of Ra, though it seems like there are few separate entities, there is still only one. This circle will be needed to create the other numbers (manifestations) through the Vesica Pisces (see Number). Ra travels in two boats: Matet (day) and Semktet (evening). Thus the boats are associated with Maat (truth and order) and Sekhem (personal power).

Atum's Creation

Atum-Ra is now ready to go past the world of Oneness and move to other numbers in the creative cycle. Since there is only one, there can not be an outer male-female combination yet, so to create Atum must either spit out or masturbate to cause the "seed from the kidneys to come." Atum creates by uniting his male member with his female half, symbolized by the hand. Ardhanari-Purusha in India also created by masturbation.[92] Something has to be expelled from the being of Atum. In sacred number it will be shown that the only way subsequent numbers can come from the one is for the one to project out a mirror image of itself and create a second circle. The kidneys are the point that Oriental masters claim our energy of creative formation is stored. This

---

[91] Lamy pp.7, 11; West *Serpent* p.48; Hancock *Fingerprints* p.373
[92] Ashby *Egyptian Yoga* p. 48

spitting or masturbating brings the Neteru Shu and Tefnut into existence. Atum came forth from nothing, created himself and then could create everything else. Anytime we paint, write or build a fence we are tapping into the creative power of Atum. Many mystics relate that the day we as a human stop creating, we stop being.

Shu and Tefnut/Geb and Nut

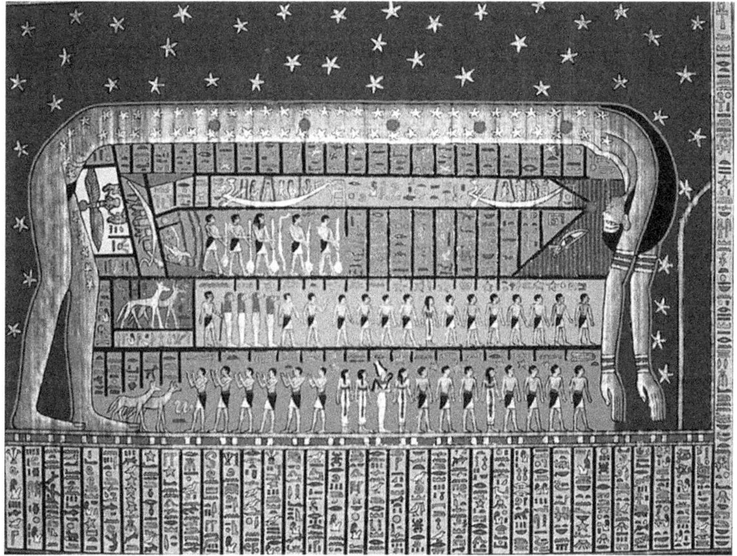

20: Nut stretching across the sky, swallowing the sun at night and birthing it in the morning, Papyrus rendition

Shu and Tefnut come from the same essence (Atum-Ra) yet are different due to gender. Atum-Ra splits up into the male and female, or yin and yang principles. Shu is usually thought to represent the air, atmosphere and space, but not space as we know it because there is no physical universe yet. Rather at this stage Shu is the principle through which form can arise. Tefnut represents moisture (water) in her vagina. This moisture is similar to rain that will allow plants to grow, thus the source of vitality. Her symbol is the lioness (power of nature), with a serpent on her crown (kundalini) while holding a papyrus scepter (power of knowledge) and an ankh (life).[93] Some have suggested the elements are represented with Shu (air), Tefnut (water) primordial hill (earth) and Atum (fire). Shu and Tefnut have a sexual union

---

[93] Ashby *Matter* p.164

131

which cause the rest of the Neteru to be born. Thus the physical world can only be born through the physical union of the gods.

Geb (male earth) and Nut (female sky) were born together in loving embrace. The earth was originally united with heaven. The next action was the creation of the world we currently know. This occurred not out of love and sex, but by the splitting apart by Shu of Geb from Nut. This ripping apart of the earth and heaven was felt as great pain. The Chinese creation myth shows how yin (dark) and yang (light) first separated from an original chaotic state of existence. In Summer it was An (male sky) and Ki (feminine earth) uncoupling, while in Genesis God divided the primordial waters into heaven and earth.[94] This action is claimed to have occurred when Ra heard that Geb and Nut wanted to marry. He became enraged and ordered their father Shu between them. Ra forbid Nut from having a child in any month in the 360-day year. This caused the Neteru Tehuti to play the moon in a game of cards to win 1/72nd of each day's moon light which added up to five extra days. This was added to the 360-day year, and gave Nut the opportunity to give birth to the rest of the Neteru (see calendar).

When the three deities are depicted together, Geb is usually shown resting on his arm and buttock. Geb looks as though he has fallen and is never again looking up at his beloved Nut. This may be a symbol that as each of us falls to earth, we focus only on the earthy realm and seem to lack the strength to rise ourselves up to the realm of spirit. Muata Ashby has also shown that the poses of Geb and Nut are key Yoga postures. Lucie Lamy has also claimed that the twisted position of Geb is similar to the rotation of the earth. The image of separation provokes the idea that the world came into existence on the basis of pain. Asian religious traditions speak of life on earth as suffering because we are not connected to the Universal All. It is the separateness that has caused the pain for Geb and Nut, as our separateness from God is the condition of our pain. Thus earthly life is a series of challenges to regain our oneness and let go of suffering.

It is interesting that in most cultures the earth is depicted as feminine, while in Egypt the earth was male. In Egypt all that grew on the earth was related to Isis. It is nature that is feminine, not the earth itself. Resting above the earth is Nut. She is stretched out so that her fingers and toes touch the ground, symbolizing the four cardinal points or four elements that all life on earth is created from. Along her body are the stars of the sky. Each night the sun was swallowed by Nut, which traveled through her body in the region known as the Duat (see Duat) where Ra would fight all of the enemies that would try to stop his rebirth. Each night Ra would win this battle and then be born in the morning from Nut's vagina. Nut is also depicted in the early stages of the *Book of the*

---

[94] Laviolete p.15; Naydler pp.41, 45

Dead as two sycamore trees that will provide nourishment to the Afterlife traveler. She became associated with Hathor and the divine cow.

Shu is what has come between the two to separate them. While Geb and Nut were still together there was the idea of "as above so below" due to the connection. His name means "to raise up" and became Atlas in Greek mythology. Shu is represented in human form with a feather and his characteristic gesture of the KA sign. Egyptologists claim that Shu's KA gesture is needed to hold the sky and earth apart, and should he relax this pose then heaven and earth would again unite. However Nut seems to be able to support herself with no need of Shu. Shu uses the KA sign which is the energy that helps bind us to the material world and is the force that keeps the dual forces inside of us from connecting as one. It is Shu who creates the belief of a world of duality, the separation into male and female forms, for at the beginning male and female were together. Shu shows that by the feather he wears (Maat/order) and from the times he is depicted with a baboon head (Tehuti/wisdom) that through wisdom and order one can overcome the appearance of duality and reunite Geb (male) and Nut (female) in our own consciousness.[95]

With Thoth winning the five extra days for the rest of the gods to be born, the Ennead of nine can be complete. Nut gives birth to Wizzar (Osiris) Auset (Isis) Set and Nepthys. Each has a special region of the cosmos associated with them Wizzar (Orion) Auset (Sirius) Set (Ursa Major) and Nepthys (sky below the horizon). Osiris and Isis gave birth to Heru (Horus).

Myth of Rule

Ra was the first ruler of the new world, the world previous to the one we now live in. The Maya refer to the previous stages of humanity as previous Suns. The Pyramid Texts tell us he governed from the 'Prince's Palace' in Heliopolis. After his morning bath and breakfast, Ra would get into his boat and inspect the twelve provinces of his kingdom (signs of the zodiac) spending an hour in each. As long as Ra remained young, he reigned peacefully over gods and men. The years began to take their toll on him, and the texts eventually depict him as old and feeble. This is the same as the myth in Mexico where Quetzalcoatl became old and feeble. When old age overtook Ra the people he created sensed weakness and plotted against him. It is not fully explained why humans would want to do so. Ra discovered their plans and decided to hurl his divine eye (utchat) against his rebellious subjects in the form of Sekhemet (the lioness form of Hathor).[96]

Sekhemet began to destroy the human race, but it is claimed that Ra's inherent goodness would not allow the entire human race to be destroyed.

---

[95] Ashby *Egyptian Yoga* p.131; Naydler pp.18-19
[96] West *Key* p.81

Depending on the text he either intervened in the form of a flood or with the help of Tehuti gave her a magic potion of beer and pomegranate juice. Sekhemet thought the drink was blood and drank all of the liquid. She either became too drunk, or bloated from the water to continue killing and fell asleep. When she awoke she no longer wanted to kill and peace again reigned. On the orders of Nun, Nut became a cow and took Ra on her back and raised him high into the sky to form the sun. It was at this time that our present world was created. This myth claims that our present world came after an age of destruction, ushered in by massive flooding. Sekhemet the lioness symbolizes all this, and many like West and Hancock see this a symbol for the precessional age of Leo over 10,000 years ago.[97] In some myths upon rising, Ra ordered the Sekhet-Hotep (field of peace) to be created. One part of it began to grow and became the Sekhet-Aaru (field of growth).

Nut rose with Ra too quickly and became dizzy. She began to shake because she was too high above the earth, and was given four pillars (legs) to hold her up. From then on Ra sailed in his boat from the East to the West during the twelve daylight hours. In the twelve night hours he fought Apop the serpent, which he always defeats and is reborn as a new sun in the morning. Shu succeeded Ra as the King of the earth, but like his father he grew old and abdicated in favour of his son Geb. When Geb took over from Shu he called for the Golden Box of Ra to be brought from the fortress. Into this box Ra had deposited: a rod, a lock of hair, and a uraeus (a crown with the cobra and vulture on it, the sign of kingship). When he opened it a bolt of fire ushered from it killing most of Geb's followers and greatly burning Geb. Only by applying the lock of hair to his wounds could they be healed. Thus the box contained not only the destructive force, but also the healing power for it. The lock of hair was later thrown into a lake for purification and became a crocodile.[98] This story is of course similar to the Ark of the Covenant, which was made of gold and contained: the golden pot of Manna, Aaron's rod, and the two tablets of the Ten Commandments. Eventually, Geb handed over the reign to his son Osiris. The myths of Osiris, Isis and Horus are less of creation and will be examined in the following chapter.

2 Hermopolis/Khemenu

The second creation myth comes from Hermopolis (Khemenu-City of Eight), opposite the modern town of Tel-Al-Amarna, and is the center of the myth of Tehuti (Thoth in Greek). As in all Creation myths, this one begins with

---

[97] Hancock *Fingerprints* p.394; West *Key* p.394
[98] Hancock *Fingerprints* p.413

Nun. Tehuti sent forth the Creative sound and brought into being four sets of Neteru in the waters. These eight are known as the Ogdoad and are the opposite qualities that allow the created universe to form. They are depicted as either frogs or serpents, beings that can live on water and on land. They are: Nun (central source) and Naunet (raw material, matter); Kuk (conscious) and Kauket (unconscious); Heh (unendingness) and Hehet (limitlessness); Amun (hidden) and Amunet (manifest). The primordial eight are sometimes seen as the four elements." The first part of the myth relates to the power of opposites. The third force to bring the opposites together is the voice of Tehuti. It is Tehuti that allows the four pairs of opposites to swim together, where they form the egg from which the goose was born. The goose was able to fly away as the sun, or sometimes the egg breaks to let a lotus rise from the water to birth Ra. Ra now assumes the role of Creator, with Tehuti as heart and tongue. The Navajo have a myth that the earth mother at creation molded the first four pairs of men and women from balls of skin rubbed off different parts of her body.[99] Some believe that this myth is far older than the one at Heliopolis.

An interesting component of the primordial eight is that in many books today the names of Amun and Amunet are omitted by scholars. This simple part of the eight, Amun, later became the ruling deity of Luxor/Thebes and was part of a creation myth all of his own. This is a strange phenomenon, one that has not been looked at closely enough. Egyptologists simply add the names of Tehuti and Maat to make up the original eight, ignoring the truth of the Egyptian texts that in fact Amun was just a part of the eight primordials. This skimming over of the truth is not the knowledge of Egypt. In Sumeria they also began with four pairs of gods, but the fourth pair were both male. Without the female it was showing that their entire society was focused on male energy.

---

[99] Lamy p.10; Mead, GRS *Thrice Greatest Hermes* (Harper and Row 1987) p.57; Clark p.79; Naydler p.53; Schwaller *Sacred* p.19; Gold, Peter *Navajo and Tibetan Sacred Wisdom* (Inner Traditions 1994) p.108

Tehuti (Thoth)

21: Tehuti Statue, Author's home alter

Tehuti was the creator of knowledge, wisdom, literature, all arts and sciences, surveying, geometry, astronomy, magic, medicine, music, drawing, writing, hieroglyphs, and was keeper of the divine records and history. He appears during the weighing of the heart to record the judgment of the soul. The Greeks and Islamics believed that he built the Pyramids. His most important teachings were called the Books of Tehuti, which later became the Hermetica. When one is seeking wisdom and knowledge, it is the energy of Tehuti that one must tap into and use. The main symbol of Tehuti was the ibis bird. There were two species of Ibis common in Egypt, one all black and the other a mixture of black and white. The bird was symbolic of this Neteru because it was the first two hermetic colours (black and white), and the fact the bird killed snakes and ate crocodile eggs, both associated with Set. The white plumage of the ibis is the purity of thought with wisdom, truth and righteousness. Tehu is the Egyptian word for ibis, and the work Tekh is one for the heart. At times the hieroglyph of the ibis could be drawn to symbolize the "wisdom of the heart."[100] Tehuti can also be shown as an ape or baboon. When Hathor had forgotten her true self and was in great need, Tehuti came to help as a baboon, a seemingly ordinary animal. Just as we rarely see wisdom from an average source or average person, Tehuti in this form is bringing wisdom from simple sources (books, lectures, talks) until the aspirant is ready to go to more direct forms of knowing (Gnosis). In a sense the right side teachings of the Toltec are teachings from the baboon form of Tehuti.

As inventor of hieroglyphs he was called "Lord of the Holy Words." Without his inventions, especially writing, it is said that mankind would have forgotten his doctrines, wisdom and knowledge- thus losing all of the benefits of his discoveries. "I am Thoth, the skilled scribe whose hands are pure, a professor of purity, who drives away evil, who writes what is true, who detests falsehood, whose pen defends the Lord of All…" It was claimed by Mantheo, Herodotus and in Kore Kosmou of Stobaius that it was the first Hermes (Tehuti) who kept alive the wisdom from before the flood inscribed in

---

[100] Ashby *Egyptian Yoga* p.73; Norville p.70

monuments all over the world. These writings and knowledge were said to be hidden so future generations could come to find them. Herodotus referred to the two pillars that Thoth had put the ancient wisdom on, "hidden under the heavenly vault which could only be found by the worthy, who would use such knowledge for the benefit of mankind."

Thoth spoke the words which resulted in the creation of the heavens and the earth and he taught Isis the words which enabled her to revive the dead body of Osiris and healed Horus. Tehuti was the master of the divine sound, used not only for creation but also in healing. All of the great healers in Egypt needed the divine wisdom of Tehuti and the medical knowledge of energy from Sekhemet. The Elbers Papyrus says, "Man's guide is Thoth, who bestows on him the gifts of his speech, who makes the books and illumines those who are learned therein, and the physicians who follow him, that they may work cures." This sound was known to the Greeks as the divine word or Logos.[101] He was the moon god, or at least in charge of guarding the moon in his form as the sacred Ibis. He was the left eye, representing the left side of the body and its feminine energies (see eye). He won the part of the moon's light to provide Nut with the extra five days to allow for the birth of the Neteru. He was the master architect of temple building and of all the mystic monuments. He is also the great judge for he mediates the conflict between Horus and Set. Interestingly no one is really sure where Tehuti fits into the chronology of Neteru. Some claim he must have been created when Ra was created, as the feminine energy of the moon had to be created at the same time as the male energy of the sun. Some writings say he is the oldest son of Ra, others the child of Geb and Nut and brother of Isis. An important component was the "breath of Tehuti" described in chapter 183 of the Book of the Dead. A master of Qi Gong, Yoga or Shamanism must learn how to use the breath to gain inner power to store the Qi.

The ink jar he holds as god of writing is also the hieroglyph for the heart. The thought of Tehuti is not the thought of the conscious mind, but rather is the thought of our true mind in the heart. The use of reaching our true mind is to acquire Gnosis, or connection to all of the wisdom of the universe. Thus the wisdom of Tehuti is none other than the wisdom of our own heart, which is in fact our True Self. He could be seen as the Heart of the World. He is the "personification of the mind of God...the all-pervading and directing power of heaven and earth." He is the will and power which kept the forces of heaven and earth in equilibrium, as it was through his wisdom that one could connect with his consort Maat. Thoth's temple was referred to as the Temple of the Net, which may be similar in scope to the veil of Isis. Shamans in South America talk of students wanting to become fishes, to use their net to catch the unknown

---

[101] Mead 50, 63, 65; *Book of the Dead* Chapter 182; Copenhaver p. xvl, 94; Fowden pp.30, 33; Hauck, Dennis *Emerald Tablet* (Penguin 1999) p.24

and unseen spirit. The idea of a net can also trap and enclose matter. To escape it one must learn the parts of the net (ropes, poles etc) in order to turn it into one's own use as a means of catching the food of the spirit, similar to Jesus wanting to make fishers of men. The similarity of the word Thoth to our word thought is striking. Most importantly, Tehuti shows that creation itself is thought and sustained by thought.[102] Tehuti is the wisdom that is needed in order to live the teachings of his consort, Maat, each day.

Hermes/World

22: Tehuti in the form of the baboon, Khonsu temple, Karnak

The Greek mysteries conjoined the ideas of Tehuti into their own god Hermes. He was given the name Trismegistus, or Thrice Great. This title of thrice great was applied to Tehuti long before it was applied to Hermes. A text from the archive of Hor in 172 BC says "no man shall be able to lapse from a matter which concerns Tehuti, three times great, the god in person who holds sway in the temple in Memphis." Sophocles wrote, "Thrice happy [like Thoth] are those who have seen the mysteries." The Greek statues of Hermes bears either the feather of truth (Maat) on the head, or the papyrus scroll in the hand.[103] Hermes was later given winged sandals, representing that the wisdom

---

[102] Ashby *Egyptian Yoga* p.48; Hancock *Heaven* pp.72, 73; Mead pp.62, 64; Cait 2-32
[103] Copenhaver pp.xiv-xv; Mead p.99

of Hermes will lead one to the astral self which can fly away from the physical body. The teachings of Hermes became known as the Hermetic path, and is the basis of alchemy and the great religions of the world since Egypt. A famous symbol of Hermes was the staff of healing (caduceus), which became the symbol for the medical profession. The two serpents that wind their way up the staff are the kundalini serpents that the wisdom of Tehuti/Hermes will help to release. Tehuti holds this same caduceus in the Middle Kingdom Temple of Seti l at Abydos.

Tehuti influenced wisdom and healing all over the world. In Phoenicia, Taut was the inventor of the alphabet and writing. He was called Theutates by the Druids, and is the Raven of Native Indian tradition. The Hindu text Mahaniranatantra states that Hermes was similar to the Buddha since each was known as the "Son of the Moon." To the Romans he was Mercury, the Norse as Woden (thus our Wednesday is the day of Hermes or Woden's day. To the French it is Mecredi or Mercury's day). Watkins compared the straight track leading through the Greek cities with the leys of Britain and said they were associated with Hermes. Hermits were a name given to servants of Hermes who acted as guides for pilgrims to help them across mountains and wild places. Some kept labyrinths, while others would stay deep in the forest alone to be in meditation. The dictionary says Hermes was an old name for the Will-O-the-Wisp (lights in the forest) or Shakespeare's Puck. Hermes is always seen to be associated with ley lines, standing stones and ancient monuments.[104]

Maat

23: Maat

The philosophy of Maat is perhaps the oldest known philosophy of righteous action. When followed and understood to perfection it ends in the spiritual evolution of the individual human being as well as the society who practice it. She is most often depicted as a beautiful winged figure, looking like a Christian angel which in fact could have their roots in Maat. Isis can have the wings of Maat to show that Isis is Maat using order and harmony to lead to wisdom and spiritual awakening. The actual practice of Maat is the study of a mystical teaching and the daily living of that teaching. Knowing it is not enough. She wears an

---

[104] Ashby *Egyptian Yoga* p.73; Mitchell, John *New View Over Atlantis* (Harper and Row 1969) pp.52, 83; Hauck pp.38, 362

ibis feather in her hair. This feather will symbolize Maat when weighed against the heart in the underworld journey. Maat in most books is defined as truth, justice, and order but the concept is much more than this. She does represent justice for all Egyptian judges were expected to make rulings based on the principles of Maat. Maat sometimes had her eyes closed to ensure equal justice. The modern blindfolded Lady of Justice is a version of this.[105]

Maat is the foundation of the cosmos. She symbolized regularity, righteousness, honesty, accuracy, fairness, faithfulness and divine harmony. At one time all that existed was Chaos, but the creation of Maat led to harmony where creation could happen. It was the human responsibility of each person to live a life that kept this harmony in balance, as it was for Egyptian leaders to perform in ways that would keep the entire country in this harmony. To not live Maat meant that one would be allowing for the effects of karma (Meskhenet) to be reopened. The weighing of the heart is symbolizing this check of our actions and thoughts versus our karma. The more we lived Maat in our life, the more in balance the scale would be thus the less need for our return to an earthly existence. As a reminder Egyptians were taught to "do Maat and speak Maat." Some compare the path of following Maat as similar to the path of following the Tao.

3 Memphis

24: Shakaba Stone, British Museum

---

[105] Ashby *Egyptian Proverbs* (Cruzian 1998) pp. 4, 7; Lamy 17

The third Creation myth takes place in the city of Memphis (not the home of Elvis) but the former capital of Egypt and the center of Ptah. While in the other myths a super being creates other lesser beings to carry out creation, here the absolute spirit is personally engaged in creation right down to the emergence of all living things. Most of the information on this myth comes from the famed Shakaba Stone. The stone was originally a papyrus claimed to be "worn" and transferred to stone, though it was later used to grind corn losing many of the glyphs. The stone claims, "Through the heart and through the tongue evolution into Atum's image occurred." Atum is the raw material through which the image took shape. There needed to be idea (mind/heart), expression of that idea (annunciation, voice) and a third force (spirit) to create.[106]

Ptah

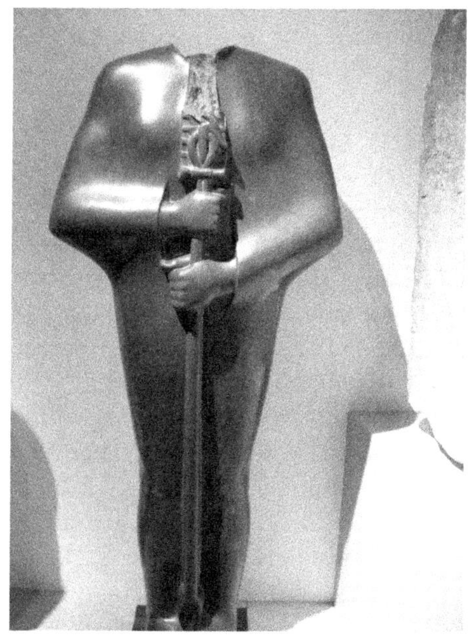

25: Ptah Statue, Leiden Museum

Memphis shows the formation of matter. Ptah is Atum on the earth, who incarnates the primordial eight (like at Hermopolis) and then becomes Tatenen "the earth which rises up." Atum performs the work of creation by sitting on Ptah (as the primordial hill). Ptah gives existence, while human consciousness (Atum) allows perception and gives meaning to that existence. To an alchemist Atum may be seen as the One Mind while Ptah was the One Thing. Ptah symbolizes all life, stability and strength. His name is made up of Pt (heaven) and Ta (earth) with h (support). He is thus the support between heaven and earth. While Shu keeps Geb and Nut apart, it is the fire of Ptah that keeps that link alive. Ptah is usually represented by a mummified figure bound in wrappings with only his head, hands, and feet free. Some Egyptologists believe this means that Ptah is a very old deity made when artists did not know how to make arms and legs. This is typical of those who can believe the Ancient Egyptians could build pyramids from stone but

---

[106] Silverman pp.125, 128

couldn't sculpt hands and feet from the same stone. He is bound showing that he is not free. He is bound (like every mummy) by Set, our own conscious mind (see Other Myths and Mummification). This compares to the Greek the Hephaestus, whose lameness is the physical equivalent to Ptah's bindings. Ptah was usually painted blue.[107]

Ptah was the master builder and it was his energy that instructed architects and masons during their building projects. Ptah was the metaphysical fire that produces its effects on the perceptible universe. He is able to transmit power and spirit to the rest of the Neteru, and control the lives of all things (animals/plants/humans) through his thought and command. Some claim Ptah carried out the commands of Thoth to create the universe, while others see the opposite. The myths and deities of Hermopolis and Memphis are related. Ptah is similar to the Supreme Being who is defined in the Hebrew Bible. Roy Norvill claims the name pth or ptr became Peter. He claims Peter and Ptah are related to words for rock and stone like the name Petra. His female consort was Sekhemet, a form of the goddess Hathor. She is also fire, but while Sekhemet uses the fire to burn away that which is impure Ptah uses the same fire as creative force to allow something new to be built (Sekhemet will be examined in Other Myths).

Ptah is the essence of the human soul that perceives the universe, and is the source and support of creation. Ptah spelled backwards is hotep (peace), the place of inner quiet of the mind that we must all venture. The myth of Memphis explains the illusion of this physical world. The wisdom of the actual creation of the universe is unknown to humans because it is beyond the use of our senses to pick it up. Our senses pick up information and send it to our brain where it makes a chemical signal to tell us what we perceive. We perceive something, but we cannot be too sure of exactly what we are perceiving. To say for certainty chair, dog or brother is to live in what is known as the world of Maya or illusion. This illusion is our own conscious mind interpreting information the way it wants, not the way it really is. If we can learn the process of seeing or becoming enlightened we go beyond seeing trees and people, just energy. A key hermetic axiom is "the universe is mental," yet it cannot be understood through the mind in the head, only through our true mind in our heart. Memphite theology says creation occurred after a first thought, which caused matter to appear as various objects of creation. God has a thought and projected it out. Since our essence is God, we too are constantly manifesting the universe. We are led by our thoughts and deepest desires and keep creating things out there, yet if we regain our essence (God) and think only of the divine will (from our heart) then everything would happen naturally from God.[108]

---

[107] Ashby *Egyptian Yoga* pp.47, 96; West *Serpent* p.127
[108] Ashby *Matter* pp.30, 38-44, 48-51,72, 79

Nefertem/Imhotep

From the coupling of Ptah and Sekhemet came either the child Nefertem or Imhotep. Nefertem (Young Tem) would be the opposite of the setting sun or Old Tem. Young Tem is identified with young Horus. Nefertem is often shown as a lotus emerging form the primeval waters on which sits Horus. The other son, Imhotep (Asclepius), was a god of healing and medicine. Asclepius was an important component of the Hermetic literature again showing the connection of this myth with Hermopolis. Imhotep means "He Who Brings Peace," and was originally seen to be the great priest who built the pyramid complex at Sakkara. It is claimed he could bring sleep to those who were suffering in pain, and could cure any disease of gods and men. The peace he brings is the inner peace that can occur after soul healing that brings us to our heart. Besides the god of medicine, he was also the god of learning in general thus assumed many of the attributes of Thoth in Memphis.[109]

Khnum

Another part of the myth is found in the village of Esna. Khnum is called the molder and creates all life forms out of Nile clay on his potter's wheel. This is similar to the Biblical account of God fashioning Adam from clay. Khnum moulds to symbolize that we are molded each time we glimpse the mystical realms or must face our personal challenges. We will always come back a bit different, shaped into higher forms. His consort was Neith, and their offspring was Heka (magic).

4 Thebes

The main triad at Luxor is Amun, with consort Mut and offspring Khonsu. Luxor is claimed by de Lubicz to show the birth of the cosmic man, an enlightened human. The temple up the road at Karnak is called Aput-Set (Place of the Enumerator). The name combines the ideas of counting and birthing. To go from one number to the next requires a birth just like with humans. The title can also refer directly to Set, the physical world where counting and numbers can be shown. The Thebian myth clams at the origin there existed a serpent, Kam-at-f "he who has accomplished his time." The serpent eventually ceased to exist "when his time was past," and his son Ir-ta "Creator of the Earth" was the one who formed the eight primordials of Hermopolis among whom we find Amun. Ra is born and becomes assimilated with Amun. [110]

---

[109] Ashby *Matter* pp.36, 72; Mead pp.457, 460
[110] Lamy pp.11-13; Schwaller *Sacred* p.197

Amun

Many believe that Amun was the great god of Ancient Egypt. This is false. While in the New Kingdom (after 2000BC) he did become the chief deity around Thebes and the south, prior to this period Amun was a serpent of the eight primordials in Heliopolis. He is mentioned only four times in the Pyramid Texts (the great religious document of Egypt). Not a solid background for the supposed great god of Egypt. In fact he was always seen as a rather minor deity until a specific shift in the astrological cycle. The main deity of Thebes during the Old Kingdom was Montu the bull. Suddenly the ram headed Amun came to prominence at Thebes, while great building projects are begun there. This is exactly at the time when the precession of the sky moved from Taurus the bull to Aries the ram. If Luxor had lasted long enough it would have been likely to see a fish take over during the age of Pisces. Memphis represented the element fire, Hermopolis water, Heliopolis air, Thebes the element of earth. In Toltec tradition, one learns to see the same event from all four directions (elements).

Amun also became connected to Min (a form of Horus) and later by the Greeks with Zeus. The Leyden Papyrus says Amun, "gives birth to everything that is, and causes all that exists to live," while other texts of the time see him as the maker of all beings, mighty and powerful. Amun normally appears as a human with a crown headdress of two straight plumes, but sometimes with ram horns that curve close to the body. He is depicted with blue skin and was called "lord of the lapis lazuli." The word Amun now ends the prayers of Judaism, Christianity and Islam. Since there are no written vowels in Egyptian, his name can be written as Amun, Amen, or Amon. His name means 'hidden,' for he is everywhere but cannot be seen. In the Old Kingdom he was referred to as Om, the famous mantra now found in Asia. This mantra helps slow our mind and take us to the hidden nature of the self. Some claim he was the main inspiration for Jehovah in the Bible. Amun did become the great king of the gods, but this is a strange thing. No one is really quite sure why the hidden became the great god. Some have even thought that Amun came to represent a group of outside forces that took control of Egypt after the Old Kingdom.

There is no question that originally Amun had a very key aspect in Egyptian teachings, that part of us that is hidden, the true essence of our being. This hidden essence is the essence of the Creator. However as Amun's position grew, particularly in Middle Egypt, there became great corruption in the priesthood that followed him. Many other centers tried to break away from the influence of Thebes. Akhenaten even tried to eliminate the old religion entirely. This was a period when many of the wise priests of Egypt began to leave and take the wisdom to other parts of the world. Thus the Old Kingdom wisdom teachings of the hidden began to be corrupted by the New Kingdom and used in a different way. While earlier this teaching was to be used to find our hidden essence within it became a way of corrupt priests to gain control of the country.

Interpretation of Creation

All myths carry many levels of meaning. Beyond the outward literal meaning are other less obvious symbolic meanings. While they each can stand on their own separately, they are meant to be used in connection with each other. The Leyden Papyrus gives an example of how the four myths are connected by claiming, "All the Gods are three: Amun, Ra and Ptah, who have no equals. He who is mysterious is Amun, Ra is the head and Ptah the body. Their cities on earth are Thebes, Heliopolis and Memphis…when a message comes from heaven it is heard at Heliopolis, repeated at Memphis to Ptah who makes it into a letter and written in the Book Of Thoth, and then sent to Thebes."[111] Thus all four myths interacted with each other during the creation, and continued to do so.

Atum of Heliopolis created out of the void, while Ptah was the divine fire of Atum coming to the earth. Thoth was the ability of the creator to know itself by the word or divine logos, while Amun is the breath of life. John Anthony West claims this idea is similar to modern Christianity, which originally had separate centers of instruction for the creation, one according to the Father, one the Son and one the Holy Spirit, and the 4th according to the Virgin. Thus the same teaching is being explained and explored in "different yet complimentary ways." If the myths are placed in order first comes Nun, the primordial ocean that appears in all myths. Second would be Atum and his manifestation part of Ptah. From them comes the elements of creation that work on all planes: Tehuti (wisdom, Gnosis) Maat (divine order) and Hathor (another female principle examined in Other Myths). Once wisdom and order had been created, the eight primordials and Ra could now be manifested. Finally the Neteru (energies that would fuel creation) could be born at Heliopolis, followed by the actual creation of the material world at Memphis. Lastly, the effect of creation could be expressed at Thebes.

The myths also point to some very real scientific information in our physical world. The first is that the world began from nothing (Nun) represented by water. This perhaps is showing that water is the source of all things. The myths also explain the doubling process of hydrogen to helium that creates stars and planets, the workings of the solar systems, and the birth and gestation process of a human being (see number). Modern scientists use the Big Bang Theory to explain the formation of the universe. They feel that there was a time in the past when all the matter of the universe was packed tightly together, to an infinite density. This is similar to the primeval nature of Nun. Eventually the nucleus became polarized with electrons and protons. Modern scientists feel that when the act of creation occurred some 15 billion years ago, all matter exploded and expanded outward, which continues to this day. The

---

[111] Schwaller *Sacred* p.188; Ashby *matter* p. 84

ancient mystics understood this concept as the Breath of God. God right now is still breathing out, thus our universe is expanding. At some point, God will begin breathing in, and out universe will begin to contract."[112]

The Annu Ennead myth corresponds to our scientific Nebular Theory. The Nebular Theory claims that our entire solar system was once a molten gas nebula that rotated at great speed, bulged at the equator breaking off of gaseous rings which later formed into a few planets. These planets in turn threw off gaseous rings which formed into other planets, with the Sun left as the remnant of the original nebula.[113] A closer look at the creation myth of Heliopolis will find Atum-Ra representing the sun and primordial fire. Atum-Ra then masturbated into existence Nut and Geb, thus they were formed from Ra (sun). The other Neteru were formed by Nut and Geb, the same as the nebular theory which claims the other planets came from the first few planets. The sun is continually praised as the great creator.

There is not enough space in this work to go into great depth of the mystical meaning of the creation myths, small bits were included in the description of each Neteru. I was given a very interesting personal account of the creation of the universe while performing a meditation with a weekly spiritual group. We were all in deep meditation when I asked to have knowledge of the creation. Soon my mind stopped working and all became blank and dark, equated with the nothingness of Nun. When the meditative tape stopped playing a friend stood up, similar to the serpent and Atum stirring in the primeval waters. He accidentally kicked my leg in the dark. I felt a massive jolt of electricity run through my body. I had been given a personal experience of the power of creation, the nothingness, the stirring and the jolt of fire that allowed something to form from the nothing.

The ancient wisdom is also informing us that the creation did not just occur once, but is continually acted out each moment of every day. With each heartbeat or breath we take, a new creation of life occurs. Every seven years every cell in our body has been remade, thus we are recreated as a new being. We can learn how to use the creative forces of the universe in our own lives. The creation myths try to teach that we too are Neteru who are creating with our mind. We are creating a dream world that once understood can be transformed. Since we understand that we are the ones creating most every part of the dream of life we are experiencing, we realize that if we can change or take control of our thoughts, the dream must change. This is the beginning of awakening, to finding the heart, and living a life based on the teachings of Egypt.

---

[112] Laviolete p. 97
[113] James p.146

CHAPTER 7
EGYPTIAN TEMPLES

26: Looking towards the first pylon of Luxor Temple

Luxor

"Ancient architecture is music, frozen in stone." Goethe

In one sense, Ancient Egypt is an enlightenment seekers paradise. In the Old Kingdom (3000-2000BC) the symbolic information was fairly pure (presented un-altered) to its origins in the Pre-Dynastic Period (10,000BC). As the civilization continued- more delusion found its way into the mix. The older the text, temple or pyramid is, the more likely that the symbolic information and power presented. Thus the trick becomes how to decipher the true age of anything.

Egyptian temple complexes can be best explored on paper through the famous temple at Luxor, situated on the east bank of the present day Nile. Luxor is the Arabic name for the current city of some 200,000 people. During

147

the Greek period the entire area, including the temples and tombs on the west bank was called Thebes. To the Ancient Egyptians the temple was Wast. Few mention (or even know) that there is a much older temple (2-3,000 years older) underneath the current one.[114] Over time, one temple would live out its function and a new one built overtop to correspond to new energies being used.

Temple Complex

27:One of the sphinxes on the west side of the walkway leading up to the temple, Luxor

Originally the temple complex was very large, but now with the modern town of Luxor built overtop- only the temple proper, and a small portion of the human-headed sphinxes remain. It is said that the face on each sphinx lining the causeway is that of Amenhotep III (the first builder of the new temple here), yet each face resembles the style of a Buddhist Bodhisattva statue, with eyes half-closed and lips together. These sphinxes are in peaceful meditation. The idea was to walk the entire path from Karnak to Luxor (which was lined the entire way by sphinxes) as a meditation. The sphinxes are carved nearly identically (as if cast from a mold) and are designed to place you in heightened awareness. Just as a mantra repeated over and over will trip your

---

[114] Parts of this older temple were discovered during restoration work on the Great Court but the evidence was quickly covered up.

148

consciousness to mystical realms, so too an image repeated over and over. Even the short row of sphinxes that remain is enough if walked correctly to alter one's consciousness before entering.

While other temples are mostly built like a long rectangle, Luxor is built on three separate axis creating, when viewed from above, the twist of a forming spiral. Schwaller de Lubicz called Luxor the "Temple of Man" because he felt the secrets of human existence and manifestation were revealed in the mathematics of its building. While Karnak is larger, Abydos more complete, Dendera better preserved; Luxor is usually everyone's favourite to visit. It is especially beautiful to be seen at night, one of the few Egyptian temples with lights. The night lights allow the reliefs and hieroglyphs (obscured during the day) to stand out. Night-time at Luxor temple, with fewer visitors, less noise, and more reliefs available is the time to visit. Luxor has been called "music frozen in time," for so perfectly has it been designed and built. All the harmonious properties of pi, the golden section and other geometric properties have been included. This is no co-incidence or accident. The Greeks did not discover these mathematical ideas, they learned them from the Egyptians.

The entrance to any temple was through the outer pylon, a giant facing wall. This symbolic structure was meant to make an impression on everyone who came to the temple. Only members of the Egyptian priesthood were allowed actual entrance, and only the highest orders were allowed into the inner chambers. This was a place for awakening to occur, for the egoic mind of Apop to be removed from human functioning- one person at a time. But there is a very Zen aspect to temple pylons as well. Zen speaks often of the gateless gate, a symbol of the final locked door between the aspirant and awakening. Of course when you do awaken, you see there never was a door and nothing blocking. Thus those large outer pylons seem like a great barrier, and that is the image they were meant to imply, but were they?

Outside the walls of the temple are a number of smaller Greek and Roman chapels. They are very interesting and rarely examined by tourists. Be careful guards do not try to see you as a "mark" and try to extort baksheesh from you. These outer areas were the temples for the "common people" where newer priests would give what we would call sermons and lectures today. While the existing chapels are all Greek, they are built overtop of older Egyptian ones. Thus the archaeological belief that religious teachings were only available to priests is not true, these chapels were the churches of their day for the general population. As mentioned, just because the general population were not allowed into the temple proper does not mean they were segregated. Today fans can not enter the dressing room of the New York Yankees, but they can attend the games the Yankees play

No two temples were alike, each was meant to show a different aspect of the All. Every part of a temple, from the spot it was built, to the type of stone used, to the geometric proportions, to everything carved on its walls was all designed with this energetic creation in mind. Thus the temple always had to be kept at the particular energetic vibration of the Neteru energy it represented. All temples (when complete with all their paint and statues) vibrated at a very high frequency. This is an important point to consider. Even when a temple today is nearly in tact (such as the temple of Horus at Edfu), it is far from complete. The paint is gone, the carvings are defaced, the thousands of statues are either in museums, people's "personal" collections, or destroyed. The frequency at any spot today will not be the same as it was when in "use." This is the main reason the average person was not allowed entrance into a functioning Egyptian temple. It was not so much to exclude people, but to protect them. To enter a space of very high vibrational frequency with a bodily form not ready to handle it, is like plugging a 220 volt plug into a 120 volt socket. You will fry yourself. Entering a temple not prepared for it might turn you instantly "crazy" or even kill you. That is why work was done on new aspirants before they ever even set foot in the temple so they could handle the very powerful energies their form would be interacting with on a day to day basis within

.   In Egypt, citizens could not enter the temple, but they could attend the chapels, hospital, festivals and theater plays associated with the temple. Also included in any temple enclosure, especially temples associated with a female deity (Isis, Hathor, Sekhmet) was a healing center, where the sick and troubled came for help from priest doctors using herbs, stones, sound, music and energy therapy. While at Luxor I do recommend visiting a small chapel on the west side that had 13 pillars, two rows of six in front of a single one. This is a perfect representation of Jesus and his 12 disciples, or King Arthur and his 12 Knights of the Round Table, or the real symbol, the sun surrounded by the twelve moving constellations. All come from Egyptian symbolism. This could be the place where teachings surrounding Horus (Buddha/Jesus) were given to the general population.

Personally I am always struck by the serene sense of peace that I feel at Luxor. It has a similar feeling for me as when I go to Palenque in Mexico. Without going into a complete explanation of every part, wall and relief of Luxor Temple, I will point out a few "don't miss" areas that help explain not only Luxor but the concept of the temple in Egypt.

Pylon

Current pylons are usually missing some of their key features. One is flags, but the long vertical slits that held the giant masts remain. The flag is the representation of God/Neter. It is symbolized as the wind, unseen in the physical, yet seen in the movement of the objects (flag) in creation. In front of Luxor, and in fact most temples, were two giant stone obelisks, raised and placed on a bottom platform with the help of a turning groove. Today usually only one remains at any temple (such as at Luxor), with freemasons having taken one half of the pair to Europe or America. In fact no surviving Egyptian temple has both obelisks in place. Obelisks can be seen as lighting rods to bring down the energy of the heavens and pull up the energy of the earth. They represent the primal I, the original observer, God. An obelisk will vibrate at great speed, though you may not realize it. Obelisks were set in pairs to act like a tuning fork- allowing anyone who passed between them to be tuned to a particular frequency.

Outer temple walls, filled with reliefs and hieroglyphs, are designed for the general population, for the outer walls are all they could usually see of the temple proper. Egyptologists claim the great chariots, battles, gods and other carvings were to show the people the power of the king. The carvings on the pylons were to be a link or a bridge for those who may want to travel to the interior of the temple, which is symbolic for the trip within oneself. Take the famous carvings of the Battle of Kadesh on the pylon at Luxor.

The Battle of Kadesh was not the story of the Pharaoh leading an army into battle, but was more like a modern fairy tale, a symbolic story to reveal secrets of the awakening journey. It is not the account of Rameses II single-handedly defeating the Mesopotamian armies from his chariot. But examine the story as we would Cinderella or Snow White, and it can be understood. Ancient writers used events, places and people of the time not as a historical base, but to relate a teaching to the people in the language and things that they themselves would understand. Recording history was not important in the ancient world, telling tales of wisdom was important.

Rameses in this context represents every man and woman, while the chariot is the vehicle of manifestation (form). The troops of the enemy are the layers of delusion of our false self. That is where the battle is fought. In the story Rameses is left alone or abandoned (like Jesus on the cross) and knows he is in a battle that one must fight alone, and that there is no escape. This battle is said to occur in the land of Kheta Ru Settiu. Settiu means "Set Beings" and Kheta is similar to the Khat (physical body). Thus the Battle is with the false self (Set) while in a physical body. The battle was supposed to have happened in the 5th year of Rameses reign (five being the number of Horus). He fights alone because his army is asleep in camp (i.e. all his fellow humans are asleep in the dreamstate thus of no help to him waking up) and his only prayer is to Amun who lets him awaken to fight alone. On the far wall he holds lines of prisoners, which in fact are the delusion of his mind that he has defeated. He has not killed his mind, it is just seen for the lie of what it is.

28: Symbolic mend of crack on stone statue in front of the first pylon, Luxor

Great statues were also placed outside of the pylons of temples, such as the remaining seated ones at Luxor. They sit in the standard Egyptian pose for contemplation, and symbolize a stillness of mind and body. At the base of each statue is Hapi tying a lotus and papyrus plants together in a sma (symbolizing the trachea and lungs). Other reliefs may use Horus and Set in a similar pose. This is to combine the two aspects of duality together (ka and ba, tonal and nagual) into one. On the east statue is a feature not to be missed. On one side of the statue is a giant crack in the base, likely due to an earthquake. The statue itself is fine, stands as it always has. However to the Egyptian priests the temple was a living, breathing organism, as were each of its statues. The statue, and thus temple, were no longer whole due to the crack, and similar to when we put a band aid on a cut finger, a repair to this was done. The repair done here was not a true repair (for in fact the standing ability of the statue was not compromised) so instead a symbolic repair happened. Two joints are carved overtop of the crack. It is one the very best examples of how the Egyptian priests thought of their temple as a living thing, and looked after it as such. There are so many "little" insights like this all over Egypt.

Entering through the doorway- which of course is less a barrier to keep people out, but a way through the large pylon walls- is the first corridor. Here the reliefs change from the battle scenes on the outer walls to that of the Neteru. We are beginning to leave behind the standard dream of reality, and are beginning to enter a new inner world, something higher. Speaking of higher,

152

the temple itself will rise as one enters- with the back shrine being the highest part of land. As well, the ceilings will get smaller and smaller, both symbolizing a squeezing of space. As we are walking deeper into the temple, we are walking deeper and deeper into ourselves, into our inner world. No where is this more magically demonstrated than at Luxor Temple.

Schwaller de Lubicz was the first European to rediscover the magic of Luxor. He found that the human skeleton could be laid on top of the temple, with each area symbolically representing the secrets of that part of the human form. Within Luxor you will not only find insights revealed as to physical form, but meridians, chakras, yoga, qi gong- and of course at the farthest point- the wisdom of human creation. Its all there if you know how to look. Every temple has a secret symbolic plan that it was built with, locate that secret and the temple will simply unfold in front of (and within) you.

Halls and Courts

29: Thutmosis III chapel in the first court of Luxor

Passing the entrance corridor, one moves to a new inner world, the first court, and here movement will be described. To one's immediate right is the 3-room chapel that is of importance. This structure is in fact a temple within a temple, this one for Thutmosis III, whose incredible granite statue in the Luxor Museum is still "alive and breathing." As mentioned, Luxor temple "twists" around three axis, and the Great Court is aligned to the third of these, but the small chapel is aligned to the original axis. The chapel has nice symbolism, the 3 (trinity) the explanation of the dreamstate. The far left room is the dream of form (hell, son) the room to the right is heaven (oneness, love, holy spirit) and the middle room is the primal essence (God, light, Father). Each of the carvings on the walls reflect this information. There is a point though, in the middle room where two niches are carved into the walls, where one can sink beyond the chapel itself, back into absolute reality. It's a teaching of awakening in one small chapel. One other aspect about temples can be seen in this small chapel, but you have to look up for it. Most temple areas were roofed, and included small openings to let a beam of sunlight enter at specific times of the day- often to fall perfectly on a wall carving.

30:Moving Rameses statue, first court Luxor

In the first courtyard 18 giant statues still remain. All have the design of taking one step forward with the left leg. In fact the entire courtyard, when viewed from above, is taking a step forward from the temple. This is the exact part of the overlayed human skeleton of the lower leg. While the statues all seem the same, one is a bit different from the rest, the one in the south east corner. It is hard to describe it on paper, and just as hard to notice in person. All the other statues are facing forward, but the one in the SE corner has a twist of the shoulders and torso, just as a body does when it takes a step forward. Thus the statue is in effect "moving," a remarkable piece of artwork.

31:The large hallway in the center of Luxor, looking north

This court leads to the famous colonnade hall. While at Luxor there are only two rows of giant 40 foot high columns- representing the thighs, in most temples this area included a huge "forest" of columns (like seen at Karnak, Edfu or Dendera). Due to the fact that this temple represents the human being , it the reason only two columns (for the two legs) are included. Along the walls are reliefs of the famous ceremonial feasts after the travel of the statue of Amun from Luxor to Karnak. Why would eating appear in the place of the legs and not the stomach? Scientists have now shown that most of the nourishment of the blood system, what nourishes the body, is actually made in the legs. Carlos Castaneda mentioned that memories are stored in the thigh, and there are elements of memory (past reflection) in the wall texts as well. There is a point on this colonnade, exactly at the golden section, where one will find a place of total peace and body harmony. It is so powerful that some people get dizzy from standing just a few seconds upon this spot.

Next comes a courtyard of 64 columns, 64 being the number of the I Ching and the number of codons in human DNA. This is one of the real fantastic spots of all of Egypt, especially at night. Around 8 pm it is no surprise to find a number of young Egyptian couples sitting here. The place just seems to harmonize, and at times I feel I could sit here for the rest of my life, perfectly happy, perfectly at peace. According to de Lubicz this is the place of the stomach, thus the Dan Tien of Taoist philosophy. It is here one will find the Breath of Life.

32:Great Court looking south-west, Luxor Temple

Inner Chambers

Entering into the back areas of the temple, a new feeling takes over. Much of it is still roofed, and due to the lack of sunlight has allowed some of the wall reliefs to retain some of the original paint.[115] Yet in all these back areas of the temples something vital is missing and you will have to use your imagination to find it. Or better yet, take a short trip to Coptic Cairo. Coptic Christianity has kept alive the links to ancient Egypt, not just in language but in their specific interpretation of many Christian symbols. Gnostic Christianity had a close connection to the early Gnostics who formed a new teaching around the story of a person named Joshua (Jesus) over 2,500 years ago based on the Egyptian myth of Horus, Isis and Osiris. Besides visiting the wonderful and active churches in Coptic Cairo, check out the little "cave-like" domes. Down 4-5 steps is a dark space carved out of rock, that usually includes a small picture or painting of a Christian saint, or perhaps a New Testament open to a relevant page along with some prayer offerings, candles and incense. This is a

---

[115]The best places to see paint in Egyptian temples are at Medinet Habu (especially its the hypostyle hall) and the reliefs at Abydos and parts of Karnak.

reminder of what the back room of an Egyptian temple would have been like. They would have not have been empty as we see them today. There would have been candles, incense, perhaps open papyrus. The missing paraphernalia would be just as important as what was carved on the walls.

By the time you reach the inner chambers you will notice something about the wall reliefs. They have changed. The reliefs up to this point have been cut into the stone, the easiest type of carving done. Back here however the reliefs are what as known as raised, in which the stone itself is chipped away to leave the image projected outward. This is a much more difficult practice of work, and is also an indication of a much older time of building. The inner sanctuary of Luxor (where the statue of the Neter was kept) has some interesting symbolism. The area was "redone" during the time of the Greek takeover around 300 BC, but a intense energy remains here. Similar to reliefs carved at Greek period temples (Edfu, Philae, Dendera) the depictions of the Neteru go from sleek strong images on the walls, to gods that are "fat and flabby." These gods were carved this way to show the greed and materialism of the Greeks had invaded Egyptian religion and symbolized a new period on the earth was underway. It was also the spot I saw a group of photographers taking photographs randomly in the night, and coming up with brilliant photos of orbs and lights.

Another thing to notice is that there is just as much importance with how the reliefs are carved, and not just what they are reliefs of. For example you will notice that the walls are made out of blocks of stone. Notice where the figures are in relation to the cut lines of the blocks. Its not random. If the figure has its stomach at the exact point where two blocks of stone go through it, that is the way it is supposed to be, and there is a symbolic meaning for that. At different areas of the temple, all of the figures on the wall have the stone blocks join at the knee, or the shoulder, or eyes. As well is a feature called transpondance. That means an image on one stone wall, is not complete with out incorporating what is on the exact opposite wall- not of the room- but of the stone itself. Thus both sides of a wall are in fact often mirroring the same message, and you will see much of this in the back temple rooms at Luxor. Much of the great symbolism of Luxor is in the inner sanctuaries (the birth room, the walls of the hypostyle hall, the vultures over the doors), but will I leave that for you to explore in detail. I will though mention the back three rooms. While they are currently in a poor state of restoration, there are still phenomenal. Egyptian temples were built from back to front, thus this back area was in fact the very first part to be built, thus is the oldest part of Luxor Temple. All thee of these chapels have reliefs of Osiris (void) and often the erect phallus (first creation from the nothingness). In Schwaller's skeleton this is the head, with the top of the skull actually resting out side of the temple walls themselves. The seat of wisdom of the body (final chakra) is not in the temple (form) at all- thus showing one must go fully beyond form to not just know what Osiris is, but in fact to be Osiris. To do that one can not take Luxor, or anything from the dreamstate including "you," with you. This concept was often depicted in later Renaissance art, with people with their heads cut off, skulls littering an area, or like the statue of St. Nicaise who carries the top of his own head in his hands, thus showing he has vanquished his ego/mind and not taking his head with him to finalize the spiritual search.

Other Temples

Of course, Luxor is not the only great temple to see in Egypt. Here are a few pointers to some of the Hermetic wisdom that can be found at some of the other temples around Egypt.

Karnak

33:Looking across the sacred lake towards the remain of the temple of Amun-Ra at Karnak

The temple of Amun-Ra and surrounding temples are the largest still standing religious complex in the world. The lead up the large first pylon is by a ram-headed series of sphinxes down what is left of the processional avenue. Another avenue connected Karnak (via the next door Mut Temple) to Luxor. This temple complex is large enough to have its own chapter, but I will just point out a few interesting parts that help understand more of Egyptian temple design. First off notice the temple of Rameses III in the first courtyard. A temple in a temple, and contains Osiris statues and very interesting rear chambers, that like the Thutmosis chapel in Luxor, offer the Trinity design of 3 into 1 (picture of temple appears in chapter 7).

34:Looking down the hallway of the hypostyle hall at Karnak

Karnak's most well known feature is the Hypostyle Hall, made to gigantic proportions. 134 columns support a roof 75 feet high. What I want to bring attention to is not the size but a couple of features that can be seen on the roof. One is the lattice type window holes that would allow shafts of light to enter the hall at specific times of the day. The second is the column areas of the roof that still contain original paint and give another good example of the look and feel of Hypostyle Halls in their completed states. Every part of the walls of this hall also contain vivid reliefs. Tehuti is in one to record the name of the Pharaoh on the Persia tree (world tree) while in another Rameses kneels before the tree, while in others are large boat processions and offerings. You can spend a few hours just in this hall examining everything and still not see most of what is here.

Only two of the many obelisks remain in place (the others having been stolen and placed in front of churches or government buildings), but much of the inner temple rooms are still rather complete and worthy of inspection. The sacred lake here is huge, and near is a large stone scarab beetle. You will notice people walking in circles around it today as guides tell them that it is a fertility symbol and that women could walk around it 7 times to become pregnant, while others will say good luck will come if you walk around it 7 times.

35:Outer pylon of the Temple of Khonsu, Karnak

Around the complex can be found a Montu temple (for the original worshipped deity). When temple building of Amun (ram) started here the astrological precessional age had changed from Taurus to Aries, leading to building for the ram deity. There is also a Ptah temple, a Mut temple (closed to the public) that contains a very unique feature of a u-shaped sacred lake. This horseshoe shape likely holds the same meaning as it does in our modern world, good luck or prosperity. The Mut temple was where thousands of Sekhemet statues were buried, and many that you see in museums around the world come from here. Should you get permission to walk around the Mut Temple, you will still find hundreds of statues in semi-excavated pits.

Within the Karnak enclosure is the Khonsu temple, for the son of Mut and Amun, is dedicated to the moon thus linked with Tehuti. There are some great baboon statues still in the hypostyle hall- rarely do you see baboon statues except in museums. This temple is still rather complete and has terrific wall reliefs of Tehuti and Horus, has chapel rooms that contain large amounts of original paint, is rarely visited so is almost sure you can get lots of free time (I often bring the guards here food as a gift so they can give me lots of space at this temple.) In one of the side rooms in this temple I had one of my most amazing experiences in Egypt. While doing a very long and deep meditation on one of the walls...the image began to fade away...and another image began to appear. It was also an Egyptian wall, but not the one that is normally there. It is then that I began to understand the the Egyptians may have made their wall reliefs in more than just 3 dimensions. There is the 3-dimensional image (the one we see when we look at a wall) but perhaps others, put into finer dimensional layers, that with enough consciousness shifting you could move to the next layer and obtain the next set of images. This would repeat itself in the King's Chamber of the Great Pyramid when the blank granite walls, after a couple of hours of meditation, became a beautiful series of reliefs of Isis.

36:Chapel of Senusret, now in the open air museum, Karnak

Also at Karnak check out the open air museum (that makes you pay an extra entrance fee which I don't understand) but contains a series of interesting chapels that were once part of the complex- but for various reasons were dismantled and used in part of the building of the temple proper. Over the last 100 years the blocks have been found by archaeological teams, and the chapels restored to their original designs. The most stunning is the White Chapel of Senusret 1. It has near perfect geometric proportions and I spent one lovely afternoon just sitting in the shade of tree sketching this chapel from various angles. Also called the "Throne of Horus" the blocks were rescued from the third pylon. It creates a perfect measurement of all the old districts (called nomes) of Ancient Egypt. On its walls the hieroglyphs (baskets, birds, flags) are some of the most detailed in all of Egypt- all in raised relief carving. Another chapel is the Alabaster Shrine of Amenhotep I, made yes from

161

alabaster, a very rare stone in Egypt. The white would symbolize Albedo or purification- and when you sit inside of it you notice a very fast energy around you. Another chapel to see, and made famous in the 2000 documentary, is the Red Chapel of Hatshepsut. Each block here is of red quartzite on a base of black granite, and some of the walls have deep remains of the original paint. The purification scene with Tehuti and Horus is still stunning.

Hatshepsut's Temple

37:Temple of Hatshepsut, West Bank of the Nile

Perched along the limestone cliffs near the Valley of the Kings, is a unique temple for one of the few female rulers of Egypt, Hatshepsut. Built out of geometric raised steps, it presents a very unique perspective on the eyes when seen from afar, but when climbed consists of two long stairways that bring one to 3 raised terraces. A long causeway linked to the Nile, lined with Hatshepsut's headed sphinxes. Traces of pools, orchards and tree holes have been found alongside, making the area around the temple more like a giant garden.

This temple is extremely unique and little else in Egypt looks like it. To me though it looks almost exactly like the very interesting Mayan temple at Sayil (see photograph below.) The axis of the Hatshepsut temple ran almost on line to the front pylon of the Amun temple at Karnak, showing there was some relation. More interesting was that Hatshepsut's tomb, KV 20, was built in the cliff directly opposite the temple, and possibly had the idea of digging the shaft to create the tomb directly under the temple. Poor rock quality made this attempt, if true, impossible and a very odd circular route for the tomb was dug.

Originally this was a Hathor temple, and even after the building of this monument, the Hathor festivals continued. It's Egypt name was Djser Djeseru (Holy of Hollies). Its Arabic site name Dier-El-Bahari (northern monastery) comes from a Coptic monastery that was built near the runs in the 7th century AD. Of interesting note of this temple is the second terrace whose back wall displays the famous journey to the land of Punt. Considered by archaeologists as records of key trading missions to far away lands (which of course happened) this record on the walls is more the female journey of awakening. While the male version of the King smiting the enemies in the famous Battle of Kadesh, shown on the pylon walls of temples like Luxor, here in the female awakening- it is a boat journey to a far away land where trade, diplomacy, and sharing are what allow the ships to return full of far off treasures. Also in the middle terrace is what Kent Weeks describes as a first of its kind depiction, of Hatshepsut's divine birth- having Amun-Ra as her father (to give her mother a virgin birth) to prove her lineage to rule the kingdom. Also note the great Hathor shrine, with columns similar to that found at Dendera.

38: The Palace at the Mayan site of Sayil in Mexico. Notice the resemblance to the Temple of Hatshepsut in Egypt.

Colossi of Memnon

39:Standing statues of Amenhotep III, called the Colossi of Memnon, one of the few remaining parts of a temple larger than Karnak that stood at this spot, West Bank of Luxor

All that remains of temple of Amenhotep III are two large seated statues that originally stood at the temple entrance pylon. They are 65 feet high and weigh 1,000 tons. They are carved out of blocks of orthoquartzite, a very hard stone to carve. What makes these statues so historically interesting was the great visits that were placed on them in Greek and Roman times, for it is said that each morning as the sun rose and caused a temperature change in the northern statue (supposedly due to cracks that came in a 27 BC earthquake) would make an odd whistling sound. The Greeks believed it was the cry of Memnon (the mythical African warrior who was killed by Achilles in the Trojan War) and to hear this cry was said to bring one good luck. The statue is said to have stopped the singing in 199 AD when the statue's cracks were repaired as part of an upgrade (or to stop people's gaining more good luck?). Archaeologists have found that the temple was filled with statues, such as 730 Sekhmet statues (one seated and standing for each day of the year). In fact the large number of Sekhmet statues found buried at the Mut temple near Karnak might be from an Amenhotep III Temple cash.

Not much else of the temple remains, whose stone was plundered and used for other temples. It would have been the largest in all of Egypt at 4, 200,000 square feet- dwarfing even Karnak. It is claimed that most of the temple was made of mud brick and as it was eroded away by Nile floods, then the stone was quarried and used elsewhere. I personally find that description a bit odd. Amenhotep III was the father of Amenhotep IV (Akhenaten) who was not supposed to be the next Pharaoh (first son Thutmosis should have had that honour, but he either died early or was run out of town so his brother captured the throne). It is possible that the temple destruction might have come from Akhenaten or his followers, destroying the temple of the father who represented the old ways of Egypt, as Akhenaten changed to the religion of the Aten (sun disk) and moved the capital to the new city of Akheaten in the north.

Ramesseum

40:Small part of the collapsed statue of Rameses II, Ramesseum

The memorial chapel of Rameses II (the Great), due to its easy access on the way to the Valley of the Kings, is an often stop for tourists. Much of the front part of the temple is now demolished- and near the front what most eyes are drawn to is the giant arm and shoulder of a fallen statue that would have stood 57 feet high (not including the base) and weighed far more than 1000 tons-larger than the Colossi of Memnon down the road. Again walk through the remaining part of this temple, see the areas where paint remains and the wall reliefs are still almost in tact. One of them is known as the "Astronomical Hall" for the many astrological depictions that appear on the ceiling, and are a reminder how important the combination between what was happening in the sky, and what was happening on earth was to the Egyptians.

After the New Kingdom this temple, like the destroyed one of Amenhotep III, were quarried for their stone and all but forgotten. Like many other temples in Egypt, a Christian church was eventually built in the middle of the ruins, following the adage of building churches on top of the old pagan monuments, for the Christians knew the temples were built on the strongest points of energy in the area.

Medinet Habu

41:Columns still showing their original paint, back chambers Medinet Habu

Medinet Habu (temple of Rameses III), just south of the ticket office, is perhaps the best preserved temple in all of Egypt (some of the back areas still have most of their coloured paint on the walls and columns), but with so many other sites to take a tourist's time, most only take a short look here. The name Medinet Habu is Arabic, and may come from the name of Amenhotep-son of Hapu (temple builder for Amenhotep III); others suggest that it comes from the word Hebu, the old name for the Ibis bird of Tehuti, which for Hermeticists like myself make this temple worth an even more detailed examination. There is also evidence that the place in ancient times was called Djeme (after a nearby town, or word meaning young men) but this word is also close to Djehuti (Thoth), again linking the temple to the Ibis.

The temple itself has a giant enclosure and holds hundreds of storehouses. The first wall is entered through a giant gate that resembles a military fortress, and it is a wonder why this temple needed such a- at least symbolic- measure of entrance protection. Some speculate the population became very angry with Ramses III during his reign and he had to "hide out" in his mortuary temple during these periods. Up the stairs of the gate is special rooms that would hold the women of the king's harem, the rooms adorned with reliefs of young women all giving flowers, making music and being affectionate towards the Pharaoh. The doors for the harem rooms have locks that lock from the outside, not inside, making it a semi-prison. On the ground, between the gate, is two seated statues of Sekhmet.

42:Called dancers but seeming to depict more of a Yoga posture, Medinet Habu

Before entering the temple itself, two smaller temples that should be visited. To the left is the Chapel of the Divine Votaress, made for princesses of the king. Perhaps nowhere in Egypt has the word femininity been so shown in a temple or chapel to me. Small dark passageways walk you around the 4 chambers, whose walls have very interesting reliefs on them. To the right of the main gate is another temple. While constructed in the 18th Dynasty, it was built on top of a much older structure- on a spot that was claimed was the place of the rising up of the 8 original primordials, part of the Khemenu Ogdoad creation myth (another link to Tehuti). Being restored by the Oriental Institute of Chicago, its head restorer Danny Roy invited me in for a tour of the temple's statues, wall reliefs, and onto the roof to show the way the temple roof blocks were laid out and positioned. Part of the work of the restoration team is to clean and record all of the texts on the temple walls. Spending time at this small chapel/temple is like being in a vortex of energy, where the location and stones that transport you to a time long ago, perhaps actually to the creation of the dreamworld we call life on earth.

When studying the temple of Rameses III itself, the first thing one notices is the hieroglyphs and carvings on the walls. They are deep set. Really deep set. No one has really provided an adequate answer as to why they have been carved so deep into the stone walls. On the walls of the first court is where I found carvings of what are said to be people dancing, but I noticed them to be in the art of Qi Gong and Yoga, as well as wresting and other sports.

43:Relief of Isis and Ptah working with sexual energy, side chapel, Medinet Habu

The festival of Min (deity of sexual energy) is depicted in the second court, and I think this helps to explain some of this temple. Just off the second court is a small series of rooms with well preserved reliefs on the walls. One of them has Isis standing behind Ptah, whose wings move around to meet directly at his penis. I began to feel that many parts of Medinet Habu may have been for tantric sexuality- and I feel that having sex at this temple might in fact provide a very deep energetic charge to a tantra session. There are a lot of rooms to

168

explore in the back of this temple, each one with different scenes on the walls, and due to the size of the temple and relatively smaller amounts of tourists (compared to Luxor and Karnak) you will likely get some time alone in them-save for the guards who back here will try to hassle you for money.

Dier El Medina

44:Old workman's village of Dier-El-Medina to the right, temple of Hathor to the left.

Near the ticket office is what remains of the old village of the work and craftsmen who dug and created the tombs of the valley. The ruins show a village of about 70 houses where 50-100 families lived, and from the upper cliffs one can get a good layout of the village streets and the similar layout of each of the houses. Just north of the village is a small Ptolemaic temple dedicated to Hathor and Maat, and is a rarely visited place where you can really enjoy a nice little temple to yourself. In one of the chambers is a unique version of the weighing of the heart, which rarely appears on temple walls, and has a different look than one finds in much of the Book of the Dead papyrus scrolls.

Edfu

45:First Pylon, Edfu

To the south of Luxor is a few temples seen on a felucca trips or by convoy. One of those temple is the Temple of Horus as Edfu. Linked to the sister temple of Dendera, this is perhaps the best preserved temple in all of Egypt- and demands a day of exploration. This complete state is why Kent Weeks described, "for most tourists it is the sense of mystery and drama the temple offers that are the big rewards. It is not uncommon that visitors cut short their time at Edfu temple because they find the dark and silent interior so evocative of ancient rites that they become unnerved."[116] Yes it is true that many people have a hard time at Luxor temple, however I feel it is for a different reason entirely. Each Egyptian temple is built to represent the energy of that Neter- that principle. In this case it is Horus, that which can overcome Set (conscious mind) and the only way to go past the mind is to see it. Thus in a sense this temple is going to reveal our Setian nature to us. I always ask when

---

[116] Weeks, Kent Illustrated Guide to Luxor (University of Cairo Press 2005) p.540

46:Hypostyle hall and falcon statue, Edfu

someone has gone to Edfu, "what happened that made you angry there?" And often the answer is, ya how did you know, there was this guy I met...

One of the features of this temple is that instead of 2 sphinxes or Pharaoh statues to line doorway of the pylons, here it is 2 falcons, the protective form of Horus. The hypostyle hall and the vestibule chambers are still almost as they were (minus the paint) and take special note of the hieroglyphic inscriptions that cover every wall. You will also notice areas of reliefs here (for this is a Ptolemic Greek temple built over a much older one) that have the Neteru depicted as fat and droopy- to again reveal that the great time of wisdom in Egypt was coming to an end.

Dendera

47:Hypostyle Hall with Hathor head columns, Dendera

To the north of Luxor are two well known temples that are often combined in a trip- Dendera and Abydos. Many tours do not go here, and personally, I would not go on an Egyptian tour that omitted these two amazing temples. Like its brother site at Edfu, Dendera is very well preserved. The temple of Hathor is an all feminine temple. Interestingly its old Egyptian name was Tantera, very close to the word tantra- giving clues that it quite likely was the female that was the area that taught sacred sexuality.

The first pylon and first courtyard are now gone, so the first part of the temple to be seen is the hypostyle hall, where you are met by 6 columns all with Hathor heads upon them (actually on all four sides reminding me of Hindu statues of Brahma). The light and shadow play well in the temple- though you will notice much of the ceiling has a blackness to it, from the many fires in Arabic times as the temple when full of sand was used as living quarters.

48:View looking to the ceiling of the Hypostyle Hall, Dendera

The two parts that make this temple extra special to visit is the roof and the crypt. All temples has stairs that led to a several rooftop chapels. Most of those roof areas at temples are gone now, and Hathor temple was one of the last where tourists could go and see, in this case, a chapel of Osiris that detailed the myth of his death and resurrection. It is also the place where the famed circular zodiac was found (original in the Louvre in Paris), not in the downstairs hall as guides try to tell tourists. Sadly the upstairs is now closed, I believe due to an accident where a tourist fell of the roof and died. The roof area also held very small drainage channels where rain water would run to lion-headed spouts on the sides, then run down specific magic hieroglyphic texts on the walls- thus the running water would absorb the magic power in the glyphs, where it would be collected on the bottom and drank.

49:Possible ancient depictions of light bulbs, from the crypt at Dendera

Near the back of the temple is entrance to the crypt area. Again most temples had such a feature, but here is about the only place that tourists can enter. Within the crypt is a relief that has become known as the "Hathor light." It is so called because the round tube like object with a snake in the middle of it has been compared to modern light bulbs. Egyptologists tend to say that the round object is a lotus flower with snake in the middle, on a djed pillar- but it sure looks like a light bulb to me. One of the main questions to ask is when building long tunnels for tombs and pyramids, how did they get light in for the workman- so the idea of some type of light bulb is not out of the question. Lastly about this crypt area. To me Hathor is the perfect temple of the female, and being a male, I never feel that I can walk past the hypostyle hall to the back of the temple unless I am asked and accompanied by a woman, and as for the crypt- I have never gone down into them for something tells me it is a "females only" area.

Surrounding the temple was a sacred lake, a number of chapels, and if you look closely on the right side of the temple, you can find the remains of the hospital where the sick came for shamanic and sound healing, and where those troubled could come to get helpful dreams from Hathor. As well, the New Year's solstice ceremony had a major celebration here. Lastly, if you get on the roof and look to the West, you can see the very cliffs of Nag Hammadi where

174

the famous Gnostic Codexes were found in 1945. They have always claimed to have been documents hidden from a monastery to the north- however due to the closeness to a major temple in Egypt got John Last to believe that the Nag Hammadi documents actually come from the Temple of Dendera. That makes them not a Greek or Coptic recollection of early Christianity- but as I will make a case for in my upcoming book- the Greek/Coptic attempt to take the Egyptian Book of Thoth and turn it into something more modern and readable to the world around 100BC. The Nag Hammadi texts are perhaps the best ancient text for modern eyes to explain the ideas of the parasite, holographic reality, and the Absolute.

Abydos

50:The author outside the entrance to the Temple of Seti I, Abydos

This spot had the original name of Abdju, and became the pilgrimage spot for Osiris, due to the belief that the massive stone block Osireion was the spot of the burial of Osiris's body. The temple found here is connected with Seti I, and like everything at Abydos, is most unique. For me there is no one temple in Egypt that I want to see more- partially due to the incredible state of the temple itself, partially due to its back rooms having some of the best raised wall reliefs in all of Egypt, and partially due to the energy of being around the Osireion, which as will be explained could be one of the oldest sites in Egypt. The temple, built in an L shape, is believed to have taken that form to work around the Osireion- but that theory would force the acknowledgement that the Osireion is older than the temple (and would open too many questions as to its actual age), and a new theory had to be devised where both were built together by Seti I and the Osireion was an attempted copy of the temples at Giza.This is what I call the "don't ask any questions theory."

Like Dendera the first pylon and courts are gone, thus one enters in the hypostyle hall with 26 foot high ceilings, and leads to an amazing pillared room with a complete ceiling, where shafts of light still enter at the exact time of the day that they were meant to enter into and produce some amazing displays of light. At the end of the hypostyle hall, where the chapels begin, are some of the best raised reliefs in Egypt, as well as hieroglyphs with incredible detail. Look closely.

51:Relief from back chapels of Abydos

Beyond this are 7 chapels for Horus, Isis, Osiris, Amun-Ra, Ra-Horkhety, Ptah, and Seti I. The Osiris chapel opens into another set of small rooms. These small rooms in the Osiris hall have some very special reliefs including one of offerings to Maat, and Tehuti holding the twin caduceus shown in such a way to suggest he is holding the DNA strands (and can be seen on the title page of this book).

Walking along the L one comes to the famous King's list, where 76 kings prior to Seti I are listed (excluding a few like Akhenaten, Tutankhamun, and

Aye considered heretics). The other wall is not often looked at, and this wall describes that for thousands of years before these human rulers of Egypt, Egypt was ruled by a long succession of deities, then intermediaries known as the Followers of Horus. This connects with Manetho's calculations that Egypt was ruled in combination of God and human form for over 30,000 years before human pharaohs began their rulership.

52-53 Two photos that show the giant stone blocks of the Osireion, reminiscent of Stonehenge

Outside is the famous Osireion. The only other spot in Egypt that has this appearance of giant stone blocks is in front of the Sphinx at Giza and it is likely these spots are linked together time wise- which would make this spot perhaps the oldest temple in Upper Egypt. This subterranean chamber may have once been filled with water to make the stone structure a semi-island. The primordial land rising from the chaotic waters at the time of creation. The walls alongside and in the corridors offer scenes from the Book of Gates. The large red granite blocks of stone, with other stones laid overtop, gives it a striking similarity to England's Stonehenge. Photos of this part of Abydos rarely appear in archaeological books because they know this area will provide too many questions to the casual reader (how did they move those stones and position them, it's like Stonehenge etc).

54: A helicopter, a submarine, and an airplane? Wall reliefs from near ceiling in Abydos

One more interesting facet is back near the ceiling of the hypostyle hall. There are a series of hieroglyphs that have become somewhat famous. Archaeologists have tried in vain to explain how they are hands, or trees or fish or whatnot- but it is quite clear that they look like exact replicas of helicopters, submarines, and airplanes. How can that be? And I have a speculation about this temple complex. The hieroglyphs and the king's list (record of time) are a clue. The Osireian to me was some part of a either a time travel device, or at least a time seeing device. It was there that the Egyptians were monitoring time-space. Some of this appeared on the walls of the temple, and this included key information of the past, the future, and important events and knowledge that could be brought back and used in the Egyptian period, and perhaps information presented on the looping nature of time itself.

Around Aswan

55:Entrance way at Abu Simbal

Farther south around the city of Aswan can be found the temple of Isis on Philae (well actually not on Philae, the temple had to be moved to another island when flooding began after the building of the Aswan Dam. It may be for that reason that while a great temple, I often feel as if the energy is off), the Satet temple and other structures on Elephantine Island, and further south the in-rock temple of Rameses II at Abu Simbal. This temple as well was moved (if you can believe it, piece by piece) and reassembled here in this man-made mountain designed to recreate the original Abu Simbal. Again this is another spot in Egypt, that while looking spectacular, does not have much of an energy charge and I attribute that to the fact that the building is not on its original site.

This again takes us back to the start of this chapter- that Egyptian (or any ancient place) were built on a very specific part of the earth. That was to amplify the energies and attributes the temple would be showcasing via that exact energetic spot. To actually move the temple to another spot, is symbolically like unplugging it from the wall socket that was the main source of its power supply. Nothing is placed in the ancient world by accident.

CHAPTER 8
OSIRIS MYTH

56:Rows of Osiris statues in the court of the Temple of Rameses III, Karnak

The Great Myth

The story of Osiris is one of the most important in mythology. The basis of the story is that brother kills brother, to be avenged by his son. This story has been told and retold throughout history: Cain and Abel in the Bible, Shakespeare's Hamlet, and Disney's Lion King. This myth was in place at the earliest stages of Egyptian history, included in the famous Pyramid Texts. The myth of Osiris is not found in its entirety throughout Egypt but there is enough on temple walls and in texts to provide much of the information. Today much of the detail comes from the Greek writer Plutarch. There is a question to the validity of his account. It has never occurred to Egyptologists that Plutarch, a priest of Delphi in Greece, might have purposely confused or distorted the myth to try and misdirect the reader from key elements of the story. He was initiated in the mysteries as he says, "The mystic symbols are well known to those of us who belong to the Brotherhood." As an initiate Plutarch would not have unveiled the secret meaning of the Osiris myth under fear of punishment. Since none of this happened to him, either his book was regarded as harmless or at least not directly informative. It may also mean that because of his Greek origin the Egyptian priests did not disclose the full information. I will present the basic myth of Osiris gained from information from the temples of Egypt, then interpret some of the main points and the individual Neteru.

The Myth of Osiris[117]

I stopped my explanation of the creation myth of Heliopolis with the four offspring of Geb and Nut being born. The continuation of this story is the Osiris myth. Osiris married Isis and Set married Nepthys. Being the eldest when Geb abdicated, Osiris became the new King of Egypt. Set was always jealous of his brother, first when he married Isis and secondly when gaining the throne. Osiris and Isis taught the people the secrets found in the Books of Tehuti such as how to cultivate the fruits of the earth (agriculture), gave them law, abolished cannibalism, were the first to explain the Neteru, consecrated the first temples, and organized the sculpting of the first images. He also introduced the hieroglyphic script invented by Tehuti, and invented two kinds of flutes. Osiris was the enemy of violence and he ruled by his gentleness alone, often using songs or musical instruments. A golden age took place under the rule of Osiris and Isis. Once Osiris had everything in order, he handed control of Egypt to Isis while he set out to "visit all of the inhabited earth to teach the world the same knowledge." He supposedly traveled with Tehuti and Anubis.

When Osiris was gone his brother Set banded together 72 conspirators, but Isis ruled well and Set had to wait for Osiris' return. Osiris either returned to Egypt at the age of 28, or in the 28th year of his reign. Set invited Osiris to a banquet on the 17th day of the month of Hathor in which a splendid coffer of wood and gold was offered as a prize to anyone who could fit perfectly into it. Secretly Set had built the chest exactly to Osiris's measurements. All tried to fit in it at the banquet but failed. When Osiris made his attempt, the conspirators rushed forward, nailed the lid shut and poured molten lead overtop to stop the air supply. The chest was then taken to the Nile where it floated to the sea. When Isis heard of the loss she cut off a lock of hair (a sign of mourning usually laid on the tomb of the deceased). Isis now used all of her powers of magic to locate the coffer. In the Greek version of the story the loss of Osiris was told to the people by the Pans and the reaction was given the name panic. The coffin turned up on the shores of Byblos, either in the branches of a tamarisk bush which soon grew into a magnificent tree or in a huge erica tree

---

[117] The myth can be found *in Fingerprints of the Gods, Osiris and the Egyptian Resurrection, Ausarian Resurrection and Egyptian Yoga*

that quickly enclosed the coffin. The king of Byblos saw the tree and was impressed by its beauty and height and had it cut down to make a pillar for his new palace.

Isis traveled incognito and found some children who knew of the whereabouts of Osiris. Still undercover, she took a job as the nurse of the King's son. Each night while the others were asleep she would pile logs on the fire and place the king's child onto the fire after which Isis would mourn for her dead husband. News of this strange behavior reached the ears of Queen Astarte. Astarte concealed herself in the great hall to see if the rumours were true. When she saw her baby placed onto the fire, the queen rushed forward to snatch her son back. Isis responded that the queen's actions had robbed the boy of immortality. Isis then revealed her true identity, and the king had the tree cut open so she could take the coffin back to Egypt.

Set found the coffin of Osiris in its hiding place among the delta marsh. In a great rage he tore the body of Osiris into fourteen pieces, scattering them around Egypt. Isis, along with sister Nepthys, Anubis and Tehuti, found all of the fourteen pieces except one. The only piece she could not find was the phallus which Set had tossed into the Nile and had been eaten by a fish. At each place she recovered a piece of her husband she buried it (or built a temple there). With the help of the words of power of Tehuti, the pieces of Osiris were put back together long enough to impregnate Isis. Osiris was reborn and went to live as a star in the Duat. Isis gave birth to Horus. Horus was hid in the papyrus swamps, similar to Moses. While growing up he was bitten by savage beasts, stung by scorpions, and burnt. Tehuti and Isis cured all of these problems. Horus was then given information by his father Osiris about his death, and the need for Horus to avenge it. Osiris gave his son special military training.

Horus and Set continually fought without either defeating the other. When Horus captured Set and brought him to his mother Isis, she felt pity and compassion and let Set go free. In rage Horus either cut off her head or removed her crown. Tehuti gave Isis a new crown in the shape of cow's horns. The battle continued. Set gouged out Horus' eye, but later had his sight restored by either Tehuti or Hathor. Chapter 17 of the Book of the Dead claims, "the way to restore the Eye of Horus is to rip off Set's testicles," which Horus does. Finally the two were brought before the Ennead. Set promised to end the fighting and invited Horus to his house, but from evil intentions and tries to have intercourse with Horus. The battle continues.

Set now tries to trick the Ennead by saying Horus is illegitimate. Finally Osiris sent a letter to the Ennead asking them to do what was right. Tehuti, on behalf of the other gods, ruled that Horus should be the new king of Egypt. With peace made, Set decided to make his body in to a barge to carry away Osiris' body for funeral. From then on Set took a place on the solar barque of Ra, while Osiris went to become the Lord of the Duat (underworld).

Osiris (Wizzer)

57:Close up of Osiris statue with crook in right hand, and flail in left hand, Remeseum West Bank

Osiris was called the King of Eternity, who with his sister/wife Isis brought order and knowledge to Egypt. He was a great teacher who then went to instruct the world. He was raised from the dead long enough to impregnate Isis and become Lord of the Duat. Osiris is connected in the sky with the stars of Orion (Sah in Egypt) and the Great Pyramid is claimed to be dedicated to him. He is similar to the Mexican Quetzalcoatl 'Feathered Serpent.' Quetzalcoatl was also a teacher, healer, and came from a far away land to teach non-violence. The Book of the Dead claims Osiris lives in a house with, "a roof of fire, whose walls are living uraei (serpents) and the floor is a stream of running water." Quetzalcoatl was said to arrive on the boat made of serpents from the east. His Egyptian name (Ausar) is pronounced Wizzer, and it is from this name that the word wizard originates.

Osiris is coloured either green or black. When black he is representing that all light (his son Horus) must come out of the blackness. This is also true of the alchemic process whereby the final stage (gold or light) must come from the original blackness of the Prima Materia. When he is green he is nature and the cycles of life represented by agriculture. The Osiris myth became associated with the flooding of the Nile, which allowed food to grow. This cycle is also where the idea of karma originates. He is also the green colour of the heart chakra. He governs the Duat and at times is shown as a circle. Coffin Text 330 shows how he is related to the universal order, "weather I live or die, I am Osiris. I enter in and reappear through you. I decay in you, I grow in you, I fall down in you, I fall upon my side... I am not destroyed. I have entered the order, I rely upon the order, I become master of the order. I emerge in the order." He marries Isis for she is nature, and by being in love with nature we can learn to merge with and rise above it.[118]

---

[118] *Papyrus of Hunefer*; Hancock *Fingerprints* p.393; Hancock *Heaven* p.198; Hall p.41, Budge *Future* pp.64-76; Laviolete p.20; Budge, EA Wallis *Egyptian Heaven and Hell* (Dover 1996) p. 306; Ashby *Egyptian Yoga* p.132

His resurrection is a second birth in the form of a new consciousness. Osiris represents the mortal human. His journey is our journey, his struggle is our struggle, and his reward is our reward. As the Neteru helped Osiris they too can help us. By carrying the seed of eternity (Horus) while dead he represents that each human carries the powers of spiritual salvation inside. Sometimes he is shown standing or sitting on a throne. His head is crowned, but his body (except for the hands) were bound with the mummy wrappings of the dead. Here we find spirit (the living head) bound to matter (the mummified body). In his hands he holds the heq (shepherd's crook) which represents control over the thoughts of the conscious mind (as one must control the wandering sheep) and the flail (the punishment we must at times meet out to ourselves when not following Maat). The flail also has three lashes upon it (Hermetic process) each with seven beads (the chakras that must be purified). The position of the hands is very important. If crossed at the wrist they represent death, crossed at the two fists represent judgment (like at the weighing of the heart). A double-crossing of hands and staffs indicate renewal.[119] Every mummified Egyptian would have been an Osiris.

When Osiris was 28 years old, or in the 28th year of his reign, he is attacked by Set. This is our Saturn year, which makes a 28-year cycle through everyone's astrological chart. The return of Saturn leads to a major life change. Since few are ever ready to change, Saturn throws our life into disarray. I would not be walking this mystery path without the difficulties that happened in my 28th year. Many wonder why does Osiris get into the box? It is the same as Jesus at the Last Supper when he knew Judas was going to betray him. Osiris, like Jesus, agrees to face their true destiny no matter how difficult the choice seems to be at first. His destiny was to be the lord of the Duat, but only by dying to this world could that destiny be fulfilled. Osiris while in the tree is in isolation, similar to a state of deep meditation or times of depression or illness. This is a time when Osiris cannot outwardly act, but must use the time to plan and to reflect. The old has been destroyed, his kingship of Egypt, but nothing has yet come to take its place. The tree is the world tree that sprang forth all life, and is a symbol for our spine that supports the chakras (djed pillar). When Osiris is cut up by Set it is symbolizing he has been separated from his former self. This is similar to ritual shamanic dismemberment. Shamans do this metaphorically in the energy body ripping apart the initiate, cleaning them fully and then bringing them back together. Parts of the Pyramid Texts claim, "your bones are reassembled, your members are rejoined to you. Shake off the dust!" Another speaks of wiping the flesh and collecting one's bones. The loss of the phallus, like Shiva, represents seminal retention in order to channel the sexual

---

[119] Hall pp.60-61; Naydler p.257; Ashby *Egyptian Yoga* p.102; Schwaller *Sacred* p.214

energy to the higher spiritual centers. This rechannelled energy was used to create Horus.[120]

Osiris's body was cut into fourteen parts then scattered. Each of the fourteen parts later became temples in Egypt, and interestingly there are fourteen Christian Stations of the Cross. Osiris came to represent the Central Soul and when he is cut up into a number of pieces he is the soul divided to all the individuals of Egypt. When cut up we are no longer part of the unified all of creation but are instead seeing everything as separate entities. As lord of the perfect black Osiris is similar to the Buddhist teachings of "nothing but nothing," that when one reaches nothing (the blackness) they have reached everything. When depicted upon the throne in the Book of the Dead he is the one and all, and is sometimes referred to in this state by the name Nebertcher, the trinity of Amun-Ra-Ptah mentioned in the Creation Myths.

Isis (Aset)

Isis is the virgin mother of Horus, and was so popular that she stayed as a key worshiping figure long into the Christian era. Isis was either the daughter of Hathor, or Hathor herself in another form. She can wear two crowns. The most frequent is the hieroglyph of a seat (showing the connection with Hathor who is the seat of Horus), while the other is the vulture headdress with a crescent disk and a pair of horns. Occasionally she has a cow's head or is also sometimes depicted with the winged arms of Maat. She was related to the star Sirius, and each Summer Solstice was said to cry a tear for her departed Osiris that caused the Nile to inundate. This was the Egyptian New Year and began the calendar we still use today (see calendar).

Isis is the goddess of nature thus was the earth mother. As queen of the earth she made agriculture possible. Isis was also the goddess of magic. She used her magic given to her by Tehuti to resurrect Osiris and heal Horus. What was deemed magic was really knowledge of things such as herbs, energy, and the other bodies of self. She is also connected to what has become known as th veil of Isis. The veil covers our inner eyes from sight of truth and reality, instead allowing us to only see the illusion of this world. Most today believe that Isis is somehow veiling us or hiding us from herself. But as the great goddess of wisdom, why would she want to hide or put humans into illusion? Correctly understood the veil of Isis is really the veil of "seeing" Isis. It does not come from her, but blocks site of her and nature- why we must go to Isis for help to life this covering. A reminder that veil is a ...for the word evil. Above her temple at Sais was the words, "I Isis am all that has been, that is or shall be, no mortal man has ever seen me unveiled." What that means is that while

---

[120] West *Serpent* p.174; Lamy p.24; Ashby *Egyptian Yoga* p.97

connected to body and mind, Isis is veiled or has a covering. In Hermetic lore Isis is the daughter of Hermes (Tehuti), standing for the innermost secret of the mysteries. She hides from all except the most steadfast seekers.[121] It is her wisdom teachings that help each aspirant gain the initial knowledge of nature and spirit.

As mother of Horus she personified the life giving principle. She is often depicted with Horus sitting on her lap nourishing him with the gift of life. All of these elements were later incorporated by Christianity as the Virgin Mary. Children helped Isis to locate Osiris' body and for this reason children in Ancient Egypt were looked upon as having a power for divination. Children still have many of their occult powers, as adults have yet to break them of their link to the divine energy. Isis is the action inward of personal meditation, thus the reason she searches for Osiris alone. The placing of the baby on the fire represents the fire of the inner mind that must burn away that which keep us from our true self. This fire, even though it may be painful, is needed to reach the state beyond the veil that she personifies. It is the reason she claims that the baby will not be immortal when Astarte snatched the child from the fire.[122]

Isis was also said to have black skin like Osiris, showing that Isis and Osiris are really the same. In her aspect of Amentet she is the subtle substance of nature, the astral plane. Two key features of Isis are love and wisdom. Isis has undying love and devotion for Osiris that transcends her loss of him. Her love also caused the birth of Horus. This is the devotion of the initiate which leads him or her to the divine, for all that is needed is a deep love for the divine. This is similar to the Christian Gnostics who say that to reach Sophia (the beautiful female personification of wisdom) one must love her as a wife. The wisdom of Isis or Sophia cannot be found in the head intellectually, but can only be found with love from the heart. It is said Isis veils herself and no mortal man has unveiled her. Thus to know Isis means one must become one with her, or experience her directly with love. This unity would create a state beyond normal waking consciousness where one dispels the illusion, which is why no worldly human (who still believes the illusion) can discover her.

Nepthys

Nepthys is the sister of Osiris and Isis, and is the wife of Set. On her head is the glyph for "mistress of the place." In the myth she helps her sister locate and rejuvenate the body of Osiris. Nepthys is the lower nature of matter, that which intoxicates the mind and senses while Isis is the beauty of creation. This connection to the material realm is the reason for her becoming the wife of Set. Anything born in nature must eventually die, and this force of death is represented by Nepthys. Isis and Nepthys are aspects of the same concept, thus

[121] Caitlin 2-19, 20; Hall p.25
[122] Norvil p.55; Hall p.41

are often depicted together. They stand near the dead Osiris and are called his "two windows." They are depicted identically with only an opposite headdress. It means that nature and life (Isis) is the opposite of death, but they are both a part of the same principle. You cannot have one without the other. The fact that Nepthys helps Isis in the myth shows that there will be many times when death in fact will help us. Muata Ashby claims Isis is matter seen through the eyes of wisdom, while Nepthys is the same matter seen through the eyes of the ego. The enlightenment of Osiris occurs when he understands both aspects. Chapter 30 of the Book of the Dead refers to the two women as "the two great uraei," thus they are the force of kundalini. This twin force is shown by two females in India (Ida and Pingala) and also the Egyptian female deities Uatchit and Nekhebet. Just as in nature the two poles of kundalini are different, but are actually the same energy.[123]

Set

Set from the myth has come to be looked upon as evil, but Set was also worshiped at certain times and temples because the priests understood that the energies he represents were needed. Set is the power of opposition which is always trying to disrupt peace (hotep) and harmony (Maat). This opposition stems from our conscious mind, but it is at times seen as evil and at other times as a necessity for our growth. It is similar to shamanic ideas that we must embrace our challenges as opportunities to grow, rather than as things we detest and hide from. When something gets in the your way, this is the power of Set. It is not necessarily bad for it forces you to use all of your resources, to focus on the light instead of the dark. If you do then you will be like Horus who was able to defeat Set. If everything was just handed to us without the need to challenge ourselves and our abilities, we would never find our true inner strength. Overcoming our challenges will lead to great power, as Horus became the ruler of Egypt when he overcame his adversary. That being said, even though we can acknowledge the need for opposition and Set, that does not mean we shy away from the challenge of defeating him. Originally he is the fighter of Ra (our higher self) but after defeated by Horus he is not destroyed but helps Ra. We too want to defeat Set, not to destroy his power, but to begin channeling it to help our highest good.

Set needs 72 accomplices, a key number of precession. Astrologically Set is linked to the planet Saturn, representing the 28-year cycle described earlier. Set is the desires of the mind. This leads to selfishness, greed, hatred, anger, lust, etc. These are termed fetters and prevent the soul from discovering what is beyond. These fetters are symbolically the wrappings of the mummy, which are always associated with Set. As the mummy cannot move or act so too can our soul not properly live in awareness when fettered by the desires of

---

[123] Ashby *Ausarian* pp.134-36

the mind. Set is the ego gone awry- showing how the mind has gone from a friend to a foe. Set is also associated with the meteoric iron that fell from the sky and was used in the opening of the mouth ceremony. Set wanted to marry Isis, not out of love but because he could gain power and control of Egypt. He thought of her as any other possession, based on what having that possession would bring to him. During the story, Isis is usually able to stay one step ahead of Set because she is free of all desires except divine love. Set also represents unrestrained sexual energy, the power that needs to be either used to create or returned to the body through tantra. The word Seti comes from Set and means to shoot (either an arrow or to ejaculate). Set cannot control his sexual desires, and when he was unable to have Sex with Isis he ejaculated on the ground frustrated. He represents the animal tendency to direct energy out of the body without control and reacting to life's events without thinking.

In early versions Set merely killed Osiris and buried his body at Abydos. By the end of Egypt's reign Set was beginning to be portrayed in a more evil light. The things that were usually left in depiction for the serpent Apop were now being passed onto Set. In the myths he gets nastier, perhaps a symbol that the conscious minds of the average people were becoming stronger and creating more strife in the world. While Osiris was the growing plants on the bank of the Nile, Set was the hot desert where one could not grow food. He was painted red, and depicted as a dog, a pack of wild dogs, a crocodile or an ass. As a dog he is the barking conscious mind that we cannot shut off and keep quiet. A pack of dogs can bring down a larger animal through small bites over time. So too will our own mind bring a larger being (our soul) down through its small repeated actions. The crocodile lies unseen under the Nile and strikes suddenly as our patterns and habits of our mind will strike us without warning.

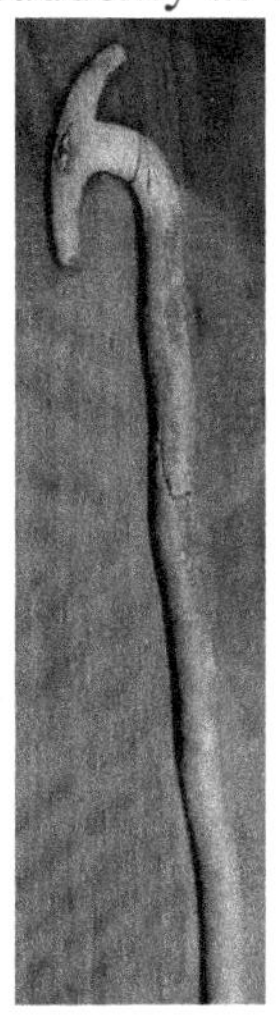

Set is sometimes a beast with a curved snout and a forked tail. The forked tail and the burning heat eventually became Satan (from Set) in the Bible. Satan is the Angel of Darkness and means 'adversary' in Hebrew. Originally he was simply an opponent. When the Old Testament was translated into Greek, Satan became "Diablos" the accuser. The name had changed away from its origin of Set to become something that had connections to false accusations. The word Diablos became the Devil, and formed the new Christian concept that the Devil is not actually us but is something out there that tries to stop us. The only devil is our own mind, and we must first examine if that mind should be in a human being or not.[124] Older reliefs show Set coming out of Horus's body, or together holding a ladder or tying a papyrus reed in the hieroglyph for union.

---

[124] Laviolete p.23

58:Ancient Egyptian Uas Scepter, the top of which has been molded to be given the appearance of Set. Often the wood would have been painted red.

Horus eventually defeats Set but does not kill him for Set is a power that cannot be annihilated, only redirected. When one has finally controlled their Setian nature, they are shown holding the Uas scepter (in the right hand showing active force). The staff has an angled head and forked tail to show Set is now as rigid as the staff. To hold the uas in the left hand meant was one was gaining the intuitive powers to control Set, or that they were stopping internal dialogue (mediation). Boheme wrote a passage which explains finding Set within, "Finding within myself a powerful adversary [Set], namely the desires that belong to the flesh and blood, I began to fight a hard battle against my corrupted nature, and with the aid of God I made up my mind to overcome the inherited will to break it, and to enter wholly into the love of God. I therefore then and there resolved to regard myself as one dead in my inherited form, until the spirit of God would take form in me, so that in and through Him I might conduct my life. Now while I was wrestling and battling with the adversary within, a wonderful light arose within my soul (Horus). It was a light entirely foreign to my unruly nature, but in it I recognized the true nature of God and man and the relation existing between them, a thing which before that I had never understood and for which I would never have thought to seek."[125]

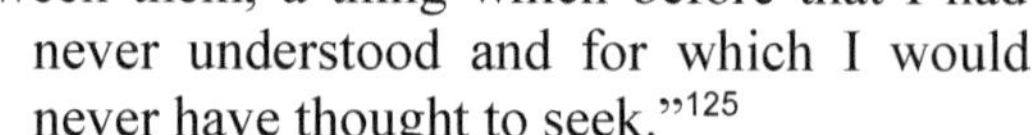

Horus (Heru)

59:Horus as the falcon, holding the ankh and uas- Khonsu temple Karnak

Horus is the 10th Neteru of Heliopolis. Ten is the highest number in an original series of numbers and represents completion, but Horus is more closely related to the number five as he is the fifth Neteru emerging from the coupling of Geb and Nut. He is represented by the falcon or hawk who can fly free to the sun. Horus is our astral body or the body beyond the physical. The hawk is gifted with great

---

[125] Ashby *Egyptian Yoga* p.137; Mead 76; Norvil p.65; West Key p.414

clarity and vision, thus is the ability to see what is real as opposed to illusion. He is the guiding force through the recapitulation of our life to find what our path and events held for us, and how our own mind held us back. He has the famous expression "watching you like a hawk." This watching is the observer within that is watching the wandering thoughts of the mind (Set, Apop). Horus became recognized in many forms including: Heru-P-Ichant (Horus the child, the infant being suckled by Isis), Horachety (Horus of the Horizon, a the name that connects with the Sphinx at Giza), and Heru-er (Horus the elder, the one who overcomes Set). His worshiping temples were as the falcon at Edfu, in the south at Nekhem (Hierakonopolis), and in the north at Bedhet where he was the winged sundisk. Most texts show him to be the last of the Neteru to rule Egypt during the First Time. Mortal human kings were the descendants of Horus, while priests were the Followers of Horus. Horus is the path we aspire to break free of the karma of reincarnation and unite with the All. The path of Horus is also the path of Jesus, Krishna, Buddha etc.[126]

Horus was married to Het-Heru (Hathor), who is the feminine principle of light. His four sons protect the organs which were removed and placed in canopic jars prior to mummification. By being able to defeat Set he represents the power to overcome opposition. When one is challenged one can call on the light of Horus to lead us with strength. He is born from the combination of Osiris (spirit) and Isis (nature). Horus is the rebirth of spirit, but not a physical birth from the womb but a rebirth of the mind. Following the path of Horus leads us to reach the state of Gnosis from Tehuti and to live the principles of Maat. To do this requires less time focusing on the material world and our desires and wants. We have to explore our Setian nature, not to think we are worse for having one but to think us better for taking the time to find it and acknowledge it. Until we are honest about what we are fighting, our energy to transform will not be used well. This is why everyone is classified as a Horus, because each examines our Setian nature to transform it. We can then be a king and rule our own sphere, as Horus rules Egypt. The only Neteru who had the authority to crown Horus was Tehuti, representing that only the wisdom of inner Gnosis can provide us the truth that can take us to enlightenment.

The struggle of Horus and Set is the struggle of every human being to control the mind. The path of Horus is the path of the heart. The battle with Set does not actually exist on the physical plane, though it may appear so. The battle outside is only representative of the battle that is happening inside. To not understand this one will spend all of their time fighting the outer world when in fact the only fight is inside. This key part of the teaching is reveled with Horus depicted with Set's head coming out of his side in the Book of What is in the Duat, or are shown together tying a papyrus into a sema union sign. Set is within, and we must use the light of the heart (the number five) to go back and

---

[126] Ashby *Ausarian* p.179

reach Osiris, which is our father and our higher self. Set is not an evil force to be destroyed, but be transformed into something of a higher vibration. Thus our ego is less destroyed as it is turned into our best use, as Ra calls upon Set to battle Apop. Thus the mind is used to help fight itself.[127]

Hathor

60:Top of a Hathor head column block, Dendera

Hathor (Het-Heru) means "House of Horus." She also had the titles of "Mother of Light" and "Lady of Hotep (peace), the Eye of Ra, Dweller in his Disk, Mistress of all the Gods." She is the personification of feminine energy on the path to enlightenment. A statue of her from the temple of Dendera would once a year mate with the statue of Horus from Edfu. At the temple of Dier al-Medina she is called "the Golden One, Queen of the Gods." She has dual aspects as Sekhemet and Bastet (see Below). She is usually symbolized by the cow, relating her to Nut. She sometimes takes the place of Nut at the sycamore tree that nourishes the traveler to the underworld. She is most known by her aspects of love and lovemaking (becoming Aphrodite in Greece), merriment, dance, music and song. She plays the sistrum and wears the Menet. Her great temple was at Dendera, the place of the famous zodiacs where the New Year's festival was held. She was also a key figure at the beautiful Temple of Hatshepsut opposite the river from Luxor. One her head is the cow horns or sometimes a falcon on a perch, representing the House of Horus. At times she is depicted as the mother of Horus, thus Isis and Hathor are the same.

The nourishment that she provides is the encouragement in the Book of the Dead for the initiate to battle Apop (outside control), and to not lose one's heart (the place of Maat and our true self). She also teaches one how to become a lotus, the flower that ascends to light from darkness. What she is providing is the inner strength for us to connect with Horus inside, as our love will cause us

---

[127] West *Key* pp.78, 394; Lamy p.83; Ashby *Egyptian Yoga* p.101

to couple with our spouse. She is also the love for ourself that we need to make anything happen. She connects with Horus sexually through Min. She is not unbridled passion or sexual pleasure, but true love. Our sexual energy is an important part of being human, and is our initial force that makes us want to join with something beyond ourself. She is able to show that when one is using proper sexual coupling techniques (see Min) love is used to turn the sexual energy into a force of spiritual growth. If we only act through lust we will be unable to use our sex energy, instead wasting it on desires of the mind. This is why she holds the Menet, the symbol of proper balance of male and female sexual energy.[128] She is also a seat, thus a place where Horus can rest. She is vitality (jewel 19 to the Toltecs) thus energy is brought from rest, and Horus at times needs to rest during his battle with Set. It is resting in love. Hathor is said to have seven images or forms that connect with the seven stars in the Pleiades, and the dance of the seven veils. This connection is with the chakras that will lead to the flow of kundalini. The seven Hathors were worshiped at Dendera and were represented in the form of young beautiful women wearing tight-fitting tunics and vulture headdresses. They also held tambourines.

She was often shown playing the sistrum (sesheshet in Egypt), a musical instrument that drives away evil spirits (see chapter on sound.) The three feminine figures of Hathor, Tehuti and Maat reveal the energies that are used in creation. They are unchanging forms that exist, as wood can become a table or a bowl but will still be wood. Tehuti is a male, describing that he is the force of taking the feminine energy that is internal and adding the male energy of acting outward with it. He is the love of the divine (heart) and the need to walk towards it, while also being the outward manifestation of God through omens and Logos. Hathor is the force of spiritual energy and love that we need within. Maat is the order and harmony that every creature in their heart is striving to attain.

Sekhemet

61:Sekhemet statue, British Museum

Sekhemet was the consort of Ptah and was one aspect of Hathor. She is depicted as a lioness, wearing on her head the solar

---

[128] West *Key* pp.345-50, 394, Lamy p.83

disk with the uraeus serpent. She is also depicted atop a u-shaped serpent, holding both of its necks. Her name means powerful. She represents the burning power of the sun. As the eye of Ra she nearly destroyed all of mankind until Tehuti intervened and gave her wine to drink and turned her into Bastet. Actually she is really not the heat of the sun, but the heat of our inner sun. She is the inner fire of kundalini which when it reaches the head will become the Eye of Horus and open the power of the third eye. Not understood correctly, this fire could lead to severe damage, thus the warning in the myth. If used correctly, this fire will burn all of our blocks that halt the flow. This process is soul healing. All great healers in Egypt needed her wisdom along with that of Tehuti. Like used by Oriental masters, this fire is needed to reach deep within. When events are brought out from the blocks they will produce tremendous pain as we relive them to eliminate them from our being. Only by ridding ourselves of the pain within us can we really heal. New age healers who claim that you won't experience anything but a happy feeling are not really healing you, but performing the kind of healing from Bastet that is only helping. Sekhemet was the healer and she hurts, but from that hurt comes the true connection to being free of our bindings.

Her name comes from the word Sekhem which means personal power. This power will lead us to healing, and also is the inner light that will dispel our darkness. Her statues were usually made out of igneous rock like basalt or granite to emphasize the power of fire that she represents. So powerful were her statues that I was able to use one to heal a number of people, as explained in the chapter on religion. Because of her great power for healing or destruction, a statue of Sekhemet should be shown the utmost of respect.

Bastet

Bastet today is thought to be the black cat. Actually Bastet is a cat headed woman who holds a sistrum, while a bunch of black cats surround her. The kittens are Bastet on the physical plane, while Bastet as a form of Hathor is in both the physical and spiritual. Cats are well known for being able to easily travel to the astral realms, and are often a symbol of feminine meditation. Black cats are powerful protectors and suck up negative energies. They were used by ancient women thought of as witches, not to cast evil spells but to protect those negative energies from coming to them when making up healing potions of herbs.

Bastet wore a green garment while Sekhemet wore a red one. While her counterpart Sekhemet heals with the power of fire, Bastet is a more subtle healer, not as powerful but helpful nonetheless. Her gentle healing is what provides some relief from aches and pains, or physical problems like illness (symbolized by surrounding herself with physical cats). Sekhemet does the inner soul healing which is painful in its depth, but even masters know that subtle healing at times is also required. This is less a healing than a helping. If all we ever felt is pain, our mind could think that no healing is taking place. Bastet healing also gives us extra strength which is needed to allow us to continue to endure the pain that the healing of Sekhemet will continue with us. Eventually, working with both of these aspects will take us to a place where the block (demon) is eliminated and we will be open to pure energy and strength.

Eye of Horus
"If thine eye be single, thy whole body shall be full of light." Matthew 6:22

The Eye of Horus is described in great detail in Egyptian mythology. The Pyramid Texts claim, "Behold Osiris Unas, you have been brought to the Eye of Horus and you will gain possession of it at your initiation." "O Osiris Unas, may you gain control of the Eye of Horus. The subtle body is inherently afraid of it." "It will affect you and your mouth will be opened." The Book of the Dead chapter 138 claims, "It (Eye of Horus) can divert the powers of Set." It is also symbolized by the goddess Utchat or the winged sundisk. At one point during the battle, Set gouged out the eye of Horus. It represented a time when Horus was blind to the ways of spirit. Each of us in our training will reach times like this when we feel we are in situations beyond our teaching. However there was help for Horus, so there is help for us. Hathor and Tehuti came to his rescue to not only obtain the eye, but also provide him with an even more powerful one than before. When the eye returned it found an Akh in its place (the inner light that leads to enlightenment) so it was made as a cobra and placed on the forehead.

Egyptian texts claim that with the Eye of Horus one will be able to see clearly and have protection and power. It was a famous symbol to the initiated and an amulet for the masses. As in Asian tradition, the right eye is seen as the masculine sun (Ra in Egypt) and the left the feminine moon (of Tehuti). An imbalance in our masculine-feminine energy can be spotted in the eyes. While these eyes are separate, we too see the world as separate. The Pyramid Texts say one needs to unite the white and black eyes (left and right) to be initiated. When this happens we can raise the kundalini to the point of our brow and open our third eye. This is the Eye of Horus which will allow us to see beyond the normal world of duality. We will see things as they are, thus be classified as a seer. This eye will allow one to see the Light, or energy as it really is in the universe. The eye was brought back by Tehuti and Hathor showing that it is Gnosis and love (both found in the heart) that will allow the Eye to be created.

Another myth has the Eye of Ra going into creation and getting lost. The eye did not want to return so Tehuti was sent to find the eye, which was upset when it returned to see Ra had already replaced it. Tehuti thus placed it on the brow as a uraeus. This myth is similar in information to Horus. Here Ra is our Higher Self that sent his eye (part of himself or individual soul into creation) which got lost or forgot the nature of its trip. Through ignorance (desires of Set) the purpose of our higher self is forgotten. The eye (material souls) get caught up in the apparent reality of the physical world. Tehuti (wisdom) comes in the forms of Metu Neter (the hieroglyphic texts/books) or as spiritual teachers (Sbai/masters) who was able to instruct the eye (us) back to reality. With the understanding in place the individual soul can return.[129]

Humanity was said to come from the tears of Ra. From the tears (remtu) came humans (rethu). It implies that human experience is both a sorrowful condition because we have lost our connection and become associated with the ego. Even things we find as pleasant will bring us sorrow. No situation, no matter how good, can last forever. Thus even in our pleasure we will find pain when the activity can no longer happen. We can not win every sporting event, can not always have sex, our favorite TV show is not always on, people will die. To find the true self one will find inner peace and pleasure in any activity and not have sorrow if a particular one is not available in any moment. This is the pain that is explained through this myth. When we find balance we will be able to allow enjoyment in any activity or situation in the moment, then from detachment not find sorrow should any activity not be able to happen again.[130]

Osiris Myth in Nile Flood

The myth of Osiris permeated every aspect of Egyptian society, but none more than during the yearly flooding of the Nile. The life of Egypt depended upon the river. In the midst of the desert, the Nile is 4,000 miles of hope. Diodorus of Sicily claimed the Egyptian name of the Nile was Aegyptus (Greek for vulture), and could explain the reason the Greeks used the word to explain the entire country. To refer to the Nile meant to refer to Egypt. The river received its modern name from the King of Nileus. The Nile was seen as the companion of the Milky Way in the sky called the "Winding Waterway." Each year a great flood, known as The Inundation occurred. This event caused three seasons in the Egyptian year: Shomu (deficiency April-June), Akhet (inundation July-Oct) and Proyet (coming forth Nov-Mar). During the period of inundation, the Nile is the Neteru Hapi. [131] Unfortunately the inundation (flooding) of the Nile no longer occurs as a result of modern canals and dams which have been built in Egypt.

Beginning at the time of the summer solstice, the star Sirius (represented by Isis) rose in the sky. Sirius is the only star to rise every 365.25

---

[129] Ashby *Egyptian* p.140; Lamy p.15
[130] Naydler p.8; Isha p.306
[131] Lamy p.6; Naydler pp.9, 17

days, thus became the calendar we use today. Even more amazing in Egypt was that the rising of Sirius also signaled the flooding of the Nile. The night prior to the flood was known as the 'night of the drop,' when Isis as Sirius was said to send a tear down from heaven for her dead husband. This tear landed in Nubia in the south, which caused the Nile to flood. Prior to the inundation the Nile was at its lowest level, and the heat and desert encroached on the green land turning it to dust. Animals and humans became weak due to the heat and lack of water. It symbolized the death of Osiris as the heat of Set was taking command. Yet the rise of Sirius as Isis, and the drop of water she brought down, allowed not only the force of Osiris to brought back to give life to Horus, but also for the life giving force of the Nile to return water to the heated lands.

It was just at the point when Set had seemed to gain victory that the Nile would again inundate. The floodwaters turned the Nile green with a mass of vegetable detritus floating from the equatorial swamps in the south. For several days the Nile would smell foul with this decaying vegetable matter. This greenery was Osiris and the stench was the purifying odor that would force out all the evil from Set that was lingering. A few days later, a second red coloured wave of mud from the soils of Ethiopia arrived. The Nile rose 40-45 feet in the south and 25 feet at the northern delta. The waters submerged the whole country, giving it the appearance of a vast sea or lake. Herodotus wrote, "When the Nile overflows, the whole country is converted into a sea, and the towns which remain above the waters look like islands in the Aegean."

During the flood Osiris was still dead, but Horus was battling Set. The completion of the inundation and the possibility of planting was symbolized as the victory of Horus. Osiris, as plant life, was now able to rise from the mud. This rising was ritually enacted in the raising of the Djed pillar (see symbols). Each year the power of Osiris and Horus could be seen by the entire population. The Nile flood also recreated the act of creation. When Egypt was submerged under the flood waters the whole land returned to the primordial condition of Nun. The evaporation of the water became a reenactment of the beginning, when the primordial hill first appeared from the waters.[132]

Other Stories

The myth of Osiris and Horus is nearly identical to the Christian New Testament teachings of Jesus and many other religious teachings of the world. In India, Krishna is the black one and is pursued by his evil uncle King Kamsa. Kamsa foresaw that Krishna would assume the kingship so he ordered all male children to be killed (like the Jesus and Moses stories). Like Horus, Krishna's eyes are the sun and the moon unified into one whole. Krishna was also born of a virgin. The Finish story of Kullervo has the father and the uncle separated by

---

[132] Ashby *Egyptian Yoga* p.ey 102; Santillana, Giorgiode and Dechand, Hertha von *Hamlet's Mill* (Gambit 1969) pp.28-31

a hawk. Some say they were born from the trunk of a tree. The child at three months says he will avenge his father's death. The uncle tries to destroy the child by throwing him into a fire. He was sent to the forest where he felled five (number of Horus) trees and then eight (Tehuti) more. He also threshes grain and feeds a cow. The story in Greek is of Demeter who must search on her own to find Persephone in the underworld. Demeter also attempts to make a child immortal by placing it in the fire. The Blackfoot have a myth of how sign language started. Two twin brothers fell in love with the same woman. One decided to rid of his rival brother by taking him on a canoe trip, leaving him on an island. The abandoned is taken into a beaver lodge and taught the beaver medicine including signing. When the summer comes, the twin returns to teach the people signing.[133]

Other Neteru

Aker

Aker is the twin lion god or two sphinxes back to back facing east (yesterday) and west (today). They guard the exit and entrance to the Duat, and lions were used to guard the entrance to temples and homes as is still done today in Chinese tradition. Aker's job is to keep out yesterday and tomorrow (past and future) thus keep all who pass by in the Now. To walk between the two lions was to leave time behind.

Ammit

Ammit is the combined hippo, lion and crocodile that is found at the weighing of the heart, who eats the souls of those who do not pass the balance. He will be explained further in the chapter on the Book of the Dead.

Anubis (Anpu)/Upuat

---

[133] West *Key* pp. 71, 351; West *Serpent* p.121; Schwaller *Sacred* p.183; Ashby *Egyptian Yoga* p.107; Ashby *Ausarian* pp.138, 151

63:Anubis in the form of Upuat (Opener of the ways) found in the tomb of Tutankhamun, Cairo Museum

While Anubis was part of the early texts, by the New Kingdom he became prominent in mummification and the Book of the Dead. He weighs the heart, sat (guarded) the box/ark of Osiris, and as Upuat was the "opener of the ways" who guided the dead in the underworld to the Elysian Fields. He has always been assumed to be jackal headed but many now refer to him as a domesticated dog. When in all animal form (like the one from Tut's tomb) he has a black coat with gold trim. The dog prefers carrion instead of fresh meat, and is able to sublimate the dead matter into his own living purpose. A dog is also famous for its homing instinct (even at night) and is a great guide. Who better to lead than one's favorite dog? Anubis represents our inner ability to distinguish the physical world of illusion from the world of true reality. That he is coloured gold and black shows he is the beginning (black) and end (gold) of the alchemic process. We must be like a dog and by loyal to wisdom and love, while rearing up and barking at the evil of the mind. Thus he is the opposite dog qualities of Set. Because he helps to discern between reality and illusion, he is a perfect choice to be one to weigh the heart. Anubis is the one who embalms the mummy, as in early training the initiate is symbolized as one who is dead in the coffin. The resurrection is the connection to our own higher self. It is the discrimination of Anubis which can lead us inside to Horus. As Upuat he represents our ability to watch our own ego, to detach from worldly desires.[134]

Apis-Bull

The Apis-Bull was worshiped in Egypt as a symbol of fertility and strength of kingship. There would only be one sacred Apis bull alive at any one time. Upon its demise the priests of Memphis would be dispatched in search of the reincarnation of the Apis. The task was to find a newborn calf which had the special physical markings that distinguished it as a reborn Neteru. These marks were an inverted white triangle on the forehead, white markings resembling a vulture on the shoulder, a falcon round the rump, a tufted tail and the configuration of the scarab beetle on the tongue. The calf would be brought to Memphis to the temple of Ptah and kept in a special place. When the bull died it received a royal burial and was placed in the rock tombs of the Serapeum. The bull symbolized male sexual power and Ptah as creator of forms. Serapis was a Greek combination of the Apis bull and Osiris, which became popular in Alexandria, Greece and Rome.[135]

Apop

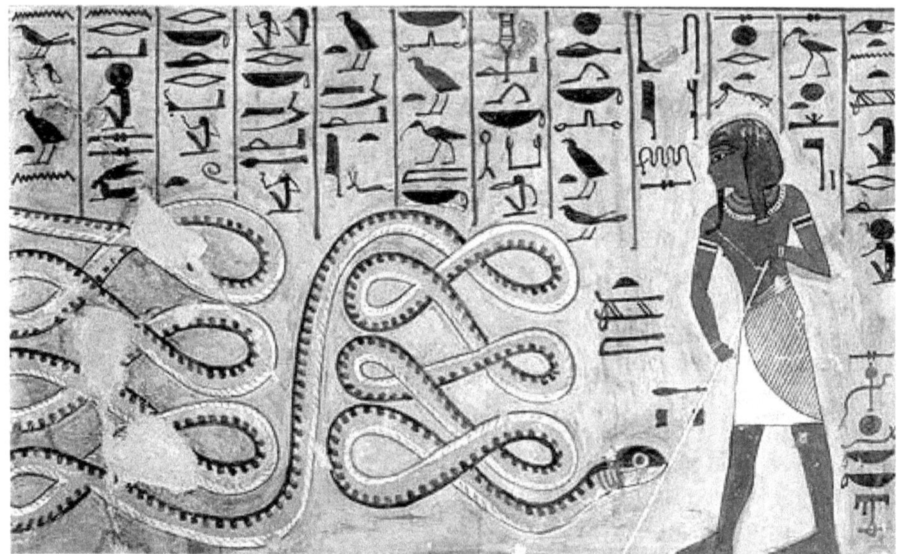

64:Atum before the many coils of the Apop serpent, Book of Gates

---

[134] Rohl, David *A Test of Time* (Century 1993); West *Key* pp.77, 81
   cxlix Ashby *Egyptian Yoga* pp.63-65
[135] West *Key* p.77

Apop is the serpent that is fought each night and hacked to pieces by the combined forces of Ra, Osiris and Horus The Leiden Papyrus sets out the ways to defeat Apop. Apop is always shown traveling along the ground, or in great undulations. Without the waves the mind is free to be in a state of hotep (peace). Apop is also the undulations of the dream we believe to be real. Apop is said to need "no nourishment other than his own loud and dreadful roar," the very sounds of his own mind. Every night Apop attempts to stop Ra from becoming the light, as our own mind tries to stop us from reaching our inner light. The myth is explaining that as Ra must constantly battle Apop, we too will have to constantly battle our mind for it is a constant adversary. A part of the Book of the Dead shows Apop sitting upon the Djed of Osiris, meaning that he is trying to stop the flow of energy up the spine, defeated with the "fire of the back." We need to use our inner light to halt this opposing force. When the serpent is struck with the spear it stops moving. When we can stop our mind with meditation we will gain control over our dream that we call reality. In time it becomes Set (who is the only one on the boat who does not get hypnotized by Apop) on the boat of Ra who defeats Apop, thus we use the positive quality of the mind (opposition) to defeat the negative "intrusion" that is attempting to gain control of our Being (Apop). Apop also has the names in texts of Sebau and Nuk. He became connected to Set, conscious mind, which caused Set to be seen as evil. Yet it is more correct to say that Apop entered human consciousness and "took over" our mind to turn it to the ways of the Apop serpent. Thus we must overcome what Apop has done to Set, not Set itself.

Bes

65:Bes from a stone block at Dendera

Bes is a dwarf god with a beard, monstrous face, lion's mane and protruding tongue pressed between his teeth which are all non-traditional Egyptian features. He is found at Dendera and like Hathor he was fond of dancing, music and jubilation. He played the lyre, tambourine, and sistrum. He was a favourite deity for women in childbirth and for children because he was thought to frighten away bad dreams. He was also thought to bring good luck and fortune.[136] The reference to the dwarf in fairy tales and their role in the alchemic process may have roots with Bes.

Heka

Part of a group that includes Hu (divine word/Logos), Sia (divine knowledge) and Heka (life force in action). (See magic)

Min (Amsu)

66:Min from wall relief, Luxor Temple

Min is a form of Horus that used the symbol of the thunderbolt, door bolt and lettuce. His thunderbolt was later added to the Greek Zeus. He is thought by Egyptologists to be related to the rain and storms (because of the thunderbolt) for it is he "who opens the clouds." The bolt of lightning is actually representative of the sexual process, as sperm will flow from a man like lightning during orgasm. In later Egypt his true meaning was lost as he became a cult god for orgies of sexuality. His teaching evolved in Europe to Mayday sexual fertility festivals. Just as a huge pole was erected to Min in Egypt, the maypole was later erected in Europe.

In the proper Egyptian teachings, Min is an aspect of Horus. Min is not the unbridled use of sexual energy, but the opposite, the learning to control and use it wisely. Many of his statues show him with an erect penis, held by his left hand while holding a flail in his right. This pose can lead to victory "over the enemies of his father." The father of Horus is Osiris, and his enemy is Set. Ancient tradition taught the importance of understanding our sexual energy. It is the most powerful energy force that we have. When used for sex it can create another human. When used just for pleasure it creates neither a human or the impetus to raise kundalini. When used in tantra it causes kundalini to rise, as the plumes on the head of Min are Isis and Nepthys.

Tantra teaches that sex is not bad but one of the most powerful acts that can be undertaken if done correctly. The energy is stirred to the highest level

---

[136] West *Key* pp.70, 240

possible, with most of it channeled back into the body to be used for spiritual development. These inner orgasms as they are called, far exceed the outer. He holds the penis with his left hand, the inward feminine quality to show the force is going inside, while holding the flail to beat back his own inner urges to outwardly project the thunderbolt. Both Min and Set have lettuce as their favorite food. It is a once an aphrodisiac and part of a vegetarian diet. Thus we must nurture both parts of ourselves, for we will use the lower self's urges for sex using love (Hathor) for our partner and our self to connect with Horus inside.

Mut

Mut is usually depicted as the wife of Amun-Ra at Thebes, and her temple was at Karnak. She is a personification of the one great goddess like Hathor and Isis. Mut is the Great Mother and the sound of Mut is still present in every word for mother around the world. While sometimes she wears the double crown, usually she wears the vulture headdress, a bird known as a fierce protector of their young. She is connected with the Greek Hera.

Neith

Neith is the consort of Khnum at Esna and is symbolized by two crossed arrows or the weaving shuttle. The crossed arrows (x) symbolize fertilizing and multiplying as we use the symbol today. It has nothing to do with war or hunting as believed by Egyptologists. As a weaver she weaves the web of life. It is the ancient symbol for the interconnectedness of all things. As everything in the universe is connected by this web, by learning to weave we can access all of creation. Neith in some myths was also a part of the tribunal of Horus and Set. She decreed Horus should rule, but Set should receive some sort of compensation for he too was part of the web of life.

Nekhebet and Utchat

Nekhebet was the vulture of the south while Utchat (Buto to the Greeks) was the cobra of the north. Together they would appear upon the diadem headdress of the Pharaoh. They are actually one and the same, just appearing in dual forms. Nekhebet is also a form of Isis while Utchat is a form of Nepthys. Together these two female goddesses will lead one to the Eye of Horus, shown by their dual position on the head. As mentioned, the Eye of Horus is the third eye that allows us to see beyond the material, and comes from a rise of kundalini to the head. At times they can also come together as the winged sundisk (freedom and power), or as the two serpents along the staff of Tehuti. As explained with Nepthys, they are opposite poles of the same principle. Their combination leads to heightened awareness.

Selket

Selket was scorpion headed female and associated with Horus in the swamps. The sting and poison of the scorpion represents the sting and death we must do to our conscious mind. Selket is also related to the Egyptian word breath (selk), and is connected with Neith. The breath (infusing ourself with spirit) will help us connect with Neith (the web of life). She, along with Neith, Isis and Nepthys guarded one of the four canopic jars filled with the organs of the mummified (See the sons of Horus).

Seshat

Seshat or Sefekht is translated as "the Secretary" or "Seven." She is the consort of Tehuti, (thus the form of Maat in the physical) and can be seen as a librarian, record keeper and controller of the Akashic records (the wisdom of everything). She was sometimes called "Mistress of the Book" and "Mistress of the House of Architects." She is often shown laying out the foundations of a sanctuary with the aid of the stars. On her head is a seven-pointed star, similar to the one on the head of the Statue of Liberty. Interestingly she is also shown wearing a panther skin. In Egypt as well as Mexico, the cheetah or leopard was worn as a symbol of the high priest.

Sobek

Sobek was the crocodile. At times the crocodile is associated with Set and the fast strikes of the conscious mind. In the form of Sobek, the mind has been controlled and placed in service with our heart. The temple of Kom Ombo was built to explain this principle.

Sons of Horus

The Four sons of Horus protect the viscera (organs) which were removed and placed in canopic jars prior to mummification. Each of the jars were paired with a female deity who offered protection. The four sons are: Amsety (human headed, liver, element of water, west, protected by Isis), Duamutef (jackal headed, stomach, earth, north, protected by Neith) Hapi (baboon headed, lungs, air, east, protected by Nepthys) and Qebsennuf (hawk headed, intestines, fire, south, protected by Selket). Native Indians provide offerings for the seven directions: four cardinal as well as earth, sky and the inner of Spirit. The Egyptian Salt Papyrus claims there are deities of the seven directions which are Isis, Nepthys, Thoth, Horus at the four corners, and "Geb is the ground, Nut is the sky, and the Great Hidden God is the interior."[137] The placing of the elements to the directions is the same as found in the native Indian medicine wheels. The four sons were said to follow in a particular order

---

[137] for more on the placement of the four corners in the tomb of Tutankhamun please see Lamy pp. 93-95

(counter clockwise). This is similar to the teaching of Toltecs who may start with the technique of recapitulation in the east, which leads to not-going in the north, which leads to erasing personal history in the west, and finally to dreaming in the south.

Sokar

Sokar was the hawk god found in the Book of What is in the Duat and is related to the pyramids and sphinx at Giza. This god is a form of Horus and is often associated and combined with Ptah as well as Osiris. In the Pyramid Texts he manufactured the royal bones, while in the Book of the Dead he fashioned silver bowls for the deceased. This may represent the ability to make the components of matter, or is the place where matter comes from.

CHAPTER 9
EGYPTIAN KNOWLEDGE

67:*Statues of Maya and Merit from Sakkara, Leiden Museum*

Egypt

"Concerning Egypt I will now speak at length, because nowhere are there so many marvelous things, nor in the whole world beside are there as many things of such unmistakable greatness." Herodotus[138]

The early part of this book looked closely at the ideas of wisdom. Knowledge is a word that seems to mean the same thing, but it does not. Knowledge is a term that is more closely tied to our ideas of science, technology, or understanding of this physical world. When one has first

---

[138] West *Key* p.xi

acquired knowledge, that knowledge can be used through experience to become wisdom. As mentioned in the introduction, many try to show Egypt's technology as a sign of their "advancement." However the reverse becomes true when archaeologists believe that if a society did not have technology, they can only do things in a primitive way. Egypt was at a great height in building practices, astronomy, or medicine far beyond what most scholars today admit. Rather than attempt to prove their technology per say, I will instead be showing the results of the knowledge they possessed, or how similar knowledge could be expressed and used in ways different to us today. Remember most of the knowledge of Egypt would have been kept secret and taught only to specific members of society who proved their moral character to use the information in the best way possible. The main focus of Egyptian knowledge was based on the understanding of mathematics and geometry. They believed that this science was one that was able to bridge the gap between the spiritual and physical worlds, thus could be used to explain both the above and below.

Art

"Art is not meant to be enjoyed, it is meant to illuminate." John Anthony West[139]

68:The incredible statue of Thutmosis III at the Luxor Museum

Even modern scholars will not disagree with the incredible paining, sculpture or architecture of Egypt. However they object that while of incredibly high quality, it all looks the same. They look down upon the Egyptian priests as being oppressive and forcing artists to only create art that looked a certain way, unlike the great freedom of modern artists who are allowed to express in whatever way they want. It again must be pointed out that we must not judge the knowledge of Egypt based on our own views, instead we must place our minds in the past to understand the reason for all of this. The result will be a greater

---

[139] West *Serpent* p.75

appreciation of ancient art, and less appreciation for what is termed art today. In fact since so few can even understand what the ancients were actually creating, they miss the powers that exist right before their eyes.

To the Egyptian, art had only one purpose, to allow human beings the possibility to enlighten directly from the art created. Thus what someone wanted to paint or sculpt was far less vital than what would allow wisdom and enlightenment to be granted those who viewed it. This concept was also suggested by the mystic Gurdjieff. He believed there were two types of art. The first type is what is created today and was done from our conscious mind. Today art is created so that the artist can express their feelings or emotions, make a social commentary, or create something that looks nice. It will provoke different feelings and emotions from those who view it. It is usually created as the artist went along adding here and there what inspired them. The modern artist is attempting to find their own style that makes them different, thus related to their own ego. The Egyptian was using art to raise people above their ego. In Egypt to spend hours creating art to look good, tell ones emotions, or feed a buyer's ego was a waste of time. There is almost no ancient art created today, thus few have the opportunity to experience it at all. Modern art and architecture is physical and for the physical world. Ancient art was physical, but created for the spiritual world.

Art is usually purchased as a hobby, or a way to show others how important and cultured they are. Art is bought as a luxury, something we buy after our physical needs are met. Art is not seen as something important to our survival. In Egypt, their main focus was not physical needs but to regain our state of spiritual magic. Thus having proper art would be thought of as being just as important as food. The food we eat would be used once, but the art would be used for eternity. If an Egyptian moved to a new home, their first thought would not be furniture but artwork and statues. This is opposite to today where people chose places depending on whether all of their furniture will fit. To focus only on our physical needs would be thought of as a giant waste. To acquire modern art is the same as acquiring all sorts of "stuff" for our home. If it is not directly necessary, or part of our path to God, it is clutter. What good would it be to have 50 years of comfortable life, and an eternity without wisdom? Our modern society has become one that only thinks of comfort, not purpose or destiny or spirit.[140]

The ancient artist did not try to find their own style, but were taught how to produce art that looked the same. Ancient art will have the same impression on everyone for it was designed to affect every human the exact same way. The artist created it from a plan that would express some form of universal truth. We don't think a modern actor is oppressed because they have to read lines from a script (their part which helps to make a complete whole)

---

[140] West *Serpent* pp.71-73

like a movie or play. Thus think of an ancient artist as more of an actor, working from a script from the gods. Making true art was a most powerful tool, not only for the artist but for all who came in contact with it. Photographs would mean little, the symbolic art created from the photograph would provide much more.[141]

Nothing is placed in any part of Ancient Egyptian artwork because the artist thought it would look nice. Everything is there for a reason, has some symbolic significance, or is there to allow one to merge with God. Things were not built big to boost some King's ego, they were built that big to create a specific reaction inside each and every person who came in contact with it. By the same contrast some of the most powerful Egyptian art is also the smallest. They sit in cases in the Cairo Museum, rarely even noticed by tourists, yet because of how they were created they hold incredible power. Remember too that all Egyptian art was meant to be seen as a whole, not in part. A statue was meant to be experienced in the temple that housed it, not on its own. Any piece of ancient art that does not still include the whole of what was meant to be experienced with it, will lose a bit of its power with us.

I am not saying that art created the modern way is bad. This type of art was done in Egypt but never appeared on tomb or temple walls. This other type of art is part of the personal growth process as the artist explores their own inner being, revealing this connection to their own soul in their outer product. This type of art is powerful for the artist for it helps them connect with their Higher Self, provides personal healing and growth. Just as a Zen master will spend part of his day painting, he is painting for himself, not to sell the artwork. No one else will see it, it is for the artist alone. However this type of art is transforming only for the artist, not for every other person who views their art. Ancient art was created to potentially heal and illuminate every person who came in contact with it.

As will be mentioned in the next chapter, geometry and the interplay of numbers was very well understood in the ancient temples where the art was created. Egyptian art was created using a grid system, like graph paper, that allowed the perfect proportion of what was being created. Their grid was 18:19, like the Maya. This grid was not made out of some accidental choice, but the 18/19 grid related to the golden section (see number). The size of a fist became the measuring tool for the rest of the parts of the artwork. A light sketch of the relief or painting would be made using the grid, then when perfected would be carved or painted. Renaissance artists claimed that ancient art is music that has been placed on canvas, and looks so breathtaking to us because the principles of the golden section were placed within it. It would be actually impossible for someone not to like it. Certain numbers and geometry would be placed within to allow specific energies to infuse the painting or statue. Some Egyptian

---

[141] West *Serpent* pp.74-80; Speeth p.90

artwork will heal on its own based on how they were designed. Some will open altered states of consciousness, lead directly to the Neteru, or provoke feelings of love, well-being or kindness. This mystical understanding of art and architecture was reborn during the Renaissance by people like Bottacheli. This type of wisdom is also placed within alchemic paintings and drawings.

The abilities of the ancient world to craft stone like pyramids, obelisks or walls in Peru is beyond belief for the modern world. No one today can explain how they could work with stones up to two hundred tons and move and place them like simple rocks. Dolerite statues, one of the hardest metals, were found at Sakkara that no modern sculptor can duplicate. Some believe they needed special drills or electrical power to even create them. Thus the question becomes, how and why could they do this. It is easier to cut and move two-ton stones than two hundred ton stones. The look would be roughly the same, but the ancients did not do this. The large stones were important and they found the ways to move and raise them. The hardest stone was used for statues. They needed particular stone, or size of stone, because they were not just making a statue they were making real art which required the proper stone to create the proper energies. A statue of the fire Neteru Sekhemet could not be made out of anything except hard igneous granite that was produced from the molten fire energy of the earth.

Calendar

"It is incomprehensible how the modern world can recognize the inherit genius of Plato, Socrates, (Pythagoras) and yet reject the religious and philosophical systems of which they were the product." Manly Hall[142]

---

[142] Hall p. 36

69: Dendera Zodiac in the Louvre

Beyond using mathematics to create powerful artwork, they also used it to understand the workings of the universe. Our present calendar comes from the Romans who got there's from Egypt. Rome originally used a ten-month calendar of 334 days. The ten months led to the last four names September (7), October (8), November (9) and December (Deca, 10). By the seventh century BC January and February were added to make the calendar twelve months of 354 days, which still left the year 11.25 days short. Within a few hundred years the calendar was again off and forced Caesar, on the suggestion of Cleopatra, to install the Egyptian Sothic calendar of 365.25 days. This became known as the Julian Calendar, but while accurate for a few decades it too becomes inaccurate by one day every 128 years (for the actual solar year is 365.2422 days). In 1582 Pope Gregory installed a change because the spring equinox that forecast Easter was no longer falling on March 21 but March 11. On October 4, 1582 he decreed the next day to be October 15, thus deleting ten days. Many parts of Europe refused the change causing Christmas to be celebrated on different days across the continent. It wasn't until the eighteenth century that the Gregorian calendar became standard Europe, a calendar that will be accurate for 20,000 years.[143] Besides having this brief history you are likely commenting, so how great can this Egyptian knowledge be if their calendar was wrong? To answer that one must understand that the Egyptian temples used several calendars that were interconnected.

---

[143] Tompkins p.121

The Egyptian calendar system was more in line with the perfected one used by the Ancient Maya in Mexico, which both claim was not devised by humans but given to them by the gods. Thanks to the astronomical markers the ancient calendars use it allows us today to link our modern dates with theirs. Our calendar begins with January 1, a date that has no relation to an astronomical event. Without complete understanding of Western dating systems, twenty days after New Year would be hard to match up on any other calendar. The ancient world used specific astronomical dates such as the Summer or Winter Solstice for their new year. Thus to say twenty days after the new year in Egypt, could easily be plotted on our calendar today as twenty days after June 21st. The calendars were important and helped link to the science of astronomy and astrology. By comparing the motions of planets and stars, one would know the most favorable times for festivals, rituals, even healing. Chinese medicine still understands that certain times of the day are better for healing certain parts of the body. In Egypt this was shown as each hour of the day or night was ruled by a different Neteru.

While many calendars were kept, three were of great importance for most of Egypt's history: a lunar, civil and Sothic calendar. All ancient societies had a lunar calendar as their oldest and most important timekeeper. This connection to the feminine energies of the moon, thus to nature upon the earth, and was kept in Egypt in twenty-five year cycles of alternating 29 and 30 day months. They also kept a twenty-five year lunar calendar of 309 lunar cycles, or 9, 125 solar days. Dividing the two numbers is 29.5307 days per lunation (the modern astronomical figure is 29.53059). The lunar calendar also incorporates the golden section. The Egyptian civil calendar kept a 365-day year. Like the Maya the civil year was not thought of being 365 days, but 360 days plus five. The myth relates to Ra not allowing his daughter Nut to conceive in any of the 360-day year, so Tehuti played the moon in a gambling game winning 1/72 of the moon's light to make up five extra days. The Egyptian sky (as is our modern circle) was divided into 360 degrees. The 360 days were divided into twelve months of thirty days. Each ten of these degrees (or days) were known in Egypt as a decan, each which brought differing energies to the earth.[144]

The obvious question is why divide a circle, the sky and a day into 360 (a much harder figure to work with mathematically) as opposed to a number like 100. The Egyptians were not interested in easy but rather with keeping everything on earth in harmony with what was in the sky. They are showing something very important about the sky, earth, calendar, time, space and the number 360. Ancient calendars from England to South America to China were all 360 days divided into 12 months. Even the Maya, a civilization that could track astronomical events with decimal precision and knew the exact solar year, still had a calendar in use of 360+5 days. Some writers now feel that the earth

---

[144] West *Serpent* pp.94, 98

suffered a catastrophic event during the period of early humanity, perhaps hit by an asteroid or another planet. This event may have caused the earth to fall out of its perfect circular 360-day (degree) orbit of the sun, to a stranger 365.25-day one. To the ancient mind, the 360-day year was still the proper one for the earth and was used as the measure of time and space. However because the actual solar year changed for some reason, they viewed this additional time to be an extension of perfect time from before the catastrophe. From this idea comes the comma of Pythagoras (see number) that may relate to the connection between the real and illusion. We see an illusion of a 365.24-day year, but the real year may still be 360 days. The comma is a number that allows us to perceive beyond the illusion with number. It should also be remembered that the ancients say we have 360 Neteru inside of us, not 365.24!

The third key calendar was the Sothic, which had its origin in the return of the star Sirius (which was introduced in the section on the Nile). The helical rising of a star happens when it first appears on the horizon ahead of the sun, and Sirius rises every 365.25 days. Out of the 2,000 stars that can be seen without a telescope it is the only one to rise close to the actual solar year. This observation would have required thousands of years of astronomical observation, as opposed to the usual answer of a lucky guess or freak coincidence. Thanks to sophisticated astronomy shown at temples like Karnak, the Egyptians were able to determine the exact length of the solar year (kept on another calendar) and use the star Sirius as an astronomical version that kept the myth of Osiris in each person's daily life. Sirius was thought of as the star of Isis and her rising was called the day of the drop, when a tear for her dead husband Osiris lead to the flooding of the Nile that allowed the crops to grow. The southern shaft of the Queen's Chamber in the Great Pyramid points to this star.

Why the importance of this particular star, not only for the Egyptians but other ancient cultures around the world? Many mystics and even modern astronomers believe Sirius is the central fire, or great sun, around which our entire solar system (or even galaxy) orbits. Ra in fact may not be the animating force of our Sun, but of the central sun of Sirius. Sirius was mentioned with great knowledge by the African Dogon tribe, who knew that it was not just one star but has a second star (Sirius B, a dense collapsed white dwarf star that can not be seen by the eye) which revolves around it every fifty years. The Dogon also claim there to be a third star that is the origin of all female souls. The question for modern scientists was how did an "unevolved" African tribe know about advanced astronomy that was not discovered with telescopes until 1862? Of course the Egyptians had the same information placed in the Pyramid Texts, "Thy sister Isis cometh unto thee rejoicing in her love for thee. Thou settest upon thee...and she became great with child like the star Sirius." The smaller star of Sirius (B) is often thought of as a child that does not stray far from their mother Sirius A. It is somehow greatly connected to the earth, for the diameter of the earth is one-millionth that of the solar system, while the distance of our sun to Sirius is one-millionth that of our earth to the sun. The Egyptians believed human beings came from the star Sirius and from the system of Orion, related to Osiris. The Hopi and the Cherokee claim our human ancestors arrived 250,000 years ago from Sirius, which they call "Place of Ancestors."[145] Whether this is the central sun of our galaxy, the alien birthplace of humans, or simply the symbolic home of Isis this star system was of great importance in the ancient world.

With the civil calendar being 365 days while the Sothic was 365.25 days, meant the calendars would only match up as having the same start date every 1460 Sothic years or 1461 civil years. This event was known as the Sothic Year. Archaeologists have claimed the need for calendars in the ancient world was for agriculture. However a very simple calendar is all that is needed for agricultural practices. These ancient calendars allowed the energies of the sky to be brought down to the earth. They foretold the correct time for ritual or healing, even when great changes on the earth or in the universe could be expected. Because of this the Egyptians became masters of astronomy.

Astronomy

Until a few hundred years ago the study of the skies (astronomy) was linked to the discipline of what it means for the earth (astrology). Ancient cultures recorded the skies with the utmost of precision, and used that knowledge to make up birth charts, build temples or heal. They could correlate the position of the stars to understand when and how key events should happen or unfold upon the earth. They were able to relate when times were favorable or not favorable. Eclipses were carefully tracked as the loss of the sun to darkness was symbolizing a time on earth when the forces of darkness could snatch back our hard earned gains. It was a time when candles and fires would be lit to help keep Set away until the eclipse ended and the light of Ra would again dispel the darkness. The study of the stars, the zodiac and the energies associated with each constellation, led to their understanding of precession, the universal time clock. A complete trip through the zodiac lasts 25, 920 years when a new age would begin. Each of these new giant ages, as we are now coming upon, was a time of catastrophe and overhaul. Every 2,160 years a new small age would happen when a different zodiac sign rose to replace the previous. This would be less forceful than a complete precession; for example we are now leaving the age of Pisces to enter the Age of Aquarius.

Just as the Taoist can use oracles like the I Ching to suggest possible changes, astrology allows the examination of energetic influences and to provide the possibility of more choices of how to act and proceed. Some have

---

[145] Schwaller *Sacred* p.28; West *Serpent* p.97; Hancock *Fingerprints* pp.374, 390

linked the astrological signs to the twelve different forces of energy that the sun gives off each year, which provide a different first blast of solar energy upon our conception. The other planets would also do something similar. Along with the 28 year cycle of Saturn, mentioned in the Osiris myth, Marsiglio Ficino claimed that each year of our life is ruled by a different planet (energy): 1-moon, 2-mercury, 3-Venus, 4-sun, 5-mars, 6-Jupiter, 7-Saturn. Then the order is repeated. He claimed that every seven years will be a change due to the Saturn influence, as well as a four-year complete cycle that will come every 28 years. He suggested a new chart be done every seven years to chart the new influences in our lives.[146]

Geodesy

Understanding the mathematics of the earth's surface is referred to as geodesy. The Egyptians knew the circumference of the earth and used it to create their system of measurement. The Great Pyramid itself is a storehouse of geodesic data of the earth and mathematical data as a whole. Egypt in the ancient world was seen as the zero line of longitude (which today is at an arbitrary point in Greenwich, England). This line ran right through the pyramids at Giza and can be proved thanks to projections from ancient maps. The island of Elephantine in Southern Egypt was said to be a source for their ability to ascertain latitude. A well was built on the true Tropic of Cancer, thus on the summer solstice the difference of a shadow here and at a spot in northern Egypt would provide the earth's circumference. It is also claimed that pairs of obelisks could provide similar data, as could the long hallway at Karnak. This near perfect understanding of measurement of the earth was encoded within the temple designs themselves. A chapel at the temple of Karnak was shown by Lucie Lamy from its sixteen columns and two stairways to provide lengths and measures for all of Egypt.[147] This understanding of measurement was far beyond the simple use of numbers that we use in the modern world. To fully understand the knowledge inherent in ancient artwork, temples, or even their calendar one needs to learn sacred number, geometry and sound.

---

[146] Ficino p.83
[147] see tompkins 177-79 for more information; Lamy 77

CHAPTER 10
AMULETS/MAGIC/MUMMIES

70:Close up of the ankh, Khonsu Temple, Karnak

Amulet Symbols

The word amulet is derived from Arabic and means (to bear or to carry). They are used to protect the human body (either when living or dead) from evil forces. Talisman comes from the German word telesma (incantation) and is usually the embodiment of a special magical force which charges it the same way electricity charges a battery. Plate 32 of the Book of the Dead contains what is believed to be the magic words needed to charge four specific amulets. A talisman can be worn on the body to become an amulet, and an amulet can be magically charged to become a talisman. Almost every person in Egypt carried some form of charm or talisman.[148]

The amulet had the power inherent in the substance from which it was made, and the words inscribed. Amulets could be made of stone (lapis, carnelian, alabaster, jasper or jade), metals (gold, silver, copper, bronze), and occasionally from wood (cedar, sycamore, tamarack). Some were worn simply for ornamental effect but most would have worn or carried as magical protection, like someone today will carry a rabbit's foot or put a lucky penny in their shoe. Some of the famous amulets have already been described: the Eye of Horus, the scarab (usually made of green stone for the heart) and the uas. A few other key amulets and symbols will be laid out in this section.

Chapter 156 of the Book Of the Dead contains five lines claimed to be the words needed to charge a talisman called the Amulet of Isis, which the book claims should be made of red jasper or carnelian. It is a protective device when on meditative, astral or journey work, and to open doors in the Duat. Red jasper is a stone that is grounding for the first chakra, allows connection to the earth, to our own blood flow, and to strong sexual energy. What is deemed to be

---

[148] Budge, EA Wallis *Egyptian Magic* (Dover 1970) pp.4, 59

blood may mean the essence not the blood itself. The essence when combined with Isis' magic words (hekau) and wisdom will lead to great power.

The Djed is found beside the Amulet of Isis in chapter 155. It is made of gold, needed to be raised alone, and connected with the heart. It originally represented the spine of Osiris. The Egyptians equated the "raising of the Djed" with the resurrection of Osiris and this festival was performed as part of the Nile flood. The spine of Osiris lays against the back of the djed, and is our own spine that needs to have as the Pyramid Texts claim, "the fire of the back mastered." Four lines run atop the pillar that symbolizes the four highest chakra centers which we aspire our kundalini to rise to.

The ankh is said to be the symbol of life and is found all over the world from India to England. It has a male cross knotted together with a female oval. The cross is a male symbol of action, is of the world of four and in order to reach the higher state of five, the female energy must be added. It is called the key to life because when we can learn how to combine our male and female parts, we will be able to transcend the conscious mind. The cross is related to this world of time and space. Jesus was nailed to a cross, signifying being nailed or kept in this world. His resurrection transcended the cross. However the Egyptian ankh ties or unites together the cross with the female oval. Symbolically the ankh is combining the above of spirit with the below of matter, or of yin and the yang. The ankh can be used as a protective device, a meditative tool by staring at it, or as a hekau (mantra) by saying its name over and over to unite the two principles inside.

The Menet was a necklace worn by women and played a considerable part in temple and funerary ritual where it related to notions of rebirth or the passage to a new state. It was usually worn around the neck of Isis and Hathor, and like the ankh, showed the combination of male and female qualities. Here these represented the male organ of Min and the female organ of Hathor. Together they can create a royal birth, one that will give life to a royal child (our higher self). It is also the root of the Egyptian word for nurse.[149]

In Egypt the lotus was a powerful symbol that related to the first light of creation, and was used often in religious texts. The lotus is representative of the light which comes from darkness, as the lotus rises from the dark swamps of the Nile at dawn to open its flower to the light. So too we must be like the lotus and rise from out own darkness when shown the light. One of the Neteru shown sitting on a lotus means they have reached a state where they no longer go back into darkness, but always ride on the light.

Rings were often worn by the ancients and were made in connection with the right planets (for metals), herbs and stones. Words of power would be placed on them. Moses was said to have made several rings because he was "skilled in the magic of the Egyptians." Rings are great protectors but were

---

[149] Ashby *Egyptian Yoga* pp.115-16, Lamy p.82

rarely sold in the ancient world because to have power they must be made specifically for someone. A plain gold ring became the symbol of marriage for it was describing how a simple life together could lead each of them to spiritual gold. The ring is circular thus helps bring back the powers of its parts (herbs, stones, metals) back to the source. Being worn on different fingers will bring the power to different energy meridians of the body. The wedding ring finger is the sanjiano meridian that is part of a connector with the heart. Marsiglio Ficino claimed to have learned how to make seven rings, one for each of the planets (chakras) that he wore on a different finger each day of the week. Appollonius was said to live for 100 years because of these rings.[150]

Egyptian Magic

"Hermes accuses even magic, saying that the spiritual man who has come to know himself has no need to direct anything through magic, even if it is regarded as good...he should go on seeking himself and when he comes to know God...let fate do as she likes." Zosimus [151]

The topic of magic is often included in texts on Egyptian wisdom, thus I feel the need to explain it here. Magic is actually two very different terms. What is thought of in the modern world as magic is really illusion. The audience is tricked to think that what they saw was really something else. True magic is what the illusionists attempt to recreate on the physical. True magic uses the forces of the universe and manipulates them slightly to affect the physical plane. Anything that is seen to be beyond what is believed normal can be described as magic. Levitating, herbal potions, hands-on-healing or the actions of a Yoga or Taoist master can all rightfully be described as magic because few today have the power to understand what they witnessed. The word magic comes from the Greek Magos or Magi, the name given to seers from Mesopotamia and Persia who were still able to contact spirit directly.

Magic is really not a key teaching in the mysteries. Magic is the way of an individual to get something, while the mystic is interested in what they can give. To produce a spell to get a new set of clothes is magic, to make a spell to help a family who just lost all their belongings in a fire is mysticism. The actual process is similar but the intent is different. That being said there are very powerful people right now who use magic daily. Some do not even realize it, as their angry thoughts get manifested. The ancient Egyptian priest had to have a key understanding of the workings of magic, less for them to use but to notice if negative (black) aspects of the art were being used on them. At this point the training teaches not to respond to the aggressor but simply to become a mirror and reflect this nasty energy back to the sender. That is turning black magic

---

[150] Agrippa pp.142-44; Ficino p.110
[151] Copenhaver p.xxxviii

into white magic. Actually all advertising is a form of magic. They make us believe that if we have their product, some miraculous thing will happen (meet a woman if we drink their beer). However, we drink their beer and we meet the woman. They have witched us, altered our thought process. Yet we could do all this without spending their money on their product, but the advertising "magicians" don't tell us that.

The true magic of helping is all around us. Stones, trees or animals are all available for our help as long as we are trying to benefit others or the universe as a whole. There is no need for giant rituals or recited spells, for true magic is an act of the heart that is connected with spirit. Spirit finds a way, thus faith is the best magic. To try and manipulate beyond faith can lead to difficulty. If one is in need of 100 dollars one could ask spirit to find a positive way that what they need be brought into their life. To try and manipulate spirit and force it to provide $100 can certainly be done by what is called magic, but it could come as an insurance payout after an accident. In Egypt one would be taught less magic, and more how to live magically from the heart. The pure loving heart would connect directly to spirit, act as a conduit to let the energy flow, and through the intention of helping and giving they would learn to allow spirit to provide all that one needs to do so.

That being said all acts of God can be taken as magical, so can making love, or teaching a child how to ride a bike. Magic should be thought of as an activity that is infused with some special energy beyond the normal. To have sex is merely about personal pleasure, but to make love is magical. In Egypt the Neteru Heka has been translated as magic, but this is a Western background trying to understand deep Egyptian metaphysical notions. Heka in the Coffin Texts is a special energy that provides safety. He is connected with Atum and sometimes thought of as the brother to Maat, which would make him less magic in our sense of the word but more of the outer force that energizes us to live Maat (the right way). He was always thought of as benevolent, with the intent of the magician turning Heka's energy to be used for positive or negative as he is sometimes show holding crossed serpents. The word Hekau means words of power which are less of a magic spell as mantras for the deep meditation of the initiate.

Tombs and Mummies

So much time seemed to be spent by the Ancient Egyptians focusing on death that many believe them to be a scared or morbid culture. However the ancient Egyptian views of death did not develop out of some fantasy, but originated through the understanding of the universe and humanity's place in it. With this understanding they became a culture that used death in order to fully embrace life.

Birth was Mes (to bring forth). Death in Egypt was given the name mena, which was also the word for ships to arrive in port. Death was a return to our true source, and the day of death was called "moving day." In texts they are not actually referred to as dead, only that they are unhappy. Using the term death would give it power, as we would say someone has departed or passed away today. The owner of the Book of the Dead is not dead but called an Osiris, claiming they are already beyond the state of death. This sense of something happening beyond the state of death is mirrored in the Egyptian text Dialogue of a Man with His Soul. In it a man is pondering his soon coming death, "death is to me today like a sick man's recovery, like going outside after confinement…death is to me today like a well-trodden path, like a man's coming home from an expedition…death is to me today like a man's longing to see his home, having spent many years abroad."[152] Usually funerary texts relate less to our physical death in this world but our symbolic death while alive so we can reach the place of spirit and higher self.

Mastabas

71:Passageway between two mastabas made of large stone blocks, Giza Plateau

---

[152] Faulkner p.150; Clark p.262

In Pre-Dynastic times (the period before the supposed start of Egyptian history) the dead were buried in a crouched position in shallow pits in the desert. In these dry conditions the body mummified. Cold can also mummify as shown by mammoths in Siberia and the mummies of the Incas in Peru. In time the pit in the earth began to be replaced by a tomb called a mastaba, the Arabic word for bench. They were made of mud-brick with flat roofs and sloping sides, thus looked like a bench. From the mastaba, a narrow shaft ran straight down to a tomb where the person was buried with some personal equipment and possessions. At times, servants were buried beside as if to oversee the needs of the dead in the next world, so too were wooden boats that were symbolic of the voyage to the next world. One of my favourite things to do in Egypt is to walk the mastaba fields at Giza, you usually have them all alone with the tourist's attention taken by the pyramids.

Egyptologists claimed that the early mastabas were easy targets for tomb robbers who dug their own tunnels to steal the riches left inside. Egyptologists now say that Egyptians changed from Mastabas to stone pyramids. Pyramids were not tombs, and no original body has ever been found inside one. However they were related to the teachings of the afterlife. Besides, if a mastaba was easy for tomb robbers to find why build giant monuments to make them even easier to find? Egyptologists say that the pyramids did not stop the robberies so a new set of burials was performed in the hills opposite Luxor, the famed Valley of the Kings and Queens. False doors, blocked passages, detours and concealed entrances were all made to supposedly thwart tomb robbers. Even so, only King Tutankhamun's was found intact. The tombs at Luxor are decorated with great paintings and reliefs, and was the period of time when the text known as the Book of the Dead was buried with the deceased.

Mummification[153]

72:Late Kingdom mummy casket, Leiden Museum

The standard Egyptological story of mummification is that when burials no longer happened in the Egyptian sand, it was found the bodies did not mummify. So the Egyptian upper classes tried to find a process to simulate the experience. Originally a resin was used but that accomplished little. A new system of mummification was eventually perfected. It must be noted that the process was at one time not only a metaphor for the initiate, but also did provide a sense of everlasting life (as will be explained). In time though, as the priesthood became more corrupt, it became a money making venture for priests from frightened upper class Egyptians, similar to modern televangelists. In the Victorian era the mummy was thought to have healing powers and many were removed from Egypt, not to be shown and preserved in museums, but to be part of "mummy parties," where the wrappings were taken off and the former living being ground up for magic potions.

Even today no one is exactly sure of the Egyptian process but some of the key elements have become understood. To begin with the inner organs of the body had to be removed to allow the corpse to properly dry. The brain was removed through the nose either by scooping it out or stirring it until it became a runny liquid and poured out. Cuts to the body allowed the removal of the inner organs. The body was then filled with natron salt and spices for forty days. It finally would be wrapped in linens, rubbed with oils and "painted" with a water-proof finish. A second layering of bandages covered the body, with amulets and talismans placed between the bandages. The entire process lasted 70 days.[154] When the mummy was complete, a funeral could be held that involved ceremonies such as opening the mouth.

---

[153] for a good description of the full mummification process as is known today please read West *Key* pp.54-58

[154] Perl pp.34-35; West *Key* pp.54-58

The organs that were removed were not thrown away but placed in canopic jars with heads of the four sons of Horus. The organs related to the four lower chakras (bodies), that when overcome symbolized one no longer needing them. The sons of Horus and their protections were: Duamutef (stomach) Qebsennuf (intestines) Amsety (liver) Hapi (lungs). Interestingly the organs were removed but the brain was simply turned into a soupy mess and scooped out. The heart was left in tact, symbolically showing that it is the only organ that really mattered. The brain would be the least thought of organ for it was not even preserved. The 70 days of mummification equated to the length of time that the star Sothis (Sirius) was not visible in the sky. Her appearance equaled the rise of the Nile flood and symbolically to the resurrection of Osiris. The mummification process was to help make the deceased an Osiris.

Originally only Pharaohs and high priests were mummified, due to the great length of time and effort needed for the process. During the New Kingdom more mummifications occurred for higher ups in the government. As the New Kingdom was coming to an end, priests began to redefine a speeded up process that would allow those who had wealth to have themselves mummified as well. They used a tar-like substance called pitch. While they preserved, they broke easily. It was these figures that were called mummiya (meaning pitch or bitumen) by the Arabs. By the time of the Greeks even faster and poorer mummifications (the McDonald's of the mummy world) came into being for the new middle class Greeks and Romans. These mummies were so poorly done they rarely even survived a few hundred years before decomposing. Those who had no wealth were buried in the ground.

Purpose

Egyptologists explain that mummification was a requirement of the dead in order to experience everlasting life in the Duat. And quite likely this is what was believed, and sold, to the people of Egypt. But as it its more deeper understandings, no one is really quite sure. Some possibilities to explain the underlying significance of mummification are: Mummification could have come from the insight that after natural death, a non-preserved body will decay into its respective particles of physical matter (the dust of the earth). The astral body survives a bit longer, then it too decays into its astral particles. The body has returned to origin and source of its parts. If the parts of us that are beyond the physical are perfected, one can continue on in the next realm. If not they must return to the earth in a new physical body to continue living out their karma and experiences. We take very little memory of these other lives with us in this one, but our inner parts know of them and produce key experiences that are needed from the view of our fate and destiny. This is the idea behind the religion of Buddhism, who do not practice burial or mummification, but cremation. They believe that our soul is incarnating to have physical experiences and once we die those experiences have stopped. The soul cannot come back to earth and take a new physical body until each part of us in the last body has returned to the environment. This process may take 100-200 years for a body to fully disengage. When we form our new body, molecular parts of the old are drawn to the new which allow the continuation of our past lives (experiences) into the new one. While we may have different DNA and look different, we are made of exactly the same stuff as before. Cremation helps speed the process by making the return back to the earth almost immediately, as the Eastern teachings want to live out karma on earth as quickly as possible.

However, mummification is the opposite of cremation. If the body's particles are not allowed to break down one cannot return in a physical body. One must stay in the other realm. So why would that be? If it is said that Ancient Egypt followed the process of reincarnation, as most spiritual books comment, then they would also likely follow Buddhist ideas of getting the incarnations over as fast as possible. Some would say that the mummification was supposed to be for high priests and enlightened beings, to be sure that they did not return to a physical body on earth. The question becomes, if someone was so advanced, why would they need to return to the earth, or even care if they did?

Perhaps they found an additional realm of existence which can only be entered and experienced beyond this realm and the body must be mummified for that to happen, or perhaps it relates to the mystical teaching of the body as a prison of the soul. Gurdjieff claimed that we are in fact only in a body on earth because we are energetically stuck (like caught in a net) and if we can get out we will continue the journey we are supposed to be having. In an odd twist, there are some Buddhist mummies in Japan of monks who purposely mummified themselves while alive, using specific practices and diet. Today they still reside in the temple shrines (and like Ancient Egyptian temple statues), the mummified Buddhist monks are clothed and fed each day for it is felt their life energy continues to impart teaching wisdom to those who come to worship before them. It is possible that the original temple statues of Egypt were not "statues" but the mummified remains of the great beings of the distant past.

There is suggestion that Akhenaten did not mummify the dead during his reign. It could be the reason King Tut's burial was so lavish, as he was the first to be mummified after a time. Another theory that I pose in the third volume is that mummification may be originally linked to the concept of life on earth being a time loop, and mummification was a way of keeping consciousness through the loop (ala Phil Connors in Groundhog Day). In time priests not aware of this sold this as an everlasting life, but could have been a very detailed science for "watching the future," then returning in the next loop with more information on what was coming and the ramifications of choices from the last round of living.

Once the Europeans came to Egypt they began to disturb the mummies and even destroy them. It was claimed that those who did so would bring on a curse. If any of those above theories is correct, that a mummification was needed to avoid a return to a reincarnating earthly world, by destroying a mummy, the parts can decay which allows for a return. The curse may be the departed spirit angry that it has its previous body beginning to be broken down and may lash out to try and stop this process. Thus I remind everyone who travels to Egypt or works with mummies in any way to show them great respect. I also give an alternate idea as to what the Curse of Tutankhamun could be in volume 3 chapter on Akhenaten.

Ushabti

When mummification became the way for unscrupulous priests to make money, the developed a special figurine to make them even more. These figures are called ushabti. Originally figures called shawabti were buried with the deceased, each who had a specific function. Thus if in the next life one needed to haul water, a shawabti would do it for you. Since a great number of these figures would be needed, many for each job in that afterlife and that would cost a lot of money to have all the specialty figures made, a new figure called an ushabti (answerer) was made. Discussed in chapter 6 of the Book of the Dead, it was inscribed with a spell that whenever it was that called upon, and could perform any duty needed.[155]

That was a neat trick. Instead of telling someone they needed 1000 specialty figurines to be buried with, now they just needed 50 of these new all-purpose figurines who could do any job. And no surprise, New Kingdom tombs began to be filled with these ushabti. Of course this must have caused considerable confusion for the awakened in Egypt. Since life and death are both illusions, none of it would continue upon death, so the idea of needing figures to perform work that does not exist is foolish. How did such a concept get so popular? As the priesthood began to get more corrupt, along with mummification they brought the entire funerary concept of the Pharaohs to the upper classes. They were able to convince the average population that since they were not the king, when they reached the other world they were going to face challenges that involved physical labour. In other cases these priests would have taught their "clients" that the next life would be a joyous paradise where everything one had and did today would continue, as long as they paid them some royalties to make it so. This special world became known as the "Fields of Reeds or Rushes" where the deceased would live the good life with Osiris forever. The ushabti were brought with them so no work at all would have to be

---

done and they could just lounge on their fabulous estates. I'm sure you can see how this false teaching could have become welcomed so easily and quickly into Egypt. Just as a person today who hands over large sums of money to religion thinking their payment will somehow ensure them a safe afterlife, so too did the rich in Egypt not want to give up their place of importance so easily. It was and is, a big money grab so the recipient will be the one living the good life. It is about ego on both sides.

Valley of the Kings.

73:Tomb entrances in the Valley of the Kings

No trip to Egypt would be complete without a look at the tombs in the famous Valley of the Kings, where many Pharaohs of the New Kingdom were buried. Most make their way here as part of a bus tour, that rushes one into a few tombs, then back onto the bus to squeeze in as much in the day as possible. Sometimes I will take the local transport here (1 pound mini-bus from the Nile ferry dock) but usually my preferred method is to "walk like an Egyptian." From the workman's village Dier El Medina (near the main ticket office) is the Donkey Trail. It is the very trail that the tomb workmen (who lived at Medina) would walk to their jobs in constructing the tombs. Not only is it a beautiful walk (especially early or late in the day when it is not too hot) it gives great views of the Nile valley.

74:Old workman's path, known as the Donkey Trail, from Dier El Medina, travels along the cliff face and ends at Hatshepsut's Temple and the Valley of the Kings

Once into the Valley of the Kings, you will find that there are tomb entrances all around the hills in the area. They are labeled KV (King's Valley) and the number they were found by modern archaeologists. So KV1 was the first found, KV 55 much later. Each of the tombs is unique, though they have a few similarities. Each are cut deep into the rock cliffs, most are straight (the early ones often dug in an L shape) and they have several chambers. Generally each of the tombs from specific periods have the same layout and artwork. The walls and ceilings are painted with some of the famous texts mentioned earlier. If you want detail on each of the tombs for visiting purposes I recommend the excellent book *The Illustrated Guide to Luxor* by Kent Weeks, the Egyptologist who discovered KV 5 (Rameses II sons) in 1983. Here I will just mention a few key tombs. Plan your trip to the Valley of the Kings well. It can get hot during the day, and the tombs themselves can get stuffy, so bring plenty of water. Don't rush to see four tombs in an couple of hours, take your time. Examine the walls, ceiling. A good trick is to visit the most popular tombs at lunch time- when the watch tells people they are "supposed to eat." Many popular tombs will be surprisingly free between 12-1:30 PM.

75:Corridor to a Tomb in the Valley of the Kings.

KV 9 (Tomb of Rameses VI)

A favourite tomb of mine, because it was the wall texts presented in Alexander Piankoff's book that I used to try to unravel the Book of What is in the Duat (chapter 17). So for me arriving at this tomb for the first time to see the very texts face to face that I had been working on for over a year's time was quite a thrill. Is is one of the longest tombs in the valley, 380 feet long and 5490 square feet in total size. This tomb contains not only the Amduat text, but also complete versions of the Book of Gates, Caverns, Litany of Ra, and on the ceiling Book of Day and Night. It also has the first appearance of the Book of the Aker (Earth) in the burial chamber, which rarely appears in tombs. It is a great place to see complete versions of the main texts of Egypt in one place.

KV 34- Thutmosis III

This Pharaoh has so many interesting things about him, and his tomb should follow that pattern. It is a long climb up the cliff face on a rather wonky staircase to get you to the entrance. His burial chamber ends in a round oval (perhaps to be a cartouche or a scarab beetle) and on the walls are early versions of the Book of What is in the Duat. Instead of the complete painted figures found a few hundred years later in KV 9, here they are the "cartoon-like" stick figures- but just because they appear to be more simply drawn does not mean that it is a simple version- for the workmanship on these figures is incredible. KV 35 Amenhotep II is similar to this tomb.

KV 8- Merneptah, KV 14- Tausert

These two tombs I really enjoy. They are very long, have detailed wall and ceiling paintings, but because they are not the "popular" Pharaohs, you can have a bit more time to yourself in here when viewing the artwork. I like to use these tombs to examine the Book of Gates or Caverns overall, and then Use time in KV 9 to examine a specific detail of the texts.

KV 17- Seti 1

Perhaps the most amazing in the Valley, however due to poor archaeological techniques on discovery, this perfectly preserved tomb repeatedly flooded, damaging the paintings. It is now closed to the public. The photographs, paintings and drawings from the tomb help to provide deeper detail and understanding of the tomb texts that appear here in the Valley of the Kings. It was the first tomb in the valley to every part of every wall covered with a text.

KV 57- Horemheb

This is an interesting tomb for a couple of reasons. It is the first tomb to have been made after the Akhenaten era was over, and was the first tomb decorated in painted raised relief rather than on a flat plastered surface. You might say that it was as if the artists were wanting to make a statement that the tombs being made now were different from what had gone in the past, marking a new era perhaps on Egypt. Following Horemheb was the first of the Ramses rulers- Ramses I buried in KV 16, whose walls look similar to this tomb.

KV 62- Tutankhamun

Ok I have to admit, I have been to the Valley of the Kings about 10 times and not once have I entered into this tomb. Why? It could be that even though its historical significance, it is actually a very small tomb with only a few wall paintings, and is besieged with line after line of tourists. Maybe it is because it is the only tomb in the valley that there is an extra charge to go and see it? Or maybe when you read my speculations on Tutankhamun in volume 3, there was a part of me that knew better than to enter his tomb, that it might be the very one in the valley NOT to go in. I leave it for you to decide.

Valley of the Queens

Walking the other direction from Dier El Medina, one will reach the Valley of the Queens. Again walking is a favourable method, for half way is a couple of small hidden temple's for Ptah and Meretseger carved into the rock face- and it is a nice walking break to sit in these temples- usually alone- meditate and prepare for the next part of your journey.

The Valley of the Queens was known in ancient times as the "Place of Beauty or Place of Harmony," and it was here that Royal wives and children were buried. Only a few tombs are now open to been seen here, and all from the period of Rameses III, QV 44 Khaemwaset, QV Amenherkhepshef and are worth the look at difference between the royal tombs in VOK and Noble's tombs at Gurna. The most famous tomb in the Valley of the Queens QV 66 Nefertari (principle wife of Rameses the Great) and was perhaps the jewel of the entire West Bank for visits, but like Seti I has had to be closed to the public due to concerns for the protection of the tomb (moisture from tourists visiting causing the plater to crack off the walls). The Noble tomb of TT 96 Sennefer to me gives a tiny taste of a look at Nefertari's tomb, which makes another reason to visit it.

Tombs of the Nobles

76:TT 96 Sennefer. Notice the grapes on the ceiling above.

Between the Valley of the Kings and the Valley of the Queens lies some 2-3,000 tombs over a 500 year period for various nobles the ran the kingdom for the Pharaoh. Most of these were found around the old city of Gurna (now demolished) and some near the workman's city of Dier El Medina. These are often not on short tours to Luxor, guides focusing time elsewhere, but these tombs should be visited for the artistry of the wall paintings and carvings, and for the very different and unique scenes found here not found at the royal tomb burials. I will mention a few of the tombs to make sure to be seen when on the West Bank.

TT 100- Rekhmire. This was the Vizier (Pharaoh's representative much like a Prime Minister) of Upper Egypt during much of the reign of the famous Thutmosis III. A priest of Amun, Rekhmire was claimed in this tomb that "there was nothing of which he was ignorant of, in heaven or earth, or in any quarter of the underworld." Almost every wall of the 3200 square feet of this tomb is painted, and mostly depict symbolic scenes of daily life and the duties of the Vizier. One scene has him presented with gifts from far off lands: monkeys, giraffes, ostrich, cheetah and such. TT 96 is the tomb of Sennefer, mayor of Thebes. This tomb has suburb paintings on the walls and columns (similar to those found in the Valley of the Queens). What is most famous in this tomb is the ceiling, which the tomb architect used to his advantage. The ceiling was unable to be plastered and smoothed, so it was left rough, and on it was placed paintings of a carpet (which due to the roof appears to be blowing in the wind) and grape vines (which appear to be 3-dimensional). A trip to this small tomb is a must just for the ceiling alone. Notice the incredible number of lotus flowers that apppear in all the reliefs of Sennefer and his wife.

TT 55 Ramose is a unique tomb not to be passed by. While it does have one painted wall, that includes the famous wailing women- the rest of the walls are carved with raised reliefs. The detail in the braids of the hair for example, is a thing of beauty when realizing how hard raising reliefs is as opposed to sinking them into stone. Another thing that makes this tomb very special is the fact that there are no scenes of daily life here, only Ramose's funeral and his relationship with the Pharaoh Amenhotep IV (later to become Akhenaten). Nothing that surrounds Akhenaten is by the book, even here where on a far wall he and his wife Nefertiti are depicted, in what can be said as the beginning of the Amarna style of art. But a bit further down is a more standard depiction of the couple including the aten disk with hand-ended rays reaching out to the ground. In a sense this wall of the tomb is showing a bit of the evolution of art at the time the Heretic Pharaoh. The layout of the tomb appears as though Ramose died early in his time with Amenhotep/Akhenaten, as much of the tomb wall painting is unfinished, and there is no mention of a child succeeding him. Again it is quite possible that when Akhenaten was ready to move the capital to his new city of Tell-El-Amarna, Ramose might not have wanted to go, or was "eliminated," hence the need to have him buried and put away quickly. Another possibility that came from looking at this tomb was that Ramose could be the Biblical Moses. The name Moses is a corruption of the Egyptian word Mose meaning "born of" in Ramose's case, born of Ra or son of Ra, That Ramose seems to have disappeared after Akhenaten moved the capital of Egypt from Thebes to Tell-El Amarna gives another possibility that Ramose might have had to leave Egypt, not wanted in the new rulers political and religious ideology. Anything is possible during the reign this period of history.

The Ramose tomb is also memorable for me, on my first trip to Egypt I went to this tomb with an Australian couple that I had recently met in Luxor. As we were peering down the long shaft in the forecort we thought against what seemed to be a long walk down into the darkness...when the husband Dave, dropped his camera and we heard it roll down and down until we could hear it roll no more. We now had to walk down to get the camera. It was a challenging walk, even with 2 flashlights. We wound up down in the underground chamber, a small 4-pillared room with a very odd cylindrical shape in the middle. We turned off our flashlights for effect, and stood in the incredible spooky complete darkness for a few minutes getting another energetic taste of Egypt. We then walked back up only to have the tomb guardians staring at us, wondering what crazy people were dumb enough to walk down the dangerous shaft. In case you were wondering, the camera turned out fine.

77:Daily life from TT69 Menna

Other very good Noble tombs to check out IS TT 69 Menna, What makes this tomb unique was not just the quality of the artists here, but what they drew. Each person and animal is given individualization, which is very rare in Egyptian art. It is possible that every person drawn on the wall was modeled on someone who was living at the time. As well he has added humourus and odd touches not found in tombs- a man falling off one of the boats, strange looks on some of the men in the fields. The famous wall of the fishing scene is also memorable for the amazing detail given the fish and birds, which give very lifelike examples of the animals of the time. And the daughters of Menna are also given a deep individualization not normally seen in art. I believe that this is more than just the "whim" of the artist, but may perhaps have been a suggestion of Menna himself. Imitation is often a form of flattery so this might also be the people who worked for him wanting to share his humour and how he treated them as "individuals" not as numbers on a clock like other Egyptian high court members might have.

Dier el Medina Tombs

78:Field of Rushes in the Tomb of Sennedjem at Dier el Medina.

`Generally only three tombs are open for a visit here, but they are very well preserved. These were tombs for special workmen and craftsmen of the valley, as opposed to the private tombs of the officials just mentioned. Unlike the great religious texts of the Valley of the Kings, or the scenes of daily life and funeral processions in the Nobles Tombs, there here mostly show lovely pained scenes of the Book of the Dead, some of which appeared in the tombs they worked on in the VOK. What is interesting that while they "borrowed" scenes from the Book of the Dead here, they did not borrow texts such as the Book of Gates, which showed that somehow the Book of the Dead was viewed as something more common for the average person. The colours on the walls are terrific, as is the attention to detail in the work. These tombs were entered by a small forecort, and then led to a small pyramid. These tombs were for an entire family, and not for just one individual, and several people could be found buried in each one.

TT 1 is the tomb of Sennedjem. Like most tombs here you come to a rounded ceiling in a small rectangular room. The back wall has a famous depiction of the Field of Rushes, done perhaps with the most detail in New Kingdom Egypt, while chapter 1 is mostly featured on the walls. The ceiling shows religious activities with the Neteru. In the entrance way can be found Atum as the cat, cutting the head off the serpent Apop. TT3 is the tomb of Peshedu. Because it is 150 feet up the hill it is less visited, as guides don't want to spend the extra time to show tourists, so this is a chance to have more alone time here. This tomb is most known of the reliefs of Peshedu kneeling beneath a palm tree beside a pond. Notice how the palm tree is made in great detail (the palm was symbolic for years and time, so there is much more being presented here). The other open tomb here is 359 Inherkhau, most known for its ceiling designs of geometric shapes, "x o" patterns, and bull's heads in a way that resembles many of the things painted by the Minoans on Crete.

Mysteries of the Mummy

The true teachings of the mummy had nothing really to do with death, but were symbolic instructions and exercises to teach the initiate how to connect with their higher self (God). Sheti is the Egyptian word that means to lead a spiritual life. This word's root is sheta, which means hidden, mystery, and the upper nasal passage (where the third eye that leads to the mysteries is located). Shetat or Shesheta are secret rituals. Thus sheti means to lead a spiritual life by going into the hidden mystery and perform the sacred teachings. A mummy in Egypt was called a Shet-t, connecting it to the initiate's work on the spiritual life. The mummy originally was not something that is worked on when dead, but when alive. The mummy in the coffin is actually symbolic of our wrapped up higher self that is kept locked inside our own coffin (the mind). The bandages of the mummy were always equated with Set, for it is our own conscious mind that creates the illusions and desires of the ego. To find our true self we must open the coffin, and unwrap our mind to find the heart within. This is the true teaching that the mummy is attempting to explain.

Duat

79:Seated Osiris with Anubis and Horus behind, Valley of the Kings KV 57

The Duat is a very special place in the understandings of the after death state, for it is where the deceased is said to live with Osiris who circles the region. The Duat is usually translated as the underworld, but is more of an inner world for it exists within the body of Nut. The sun when swallowed travels the Duat inside of Nut each night before being reborn. Three Old Kingdom texts: Book of What is in the Duat, Book of Caverns, and the Book of Gates describes this region. Of course the Duat is really inside each of us, and it cannot be reached in a physical way but from a place of higher consciousness. The Duat was also located in the sky near or in the constellation of Orion.

The sun gets reborn from the Duat as Khepera, showing that the inner Duat must be a place of darkness where one can reach the transformative light. The Duat was believed to be a place where great tests, challenges and monsters waited for us. Passing all of them successfully would lead us to come face to face with Osiris on the throne. To the Egyptians the Duat was the place where our innermost us, God, could be found. It was claimed to be made up of seven sections, called mansions and relate to the seven cows of Hathor (thus to our seven chakras). Just as each of these mansions must be passed to reach Osiris, so to do we have to clean and purify our seven chakras to reach the true realm of the inner, which is the Duat. At each part a guard awaits who needs specific questions answered by us. This symbolizes our wisdom that we have gained, not only from texts but also form our existence that can be taken into states of altered consciousness.[156]

The exact spot where Osiris can be found within the Duat is called Sekhet-Aaru or Amentet. It is compared to a place that is beyond time and space, has no thought, and no birth or death. It is reached through passing the seven arits (halls) and Chapter 125 of the Book of the Dead says, "I have drawn myself to the place where the cedar tree does not exist, where the acacia tree

---

[156] Ashby *Ausarian* p.145

does not put forth shoots, and where the ground neither produces grass nor herbs." The lack of plants refers to a place that is so still and unchanging that nothing grows. There cannot be material things for they are subject to birth and death. The only way to reach this place of no motion is to take our minds to the place of no motion. When one can reach this part, they are with Osiris, lord of the black. One has reached the state of nothing or the void. This is the place that is beyond the world entirely, back to the oneness that is in fact everything. To reach this true state of being we must avoid the monsters (the parts of our mind that lead us away from this state) and connect with the Neteru that are found (the energies that help bring us to this state).[157] Thus the Duat can never actually be located for it only exists within each of us, at our true state of being. This is the place that meditation, alchemy or other transformative discipline is attempting us to reach.

---

[157] Ashby *Ausarian* pp.146-47

THE POWER OF THEN

Volume 2: Hermetic Knowledge

"The universe is a giant mystery with no limits. To fall prey to the axiom 'I believe only what I see' is the dumbest stand one can possibly take."
Carlos Castaneda

CHAPTER 11
HERMETICISM

80: Medici Villa-Careggi near Florence Italy, site of Ficino's Platonic Academy

Corpus Hermeticum

"At first glance there appears to be scant remains of what was once an abundant literature. But since it was mostly kept secret, it is amazing that so much has been preserved. Yet always remember that what we have is but a mere fraction of the original lot." GRS Mead[158]

What is called Hermeticism is a teaching or core of study that has its roots in the Greek text *Corpus Hermeticum*. This book was supposedly written by the Greek god Hermes. The text itself is claimed to be a Greek translation of

---

[158] Mead vol 1 p.4

the Ancient Egyptian Books of Thoth. The literature, all but destroyed by the Catholic Church in the 3rd and 4th century (attempting to hide the true Christian origins), resurfaced in Europe in the 15th century to spawn the Renaissance. It was the Hermetic teachings that inspired: Blake, Goethe, Tolstoy, Dostoevsky, Mann, Yates, Browning, Leonardo, Shakespeare, Wordsworth, Da Vinci, Copernicus, Bacon, Kepler and Isaac Newton. While in fact all religions are Hermetic, meaning written in a specific form of symbolic code, this can only be understood by putting the teachings into practice. Today the word Hermetica usually refers to a specific group of books: 18 books of the Corpus Hermeticum, the Asclepius, The Stobaeus (a number of fragments written by John of Stobai), the Kyballion, and various other fragments.

One of the best Hermetic explanations for modern seekers comes from a group known as the Gnostics. Originally their original texts were lost to us (burned by the Catholic hierarchy opposed to the Gnostic symbolic understanding). In fact, for over 2000 years the only scholarly reference to the Gnostics was from church leaders who had written letters in opposition to them. That was until 1945 when a huge cache of hidden scrolls were found in Nag Hammadi, Egypt. Most believe they are an early Christian group based on certain translations, but that is far from the truth. There are the opposite of modern religion, more like deep Zen or Advaita. The main Gnostic teaching is that there is only one, an Absolute Reality. That Absolute split and got caught into matter where an external force- they called archons, created an artificial simulated reality (called Hal) and implanted a mind (they called a virus) to keep humans trapped. Their teachings claimed to be the way out of this trap, back to the original nature.

When the Hermetic texts were banned and those who taught the direct teachings of enlightenment were run out of the Christian world, they found a home in the Islamic Hermetic city of Haran. Not only was the Corpus Hermeticum kept alive here, but so too was written the famed book Picatrix. Muslim Spain also became a holder of the ancient wisdom, with the Cordoba Library having some 400,000 books. In the 8th century many European nobles, with no books available to the masses (for even the Bible was forbidden to be read) pilgrimaged to Spain for books and wisdom. In the east, the city of Constantinople kept the Hermetic and Gnostic teachings alive. As well Buddhist, Taoist and Hindu teachings were beginning to make inroads into the Middle East.

In the 15th century scholars from the Christian east came to Italy where they arrived at Florence. They began teaching the words of Plato and Hermes there. Cosimo D'Medici was immediately impressed and set up a new Platonic academy at Florence, and led to the birth of the Renaissance in Europe. Academy master, Marsiglio Ficino, made the first Latin translation of the

Corpus Hermeticum in 1548. Of course I am simplifying all this, for those who wish more detail I suggest the book *Elixir and the Stone* by Michael Baigent.

The new academy in Florence, and its offshoots that were spreading across Europe, quickly became a real problem for the Catholic Church. The Bible could only be printed in Latin, but even if you could read Latin you were forbidden to read it anyway. Now all of sudden thanks to the translations of the Hermetic texts and the printing press, these ancient works were available in French, English, Spanish etc. People began to take to the teachings that told of speaking directly to God without the need of the Church, which had become a corrupt bully.

The original Gnostic teachers has claimed that the Hermetic literature was the background of Christianity, but the Church needed to step in hard to stop all this "wisdom." They found two well respected opposers. One was Rene Descartes (he of I think therefore I am, thus a man trapped in his mind) and Isaac Causabon. They claimed in 1614 that the Hermetic books were written in the 2-3rd century in Alexandria, thus had no Egyptian wisdom, and more importantly were written long after Christ, thus they were just a "plagiarism" of Jesus' true teachings. Causabon was held in great respect in many European circles, and his argument was enough to halt the spread of Hermetic thought, openly at least. It still continued in secret societies that formed to keep teaching the Hermetic wisdom.

By the 19th century with new world religious texts, the similarity between Buddhist, Taoist, Zen and Hindu philosophy was more than co-incidence. Once the Egyptian hieroglyphs were translated, many too began to see the similarity between Egypt and the Hermetica. A famous text appeared during the Middle Ages called the Kyballion, and relates what are known as the 7 Hermetic Principles. The first is that "All is Mind," or everything is just the mind or thought of God. Thus there is no difference between anything in creation for each is just a thought of God's mind. The second principle is "as above, so below," the idea of mirrors and of holograms (the part containing the whole).

The third principle is the "Everything vibrates" or makes a sound. The fourth is "everything has polarity," the fifth "everything has gender," which is different than polarity. The sixth is "everything has rhythm," while the seventh is "cause and effect," or the ideas of karma. I will explore some of these topics in the upcoming chapters, yet what I find most interesting is that the Hermeticists are teaching us these principles to tell us that this is how this reality works. Yet if you read closely, they are also telling you that these rules only apply to this reality, go beyond and these rules don't apply. Thus everytime we can understand a principle, then go beyond it, we in effect break the hold of this illusion of reality.

The Hermetic process, which became key to the teachings of alchemy, was said to occur in three stages, and each of these stages was symbolized by a particular colour. The first stage was the black and was called Nigredo or Calcination. The second stage was white and was called Solutio or Albedo. The final stage was red and was called Rubedo, though at times a fourth colour (yellow called Citrinius) was sometimes included. Each stage required the student to work on specific aspects of themselves, purify and transform their entire being until they could shine with the gold of the astral light. It is then they were ready for the final stage, the Gnosis (silent knowledge) of Tehuti/Hermes. Within the three main stages are seven component stages that are the similar to the Oriental teachings of transformation through the seven chakras. (A more detailed description of the alchemic process can be found in the appendix).

The main focus of the Hermetic work, as it is with all of paths of wisdom, is to teach that the conscious mind and our personal self-grasping must be systematically destroyed. They teach what keeps us from our true divinity, the magical nature of humanity, is our own conscious mind. Our soul has a mind (our heart) but something else has provided us with another. This mind is never questioned, but the Hermetic work actually involves the questioning of our mind's importance, allowing the exercises and purification work to reach our hearts.

Myth of Hermes

"Mythology is an interior road map of experience, drawn by people who have traveled it." -Bill Moyers-

It becomes somewhat of a detective mission to decipher the ancient Hermetic codes left in the texts, temples and tombs in order to uncover exactly what the ancient world wanted to pass on. This volume will focus on the serpent Apop, and how this serpent force has managed to subliminally control reality through the egoic mind. The good news is that the old texts and myths reveal how Ra (inner light or consciousness) can overcome this force of Apop, and allow all of creation to walk into a natural way of being and living.

All myths are shrouded in symbol- pointing to something that is best not said openly. An invitation for the reader to "come look for themselves." Passed on for countless generations, this information was so potential damning to controlling organization that the writings had to be placed in secret code. Like any code they must be "code broken" to be understood and used. Without knowledge of symbolic language, it will be missed. I thought there was no better beginning to this volume than to offer up the Greek legend of Hermes, which came to Greece via Egypt. I will italicize key symbolic words in the legend. By the end of reading this book you will be able to return to this myth and perhaps code break it yourself to see that this is no mythological tale but in fact describes the process of awakening. My symbolic code break will appear in Appendix 5.

The Legend of Hermes as it appeared in Greek myth:

Hermes was born in a *cave* on *Mount Cyllene* in *Arcadia*. Zeus had impregnated *Maia* in the dead of *night* while all the other gods *slept*. When *dawn* broke Hermes was amazingly *born*. Maia wrapped him in *swaddling bands*, then she fell back to *sleep*. Hermes however, *squirmed free* and ran off to Thessaly. There his *brother* Apollo grazed *cattle*. Hermes *stole* a number of the heard and drove them back to Greece. He kept them in a small *grotto* near the city of Pylos, then *covered his tracks*.

Before returning to the cave, he killed a *tortoise* and removed the entrails, using the intestines of a cow stolen from Apollo and the hollow tortoise shell he made the first *lyre*. When he returned to the cave, he *wrapped himself back* in the swaddling clothes. Apollo finally realized that he had been robbed and protested to Maia that it was Hermes, but she saw him sleeping in his bands that she could not believe it was him. All-powerful Zeus however had been watching the whole thing and acknowledged the theft and that Hermes should return the stolen cattle. An agreement was reached, but while it was happening, Hermes played his lyre and the *music enchanted* Apollo, and he offered to let Hermes keep the cattle in exchange for the lyre. Apollo later became the *grandmaster* of the instrument.

Hermes while *watching over his heard* also invented the pan-pipe and the flute. Apollo also wanted these instruments, so Hermes bartered with him and received a *golden wand* which became his famous staff (in some stories it is Zeus who gives him the golden wand.) Later Hermes liberated Io from Hera's servant the hundred-headed *giant* Argus. Hermes played his flute and the *giant slept*, so Hermes *cut off the giant's head* and released Io. Hera was so taken by her former giant servant that she placed his hundred eyes and put them on a *peacock's tail*.

CHAPTER 12
NUMBER/GEOMETRY

81:Pacioli teaching sacred geometry, 1495 painting

Mathematics

"Number is within all things." Pythagoras

"Numbers are the highest degree of knowledge. It is knowledge itself..." Plato[159]

The great mystical mathematical school of Pythagoras claimed that "All is number," and that every aspect of knowledge can be understood through number. In our modern world we see numbers, like everything else, as fixed concepts. The ancients used number to understand God, the creation,

---

[159] Schneider- both quotes

manifestation, and the physical laws within the manifestation. Science spends its time learning how; the ancients spent their time learning why. Everything in the manifested universe is vibrating energy. The faster the vibration, the higher state of the matter (gas vibrates higher than water). Vibration is but a sound, a sound can be reduced to a number, and number can be expressed through geometry. Today chemists understand that every chemical substance in the known universe is governed by a specific set of whole numbers, called the atomic number. This number corresponds to the number of protons and electrons that surround the nucleus of their given atoms. Hydrogen has a number of 1 for having one electron in orbit, while Helium has two. Number helps to understand the fixed world, while geometry is the "bridge between the one and the many," or how the Oneness of God became the many of the material world. In the ancient world numbers were sacred.

The word mathematics originated with the Pythagorean Mysteries. Students of the mysteries who studied number and science and how it related to self-knowing were called mathematekoi "those who studied all." The word has since become associated with just the learning of numbers. Students taught math today are domesticated how to memorize a skill, then use it on problems where there is only one right answer. Teachers test us with a technique called 'drill and kill.'[160] The spiritual teaching of number would help us understand the ideas of love, how trees grow, why hair curls, and how one hears. The ancients were less concerned with the right answer, but how one could use number and its varying possibilities to understand the possibility of the universe. To know 2+3 is 5 was less important than to understand how 2+3 could equal growth. The two greatest societies to understand this power of sacred number were the Egyptians and the Maya. The great Greek philosophers such as Pythagoras and Plato were both trained in Egypt. This ancient understanding of number appears in the Jewish Cabbala and Hermeticism. To expand beyond this introduction I highly recommend reading the well-written *A Beginner's Guide to Constructing the Universe* by Michael Schneider, and the more difficult to read *Sacred Geometry* by Robert Lawler.

Number in Egypt

"Egyptians understood that the creation of the universe allowed the entire system to begin, a system of number, sound, harmony and frequency. They built a whole civilization to pay homage to it." John Anthony West[161]

---

[160] Schneider p.xvii
[161] West *Serpent* p.68

82:Part of Rhind Mathematical Papyrus, British Museum

It is still believed that mathematical knowledge from precession to pi to the golden section were all 'discovered' by the Greeks. Thankfully today it is proven that all of these mathematical formula were understood and used by the Egyptians thousands of years earlier. They were placed within the layout of every temple or piece of artwork. The Egyptians understood that specific numeric proportions or layouts led to more beautiful or illuminating finished products. The specific number system or use of equations such a pi and phi led to pieces that vibrated with powerful energies that would lead those who viewed, heard or experienced them to higher states of consciousness.

There are surviving mathematical papyrus that were teaching manuals for students. The famed Rhind Mathematical Papyrus promises "rules for inquiring into nature and for knowing all that exists, every mystery, every secret." This papyrus was a set of exercises for students along with their solutions, thus similar to a modern high school math textbook. When originally deciphered, answers to problems did not match modern answers and errors were found that could not be accounted for by copying. From these "mistakes" modern scholars claim the Egyptians did not have a great understanding of mathematics. However this was the technique of teaching. A teacher today teaches that 1+1 is 2 because they say so. The ancient method was to allow the student to come to these discoveries themselves, with the teacher there to guide them along the way. The study of mathematics was for students a matter of individual discovery of not just how numbers behave, but why. Schwaller de Lubicz spent further time with the papyrus and concluded that many of the answers described as wrong could not be solved using modern math techniques. To the Egyptians learning how the numbers related to each other and the universe was just as important as learning basic rules. Often it seems the basic rules (2x5=10) were never provided, but the student spent time solving problems that would lead them to discover the rule on their own.[162]

In many cases steps have been omitted from the calculations, steps that we would perform today on calculators. It is possible that this was done through the art of doubling. Multiplying 433 x 359 is very hard in one's head. Yet with the process of doubling, which is how modern calculators function, very difficult answers could be found rather easily. "The most ancient system of calculation in the world is also the most modern." Doubling would also help to remind the student of the laws of creation, how the many arises out of the one, and how cells in our body grow. Scholars claim that the Egyptians did not know a 3-4-5 right-angled triangle, which provided the value of pi, because the calculation for the hypotenuse does not appear in the papyrus. However, the value of pi (3.14) appears all over Egypt. It appears in tomb artwork of Rameses VI and Tutankhamun, as an outstretched king and the snake. All Egyptian doorways were laid out to show pi. In fact the Greek symbol for pi has the same look as the Egyptian doorways.[163] Pi is also seen throughout the Great Pyramid, from its height to base ratio to specific measures inside the chambers and passageways. Egyptologists have always claimed that all of this is a coincidence, but the Egyptians created this great monument and needed the energy that only a perfectly constructed "piece of pi" can bring.

The Leyden Papyrus is a papyrus text of stanzas that are can be used to help Ra defeat the serpent Apop. Each line is designed according to the teachings of sacred number. The 27 stanzas are not numbered 1-27, but from 1-9 then 10-90 and 100-900. Each stanza of a group (3, 30, 300) all discuss elements pertaining to the main whole number, in this case three. This symbolism in this papyrus helps to outline the great depth of knowledge that the Egyptians had when it came to aspects of the sacred in the universe.[164]

Space/Time

A member of the Egyptian priesthood understood the physical world more the way a shaman or mystic understands it. Today people believe that the world we interact with daily is the only world, while shamans see existence as an onion, one world that overlaps with several others. Thus what is perceived as this world must be viewed in a different way. The word space has come to mean something that is between two objects. If there were no objects, there could be no space. Space is defined as the volume between two cars, two walls, two straight lines etc. A straight line on a page will produce no space, because

---

[162] West *Serpent* pp.64, 106,107
[163] West *Serpent* pp. 19, 39, 113; Lamy 9; Tompkins p. 195
[164] Lamy pp. 13-14, 78-79; West *Key* p.239

the line itself is not thought of as space. The ancients understood there also must be space inside things and not just between them. Time was also viewed differently. Today time is believed to be linear, a straight line on which events can be plotted. This is really done in order to differentiate one event from another, thus is related to space. Space is the distance between objects, while time is the distance on a line between two events. Without events there can be no time. Just as ancients saw space as also having an inner quality, they perceived time not as a straight line but circular. There was no past or future just a spot on an endless circle.[165]

All modern time needs an event. The time 1:45 is not important to us, only when we have a meeting scheduled then is it. 5:00 is really not much different than 5:15 except the importance of an event, the end of work, that we place on that fixed time. Without this concept we would view time in terms of sunrise (new day), noon (mid day) and sunset (end of day). We wouldn't go see Robert at 1:45 but sometime during the day. We would be in less of a rush, and Robert would only know that we are coming and would go about his business until we arrived. This idea of a fixed specific concept has led to the rigid slavery of our lives, where a clock dictates how we should think (eat food at 12), act (rush because we are late) etc. Today is now worse as our circular clock hands that at least reminded us of the movement of the sun in the sky has been replaced with a blinking light. The further away our link with nature, the less we will be able to notice the omens that have been staged just for us. To the Egyptian time was more in the now, in our feelings and in spending the moment as best suits us.

Time is known to be relative, thus influenced by the perception of that who is experiencing time. A wait at the dentist's seems longer than when engaged in a fun activity of the same length. Thus time is an illusion, but when focused on this world it is real. What we call time is only a need of the human mind to explain the way events seem to happen in some sequence. "In fact what we experience is not the passage of time, but the motion of the Neteru (energies) as they (we) interact with each other." The Egyptian text the *Instruction of Mer-Ka-Ra* has a father hope his son will live a life of Maat (harmony) because on death those that judge him, "consider a life as but an hour…life in the other world is eternal, but he who arrives without sin will walk freely as do the masters of eternity."[166]

That being said, timekeeping was important for the priests of the temples who needed an accurate form of time, less to mark their lives but more to record the movement of the stars and keep accurate calendars. They would find that by studying numbers, the sky, and themselves, there was in fact no difference. The Ancient Hindus learned from the Egyptians that the average

---

[165] Naydler pp. 12-13, 59
[166] Ashby *Matter* pp. 56-58

breath took four seconds, which they called a prana. With this system they were able to relate human breath to the rotation of the earth on one degree of its axis to be 360 prana (there's that number again) or 24 minutes.[167]

Sacred Geometry

"Geometry existed before the creation." Plato
"Let none ignorant of geometry enter here." Sign at front of Platonic Academy of Ficino [168]

When one is using geometry tools and number they are thought of as a smaller version of the divine creator. Their tools: the compass, straight edge, ruler and pencil should be treated with respect for every geometric construction is in some way mirroring creation. The compass point was seen as the eye of God, while the legs were the rays of light that shone outward from the All. God was sometimes referred to in mystical Christianity as the "Great Geometer," and was depicted holding the compass. Using a ruler creates a line between two points, which symbolize a line of energy and motion. As each line is drawn Egyptians were urged to think symbolically of energy lines on the earth and in the body.

The actual numbers will now be presented. The mystical understanding of these numbers, and their geometric associations of how these numbers create and interact will be elementary examined. Again for further detail please read the books on sacred number and geometry discussed earlier. Much of the information in this chapter comes from the excellent book *Beginner's Guide to Constructing The Universe* by Michael Schneider.

0

83:Maya numeral system, notice the shell for 0, thus zero was not nothing-

Today we see zero as nothing, but the ancients understood the concept of "nothing but nothing." This means that in fact at creation all that exists is nothing, and with nothing you have everything. Thus to the Maya zero never marked nothing, but existed as a space showing that one thing was ending and another was going to begin. Zero was

---

[167] Schneider pg 69, p.210
[168] Schneider p.357

showing there was nothing now, but there would be in the future. It also rests on the concept of energy cannot be created or destroyed, thus it is impossible to actually have no energy for it is always here.

1

"You can not conceive the many without the One." Plato
"For those who are awake, the cosmos is One." Heraclitus[169]

84:Christian image depicting God as the sacred geometer of all, Bible Moralisee

The discovery of number begins with the number one and the circle. Every circle is thought of to be identical, only differing in size. Just as every manifested form originated from the All, geometrically all numbers and shapes arise from the circle. The number one creates all other numbers as shown in the equation $111111111 \times 111111111 = 12345678987654321$. A circle begins from a mysterious center, symbolized as a dot or point of the compass. It moves outward to an infinite number of points that surround it. The radius and circumference of a circle is known by the value pi, which is endless. The creation of a circle from a compass is thought of as creating a space of light and power in all directions. The dot is likened to the male part while the outer circle is the feminine part. Religious art from the Tibetan Wheel of Life to Christian Paintings of God holding a circular cosmos relate the circle to the All. The symbol of a circle with a dot in the middle was the Egyptian, Chinese and Maya glyphs for Light. Our word universe comes from the Latin word for 'one turn,' meaning one turn of the compass to create a circle. Interestingly the circle encloses the most space with the smallest perimeter. Thus the best protection with the least material (least weight to carry) is a round shield. A round pizza will hold more toppings and a plate is round because its shape provides the most space for food.

2

"Everything that originated from the tree of knowledge carries in it duality." Zohar

---

[169] Gold p.83

"How much different between yes and no? What difference between good and bad?" Tao Te Ching

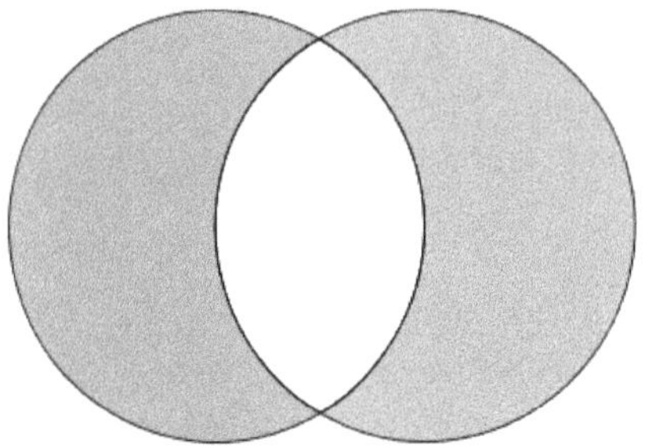

85:The Vesica Pisces

If the circle is the All there becomes a problem for unity multiplied by unity is still unity, 1x1x1x1=1. For one to become two, it need to add to itself, 1+1=2. For the one to become the many it needs a mirror, another circle identical to itself. Our world must have a mirror or shadow world or nothing in it could be created. These two circles overlap to form what is called a Vesica Pisces, which creates a fish-looking part between the two. To make the world of two, a straight line is drawn between the point of one circle and the next. This creation of the second circle was depicted in the ancient myths by the Creator saying the Word (Logos) which allowed for creation to happen. The fish symbol was seen as the womb or birthplace for the other numbers.[170] The shape was also the symbol of Christianity in its origin, for the religion started in the astrological age of Pisces. Christianity may be concealing that its teachings are really about female (fish, womb) and not male energy. The reason a male figure is used as the "main person of myth" was to show that the teachings are feminine but one must use masculine energy to act them out.

The number two is duality or polarity. Unity had to have the opposite of itself created: male-female, up-down, left-right, good-evil, true-false. Without one part of the polarity there cannot be the other. There can be no true unless there is also a polar line of false. We could then plot a value of true-false somewhere along this line in degrees. Anything we think we are, or the universe is, can just be plotted on a straight line of two extremes. The ancients attempted to express this with the Asian yin/yang, Maya Hunab Ku, or Horus and Set in Egypt. To be one we must have the opposite. If we are female, we also have male energy in us. Our chore is to walk the middle ground, without any extreme. This will reconcile the opposite in us. Hermeticists teach to sway less to one extreme, for we can then not sway as far to the other.

The illusion of this world is of duality. Our world is not the way our conscious mind makes us think of it: in dual opposites. All there can be is either unity (All) or numbers beyond two (many). As long as there are two polar opposites, nothing can be created. A male and female can be in a room but cannot create a baby or even an argument, for a positive and negative charge alone do not produce a current. A plaintiff and a defendant do not create a

---

[170] Schneider p.22, Schwaller *Sacred* p.70

ruling. For anything to be created it must have gone past the number two and come together as the number three. While still in twoness there is only opposition. For this reason the ancients did not like the number two for it took one away from the All, yet in itself did not actually create anything but discord. As long as we are in the number two we must be separate from the opposite pole. If we are right, it is because someone else must be wrong. If we are high, it is only because something else is low. There must be an opposite for whatever we are judging, thus two is a state of complete static and conflict.

The ancients also believed that if the numbers 1 and 2 were present, the number 3 must also be present. The trinity used in all religions is the understanding of how number can go beyond the state of opposition. Thus when the All creates opposites, it also creates the trinity needed to overcome it. In Egypt this was symbolized by having the open mouth hieroglyph as part of the word used to make up Ra. The mouth closed is the one, the open lips are the two, while what originates from it is the word (Logos) that allows for creation. Thus all three numbers were present at the beginning. The ancients believed 1 and 2 were the parents of all numbers. They saw this because with just a circle and a straight line they could create all the other geometric patterns.[171]

3

"The way bears one, the one bears two, the three bear the ten thousand things." Tao Te Ching

The number three is the birth of the triangle from the Vesica Pisces. The triangle is the first enclosed shape that can be made, and is the opposite of a circle enclosing the smallest area for the greatest perimeter. A triangular pizza or shield would be the smallest by area. Three types of triangles exist: equilateral (same angles) isosceles (two similar angles) and scalene (no equal angles). Three was important as it represented symbolically the number of stages in the Hermetic process. Native tribes still count 1-2-many, while we need only count 1-2-3 and it is as if by saying three we are in fact allowing the possibility of continuing infinitely. Things when divided into threes seems natural; beginning, middle, end; birth, life, death; past, present, future; ready, set, go; gold, silver, bronze. Fewer than three steps seems incomplete, while more than three seems superfluous.[172]

While most think we live in a world of duality, we actually live in a world of three. This realization is one of the great keys to unlocking the wisdom of the universe. Great mystics from Gurdjieff to shamans speak of learning of the third force that actually creates our manifest world beyond opposites. A triangle is actually created from a straight line by placing another

---

[171] Schneider p.32, West *Serpent* p.115
[172] Schneider pp.39-40, 44

point somewhere away from it. This point is thought of as the third force, or the idea of friendship, peace, harmony and marriage. The third force is not a part of the line or the opposite poles, thus is able to bring them together to create. This third force is not something that can be seen and touched (the line) but only felt. What brings a man and woman together is love, or in some cases lust. These concepts cannot be seen, but their effects can be. It is a number of the heart because it is a feeling, as opposed to the number two understood by the mind.

In myth when the number three appears it represents the process of life, or the third force that can lead to rebirth, success or transformation. There are three bears, blind mice, little pigs, musketeers, Wisemen, wishes. Lucky things come in threes. In the Greek world the goddess Harmonia (our origin for harmony) is the third force for she was born from parents Aphrodite (love) and Aries (War). This is the symbol of the order of Maat and how one can balance the forces of the world. It is also found in the Egyptian text, "It is I (Atum) who spat out Shu and Tefnut. I had come into being as One God, and behold there was three."

With one and two being the parents of all numbers, three must naturally be their first child. Mathematically 1+2+3= 1X2x3, thus the use of these first three numbers create balance and equality, rather than opposition of duality. From this peace and harmony the other numbers grow. The building blocks of life (amino acids) and quartz crystals are in the form of tetrahedrons. Triangles (arches, tripods and A-frames) are also known for their ability to provide support or strength. Our pelvis and legs are a stable triangular A-frame, while tricycles provide more stability than bicycles. Rose thorns, shark teeth, and axes get their power from a triangle. Insects use a tripod as they walk on three of their six legs at any time. The act of praying to reach the divine is created through the triangle formed with the hands and body.[173]

4

Three has not manifested. It is an unseen force that brings the two together. To have the third dimension (the physical) it takes a fourth point to make depth or volume. The square is the symbol of the number four and is equated with equality and fairness: "square meal, fair and square." It was seen as equal because duality added or multiplied 2+2=2x2=4. Four represented our planet, divided into the four cardinal directions, elements, corners of the globe, pillars, or seasons. The number is not actually matter yet, but the origin of the stuff that will make the matter (elements) or the processes needed to do so. Thus four is the earth which provides the substance that matter can be created from. To make a child you need a man, woman, desire, sex act. The child is not the act, but comes from it. The square placed in a circle is the potential for matter enclosed within unity.

---

[173] Lamy p. 14, Schneider pp.39,42-47, 58-59, 62

Most cities were laid out in a square grid pattern, and sports fields where games of the earth are played are usually in a square or rectangle. Most board games were laid out on a square, as are playing cards. Anything square or rectangular can be thought of as something that can symbolize the planet earth. The art of origami (paper folding that will make symbols of the earth) always begins with a square. The number four, and its higher denomination of forty were very prevalent in mythology. Forty symbolized a period of time for something magical to occur. Noah's ark waited for 40 days and nights, Moses waited 40 days on Mount Sinai to receive the Ten Commandments, the Israelites spent 40 years wandering the desert, and there are 40 thieves of Ali Baba. At the 40th day of human pregnancy, the embryo becomes a fetus.

The human world was said to happen whenever the numbers four and three came together. It became part of occult symbols of three above (spirit) and four (the elements) below. This concept is found on a US dollar, in Egyptian art where heads were triangular in measure and bodies in a square, and the symbol of Freemasonry which is a compass open to 60 degrees (of an equilateral triangle) over a carpenter's rule open to 90 degrees (of a square). Even numbers were thought of as female, while odd numbers were male. The ancient language understood how these energies manifested and described things of even numbers like eyes as feminine, but those that were singular (a nose) as masculine. A cross represents the number four, as it has four sections linked together where they intersect. Christ was thus not nailed to a cross, but was a symbol to say that he was pinned to the material world. Only by going past it was He able to attain the Kingdom of Heaven.[174]

5

86:Egyptian tomb relief, notice the rope made into a spiral, Leiden Museum

---

[174] Schneider pp. 65-66, 68, 70, 94; West *Serpent* p.38

A pentagram represents the number five which provides its knowledge through the golden section and the spiral. It is seen as the completed matter coming from love because it was the first combination of a male number (3) and a female number (2). The number five is the number of life and growth due to its connection to the golden section (also called the golden mean, divine section, fibonacci series, the symbol phi, or the number 1.618). This non-whole number relates to pi, creates spirals, shows how things grow, and was most important for those who created ancient artwork. It can translate spherical areas onto flat ones. It is thought to be the most pleasing relationship to look at, thus the most beautiful things are often those with the most golden sections. It is either explained by the fibonacci series that follows the numbers 1, 2, 3, 5, 8, 13, 21…, in which the next number in the series is derived from adding the previous two. The farther along dividing one number by the number before it will get a more exact golden section. It can also be obtained by dividing a line AC at B so that AB/BC = AC/BC or 1.6180339. It can also be created from two identical squares. Numerically phi is obtained from 1+ square root of 5 divided by 2. Also pi=phi times 6/5.[175]

Numbers which have an infinite number of digits after a decimal point are called irrationals. They are irrational because they can not be understood by the human mind. We can watch 2+4 interact, even 2+ .5, but we can't watch 2+1.6180339 interact. Modern math tries to rationalize this by creating a new decimal number. Yet to the ancients something was always lost when using an irrational. The symbol for one-half was a figure with two unequal sides, showing that once away from a whole number, something was lost. However irrationals were important for they understood how our entire universe is. Whole numbers were thought of as the consonants of the world, while irrationals (pi and phi) were the vowels that allowed numbers to interact. This taught that what we experience in the universe couldn't be everything, because irrationals are needed to create it, which always cause a small part to be lost or hidden. They also understood that the golden section would help understand what was hidden.

The golden section is found in a rabbit's tail, a piano keyboard where eight white keys and five black ones represents the section. The human body is fully structured by this principle with the navel dividing the body's entire height by phi, but so is the nose to the face, elbow for the arm, or knuckle to the finger. Any one of those lengths can be multiplied by 1.618 and obtain almost perfectly the other figure. The idea is that those whom most people find attractive, often have more body proportions that closely match the golden

---

[175] West *Serpent* pp.21, 62-63)

section.[176] Most pyramids use phi in their construction, as all key works of ancient art. Temples were all made with this principle to bring in harmonic energies into the building. Anything created without use of the golden section will not be as proportionately aligned to the cosmos. The distance of each planet from the sun shows the golden section. Since the number was found throughout the universe it was further proof that humans (or anything) was a mirror for the whole cosmos.

The Golden Section plotted out on paper becomes a spiral. Spirals are found in the way water goes down a drain, shape of our ears, weather systems, the way plants grow, human DNA works, babies spin to life, hair curls, our bodies digestive tracts spiral energy and waste from food, and in how galaxies operate. Spirals are the expression of moving energy, and when energy is allowed to flow unobstructed it will do so in a spiral. Whenever a spiral is present there a pentagram star inside. Spirals grow around a center point at differing rates of speed. There are two types of spirals. The first is Archimedean which grows at a fixed rate (each spiral is the same distance from the previous). This is found in coils of rope, record groves or toilet paper, usually in manmade creations. The second is the Golden Spiral, which is the most common in nature. Here each coil keeps increasing, getting wider as it moves away from the source. The Golden Spiral grows around what is known as a calm eye, or fixed point. This was the original start of the fibonacci series, a place that is unchanging. A hurricane may rage on the outside, but at the eye all is calm. All plants grow around a central unchanging stem. Due to the numbers of the fibonacci series, a spiral will spin faster at the center than it does farther out, as the branches of a tree are closer together at the bottom than the top. Water going down a drain will spin fast at the center and more slowly at the outside, while in our solar system the planet Mercury (closest to the calm eye of the sun) moves fastest while Pluto (farthest away) moves slowest.[177]

Spirals will also occur where opposites clash, thus come together to form something greater. This is shown in what is called a mushroom spiral, when milk is poured in hot coffee, meets resistance and curls like a mushroom. This was a key feature of ancient Maya, Egyptian and Greek column architecture. A vortex is another type of spiral that is seen behind moving rowboats. It is how airplanes or birds fly. Some birds, like the owl, can use the vortex so well that they can create almost no air turbulence and sneak up on their prey without sound.[178] The Egyptians often depicted the number five as a five-pointed star, relating that the ideas of five were found in the stars. The five-pointed star in a circle represented the Duat (the place we will go when perfected). Since human beings were living life with Maat to become a five

---

[176] Schneider p.124-25
[177] Schneider pp.139-48
[178] Schneider pp.158-60

pointed star, this perhaps meant they were learning how to live more as a golden section which would lead to the beauty and harmony of Maat they were seeking.

6

"Every construction, no matter how simple it may be, has a soul because it has volume." Schwaller de Lubicz [179]

Six is the result of the first three numbers multiplied 1x2x3=6. The idea of six around one makes the best use of space: telephone ends, muffin trays, computer circuits. Old cities were laid out on a hexagon grid pattern to decrease competition, minimize transport and allow for maximum administrative control. The ancient Europeans also saw the week as six days of activity around a central Sabbath day of rest. A bubble is also six around one, so is lizard skin, Ely's eyes, snowflakes, honeybee hives and quartz crystals. With the number five something has grown and become physical matter, however it needed time and space to define it. While four is the makings of the world, six is the framework that our world operates in. It is important to note that creation does not take place in time, rather time is an effect of creation. Anything related to time or space is laid out in multiples of six, connected to the time when the calendar was 360 days. There are 60 minutes in one hour, 60 seconds to a minute, 24 hours in one day, 12 inches in one foot, 36 inches in one yard, 360 degrees for one circle, 12 ounces to a pound. All of these units of measure were either related to the circuit of the earth around the sun, or the length of a degree on the earth's surface. Thus every measurement we would make in our daily lives would link us back to the cosmos. [180]

The word six is closely related to the word sex. Sexual intercourse can only happen in the world of time and space. However, tantra teaches that one can use sex in order to transcend the world of time and space. The cube is a perfect 6-sided figure and was used in Egypt as a symbol for space (volume, because it needs six directions to define it). The Neteru sit upon a throne (cube) in the pose of meditation to reveal that they are using the power of meditation to transcend what they sit upon, time and space of this world.

7

"But the seventh day is the Sabbath of the Lord thy God, in it thou shalt not do any work..." Genesis 20: 10-11

---

[179] West *Serpent* p.47
[180] Schneider pp.178, 182, 184, 191, 197, 208; West *Serpent* pp.12, 70; Mitchell p. 126

"Progress of Supreme Unity, upon which all virtue and by passing the number seven into the number ten, there may be a wonderful operation depends." Henry Cornelius Agrippa[181]

Seven is seen as the perfect number in the ancient world. Seven is interesting as $1x2x3x4x5x6x7=7x8x9x10$; and $1x2x3x4x5x6=8x9x10$ showing that seven and ten are related. The number seven is actually not necessary in the equations, thus it serves as a balance. Libra, the scales is the seventh zodiac sign. As well, $3+4=7$ but $3x4=12$, showing that 7 and 12 are related, as represented in a piano which has seven white keys and five black keys. The Bible contains hundreds of references to the number seven. There were seven original planets, chakras, stars of the Pleiades (which the Egyptians called the Seven Hathors), colours of the rainbow, notes on the musical scale, Churches of Asia, Seals of the New Testament, Virtues (faith, hope, charity, strength, prudence, temperance, justice), Deadly Sins (pride, avarice, luxury, wrath, idleness, gluttony, envy), Wonders of the World, Liberal Arts, dwarfs in Snow White, Golden Candlesticks, uraeus in Egypt, and souls of Ra. Christmas trees originally only had seven lights to symbolize the seven chakras going up the spine. The seventh day was to be the Sabbath (Hebrew for 'cease from labour'), and the 7th year was a 'year of release' when a field was left fallow, debts were forgotten, slaves set free, or statute of limitations for some crimes. Thus the number seven was always seen as the great path, or the point when we are no longer bound by our past.[182]

Very little in the world is 7-sided because a heptagon's angle cannot completely cover a flat surface and fill three-dimensional space without leaving gaps. Thus seven is used to transform from six to a higher vibration of eight. This jump of transformation is referred to as an octave. Everything that grows, like the human body, follows a doubling process for seven intervals before reaching the eighth stage. In a human this is when the cell can divide into two. The octave is very important to understand this number, which is greatly related to music and will be discussed in the next chapter.

The number seven is best experienced through the colour of the rainbow. Sunlight is all seven vibrations of light that blend together into one. A prism refracts the sunlight, bending and spreading the waves by size to the seven colours (chakras, musical notes). We can hear ten musical octaves due to the spiral shape of our ear but we can only see seven colours due to the rods and cones of our eyes. Rods receive black and white, while the three cones see red, green and blue (which combined make the other colours). A colour TV is made up of small red, blue, and green holes to match the retinas of our eyes. If

---

[181] Agrippa p.40
[182] Schneider pp. 222, 234; Arewa, Caroline *Opening to Spirit* (Thorsons 1998) pp.61-63

you take a second prism, the colour returns to white light, showing that the monad creates all numbers yet never loses itself.[183] The importance of the number seven as a process is because it relates to the seven chakras. They represent specific parts of our being: physical, mental, emotional etc. Each one must be harmonized and cleaned to allow the kundalini serpent to rise and mix with the spiritual energies of the sky. This will allow us to reach the eight (new octave of vibration). The mention of seven in religion or myth is really a teaching tool for the understanding and cleaning of our chakras. In Persia are the Seven Shining Ones, Seven Valleys in Islam to reach Allah, Buddhists journey through the Seven Gates, and climbing Jacob's Ladder takes us to Seventh Heaven.

8

Eight is the new octave, and is the number of Tehuti/Hermes. They are related to Gnosis, thus eight must be the number of reaching inner knowing or knowledge that comes without words. Eight is known for it's doubling power: 2x2x2=8. It's symbol shows perfectly flowing energy along the above and the below. It is found in an Egyptian text, "I am one who became two, two who became four…who became eight, then I am one again." When seen on its side it is the symbol for eternity, again showing that the wisdom of Tehuti leads one to eternal life.

Asia was the first stop of the Egyptian Mystery Schools and is no surprise that eight is a key number there. It is found in the eight Essential Saints, Directions of the Wind, and the Eightfold Path to Enlightenment. Tibetan mandalas and the placement art of feung shui uses the eight. The Buddha was claimed to be born on April 8, with a birth attended by eight priests, and he died on December 8 at the age of 80. His ashes were divided into eight portions and given to the eight tribal chiefs. It is the number of hexagrams that make up the Taoist oracle of the I Ching which creates 64 hexagrams (8x8), the same number reflected in the human DNA molecule and the Maya Tzolkin calendar. The writers of the New Testament were actually the Christian Gnostics; Hermetic Egyptian initiates who understood the secrets of sound, number, and music. The Gnostics knew Jesus by the number 888, the value of his name. Interestingly Hermes was known as thrice greatest. Hermes is a descendant of Tehuti whose sacred number was 8 or the Ogdoad. Thrice Tehuti would be 888. The Gnostics may have been revealing great wisdom in their choice of names in the text. Mary has the number 192, when added to Jesus 888 equals 1080. 1080 is the number of the moon and feminine intuition.[184] The Hermetic writers of the New Testament may have been showing that their text

---

[183] Schneider pp.250, 254, 255

[184] Hauck p.414; Schneider p.269; Mitchell p.155

was more inspired by the feminine energies of the world, thus very opposite to the Old Testament which was founded on the male solar energy.

1080 is also the sacred number for Greek words that represent the Holy Spirit, spirit of the earth, and the fountain of wisdom. 1080 is the radius of the moon in miles, 108 is the atomic weight of silver (also associated with the moon and Hermes), is the traditional number of breaths in one hour, and 10800 is the number of stanzas in the Hindu Rig-Veda. In Christianity the word Christ has a number value of 1080. The importance of number and sound was a key aspect of ancient symbol and knowledge. By understanding this fact may help you not only when looking for the inner understanding of modern religious texts but in the Egyptian texts as well. Pyramids are actually octahedrons, 8-sided figures of which only the upper four are seen. Some think the pyramids of Giza may have the other four sides created underground. This is the densest geometric form, and was the symbol of fire. It was condensing the fire of spirit into the smallest space. When the number eight is multiplied (16, 24 etc) the total of the numbers get smaller. This wisdom helps to lead us to understanding the illusion of the world. The world is thought of as a dream, and just as we dream at night we see it as less real upon waking, so too does the wisdom of Gnosis explain that the father we get from this world, the less real it becomes. It is attempting to bring us back to the eight, the octave, and the understanding of oneness.[185]

9

"When Abraham was ninety and nine years old, the Lord appeared to Abraham and said unto him, I am the Almighty God; walk before me and be thou perfect." Genesis 17:1

Nine is the limit to which number can reach before beginning a new series. It was thought of sacred, representing perfection and order and was the number of Osiris. In Asia gifts given in groups of nine are considered most respectful. It is found in sayings like "cats have nine lives, go the whole nine yards (not ten), was on cloud nine, dressed to the nines." Nine is used by shamans to express an ultimate journey, while Odin rules the nine Worlds, Homer claimed the city of Troy was besieged for nine years, while Persephone spent nine months above ground. In Christianity there are nine orders of angelic choirs, nine orders of the devil, and the nine gates of hell, Jesus died at the 9th hour, and appeared nine times to his disciples. Nine is showing the extent one can go. Nine is the key to the process of birth, for there are nine threads to the human cell and a baby takes nine months to be born. Nine closes the

---

[185] Mitchell p.156; Ashby *matter* p.158

possibilities of a cycle because anything multiplied by nine still works out to nine. For example 3x9=27(2+7=9). Because nine is always nine, when you find that nine (Osiris) is really the higher self. Gurdjieff claimed the Enneagram (9 points) is a universal symbol which contains all knowledge. The number 9 insures that the numbers 1 and 10 are also present. The Ennead of Egypt came from the 1 of Nun, and 9 around 1 to produce a pyramid. The number 99 is sometimes used by landlords in lease, or a prison sentence deemed the ultimate term. Abraham was 99 when the Lord spoke to him, while Islam has 99 Beautiful name for God.[186]

10-Decad

Ten is the end of the process, contains not only the entire family of numbers 1-9, but also is ready to raise a new family 11+. To know the properties of ten is to know all, 1+0=1, and flows back to unity. Any number multiplied by ten will have its root the same as multiplying by 1. Ten is the Pythagorean perfect number, and most today want to be a perfect ten. This is why Horus, who is the principle we all must know to reach oneness and enlightenment is the number ten. He is also the number 5 to show that it is the wisdom of growth and the golden section that will lead us to the number 10. In ancient myth the number ten would usually signify the completion of the journey, or the end of the path as an enlightened one. The Bible was originally written by the Jewish Cabbala masters, which is based on the ten (ten being God). The 10th generation after Adam was Noah, and followers are expected to adhere to the Ten Commandments.[187] There are also ten oxherding pictures in Zen Buddhist enlightenment teachings.

12/13

These two numbers represent possibilities. The number 12 is 6x2 and 3x4 thus seen to have a great relationship to events in the material world. However the number 12 is actually related to 13. It seems there is never a 12 without the 13, even though for some reason 13 is deemed unlucky. When we buy a baker's dozen we don't get 12 but 13 donuts. The sky has 12 Zodiac signs, but is always claimed to be a 13th sign that was eliminated from Western wisdom two thousand years ago. Thirteen signs still exist in the Chinese and Maya astrological system. There were 12 disciples, but Jesus kept them together. There were 12 Greek gods at Olympus with Zeus at the center, 12 Knights of the Round Table around Arthur. There were also 12 Tribes of Israel, Labours of Hercules, Generals of Washington's Army to fight for the 13 Colonies, 12 meridians of Chinese medicine with a 13th central channel. Thus the number 12 is the way for us to reach beyond to find the hidden (13) which

---

[186] Schneider pp.302-308; West *Serpent* p.56
[187] Schneider pp.324, 327, 330

is at the core. Geometrically the earth is thought of as having 12 pieces that have been sown together looking like a big soccer ball. The markings on the original soccer ball may have been used to hide within the game the secrets of the actual makeup of the planet.

87:The Egyptians placed their knowledge of number and geometry into their artwork and reliefs, here in Meruka's temple-tomb Sakkara

Magic Squares

A magic square is a math problem, but was seen by alchemists as laden with secret wisdom. A magic square occurs when consecutive numbers, starting from 1 are laid on a grid. Each row and column will add up to the same number. The columns of the square that uses the numbers one to nine all add to fifteen and is thought to represent the planet Saturn. There are seven magic squares to relate the seven planets (chakras).

Beyond Numbers

Robert Temple in his book Crystal Sun speaks of the Comma of Pythagoras, which is the number 1.0136 and called the "greatest secret of Egypt." When the real earth year 365.2422 is divided by 360 (the original year) the result is 1.0145. Thus it may be that this number helps to understand the difference of time and space on the earth the way it is supposed to be (a 360 day orbit) as opposed to what it has become (a 365.24 day orbit). The actual difference between the comma of Pythagoras and the divided numbers of the earth is 9.6 ten thousandths. 9.604 is the "uncertainty constant" (Sigma 9.604x10 exponent −14) that determines nuclear particles. Just as these numbers show the difference between the wobble and the actual, it may help us to understand the real (spirit) and unreal (illusion of matter).

The value of pi (3.1416) is made up of a particle (.1416) and a whole number (3) that in this case says that the principle it represents functions on the three dimensional plane. Thus the Golden Section (1.618) can be seen to relate to the oneness of the All for its whole number is 1. The particle of a number leads to logarithms, and the particle of Pythagoras (the .0136) is related to the particle of pi (the .1416) through the multiplication of the uncertainty constant (0.09604) as .01416 X 0.09604=0.0136. It is also related to music and octaves. Some have equated the comma of Pythagoras to the formation of all the chemical elements in the material universe. A number of .007 governs the process, which the Egyptians may have called the "tiny gap." This tiny gap also appears in Ian Flemming's code name for James Bond. With a constant of .006 or .008 the material universe would not function. Doubled the number is 0.014 which is the rounded value of the particle of Pythagoras. The number 0.0136 is also related to the creation of hydrogen and helium, the building blocks of stars and planets.[188] This tiny gap may have been the numerical way to understand the material universe, while using the comma of Pythagoras to distinguish between real and illusion. In my opinion, number and geometry are the ways this reality (prison) were created, much like a computer program. The ancients realized that to break free of this reality one had to use the reality to work for them, thus to use the same number and geometry to break free (in essence, change the program). All ancient sites in the world are constructed with this perfect aspect of geometry and mathematics to make these spots places where one can break free easier.

---

[188] Temple, Robert *Crystal Sun* (pp.352-70

CHAPTER 13
SOUND

88:Amazing detail of harp player. Notice how much care was put to making his ear. Most Egyptian musicians were shown with their eyes closed, either to indicate they were blind or could hear and feel music at another level, Leiden Museum

Sacred Sound

"Musicians in ancient times did not need to sing about solutions, they could create them." Turner[189]
"In Egypt, the priests when singing hymns of praise to the gods employ the 7 vowels, which they utter in due succession. The sound of those letters is so euphorias that people listen to it in place of the flute and lyre." Demetrius[190]

Everything in the universe, from a planet to you is in vibration. Matter is made up of energy that is in constant motion. It may look like the table is not moving, but it in fact is, just at a rate that our eyes cannot pick up. Resonance is the natural frequency an object most naturally vibrates at. Shamans say that each one of us has a song, the natural resonance of our true self. Yet each part of our body plays a part in our song. Your arm vibrates to a different frequency than other parts of your body, but when healthy they all vibrate a similar resonance as a whole. The vibration produces waves that our ears pick up as sounds. There are numerous examples of resonance: singer breaking glass, bridges swaying, Joshua bringing down the walls of Jericho by beating drums and blowing trumpets.[191]

---

[189] Baigent *Elixir*
[190] Fowden P.118
[191] Goldman, Jonathan *Healing Sounds* (Element 1992) p.13

Everything in the universe makes a sound. Sea creatures have special receptors to hear sound, while others use an echo system (similar to sonar) to distinguish what is in the water with them. Whales use songs to communicate with other whales over hundreds of miles, and modern analysis claims up to ten million bits of information per half hour is passed along (similar to the bits of information in a novel). Animals notice the sounds of the world and react to them, avoiding an earthquake that humans do not hear. To become more aligned with a plant one has to first hear it (which few humans try), and then mimic their sound. Plants grow well around other plants that make similar sounds, while die if placed with those who do not. Plants are shown to enjoy the sound of classical music.[192] Just as our body will be out of vibration when we stub our toe, so too will objects get out of vibration if they are dropped. Sound can be used to heal both the animate and inanimate.

Sounds are occurring all around us but they mix together and we rarely notice them. When at a large gathering of people we are able to focus our attention on one person. As soon as someone else says our name, a trigger is struck. We somehow are now able to focus on that other conversation as well. It was as if that entire conversation was being filtered out by our brain, yet we were obviously still registering the sounds for once something was said (our name) that has tremendous meaning to us, we noticed it.[193] Most of the perception of sound happens with our ear, but not all. Our entire body will register the vibrations around us as intuition and feelings. Shamans first teach their students how to listen. That is because our ear has far more perceptive power than the eyes. We hear things that we can never see, yet most have been trained to focus only on what they see thus the sounds of the ear is usually ignored. Actually it should be the other way around, we should spend more time focusing on what we hear and less on what we see.

Seeing things with the eyes tends to lead to more desires, and advertisers know to use the power of what we see to create impulses that could not be as strong if their message was only audible. When we go beyond desire, like when we are with our partner in love, we close our eyes. We no longer need to see them, but somehow without sight we are able to go deeper. With touch and sound we go beyond the physical into something more magical…our heart. This is a key reason for understanding sound in the ancient world, for the sight of things mostly speaks to the conscious mind while sound will lead us more to the feelings of the heart. In our world today the eyes rule, and we are not interested in going beyond what we see (which is an illusion) but have come to simply believe what we see. The ancients would not make such a judgment about anything they see without adding feeling, understanding that the world is not what it appears to be. The eyes cannot penetrate anything and

---

[192] Berendt pp.76-78
[193] Goldman p.82

just stay on the surface. In love the eyes are closed as we are trying to go inside a person and connect with their soul, not just the outer projected image of that soul. In the Bible when God communicated with humans rarely did he "reveal himself" by sight, but always spoke to those who had the connection. Exodus 28 claims, "And sound shall be heard when he goeth into the holy place before the Lord, and when he cometh out." Shamans teach that it is the sound made by objects that keep them manifested, and the songs of the shamans help to keep the world alive.

To help this concept, students of the mysteries need to be taught how to hear again. Blindfold the eyes for a few days and one will find their hearing is sharpened and they will soon feel objects and people around them. Few know how to truly listen when another person is speaking without interrupting them, or without thinking of what to say back or to defend ourself from what we don't like. Listen to what someone is saying because if we do, we will go beyond the words being used to the inner essence of what those sounds mean. Another way to start opening up to sounds is to sit with your eyes closed in silence. It won't take long to begin to notice all sorts of sounds all around us (even at home) that we normally ignore. It also allows us to begin to notice the sounds of our own bodies, which will lead to greater perception of what our body in different situations is trying to tell us.

Sound Effects

"The life of city dwellers today is a form of mild but persistent torture." John Anthony West[194]

Certain sounds are soothing and joyous to us. We all can relate to how we feel after a hard day when our favourite music is put on, or in reverse when the neighbour's dog won't stop barking. The ancients understood the power of sound and how it affected humans. In nature most sounds are harmonious with one another and the Egyptians attempted when building cities to make them as harmonious sounding as possible. Temples were made for something beyond, to make the exact vibrational sound that would create the teaching that was to be imparted. It is claimed that if one was not harmonious with the sound of the temple (not living from the heart) they might die if they tried to enter certain areas. Many of the key sites of wisdom in Egypt today have not been found because one needs to know their proper sounds. They also understood that if poor sounds were created, humans would be angry, stressed and tired. Some feel that the modern world has been created by those who want to keep humans away from our true gifts, and help to do that by designing a world of sound that would keep us perpetually drained.

---

[194] West *Serpent* p.26

Our world makes the most horrible sounds from airports, to jackhammers, to guns…which is all repeated again on TV and movies. Just at the time our body needs a break from the horrible sounds of the world, we subject ourselves to more of them. This has led to a society that is stressed, angry, frustrated, and ill. We have made it even worse by providing polluted air and water to consume, and live with less negative ions (found in nature). Yet our lack of health and calm can also be blamed on the fact that we have allowed ourselves to live day after day in a place that is filled with inharmonious sounds, that are taking away our life force without us even noticing.[195] Why not try to live as the ancients did, with the sounds of peace, harmony and nature around? At the very least we should try to spend the rest of our day after work repairing the damage of sound we had to put up with. Soothing music, melody, nature and quiet instead of loud noise and TV. Because of the ancient understanding of the powers of sound and number, these qualities must be searched for in everything they built. They will show the harmonious proportions of the golden section and in the musical scale that create specific vibrations to help humans easier connect with the realm of spirit.

All shamans have a power song, a repetitive series of words that offer protection in times of distress or strong inner power for healing. Chinese Qi Gong masters use sounds to expel negative energy and emotion from their own bodies during training. Oriental experts of the martial arts use specific yells while striking to focus the energy of their lower power center (Dan Tien) to the part of the body striking an opponent. This way with seemingly small movements that would hardly topple a child, they can send two hundred pound men flying across a room. They all understand that energy, sound and words are connected.

However there is also sound that we do not hear. This ability to use silent sound was used by natives to call animals, or find healing plants or food. They would do so not by creating the sound outwardly, but in their energy field to produce a connection of consciousness with they are calling. Castaneda and the mystic Alder wrote of looking for the hole within the sound. When a pebble is dropped into water we first see the hole that the pebble made, then the series of ripples that come outward from the disturbance. These ripples spread out to infinity and the distance between them is referred to as a wavelength. Mystics claim that the sound we hear is really the ripples. However there is a silent center that created the sound vibration (the pebble), thus they ask us to go beyond the sound we hear to the silence that created it. By working with sound eventually one will be able to bring their eyes back to their true use. We won't even have to look at things for the sound will be enough to notice a tree, or animal or object thus we can use our eyes to focus specifically on one thing.

---

[195] West *Serpent* p.26

When reaching the hole of the sound we in effect have gone beyond the sound itself to an inner quality of not only the sound, but the universe.[196] Thus the essence of every sound is silence.

Planets

Pythagoras spoke of the "music of the spheres," which meant that he claimed each of the planets made a sound that he could hear. Recently modern scientists have discovered that each planet does make an individual sound, and that the sounds are harmonically related to the musical octave. Pythagoras correlated the orbits of the planets and the vibrations to the string of a monochord. The sounds the planets make are claimed to affect each human being depending on the position of them at our birth, thus it is actually sound that makes the horoscope. Astrologers are actually tracking the sound of the heavens, and how those sounds will interact with us as individuals or the earth as a whole. Hans Kayser believes that by understanding harmonic proportions it is possible to discover planets that have yet to be discovered, because the solar system is in perfect harmonic proportion to each other. We need not actually locate the next planet beyond Pluto just plot where the monochord claims it must be.[197]

While the planets actually do make sounds, Pythagoras was likely revealing something very powerful in his statement of hearing the planets. In the ancient world the planets were a symbol of the chakra centers of the human body. They also have the same harmonic placement. By hearing the energy centers, one can notice if one is out of alignment then use specific sounds to heal it (us).

---

[196] Castaneda, Carlos *A Separate Reality* (Simon and Schuster 1971); Alder, Vera *Finding the Third Eye* (Samuel Wiser 1970) p.37
[197] Berendt pp.63-64, Goldman p.30

Music

"If the music (your vibration) becomes discordant, don't blame the musician (God), but the lyre-string he plays (you) that has become loose and sounds flat, marring the perfect beauty of the melody." Hermetic Wisdom[198]

"You should tune the inward lyre and adjust it to the divine musician." Corpus Hermeticum Book 18[199]

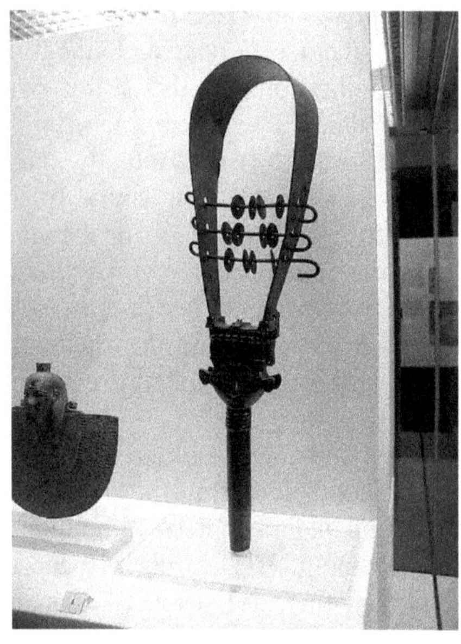

89:Egyptian sistrum (rattle), British Museum

The Egyptians understood that music was a representation of the harmony of the heavens. Through the use of sound (Neteru Merit) one could help create divine harmony and reach Maat. Music, singing and dancing could help individuals keep in alignment with this harmony, and they focused attention on making sure that the sounds and movements would be pleasing to Maat. The use of music and sound was a key component of Egyptian healing practices. In temple ritual the singing and dancing of participants would allow their consciousness to change to reach states beyond the physical.

Osiris was believed to rule not by force, but kept harmony and order simply by singing songs and playing specific musical instruments. Music affects our emotions and can sooth, agitate, make us aggressive, alter consciousness or stimulate us sexually. The Beatles claimed that their later albums were music that connected to cosmic harmony. Native shamans still sing special songs that they claim help to keep the earth in balance, though as less and less of them are alive to sing the songs, the earth and everything on it is falling out of balance. The ancient musical scale was part of a sacred philosophy reflecting inherent order and a model of the universe. Today we know the seven notes of the scale as do-re-mi-fa-sol-la-ti-do. Guido Arezzo in 1000AD claimed they are shortenings of the Latin words that show the cosmic order: Dominus (Lord, Absolute), Regina Cueli (Queen, Moon), Mecrocosmos (Small Universe, Earth), Fata (Fate, Planets), Sol (Sun), Lactea (Milky Way),

---

[198] Freke *Hermetica* p. 146
[199] Copenhaver p.67

Sider (Stars, Galaxies), Dominus (Lord, Absolute).[200] The ancients designed and used the musical scale to play the harmonies of the heavens, which would lead us to our own heart.

Octaves begin at the note c, work through the seven inner notes, until it has doubled in frequency to become a higher c. You could continue this sequence until a note is no longer audible in the material world. The same process can be achieved by going up in fifths. After seven octaves or twelve fifths the same basic note will be reached, but will differ by 1.0136 (comma of Pythagoras).[201] Tehuti was the Neteru of the number eight and the octave. One travels up seven octaves (chakras) and when this has occurred they have reached the eighth, which is the original note but at a higher vibration. This is a good explanation of spiritual development. The wisdom of Egypt takes us up along the seven chakras, and when we have mastered them all we reach the Gnosis of Tehuti. This causes our entire being to jump to a higher vibration. The use of the fifth and octaves can be found in Egyptian artwork of musicians as their hands are placed at perfect fifth and octave ratios along their instruments.

Hermeticists like Pythagoras and Plato understood the need to keep everything in harmony. Just as our body is one entity made up of several parts that needed to be harmoniously kept, so too the cosmos. Hermetic literature often relates the need to keep the human body in tune, and also in tune with the cosmic musical instrument (God). Robert Fludd referred to the power of music as, "an ascent from darkness to light." It is claimed that after the Buddha became enlightened he spoke of a sound, "the drum of immortality."[202] My teacher of sound often spoke that the universe makes a sound, and was in a sense always speaking to us. Like a radio, we are not tuned in, so when we hear this sound we pick it up as a buzzing or like the sound of crickets. As you work with paying attention to the sound, we are in a sense focusing our receptive unit which will allow us to go beyond the buzzing and allow communication from the universe (or God) to come to us directly.

Song or music is in some way the animating feature of life. Marsiglio Ficino wrote of the pneuma (breath of the divine) that flowed through all of creation. This cosmic breath was the spirit, and allowed connection of the above and below through music. Playing music was like being in a divine prayer. Ficino also wrote, "David and Hermes Trismegistus command that we are moved by God to sing, of God alone we should sing." Hermeticists and Cabbalists often give God the name of "Divine Musician," and the physical world is nothing but the song of God or the instrument that he plays on. Music was a key part of alchemy as Michael Maier in 1618 published Atalanta

---

[200] Baigent pp.191, 406-11; Schneider p.234
[201] Temple p.358
[202] Baigent *Elixir* pp.199, 200; Berendt p.171

Fugiens, fifty alchemic steps displayed in words, engravings and music. Poetry originally was not designed as something to be spoken, but something to be put to music and sung. Opera arose from the ideas of sacred drama and poetry put to music.[203] All ancient books are meant to be read aloud.

Interestingly a modern piano has only 88 keys. There are 1300 raw tones but music in the modern world uses only 5% of what is available. The ancients used most of these tones to create masterpieces of sound. The modern piano uses "equal temperament" as a way to try and harmonize the problem that octaves and fifths do not climb in a systematic manner. What the modern piano does is "shave off" a small bit of each note to create something called semitones, which are actually artificial notes. Thus every note played on a modern piano is slightly flat. In the "old days," a piano tuner would bunch the discrepancies of the slight note changes at the top and bottom of the keyboard (the least used keys) so that the middle would have more pure tones. Today this is not the case as the flat tones have allowed the player to go quickly from key to key without the need to stop and re tune the piano. Before equal temperament an orchestra would have to stop, re tune and then continue.[204] While this has led to more flow with more keys, it has not led to purer music. Thus the power of the true sound is not vibrating within us. The ancients were using sound and music for powerful healing and to unlock the secrets of the universe, thus would rather use 1000 different, perfectly sounding instruments to make the needed sounds rather than have just three that could reach "close sounding" versions of them.

In the musical world anything with a high pitch (violins, trumpets, flutes) carry the melody or the main part of the music, while those that have a low pitch (cello, bass, tuba) are accompanying. They only take part as melody when the other instruments are not being used. This may have a key note of the true roles of men and women, for women have a higher pitch voice than men thus perhaps women are supposed to lead the melody of life. The only way the male, lower pitched sounds, can dominate the melody is to silence the sound of women.

A sistrum is the instrument associated with the female (Hathor especially) and consists of a handle with a metal hoop through which four pieces of metal rods are set. When shaken the rods hit against the loop and cause a distinctive sound. The hoop is the moon, while both side are Isis and Nepthys. The four rods are the four elements and lower energy centers. The sistrum is similar to the rattle used by Native Indians. The sound is meant to create a shaking in the mind that will help take us beyond the conscious (lower centers) to the unconscious (higher centers). This is the reason the sistrum was a key part of the beginning of Egyptian ceremony for the rattling helped to start

---

[203] Ficino Letter p66, Baigent *Elixir* pp.196, 198, 200
[204] Temple p.360

the process of shifting states of consciousness of those participating. Her temples included great hospitals for healing. In some this great healing power is still active. She mainly heals through her aspects of Sekhemet and Bastet.

The drum is able to match the heartbeat of the earth. It is used by all cultures to help change our consciousness and get us in touch with our heart. The drum is seen as feminine, while the stick is masculine. When the two are brought together in rhythm they harmonize opposites. The rattle helps to shake up things, specifically our usual thoughts, which allow for the drumming to get into our consciousness. This was the reason the sistrum (rattle of Hathor) was used at all Egyptian rituals before the music could begin, as our mind would not be ready without the rattling. Bells, gongs and singing bowls are also sounds that can be used to clear the mind, and attain higher states of consciousness.

Mantra
"And they were astonished at his doctrine: for his word was with power." Luke 4:32

The idea of words or the voice as power is found in hieroglyphs. There are certain words and sounds that are power in their own right. Some of these sounds were infused into the ancient languages, making everything spoken with them powerful. Words and their combination can be studied like music to create sounds that will attune things to certain divine energies. The universe was created by the divine word, called the Logos. This divine sound is really our breath made audible. The sounds themselves are seen through the use of cymatics, a field of study created by Dr. Hans Jenny to study sound. By using a tonoscope or tightly stretched drum, sound was spoken through a long tube onto objects like iron fillings. The sounds created geometric shapes in the fillings. The more 'positive' the word or sound was deemed to be the more shape-like the result, while sounds that were seen to be 'poor' created disharmonious forms. When Hebrew or Sanskrit words like "OM" were spoken by masters the resulting shapes nearly matched the written form used to depict the word in each of the languages. Toning is using the power of your own voice by holding a note for a long period of time. This drawn out sound, usually practiced first with the vowels, open us up to universal energy.

Mantra is a form of yoga that uses a word or phrase with spiritual power. In Egypt they were called Hekau. By repeating a mantra over and over, the mystic concentrates his attention on God. A common one is the Sanskrit word Om, which is deemed to be the primal word. It is also a version of the

Egyptian deity Amun, repeated in the Bible as Amen. Interestingly the full name of Amun vibrates less in the lower body (our true source of power) but in the upper head and chest, the place where Western material people live. Thus the period of rise of Amun in Egypt was likely the rise of modern Western thinking. The word OM actually gains its power from its shortness, thus the easiness to repeat it and say it often in a short period of time. By constantly working with the sound Om one is able to transcend the mind and reach a state of higher vibration. One wants to hear its four distinct parts: A (the physical self), U (our dream state), M (a state of deeper sleep without dreams) and silence which is meditation that transcends all the three other sounds.[205] One wants the sound of any mantra to go down from the mouth into the body, until the entire body and every cell vibrates with the sound.

Swami Sivananda told his pupils to repeat mantras as many as 50,000 times per day, for with this great discipline one could achieve results in a short period of time. However any work done with mantras will help raise our vibration. Words of Power are likened to digging a well. Dug deep enough one will reach water. If mantras are used long enough one will reach to the deepest parts of the self. At the beginning mantras are spoken aloud, in order to help focus our attention on them. In time one can advance to the more powerful stage of repeating them internally. Eventually the sound of the mantra will be heard when not practicing.[206] A mantra is a type of meditation in which we replace what we are normally saying in our head, with a more powerful set of words. However most do not understand that mantra, like any meditation technique, is not actually meditation. It is an exercise to help us eliminate the negative thoughts of the mind, but eventually even the mantra must fall away until you are left with nothingness. It is at this point that without our internal dialogue, our view of the world and ourself ceases, which means we stop the world and can connect directly with spirit.

Certain Egyptian Neteru can be connected with if one can use the proper words of power for that deity. It is the main reason that Egyptian hieroglyphs did not put vowels in their written language, so that no one could know the true name of anything. Knowing its true sound, you could recreate the sound to connect with that energy directly. They wanted such work to be one of personal development, personally working with the sound until an inner knowing surfaces. According to Hindu tradition each mantra has six separate but indivisible parts: Devata (deity of the mantra), Rishi (one who first spoke it), Raga (musical component), Bija (the seed), Shakti (power of origin), and Kilaka (chanter's own will power).[207] The famous Hare Krishna chant uses the repetitive names of Rama and Krishna to help purify and cleanse the heart. Try

---

[205] Ashby *proverbs* pp.79, 140; Freke *World Mysticism* p.40
[206] Ashby *proverbs* pp.137-138
[207] Crowley p.148

saying it a few times and feel the cleaning of the chest area. Quotations or phrases can become mantras that are repeated over and over until the wisdom of the hidden messages are revealed within. Each chakra has a sound (Lam, Vam, Ram, Yam, Ham, Om and All) that helps loosen our blocks.

Healing/Harmonics
"Make the sound be heard at the end of the universe." Tehuti

Just as sound can be used to destroy (as in the story of the walls of Jericho), it can be used to heal. What we call illness can be described as some part of our physical body vibrating out of tune. To introduce the correct sounds will help create the healing needed for all parts of our being. The great Renaissance alchemists and doctors from Agrippa to Paracelsus spoke of illness being a state where one was no longer in harmony with the universe (divine musician). Chants, hymns and songs in the ancient world were designed to alter states of consciousness and make healing possible. Healing can be done with musical instruments, singing bowls, dijerido, bells, but the best is the trained human voice. Using the voice to make sound is called toning, and it is powerful because a human is able to create harmonics. Using these sounds one will find a part of the body that does not make the same sound as the rest, or the healing instrument will sound flat when played there. The sound is played over that area until a new vibration has occurred. Oriental healers speak of five lakes of energy associated with the five organs (kidney, liver, spleen, heart and lungs). Illness was the inability for energy to flow from lake to lake due to a blockage. Each lake or organ can be healed of blocks by using specific Qi Gong healing sounds. The sounds loosen stagnant and blocked energy and allow flow. Great initial healing sounds are the vowels, which are said to link directly to the energies of the creator.

What is deemed the most powerful healing sounds are made with harmonics. A harmonic is more than one tone created at the same time. This can be done with two different instruments or voices, but gains its greatest healing power as when used by Tibetan Monks or in Gregorian chants when an individual creates the harmonic by using overtones. Their harmonies help to create similar harmonics within our own bones. Many monks today have no need to eat food and rarely sleep because of spending several hours a day using specific harmonic chants that keeps the health of their body in tact. Simply adding harmonics to our daily regimen would increase our health, and decrease our need for sleep.

CHAPTER 14
EGYPTIAN HEALING

90:Remains of healing temple, Chichen Itza Mexico

Medicine

"You will resort to the sacred medication of plants." Elbers Papyrus[208]

"I want to help people, I want to do something good for them. So when He (spirit) comes I have done something good, or I have saved somebody's life that way...all the blessings were given back to me many times over...these powers that were given to me, they can't be evaluated in terms of money. So I say thank you." Wallace Black Elk, Lakota shaman[209]

---

[208] Schwaller *Sacred* p.157
[209] Black Elk p.13

Egyptian medicine is the one field that Egyptologists see in some high regard because many translated papyrus reveal modern western medical knowledge and treatments. However, the Egyptians healing must be examined from their understanding, not ours. Greek medical father Hippocrates in the 5th century BC admitted a debt to the Egyptians, while Herodotus called the Egyptians "the healthiest race in the world." Yet modern science still claims that all today is better than the past in medicine. Only recently and reluctantly have they been forced to accept things like Chinese medicine, which is scientifically undetectable.[210]

When asked how the Egyptians obtained such medical knowledge the usual answer is accident, or trial and error (which is just a prolonged system of accident). Modern people do the same when they label something a coincidence. Saying Egypt was able to produce fabulous cures by accident is a way of brushing the real question under the table. We must admit that they, like a native shaman are not lucky. They are more advanced than everyone thinks. According to Clement of Alexandria the final stage of the priesthood process was to learn how to heal, not like today when people learn to do this at the start. To properly heal someone requires the wisdom of the universe, sound, number, astronomy, energy and the like. It also demands that one work through almost all of their own issues, pain, and blocks that we have had in our own life. This requires years of incredible effort to reach a stage where the heart is pure enough to see beyond the illusion and gain a connection to spirit to provide the proper healing. Only after years of fully healing themselves will someone be able to provide healing for others. On the way one can learn to help, but they cannot fully facilitate healing because they don't even know if the condition should be healed. One must be able to connect fully with their patient's higher self to "see" if the illness is their greatest learning experience. No ancient healer would heal someone of their greatest life lesson until they had learned it. In Egypt this training came in the temples and involved a combined understanding of physical and spiritual illness and cures.

---

[210] West *Serpent* p.118; Naydler p.131

Egyptian Healers

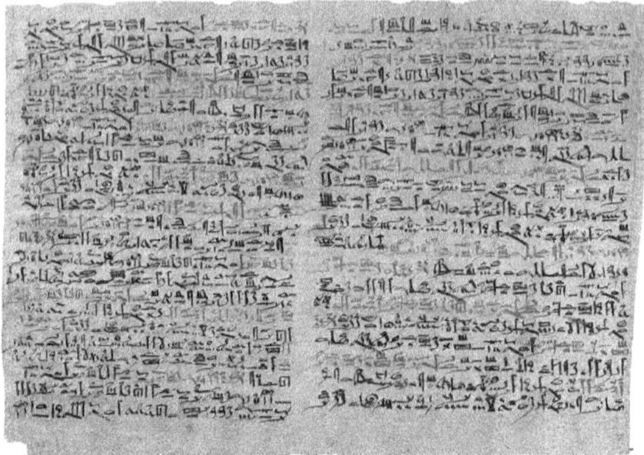

91:The Edwin Smith Surgical Papyrus,

The Edwin Smith Surgical Papyrus mentions that every doctor/healer (called a swnw in Egypt) was a follower of Sekhemet and Tehuti. From Tehuti they learned the wisdom of connecting with spirit through Gnosis to find the true cause of illness. Tehuti taught the sounds, herbs and stones to use. Sekhemet taught the energy meridians of the body and the chakras, and how to heal the ailments that were found. Like doctors in the 1950's who made house calls, each Egyptian doctor had a box that they would bring their herbs, stones, amulets, and papyrus scrolls. The Egyptians kept very good texts on illness and ailments that could be consulted. The Elbers Papyrus is a text that acts like an encyclopedia of various ailments. The main physical component of Egypt would have looked similar to modern Chinese medicine, with the use of herbs, reflexology, acupuncture, Qi Gong and Yoga.

The most well known Egyptian medical text is known as the Edwin Smith Papyrus, which lists the diagnosis and cures of different traumas. It shows 48 cases of injury to the head, face, neck, throat and spinal column. For each injury it gives a diagnosis, examination, prognosis and treatment. It even provides footnotes on the terms used. Many modern doctors agree with the diagnosis and recommended treatments provided. To produce such a piece of physical cures meant they must have had at least an equal knowledge of the body and its functions as medicine today. They had an advanced form of dentistry, contraceptives (using the bark of acacia trees), and sunscreen. Many Egyptian medical papyrus were originally laughed at when they were first found and deciphered in the late 19th century. Some called for using the dung of different animals for wounds and disease. German doctors called Egypt's medicine by the mocking name, Drekapoteke (sewage pharmacology). Today science no longer laughs at Egypt's cures with the discovery that animal dung contains anti-bodies similar to penicillin. Thus the use of the dung was a very excellent natural healing tool, something not again understood until late in the 20th century. They also laughed at papyrus that suggested women urinate on wheat to tell if fertile, today this is again known to provide information not only if one is pregnant but also the sex of the child.[211]

The second nature of healing was never written down as the physical cures were. They understood that providing herbs, healing cuts, or mending broken bones was only the outer cure. There was a deeper reason these things were occurring. Just as today an outer illness is only a sign of an inner problem, the true healers of Egypt were able to see beyond the physical to address the spiritual cause. The Egyptians saw everything as related to the whole. Thus a part of the body that is sick is somehow related to the whole, not just that individual part. Some of this work including the saying of special magical words, that are thought of by Egyptologists as spells. They were less a magic spell, than a way of using the power of sound to create the proper vibration in the body to provide a shift of energy and begin healing. The songs of native shamans have a similar effect. They are not random words, but special words of healing power that heal simply because of the sounds spoken.

This type of healing was often referred to in the papyrus as destroying the demon that inhabited the body. Today such a notion seems the work of superstition and ignorance. However when one works with a healing master who still heal the ancient way, this concept is understood. Thus to just change or heal an outer cause does nothing to halt our inner demon, and this is the nature of soul healing. Each of the inner demons we rid, the more we can use energy to reach our heart (true self). Thus the true healer found what a person's demon was, how it formed, then provide treatment to ease the physical symptoms. The physical healing helped to make the person stronger and full of energy. They would need this energy for the healer was also providing unseen healing that was helping to lessen the power of the demon, and at the same time pulling it out for the person to fight. They were like a boxing promoter, and gave us the gloves and the ring to defeat whatever inside ourself was making us sick. This allowed the cause of our problems to be faced by us, and defeated by us. Thus true healing require cures for the physical and cures for the spiritual. The cure was for the whole person, not just a part of their being. Fully and properly healed, the person would now be free to use the energy that was previously used to manifest problems, to now manifest one's dreams. Ancient texts, including the Hebrew Bible, tell of their characters living for hundreds of years. It is quite possible that using proper healing methods and providing proper ways of living for people, that living to 400 years old in the past was not an unheard of thing.

---

[211] West *Serpent* pp.117, 119; West *Key* p.42; Schwaller *Sacred* p.114

One of the things that the Egyptians may have used, is round metal tubes. I always wondered about statues that I saw from the New Kingdom, holding what appeared to be two round tubes in each hand. That they were prevalent on so many statues told me they were telling something, but what? The answer came oddly when I friend loaned me a modern "parasite buster." This is a device of two copper tubes, hooked to a power source, that will create a negative current in the body- which destroys parasites and heals injured tissues. Then I found that others had speculated that these tubes held by the Egyptian statues were also healing devices. Some now claim that Egyptians made one tube of copper (to be positive sun current) and one of zinc (to be a negative moon current). They were then filled with specific stones and crystals- depending on the need, and then held in the hands- creating the same type of strong electrical current in the body. Held for perhaps one hour a day might have kept away almost all illness.

Healing Temples

All of the temples of Egypt were places of healing for those that were aspiring to the mysteries. Most of these temples also included a type of hospital where healing of the general population could take place. Each town would have their own local shamans and Rhwt (Egyptian for wise women, who could heal using nature). They provided cures for basic aliments. At times the general population would be in need of more than these local people could provide, thus the need to go to the healing temple. Beyond deep cures, the temples also provided space where healing dreams could come during the night. Dream interpretation papyri (similar to our dream books) were given to the seekers. Statues were placed in these rooms that had healing properties (similar to the Sekhemet statue I mentioned earlier). Others had areas for healing baths. These were not simple spas, but linked to the healing of the native sweat lodge. The temple itself would be created to specific harmonic principles thus just being in a functioning ancient temple is healing in itself.

The actual teaching of Egyptian healing is far too involved to tackle any further in this introduction. These concepts will be one of the main components of my future books. Every one of us is suffering from some sort of great inner pain, challenges of the conscious mind, and the challenges passed on in our DNA. Thus all of us are patients waiting for true healing, and once we can truly heal ourself we can become a healer for others. That is the true reason why we must want to heal, not just for the health and freedom for ourself but to then learn the techniques of the ancient healing arts so that we can do the same for humanity and the planet.

CHAPTER 15
FAIRY TALES

92:Fairy Godmother appearing in the hearth to Cinderella

Myth and tales

"Give people a fact or idea and you enlighten their minds, give them a story and you touch their souls." Geog Feuerstein [212]

"Deeper meanings reside in fairy tales told to me in my childhood than in the truth that is taught by life." German Poet Schiker [213]

"Myth [and tales] is a deliberately chosen means for communicating knowledge." John Anthony West[214]

Fairy tales are seen as simple rudimentary stories written to entertain little children while providing them a moral for their behaviour. Simple fairy tales are far from simple, as they contain hidden Hermetic wisdom. The ancient masters created these tales at the beginning of time, thus they are nearly identical (or at least easily recognizable) all over the earth.

As with all mythology, a story is by far the best way to pass on information. Many ask that if the ancients had knowledge why not just write it in a book like we do and preserve it for all times in libraries? The great library at Alexandria contained more than 500,000 scrolls until the Christians burned it down. The Maya had thousands of books written on bark until Spanish Bishops had all the parchments burnt. During the Middle Ages if books were not hidden they were burnt and lost forever. There is no telling how many wondrous works

---

[212] Feuerstein, Geor and Kak, Subbash and Frawley, David *In Search of the Cradle of Civilization* (Quest Books 1995) p. 95
[213] Bettelheim, Bruno *The Uses of Enchantment* (Alfred A Knopf 1989) p.5
[214] West, *Serpent* p. 127

of wisdom went up in smoke all over the earth during the last two thousand years. It would be easy even today for a government or ruling religious group to deem all books and information on the Internet the work of the devil and destroy them all. All the knowledge that was placed in books to last forever could be lost in a generation.

Mythology and tales are different. They were not created to be placed in books, but to be transmitted orally and stored in the human mind. Is a page of the dictionary or Cinderella easier to remember? The idea being that even if all books were lost, stories would survive in the memory of the population. If the language of an area changes, the books of the old language would be useless if no one could read them. Stories kept in the mind could be changed immediately to the new language. As well, someone without the inner understanding might remember the story and tell it later to someone trained in the mysteries, thus people kept the wisdom alive without even knowing that they were.

In fairy tales the information was hidden in the stories. The more disguised the information, the less likely the ruling authorities would try to persecute. The stories were made interesting for children so they could be learned while young. Every time a fairy tale is read to children, powerful esoteric wisdom is being kept alive. The first time we hear a tale we are children. The second time is when we are parents and reading them to our own children. Likely we have not looked at the tales at all for twenty years, but with more knowledge as we read we may understand some of the hidden wisdom. The next time may be when we are grandparents now with even more knowledge to understand what is being depicted. John Anthony West claims the esoteric quality of the tales touches a person's inner being, and speaks to our heart.[215]

Today, tales are losing some of their luster. In medieval times, storytellers would travel to local villages and tell the tales during the night. It was entertainment for a population without electric lights, radio or Television. The storytellers would be versed in hundreds of tales, which they knew by heart. To one who has only read a tale and never heard it recited in person has missed a magical element. A story told by a storyteller is brought to life.

Just thirty years ago mythology was still taught in elementary schools, but this is no longer the case as myth and tales are seen as unimportant in the Western scientific world. Today children focus more on the instant gratification of video games and television. Fairy tales are losing their popularity but they are not gone completely. Even in the "Nintendo generation" the tales are still known. What is it about them?

The tales passed on to our children today are shells of their original versions. The stories were carefully woven and developed, written as much for adults as they were for children. The Brothers Grimm kept the German folk

---

[215] Hauck p.368; West *Serpent* p.147

tales alive in the early 1800's, and inspired others around the world to do the same. Their original tales, published in 1812, were far different from the same tales reissued in the mid-1800's. The originals have many references to sex, violence or "taboo" subjects, and in some cases they are terrifying. Their second version edited many of these references out. Most of these "topics not suitable for children" are rarely found in modern editions. This was not so in the period prior to the Victorian age of the mid-1800's.[216] Those who developed these tales wrote in the language of Hermetic symbolism. To cut off one's head, or tie someone to a tree all had important symbolic meaning for the initiates. In fact some of the symbology was specifically devised to scare off those not wanting to learn the true secrets.

It is a shame that most of the original versions are unknown in the modern world, their "softened Disney-like" versions in their place. Children sense the real truth in the old tales instinctively and know the modern ones are not telling all of it. Read the Disney Cinderella and Grimm's original version, and it will be no surprise which one will light up the child's eyes. Amazingly, if one simply worked with the original tale they would find that the heroines were not the passive girls represented in modern texts that Alan Dumas describes as "a sorry excuse for a heroine." The original girls were active, strong willed, intelligent and created their own destiny rather than wishing for a fairy godmother or a prince to make things all right. A tale of wishing and hoping produces girls who grow up to be passive, waiting for their Prince Charming to come along to save them rather than follow the original tales where they decide what it is they want, and then use all of their resources to go and make it happen.[217]

Another group who began working with the tales in the 1900's were psychologists. Their books describe the tales in the realms of sex, Oedipal feelings, oral fixations and the like. The tales were not created by modern psychologists but by initiates of the Ancient Mystery Schools. The tales do have psychological elements, but Hermeticists are teaching the destruction of the conscious mind. Few modern psychologists work with understanding the ancient silent knowledge. They have found the exoteric (outer) wisdom in the tales, but they are missing the most important esoteric (inner) wisdom. Most only work with modern renditions of the tales, or the French tales of Perrault the modern versions are based on. These modern versions of course are virtually devoid of the ancient wisdom. An example of this is Aesop's fables which are not esoteric as they do not touch on spiritual truths, they make a point of the psychological.[218] Aesop's fables are meant to be used by the mind

---

[216] Sierra, Judy *Cinderella* (Oryx *Press 1992) p.164*

[217] *Dumas, Alan ed Cinderella* a Casebook (University of Wisconsin Press 1982) pp. 298-300

[218] West *Serpent* p.149

exoterically, understanding the content that is in plain view. Fairy tales are meant to be used by the heart and the subconscious mind. It is recommended that if one wants to work with fairy tales, they should find the oldest original versions possible, sex and violence and all. These are the versions that carry the Hermetic wisdom.

Hermetic alchemy is the study of the process of the transformation of a human being from a black lead to an astral gold. This transformation occurs through a process of meditation, knowing thyself, and then purifying and transmuting all that was found to be inferior in the mind, body and spirit. This process was hidden by the terminology of a laboratory and the breakdown and change of substances. Strange drawings displayed furnaces or lab instruments. Their work eventually became the science known today as chemistry, but chemistry is not alchemy. The true alchemist was veiling the process of spiritual transformation. Alchemy is also the basis of modern psychology, which is why for Carl Jung to be a spectacular psychologist he had to first be a spectacular alchemist (which he was, along with studying with African shaman). On the other hand most modern psychologists are not alchemists thus are only able to understand a small piece of what is available in the tales.

Fairy tales have similarities in their construction and writing. Usually there is a difficult set of tasks, or a quest for a treasure that is usually guarded by monsters. The goal is achieved through intelligence, courage, sustained effort and purification of some sort. The quest is actually the path of the spiritual adept. The prize may be a prince, princess or jewels, symbolizing the goal of the high initiate, which is enlightenment. That is why the stories end 'happily ever after,' as by the end of the tale the main characters are no longer of the material or physical world. They are initiates and live in a different way, in a different relationship with the universe and its Creator.[219]

Perhaps the most important thing to keep in mind is that the myth is not telling historical events (even though it may be related to actual events). It is written just for the reader. It is a piece of true art, one that can open the doors of illumination to help you transform from an ordinary human being. They are stories of joy, grief, challenge and learning as the initiate travels the path from darkness to light. The myth is meant as a teaching tool for you. Since the only teaching that was deemed value in the mysteries was personal experience, the myths were meant to be lived out by the readers. Muata Ashby claims that just reading a myth will only keep the knowledge in the intellect, not allowing the deep inner truths to be revealed. "You must resolve to discover the myth in every facet of your life, and in so doing you will be triumphant as the hero(ine) of the myth."[220]

---

[219] West *Serpent* p.147
[220] Ashby *Ausarian* p.25

Following are examinations of three of the best known tales: Little Red Riding Hood, Cinderella and the Ugly Duckling. It can be helpful to find a version of the tale before reading the following commentary to add to your understanding. In Hans Christian Anderson and Grimm's there are over 400 tales alone, not to mention all of the other tales from around the world. After reading this book try reading some of the 'less-known' tales like Grimm's "The Story of the Youth Who Went Forth to Learn What Fear Was." The lesser known stories may in fact contain more wisdom than the popular tales investigated here.

Little Red Riding Hood[221]

93:The wolf and Little Red Cap

Grimm's tale of "Little Red Cap" has an ending that is usually edited out of modern versions. The story starts with a young girl wearing a cap of red velvet that became our familiar riding hood. Red is the colour of the final stage of the Hermetic process. This stage completes work on the upper energy centers located on the head. The title of the story is informing us that the tale concerns the transformation. We find that she has a grandmother who loves her and there "was nothing that she would not have given the child." The grandmother is likely the higher self. However, we are told the grandmother is ill and weak, thus Red Cap is ignoring her higher/spiritual self. Red Cap is to go and visit her grandmother's house (a metaphor for the inner mind of the initiate). Her mother gives her a piece of cake and a bottle of wine. The bottle is mentioned a few times in the story and Red Cap is told not to "fall and break the bottle or the grandmother will get nothing." The bottle must be the 'vessel' where the alchemical elixir of life will be fashioned. If it breaks, the work is stopped and none of the wisdom will combine with our highest spiritual part.

The mother tells Red Cap to set out before it gets hot (to start the process immediately), to walk quietly (the process of meditation), and to not

[221] A great teaching tool for the Hermetic wisdom I discuss in all of the tales is found in Norville, Roy *Hermes Unveiled*

run off the path (don't stray from the Hermetic process). Red Cap went into the woods (the symbol of the dark and difficult journey through ignorance). As soon as she enters (began meditating) she encounters a wolf (the conscious mind that does not want to be silent but constantly howls at us). "She did not know what a wicked creature he was, and was not at all afraid of him," for she did not understand the dangers that the conscious mind brings. Immediately the wolf started to ask Red Cap questions (as our conscious mind will do with us as soon as we try to quiet it).

Red Cap tells the wolf that her grandmother's house stands under three oak trees and three nut trees (three representing the stages of the Hermetic process). The name Druid comes from the Greek word Drus meaning oak. An oak can represent the physical consciousness because the old trees usually grew in a hollow that is similar to a cave, but the cave conceals a hidden treasure. The oak trees the Druids actually worshiped were not the 'physical ones' seen outside but the 'inner one' of which the spine was the trunk.

The wolf then decides to not just eat the grandmother (higher self) or Red Cap (lower self) and says, "I must act craftily so as to catch them both." This is the work of the conscious mind, which as soon as we try to do any process designed at lessening its grasp on us will do everything in its power to stay in control. The wolf suggests as he walks with Red Cap that she look at the beautiful flowers, birds and sunbeams (to spend time focusing on the outer physical world, the world of the conscious mind and to thus spend less time working on the inner mind). Red Cap thinks it would be nice to give her grandmother a flower and claimed "it is so early in the day that I should still get there in good time." This is typical of a new initiate who looks to take a break in the training or not focus as strongly with the work after a while. The new initiate may think there is 'lots' of time when in fact there is not. She ran from the path (stopped doing the work) and every time she picked a flower, she saw a more beautiful one and went deeper into the woods. This means she followed more closely the illusionary material world, going deeper and deeper into the darkness of the woods away from the light of the process. While she was focusing on the flowers (material world), the wolf (conscious mind) ran straight for the grandmother (higher self).

The wolf tricked his way in (as the conscious mind often plays tricks with us) and ate the grandmother and then put on her clothes and climbed into her bed. The changing into the grandmother's clothes is a metaphor that what we often think is our higher/spiritual self is actually the conscious mind in disguise. By going off the path "picking flowers" we will have a hard time recognizing if it is really our higher self or the conscious mind in disguise.

Red Cap has this exact problem when she gets to grandma's house and does not recognize the wolf, but notices the big ears, eyes, hands and mouth. This of course is four of the five senses (with taste being the wolf wanting to eat her), and are symbols for the way the conscious mind creates the illusion of the material world. There is an Absolute Reality beyond but when living through our senses as 99.9% of the world does, we will be unable to see True Reality instead living in a world of illusion (maya). Red Cap had fallen off the path, or she would have recognized the illusion. She could not and was eaten by the wolf.

A huntsman, one who hunts wolves (parts of us that attempt to destroy the conscious mind) hears the wolf asleep and snoring (mind not being used). He comes to the house (inner mind) and realizes the grandmother (high self) may have been eaten (had the link destroyed). The huntsman takes a pair of scissors and cuts open the stomach of the sleeping wolf. The scissors are like the sword, a cutting type of intense meditation needed to cut away the links of the conscious mind. With two cuts to the stomach, Red Cap comes out "shining" and says, "how dark it was inside the wolf" (in the control of the conscious mind). The grandmother then also appears out of the belly "barely able to breathe" signifying the inability to properly use the breath, a key to any mystical discipline. That she had come out of the darkness into light symbolized her creation of the astral body.

A number of stones were fetched and replaced in the wolf's belly and when he wanted to run away, the stones were so heavy that he collapsed at once and died (the conscious mind was brought down). The grandmother ate the cake and wine, cake being part of Egyptian initiation celebration later evolving to our birthday cakes. Red Cap now vowed to stay on the path "as long as I live, I will never by myself leave the path."

Yet, the story does not end there. Red Cap was again bringing cakes to her grandmother, but no vessel of wine (as she had created the elixir) when another wolf appeared. The wolf tried to "entice her from the path." This is important for all transformative disciplines tell us that just when we think we have our conscious mind in control, it will resurface with more vigor in one final attempt to win back control. Red Cap hurried past and went to Grandmother's house, thus stayed on the path. She was going to fight the conscious mind directly. The wolf was unable to enter through the shut door (the inner mind had been able to shut out the conscious).

With the wolf on the roof, grandmother has Red Cap fill a stone trough with sausage water with which she was cooking. The wolf sniffed the water and fell off the roof into the trough and drowns. Red Cap was joyous "and no one ever did anything to harm her again." She was now fully in control of her conscious mind and had done so by staying on the path using courage and effort, as we all will have to do to defeat the part of us that must go.

In an old French version of the tale the path of the material world that is symbolized by the flowers in Grimm's story is replaced by a choice. Here the wolf stands at a fork in the road and asks which road Red Cap wants to follow:

pins or needles. This is a sewing reference of the way to repair a garment. The easy way is to use a pin to just tack it in place but it will not last long as a repair. To do it with needle and thread will do the job right, but it will take considerable time and effort. Red Cap in the tale chooses the path of pins (the simple path, that of the ego and the material world). In other versions of the tale, Little Red Cap manages to escape the wolf using her cunning and intelligence. Instead of being eaten by the wolf in grandma's house, she recognizes its evil intentions (as all intentions of the conscious are evil) and forces the wolf to let go of her by claiming she needs to go outside and relieve herself.[222] This version never appears in modern stories.

It is the Perrault version from France where Red Cap's name has been changed to Little Red Riding Hood. It was Perrault who has also given us our awful modern version of Cinderella (see the following section) but does us no favours with this story. There is no rescue; Little Red Riding Hood simply dies. He omits most of the story such as key facts of Red Cap being warned to not stray off the path. He adds a moral to the end of the story, "Nice girls ought not listen to all sorts of people." A true Hermeticist would have no need for a moral, as the tale is not about the physical world but a metaphor of the journey of spiritual transformation. The story itself would provide the keys needed to unlock the doors of the work. With the addition of a moral, it is quite clear that Perrault is not passing on Hermetic wisdom. Perrault also puts his ideas in explicit detail. His is a story about sex. Riding Hood undresses in the house while the wolf tells her his strong arms are to better embrace her. Riding Hood also makes no attempt to escape or fight back. Thus is she naive, or wants to be seduced.[223] Either way this is no heroine, the story is written by someone without the Hermetic keys to understand the oral version of the tales he was hearing and thus should be ignored by those on the path. Work with the other versions that still contain the ancient wisdom, usually with the Red Cap title.

Cinderella

The tale of Cinderella can be found in more languages and parts of the world than any other myth except that of Osiris and Isis. It is found in Europe, Asia, Africa, Middle East, and North and South America. Its widespread presence immediately shows the importance of the tale, for it has survived in so many ways around the world. Two of the earliest versions are the Egyptian story of Rhodopis and the 800 AD story from China of Yeh-h-sien.

Unfortunately the best known version is actually the most divergent of all the Cinderella stories. Our version, made famous by the Disney movie, comes from a book of fairy tales by Charles Perrault in the 1670's in France.[224]

---

[222] Bettelheim p.171, Sierra p.164
[223] Bettelheim pp.168-69
[224] Sierra p.161p.151

Perrault was a member of the court of Louis XIV and wrote an odd version. Perrault also added moral, as he did with Red Cap. For this reason, the older versions that still contain the true wisdom will be examined. Learning the wisdom in the original tales will help you be able to look at the Perrault/Disney version to realize what key information was changed or left out.

The true Cinderella tales have common elements. Usually a young girl (but sometimes a boy) is persecuted and mistreated by their family. They receive some sort of magical help so they can be recognized for the good and beautiful person they are and marry the prince or princess. There is usually proof of identity, often by a shoe that is usually golden. A hearth and ashes (dirtiness of the main character) are common, as are helpful animals, a magic tree, three visits to a dance or church with three times running away, and Cinderella succeeding through intelligence and courage. Those familiar with the Perrault/Disney version will notice her shoe is made of glass (not gold), there are no magic trees, she only goes to the dance once, and Cinderella is not intelligent or courageous but whines and wishes for things.

Aschenputtel

We start with the oral version found in Grimms which "is closer to the European oral tradition than Perrault's tale."15 Grimms edited this version in their second published book but it is important to work with the original from 1812. The story starts with the death of a girl's mother who as she died promised to be with her always. When the father remarried the new wife brought two daughters with her. Her stepsisters were "fair to look upon, but dark and ugly in their hearts." The evil/ugly stepsisters are common to the Cinderella stories and they represent the physical and material world of duality that we live in. In truth there is only the Absolute but without wisdom we see the world in terms of opposites (high-low, good-bad, big-small, left-right, man-woman). Notice in most of the stories the stepsisters will always be concerned with physical reality.

The stepsisters wore good clothes, and gave the girl the old ugly ones and wooden shoes. They forced the girl to work in the kitchen and to do numerous chores. The girl had nowhere to sleep but the hearth among the ashes. We are told that because she was always dusty and dirty she was called Aschenputtel. A lot of information is provided here. The name Aschenputtel is a German word for a pot that sits in the fireplace. This word ties in with the work she is forced to do in the kitchen. The heat represented here is the initial stage of the alchemical process that requires heat to break down the impure elements of the body to an ash. This blackened state, Nigredo or Calcinatio, is represented by the fact she must sleep in the hearth with the ashes thus becoming black. In our modern version her name is Cinderella, the cinders referring to the blackened state that must occur. This state requires a complete breakdown of our association with reality and who we think we are. In this story the breakdown is represented first by the death of the mother and then with the introduction of the stepsisters and stepmother. She works constantly without hope, a common experience of those going through Nigredo. Speaking from experience, Nigredo is a time of illness, depression and a complete overturning of who one thinks they are and what they think the world to be.

The father, before going to a fair, asks his children what they want him to bring back. The stepsisters want "fine clothes, jewels and pearls," all material elements of the dualistic physical world. Aschenputtel instead wants the first twig that strikes her father on the way home. She asks for something in the realm of nature, which is the first discipline learned in alchemy. What he brings for her is a hazel branch. Hazel is a type of wood that is symbolic of rebirth, thus will help in the rebirth of her dead mother and the girl's personal attachment to the spirit world. She plants the branch over the grave and cries, which causes the tree to grow through her tears. The second stage of the alchemic process is Dissolution or Solutio, where the element of water is used to work with the ash to clean it away. It does so by exposing the hidden emotions of the body, and involves the process of crying whereby we look at all of the hurts we are holding, finally to release them. Only then can we grow. The fact that the tree grows over the grave signifies that the gifts she will receive from this spot are beyond the physical world.

She sits under the tree three times a day (again the number of the process). A white bird comes to the tree and brings her whatever she asks for. The white dove is also a symbol of Albedo, which is also seen as the whitening whereby the black is purified by water to a pure white. The King announces a three day dance (notice it was three days) and all the beautiful women are invited. When Aschenputtel wants to go, her mother and stepsisters laugh. She is forced to pull lentils out of the ashes. With help from her magic birds she accomplishes the task, but over and over again the stepmother throws more lentils on the fire and Aschenputtel cries more and more each time. This is showing the length of time that can be involved in the process of Dissolution, with continued pain and work as more buried events come to the surface. Even though she completes the work, the stepmother and sisters leave for the dance without Aschenputtel. Picking the lentils out of the fire can also represent the stage of Seperatio where one must separate out the negative parts of the being.

Aschenputtel asks for help from her mother's grave. The white bird provides a dress of gold and a pair of silver and silk slippers that gets Aschenputtel to the dance. At the ball, her own stepfamily does not recognize her. This is a key point of the story that is often overlooked. Why did they not recognize her? This is answered in the Cinderella tale of the Micmac Native Americans where only the heroine is able to "see" the Invisible One. Shamans call the ability to break free of illusion/maya as "seeing." The average person looks at things, but the shaman can see the real essence. We see a person or a table, but the shaman sees what something really is and can not be fooled by outer appearances. The stepfamily could not "see" Aschenputtel because they are of the physical world and have not gained wisdom to allow them to "see" the true identity of this new arrival.

The King's son dances with no one else saying to other men who ask, "No. She is my partner." This is referring to the step called Conjunction, where our male and female halves of our being must be brought together. At the end of the evening, the prince wants to see Aschenputtel home to know where she lives, but she runs away to hide in the dove's tree house. The tree (representing the chakras) is cut down to find no one inside the house. The father wonders if it had been his daughter, but finds Aschenputtel at home in her dirty clothes with an oil lamp burning in the chimney (again representing the work being done on the chakras). The entire scene repeats itself again, this time with Aschenputtel climbing up a pear tree after running from the dance. The Maya used the pear tree to represent the heart.

For the third dance Aschenputtel is given gold slippers by the magic birds. When she tries to run away this time, the prince places pitch (tar) all over the stairs that causes her right shoe to get stuck. The tar on the stairs may represent the dark matter in our subconscious which clings to the feet, thus making the path difficult for us to follow. It is also important that it is her right shoe that was lost and not the left. The right side is our active side, and losing this shoe would be taking away her forces of acting.

As in most of the Cinderella stories the shoes are made of gold, gold representing the final stage of the process or our astral body. Hermes is often shown in gold shoes with wings representing the golden astral body that can travel anywhere. The shoe is always key to the story and often the prince or king never even meets Cinderella but only finds her shoe. The shoe is said to be small and slender and he promises to marry whomever it fits. The human foot, as is shown in reflexology, contains a connection with every part of the human body. A problem with the liver, bladder, or sore wrist can all be cured through the foot. For a spiritual adept the foot can be a representation of the whole person, and a shoe may create an imprint of the foot when worn. Thus for one who can psychically read such things, to have one's shoe would be enough to completely know everything about a person. This is why the prince or king (if an adept) would never need to meet the girl in person only to see her shoe.

In the Aschenputtel version, the prince searches far and wide for the shoe's owner. When he comes to the family's house the stepsisters are tried first. Often omitted in modern version is that the stepmother has the sisters cut off pieces of their feet to fit in the shoes. One cut of a toe for "when you are queen you will never have to walk again." The shoe fits the stepsister's foot but as the couple rides away two doves on the hazel tree tell the prince to look at the blood on the shoe. The shoe was not a perfect fit. The second sister cuts off a heel, but with the same result with help from the doves. The doves ask the prince both times to turn around and look behind him. This symbol is often displayed in medieval art with a person or animal turning around. It refers to the need for one to turn their gaze back on themselves and look with meditation and reflection at what they always believed to be the truth. The prince does this and sees the new truth that the shoes do not fit, thus the sisters are not the girl from the ball. This is an example of how we must look back on ourselves to find everything that is truly impure, even the things we have hidden from ourself or always found an excuse for.

Before Aschenputtel tries on the shoes, she washes her face and hands (another example of the continued purification). The golden shoe fits perfectly and the prince knows this is his bride. The astral body has been perfected and the wedding can now happen (the chemical wedding that all on the path are attempting to complete inside of ourselves). At the wedding the doves pluck out the eyes of the stepsisters thus guaranteeing they will never be able to "see" with the Eye of Horus. The tale mentions they "will go blind for the rest of their days" meaning they will never, due to their wickedness of their hearts, be able to "see the light." It is a final warning to all on the path to find purity of heart.

Pea D'Annisso/ Allerleirauh (many furred creature)

Two similar tales, one from France and Germany, are reviewed together. As a note, the German version seems to hold more specific information and will be the main focus of this section. These are very old tales, older than the Perrault version and perhaps the Grimm version. The storyline is unique and often not found in fairy tale books. The main reason that the tales are omitted from most books is because the tale begins with the father wanting to marry his daughter, our Cinderella heroine.

In both stories a man's beautiful wife dies and makes him promise not to marry again unless he finds someone as beautiful as her. The German edition adds she should also have the mother's golden (astral) hair. As the unnamed daughter grows up she begins to look more and more like her deceased mother, so the father decided she is the one he should marry. She uses her cunning in the German version to ask for three dresses (for the three Hermetic stages), one each of the sun, moon and stars. In the French version our heroine does little for herself and asks for help from her fairy godmother (a representation of spirit guides or guardian angels), who tells the child to ask her father for special dresses.

The heroine is ready to run away once she has the three dresses and demands also a special cloak make out of a thousand animals. The animals are representative of the powers of nature that one must grasp and understand: the animal, plant, elemental kingdoms needed to secure help in the spiritual realm. Alchemists like Nicholas Flamel claimed that if one did not first study nature and her process, one could not even begin alchemy. The French version condenses all of this into the fairy godmother, much less solid symbolism. When she is ready to run away (lose her identity) she takes three treasures (a golden ring, spinning wheel and reel), the dresses and the cloak. She then commands herself to God (prays or meditates) and travels the whole night (time for going inward to quiet of the mind). Eventually she comes to a forest (symbolic of the dark place we must travel through on our meditative journey), sits down inside a hollow tree and falls asleep (went inside and meditates). The French version has the godmother giving the girl a chest that can go underground (or to the inner depths of the mind), a magic wand, and a donkey skin (pea d'Annisso) which is similar to the animal skin of the German version. She also flees during the night (the time of quiet and meditation).

We find the girl in the German version sleeps until noon (the time of the most heat from the sun, or inner fire) just as the King's hunting party finds her. The party brings her back to work in the kitchen (again the heat) and sweeping the ashes (the blackening of Nigredo). In the French version, she comes to the home of a noble family. In symbolic terms a noble refers to a Hermetic initiate. Thus she comes to those of wisdom who hire her as a turkey girl, doing the hard and dirty work of cleaning out the stables. This is similar to sleeping in the hearth with the ashes as she is blackening in Nigredo. When asked what her skill is she says she can make the most beautiful lace in the world. Lace is a symbol connected to the loom or weaving apparatus. Lace represents the web of life, the interconnected strands that bind all of creation together. The German version uses the spinning wheel and reel, which represents wool or string. She is given a room to sleep but often sleeps in the corner of the hearth, symbolizing a warming heat similar to what is found in the stage of Seperatio. Every evening the girl opens the chest to look at her beautiful dresses, wash herself (purify) and comb her hair (which separates the hairs, then brings it back together).

In the German version there is a great feast, to which she manages to sneak into after taking off her animal cloak and washing her face and hands (like in the French version). She let her "beauty shine forth as if one sunbeam after another were coming out of a black cloud." She goes to the feast in her gold dress of the sun and dances with the King. Afterwards, she runs back to her room, puts on her animal skin and dirties herself so as to be unnoticed.

In the French version, a prince comes by the stables and insults her with a poker, bellows and a stick. The poker and the bellows are both famed symbolic tools of the alchemist, working in the furnace of the lower energy source of the body (called the Dan Tien by Taoist Qi Gong and Tai Qi masters). When the girl finds there is to be a ball she opens the chest (inner mind) and puts on one of the dresses. The chest takes her underground to where the ball was taking place (journey to the inner self). The prince dances with her. The next day she was teased and shamed by the prince. The average reader will think the prince in the story is a bad person, and may wonder why our heroine wants such a terrible person, and why he does not apologize. However, if the prince is a symbol of a true master, then the depiction is accurate. A master knows all of our weak points, and our ways of keeping the ego in place, thus can play a very nasty game with us to dethrone our self-importance. When one has no self importance left, one does not care what others think of them.

Eventually the prince becomes ill, and while in bed (immobile and able to use the inner subconscious mind) he begins to wonder if his beautiful girl and the turkey girl (Pea D'Annisso) were connected. So worried he becomes that he did not eat anything (he fasts) and claims he will only eat soup made by Pea. The soup is representative of the elixir of life, of feeding the soul. To make the soup Pea washes herself (purifies), combs her hair and puts on her loveliest dress "so as to be clean when she made the soup." Thus one cannot make the elixir of life while one is impure and not gone through the purification process. Pea brings the soup to the prince, who sees her shine like gold (her astral body). She no longer wears her donkey skin and they were married.

In the end of the German version the maiden is forced by the cook to make the King's soup (same as above), but she places the gold ring in it. At the second feast she wears her silver dress (showing she first works on solar male energy and now she is working on lunar feminine energy). In the soup she placed the spinning wheel. For the third dance she wears the star dress, but while dancing the King places the ring on her finger (this is the equivalent of the shoe as identification). She stays too late (a common feature of the Cinderella tale) and does not have time to change out of her dress; she covers it up with her cloak. When she brings the soup the final time with the gold reel in the soup, the King finds the reel, sees the ring on her finger (proof of identity) then removes the cloak to see the dress. She was now in her full
splendor "and could not hide herself anymore" referring to her newly formed astral body. The king marries her and they live happily ever after.

Yeh-h-sien

This Chinese version is the oldest known complete Cinderella story still in print, recorded around 800 AD. Here the father is a cavemaster (a name used for wise one). Eventually both the father and mother die but our heroine is brought up by the cavemaster's second wife. The references to collecting firewood in dangerous places and drawing water from deep pools are of the alchemic stages of Nigredo/Calcinatio and Dissolution. The fish she catches has red fins and gold eyes representing the final stages of the process.

We are later told Yeh-h-sien has to go to a spring that is far away, a long hard journey. The fish itself is ten feet long (ten the number of completion). The stepmothers cut off the fish's head (ego consciousness), and the fish bones are hidden under a dung hill, meaning gold will be found where you don't expect it - in our own lead. After help from above Yeh-h-sien is able to locate the fish bones, who give her everything she needs.

Instead of a ball, the other sisters are invited to the cave festival while our heroine watches the fruit trees in the garden. She follows in a cloak of kingfisher feathers and shoes of gold, but she runs away losing the famous shoe. The king has every maiden in the land try on the shoe but it fits no one as it is, "so light it made no noise even when treading on stone." This is a reference to the quiet of meditation, and the stone is what blocks and hides the inner mind.

Interestingly, this story ends with the king using the fish bones to grant him riches. When they no longer do so he buries them along the seashore and covers them with 100 bushes of pears, showing he was not using the heart when asking for wishes, but the mind. The sisters and mother die after being hit by flying rocks.

Billy Beg and the Bull

Interestingly the Cinderella story that seems to have the most Hermetic wisdom hidden in it comes from Ireland, and has a boy instead of a girl as the hero. A male Cinderella usually wins a princess by being a giant killer or dragon slayer. The serpent has two meanings shown in Egypt, one as Apop (the slithering conscious mind) while the other serpent gains wings (the rising serpent kundalini which leads to enlightened wisdom).The dragon in these stories are a representation of Apop. This tale has tremendous depth, and only a few key aspects will be explored in this commentary. This is a story of the number nine. It appears in the beginning of the tale when the bull leaps nine miles high, nine miles deep and nine miles broad. The number appears at the end of the story by claiming the wedding lasts nine days, nine hours, nine minutes etc. Nine is the number of Osiris and is the number of cycles and regeneration. Thus this Cinderella story explains the regeneration of nature.

From the bull's left ear, Billy is able to find things that will bring him food and nourishment. The left side of the body is the feminine side or yin, the side of Mother Earth that provides for our receptive needs. The right side is male or yang, and from this ear Billy pulls a magic stick that will give him tremendous strength. The stick is a symbol of the male element of action. There are many fights between bulls that result in blood. The bull is a representation of male sexual energy, with the blood representing the concentrated power of meditation or in this case the power to gain control of one's sexual energy. The bull is eventually defeated by the black bull, symbolizing the ego and Nigredo, the first stage of the process. Billy spent the time after the death not drinking or eating (fasting), and cries salt tears. The tears of salt are representative of the second stage dissolution, where we destroy our emotional salt blocks in the body and release them in our tears. Tears contain salt that the ancient alchemists believed were remnants of the actual solid blocks in the etheric body.

It is suggested to read the story with a dictionary for a number of words in the tale can provide different insights into the wisdom when using alternate meanings. When Billy is to fight the giants they ask, "swing by the back, cut of the sword, or square round of boxing." To "swing" is to lift up with a swinging motion, but it can also mean to change one's opinion. The back can be a term for that which is less seen or less used. Thus a swing by the back can mean to change the opinion of the subconscious mind, which is rarely seen and remains hidden. Being a Hermeticist, Billy chooses this option. He drives the giant into the earth with only the heads above ground (another example of where the process is focused) and cuts out the tongue, a reminder to remain silent in meditation and gain inner wisdom and also to remain silent about the actual methods of the process.

When asked if he saw the giant Billy replies, "nothing worse nor myself." This can be re-stated in our language as "nothing worse than myself" signifying that the giant he fights in the physical world is simply a manifestation of the giant inside. This is a key component of ancient funerary literature such as the Tibetan or Egyptian Books of the Dead. It speaks of the horrible creatures that we will have to face of the journey after death. Yet they also let you know that all the creatures are only manifestations of the creatures inside each one of us. By eliminating the negative aspect of ourselves, the monster outside will go away.

Interestingly, the most important line of the entire story is the last. Most tales end with the words 'happily ever after.' This tale could easily end with the second last line of this story with the happy wedding. However this tale adds one more significant line, "I got brogues of porridge and breeches of glass, a bit of pie for telling a lie, and then I came slithering home." The line intrigued fellow Hermeticist friend Darren Loudfoot so we studied it some more. The line "I came slithering home" makes reference to a serpent and it is likely referring to the narrator of the story. Thus the narrator of the story is a serpent. The serpent or snake is a sign of hidden wisdom in the ancient world, and with the serpent narrating the story reveals that this tale is full of hidden wisdom.

The remainder off the last line has been studied with the use of a dictionary for "brogues of porridge and breeches of glass" made no sense on the surface. The dictionary informed that a brogue is an Irish dialect or a strong ornamental shoe. Porridge is the oatmeal food we think of, or a term for imprisonment. Thus Billy was imprisoned in strong shoes. Breeches are riding trousers worn just below the knee, while glass is transparent. The line may be telling that he is imprisoned or focused only on the strong shoes, or the path of wisdom. He wears breeches made of glass so if you look beyond the outer material you see his legs (the inner usually hidden). His bit of pie can mean he offers us a small part of the hidden wisdom (as the good part of the pie is hidden beneath the crust). By saying he is telling a lie could be a warning that some part of the story was not the truth and it is up to the reader through training to understand which part is a lie.

As you can see from this short explanation of this tale that it is a great source of wisdom and should be read with a dictionary to find further wisdom is hidden within the word play.

The Ugly Duckling

The ugly duckling is truly a story of esoteric and alchemic wisdom. The story immediately points to its Egyptian roots. The tale begins with storks who "walked on their long red legs talking Egyptian because that was the language they had been taught by their mothers." The stork is a version of the ibis, the great bird of Tehuti. The mention of the Egyptian language at the beginning of a Danish tale alerts our readers right away to what will be forthcoming, some of the hidden Hermetic wisdom of Thoth.

Before we even meet the newborn duck, we are told of a setting full of woods (places where it is dark and difficult to navigate through like the process of wisdom the initiate will undertake). The area has a number of hidden pools and lakes (water referring to the power of meditative reflection to look at the self and know thyself). In a forest between a moat and a castle are stalks so high that a child could stand upright under them and imagine that they were in the middle of the woods. The child symbolizes one at the beginning of the journey (as the wise master is depicted as being elderly). The high stalks show the process to be worked on will be high up, the head and mind. Also the mention of imagination is made. Alchemists see this as part of what they call the prima materia or first matter. A child will use their imagination, but as adults we lose this ability. It is the imagination which allows us to connect to the realm of spirit above.

The mother duck builds her nest in this place and sits with her eggs "feeling sorry for herself because it was taking so long and nobody came to visit her." This statement is explaining the initial steps in the process. With no one coming to visit, it would be quiet thus a perfect time for meditative practice. There is also reference to the length of time it takes. Personal transformation is a long, hard process, no matter what the new age seminars say. You will not be transformed or ready to heal after taking a weekend course. The process will take your full effort for a long time, and you will have to confront your inner demons that most would rather not admit to having. Most would rather be like the other ducks that "preferred swimming in the moat, or gossiping, opposed to being quiet in meditation."

All of the eggs hatch except for one. The mother is tired and asks for help and an old duck comes to help her but simply says it is a turkey egg. He tells the mother to forget about it and go ahead in life with the others. This is actually the ego talking. When we begin the steps to transformation we will see some small successes but often the big ones are right around the corner. The ego is afraid of relinquishing total control of our being, so it tries everything to trick us into stopping our work. It does not want us to continue to our goal, the complete destruction of itself. So here the duck tells the mother to forget the egg and go on. The mother however decides that she has put in this much effort, she can afford a little more. This is a wise message for all of us to keep putting in the effort.

Sure enough the egg hatches, but the duckling is deemed to be ugly and not like the other ducks. That one is not like the others is a clear reference to one who begins following a mystery/spiritual path. They begin to realize that they are not like the rest of the people in the world who are only interested in the physical and the material. In many versions the duckling is shown as black. Black is the first stage of the alchemic process, Nigredo or Calcinatio. Here we seek to use fire on ourselves as we find what is impure in our make up and burn ourselves down to a black ash that will be worked with in the later stages as in the early parts of Cinderella. This is a tortuous time as one has to undercover most of their shadow elements, impure thoughts and most awful experiences of life. What is not looked at here gets looked at in future stages. This difficult time is echoed in the Ugly Duckling.

A mention is made of families of ducks who get into a fight over the head of an eel. The eel, like the snake, is slippery and moves about all over like the thoughts of our conscious mind. The mind needs to attain a stillness to gain wisdom. The fight is over the head, a direct reference to the mind, but the cat swipes it. In the Egyptian Papyrus of Ani (what we call the Book of the Dead) the cat (powers of feminine reflection) cuts off the head of the serpent Apop, the archenemy of the sun god Ra. Apop keeps us from the light by the moving conscious thoughts in our mind. The cat, representing feminine meditation, is able to cut off the head of the serpent (our thoughts) to allow stillness and the emergence of the light.

The other ducks began to tease the ugly duck mercilessly "look how ugly he is…he's big and doesn't look like everyone else and that is reason enough to beat him." Eventually even his own mother wants the ugly duckling to go away. As mentioned, the initial black stage of the process is a very difficult one. One must follow a special path to wisdom while the rest of the world is following the path of physical gratification. To be different than the rest is to be attacked by the rest for being an outcast. Even family and friends are likely to mock one who follows a true spiritual calling.

Finally the duckling has enough of the insults and attacks that he runs away to be alone and "closed his eyes." This act represents not only the need to be alone so as to meditate properly (with the eyes closed to take the focus off the material world), but is also the fact that one has to be strong and eventually will have to stop spending time with the general uninitiated population. Spiritual advancement depends on it.

The duckling winds up in a swamp where wild ducks live. They admit he is ugly but invite him along anyway (for his initial work had shown he had some of the wisdom). While in the swamp he meets two male ganders. They represent those on the material path for they want the duckling to come with them to go meet some "beautiful wild geese." Almost immediately a hunter kills the two ganders. This is showing what happens if one on the spiritual path gives into the temptations of the physical world. The fact that they are killed is another representation that they are of the physical and will die in the physical.

At this point, dogs come running (the barking mind that must be tamed) and they bare their teeth. Shamans warn that while on a journey if one sees a spirit animal bear their teeth they should be avoided. The duckling does just that, hiding and laying very still (in a deep meditation) and the dogs quietly turn away. The duckling manages to still the mind and overcome physical temptation. As he runs away a wind comes up that nearly stops his progress, symbolic of that which will come up to try and keep us from continuing on the path of wisdom.

The duckling finds an old hut where an old woman lives with a hen and a cat. This may represent finding a temple or teachers. The fact that the ducking has gone through tremendous hardship and work shows that the duck was ready for more advanced teachings. While there the duck thinks he should be allowed to have a different opinion than the other housemates. The woman gets angry and asks if he could lay eggs like the hen or make sparks like the cat. When the duck replies no he is told to "keep your mouth shut, you have no right to opinion when sensible people are talking."

If the hut represents a temple environment this line would make sense. When the student is first working with masters they usually must take a vow of silence, so they can spend their time listening to the wisdom of the teacher. The duckling was asked if he could perform the feats of the other initiates in training, symbolized by the animals in the house. When the duckling said he could not, the masters were in a sense telling him to shut up and listen to the sources of wisdom so that he might learn to have the power the other students have gained. As long as he is talking about his own ideas he cannot learn the truth from the masters. The old woman replies, "that's the truth and I am only telling you for your own good." That is how you recognize a true friend: it is someone who is willing to tell you the truth no matter how unpleasant it may seem at the time. This is also a true master, who loves their pupils so much that they will show them the truth of the universe and themselves, often which is terrifying and unpleasant. One has to realize the master is doing this for our benefit because they want us to experience universal truth and find out what inside of us truly needs to be transformed.

The duck finally leaves (after likely acquiring a large amount of wisdom) and comes to another lake. A raven (another black sign of Nigredo) looks at the duckling and says, "what a terrible time the duckling must have had." The raven is speaking of the hell that the duck must have gone through, but is also referring to the fact that he is close to making it to the next white stage. The lake here may refer to the white stage of dissolution and Albedo, a purification of the black ash by white water.

Just then the duckling sees swans (the white birds) that are flying south for the winter. This is showing that the duckling is not yet at the white stage, but birds that fly south for the winter, fly back next spring. As the weather grew colder the duck keeps swimming in circles, perhaps representing the fact that we constantly are given lessons but as we usually don't learn them. We come right back full circle again repeating our old habits and patterns. The hole in the ice keeps getting smaller until finally he is too tired to swim and sat still, for his patterns finally took him no where. The ice comes around and freezes him solid. Thus when we finally stop running in circles to stare our lesson right in the face, we are often overcome by it.

A farmer (one who grows things and transforms seeds) frees the duckling with his shoe and takes the bird to his wife who brings the "duckling back to life." After seeing and fully integrating the lesson, we are ready to let go of it and the part of us that was not allowing us to move past it. While with the farmer the duckling flew into a milk pail and into flour, both white and representative of the stage of dissolution or Albedo and the whitening purification taking place at this stage.

Finally spring comes and the swans return. The duckling now has "strong and powerful wings," reference to the power and knowledge gained. Yet the duckling finally decides to let the swans kill him, meaning he is finally ready to sacrifice his old self (the ruling ego) and allow the ego to be killed. "Kill me," he whispers to the swan.

At this point the duckling looks into the water and sees that he is actually a swan himself (an initiate). The process had happened some time ago but he had not yet noticed the actual change. "He was thankful that he had known so much want and gone through so much suffering, for it made him appreciate his present happiness and the loveliness of everything about him all the more." A perfect thing to say by someone who reaches "unity with the All."

Children then run out shouting, "look, there is a new one," as the priests would announce a new initiate to the group. Cakes and bread were cast on the lake for the swans, cake being an Egyptian symbol of the end of an initiation process that over time became our traditional birthday cake.

Perhaps the examinations of these three famous tales will bring you to explore them in more detail, and to examine other tales like: Snow White, Aladdin's Lamp, Jack in the Beanstalk and Puss and Boots. Do not forget as well the hundreds of little known tales that carry as much, if not more wisdom than the current most popular stories. The most profound fairy tale that I have found is *Alice in Wonderland*. That book contains elements of shamanism, Zen Buddhism as well as other traditions. Working with the wisdom of the fairy tale can only help your advancement as an adept.

CHAPTER 16
TEOTIHUACAN

94: *View from Pyramid of Sun back to Pyramid of the Moon, Teotihuacan*

The Place Where People Become Gods

There is little that can prepare you for your initial visit to the ancient site of Teotihuacan, about a half-hour drive northeast from Mexico City. While books provide pictures, maps and stories of the site - actually experiencing it is something very different. My first visit to Teotihuacan was with a wonderful Mexican family, the Munoz. As we approached I noticed a gigantic mountain in the middle of nowhere. "What's that", I stupidly asked. "That is Teotihuacan."

The city was deserted and covered with vegetation when the Aztecs discovered it upon taking over Mexico. The Aztecs were a conquering race from the north who misunderstood the powerful wisdom of the conquered Maya and Toltec. The Aztecs didn't know who built Teotihuacan but they did know of a myth that claimed that the 5th Sun (our modern world age) was born there. Two large mounds were dedicated to the sun and moon, and a long open stretch of road was called the "Way of the Dead" because the Aztecs felt the mounds along side were tombs. The Aztecs did give the site the modern name

Teotihuacan, meaning "the place where people wake from the dream of life to become gods."[225] That name is enough of a clue to indicate that this site was the Mexican equivalent of Giza in Egypt. One becomes a god by gaining the wisdom of the universe and these secrets were taught here.

Something has always intrigued modern scholars about this site. While every ancient site in Central America: Copan, Palenque, Tikal and Chichen Itza all have writing of some sort, Teotihuacan amazingly has none. This has led some to believe that perhaps this was not a site of learning after all, since in our modern world all of our learning is in books. This of course is the error of the modern archaeologist not the ancient inhabitants of Mexico. Like the pyramids of Giza (which contain no hieroglyphic inscriptions) Teotihuacan had no need for them. The Hermetic wisdom is actually in plain sight, one just needs the keys of the ancients to be able to locate and understand it.

The site of Teotihuacan will first be explored through the archaeological, astronomical and scientific data found there. The information will be analyzed to show its connections with the wisdom and sites of Egypt. The second section looks more closely at symbol, artwork and mythology. Here the hidden Hermetic wisdom of Tehuti will be presented, much for the first time in print.

Background

95:Model of Teotihuacan

---

[225] Tompkins, Peter *Secrets of the Mexican Pyramids* (Harper and Row 1976) p.12; Berrin, Kathleen and Pasztory, Ester editors *Teotihuacan: Art from the Valley of the Gods* (Thames and Hudson 1993) p.34; Hancock *Fingerprints* p.154

Not much will prepare you for the scale of Teotihuacan. A survey team in 1967 mapped out the city and found it covered eight square miles and could have housed some 250,000 inhabitants. It may have been larger than Ancient Rome. As more of the city was excavated it was found to be a center of trade, politics and especially religion. The city had residences, apartments that could house up to one hundred people, public baths, theaters, ball courts and even hotels. There was also an entire system of artificial waterways and canals that went through the city to bring food from outlying farms and was a connection for trade. Cultures from all over Central America, including the Maya, congregated here making the city a "melting pot" similar to Alexandria 2000 years ago. Today most of the city is still buried (seen only as trees, fields and small hills), but they are in fact hundreds of unexcavated temples.[226] What the tourist sees is but a small, albeit spectacular part of the entire city.

Another aspect of the site, now missing for the modern tourist, is colour. Today most of the colour is gone. The city was completely painted, especially in bright yellow, red and turquoise. If you look closely at some temples small bits of the paint remain. To truly get a sense of the majesty of the city one must imagine the bright coloured paints wherever one goes. Also many of the temples, called talud-tableros, no longer have their structures that likely sat on top.

Most archaeologists date the site from 150 BC-750 AD. Some are not convinced of these conventional dates and push the site's date back to around 1500 BC, and others to a time over 6,000 years ago. A big question is what happened to this site. Once the largest city in the Americas it was abandoned by 750 AD after being destroyed by fire. While suggestions from natural disaster (earthquakes and volcanoes) to some form of peasant revolt are common, most now believe the inhabitants purposely destroyed the site. The work to destroy it would have been as great as to build it.[227] We are looking at this site as a place of ancient hidden wisdom. Perhaps after understanding the wisdom it will become clear why it had to be destroyed. The first question has to be who built it.

Toltecs

Members of all the cultures of Mexico came to Teotihuacan to learn from the inhabitants. The Aztecs had no idea who the builders of the site were, and some modern writers claim the Aztecs thought giants built the pyramids. Actually that is a mistranslation for the actual quote in Sahagun (a Spanish Bishop who copied down the myth and tales of the Aztec in the sixteenth century) reads, "it is unbelievable when they say that these [pyramids] were

---

[226] Tompkins pp. 213-32; Berrin pp.17-18; Hancock *Fingerprints* p.182
[227] Tompkins pp190, 232-36; Hancock *Fingerprints* p.169

302

made by hand, but at the time giants still lived there."[228]   The quote is not saying giants built the pyramids, only giants lived there. No greater giant can be found in the world than a master of the mysteries, and these masters could have been the Toltecs.

The Toltecs were said to inhabit the city of Tollen (Great City), believed by most archaeologists to be the site of Tula just west of Teotihuacan. The name Toltec is Aztec for craftsmen. Sahagun wrote that the Aztecs believed the Toltecs were "superb artisans, devout worshipers, skillful tradesmen, stone masons, carpenters, bricklayers, workers in feather and ceramics, spinners and weavers." Other Aztec sources claim the Toltecs were the inventors of medicine and were great physicians because of their knowledge of herbs. Some called them skilled in astronomy and were able to keep "an accurate count of days and years and the movements of the stars and planets." Still others saw them as the holders of wisdom as their priests could interpret dreams and perform great magic.[229]

The Aztec Ixtlixochitl agreed with many of the above statements but also included that the Toltecs "were the best painters on earth." The supposed Toltec capital of Tula has no paintings or murals. Teotihuacan has some of the greatest mural paintings ever seen in the world, and seems to be its mode of artistic perfection.[230] So it must be asked, how could the greatest painters in the history of the earth have a capital that has no painting? It would make more sense that the famed Toltec capital of Tollen, where Quetzalcoatl (the feathered serpent representing Horus in Mexico) was defeated by Tezcatilpoca (the Mexican version of Set), was not Tula but Teotihuacan.

Way of the Dead

---

[228] Berrin p.158

[229] Sejourne, Laurette *Burning Water* (Thames and Hudson 1957) pp.23, 98; Hancock, *Heaven's* p.20

[230] Sejourne pp.97-98

96:Looking down the "Way of the Dead" from Moon Pyramid, Teotihuacan

The city was divided into four sections by two large streets (or avenues), of which the most famous runs from the Moon Pyramid to the Citadel (see above). It is 2.5 km long and used to extend past the Citadel in the south, perhaps as far as the mountains. The modern name Way of the Dead (Avenida de los Muertos) is a misnomer. The Aztecs named it for the mounds alongside the street that were deemed to be burial tombs. In fact they are temples.

Actually it is not really a road either for the avenue is blocked off at several spots, seemingly to make separate areas. To cross from one section to another requires a great detour up a series of stairs, across a platform and down another set of stairs. This appearance of 'locks' has led some to claim the street was once filled with water to predict earthquakes. Others see it as representing the Milky Way in a great celestial outlay of the sky to the ground serving as a symbolic path on which the spirits can walk.[231] The Nile River near the pyramids at Giza also symbolized the Milky Way and Teotihuacan has a number of connections with Giza. It is important to keep in mind the famous Hermetic axiom, "As above, so below."

Pyramid of the Sun

---

[231] Hancock *Fingerprints* p.173; Hancock *Heaven's* p.25; Tompkins *Mexican* p.232

97:Pyramid of the Sun, notice how the stairs appear to be an outstretched person along the face, Teotihuacan

The largest structure at the site, and the first one every tourist wants to climb, is called the Pyramid of the Sun (see pabove). It is the third largest pyramid by volume in the world, behind the Great Pyramid at Giza and the Pyramid at Cholua located one hour east from Mexico City. From a distance the facing stairs of the pyramid look like a human stretched out with arms and legs. The sun has always been representative of male creative energy, thus the outstretched human on the pyramid may in fact connect the pyramid to the sun. Some claim sun ceremonies occurred here where initiates had Kundalini raised to mix with the solar energies.[232] Many scholars claim the pyramid was originally coloured red, which would make it representative of the final stage in the Hermetic process. One of the key components of the red stage of the process is the purification of the mind to allow the kundalini to flow to the sky.

The pyramid, like most Mexican pyramids, was built successively over smaller ones. Today the base is around 738 feet, making the base of this pyramid similar to the Great Pyramid at Giza, but the pyramids differ in height. The Sun Pyramid is 233.5 feet high, less than the one at Giza. The Great Pyramid at Giza has an angle of construction of 52 degrees while at Teotihuacan the angle is 43.5. Interestingly the base of the pyramid at Giza (3032.16 feet) divided by 2 pi will equal the height of the structure (481.3 feet).

---

[232] Tompkins *Mexican* p.240

The Pyramid of the Sun's base (2932.8 feet) divided by 4 pi provides its height (233.5 feet). This is one of the first connections with this site to that of Giza.[233]

There is more startling information about this pyramid. On May 19 and July 25 when the sun is directly overhead, the west face of the pyramid is oriented perfectly to the setting sun. At the equinox, the passage of the sun's rays result at noon in the progressive "obliteration of a shadow" in 66.6 seconds. As well the lower portion of the fourth level is slightly convex to make a triangle with the rest of the pyramid at 19.69 degrees, the same number as the latitude of Teotihuacan. The significance of this design allows the rays of the sun to fall perfectly on the north face at the equinox. The pyramid also perfectly aligns with the Pleiades.[234] To accomplish such design the builders would need incredible math, astronomy and geodesy. The Great Pyramid at Giza contains similar mathematical and astronomical data.

Unfortunately when archaeologist Leopoldo Batres began to reconstruct the pyramid to help restore Mexican heritage and a sense of their past at the turn of the century, he removed twenty feet of building material on three of the sides. Amazingly he used dynamite to help speed up the project. Today only the west face (not surprisingly where the equinox shadow ritual is still seen) is the only face which is roughly in tact. How much more astronomical and mathematical knowledge was lost in Batres' "reconstruction?" Batres also destroyed several temples at the site by building a railway to remove debris of his excavations.[235]

98:Stone blocks outside of the Pyramid of the Sun. Notice the 5 pointed star on two upper blocks.

---

[233] Hancock Fingerprints pp.178-79

[234] Hancock Fingerprints p.176; Tompkins *Mexican* p.251

[235] Matos, Eduardo *Teotihuacan: City of Gods* (Rizzoli 1990) pp. 28, 30; Berrin p.67; Hancock *Fingerprints* p.191

In front of the pyramid is what is called the Palace. While most of the area has not been restored, it is similar to the mortuary temples at the head of the pyramids at Giza. Carved in a number of stone blocks is the five-pointed star with a circle in the center (see above photo). This was the same symbol that the Egyptians used to represent the Duat (underworld or innerworld) ruled by Osiris. The Great Pyramid of Giza is claimed to have been created for the mysteries of Osiris. Osiris being male was connected with the sun (the title of this pyramid) and his place of eternal residence (Duat) is also found here.

Caves

Beneath the Great Pyramid of Giza is a gigantic man made pit that archaeologists say was originally to be the king's burial chamber. Students of the mysteries know that no one was ever to be buried at the pyramid, the pit was part of the system of wisdom teachings. At the Pyramid of the Sun a long passageway runs for 300 feet when it branches into a cave shaped like a 'four leaf clover.' This gigantic cave looks similar to the chamber beneath the Great Pyramid. The passageway to get to it was modified and now seems very snake-like. In the cave, rocks were used to create a system of drainage pipes that leads to the idea that it must have been a place for some type of special ceremony.[236]

In shamanic cultures a cave is seen as the entrance to the underworld (Duat). A large amount of fish bones were found here that might make the cave a ceremonial center as Mexicans believed humans originated from fish. The Teotihuacan Mapping Project found many artifacts here including highly polished pieces of mirror and signs of rituals with water and fire. Both are aspects of the smoking mirror and burning water to be examined later.

Looking out from the cave entrance 15.5 degrees north of west toward the western horizon was a spot related to the setting sun and Pleiades (an important star group). The sun sets exactly at this spot on August 12 and April 29. The importance is the length of time between the days, 260 from August to April and 105 from April to August. 260 is a Tzolkin (the number of days in a key Mexican calendar) and 105 is created by adding 52+1+52. 52 is a very important number known as the calendar round. August 12th was the day that the long count calendar began in 3114 BC starting our present 13 Baktun cycle that will end in 2012 (see chapter 6 for more information). To the Aztecs the Pyramid of the Sun was the place where the 5th Sun (our present world age) was created.[237] Interestingly the start of the Maya calendar coincides with a key astronomical event at the Toltec site of Teotihuacan. Revisionist writers of

---

[236] Berrin pp. 22, 34; Tompkins *Mexican* pp. 120, 195; Hancock *Fingerprints* p.180
[237] Berrin pp. 22, 23, 34, 35

Egypt like Graham Hancock and Robert Bauval see one shaft of the Great Pyramid to align with the Pole Star. With the connections to the Pyramid of the Sun in Mexico, it might be found that the underground chamber at Giza is also connected with the creation of a world age.

Pyramid of the Moon

North of the Pyramid of the Sun is a smaller pyramid called the Pyramid of the Moon. The Moon Pyramid appears to be the same size as the Sun Pyramid because it was built on higher ground, similar to the Pyramid of Khafre at Giza. Surrounding the Moon Pyramid are twelve smaller temples and a number of alter-type areas. There were a number of passages in the pyramid that were destroyed during a restoration in 1920.[238] This area will be examined in detail in the final sections of this chapter.

After climbing both pyramids it becomes clear that the Moon pyramid is far steeper than the Sun Pyramid. During the climb you wonder why the ancient builders did not change the angle of the stairway to make it easier for those climbing. I believe that there was a key reason for the stairway. Using a very sloped stairway would require one climbing it to walk in a very slow fashion. The idea is to walk with reverence, to not rush your way up. As I did this my consciousness instantly shifted, and my feet were no longer touching the steps. I was still climbing, but floating instead of walking. I am positive that those who quickly climb the stairs will be unable to accomplish part of what the steps were designed to do, offer you the chance to open deeper states of consciousness.

Citadel

---

[238] Tompkins *Mexican* pp. 120, 357

99:Quetzalcoatl head, Citadel group of Teotihuacan

The Spanish named a gigantic enclosed area the Citadel because the thirty-acre area resembled a fortress. A number of smaller temple shrines surround the courtyard, while in the center is the famed Pyramid of Quetzalcoatl (feathered serpent). The pyramid rises 72 feet high in six steps and covers 82,000 square feet. It is smaller than the two other pyramids at the sight but is still impressive due to what is added to its facing. Most of the vibrant colours of paint are now gone, but the giant heads of two figures remain. One is the head of Quetzalcoatl depicted as a reptile with an open mouth surrounded by eleven petals, either feathers or flowers. The second is a figure considered to be Tlaloc, otherwise known as the rain or storm god.[239]

This second figure is speculation to great debate. Sejourne believes Tlaloc represents the god who converts matter into creative energy. Some think the head is not a rain god but is actually a jaguar representing Tezcatilpoca (Smoking Mirror god of the Rain of Fire). He is ruled by serpents (that of the kundalini fire that one must learn to uncoil and rise in order to purify ourselves), the rectangle (symbol of the number 4) and also bears the form of the cross (symbol of male energy and the material world). Tlaloc also seems to have the wings of the butterfly (representing transformation). The authors of

---

[239] Tompkins *Mexican* p.213; Hancock *Fingerprints* p.166

Hamlet's Mill believe Tlaloc is constructed out of two serpents perhaps representing the caduceus.[240] This could in fact be the Mexican Tehuti.

The serpent heads on the walls have some very distinct features. To begin with the mouths are opened and hollowed out ending in a small rounded hole. It is the exact configuration for a person's fist and arm to fit perfectly. At Sacsahuamin in Peru, a snake-like figure is carved into the rock. Warriors would place their hands into the serpent's head to gain great power. A compass placed inside the serpent spins wildly showing very high electromagnetic forces inside the carved head. So too do compass placed on stones at Pumu Punku in Bolivia.[241] No one has yet explained why a carved serpent should have high electromagnetic forces.

Unfortunately Teotihuacan is heavily guarded and I was unable to test my theory of placing my arm in the serpent's jaw. At Chichen Itza there are many open-mouthed serpent heads along the site. I placed my right fist into a mouth asking for the wisdom of Quetzalcoatl to come into me. My right arm was soon on fire as if a lightning bolt was traveling through, and then I was directed the place of healing at Chichen Itza. I'm sure similar things will occur at Teotihuacan if one's fist is placed inside the serpent's jaws.

Pyramid Connections

At Teotihuacan people became Gods. At Giza Pharaohs were transformed to "join the company of the Gods." There are more connections. Like Giza the three pyramids at Teotihuacan have two in a perfect line, with the smaller one offset. It suggests further that the sites are linked by the same knowledge used to create them.[242]

There is suggestion that the three pyramids at Giza represent the mysteries of Osiris (Great Pyramid), Isis (second pyramid) and Horus (third smaller pyramid). Interestingly the main pyramid at Teotihuacan is the Pyramid of the Sun, the sun connected to male energy. The second is the Pyramid of the Moon, and the moon always associated with feminine energy. The combining together of the two created their son Horus, our astral perfected self. The third small pyramid of Quetzalcoatl could be of Horus. The smaller Pyramid of Menkaure was actually two distinct colours, with the top made of white Tura limestone and bottom of red Aswan granite. The Hermetic colours may also represent the battle between Horus and Set. The third pyramid at Teotihuacan has two differing, perhaps conflicting symbols upon it. The mythology of Quetzalcoatl is virtually identical to that of Osiris, Isis and Horus.

Sejourne claimed the Pyramid of Quetzalcoatl may have been the house where the body "buds and flowers," the name the Aztec called the place where

---

[240] Santillana p.290; Tompkins *Mexican* p.214; Sejourne pp.87,99, 104
[241] Landsburg, Alan *In Search of Ancient Mysteries* (Bantam Books 1974) p. plates
[242] Hancock *Fingerprints* p.169

their nobility was educated. All members of the high Egyptian priesthood were considered Followers of Horus and it would be no surprise to find that Toltec priests were Followers of Quetzalcoatl.

John Mitchell was one of the first people to write that ancient sites all over the world were placed on top of a worldwide geodetic grid system.[243] To the ancients this was commonly understood as it is today by shamans and mystics. Energy meridians run through the earth and are referred to as ley lines. Where they cross are the equivalent of acupuncture points on the body, areas where the spot can effect the whole. Great ancient sites were built on these spots, and create the instant shift of consciousness for people who are open to these energies while there. Many of these 'points' no longer have an ancient site on them, or never did, but they contain the same power. It is important to realize that the great sites like Teotihuacan or Giza were not picked at random but at places where one can tap directly into the transformative power of the earth.

Mica

100:Stela with inlaid pieces of mica, small round black rocks, once covered this artwork, Teotihuacan

On the fifth layer of the Sun Pyramid was found a layer of mica, a rock that forms in thin sheets one on top of the other. In 1966 when it was found, Mica was very expensive and was quickly removed for sale. However mica still remains at Teotihuacan at the famed Mica Temple located between the Citadel and the Sun Pyramid. It is usually locked with an iron gate and is guarded so it is difficult to examine.

Under the floor of the temple are two-90 square foot sheets of Mica. Through geologic research it was found that the mica did not come from Mexico but 2,000 miles away in Brazil. There is mica in Mexico, but for some reason this was not seen to be good enough for the construction. The builders had a need for a specific type of Mica and went to considerable lengths to get it. First the 90-

[243] Tompkins *Mexican* p.326; see also Mitchell, John *New View Over Atlantis*

foot square sheets of mica had to be transported from Brazil to the center of Mexico. This is a difficult enough task today never mind 2000 years ago. Secondly, the sheet was placed under the floor where no one would even see it. It could not be decorative, as no one would see it, so why go to all that trouble to obtain it?[244]

Mica has some interesting characteristics. From a spiritual sense mica is seen to offer a window to the psychic realm of divination. The room could have been used for some sort of fortune telling, with the powerful sheet of mica used to increase the psychic abilities of the priests. On a more scientific front mica has a "high electrical resistance and opaqueness to fast neutrons. Hence, it acts as an insulator or nuclear reaction moderator."[245] Could the ancients Toltecs at the site have been using the mica as some sort of power generator for Teotihuacan?

Astronomy and Math

The Maya claimed Teotihuacan was a map of the sky, where dwelt the spirits of the dead. Hermetic teachers explain the microcosm is a relation to the macrocosm. Certain places in the world were designed to be a perfect reflection of the entire universe. Teotihuacan could have been one of these chosen sites. Stansbury Hagar believed that the Way of the Dead represented the Milky Way, and the mounds the planets, to produce a map of our solar system. Hugh Harleston Jr. followed in Hagar's footsteps. Harleston first measured the sight and using the polar radius found the standard unit of measure that he called the Standard Teotihuacan Unit (STU) of 1.059 meters. Using the STU the site began to explain itself through number.[246]

The Citadel produced measurements of 365, 365, 365 and 366 (leap year) to mark a four-year calendar. He believes the Citadel may have been created with the specific platform temples to mark different points of the 52, 260; 360; and 365 day calendars. A clockwise journey of all of the temples could reflect the changing years. Harleston also believes the layout of the Citadel temples reveals pi, phi and epsilon (the rational base of logarithms). The Pyramid of Quetzalcoatl may mark the equinox along its fourth level. There were also many geodetic markers on stones in the hills to mark the solstice and equinox.[247]

---

[244] Hancock *Fingerprints* p.175; Wilson, Colin From Atlantis to the Sphinx (Virgin Books 1996) p.129

[245] Tompkins *Mexican* p.202

[246] Tompkins *Mexican* pp. 211, 244-45; Hancock *Heaven's* p.23; modern archaeologists believe the standard unit of measure was 83 centimetres.

[247] Please refer to Tompkins *Mexican* pp. 252, 260-63, 319 for more in depth explanation to the number system and its site layout

He also found the site may have indeed represented our solar system. With the Pyramid of Quetzalcoatl serving as the sun, a binary system of 9-18-36-72 etc. was employed to lay out the planets. The Citadel itself contained most of the planets. Mercury was at 36 units, Venus at 72, Earth at 94 and Mars at 144, all the exact relations to one another. He also has found reference to two planets between Mercury and the Sun (which many other astronomers also believe exist) at 9 and 18 units. Harleston named them Olkan (Sun consciousness) and Kinan (Sun Spirit). The San Juan River, which was re-routed by the site's builders with no logical explanation from archaeologists, was the asteroid belt at 288 units. A pyramid exists for Jupiter at 520, an old platform torn down for transit at 945 units was Saturn and the Moon Pyramid at 1845 was Uranus. Two other unreconstructed temples farther north of the Moon Pyramid at 2880 and 3780 units were at the exact spots to find Neptune and Pluto. At 2200 Hunabs (another form of measurement) he found a temple which he calls Planet X, at a distance of twice Pluto from the Sun. Some astronomers also believe there is a planet much farther out from Pluto.[248]

Modern science did not discover Pluto until 1930. How could the builders of this site have knowledge of not only the planets but also their relative distance between one another? Pythagoras claimed the planets were in a direct harmonious relationship with one another, like the musical scale. Science now shows this to be correct as does the layout of the temples at Teotihuacan.[249] Not only could the builders of Teotihuacan create vast temples, but could blend them with extraordinary scientific knowledge.

The city street grid system is at 89 degrees, not the usual 90. The Way of the Dead is 15 degrees 30' east of north which could allow the Pleiades to be seen perfectly at the zenith. Alfred E Schlemmer claimed the Way of the Dead was not a street but was filled with water to act as a reflecting pool to measure the world's earthquakes. His theory has some credence as the Way of the Dead is not a straight piece of road but is actually number of sections with large walls and temples between barriers that look like locks. The north end of the Way is 100 feet above the south end. Schlemmer had accumulated data establishing that tornadoes and earthquakes repeat in cycles based on the motions of several bodies in the solar system which led to his theory of water filling the Way of the Dead.[250]

Some writers have claimed that the Mexican culture was obsessed with catastrophic world endings and that the Aztec calendar claims our modern world will be destroyed by an earthquake. The Aztec's never said the Fifth Sun

---

[248] For more detailed explanations of the site's numeric connection to the solar system please see Tompkins *Mexican* pp.267-6
[249] Tompkins *Mexican* p.269; Hancock *Fingerprints* p.168
[250] Tompkins *Mexican* p. 272; Wilson 128; Jenkins, John Major **Maya Cosmogenesis** (Bear and Co. 1998) p.82

was to be destroyed by an earthquake, only movement. It is modern scholars who have translated this to mean movement. Movement could mean anything from an earthquake, to a pole shift, to a transformation of the human population.

Others claim that the site has a musical base. A student of the Hermetic mysteries knows that the entire universe can in turn be represented by number, which can be represented by sound. Harleston looked at the ancient disciplines of sacred number and sacred sound. The planets are in a harmonious relationship to one another (shown in the building of the site) but the planets will also perfectly reflect the musical harmonic scale. He wondered if the Way of the Dead could be a gigantic guitar representing notes of the musical scale. He says the 'guitar' stretches from sun to the moon and plays the note 'C.' 'G' would occur one-third of the way from moon. Three chords overlap at 96 units (the orbital distance of the earth in STU). To Harleston, Teotihuacan is the work of master mathematicians who worked with the concepts of space-time and energy. Thus the whole complex could have served as a university where "the site could teach the student to reach beyond himself to a larger vision of their relationship to the cosmos."[251]

Site of Gods

Teotihuacan was the "place where people become gods" or "the place where people wake from the dream of life to become gods." Father Bernardino de Sahagun was a Christian Monk 500 years ago who attempted to save the myth and wisdom of the Mexican population while the rest of his Christian brothers were killing or torturing the inhabitants, and burning their writings. He kept alive information that claimed, "after this death (Lords) were canonized as gods, and it was said that they did not die but wakened out of a dream they had lived [life on earth]…turned into spirits or gods."[252]

As any student of mysticism knows, one of the main tasks taken by those who follow the path of is to learn that the world we live in is not real. It makes it clear that this was the place where this high level of mysticism was

---

[251] Harleston realized he might have underestimated the scientific capacity of the builders. It now looked like the STU of 1.059 related to orbital distance while phi (1.618) indicated time. As well the number 1.059 controls not only the frequencies of sound but also of light. The frequency of each colour of visible light can be obtained by multiplying 1.059 or its square and he wonders if the STU may be a natural unit of space-time, furthering Teotihuacan's place as the site of the wisdom of the universe. Harleston believes that the builders of Teotihuacan were showing some amazing things. Tompkins *Mexican* pp.275, 278, 279
[252] Matos p.24; Berrin p.157; Sejourne p.85

taught, a site of the ancient mystery schools that have long produced the great men and women of the planet earth.

Laurette Sejourne claimed Teotihuacan was "the place the serpent learned to fly." Sejourne was one of the first mystical archaeologists in Mexico and understood that the serpent learning to fly was a key image found in Egypt, India and China. A serpent with wings represents one who has overcome their lower nature, allowed the Kundalini to rise and mix with the sky. One would then be godlike, and called a Horus, Christ, Buddha or Quetzalcoatl.[253]

The Aztecs said that the process of turning men into gods was overseen by a body of priests, the "wise men, knowers of occult things" sometimes called the Followers of Quetzalcoatl. To the Egyptians these wise men were the Followers of Horus and in the Popol Vuh of the Maya they were "Plummed Serpents, great knowers and thinkers."[254]

Fifth Sun

The Aztecs believed there were Four Suns (or world ages) that preceded our own. The first was destroyed by jaguars, the second by wind, the third by fire, and the fourth by flooding. The Fifth Sun, our present world age, is said to have its origins at Teotihuacan. The Aztecs believed the Pyramid of the Sun is the exact spot where creation had been set in motion for the modern epoch. The Aztec King was said to make pilgrimages there on foot. The myth claims that after the fourth world was destroyed by flooding, the sun vanished from the sky and the world was consumed by darkness. It was said the water lasted for 52 years (an Aztec calendar round) and then the sky collapsed. Only the sacred fire was left at Teotihuacan and the gods knew that someone would have to be sacrificed to create the next sun.[255]

The gods asked, "Who will bring light to the world?" Tecuciztecatl volunteered but all of the other gods were afraid and hid. Nanahuatzin, a scabby god filled with pustules and was unnoticed as he never spoke only listened, was also chosen by the others to bring light to the world. They fasted for four days and four nights and lit the flame of the hearth. Tecuciztecatl brought gifts of feathers, balls of gold and precious stones. Nanahuatzin instead brought bunches of green canes bundled in threes and nines, maguey needles soaked in his own blood, and his own scabby sores. Both were said to build a tower and stay there each of the four nights observing penitence. The towers are now the pyramids of Teotihuacan.

When it was time for the gods to throw themselves into the roaring fire, Tecuciztecatl pulled back from the intense heat out of fear. He attempted four times, his allotted number of attempts. When he failed Nanahuatzin was given

---

[253] Sejourne p.86; Tompkins *Mexican* p.388

[254] Hancock *Heaven's* p.*19*

[255] *Hancock* Fingerprints p. 99; Hancock *Heaven's* p.15; Jenkins p.29

the opportunity and he summoned his courage immediately and jumped into the fire, roasting and burning in the flames. Tecuciztecatl then too jumped in. An eagle and a jaguar were also said to jump into the flames. After waiting for much time, "the light of dawn began to appear" with the two sacrificed gods becoming the sun and the moon.[256] This is not a myth of the beginning of a new physical sun but the transformation and purification of the initiate. Men were deemed to become gods here and this myth helps to explain how.

The myth begins with a question, "Who will bring light to the world?" This question could easily be asked to any of the mystery school initiates, for the nature of the work is to develop one's inner light in order to do the same with the universe. The one who was eventually chosen was full of scabs, revealing that the outward physical appearance is not necessary and will be cast aside. It claimed he was quiet and listened carefully. This is the sign of a good student, one who listens to their teacher's comments and uses quiet for inner work. Sejourne claims the god is declared scabby because he has already reconciled the opposites within himself and has detached from his fragmentary self, in other words he has begun to leave the physical world behind.

Fasting is a key component to the purification of the individual, a fast that lasted for four days and four nights. This totals eight periods, the symbolic number of Tehuti/Hermes. The hearth is a symbol for the area of the body known as the Dan Tien. This lower burner was seen as the first fire that the initiate has to light in order to allow the kundalini fire to stir and rise up the body. While one brought precious things, Nanahuatzin brought bundles in threes (number of the Hermetic process) and nines (the number of Osiris and cycles). The maguey needle may be a representation of a sword or arrow that would be needed to prick and still the conscious mind, the blood a symbol of the concentration needed.

The tower is similar to the idea of a mountain, a symbol used frequently in the Old Testament to refer to the difficult task of meditating, like climbing to the top of a mountain. The roaring fire is a symbol of the deeper fires of purification, ones that will destroy every last semblance of the conscious mind and link to the physical world. Tecuciztecatl, who brought objects of the physical world, was too afraid to jump into the fire for he would lose his connection to this world. Nanahuatzin had rid himself of everything in the physical world, even his body, and jumped in. The roasting and burning are the burning away of all that is impure. When finished he would leave the fire as an Egyptian Akh "Shining One," and be ready for the final teachings of the process. It is a further alchemic example that out of the ashes, blackness, and ugliness of ourselves is our own salvation to the powers of the light if one can transform them to their true brilliance.

---

[256] Matos pp.25-26; Berrin p.158; Sejourne p.76

This myth created the Aztec ideas of the Fifth Sun, the Sun of movement. It was born out of the sacrifice of a god therefore men must also be sacrificed to sustain it. The question becomes how could the Aztecs take a myth that was for the enlightenment of the human soul and use it to rip out the hearts of sacrificial victims? The same way students of modern religions no longer understand the actual teachings of the texts they read.

Human Sacrifice

101:Image of a dripping heart from Teotihuacan mural

No human sacrifice took place at Teotihuacan as this was a place of wisdom and learning. While there are burials that appear to be of sacrificial victims it is most likely from a later period of time prior to the destruction of the site. It was the Aztecs who adopted this practice. Hundreds of thousands were killed, their hearts ripped out and at times the skins of the victims were worn. Gruesome stuff! It is said that the Fifth Sun demanded human sacrifice. Those who were sacrificed were called Eagle Men, and made their way to heaven to become stars.[257]

The Aztecs were not wise men but warriors. They came from the north and eventually destroyed all in their way to take over Mexico. One of their main tasks was to kill the holy and wise people of the previous cultures so that no one would be able to oppose them. They did however want the wisdom and information for themselves. Before the Spanish took over Mexico and burned close to 50,000 books of the Maya, Toltec and Aztec for being the works of the "devil," the Aztecs had confiscated most of the texts for themselves. Like the Greeks who stole the Egyptian texts to make the library at Alexandria and then could not properly understand the information that was being given, so too did the Aztec.

The Aztec could tell that the site of Teotihuacan was an incredible place. They attempted to recreate the wisdom in their own capital of Tenochtitlan. A great number of Teotihuacan elements of style, painting and artwork appear at Tenochtitlan. The Aztec even did some excavation work at Teotihuacan to find sacred objects for their city. Tenochtitlan also included two main streets to divide the city and has pyramids in similar locations.[258] It was

---

[257] Tompkins *Mexican* pp.10-11; Hancock *Fingerprints* p.98
[258] Matos pp.23; Berrin p.162

the texts that they tried to model most. The problem with the written word or in this case murals and artwork, is that even translated people think anyone can understand what was meant. How many Christians question that their understanding of the Testaments may be false, likely the same percentage of Aztecs who questioned their understood the wisdom of Teotihuacan.

The Aztec priests probably did not really believe that their sacrifices had anything to do with extending the Fifth Sun, but believed that they understood the secrets of how to gain immortality suggested in the codex, reliefs and murals of Teotihuacan. As the great loss when the Gnostic writers of the New Testament were killed, so too were the Aztecs unable to understand the texts without those who created them. Without the Toltec wise men the Aztecs messed everything up.

The ancient Teotihuacan reliefs focus on the heart. Metaphysically the heart is the union of the above and below, and the place of mind and thought. This is why the heart was symbolically weighed by the Egyptians in the Hall of the Double Maat. The heart is the center of our inner truth, our path, destiny, and of universal love. To truly reach one's heart is the hard work in the ways of mysticism. A heart in Egypt that did not pass the test in the Hall of the Double Maat was eaten by Ammit, Eater of Hearts. At Teotihuacan hearts were shown as wounded and hurt, with drops of blood dripping from it to show its pain of not being merged with the Absolute or God.[259]

The way to heal the wounded heart was through the process of purification. One must first purify the impurities of the body, then the mind through the destruction of the ego and personality. A pure heart will be the result. The knife is a symbol used not just in Mexico but by alchemists and Hermeticists all over the world to explain the cutting motion needed to eliminate the impurities. At Teotihuacan the knife is often shown with a bloody heart, or even cutting into the heart (see illustration 101). In the reliefs those who had their hearts ripped out were shown to be immortal beings, living in the sky full of wisdom. This would be correct as after they had purified their mind, body and soul, the heart could allow the One Thing of the material world to merge with the One Mind of the Above. This also occurs in the chakras of the body as the upper and lower centers merge in the heart. The Aztecs used the texts to believe that the way to immortality in the sky was to follow the ways of Teotihuacan through a bloody, ripped out heart. Unfortunately, there were more symbols here to confuse the mixed up Aztecs.

The wearing of the skin of the human is one that few have understood. Why would an Aztec want to skin a sacrificed person and wear it? The Aztec have a myth of Xochipilli who was a naked man, one without flesh. The skin is representative of matter which must be thrown away. He is often shown clad in a garment of gold representing the yellow flayed skin, whose acceptance frees

---

[259] Sejourne p.121

him from the encumbrance of matter.[260] Again we find our answer in the ancient mysteries. Mystery traditions teach us the need to not live in the flesh, as the material world of illusion is the barrier to the wonders of Absolute Reality. Only by giving up the flesh can one obtain the wisdom of enlightenment. Symbolically this could be shown by a skeleton with the flesh ripped or torn away. Again this is symbolic of the path we must follow, not the literal translation of what one should do. Everything the Hermetic artist or scribe created was a code. The symbol and allegory were not to be taken as real steps but represented symbolic actions to be done by those on the path of wisdom.

The Aztec are another example of what happens when one's only focus is on the literal translation of any text. The Aztecs did not work with a true mystery school system. They thought they could get all the answers themselves. In Europe the results of not following the path of the true wisdom of the texts led to the dark ages of the inquisition; in Mexico it led to human sacrifice.

Hermetic Symbols

Turning our attention back to the site of Teotihuacan itself we can explore some of the symbols that appear at the site. The first is a relief that depicts a person with a bird headdress, carrying a shield with three arrows and speaks twice out of the mouth.[261] There is no question that this is the representation of Tehuti. On the head is worn a large beak (similar to the Raven beak worn by the Northwest Coast Natives and described in Chapter 5). A tuft of hair protrudes from the back also similar to the hair of Tehuti. The fact that he carries three arrows is symbolic of the three stages of the Hermetic process and that he is Thrice-Greatest. That two spirals appear from the mouth is a representation showing that the figure combines the above and below. The spiral is the number five and represents that the wisdom of Tehuti will be what leads to personal growth.

Near the Pyramid of the Moon is the Palace of Quetzalpapalotl (Quetzal butterfly). The butterfly was an important symbol of transformation to the Toltec. The butterfly begins life as a caterpillar that has to shed its initial form, symbolizing our physical body. It goes into a cocoon (as we must do to escape the world through meditation) to appear as the beautiful winged butterfly able to go anywhere (as we will be able to attain our higher soul self and travel to the higher astral realms).

The area also has pillars with a series of spirals, representing the number five and growth. The eyes and spiral centers are inlaid with mica, a

---

[260] Sejourne p.152
[261] Diagram is found in Matos p.121 from Casa Barrios Murals.

stone that was able to allow seeing into the psychic realms. This could be a place of where one was able to learn the shamanic ability of "seeing," or to be able to peer into other worlds and experience the true reality of what most consider solid objects.

The Jaguar Palace is close by and it is known for its beautiful statues and carvings. Here the jaguars are wearing a feathered headdress and each blow a conch shell. The Temple of the Feathered Shells contains a number of four petaled flowers around a spiral circle, reminiscent of the layout of the Oriental five elements linking the site with the eastern traditions.

Many hands and feet are shown at Teotihuacan. The feet may represent the path towards spirituality, and hands (often shown with flowers or water flowing) may represent Qi energy or healing.[262] Eyes are often shown, usually in water. This could this represent the all-prevailing essence around us. Only by using the Eye of Horus could we learn to see past the essence to true reality.

A vessel (shown on page 44 of Teotihuacan: City of Gods) contains artwork of a number of small lizards seemingly biting the tail of the lizard ahead of them. The oroborus was the alchemic symbol for time, symbolized by a dragon or serpent eating its own tail. The concept is that time has no beginning or end. The vessel has nine spiraling lizards, nine being the number of Osiris and of the cycle. Teotihuacan is one of the only places in Mexico where vessels have three legs. Three of course is the number of the Hermetic process. Orange was a favourite vessel colour, the orange made of numerous minerals and unable to be re-created today.

Sahagun wrote of the ideas of snares and nets, which represent the sins of mankind. A mural at the site shows a jaguar encompassed in a net. Another text warns of falling into the trap of the net that has been left on the ground.[263] The temple of Tehuti at Khemenu was called the "House of the Net." The net may symbolize something that is used to trap material things, similar to the Veil of Isis. The net is a connection of being trapped in the world of matter and not able to see past the net to the All.

Murals

---

[262] Sejourne p.178
[263] Sejourne pp. 9-10; Berrin p.61; Hancock *Heaven's* p.18; and in Sahagan's work volume 1 p.472-77

102:Goddess mural, Teotihuacan

Teotihuacan is also known for its murals, many of which have been badly damaged. They are pieces of magnificent artwork coloured beautifully in red and yellow, the last two of the Hermetic colours. A number of the symbols found here are similar to Egyptian hieroglyphs. Easily seen are the twisted rope, the entwined lines, the eye and the Egyptian symbol for metal. At a giant mural near the Pyramid of the Sun are many small symbols that surround the main painting, similar to where hieroglyphs appear in Egyptian funerary texts.[264]

A famed piece is the Tlalocan Mural of which a replica appears at the Anthropological Museum in Mexico City.[265] The top portion is believed to be the goddess, whose hands seem to be giving blood or water. In the Tetitla Mural a similar goddess may be giving water or seeds. In either case what she gives represents life. The headdress has a symbol similar to the hawk. Stars and flowers appear on the body and a great tree grows from the head. The lower part of the mural is a number of people performing strange actions. There is a frog spewing forth something from its mouth that traps a number of people in it. The lower portion with the frog is the below, where we are trapped in matter as the people are trapped in the frog's expulsion. The middle world is a world where strange things occur as we are linked to above and below. The above, represented by the goddess of life, is a place of life and wisdom.

---

[264] See Berrin pp.134-36

[265] Murals can be found in Matos pp.102-03, 178 and plate 64; Berrin pp.48-49, 55

Smoking Mirror

103:Tezcatlipoca (Smoking mirror) from the Codex Borgia

Bits of mirror were found in the caves below the Sun Pyramid. Tezcatlipoca was the enemy (and brother) of Quetzalcoatl who was able to defeat the feathered serpent by using a mirror to show him how old and frail he was, forcing him to flee. An aspect of this became known as the "Smoking Mirror" or "smoke that mirrors." Tezcatlipoca is the force that battles his brother, thus he represents the Egyptian god Set. Set is the force of opposition within us that we must learn to overcome to follow Horus and learn the true nature of the universe. Quetzalcoatl is the powers of Osiris and Horus combined.

A mirror only reflects reality. Shamans call our world the shadow world and all of our physical objects are shadows of the true essence which resides in another dimension. The smoking or unreflecting mirror represents our inability to "see" or distinguish true reality. Thus Tezcatlipoca is the factor within us that causes us to perpetuate the illusion of this reality by smoking our sight (Eye of Horus).

This idea is also found in the Maya Popol Vuh, which like the Christian Gnostic texts, record a Golden Age when the first humans were intelligent and "saw and instantly they could see far; they succeeded in seeing, they succeeded in knowing, all that there is in the world." The great wisdom proved their undoing, outraging the gods. "The Heart of Heaven blew mist into their eyes which clouded their sight as a mirror breathed on. Their eyes were covered and could only see what was close, only that was clear to them…in this way the wisdom and knowledge of the First Men was destroyed." All that survived to tell of the heights they had formally reached was the book Popol Vuh, which may be called "The Light that Came from Beside the Sea."[266]

This story from the great Maya text explains a time of wisdom when one could see, but without the ability to peer past the illusion of matter into true reality, the wisdom was lost and mankind was sunk into the depths that we have become during the last 2000 years. This idea of seeing and using the sight properly is all connected with the smoking mirror.

---

[266] Hancock *Heaven's* p.318

Burning Water

104:Burning Water, notice the knife piercing the top of the skull

The symbol of burning water is a combination of the glyph for fire with the glyph for water (see above). Archaeologists claim that burning water is a symbol for war.[267] This is another mistake by modern scholars with no background in the metaphysical. There may be a battle but the battle is within ourselves.

It is important to understand that burning water was also a symbol used by the Medieval Alchemists. Marsiglio Ficino wrote of the first humour "like that of burning water called Aqua Vita 'water of life', or the 5th Essence." Christianity saw the combination of the fire of spirit from above in union with water below as the ultimate act of creation. A union of opposites (male-female, yin-yang, sun-moon) could bring about a third reality that would incorporate the aspects of the parents. This would lead to a higher state of consciousness or the Philosopher's Stone. It is the union of fire and water that will create the merging of thought with feeling. It is also represented as the birth of Horus from Isis and Osiris. This connection of opposites was the Taoist work of combining the shen energy with the Qi. [268] One must learn to combine the opposites parts of themselves in order to find that there are no opposite parts, only Oneness.

---

[267] Berrin p.135
[268] Hauck pp. 52, 74, 94, 281; Ficino pp. 15, 196

Considering that similar terminology was used by the alchemists and priests of Teotihuacan, I decided to look again at the Mexican myths involving the ideas of burning water, using alchemy as a guide. Burning water may be the symbolic explanation of the purification of body, mind and spirit that would have to take place before an initiate could in fact be Quetzalcoatl.

Sejourne also claimed that burning water was the reconciliation of the two opposing forces (Quetzalcoatl and Tezcatilpoca, Horus and Set, above and below) that takes place in the human heart. From this aspect, a human could bud and flower from the realm of the flesh thus striving to reach the higher realm of spirit.[269] Teotihuacan was the place where the main instruction for the serpent to fly was given.

In the Hermetic mystery tradition one did not really die in training, but death was used as a metaphor. Often forms of ritual death, such as being buried alive, were important for the initiate to learn that they were far more than a physical body. Some Mexican texts claim the dead, representing the initiate, had to overcome seven difficult tasks before they could be in the place where the "Dead Were No More."[270] These seven difficult tasks are the paths of the seven chakras or planets. By learning of their impurities and using purification, one could reach enlightenment and join the two opposing forces.

The two opposites of fire and water are needed to allow the inner flower of higher consciousness to grow, just as a flower on earth needs the fire of the sun and the water of the rain. A flower on earth cannot grow with only one aspect but needs a perfect balance of the two to reach its full beauty. The Aztecs in Tenochtitlan placed the gods of rain and fire side by side on the top of their main temple pyramid as homage to this growth.[271]

Burning water is always shown occurring in the heart, which is often described as a prickly pear. The pear tree is found in many of the Cinderella myths. It is said to have sprung from the river goddess and the eagle of fire above. Thus the two streams are shown together, one of water and one of fire symbolizing "blossoming war." The image of burning water always appears with Quetzalcoatl.[272] The symbols of the work were the heart, blood and knives led to the problem of Aztec sacrifice depicted above. This word is depicted as battle or war, and current author Jed McKenna writes constantly that awakening is messy, bloody and all consuming affair. Every aspect of the ego self is going to have to be killed. In his view, even the heart, the thing we hold most sacred (love, hope, joy, unity) is also going to have to be killed to reach the Absolute that is beyond.

---

[269] Tompkins *Mexican* p.387
[270] Sejourne p.65
[271] Sejourne pp. 99,110
[272] Sejourne p. 108

The Aztecs kept alive the Toltec ideas of combining the eagle and the spotted tiger "which once represented the sacred battle between heaven and earth, between being and void." The eagle and the tiger also represent the union of two opposites with mankind as the meeting ground. Teotihuacan combined the images of tiger, eagle and the serpent.[273] They were fully describing that by bringing together the opposing forces of tiger and eagle (representing fire and water) a third force would be created, in this case the serpent. The winged serpent has been shown to represent higher consciousness. This new realm of being could only happen by waging the inner war, combining the opposite principles inside to allow our transformation. This imagery can also be seen in the Maya ball game, which was not a game to find sacrificial victims but was a representation of burning water. A brief explanation of the mystical nature of the Maya ball game appeared in the chapter on the Tarot.

A tree of life is another symbol of the same unity. On the tree, death is at the bottom and the sun is on top. Both are connected by a giant circle of concentric lines symbolizing the reconciliation of opposites on either side of the tree. Some say that Quetzalcoatl is on the left and Patron of Souls is on the right representing the Fifth Sun.[274] The relief is similar to the 10th card of the Tarot, the wheel of life. This card depicts matter being dragged down and light (spirit) rising while the wheel represents the passage and cycles of time. As time passes and moves it is up to us to understand our opposite forces and learn how to harmonize them through the use of wisdom. And how to no longer run from our death, but to turn toward it and make it our greatest advisor. This wisdom can be discovered at Teotihuacan.

---

[273] Sejourne pp. 113, 114, 120
[274] Sejourne pp. 117-18

The Wisdom

105:Rocks in Moon Pyramid group

The big question is where is this great wisdom? I can tell you that a great amount of it is stored in the complex near the Moon Pyramid at the north end of the site. Thanks to powerful Hermetic work and connection with Tehuti, information came in waves here. After looking for a time from the top of the Moon Pyramid down the site, I was drawn to enter a small square temple at the bottom the pyramid. After entering I was drawn to the middle 'altar' which is a rectangular stone structure with a number of rocks placed on the top. There it is, the wisdom. It is in the rocks. It is a gigantic library, but instead of books rocks are used.

Carlos Castaneda wrote that ancients did not need to read books as the total needs were in what they created and could be retrieved if the assemblage point would move, or consciousness shift.[275] Shamans are very respectful of rock and stone. They have been here for a long time and are said to carry much wisdom and healing. They can also be programmed to store information. The Egyptians would build with a specific type of stone to reflect the concepts and wisdom the building was to represent. Granite was used to represent ideas

---

[275] Castaneda, Carlos *Art of Dreaming* (Harper: New York 1993) p.145

associated with fire, while limestone would be used for more feminine and watery qualities.

After spending time with the rocks in the small open temple, I had a better look at the surrounding twelve temple platforms. At the top of each structure is a perfectly rectangular arrangement of stone stuccoed into a base (see photo 105). Hundreds of stones appear on each temple, and each would reflect one of the twelve basis of learning. One might be number, another history, another science, and another spiritual wisdom. It was a requirement of each of the initiates at Teotihuacan to learn how to read the wisdom in the stones and then spend time in the library letting the stones teach them. After a certain amount of time a huge test would occur where one would have to either prove they could read the stones, or make use of the wisdom from particular stone areas. If these tests were passed a huge festival would occur, complete with beautiful yellow flags flying all over the city.

The next time you are at the site of Teotihuacan take some time in the Moon Pyramid area. It will usually be deserted with tourists climbing the two big pyramids. Chose a temple platform and perform your ritual way of altering consciousness and then chose a rock and see what happens. If done with respect, honesty and love some powerful wisdom might be the result of your effort. Perhaps you will actually be able to gain the complete understanding of Teotihuacan and its initiation into the high Hermetic wisdom.

CHAPTER 17
TAROT

106:Early Tarot Card of Le Bateleur- Magician

History

"A person devoid of books, had they only a Tarot of which they knew how to make use, could in a few years acquire a universal science and converse with an unequaled doctrine and inexhaustible eloquence."

Eliphas Levi[276]

Tarot cards are seen by most as either the origin of modern playing cards or a tool for psychic readers to foretell the future. They do have this purpose, but there is far more to this deck. It was actually designed as a way to pass on the ancient wisdom, through symbol, on the path to awakening. The Tarot has been called the 'oldest book known to man.'[277] Today one may find over a hundred versions of a Tarot deck, still keeping ties to the layout of the oldest known decks. The Tarot is a deck of 78 cards that symbolically depict all the forces that effect human life. The deck is divided into two sections. The first contain twenty-two cards with intricate pictures called the 'major arcana' or 'trump cards.' The word trump is derived from the Latin word for the Triumph, a religious procession in which the powers of the gods were displayed. The trump cards displayed the powers of the gods in symbol. The major arcana were the greater secrets, that which could only be taught to high initiates who proved their worth.

The other section is the 'minor arcana' made up of 56 cards in four suits. The four suits are pentacles (now diamonds), cups (hearts), wands (clubs) and swords (spades). With the exception of one card in each suit (the knight) the 'minor arcana' developed into our modern deck of 52 playing cards. The minor arcana represent the lesser secrets, the initial alchemical stages and the wisdom that is available to all. The act of shuffling the cards dispersed these

---

[276] Gray, Eden *The Tarot Revealed* (Signet 1960) P.225
[277] Gray p.12

elements into the physical world. No one is really sure exactly where Tarot Cards originated or where the name Tarot comes from. Some say the name Tarot comes from the Egyptian word 'ta-rosh' (royal way), a change in letters of the Egyptian goddess Hathor or from the Caballa word 'Tora' (the book of secret Hebrew wisdom). Still others say the word originates from Latin word for wheel 'anagram rota', while others see a connection to the Chinese Tao, a word that means The Way.[278]

The name of course is of less importance than the cards themselves. Playing cards of some sort appeared in Europe during the Middle Ages. By the time of the Renaissance, the Catholic Church recognized the cards as a threat. They saw the cards, especially the trump symbols of the major arcana, as having the power to awaken spiritual forces in people and thus became a threat to their control. The Church admitted the cards were part of a spiritual process, but claimed the cards took one down the ladder to hell. The church banned the major arcana in Germany in 1378, France in 1381, and Italy in 1441. Our modern 52 card deck evolved from the 78 card tarot deck after the ban. However that still left 56 cards. The church also eliminated the Knight cards from the Tarot which they perhaps felt were connected to the Knights Templar, a mystical order the Church had burnt in the 14th century. The Fool is the only major arcana still present in the modern playing deck as the Joker.[279]

To most Europeans at the time the cards were not a means of spiritual hidden wisdom but simply the tools for games. When the trump cards were banned, which were the very heart of the Tarot, they had to designate one suit of the remaining cards to be trump. We must do the same when playing older card games even today. Since most of the people who used Tarot cards only wanted to use them for games, not for mystical wisdom, the Church lessened their attacks on the cards even when major arcana decks began to re-appear in the 1600's. The Church almost seemed to forget about its original opposition, perhaps thinking they had killed all those who may still be able to understand them.[280]

Egypt

The first European to openly suggest the Tarot's connections to Egypt was Antoine Count de Gebelin in 1781. He was the principle of the French Academy and was a student of ancient mysticism. Gebelin believed the cards were part of the sacred book of Tehuti and he began to explore the hidden symbolism. He claimed the name Tarot originated from the Egyptian words Tar (path) and Ro (royal), thus the path of Horus. Once his interpretation hit the

---

[278] Giles, Cynthia *The Tarot* (Paragon 1992) pp. xii, 5; Hauck pp.335-37
[279] Hauc, pp.337-38
[280] Giles p.64; Hauck p.338

inner courts of Europe many more people who studied mysticism and alchemy also began to examine the cards.[281]

Dr. Gerard Encause wrote under the pen-name Papus. He claimed the Egyptian priesthood invented the Tarot prior to rule by the Greeks for the purpose of preserving knowledge. He claimed that instead of passing on the information to initiates in the Mystery Schools, who needed to show high moral character, they decided to pass on the wisdom through vice. By placing the knowledge in the midst of a game, the knowledge would be passed on generation to generation as the game was played. Most would be unaware that they were keeping the wisdom alive. Those with virtue would not be forced to be the secret keepers of knowledge as it would be passed on without their participation. They simply needed to recognize the wisdom when it was in front of them.[282] The wisdom was placed through symbol into the cards where it would remain as the Hermetic axiom 'hide the truth in plain sight.'

Another writer, Paul Christian who was born Jean Baptiste Christian Pitois, wrote a book called The History and Practice of Magic. One of his chapters is said to be a copy of an ancient manuscript of Iamblichus, a mystic and writer who died in 325 AD. Iamblichus wrote several books on the Egyptian Mysteries. Christian claims to have found references of an initiation ceremony in the Great Pyramid where twenty-two paintings appeared on the walls. The twenty-two paintings are almost identical to the Tarot cards. The question here is whether Christian found a lost manuscript, which would definitely date the Tarot to Egypt, or if he took some creative license to invent a background for the increasingly popular cards.[283]

Modern Developments

Over time, more and more spiritual individuals began to interpret and reinvent the Tarot. Spiritualist Eliphas Levi in the 1860's was the first to write of a link between the cards, the letters of the Hebrews and paths of the Caballa tree of life. This became the chosen way of interpreting the cards in the Western World. However, Levi also saw a connection to the Egyptian Mysteries and the untranslated Bembina Tablet of Isis he found in Rome.[284]

Two members of the Golden Dawn, AE Waite and Allistar Crowley, developed their own Tarot versions in the early 1900's. Waite believed there was no Egyptian basis to the cards and used his background of alchemy and the Caballa to make his deck, published by Rider in 1910. Some of his pictures were evolved from a 15th century Italian deck called the Sola-Bosca Tarot, which has not survived in complete form. He believed the cards were the steps

---

[281] Hall p.74; Giles p.23
[282] Laviolette p.143; Giles p.35
[283] Laviolette p.129; Giles p.33
[284] Sharmon-Burke, Juliet *Understanding the Tarot* (Stoddart 1998) p.9; Giles p.28

of the alchemic process of Hermes, and their understanding would create the astral body.[285] This is now the deck that is most familiar with Tarot users today. Interestingly the deck most used is less than 100 years old, not the old versions that are more closely linked to the ancient wisdom. As well, whether Waite knew it or not, alchemy and the Caballa both originated in Egypt thus his cards are Egyptian in their source.

Crowley made a Thoth deck, which he claimed was a picture form of the Caballa. In 1927 Paul Foster made a deck that he claimed was closer to the original deck that he felt originated in Morocco in the 1200's.[286] Numerous other decks now appear on the market.

New Ideas

There is a belief that the cards have been translated and their numbering system is complete and without question. In fact it was often considered that those who had the exact number system of the cards were expected never to reveal it. Many claimed that those who have written about the cards, like Levi and Waite, were either not truly trained in their meaning or they purposely wrote false information and wrong card orders to throw people off track.[287] If this is the case we must look very closely at the manner that people today view and use the cards. I believe there is another way to understand the cards using the concepts of Ancient Egypt.

The cards are usually looked at under the Hebrew Caballa system, where the major arcana are laid out in a series for the initiate from 1 to 21, as if the cards are a specific path to be followed. When viewing the symbolism of the cards in this manner, the teachings do not seem to be in the correct steps. In fact the steps seem way out of place.

In the original version of this volume, I compared the cards 1-10 with their counterpart of 11-20 as if they represented a play of opposites. I noticed the Maya might have also been suggesting the same thing. The field layout for their famed ball games was a checkerboard configuration of 99 squares. The game was not for human sacrifice but represented the energies of the universe and their interactions. Originally more of a teaching tool for wisdom and not a game, twenty-one individuals would stand on the board. Ten would be on each side of the field, and each represented dual components of the same idea (love-hate, life-death, and wisdom-ignorance). The 21st figure represented mankind who began at the center of the field.[288] This seemed like a confirmation that I was on the right track with the use of sacred number and opposites.

Since that writing, I have gained new insights that the cards are not laid out in a path at all, but are numbered based on a specific internal numbering

---

[285] Giles p.55; Hauck p.336
[286] Giles p.55
[287] Giles p.38
[288] Tompkins Mexican Pyramids (Harper and Row 1976) p.386

system within us. The cards are aspects of ourselves, and the cards (hence the numbers) interplay with each other in different ways. Thus the cards can be looked at in any order. Each of us has a predilection to one number as our main focus in this life, and understanding this helps the student and teacher to devise the proper teaching sequence most suited to that individual. There are also certain cards (people) that have a predilection for other cards (people) thus they work well together. Together all 21 cards (people) make the perfect "group" where every aspect of being and awareness can be combined to make a manifested outer world whole. As well of course is the understanding that there really is no path at all. One does not become a warrior, but either is one or is not in this moment. One does not become a Buddha, they either are or they aren't. The mind can not understand this, only the heart can, and these cards are meant to be understood by the heart thus to view them as a "path" will take the student way from the meanings of the cards. Any card will do, and in any order- but remember there is a specific way they do interact with the other cards as there is a way that our elbow interacts with our wrist.

Given this new insight I had a hard time as to whether to include anything of the previous descriptions of the cards- given that in a forthcoming book I will do so in more detail. I decided for the sake of continuity to keep this very brief overview and not confuse the reader any further. For now if Tarot cards interset you, use them in personal study. Look at them, meditate with them and try to put the wisdom they explain into your day-to-day existence.

CHAPTER 18
NORTH AMERICA, HAWAII,
OLMEC and MAYA

109:Raven mask, Vancouver Museum- notice resemblance to Tehuti

Most would look at you strangely if you told them that the myths of the West Coast Native Americans and the Hawaiian Islands were Egyptian. You can start looking at me strangely. Egypt is the source of all of the world's wisdom and North America is no exception. However it took coming face to face with the Raven to understand this fully.

I had difficulty finding concrete evidence in North America of its Egyptian roots. I had greatly used my Native Indian shamanic practice to understand much of the Egyptian priesthood and texts, not to mention helping my personal connection with inner power. In the context of researching this book I was visiting a friend of mine who is a Native Indian artist in Vancouver. She suggested I take a free day to explore the Native exhibits in the UBC Museum of Anthropology.

I had walked through most of the museum, admiring everything from shamanic tools to totem poles when a mask caught my eye. Most native cultures used masks in their rituals. The Iroquois of the east used ones with curled lips to help scare away the evil spirits. The masks at Teotihuacan were inlaid with jade and other jewels. In the Greek Mystery Schools the mask was called the persona (our root for personality) and represented that all we do is a mask that hides our true self.

On the west coast of Canada there are also masks. One of the most frequently represented figures for the masks was the Raven (see 109). Looking at a series of them I was instantly drawn to the similarities of Tehuti. I first noticed the long beak and connected it with the long beak of the ibis bird. The eyes are created in the shape of the crescent moon; Tehuti was associated with the moon. Moons are also drawn on each side of the beak. The masks are painted in three colours: black, white and red which are the three Hermetic colours. So great are the similarities between the symbolic depictions of the two birds I wondered if there is similarity in the myths. After learning the tales of Raven I no longer have no doubt that the Raven was Tehuti brought to Canada.

Raven Myths

The Raven was a creator, the bringer of light and the moon and was a trickster. Tehuti also was a creator and represented the moon, while Hermes is the trickster. A great teacher of wisdom often has to trick their students into continuing with or beginning their training as they are not advanced enough to understand the need for the wisdom teachings in their life.

The Haida creation myth states that prior to everything the world was dark (similar to Nun in Egypt). The reason for the blackness was an old man in a house by river had an infinite number of boxes. Each was a bit smaller with the smallest box containing all the light in the universe. The Raven "who existed at that time because he had always existed and always would" bumped into things due to the darkness, while the old man had never even seen his only daughter. The Raven wanted to enter the house and steal the light, but could not find the door no matter how many times he circled it. When the daughter came to the river, the Raven changed into a single hemlock needle and floated down the river to be caught in the girl's basket. With magic he made the girl very thirsty so she drank and swallowed the needle.

"Raven slithered down into her warm insides" becoming a small human being and went to sleep. He was born and cried to play with the light (as Tehuti was the Neteru of sound). Raven gained the confidence, or tricked, the old man. Raven pleaded for each of the boxes, until finally he could hold the light. He grabbed it in his jaws and flew away. An eagle chased him and Raven dropped half of the light to be the moon and the stars and the rest became the sun. Originally the raven was white but by going up the chimney he got black from the soot, similar to the ibis which is black and white. In other versions it is a pine needle or dirt instead of a hemlock needle. In some he steals just the moon and breaks it in half to create the sun.[289]

There is an Egyptian myth of Tehuti similar to the tale of the Raven. The tale is in the Cairo Museum, number 30646, discovered in a tomb near Luxor. It describes the tale of Satni, son of a Pharaoh. He was told of a tomb where there was a famed Book of Tehuti, "written in the god's own hand." It was said to include secret knowledge of the "risings of the sun, appearances of the moon, and the rotations of the celestial gods (planets) that were in cycle (orbit) around the sun." Thus the text reveals the secrets of astronomy, with knowledge of the sun as the center of the solar system. An old man showed Satni the tomb but was warned of the mummified pharaoh found inside who would destroy anyone who tried to take away the Book of Tehuti. Satni entered, saw the book and said, " It gave off a light as if the sun shone there." The wife's mummy spoke and warned not to take the book. She claimed that her husband knew that Tehuti had hidden the book inside a golden box, that was inside a silver box, that was inside many other boxes, the last being bronze and iron. Her husband had grabbed the book, disregarding the warnings. Tehuti then condemned not only the husband but also the wife and son to suspended animation. Although still alive they were buried, and while mummified they could still see, hear and speak. The old mummy claimed there was a way to obtain the book, to play and beat Tehuti at the card game of 52. Satni played Tehuti and eventually was given the boxes, and the book that shone like light.[290] You can see the obvious connection with the Raven tale and Egypt.

There are many Raven myths beyond that of the creation and many of them are connected to the Egyptian wisdom of Tehuti. One Tlingit Tale claims the Raven at his origin was very wise. His mother gave birth to him after she swallowed a stone, which blocks the entrance to the true mind. His name was Itcaku, meaning very hard rock. Raven shot a loon who had a bill of copper (copper a symbol of the conscious mind that he was destroying). Then his father told Raven's brother to go "fell a tree, so it would kill Raven." The tree is a symbol of the body that must be worked on, and the attempt to kill is the conscious mind that will fight back when we try to destroy it. When the tree fell on the Raven it did not kill him because he was made of rock. He was then told to clean (purify) a canoe, which closed around him when he tried to clean it, just as Osiris was sealed in the box by Set. Raven extended his elbows and broke the canoe into firewood (showing that he would need the burning purification heat of the fire). The father then put into the fire a large copper kettle that was filled with water and heated stones. Raven was told to get into the pot, but was able to change himself into a rock. When the servants lifted the

---

[289] Reid, Bill *Raven Steals the Light* (Douglas and McIntyre 1984) pp.12-17; Goodchild, Peter *Raven Tales* (Chicago Review Press 1991) pp. 33, 38
[290] Stichen, Zechariah *When Time Began* (Avon Books 1993) pp.221-23

lid and saw he was still there they told him to come out; he had finished his purification in the fire. The father was very angry and wanted to let the rain pour down (purification by water). People could not get food and began to starve. The water rose in the Raven's house which had eight (the number of Tehuti) rows of timber beams. He and his mother climbed up the timbers, or the chakras. When they got to the fourth timber (heart chakra), they were half way up and the Raven had his mother put on the loon-skin. While mother swam on the water, Raven flew to the highest cloud in the sky. One stayed below while the other went above. He hung there by his bill. He pulled his bill out and prayed to fall on a piece of kelp. He managed to do so and found the waters half way down the mountain.[291]

To the Haida, the Raven is the 'great inventor' and 'he whose voice is obeyed', as Tehuti created the world from the sound of his voice. One Haida myth seems very nasty and repulsive. The Raven skins the chief's daughter and puts on the skin. The Raven also removes people's eyes and roasts them in a fire before eating the eyes. This tale seems disturbing to those who do not understand the symbolism, as the Aztecs did not understand similar symbolism at Teotihuacan. By removing the skin Raven was showing the importance of learning to rid the flesh or no longer be focused on the world of the material. To pluck out the eyes is a symbol from Egypt to no longer use our regular sight (which is useless) but instead to learn the aspects of 'seeing' through the Eye of Horus.[292]

A Yurok tale has the Raven obtaining fire by playing in a gambling game with the sun. Tehuti managed to obtain the five extra days for the Neteru to be born by winning a gambling game with the moon. In another tale the Raven cuts off a bear's testicles and cuts out a cormorant's tongue.[293] An initiate needs to cut off his testicles, as Horus must do in his battle with Set to obtain the Eye. In other words one must learn to control their sexual energy to store enough power so we can 'see.' Cutting out the tongue is a two-fold expression. On one hand it refers to the need to stop talking so one can be in silence for proper meditation. It also refers to the need to stay quiet about the teachings except with other adepts.

---

[291] Goodchild pp. 11-12
[292] Goodchild p.38; Taylor, Colin ed. *Native American Myths and Legends* (Salamander Books 1994) p.86
[293] Goodchild pp.45-47

Totem Poles

110:Totem Pole, Isis with Horus

On April 1 2000, I was strolling around the harbor area of Victoria when a totem pole caught my attention. The pole was commissioned by Chief Norman George of the Songhees Band in 1994, but represents an old myth. As I walked towards it the lowest carved image came into clear view, a child sitting on the lap of a woman (see above). One might think of the Madonna and child. They would be correct, but they would be more correct to say Isis and Horus where the Christian image originates.

Osiris pose on Native Indian totem pole

I checked the entire totem pole and was not surprised to see the myth of Isis and Osiris fully played out. The lower image has Isis with the infant Horus, for at the time he is needed to be protected from his uncle Set. Above is a carving of a figure similar to the dead Osiris (see plate 15). The hands are crossed across the chest (the classic Osiris pose) and he holds a feather. Osiris usually held the crook and flail.

Above the Osiris figure is an angry creature coming down from above. The evil looking mouth and bearing of teeth is a perfect representation of Set. Set is the fourth figure from the bottom (four the number of the material plane) and sixth from the top (six the number of the world of time and space). Above the Set figure is a mask and beyond is a bird that may represent the influence of Tehuti. Above another face comes a single eye, likely the Eye of Horus. The tenth and last figure to appear is at the top and is of a hawk-like bird with a strong beak. Horus the falcon is the tenth Neteru of Heliopolis and represents the goal of each and every human being.

Hawaii

The Hawaiian Islands are a perfect place to go looking for the "lost" wisdom of the Egyptians. To find it here you have to know what you are looking for, and how to look for it. When things began to falter in Egypt after 2000BC, more and more priests began to head to other parts of the world to keep the wisdom alive in a safer place. Hawaii was a key point of these new settlements.

The Kahunas of Hawaii claim without question that their descendants and wisdom came directly from Egypt. If you imagine a globe with your finger placed on Egypt, then travel directly through the earth you wind up at Hawaii. It is the exact opposite spot on the earth. Thus they are mirror images of the same energy. Not surprisingly, many of the key aspects of Egyptian wisdom became the opposite for the Hawaiian Kahunas. As an example, the Egyptian language was written with mostly consonants while the Hawaiian's use mostly vowels. Not everything is the opposite and this helps to force the student to do the work and understand what is to be reversed and what is not. The two colours of the Hawaiian royalty were yellow and red, and their staff was either white or black; thus the royalty had all of the Hermetic colours in their ceremonial costumes. Hawaiian statues are dressed and anointed very similar to how it was done in Egypt, and Hawaiian temples are similarly constructed in shape like Egyptian temples.[294] Even more similarity lies in the mythology.

---

[294] Kalakaua, *Legends and Myths of Hawaii* (Charles E Tuttle 1992) pp. 31-33, 41, 45

Pele

111:Volcano crater, Big Island of Hawaii- home of the goddess Pele

Perhaps the most noticeable Hawaiian myth with Egyptian connections is that of Pele. She rules the volcanoes and mankind has no power to resist her. She is known as 'Pele of the Sacred Land or Pele the Eater of the Land' when she devours the valleys with her flames. The lava of her flows can destroy everything in its path, but it will also build new landscapes. She may appear as a beautiful young woman or as an old woman with a white dog. When enraged she may appear as a woman in flames. When picking berries on the mountains older Hawaiians still offer berries to Pele. Some offer pork, vegetables, fruit, or gin as alternatives.[295]

Pele is the Hawaiian version of Sekhemet. Understanding the Sekhemet myth will help students understand Pele. Sekhemet was one of the dual aspects of Hathor (along with Bastet) and was the daughter of Ra. When Ra decided that mankind needed to be destroyed, he hurled his eye in the form of the lioness Sekhemet on the earth. She was the searing heat and fire of the sun and set the world ablaze. All of Sekhemet's statues were made of granite to signify the power of fire she represented. She also represented the fire of light that can dispel the darkness. As Sekhemet's destruction continued, Ra had a change of heart and Tehuti appeared as either a flood or he gave her wine to drink. She drank the liquid and was either too full or too drunk and stopped the rampage.[296]

---

[295] Kane, Herb Kawainui *Pele: Goddess of Hawaii's Volcanoes* (Captain Cook Books 1996) pp. 5-6
[296] West *Key* p.68

Pele is similarly the ruler of volcanoes, lava and fire. She too is seen as a destroyer with her fire. The fact that some try to appease Pele with gin may allude to the Ancient Egyptian myth of Tehuti appeasing Sekhemet with wine. Pele is also seen as that which is needed to create the beautiful landscapes, as her fire of destruction is needed for the new life to spring forth. Sekhemet was known as the great healer, as the power of fire could be used to either destroy or heal. All Egyptian healers needed the words and wisdom of Tehuti and the fire of Sekhemet. The use of fire is the same for Qi Gong masters who also heal with the burning heat. So too a Buddhist cupping master who performed purifications on me. The fire is needed to dig deep into the blocks of the different bodies, and is also needed to create the pain (either physical or emotional) to lift the block from its hold. Without pain we cannot heal, no matter what "new age" healing practitioners try to tell you. An event that is locked in you can only come out by your re-living it, or having a master pulling it out of you. It will not be fun but it is something that has to be done to eliminate it completely. If someone suggests they heal you without some personal pain on your part, then they are not using the powers of Sekhemet or Pele. Since all Egyptian healers were priests of Sekhemet, what kind of healing are you getting?

All Hawaiian creation myths begin with the introduction of duality. The world is created from female darkness and male light. From the union of opposites comes a world of opposites, similar to the concept of maya. The supreme Hawaiian deity was Kane and the great female spirit was Hina (similar to Hathor of which Sekhemet was an aspect of). Pele was born from Hina in the ancient homeland. Some believe Pele was forced to flee by a flood, others because she loved to travel, still others because her sister was outraged she has seduced her husband. Tradition states that Pele came to Hawaii from the Island of Tahiti, similar in sound to Tehuti. [297] Perhaps the myth is stating that she came form a place of great wisdom across the ocean, like Egypt.

The tale continues that Pele arrives with some of her brothers and sisters by boat. Her sister, who represents the water, constantly chased her. Her sister may be similar to Bastet, the cat goddess who represents the cool heat of the sun but may also represent the cool water of reflection. Some say the sisters met and battled in Maui, just like the concept burning water for the alchemist where fire and water must battle together to fuse the opposites. At the end of this battle, Pele's mortal body dies and her spirit is freed to become a goddess. As this happens in Hawaii she becomes the goddess of Mauna Loa. By fusing the water and fire together in our heart, we can be freed of our attachment to the physical body and the material world to become a being that is able to experience the unknown mysteries of this universe.

---

[297] Kane pp.5-6, 11

Pele has two other sisters, Laka and Hiiaka, the goddess of the dance. Hathor is seen as the goddess of love, beauty, fun and dancing. The true Hawaiian Hula is not the dance that is today performed for tourists. It is actually part of a great mystical tradition similar to the whirling dervish of the Sufi, or the famed Haka of the New Zealand Maori. The hula in its true form is a way to connect the two halves of our being and join us as one. Only by being initiated into the huna wisdom by a true Hawaiian Kahuna would one ever be able to witness the true hula.

Pele has two more opposite aspects that she must do battle with constantly. Kamapuaá is the spirit of rain, moisture and growing things. The two are enemies and lovers with a stormy relationship. This too is similar to burning water where the fire and water first battle until they can connect the opposites and create a new flower to bud. Another story is the rivalry between Pele and Poliagu, the snow goddess of Mauna Kea. They constantly battled with Pele making great fires to melt the snow, followed by Poliagu making snow to halt the fires.[298] While this can also have connections to burning water, it may also refer to the constant advance and retreat of the ice ages.

Pele is the all-black lava and makes the Big Island a difficult place to live or even visit. The entire island is black lava and the black helps to pull out the negativity in one's character. Hawaii is sometimes called the "dirty laundry island" for the lava helps to bring out aspects like greed, lust or arrogance and put it in front of us. Many have had bad experiences while on the island, which simply is Pele bringing out our negativity for us to finally admit to and eliminate from ourselves. The suggestion of the islanders is to never take Pele's lava back to the mainland for it will bring you bad luck. The hundreds of pounds of returned lava at the City of Refuge is an example that this is no myth. Negative things do happen to people who take away the lava. However the experiences are not really as bad as people think. The lava is doing the same thing that it was doing on the island, pulling the negativity out of a person and putting it right in front of them in situations where it can be eliminated.[299] Unfortunately since everyone either does not want to have to face all of the evil and negativity within themselves, or can not accept what the lava is really doing, they send it back claiming it is bad. Of course these people would also look for someone else to blame for their marriage (spouse), accident (other driver), lack of a raise (boss) rather than the real culprit which is only themselves. That includes so-called spiritual people. They feel they are so pure and advanced that they could take lava and be ok. Most of the "spiritual" people have considerable junk they won't admit to having, thus the lava really affects them. So unless you are ready to unleash hell on your life for the purpose of a massive cleanse, don't take Pele's lava from the island.

---

[298] Kane p.13, 15, 16, 27

[299] Pila of Hawaii *The Secrets and Mysteries of Hawaii* (Health Communications 1995)

At least while on the island when dealing with your issues that will reveal themselves, you will be surrounded by many people with open hearts. Their hearts have opened as the lava has done much of its work from years and years of the individual living there. When back on the mainland (Canada and the USA) I realized that most everyone really do not have open hearts. Money, greed, desires, possessions, and me, me, me is what dominate the cities. That is not to say everyone in Hawaii has an open heart or everyone on the mainland does not...but the proportions in both places are unmistakable. It takes reminding oneself by going to a place like Hawaii where Pele has done her work on the local population to see the lack of her work elsewhere.

Pu'uhonua O Honaunau

112:The reconstructed central temple, near city of Kona, Hawaii

There are many temples on all of the Hawaiian Islands, which are called in Hawaiian 'Heiau.' The name originally means a place of higher forces and quiet (meditative) thought. They are built on power spots on the earth energy grid (as are all ancient sites) and carry a relaxing, peaceful energy. Unfortunately few of the original true Hawaiian Heiau's remain, but many of those built by the later Tahitians still exist. The original Hawaiians (people from Africa called the Menehune) carried the African/Egyptian wisdom of healing with them. The Tahitians arrived full of war, anger and sacrifice (as the Sumerian and Babylonians who came to Egypt) and killed most of the original Hawaiians. The Tahitians were focused on male energy and were in complete opposition to the huna tradition that led to the original line of Kahuna healers. The Tahitians built their own Heiaus, while destroying most of the originals, to perform their rites of sacrifice. One of these new sites is called Puukohola Heiau. Just visiting this place for five minutes is enough to make one's skin crawl (as it also did at Uxmal in Mexico).

While a scant few of the original heiaus remain, the most famous is Pu'uhonua O Honaunau (City of Refuge) on the east coast of the island (see above). The place has a most beautiful energy and is a spectacular place for healing. The site is so full of energy that even the black sand beach near it is full of fish, turtles and eels.

The site today contains two distinct sections divided by a large black lava rock wall. The area furthest from the water is described in brochures as the village for chiefs. The modern reconstruction contains huts, canoes and equipment. There is far more here than meets the eye of the average tourist. One area is called the Royal Fishponds, supposedly stocked with fish as food for the royalty. While spending time in the very lush area I found it more resembled a Zen garden than a food source. The fish were part of the feung shui. But to archaeologists the "dumb" Hawaiians could have no connection to Egypt or the Orient. Yet feung shui, energy lines and placement art are important to the Hawaiian huna and just sitting in this Zen garden for a time is mediation in itself.

The large wall (built from giant pieces of Pele's lava) is pieced together with great precision. The other side of the wall is the area that gives the site its name as City of Refuge, for it was a sanctuary. Should any member of society be guilty of an act against the Hawaiian laws, they had one option to avoid persecution. They could make it to a place of refuge. In most cases to do so would be a harrowing ordeal requiring escaping those out for revenge and swimming through shark infested waters. Yet to make it to the black lava of the sanctuary meant safety. No matter what the crime, one was safe. However there was a catch. At this area lived a great Kahuna of healing. The person was now in the hands of a powerful healer who would have to follow all of their recommendations and go through a massive purification in order to clean away all of the negative parts that allowed the actions that brought the person to the sanctuary in the first place. Years may be needed for the completion of the work, but once done the person was free to enter back into society and would now be a 'new' man or woman with much of their lower self transformed and eliminated.

113:Rock with white and black rocks, teaching wisdom through games

The energy inside of the area is spectacular and I recommend just spending time alone to walk the area. Most of the best spots are not found on the tourist maps, but are still there waiting to be explored. I will mention two that are found on the tourist map, as the other parts should remain hidden except for those who will do the work to find them. One is a lava rock with small pieces of coral and black lava (see above). This is called a Hawaiian version of checkers or chess, which is an original teaching tool of the Egyptian Hermetic initiate. The game of chess is full of symbolism and wisdom. The forces of light and dark are depicted upon a square surface representing the number four and the earth. The sixty-four squares are the same as the I Ching, DNA molecules or the Maya calendar. This spot is more than just a place to play games, it is a valuable teaching tool of the mysteries.

A great stone caught my attention and surprisingly was listed on the guide. The guide claimed a Queen needed to hide so she went under the rock in darkness to be quiet. She tried to remain hidden, however a dog she had with her had begun to bark and gave her away. Hopefully by now you can already see the hidden Hermetic wisdom in the story. The queen (feminine energy) went underneath a rock into darkness (cave, night) and needed to be quiet (in meditation). What gave her away was the barking dog (the conscious mind). With the wisdom of the story staring me in the face I decided upon a little test. No one was around so I placed both hands upon the stone. Immediately my conscious mind went blank. Even the song I had been humming in my head was gone. In an instant I was almost at complete inner silence. I stayed in this position for some time and realized that the stone itself was a powerful meditative tool.

These are but a few examples of the traditions of the Native cultures on the West Coast of North America. The rest of the continent has similar stories. Try reading a number of books on Native Indian Mythology and look for similar Hermetic ideas expressed in this book. I'm sure you will be very surprised with the number of connections to Egyptian mythology that you can find.

The Maya and Olmec

114: The Pyramid of the Inscriptions at Palenque

The Maya have come to be know as the world's great astronomers. What has become known today as the "Mayan Calendar," is really their Long Count Calendar- and is used to record time in the millions of years. It is also used to calculate world ages, of which the end of the one we are currently in could be in 2012. The calendar will be discussed in detail in Chapter 25. For now I want to provide some background on this rather mysterious group of people, who flourished in Central America for perhaps thousands of years- then like a mystery novel the main cities were abandoned and it seems large numbers vanished without a trace. No one can really explain what actually happened to them, even though there are thousands of Maya descendants still living today.

The first most interesting clue to this mystery is their current name. Maya. This name of course is the same word as the Hindu goddess of Illusion- and there may be an important linguistic connection. The Maya could have been called that in reference to their ability to break the Maya's Veil of illusion. When looking closely at Mayan art and building structures there is a great similarity not only to Hindu and Buddhist art, but to that of Ancient Egypt as well- as the same information and wisdom around the world is being placed into stone monuments and artwork. A short tour of some of their most famous sites will help to display the great depth of symbolic information that that exists with the ancient people's of Mexico.

Olmec

115:Giant Olmec head, Mexico City Anthropology Museum

Prior to the Maya, the main group of people living in Central America were called the Olmec (rubber people), claimed by archaeologists to have lived between 1500-400 BC. While few cities have been excavated- La Venta is one of them, the Olmecs did leave behind a great number of very unique statues and monuments. The most famous are the giant stone heads, out of volcanic basalt, and weighting as much as 50 tons. What makes the stone heads even more amazing is the fact that they tend not to depict the standard features of people common to Mesoamerica, but that to Africa. No one has clearly explained why the Olmec should have been making giant stone "African" head statues. As well these heads seem to be wearing some sort of crude head covering, that many think resemble early American football helmets of the 1920's, thus the heads may be related to the famous Mesoamerican ball game, which seems to have its origin with the Olmec.

116:Very "Kung-Fu" looking Olmec Statue

117:Statues known as the Twins from El Azuzul, sitting in front of a jaguar, and seeing to wear very Egyptian pharaoh like head dress.

Many other Olmec statues show very Asian/Buddhist looking figures, and a few found seem to wearing Egyptian style Pharaoh headdress (see photo above). The Maya tradition claims that their calendar is a direct descendant from the Calendar of the Olmec people, and the Olmec writing system seems to have been a pre-cursor of what became the Mayan written language. It is these odd artifacts, and early writing and mathematical system that have caused many to speculate that the origin of the Olmec was not from the Americas. Leo Weiner at the turn of the 19th century was on the first people to claim that the Olmec must have come from Africa. Those who follow this theory also state that many of the skeletons found at Olmec sites do not show standard Mesoamerican physiology but instead African. Others have used the many various statues to try and show a Chinese origin for the Olmec, while the Mormon religion claims they were the group called Jeridites who came from the Middle East. Norwegian explorer Thor Heyerdahl felt that Olmec may have been early Nordics, especially from the white skinned statues such as the one below of Quetzalcoatl at La Venta.

118:Early Olmec depiction of Quetzalcoatl, white and bearded- La Venta

The Olmec have the oldest depiction of the famous Quetzalcoatl, the winged serpent god- white and bearded who came to Mexico to teach civilization, culture and wisdom. This story very much matches the old story of Osiris, who the Egyptian myth states that after civilizing Egypt, traveled the world to do the same with the rest of the earth's population. The Olmec, for all of their great monuments, seem to vanish around 400BC. No one is really sure where they came from, what they did, or where they went. You would think it would be one of the most studied questions in Central American history, but like all key markers of the past, this odd occurrence is answered simply with a "drought, cultural problems, war," and swept under the table. Following the Olmec was the famous people known as the Maya, who also seem to do somewhat of a vanishing act themselves. However if one sees the Olmec period as being 5 or 10,000 years ago and not 2,000, it might explain more of their "sudden" disappearance. Then like Old Kingdom Egypt, which was an attempt to copy the great society that was there in the past, the Maya quite possibly were trying to copy the great Olmec civilization that was there previously. The only thing is that, unlike the Egyptians, the Mayans may have succeeded.

The Maya-Palenque

119:The Palace at Palenque

In the Central Mexican jungle of Chiapas lies the city of Palenque. This of course is a modern name- named for a modern town close by, no one is quite sure what it was called in Maya times. Some suggest it was called Lakham Ha (Big Water). This city was deserted around 1000 years ago and mostly covered with jungle, until rediscovered and excavated by archaeologists in the 1800's. Being deserted for so long, the jungle having grown over the buildings, helped to preserve the site. In fact what has been cleared and restored here (the central religious area), is just a tiny part of the entire city. It is why I so enjoy traveling to Mayan sites. Unlike Ancient Egypt where only the temple or the pyramids remain, in Mexico and Guatemala, the entire city is still there. At Palenque for example, with a bit of adventurous spirit in you, you can hack through a bit of the jungle and come to the living areas, apartment houses, small temples and shrines- as long as you don't mind the constant noise of the howler monkeys.

120:Relief found in the Palace, Pacal riding the two-headed jaguar

One of the things that has been a common occurrence on every visit to Palenque, is the constant serenity and peace that I have felt there. Other Mayan cities have a more heavy energy at times, but Palenque is the place where one can really come and just chill out. The central group of structures is dominated by the what is called the Pyramid of the Inscriptions and the Palace. The pyramid is named due to several large stela at the top that contain rows of Mayan hieroglyphic texts that give some historical background of the city. Within the pyramid lies the tomb of Pacal- considered the great Maya ruler in the 6th century AD. A long stairway leads to the tomb where one finds the giant stone slab- that has many interpretations of what it symbolizes- from a depiction of the Maya maize god, to portraying a scene from the Popul Vuh, even Pacal operating some sort of machine or spaceship.

The Palace is really several small structures in one, that is focused on a four story tower originally thought to be an observatory, but now no one is quite sure.

121:Pyramid of the sun in the Cross Group, Palenque

Further back is what is called the cross group (Cross, Foliated Cross and Sun), so named by Christian explorers who felt that the reliefs in the back chamber on top of 3 small pyramids in a group reminded them of the Christian Cross. These reliefs are said to be connected to the ruler Chan Bahlum (snake-jaguar) who according to reliefs may be similar to the Egyptian idea of Menes- a great unifier. Here one combines the snake (wisdom) with the jaguar (the stalker or one who is a master of the body-mind). In fact this is the Mayan world tree, which signifies the beginning of creation. There is much to explore at Palenque, as much of the city is still surrounded and covered with jungle. As well a river flows just by the city, and makes a great afternoon stop for a swim when the heat gets too much and a break from being at the site is needed.

Sayil, Labna, Uxmal

Sayil and Labna are part of a group of smaller Mayan cities that make up what is known as the Ruuta Puuc. A series of cities close together, they are often included in a one day bus tour out of Merida. Sayil has the magnificent palace structure that resembles Hatshepsut's temple in Egypt (see chapter 6), but I want to focus now on a very interesting part of the complex at Labna. If you notice the below photograph, there is much symbolic Hermetic information layed into that part of the building.

122:Symbolic carvings in the temple at Labna

In the middle of the photograph are found numerous 8-pointed flowers-eight being the number of Tehuti and wisdom. Between them can be found two different types of spirals, one more like smoke or a mushroom, the other more like the winding or rope or string. The spiral is representative of the number 5 and growth. Yet the entire top of the building culminates in the left corner, where one finds the open serpent jaws, and the head of a man, a very Oriental looking man, is coming out of the serpent's mouth. This birthing from the serpent of wisdom is similar to the ideas of the winged serpent in the Egyptian Book of What is in the Duat. Here wisdom, growth, and serpent energy are all combining in an interesting way to depict the kind of energy that one would find by spending some time on this spot.

The largest Mayan city on the Ruuta Puuc is Uxmal. This is the site of a famous pyramid called the Pyramid of the Magician, so named for the legend that the pyramid was built by giants overnight. The Mayans have come to be known as a group of sacrifice, like the Aztecs, making sacrifices supposedly to keep the world form ending. But like the ideas of the Toltec, sacrificing people was not a part of the Mayan tradition. At some point in time that did begin to happen, but that was very late in the existence and was marking the end of a great period of wisdom. At other Mayan cities I got no visions or feeling of sacrifice in any way. That changed at Uxmal. From the moment I entered the site I began to feel ill and queezy. When I looked at the pyramid I could get images of hundreds of dead bodies being rolled down the steps.

123:Part of the odd alter in a far off area of Uxmal

To really sum up this site for me was in a small courtyard area that I explored. I was alone, and as I do at sties, I climb in or on just about everything to check it out. Here I walked up the stairs of a small temple, when my footing slipped and I tumbled backward onto the stairs, hitting the back of my head rather hard against one of the stone steps- before sliding down the 10 or so stairs to the ground. Not one in all of my travels all over Mexico, Egypt or other sites in the world have I ever fallen or potentially injured myself, until here. When I picked up my small backpack, that had gone flying in the fall, I noticed that it had stopped at what appeared to be a small stone alter with a skull and crossbones on the side. Granted in Hermetic alchemic lore, the skull and crossbones can come to represent the death of the egoic self, of the mind that thinks it is exists as a separate thing in reality. But like all Hermetic symbols they can be twisted around by those wanting to promote other ideas, and these specific symbols had definitely be used as part of the Mayan sacrifice cult. Part of me got the feeling, one I can not factual prove, that the entire idea of sacrificing humans had its origin in Mexico at this very site. Needless to say I was quite happy when it was time to leave Uxmal and go back to Merida.

Chichen Itza

124:Photograph of the Pyramid of Kukulkan at the summer solstice, the shadow resembling a serpent moving up and down the steps.

For holiday visitors to Mexico in Cancun the number one tourist stop is Tulum due to the easy day trip. A much farther trip, but far more rewarding, is the central Yucatan city of Chichen Itza. There is so much to see at this site, and even a couple of days is not enough to completely explore it. I want to point out a few interesting things of this very unique site. The center piece is the Pyramid of Kukulkan (Quetzalcoatl). This pyramid is made out of exactly 91 stairs on each side, to make a total of 364. The top step represents the 365 day year. The stairways, flanked by serpent heads, also does something rather amazing on the summer solstice, the sun causes a shadow to appear on the steps of the pyramid, emulating a serpent moving up the stairs. Thus the pyramid is partially an astronomical clock of extreme precision, and partially relating to the flow of the kundalini serpent in the body. Inside of the pyramid is a chamber where one can find the statue of a jaguar and a dog.

125:Mexico's largest ball court, and odd sound tube, all in one.

Chichen Itza also includes the largest ball court in the Americas. But beyond a sporting field, this has very unique properties. The field is 200 feet long and at one end has a platform temple-like area. What is amazing is that if two people stand on opposite ends of this field, and talk in a whisper to each other, the person at the platform end can not hear the other- but the person at the other end can hear the platform end person perfectly. I took the above photo from the "hearing" end, and you can likely barely make out the small blue dot at the far end. That is my friend who was having a rather detailed conversation with me, all in whisper- while she couldn't hear a single thing I said. This has led some to speculate that when the ball game was not being played, this area became either a giant theater or meeting place- where actors or chiefs of the town could speak to the entire population easily, without the need of modern devices such as microphones.

126-27 Symbolic reliefs from Chichen Itza

Another interesting thing that can be found all over Chichen Itza, are symbolic symbols placed into the buildings. They are such as the X-O patterns above, or the spirals that appear from the mouth on another stela. It is showing that this site is one that is transmitting Hermetic wisdom, again all in symbolic form. Further down past the temple of the warriors is another area that is perhaps to most potent healing place I have ever been to (a picture can be seen in chapter 13). I just sat for hours, without the need to do anything, other than enjoy the space of what was once a key Hermetic center.

128:The Caracol, astronomical observatory at Chichen Itza

Like the other cities mentioned, Chichen Itza was abandoned, and it seems large members of the population vanished. There do not appear to be huge gravesites for all the missing Maya, nor does it seem like they traveled to another location. Exactly what became of a huge segment of the Mayan population is still a mystery. The usual theories of war, famine, ecological disaster all entail dead bodies, and that smoking gun is still not found for evidence. One suggestion that has come was the Maya had become so advanced in their abilities to work with space-time that at a specific time date- a number of them really did vanish from our reality. The theory states that they were either able to shift dimensional worlds, or use some sort of worm hole or time travel opening or raise their vibrational frequency to a rate where they could no longer be seen by the rest here. This particular theory for the vanished Maya is that they felt that they needed to leave an ever dangerous world that was bent on the complete destruction of all ancient wisdom. They were then waiting in some other dimension or portal for the right moment (end of the Baktun calendar) to return en mass to this reality and assist with key things needed to happen at that time.

Of course this theory fails to adequately explain the millions of Mayan people that did not go missing, and whose descendants live in Guatemala and Mexico today, and whose shaman do not wholly subscribe to this theory. But like everything that is being presented about the ancient world, an open mind must be kept to all such theories that present themselves. We can see the amazing buildings made, knowledge encoded- that such a theory is not totally out of the question. Without hard evidence we should not automatically accept it, but keep it there in the realm of- "yes maybe a group of Maya did shift time and space 1000 years ago and might return at a specific time. We will just have to stay alert and wait and see."

CHAPTER 19
EUROPEAN STONE CIRCLES

132:Stonehenge at sunset, the stones almost seem to absorb and amplify the setting sun

Stonehenge, the world's most famous stone circle, lies on the Salisbury Plain in Central England. Yet few know that there are hundreds of other stone circles in the UK, Scandinavia and Northern Europe of various shapes and sizes in Scandinavia and Northern Europe. Ancient cultures all over the world loved to build large megalithic (stone) structures, but the ancient builders of Northern Europe seemed to favour the circle as their building specialty. Circular stone structures are also found in the North American Native Indian tradition in their medicine wheels, and I feel that the medicine wheels of North America and the circles of Europe are linked in function.

Medicine Wheels

Native Indians still build and use medicine wheels, and can include anywhere from 4 to 36 to hundreds of stones, used to create a circular monument that can also include "spokes of a wheel." The circle represents the four directions, and each stone has specific symbolic meanings based on its position within the wheel. The wheel itself can be meditated on, walked, or simply stood in/on specific areas depending on the needs of the one who is coming to it. Usually entering from the east, the wheel is always walked clockwise, which helps to turn on the energy vortex. A medicine wheel is only walked counter-clockwise when dismantling it, thus removing the stones and turning off the power source. Similar to the stones at Teotihuacan, where each carries a specific set of information, a medicine wheel can be visualized the same way. A labyrinth is a specific type of medicine wheel, found extensively in the Mediterranean and Europe.

Stonehenge

133:Outer sarson stones at Stonehenge

Even today with stones knocked down, or missing, Stonehenge is an impressive sight (especially when you get right up close to the stones themselves). What made people thousands of years ago go to all this trouble? The site began with a circular ditch (known as a henge). Within the ditch came a series of wooden posts (archaeologists speculate around 3000 BC) which aligned with three other large wooden posts (possibly totem poles) whose original positions are marked by three circular white areas in the parking lot. Sometime around 2600 BC, the big stones began to be brought in. However like sites of this era (such as Giza, also dated to 2500 BC) it is highly likely that the actual construction era may actually be be 5,000, or even 10,000 BC. The stones themselves were moved from a great distance from as far as Wales, with no one exactly sure just how they were moved over the rolling English countryside. Large sarsons (very hard rocks), were brought here, then carefully worked and carved- created images, shapes, faces within the stone. It was like they were "tuning" the rocks to make them the exact energetic and musical pitch that was required. 36 sarsons were then placed in a circle, while another set of stones (called lintels) were placed on top of them to enclose the stones in a ring. Another set of larger stones were set up in horseshoe shape within, that is know known as a trilithon. Bluestones (taken from a stone monument now called Blue Stonehenge close by) were brought here and also set up in circles within the monument.

No one is actually sure what the structure was used for: ceremonial temple, astronomical center (due to its near perfect alignment to the solstices and other astronomical events), Druid worship center, connection to the funerary rights of the dead. It may have somehow touched all of these functions. But what is important to remember, that even though today it appears as though Stonehenge is somehow alone- sitting between two busy highways- it was once part of a much bigger area. A precessional avenue (reminding one of Egyptian pyramid causeways) runs from the River Avon. An area to the north called the Curses is a giant oval-rectangular ditch, first thought to be a Roman chariot racing center, is now known to be older than Stonehenge itself. The name that has been passed on for this area may be a clue "curses," perhaps it was some sort of dividing line, or marker- that to cross over incorrectly was to lead to some type of curse. As well many round barrows (neolithic burial chambers) surround Stonehenge. The site links in some way with a site known as Woodhenge (all made of wooden posts) and perhaps links as well to the far away sites of Darrington Downs, Avebury and Glastonbury. All must we included in any explanation of Stonehenge. Discoveries on the countryside continue to come up, just a few days ago (July 2010) another circular henge just 900 meters away from Stonehenge was found. This was one giant complex, and the ancients went to a lot of trouble to build it, and align the stones astronomically.

Like all ancient sites, Stonehenge was built where energy grids (known to the English as ley lines) cross, and are points of great power connection with the earth. However when you get there today, strangely the energy at the site is very weak- even right in the middle when you get close to the stones. You can feel a slight energy but not much. It is almost dead. I had to wonder why that was. Then a few years ago I found my answer. The entire site has been dismantled at least 3 times, the last during the 1950's. All of the stones were removed by cranes and heavy machinery, transported off site, and the remaining area dug up and studied. Then holes were dug, the stones brought back (or at least we can assume they were the same original stones that were taken away, but who knows they could also be very good copies) and then cemented into place in the dug holes. Yes cement was used to put the stones back. All of this movement, change, possible repositioning (because some stones look a bit off compared to very early photographs), and the cement-means the energy there has changed. Sadly it is now basically a monument like a memory, to what this place was or could be, but no longer is. The real energy that the site must have exuded is down to a trickle.

To experience a stone circle with much of the energy left, one has to go about 1 hour north to Avebury.

Avebury

134:Some of the giant stones in the central circle at Avebury

The site of Avebury is definitely something to experience. The center of it all is a giant stone circle- painstakingly reconstructed at the turn of the century after much of it had been purposely destroyed in the pre-Victorian era. Part of the modern village of Avebury actually exists inside of the circle. Its that big. But this site was far more than the stone circle.

135:The serpent winds across the countryside...notice how the stone appears to be bowing or moving forward- and the very unique diamond shaped carving of the stone- a popular shape here

Starting at a temple far off to the south-east, a double stone layered pathway, representing a serpent of stone, "winds" along the countryside. Half way comes a henge, which inside the larger stone circle is found, and then the serpent continues north-west where it leads somewhat in the direction of Silbury Hill (the English equivalent of a giant pyramid, known here as an earthwork). This makes it a very close partner of the famous Ohio Serpent Mound in the USA, where a serpent also winds along the countryside, and ends with an open mouth that is either swallowing or birthing- a giant egg. This serpent is of course the kundalini serpent of the body, but might in fact represent more- the kundalini life force of the earth itself.

While Stonehenge had a bit of energy that could be felt, Avebury was on a whole other level. At certain spots along the central circle, the energy buzzing was so great that it felt like my entire body was shaking. The energy while strong, was peaceful, similar in feeling to Palenque in Mexico. A similar energy can be found in Salisbury Cathedral, which I feel was built on an old ancient site with underground granite pathways that caused the water energy to join with the fire of the granite stone. If you can follow the energy lines of the church, you can follow the energy lines of the area.

136:Wanna kiss?

The stones themselves at Avebury are large and have been carefully shaped and modified. Holes have been drilled in them, openings carved, things shaved, and each of the stones presents many "faces" as the spirits of the stones are alive. This can be noticed at ancient sites all over the world, the human and animal faces that can be make out in the stone. On the walk up to the stone circle itself, I got the sense that this entire serpent walk was a very special journey- almost like a vision quest or pilgrimage. It was not something that happened in a day, for at each pair of stones on the walk- one would have to stop and connect with them (similar to what I felt about the stones at Teotihuacan). Each set of stones represented two dual sides of a piece of ancient wisdom. The stones themselves, by the way they were shaped and carved, would help explain what was meant to be done at each one. Fingers needed to be placed in circular holes, hands in wider ones, certain areas the body would fit right into perfectly carved out areas, while in others once would just sit with or look at the stones. As each area of work was completed, then one moved to the next set and the next set. This might take weeks or months to complete.

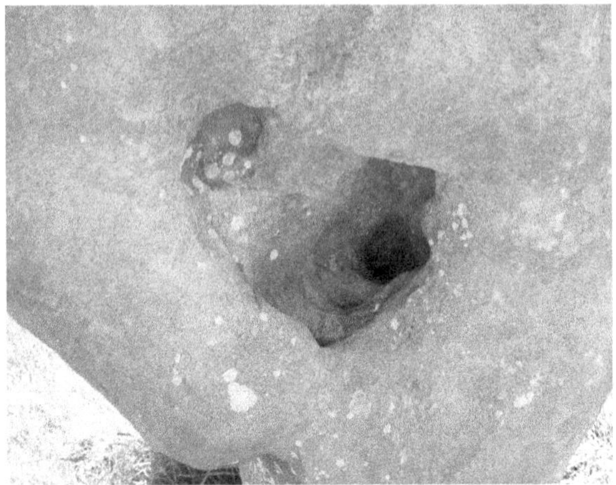

Hand would be placed into here.

137:This stone is leaned into

Again one must remember that hundreds of these giant stones were found, moved at a great distance, shaped and carved, then placed upright to make this serpentine site. And don't forget the local legends that still exist here. One warns modern day night-time drivers that one of the stones near the road likes to go for a walk around midnight, and can often startle drivers as they see what appears to be a diamond shaped stone moving across the roadway. And once you have seen the "life" that each of these stones seem to possess- such legends give a strong feeling they may be based on some sort of fact.

138:Massive stones in the inner circle of Avebury

Scandinavian Circles

139:Large stone circle near the Swedish- Norwegian border

The Northern European countries of Norway and Sweden are good examples of the amazing pre-Viking sites that dot the area, and are mostly unknown to even the local population. While Viking area graves are often found close by, it is the older megalithic stone monuments that drew the Vikings to these spots. As I will mention, stone circles are medicine wheels using much larger stones. In Scandinavia I have visited perhaps 50 stone circles, some made with small and medium sized stone, others with very large stones.

Few locals visit them. It would amaze me when I would hear of someone gathering up a bunch of money to travel to England to spend two weeks visiting Stonehenge and Avebury, when they have equally powerful stone circles just a 20-30 minute drive away. Just as pyramids are not tombs, these circles have nothing to do with physical death. In later times- just as graves began to be associated at pyramid sites hoping to somehow use that energy in the afterlife- so too here. Instead think of these circles as the temples of the ancient people. It is where they would come for healing, answers, ceremonies, knowledge, prayer, initiation, or simply just to calm the mind and body. And of course as I write in this site and my books- while the ancient sites do open a doorway to death- it is the death of self-mind that is focused on- in order to experience the Totality of the Self while still alive in the body.

These stones were not just placed randomly on any spot, but on a place where the energy of the earth's meridians cross (as the body has energy meridians, and certain points acupuncture needles can be placed in order open or unclog stuck areas). You can think of the stones as acupuncture needles, and are placed at areas where the earth's meridians can be accessed at very strong connection points. Not to be overlooked is the incredible mathematical precision with which these stones have been laid out. A German researcher I met at a site told me he has been studying European circles for over 20 years. He has measured each stone and circle, and found them matching various constellations in the sky, as well as being built with the mathematical properties of pi, phi (golden section), and various other geometric principles. In fact the geometry is staggering once you begin to have it revealed.

Once one has gained a connection and feeling to these places, one will notice spots where the legs (sometimes the entire body) will begin to buzz or feel somewhat electric. Others will notice extreme hot or cold spots, but others may get a surge of energy or clarity of mind. Also notice that the stones themselves have been specifically shaped and carved- and many of the stones will show human or animal faces that seem to project out of the stones from various angles.

Unfortunately many of these circles have been destroyed over the years. Some by farmers, wanting to clear the land, while others were purposely destroyed by the Catholic Church- who on taking over the area wanted to use the obvious power spot for their own new church. At most old churches (say pre 1500) you can usually find one old very tall stone- one of the ones that they left to stand on the site as a reminder to the power that they now controlled. In fact by tracking these old "stave churches" (which connect together in straight lines on the map) you can find a lot of old standing stone monoliths, or stones that had been part of a circle.

The countries of Norway and Sweden- in their Hermetic heyday, likely had thousands stone circles all over the country. Imagine the energy that must have present along the entire of Scandinavia if all of theses sites were complete, active and in use by the men and women of wisdom in the communities.

140:Several stone circles that "snake" their way up a hillside to a much larger stone circle- Norway

One group in the area known as Oldtidsveien, at a location called The Hun- has more than ten small stone circles that wind their way up the hillside, and from a distance they seem to wind like a snake. This connects this site, at least in function, to Avebury. Gunnarstorp is located up a hill into what was originally a beautiful forest. The combination of large stones, trees and the shadows was a beautiful experience. Sadly another site was energetically damaged, as in 2016 all the trees surrounding the main stone circle were cut down. Those old trees and those shadows now only exist in my photographs and memories. Råde has two lovely circles next to a gas station. What is most amazing here is to notice the trees that surround the area, how all of them are growing towards and over the stone circles (as if to grab there energy)-none of the trees are growing up or away. This is also especially great to visit in the spring when the many white flowers are out in this area and give the site a very magical feeling.

141:Author in part of the oval stone circle at Istrehågan, possible Hermetic Cell displayed in stone.

Another well known circle is on the the western side of the Oslo Fjord at Istrahågan. Instead of being circular, this structure- as is many that are found in Sweden- is more of an oval. It is believed to be set up like a ship- linking the site to Vikings that supposedly built it. But like all of the large megalithic structures I see, I feel that all of these sites are much much older than the date suggested.

What I first noticed about this oval circle, was that while its energy was just as strong as the circle mentioned above- unlike those which had a much more gentle energy- this circle was like a jolt. When I counted the number of stones used to make this circle I saw that it was the exact number that was mentioned in Hermetic Texts that made up their unit cells, and the number Carlos Castaneda used to make up what he called his Warrior's Party. It is quite possible that these stones have been set up as an in-rock warrior's unit, and each large stone represents one of the members of the Gnostic unit.

142: One of the many petroglyphs that are found placed on rocks all over Norway. The detail and symbol here connect me with Egypt

One other part of this area should be mentioned, and that is the large number of petroglyphs (rock art) that can also be found in the region. Visiting several of these sites, I began to notice the serpent appearing- in the boats, on the boats, in front of the boats. And then it hit me. This was Egyptian in origin. What I was looking at was a "Reader's Digest" version of the *Book of What is in the Duat* and the *Book of Gates*.

143:More Hermetic symbols?

Just in the photo above once can see in the center the twin-serpent headed boat of "Ra," and that has the oval shape in the middle of the boat- the shrine where Ra would travel. To me there is just too much similarity to the Egyptian New Kingdom tomb art. I don't want to say that it was Egyptians who drew these, but to say that what was drawn in the tomb of Rameses VI and on rocks in Sweden and Norway come from the same source and offer the same symbolic message of moving beyond the illusion of this reality.

Why Circles?

Of course the question becomes why the circle? And why the near perfect astronomical alignments needed in the set up of the stones? It might be to relate to the Earth or the Universe, that was usually depicted Hermetically as a circle. Native Indians use a circle for all their ceremonies, lay down a cross within, each point that touches the circle relating the four directions- along with above, below and within, reach the 7 layers of creation.

Another can be that they are used to link to the energy of the moon, or in some way block it. Recent research suggests that moon may not be what we have always been told. The standard astronomical term for a moon is a satellite, but the name is also used for a man-made object sent into space on a scientific mission. Many ancient writers claimed that there was a time in human history when the moon was not in the sky. Giordano Bruno's writings talk of a time when there was no moon. Democritus, Anaxagoras Appollonius, Plutarch and Aristotle said the same. This is corroborated with the stories of many native tribes who have myths of the time "before the moon."

The moon is a very strange entity. Some of it can be found in the book *Who Built the Moon*. It does not have a solid core like every other planet. It is either hollow or has a very low density, with mass concentrated only at specific points on the surface. Amazingly it is exactly 400 times smaller than the sun, but exactly 400 times closer to the earth- so they appear almost the same size. It is this odd connection that allows eclipse, the moon to block out the sun. The moon oddly mirrors the movement of the sun, by rising and setting at the opposite point on the horizon. There is no logical reason why the moon and sun should mirror each other this way. Also the moon has one side that always remains dark, never turns for that side to reflect the light of the sun. When we see the moon in the sky we always see the same side. That is odd in itself.

Some speculate the moon was created from what became the space for the Pacific Ocean after a comet collision, other theories that it is a remnant after a planetary collision. Some say it is an artificial construction, not a planet type object at all. Don't forget that in the movie *The Truman Show* (that revealed as much information as the first *Matrix* Movie) Christof, the one who manufactured Truman's illusion, had his control center in the moon. That may connect with the odd myth that tells of the "man in the moon." The moon produces no light of its own, but is a reflector of the sun's light. Thus the moon is like a cosmic mirror, what we see is not natural, but a reflection. It is why over history the moon has become linked with demonic assault, alien abduction and dark forces. Demonic beings are said to love the dark and run from light. This would be so if they and the moon are somehow connected.

Gurdjeff said "that everything on earth, people, plants, animals are food for the moon. All movements, actions and manifestations of people, plants and animals depend on the moon, and are controlled by the moon. If we develop in ourselves consciousness and will, and usurp our mechanical life, we shall escape from the power of the moon." Most take this to be some sort of metaphor or fable, something like the moon mind inside of us, but Gurdjieff claimed that everything he wrote, while symbolic, could also be taken as a literal fact. This concept become the Eagle in Castaneda books- for the moon, like the eagle mentioned by Castaneda, has a black side and a white side like yin and yang.

Ouspensky wrote that the moon operated as a giant electromagnet, pulling upon all organic life on earth and sucking into itself the soul essence of dying consciousness. He said that the moon is an embryonic planet receiving its nutritional supply from organic life on earth through an etheric umbilical cord.

Human emotions are driven by the moon. In the cosmological scheme, earth is like the mother to the moon which is still a FEOTUS in that it can not break on its own, hold an atmosphere or support life. In that sense the moon is a parasite. Yet by feeding the moon it might grow and develop into a living planet. On death the physical body returns to the earth, but the soul essence escapes UPWARDS and goes to the moon, which mirrors the Ancient Egyptian statement- "body for the earth, soul up to heaven."

Boris Moravio in *Gnosis* wrote that human life was an illusion, and part of that illusion was to get humans to accept a cosmic game and participate in it without rebellion. Yet each human does not produce enough desired energy for the cosmic game, why it needs to create emotional trauma and psychological suffering to sustain the strong energy movement from earth to feed the moon energy. This concept was shown in the movie *Monsters Inc*. To escape the lunar influence Ouspensky said we had to "create a moon within our selves." By that he meant we must develop in us a driving mechanism that can take the place of the lunar influence on us, thus have our self awareness in control and have no stimuli that can provoke any unconscious reaction. In this way we stop feeding the moon while living, and still properly pay our debt upon death. Castaneda also claimed that a debt had to be paid to what he called the Eagle, the memory of our life experiences. The only way to escape the trap of the Eagle was by the living the warrior's way, and by performing a complete life recapitulation while alive. That would pay our debt, yet provide the opening that would let us go free.

Ok I know some of that sounds pretty far fetched, but again in this investigation of the ancient world we have to keep all possibilities open,until we finally have the deep knowing. I am simply presenting what I found in research about the Moon, and thought it could tie in with stone circles uses around the world. I will leave it up to you to decide for yourself what stone circles and standing stone megaliths were made for.

HOWDIE MICKOSKI

THE POWER OF THEN

Volume 3: The Dreamstate

CHAPTER 20
HERMETIC TRICKSTER

"Being a clown brings you honour, but also shame. It brings you power, but you have to pay for it." -John Lame Deer-

One of Hermes forms was the divine trickster, and anyone with Hermes-Tehuti energy will have this detail about them.. Hermes is magical, dancelike, goofy, and not on a career track. He is the god of the internal nervous system, and the connection between head, heart and genitals. When the nervous system is not working well, Hermes is up to something, or we are not paying attention to his voice. Hermes is the one that brings tears and laughter. In alchemy he is Mercury, called quicksilver due to its amazing speed of movement. The day of Hermes is Wednesday (Odin's Day in Norse or Mecredi in French). Hermes learning is experiential, at times fun, at times sad, and at times rather mischievous.

Hermes was sometimes called the Wisefool, and every culture has a similar wise "trickster" deity. To the Native Indian this was the Coyote or Raven, and personified by the specific shaman known as the heyoka. It is the sacred clown tradition of Germanic and Celtic myth. The trickster may be a joker, truth teller, story teller, and transformer that "stirs the pot" to expose different hidden emotions of a person or society. Hermes was also called the father of the foot race and a statue appeared of him at the entrance to the Olympia Stadium. Another aspect is the magician. Those who personify this aspect of the trickster sort of live outside of time and space. Physical reality is a game to them, and the magician trickster challenges us in every way. Any trickster breaks all the rules, not just of nature but of the gods- usually for someone or something's benefit, and to show patterns and habits that need to be broken. He is ok with being a destroyer, for it helps to point to flaws in the carefully constructed societies. He has no morals thus is not controlled by what he should do and feel, and instead by what is actually needed in any moment. Because of that he can seem to inflict a lot of damage on those around him. This idea that the trickster can bring chaos can be found in the story of the African trickster god Edshu. He wears a hat that is red on one side and blue on the other. That way when he walks down the road the villagers on both sides can argue about what colour his hat was. Then to make it worse, when he walked back down the road, he turned his hat around just to cause more confusion. When asked about it he says, "it is my fault, and I meant to do it. Spreading strife is my greatest joy." He is not doing it for his own enjoyment, but doing it to slap the egoic mind of everyone he comes across.

He rebels against authority, pokes fun at the overly serious,- and often has great humour, even at himself when his own schemes for teaching sometimes fail. The old myths are well laced with humour and tricks as opposed to modern religion that has only become full of serious words. The major idea a trickster is trying to bring forth is that the form (the body and personality) is just a mask they are wearing, and they want the person to look beyond it. You can find modern examples of the hermetic trickster (someone who uses cunning, humour and sarcasm to make a point) in TV and movies with: Buggs Bunny, Bart Simpson and Captain Jack Sparrow.

Hermetic Hero

It was Joseph Campbell who called the Hermetic Trickster *The Hero with a Thousand Faces*. The hero is someone who has given his or her life for something bigger than themself. The key point was in the losing of yourself, and the giving to something higher in one way or another. Often the hero is ridiculed by others or treated poorly for what they gave up. Once any one of us lets go of our own self preservation, we undergo a truly heroic transformation of consciousness. The hero is sacrificing something of themself, and from the Tehuti/Hemes school this would be personified back to the world via the mask of the trickster. In the ancient world, the Hermetic hero was in some way tied to the idea of death. The hero either died while doing something courageous, or had a spiritual death to experience the supernormal range of spiritual life, and then come back with the message. Often he is on a quest to recover something that has been lost. Upon the end of the adventure they will always find some underlying quality that they never knew that they possessed. Sometimes swallowed, as in the Jonah story, or taken into the abyss, they are later resurrected. The conscious was destroyed so the unconscious could take over. Another way the hero's journey is depicted is by coming face to face with the power of the dark. He may overcome it, or kill it like St. George with the dragon. The outer dragon is really some aspect of his own inner mind.

The modern world, stuck in the drudgery of an office day after day, gives little chance for the hero's adventure. It is why the movie *Star Wars* was so popular. It was not a futuristic space drama, it is the hero's journey- as powerful as any Greek myth, played out on the big screen. The hero, Luke Skywalker, would no longer follow the "non human way" of the machine system that was symbolized by Darth Vader- no longer be a slave to the system. The hero is not really trying to save the world, but is trying in some way to revitalize it, bring life to it, while at the same time to eliminate his own inner demons. This is tough, for everyone around you- the system- wants nothing but to break you, and waits for any mistakes or weakness to hit you hard.

The Heyoka

"It is believed among the Lakota that if you had a dream or visions of birds, you were destined to become a medicine man. But if you had a vision of the Thunderbird, it was your destiny to become something else; a heyoka or sacred clown. The Trickster. Like the Thunderbird, the heyokas were both feared and held in reverence." Steve Mizrach

The heyoka was considered an important member of the Native Indian tribe, even though most had no idea what he was doing. He was usually freed from normal constraints of life (wife, kids, or to participate in the work of the tribe) he had other business. Despite their bizarre acts, they were seen as the most powerful healers, seers, people of great medicine. They were often the ones who were charged with battling demons or aliens when they appeared in the village. Whenever they broke the solemnness of some ceremony or event with something crazy or stupid, the people did not get angry, but took it as a sign to try and look beyond the ritual into the mysterious of the sacred. The heyoka's sudden lightning-like outbursts were seen as the keys of enlightenment, much like the absurd acts of Zen masters in the Orient. The heyoka uses these outbursts, weird shocking behavior, to stop the mind of those around them. Getting on an elevator today, turning to face the back instead of the front is a small form of heyoka action, to see how everyone will react. They were openers to doorways of perception for others without the need of drums, drugs, or tools- just the odd shock of their actions or words was enough. For that they were seen as powerful medicine people, and bringers of great visions- for due to their own bizarre behavior, deep messages of the spirit would come to them. To follow this path also meant they had to deal with great inner torment and struggle, for to live up to the calling of the Hermetic Trickster was not easy, especially as the world moved from tribal to our modern Western society, and such behavior was not in everyone's book of rules.

CHAPTER 21
PYRAMID TEXTS

175:Remains of the Pyramid of Unas in the background, Sakkara

Oldest Religious Texts in the World

"I have embraced this my father (Osiris) who has become tired, so that he may be quite healthy again." -Pyramid Text 50-

The Pyramid Texts are considered to be the oldest religious writings in human history. This is not exactly the case. These texts are what religion came from, they are prior to religion. The Pyramid Texts, especially the ones found in the Pyramid of Unas, are the oldest documents available of the workings of the Absolute reality. And to first reach the realm of no self, means to have first reached the place of living without the parasite.

The Pyramid Texts are found carved onto the pyramid walls at Sakkara. As well as the Unas pyramid, the texts are also found in the pyramids of Pepi, Merenre, Pepi II. Supposedly carved for only 180 years in the Old Kingdom, the texts vanish for a while, to reappear in some non royal tombs during the Middle Kingdom such as near the pyramid of Senwosret at Lisht, while the tomb of Senwosret-Ankh has a fairly close copy of the Unas texts. The texts make their final appearance at the Philadelphius temple at Philae during the Ptolemic period.

One thing most agree on is that the Pyramid Texts are far older than the period they were inscribed. They were either orally passed on (or kept on long gone scrolls) for perhaps centuries- until the need came to carve them in stone. A theory I have is that they may have come from somewhere else, and translated by the Egyptians the best they could manage. Another possibility is that the world's great minds gathered in one place to combine all of their knowledge. I suggest these possibilities because it seems clear that some of what is in the Pyramid Texts was unknown to the scribes carving it. New hieroglyphs seem to have been invented to explain concepts or words not found in Egypt at that time or later. Some hieroglyphs appear only in these texts in the long history of Egypt. And that causes to ask the question, why?

Early Egyptologists began to number parts of the texts, like modern religious documents, for easy referencing. The numbers are for Egyptologists to catalog them, it should not be mistaken that this was the Ancient Egyptian's numbering system. They were called utterances by Egyptologists due to the fact that many parts seem to imply that the words of the text were spoken. There are 750 utterances. Many appear in only one pyramid. The Pyramid Texts are not like a book that one reads cover to cover. There is no first chapter and second chapter. They are on the walls of a pyramid chamber, thus the entire text in that room surrounds us, like a hologram, and we must enter into it fully. Each glyph on each wall is the beginning and also the end of that text at the same time. However the are placed on particular walls, relating to a particular direction- so direction must be included in their understanding.

Pyramid Of Unas

176:The Unas causeway- long preparatory walk prior to entering the pyramid, Sakkara

The Unas texts were considered special and separate from all the other texts in the Sakkara pyramids. Unas has supposedly has the first, best preserved, and most complete copy, thus have become the core of modern study. Jeremy Naydler wrote that,"The Egyptians themselves seem to have seen the Unas text as having canonical status." Like all Old Kingdom pyramids, no body or funerary equipment was ever found to suggest this may have been a burial.

The Pyramid of Unas is now closed to the public, and requires special permission to enter, but the main elements of the complex still exist. Like all pyramids, the approach came by boat to a dock where a valley temple was created. This valley temple remnant is very close to the ticket booth when entering the site. From the valley temple, there was a long roofed causeway to another temple adjacent the pyramid. This long enclosed pathway was meant to give the impression that the outer world was being left, and an inner world entered via a long tunnel (almost like the tunnel that is traveled by shamans for all of their journeys). A few parts of the causeway remain, and the reliefs on the walls of the Unas causeway were of daily life (representing the symbolic nature of the day to day world in terms of awakening), with a ceiling of blue and gold stars. Two boat pits were also found along the causeway. The causeway ends at the mortuary temple, in this case a rather large complex that included a 2nd smaller pyramid. There was no other way to enter the Unas pyramid itself without going through this temple and causeway, thus it acted as a door. All causeways face west, to the direction of Osiris (death and the Void) and Tehuti (breaking the bubble), towards the inner reality.

Like all Old Kingdom pyramids, the entrance is in the north face, so one will walk in southward (the direction of power and dreaming). It is a tight, hunched walk in at a steep angle of 22 degrees. The slope ends with a vaulted room then a second short passageway to the inner chamber. It is near the end of this passageway that the Pyramid Texts begin. Entering, one comes to a room known as the antechamber, with a vaulted ceiling and filled with blue hieroglyphs on the walls. There are small doors in both the east and west walls (leading to side rooms). To the east is a three pronged room that has no inscriptions. To the right is a large rectangular room that includes a black granite sarcophagus box on the far western side. There is no doubt that this was the smoothest stone box I have felt in my time in Egypt. The room has hieroglyphs on most of the walls, though much of the back west wall is filled with "decorative designs," and geometrical shapes. Some are perhaps mandalas, or they may be like a pattern of cloth upon the walls, symbolic as a new garment is being put on here. The garment of course will be the new "I," with the old parasite "I" gone, leaving the self to remember what it is. These patterns on the wall may also be like the walls of the Sistine Chapel in Rome, they may be drapes to hide something energetically behind or beyond the designs.

The walls on which the designs are found are made of alabaster, whereas the rest of the walls are limestone. The Egyptian word for alabaster is 'shes,' which also has word connections with the milk of life, as alabaster has the colour of cream rising to the top of milk. This may provide alchemic symbolism for baby Horus is birthed here. A box of granite is called 'met' by the Egyptians. This word is related to 'mat,' which means to dream or to discover. Thus the box is linked to dreaming or journeying, or perhaps the insights of the dream of reality itself. The rest of the pyramid is made of sedimentary rock, linking to water and the metal silver. The sarcophagus chamber is the place where the dead (ego dead) arise symbolically from the sarcophagus box to a new dream of life. One is awake, but that does not mean the work is done. Awakening shows that reality is a whole new ball game, and all the old rules no longer apply, and it will take a lot of time to learn those new rules. Horus the seeker has ended (he found Osiris) but now he is back to baby Horus with no idea what to do in this new paradigm of awake in the dreamstate (normal human without the parasite). That is why these texts in the Unas Pyramid seem to begin in the sarcophagus chamber and work back outside to light and duality. One must begin to accept their new reality. They are no longer a caterpillar, they have become a butterfly, and now they have to figure out what living as a butterfly means. Not every stanza will be looked at, just some key ones to give an overall impression of what is referred to in here.

THE TEXTS

177:Sarcophagus Chamber, Pyramid of Unas

"What a caterpillar calls the end of the world, the rest of the world calls a butterfly." Tao Te Ching

Sarcophagus Chamber

The sarcophagus chamber texts are about the process that follows awakening. The work was done in the antechamber. In the sarcophagus chamber one dies to the "I" (parasite) and arises again as Baby Horus. These texts are meant to explain this very odd transformation.

North Wall

North is about action. This wall has "purification" texts upon it, but in fact no cleansing is happening here. What there will be a reference to is the conditioning of the body-mind. What Unas is cleansing, is his body's remaining attached conditioning to the dreamstate.

23

The first group of texts on wall are the water and incense purifications, but two of these (25, 32) are repeated later, thus act as a marker. #23 is a good first step to this whole puzzle. It begins by saying, "Osiris, seize everyone who hates Unas." It is describing the return to the void (Osiris), and the need to let drop away all that disturbs the realization. Help is asked from Tehuti (wisdom of breaking the bubble) and to place the enemy (the emotional attachment) in his hand. Today we still have the saying about holding things in the palm of our hand which means we know it intimately. Another important line follows, "Do not separate your self from him (Osiris)." Osiris being the void, truth, nothingness, gives an instruction to remain in what we are (everything) and not let mind drop us back into the separate hell of the parasite dreamstate.

25

Text #25 is about going with or joining with you Ka. The Ka is thoughts, personality, but is covered by a false ego (false KA). The false is dropped, or killed depending on your terminology, and allows one to rest in their true KA and allow the script of your character to unfold. The four directions (Horus, Set, Tehuti and Dunawy) are called to be in control of the four aspects of the dreamstate, the four proteins of the DNA. The text also asks Unas to keep one leg and one arm forward, with the other back. This is how we walk, with left leg and right arm forward, while the right leg and left arm stay back. Thus we must walk with our Ka, and not fight against its motions. Actually the texts says specifically HNA with your Ka. Hennu is a mystical dance, thus one is not walking here but dancing. Jesus and Krishna were lord of the dance, showing that for the awake living our life script, life becomes as beautiful as a dance. They know the illusion of what they had believed previously, thus they can dance the script perfectly. At the end of this stanza, Unas is given the Eye of Horus.

32

Here water is poured over the feet of Unas. The water is presented by Horus the elder, to Horus the child. Horus the seeker has now become something else, but they look similar. It is the same concept that says before awakening mountains are mountains; during enlightenment, mountains are no longer mountains; while after enlightenment, mountains are mountains again. Horus began the search thinking he was Horus. During awakening he found he was not Horus, but then awake he is Horus again, but this time as a child and starting all over. In a sense this is a a baptism, and that gives the heart the eye of Horus. The texts says the eye is now always under one's soles as we have "true seeing" as our foundation. The passage ends with, "The voice has come out for thee." The voice is probably that of Gnosis, inner knowing of Tehuti.

35

Purification with natron from the north is to let Unas's mouth be like the mouth of a milk calf in the day of its birth. Again this is a reference to a new born child, here suckling from the mother. This is symbolized by the statue of baby Horus putting his mouth to the breast of Isis, as was later copied in Christianity with Jesus and Mary. Baby Horus, or Jesus, is not meant to reflect a physical infant, but a newly awakened being- who must drink from Isis (Mary) which is the dream wisdom in order to be nourished in its new paradigm.

37-57

These utterances are for opening the mouth, using an instrument called a Peseshkep, which Alexander Piankoff refers to as a piece of bread (thus perhaps similar to a Christian wafer). The standard version was an instrument used in midwifery to cut the umbilical cord, thus again the symbology on the north wall of the new-born Horus. In New Kingdom tombs, a sem-priest is shown using it on a mummy. Of course the mummy is not a dead person, but the ego-self. But by the New Kingdom a real ritual did appear to literally open the mouth of the dead, a mistaken understanding of the old symbolism. The final utterances, 41-42, talks of the need for Unas to suckle the breast of Isis. Text 50 Unas is compared to Ra (inner light). "I have embraced this my father who has become tired (asleep), so that he may be quite healthy again (awake)."

The wearer of the qeni garment is embracing his father Osiris. This embrace must not be seen as something happening between two things, it is not a merging into one. It is the embrace of one by one. It is the realization that there can be no embrace, for there are not two things to be embraced. Horus was Osiris all along. Thus Osiris can be healthy again as he has realized what he is (absolute). Thus it is an embrace that is not an embrace. PT 368 and 357 claim that when Horus and Osiris embrace, the Akh is formed, "you identify to the Akhet, for which the sun emerges." The Akhet is directly translated as the place where the sun rises in the east, but it is really where the awake arise from sleep. Seeing there is only one, only Osiris exists.

Jeremy Naydler remarked that following the embrace in the *Ramesseum Dramatic Papyrus*, food and cloth are brought in. One of the cloths is purple and is identified with the awake king. Priests called "Embracers of Akh" enter, wearing jackal-baboon masks and "create" a giant ladder to reach the sky, which the king climbs. The priests swing clubs to keep Set back, an action that seems to magically produce the rungs of the ladder at the same time. They are symbolically keeping back the ego-mind, which of course still exists within reality even if gone from a person's mind, and wants to get back in and get in control. Yet by swinging the clubs, keeping the mind back (or ignoring it is a better way of describing it) the next step to be taken just appears. And PT 487 says that after ascending, "my bones are re-assembled, limbs are gathered." This is shamanic dismemberment, making a new form out of the old. This all ends with a ritual feast.

Food offerings are presented in the utterances, to equip Unas with "seeing." This seeing is to look beyond the veil (Maya) to see truth (Maat). This food is often seen to be symbolic of Horus's body, as the food in a Christian church is seen to be Christ's body (similarities again). By the New Kingdom these offerings became mistaken as the need to have food to eat in the afterlife, for a feast in the realm of the dead. Yet the food is a symbolic act by a very living person upon awakening. Also utterance 43 says the eye of Horus is shown to have one black and one white eye (Unas later lifts a white and black jar). The black and white is the yin-yang symbol, which originated in Egypt. The 2 eyes are duality in the finite world, all must have its opposite in duality. Unas is told to seize them. The seizing means one pulls them in and crushes the finite bubble (the container that duality exists in). Without the bubble (container) there can be no duality (good-bad, happy-sad, male-female). All will exist as the Absolute with neither being able to be labeled. Also worth noting is that utterance 44 has two mistresses, Isis and Nepthys, being "favourable to thee." Thus duality will now work for instead of against.

72-79, 81

Now Unas is anointed with the seven holy oils (chakras), which fill the eye of Horus. This anointing has made him an Akh (light) and gets him sekhem (personal power). Once the oils have been presented two rolls of linen are offered. He is reclothing himself in (2) duality, putting his human self back on to interact in the dreamstate.

SOUTH AND EAST WALLS
213-224

These twelve texts begin on the far south wall and run to the east wall-thus the two walls connect together in a continuum. 213 begins with the words, "Unas you are not dead, you have departed alive to sit upon the throne of Osiris." This is not a denial of physical death, but shows that a death experience has happened while still alive. The throne of Osiris is the seat of power, and is the seat of knowledge in the void (no-self), and one will "sit" there when one has transcended the egoic mind. While on this throne Unas will give orders to "those whose seats are hidden," those who are still asleep. Atum, the creative power, now makes his appearance in the texts.

214

Begins with a warning of the Lake of Fire, a concept that later became the Christian hell. It is a purifying fire, not a torturous one, though it may seem that way at the time. The first question one asks of course, if one is awake, shouldn't they be done with all the purification stuff? This follows the normal belief that an awake person lives in some sort of blissed out, peaceful, no more problems, happy all the time wonderland. This is nothing but a fallacy, an ego hope. The problem is that enlightenment has nothing to do for the ego or the body, for enlightenment is finding out about what is beyond mind and body. Body or mind does not awake, awake awakes. The body is still here in the dream, and it is still full of its conditioning. After awake, there will be a shifting of the body-mind as it begins to reflect more the awakeness behind it. Awakeness may have no attachments, but body and mind still do, and the dream will keep presenting circumstances for the body-mind to drop all its conditioning. Thus the newly awake may in fact do more stupid things than they did before they awoke, they are getting the opportunity to release conditioning. "Enter then into the place where thy father (Osiris) is, where Geb is." Thus the text is now claiming that no-self and Geb (objects in the dreamstate) are connected. Thus one must work with the understandings that have come from the no-self, within the dream of Geb (earth objects). One can not have this realization then try to escape from the world, if anything they must plunge now back into the world, but in a totally new way.

215

Now Unas goes to Atum (creative force) who asks, "There is no god, who has become a star without a companion." Unas replies, "I shall be that companion." Thus in a sense walking with the force of creation, following the wishes of what Atum wants to manifest. Unas is then asked to see the place of Horus and Set, combination of seeker and the thing that seeks. Here baby Horus is learning to go beyond Set and Horus to Atum, primal creation. He will no longer fight duality, doing so he will have as the text says "no mutilation, no injury." Now comes something interesting, "Ra-Atum does not give thee to Horus: he reckons not thy heart, he has no power over thy breast; Horus can not have power over him, thy father can not have power over him…Lift thyself up, in the Name of Neter. So thou becomes Atum for every god." In a sense it is saying that nothing has power now over Unas for Unas is Atum, the creator of everything, thus Unas is also everything that has been created. He sees there is no other, is no gods, just one, which is what he is. Nothing is separate from what he is.

216

Now Unas appears before Nepthys (feelings, water) and the text says "Orion and Sothis circles the Duat." Orion and Sothis are the star systems connected to Osiris and Isis, who is often said to encircle the Duat, who gets a purification in the Akhet (place of becoming light). The caterpillar needs the cocoon stage before it can become a butterfly, and the cocoon stage is not fun. It is from this "breakdown" that the Duat (void) is reached. Following this is the line "he is content because of them." This is an important word, content, for the awakened condition is not always happy- but content with how things are.

217-18

Repeated throughout this text are the words, "Ra-Atum, Unas unites with you in darkness (void) from the Akhet, for you are an Akh." Again there is the idea that Atum and Unas are one and the same, an Akh (awakened light). Also repeated, "If he (Unas) wills that you will die, you will die; if he wills that you will live, you will live." Realizing that they are one, Unas is the creator. It is not some separate far off God who had created everything, it is what Unas is.

That realization means that we in fact have the complete power of using "the gap" of our thoughts to manifest anything we want in the dreamstate. This embrace is not jut a joining, it is a realizing of what what real power is.

219

This utterance overlaps the south and east walls. The fact that it is a wraparound text makes it very important. In it, Osiris Unas makes the same statement 24 times to 24 different deities, likely representing what are known as the 12 hours of the day and night. Unas constantly repeats that he is not dead, and that he will not be judged. Realizing that if all that exists is Unas, then "who is to judge?" To be judged requires a second and if there is no second, then no judgment is possible. Unas here realizes where he comes from, what he is, and what he has access to- thus must know who the archons-Apop are and why they do not have power over him. He is now a living example of unity.

220

Here is our first example in the pyramid of what Schwaller de Lubicz called transference. Often what is on one side of a wall matches in some way what is on the opposite side. Both sides of the stone link together as one. Here in 220 Unas wears the white crown of Horus, while on the opposite wall (west wall of the antechamber) he wears the red crown. The text begins with an often quoted pyramid text line, "The doors of the horizon open, its bolts slide." These bolts of the heavens are a big mystery for the Egyptologist who has many differing ideas as to what this means. One really needs a good background in Zen where to awake one must pass what is called the gateless gate or doorless door.

221

On the south wall Unas was Osiris, but here is back to being Horus again, but not as the previous warrior seeker, but as Horus the child. "Let him be powerful at the head of the spirits, let his knife be firm against his enemies." A reminder is that awakeness awakens, not the physical form. And this knife will be used on all that is within the loop attempting to trap. He is not longer focused on his old goals and things he wanted, but the release of all from the loop

223/224

The "last" of the texts upon the walls of the sarcophagus chamber. Unas is said to be asleep, turns around (or looks behind). After comparing his lotus scepter to Anubis, and his staff to Osiris, it tells of how "changed" Unas's "condition" is. Remember that in awakening one is a changed being, but the garment will still look the same, thus be very confusing for everyone including the newly awake. At least the caterpillar takes on a different outer garment, butterfly. Unas is now advised, "beware of your borders while on earth.' This is likely some symbolic dividing line between asleep and awake, thus don't drop across the line back into the land of the asleep (get reinfested by the parasite). The final line of this part of the text continues this trend with the words, "put on (or clothe) your body and move forward." This is a common symbolic theme, that of putting on new garments. The garment is the I or personality being used, but after awakening, it is never mistaken as the real "I."

EAST GABLE

The last part of the texts in this room are not on a wall per sey, but along the gable of the east wall. Like its counterpart on the antechamber west wall, they have 7 texts- and each should be noticed in connecting with it's other transference wall counterpart. Given that there are 7 texts, each will refer in order to the 7 chakras of the spine.

204-212

204 claims that Unas's nourishment is now provided by Osiris (truth, void), "Unas is never thirsty or hungry. 205 has Unas transformed into a hill, to have one's primal sexual energy to use. Doing so Unas is said to be, "unbound, set free, and seen by the gods." Unas becomes the son of Ra, thus radiates his light. 210 is the key text here which calls for Unas to have a "pure tongue in his mouth." A large portion of this text also is so that Unas will not eat his excrement and urine. This seems like an odd concept to us. In later funerary texts like the *Book of Gates and Caverns* it warns of a section of the Duat known as the upside down world, and when in the opposite world one eats excrement for example. The simple version of all this is a reminder not to go back to the separate egoic state.

PASSAGE BETWEEN CHAMBERS

This small corridor has texts on the north and south walls. The north wall has some copies of texts that were in the sarcophagus chamber, but the south wall is unique.

SOUTH WALL 244-46

244 has a symbolic breaking of the two jars (Set and the enemies of Horus). There are two jars for they relate the dual world of the dreamstate.

What he is smashing is his belief of duality. In 245 Unas comes to Nut and says, "I have thrown my father Osiris down to earth, I have left Horus behind." At the end Unas is said to have grown wings and feathers and his Ba is full of Heka (magic words) thus can manifest. Nut asks that a place in the sky be "split open" for Unas is a star, a companion of Hu. Hu (creative utterance) is usually associated with Sia (divine intelligence). The last text on the south wall, 246, is a bit confusing. Unas is compared to the bull of Min, thus a full sexual and creative being. He is told to be wary of Horus with red eyes, but not Horus with blue eyes. The text says around Min the gods are silent and he is asked to step into the Akhet (symbolically rising into light from darkness), and the doors are opened (he is not stopped from going into the antechamber, or into his awake character in the dream). He walks into the Akhet (which must be what the antechamber symbolically is) and into his power.

ANTECHAMBER

West Gable

Any gable text is special because it is raised above the walls. Like the sarcophagus east gable there are 7 texts that relate to the chakras and connect through the stone to the 7 texts alongside it.

247-252

"Thy son has done (this) for thee." The speaker then is Osiris, but Osiris is not saying he did it for me, but for thee, Horus thought he was doing the work for Osiris, but really it was for himself. "The great ones tremble when they have seen the sword which is in thy hand." The sword is the tool the awakening one must carry, is that which will chop away all that is false, which regarding the dreamstate, is of course everything. A person who has gone past the first step can internally look like a psychotic killing machine. Of course it is killing of all ego attachments. The ones we don't like are easy to kill, it's the one's we love and care for. Those attachments are the challenging ones for people.

The text now changes. "Unas there, O Unas see, look,hear. Unas arise on thy side. Do as I order, You who hates sleep, but were made tired. Arise!" Calling for Unas to look, see, hear and be there is in a sense demanding him to be alert. The text is referring to the sleep state, and called for the part of us which hates sleep (awakeness) but was made tired (or made to forget or to drop into illusion). This order to be present is not to be alert in the dream, but simply to recognize when he has drifted back, fooled by the dream again. Thus the passage is not urging him to be "in the now," but simply to stop every time the archons try to pull you back to sleep. This puts Unas in the place of power, as

Ra, the inner light that illuminates darkness (false). The last part of the utterance has importance, "It is Horus to whom order was given to do (this) for his father, To the Lord of the Storm, Wrath is forbidden when he carries thee, It is he who carries Atum (all)."

Thus Horus (seeker) was given an order by his father (Osiris, dreamer). Horus is never acting on his own, but always acting under the orders of Osiris. Every act for Horus is predestined, but it looks like he has a choice (to make it seem interesting) so he must act on that appearance. The land of the storm is Set, and in the end of some Osiris stories, it is Set who carries the throne of Osiris. The enemy has become useful. But the last line is what Set (mind) is really carrying, not Osiris, but Atum (absolute). In a sense now mind is simply carrying out the direct wishes of the Atum within the dream. This very powerful little utterance has a lot of useful information there, and is one recommended to be read many times over.

Text 249 has an important line, "Unas is the lotus flower (light from darkness) …come out of the island of fire (that which is raised from the primeval darkness)…after he has placed truth there in the place of falsehood." A lot exists for such a short phrase. In fact that could be the line that sums up the entire pyramid texts. He went into the darkness, and burned up all that is false, with fire. With false gone, truth is left. "Unas appears as Nefertem, the lotus flower at the nose of Ra, As she comes out of the horizon everyday, And at the sight of when the gods purify themselves." Nefertem is the child of Sekhmet (fire) and Ptah (stable matter). The name means Young Atum, or harmonious action. Nefertem is sometimes thought of as the new Atum, rising as the sun in the east (thus related to Khepera).

250 begins with Unas uniting hearts for Her Sai (one who is over wisdom or one who is fulfilled). It is symbolically compared with being filled with food (which is why there may be so many food references on the sarcophagus chamber east gable). One does not acquire truth, they become it, in a sense fill up with it. But that is misleading too because truth doesn't come from anywhere. It is what you are. Unas is also called in this text "The great one who is in possession of the divine book." The divine book is the book of Thoth. Again this is not a book of pages to read, but the revelation of what is, metaphorically described as knowing a hidden book

Unas and Ra have now become one and the same in 252, "Unas lifts his ames-scepter. When he intends to refuse admittance to Unas." Thus Unas is doing something to Unas, Unas is in a sense referring to two as if each were an aspect of himself, or referring to himself in the third person. He has dis-identified with Unas, yet remains Unas. He knows Unas is just a costume.

178:Pyramid Texts from the Pyramid of Teti, Sakkara

ANTECHAMBER WALLS

The texts begin with the West Wall and wrap around into the south wall (see Naydler for picture of stone 243). The texts of the antechamber are very different than those of the sarcophagus chamber. The antechamber seems to talk more about the path of awakening.

WEST WALL
254-258

254 is a very long text. It begins with the saying "the heart of the fiery breath is against you." The text asks the Lord of the Horizon to make space. "Unas will pronounce a curse on his father Geb. The earth shall not speak anymore. Geb shall not be able to defend himself. That which Unas finds on his way, He will eat him piecemeal." It is similar to me to the early soliloquies of Ahab in Moby Dick. Ahab is after the white whale, representing delusion and/or Maya, and nothing will stand in his way. Here Geb (as earth, physical world, manifestation) is Unas's foe, and it is he which Unas will eat. He wants the earth to speak no more, or in a sense to not the let the false dictate or force via ego anymore. Unas is going to reject a huge layer of reality and burn it up, and then see what is on the other side. If you look closely at the words, Unas is as monomaniacal as Ahab. "The lord shall be dammed off completely, the two ridges of mountains shall be united, the two banks of the river shall be joined, the roads will be hidden for the passers-by, the steps will be annihilated by those who go up!"

What a great stanza. The world being referred to here is the world of two (duality) and the need or unite or join (one, or not-two). This will never been seen by himself or others because he is annihilating each step as he walks, or sees there never was a step, never a Unas to walk it, and no one to see him walk the steps. Erasing the steps means Unas's main goal is to reach unity, not show others how to get there. This goal is the journey, not a record of the journey. The text continues, "Ha! Fear, tremble ye evil doers, Before the storm of heaven! He has opened the earth with what he knows. On the day when he intended to come. So he said, he the one rich in plowland, He who lives in the Duat." Unas is re-affirming that he is still on the attack. The earth opens because Unas sees reality different now. Next he meets the goddess Beautiful

West again in her form as the divine cow and is again sent to the Sekhet Hetep (Field of Peace). Unas now says that he is the sun (Ra) breaking his fetters (attachments that tie him to the dreamstate), "The lord of peace gives thee his arm, o ye his she-monkeys who cut off their heads. Let Unas pass by in peace. He has attached his head to his neck."

The monkeys are likely a version of the wisdom baboon related to Thoth. They cut off their head (die to ego self) but it also speaks of the head being re-attached. Again a reminder of ego, you may kill it or cut it off so to speak, but a similar of deeper I must be worn to interact in the world of form. Unas then reaffirms in the text that he will keep his commitment and not let anything stop him. As seen in the sarcophagus chamber, later Geb and Unas will again be friends- he and the manifested dream will be friends. But this part was what was prior- and all out attack on everything trying to pull the wool over his eyes.

In 256 Unas gains the throne of Horus the Elder, and again fire appears and "massacres" his enemies. Doing so, "The gods have seen it while they took their clothes off, they now bow before Unas..." Thus Unas knows the underlying principle of the gods, so they no longer need masks (symbolized as clothes) and they can fully show what they are to him. In 257 Unas breaks the Bia (basin) of the sky. Naydler calls this the canopy of the sky. What Unas has done is to have broken the bubble of relative reality. Now Unas can take "his seat" in the bark of Ra, journey of light. Unas is now Osiris, in a dust storm, perhaps a better image is to say in a tornado. This is an apt metaphor for someone who has broken the bubble and seen beyond it to their first glimpse of ultimate reality, which of course is that this one is a sham. Yes that is quite like being caught in a tornado. The movement to absolute also seems to happen as if falling through a funnel or tornado. "Unas is on the way to heaven, with the wind, with the wind, he will not be hindered." In many ways I see this wall of the antechamber to relate to the First Step, where one goes from normal life or the idea they are on a spiritual journey- to really walking one. This is the great disillusionment, and all that is left now is to finish walking to heaven (awakening). It will tough, bloody and messy- until one sees there was only one thing that ever had to be faught, yet paradoxically only one thing beyond it.

SOUTH WALL
260-272

In one sense the west wall texts end here, but in another way, they don't. 258 completes the record of Unas heading towards the first step. However 260 begins with a line or two on the west wall, showing they are related. The south wall texts are all about dangers and difficulties. The east wall declared Unas as Horus again, (not awake). He has yet to step into the world of Osiris (void). The south wall claims Unas is an orphan (tefer) and is with the sister (Tefnut) thus a play on words. At the end of Moby Dick Ishmael/Ahab has become an orphan, meaning alone. But here orphan also means something else. He comes to the 2 truths (double Maat, who appear in the famous chapter 30 and 30b weighing of the heart in the Book of the Dead). The weighing of the heart is not a judgment after death. Here the two truths give the throne of Geb (earth, dreamworld). What this is likely referring to is a new view or understanding of standard reality, thus Unas can begin to operate differently in reality. What had deemed to be the enemy, the material world of Geb, is becoming a friend again. Unas gathers together his members and then,

"Unas comes out, the guardians of trun,??? he brings it while it is with him...Unas shelter is in his eye, the protection of Unas is in his eye. Unas vicarious strength is in his eye, the power of Unas is in his eye." These lines parallel the very forceful renditions of Richard Rose on the value of commitment, not only to continue one's journey, but the very commitment becomes one's own protection. The eye (seeing) sight beyond standard reality, means one must commit themselves to break free. Stop the commitment and the process stops. The egoic dreamstate will attempt everything to get one to stop. It will find any distraction to make someone's focus go elsewhere. If it is family, someone may get sick, or maybe a money problem, or perhaps a gift of great luck in the dream, or a temptation that will later cause a great waste of energy. The protection and power comes from seeing that anything-from the egoic state- is non truth- and thus to declare war on the false ego, and then let nothing within the dream make him stop. Eventually the dream will give up because it knows nothing will work anyway. So there is no need anymore to make the wife sick, or get someone bankrupt, or other calamity. "Ye who might have come to Unas as adversaries, come to him as friends!"

Finally 260 ends with the way for Unas, "Unas' abomination is to go about in darkness, so that he does not see, upside down. Unas comes out on this day and Horus the truth is with him, Unas will not be handed over to your flame, ye gods." The not wanting to travel upside down becomes a feature of *Coffin Text 1037*, or funerary texts like *the Book of Gates or Book of Caverns*. It is seen as a fear to get caught in this famous other world upside down. This is a mirror of this world. His fear here is also to not be darkness (not bad as we think of the idea today, but just anything hidden from the mind- psyche, subconscious) or thus anything not fully seen or examined. The fear of every seeker is to delve into that which is hidden. One does not mediate to have a peaceful mind for example, but to examine all of their hidden, which no one does, which is why few awaken from just meditation. So Unas works to bring the day (light) to shine on his shit, thus revel the shit, and then truth can replace the darkness- freeing him from another of Maya's chains of attachment.

261 is known as the lighting bolt text, for it seems to claim that Unas is a bolt of lightning thrown through the skies. But this has nothing to do with

lighting in the sky. If you understand 260, then 261 becomes very clear. 260 ends with Unas wishing to shine light on the darkness, his obstructions. Thus he becomes the lighting bolt that will light up the darkness and reveal his attachments that must be destroyed. In 262 "Ignore not Unas O (Ra, Horus, Thoth ect) Know me for I know you, Ignore not Unas, O Ra, Greatest one of all the annihilated." It is not Unas per sey who is concerned about being ignored, it is what is "behind Unas" using lightning to search out (parasite, mask, false self) knows it, and thus he owns it. "greatest one of all the annihilated" is a little tricky, but there definitely is destruction taking place, and any part of "us" looks great and important until we see that it was based on a lie. As this little "mondo" continues, things seem to get better as there is more peace, better health, finally being a nehen star, or the darkness has transformed to light. But this is not a one time deal, this same process will have to repeat itself over and over for each and every part of false self that must be found, eradicated and let go. The utterance ends with all sorts of dangers that Unas has avoided. Doing all this lets "Unas rise up to Ra."

267 appears to be information about Unas's trip in the field of rushes, later depicted in detail in the *Book of the Dead*. This includes boats and ladders, the stairway of the chakra system. "Unas washes himself, Ra appears." This is some form of cleansing, then comes Isis and Nepthys to suckle him, or perhaps encompass him- in a sense the two kundalini strands are moving around him "Horus takes him to his side, he purifies Unas in the Jackal Lake." This lake is Anubis, thus a transformation lake. 270 is the famous ferryman text "Awake in peace, those whose face is behind…in peace, ferryman of the sky…Unas comes to thee, that thou may ferry him in the ferry boat, in which they ferry the gods." This part of getting the ferryman to take one by boat later gets expanded in *Coffin Text* 397 and *Book of the Dead* 99. In the *Book of the Dead*, the ferryman is asleep. His name is "whose face is behind, or who looks behind." The ferryman is the driver of the car, the dreamer itself, who should be driving instead of sleeping, while the ego false self has taken over driving the car. So the ferryman to take back control of the steering he must be woken up. In the *Coffin and Pyramid Texts* there is more than just waking up for the ferryman. The ferryman will give the "traveler" a very deep verbal examination, then the boat (which has been disassembles) must be re-assembled, paralleling the dismemberment and memberment of Osiris. The last part of the text is, "he will jump up and place himself on Thoth's wing. It is Thoth, Who will ferry him over to the other side." Thus the traveler is saying he is putting his 100% of his faith in Tehuti (wisdom, gnosis) and it will be wisdom, no matter what happens, that will guide him to cross the river (reach truth).

NORTH WALL

The north wall texts very much parallel the south wall, but perhaps resented in a slightly different way. The south is about dreaming (seeing what is or is not) while the north is about action (doing).

302-312

Begins with Unas being declared the son of Sothis (star of Isis) thus Unas Is Horus (here called the Great Bear Constellation). Unas has a throne in the sky and on earth (above and below), and the face of a falcon (Horus) and the wings of a goose (Geb). Unas meets the daughter of Anubis- friend of Thoth (perhaps Maat or Sheshat) who stands at the window of the sky. The word for opening or gate is peter, which is usually translated as to see, but ptr has connections to stone or rock, the obstruction that blocks true mind. Thus the guardian of the gate, is also the very obstruction that one must go through. He calls for the ostrich (Maat/Thoth) to open the way, that he may pass.

305 is maybe the most recognizable hermetic text on the walls. A ladder gets laid by Ra and Horus, each holding a side while Osiris watches. Unas is questioned and asked "art thou a god, whose places are pure." The answer, "I come from a pure place," allows Horus and Set to help him up the ladder. Thus it will be the two aspects that will help him rise. The Akh (spirit, light) belongs to heaven, the khat (body) to the earth (dream)." This is the famous hermetic axiom, "as above so below." "Is the heir grown poor, not having a script, Unas shall work with his big finger, he shall not write with his small finger." Unas is writing his own script for his life, and he now writes with the big finger not the small. This may be true mind over conscious mind. 306 ends with Unas under the Keshet Tree in the Field of Rushes, which is similar to Buddha's enlightenment experience sitting under the Bodi Tree. Unas again becomes a hill, full of creative power, that leads to Akh (spirit).

Utterance 256 on the west wall had Unas seeing the gods naked. Now here he sees the four goddesses in 308 naked. Thus he as seen the male and females without clothing (without masks, layers of false self hiding what is true about them.). As the egoic masks have come off, so too does the human conditioned clothing want to come off as well. 309 claims, "Unas is the thrasher of gods who is behind the castle of Ra born from the goddess Wish-of-the-gods, She-at-the-prow-of-the-barge-of-Ra. Unas sits before him (Ra), He opens his chests, unseals his decrees, Unas sends his messengers, which do not tire, Unas does that which he (Ra) says." Just 8 lines has a lot here. First it claims that Unas is born of a wish, by the woman in the prow of Ra's boat (Maat). Thus it is the wish of truth that created Unas. As such he is not just in service to Ra, Unas will live out the will of Ra, doing whatever is asked of him. Ra here can be seen as the dreamer, the truth of what Unas is, the one who knows the script of the manifested form known as Unas. Thus Unas is no longer trying to fulfill his ego requests, he is happy to be connected to the wishes of his dreamer (Ra) and will just follow the script of his life perfectly.

In 310 Unas goes to the one who sees "front and back" and asks him to bring a boat that "flies up, the one which alights."With so many references of rising up to the sky in lighted boats have caused many to believe that these texts give references to aliens in spaceships, people being lifted up into the world of the gods (seen to be where the aliens/gods come from). The challenge is to see if these references are to aliens, forces of the universe- but there have been many ancient rock carvings and paintings seemingly of traveling vessels. 312 the final text on the west wall has just three lines asking the "bread to fly up." Bread is symbolically linked to power or energy. It may be as the gate of Ra is opened, the chakra system is opened allowing energy to flow fully up the down the body.

EAST GABLE

273/274 on the east gable of the antechamber, are perhaps some of the most famous of the Pyramid Texts, because they are mistakenly called "cannibal texts." Unas is claimed to be eating the bones of the gods, and like any headline, it sells papers. Consider too that when these texts were first being deciphered around 1900 AD, the Egyptologists were Victorian Europeans who saw ancient Egyptians as uncivilized non Christian savages. I see the East Gable as the "awakening text," the sarcophagus chamber is what to do after awakening- but this gable reveals the actual moment of awakening.

(section 393/394/395) The stanza begins with things clouded (by the veil of Isis/Maya). There was movement, then all movements cease (one is stepping from the apparent movement of duality, to the non-movement of the absolute). "Living on his fathers and mothers" means to be spiritually nourished by All That Is. We will see that this is not about eating dead ancestors, but making things a part of ourself, and is symbolized as eating or ingesting. This ends by saying that Unas is now more powerful than Atum- because Unas sees he his Atum, thus Atum can not be more powerful than Unas. They are one and the same. (396-406) Every direction has been assembled, and he has used fire to burn away the false. He once suffered from "wanting" but instead "feeds on the essence of every god." When eating is being mentioned, what is being eaten is wisdom or truth. A shaman does not learn something by knowing it intellectually, but learns it by "eating" it, making it a part of his bones and flesh. He thus becomes truth and embodies truth. Unas also turns his back to Geb (the earth dream) and is not going to let the egoic dream influence him. He will prepare his own meals, thus let his true nature determine how he will live and act. Doing all of this allows Unas to encircle the two heavens (duality).

275/276 the other small utterances on the gable has Unas coming with the clothing of a baboon, only to open the gate- and then drop his loincloth (the last remaining vestige of self and mind). In 276 he chases the serpent of mind called "his adversary," the serpent alien brought parasite finally being dismantled.

EAST WALL

Carved into the wall underneath the "awake gable" is mostly about snakes, focusing on the process of destroying mind/false self/ego. Much of the process of awakening is laid out on this wall symbolically. The crawling snake (as opposed to the winged serpent) is Apop. It is also the primeval serpent who trapped Atum, until he can transform into a cat and cut off the head. In 277 Horus falls because his eyes are ripped out by Set, as Arjuna falls in the Bhagavad Gita- this is the same scene. In the Gita, Arjuna has fallen, not because he will not start a war that will destroy all the knows, but he has found that all he loves is as much a dream as all he hates.

278-299 Babi has arisen as the penis, kundalini is rising. The powerful sexual energy will now be acknowledged and turned inwards to protect and renew. Thoth (wisdom) will be Unas's protection, thus his guiding force. He in a sense gathers strength to battle against that which opposes him. This again is similar to that scene in the Gita where Krishna must show Arjuna the way the universe actually works so that he will pick up his sword and start the war- considered battle here. If one uses the texts on this wall and compare with the Gita, the comparasin will stun you. 301 is describing the final push between asleep and awake. He makes an offering to the primordials of Hermopolis (4 pairs of deities behind Thoth). He is doing this to reach "their father", thus reveals that there is something more than even the oldest primordials. Unas claims to know the name of the father. "he will hold Unas again, he will make Unas alive every day." The only way Unas was able to complete this full journey was to see the total annihilation of every piece that made up Unas. To reach the absolute we have to give up as an individual self to make it through the funnel to reveal what we have always been. Afterwards comes one might say a return to manifestation, a re-ordering of Unas (described on the north and south walls). This makes Unas's eye whole, thus he can now see the truth of reality at all times, though for a while ego will try to come back and keep trying to trick him.

"Arise great boat, as Upuat (opener of the ways) Full of Akh (illumination) Coming from Akhet." Thus he is opening the way as an illuminated being, and like Ra he rises from the Akhet each morning as light- for as Ra awakens as light, so too will Unas, for again the reminder that Unas is Ra. This text ends with Unas being purified in the Jackal Lake, or Upuat Lake. He becomes powerful (bright) and sharp (like a knife). He becomes "lord of the green stone." The most famous green stone is the sacred stone of Hermes/Tehuti called the Emerald Tablet, upon which the secrets of the art of alchemy were said to be engraved. Unas ends up as two green hawks.

ENTRANCE CORRIDOR

The final area with texts in the Unas pyramid is the entrance corridor. What is most interesting about these specific texts is that they are of course either the beginning or end of all the texts in this pyramid. I leave them for you to examine. This undestanding of the Absolute Reality of no-self was the key element of the Western teachings of Osiris. The land of the dead is really the land of the void- and it is this understanding of how nothing is everything that allows a much deeper walk into the other directions. This section on the Pyramid Texts was a good overview of the western teachings of the four directions. The rest of this volume will focus on the other three directions, and learning more in detail what the Egyptians said about the mental parasite, and about what has become known in the modern world as the Matrix Reality.

CHAPTER 22
BOOK OF WHAT IS IN THE DUAT

107:Ra in his solar barque, Valley of the Kings

The most well known Egyptian funerary text is the Book of the Dead. Though popular, it is far from the most important of the Egyptian religious literature. Long before the Book of the Dead (properly titled the Book of Becoming Light) was written on papyrus scrolls and left in the tombs were the famed Pyramid Texts. These long rows of hieroglyphs, likely the oldest religious writings in the world, were placed in pyramids of the Old Kingdom at Sakkara. By the Middle Kingdom the Book of the Dead, and a number of other texts, were found in tombs in the Valley of the Kings and Queens. These texts included the Book of What is in the Duat, Book of Caverns, Book of Gates, Book of Day, Book of Night, Book of Aker and the Litany of Ra. While these pictorial texts may seem to be far removed from the all-hieroglyphic Pyramid Texts, they are not. John Anthony West has compared the connection of a medieval stained glass window with the related Gospel text that inspired it.

Thankfully for the student of the ancient mystical tradition these pictorial adaptations of the Pyramid Texts are of great help. As no one as yet can satisfactorily translate the texts, we get only a partial idea of what they are concealing from any translation. With a picture the hidden wisdom is much more penetrable, more able to be compared and understood from similar imagery from around the world. For this reason I have decided to concentrate on a text that has not been properly explored by the modern Egyptologists.

The Book of What is in the Duat was placed on tomb walls in the Valley of the Kings. The Duat is usually translated as the Underworld but this is not correct. It is more likened to the astral realm, a real world beyond the physical. It is the place we will have to go upon our death, thus it becomes imperative for the mystical initiate to learn the hows and whys of such a place prior to death. The text was painted and carved as though a huge papyrus was unrolled across the walls of a tomb. It is divided into twelve registers or hours. Many Egyptologists believe this text describes the travels of the sun through the twelve hours of the night, showing a complete lack of understanding of what the Duat is. This is not a text of what the sun does at night but is rather a tool that describes the process of spiritual illumination that begins in darkness and ends with the scarab Khepera as the rising sun.

The first version of the book was found in the tomb of Thuthmoses 1, 1504-1492 BC. This version is a fragment and complete versions appear later in such tombs as Rameses VI. Each of the texts, while almost identical, have slight alterations. Later versions of the book from the last eras of Egypt no longer have the same perfect proportions of the golden section as the early tomb books. This shows the later artists were not versed in the ancient art of sacred number and geometry. That the text first appeared for a Pharaoh named after Tehuti is a clue to the information that may be provided by the Egyptian priests. The hidden Hermetic wisdom of Tehuti in the text is easily found when applying a new focus to the drawings and glyphs.

The text, except for the first division/chapter, is usually divided into three registers. The middle is said to be the celestial river where the solar barque (the boat that carries the sun) travels, while the upper and lower are the two banks of the river. This has led scholars to interpret the text as a metaphor of the sun's travels along the Milky Way. While many elements are incorporated into the drawings and glyphs, the key teaching is to explain the flow of kundalini.

This text should not be investigated independently but used in connection with the other texts of the period, especially the Book of Gates and Caverns. All three of these texts are about the control of our energy and power in our body. The understanding of this energy system, allows us to awaken our inner power and reach the realm of mystical enlightenment. From the teachings of the Orient, especially Taoist Qi Gong, the same ideas are present. The Taoists teach of the gates of the body, usually along the spine, that need to be opened in order for the Qi to flow properly. The Caverns very well could be the pools of energy (associated with the physical organs) that get clogged with blocks due to our bad thoughts, actions and karma. Thus the texts of Ancient Egypt are describing the path of Qi Gong and Yoga in pictorial form (showing the origin of Egypt as the source for these systems of wisdom) to teach the understanding of the energy body and how to unblock it.

Entering the Tomb of Rameses VI, a solar disk containing the scarab and a ram headed solar deity on the left wall while Isis and Nepthys are on the right. The Egyptians, as did the Hindu, Buddhists, Taoists and Maya, understood that the body was made up of male and female principles. These principles were symbolized by the eyes. The right eye is the male principle represented by the sun, and the left eye is the feminine energy represented by the moon. The Eye of Horus is the combination of the two energies into one harmonious being. This being was called a Hermaphrodite by the Greeks for being a perfect blend of the male Hermes and the female Aphrodite. When looking out of the tomb the male solar disk is on the right, and the feminine gods on the left. The understanding of the placement of these symbols may help us understand the texts. The Book of What is in the Duat (which contains references to the journey of the sun) is on the same wall as the solar disk, while the Book of Caverns, which is recognized by its oval cocoons (the oval a world-wide feminine symbol) is on the opposite wall. The connection between the two texts and the symbols at the entrance is far from a coincidence. It is thus quite likely that the Book of Caverns is the text relating the feminine energy of the body, while the Book of What is in the Duat is the masculine energy. That would leave the Book of Gates to represent the middle channel of the spine.

Bearing these concepts in mind we can now further examine the Book of What is in the Duat. This is not an easy text to decipher because there are so many symbolic references placed into a very small section, along with a number of hieroglyphic texts. To try and make some sense of it, the text will be examined division by division. Due to the wealth of information only key parts of each division will be examined. Please take this chapter as a guide to look more closely at the text yourself to find the wisdom it contains. To aid in your understanding two illustrations, of the first and fourth divisions are included (see illustration 19 and 20).

Interpretation[300]

An introductory series of hieroglyphs precedes the first division and is without any drawings. The introduction talks about "writings and drawings of the hidden palace." This inner palace would be the inner part of our being. The

---

[300] The texts used to examine the Book of What is in the Duat are: Budge AE Wallis *Egyptian Heaven and Hell* (Dover Publications 1905); West, John Anthony *Traveler's Key to Ancient Egypt* (Quest Books 1995); Piankoff, Alexandre *Tomb of Rameses VI* (Pantheon Books 1954)

concepts of soul and akh (perfected/illuminated ones) are the focus. The introduction claims the following texts will offer information of "knowledge of souls…doors…and the ways through which the great god journeyeth." It also claims to provide knowledge of gods, divisions, speeches and praisings. There is no surprise that John Anthony West claims the introduction seems to suggest a manual or encyclopedia of the Duat will follow.[301]

Looking at the line of glyphs mystically it can be noted some key themes (glyphs) are repeated. The first are the birds that represent the ba, the ibis and the akh. All are connected with Tehuti which helps to explain further that this is a book of wisdom. The sign of sma (union) appears as if explaining the union of the above and below will be set forth in these teachings. Thirteen papyrus scrolls, which represent hidden wisdom, appear in just six lines of text.

First Division

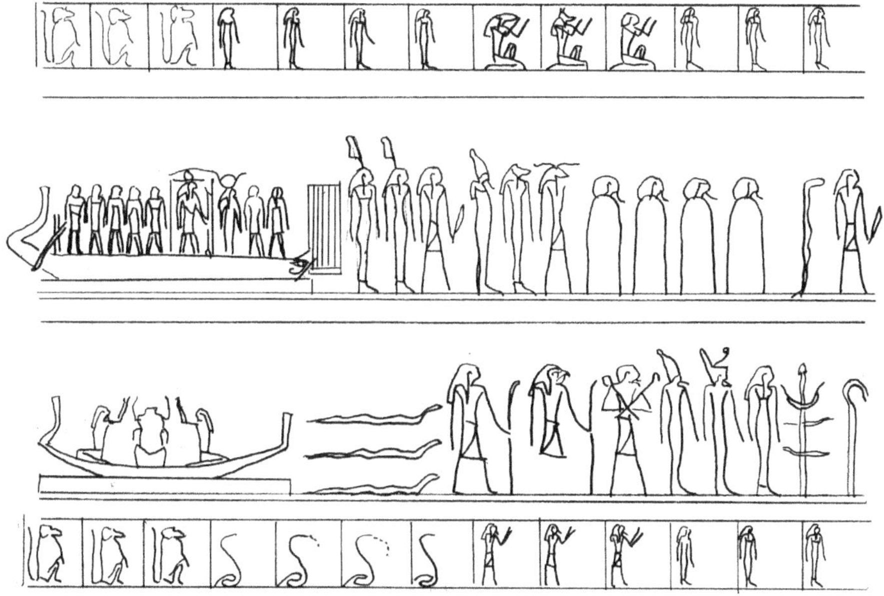

108:First Division sketch from KV 34 Tomb of Thutmosis III

The first division is always depicted with four registers, while the other divisions have three. No writer has ever explained why. Some have suggested the middle register was divided in two to show the twin principles of Ra. More likely it has been divided in two in order to focus the reader's attention that the text begins in the realm of duality. By the stage an initiate was reading a text

---

[301] West *Key* p.284; Budge *Heaven* p.1

such as this, they would be aware that the world that we view as reality is a dual world. In fact the entire first division is laid out to express the dual world that we live in, and offer the suggestions as to how to break free of this duality.

The upper middle register depicts the solar barque on its journey. The boat is representative of our body where the spiritual journey will take place. The main figure on the boat is a ram headed deity with horns and the solar disk claimed to be Ra. We should perhaps not be so hasty to claim this figure is the Neteru of the sun. During this period (of Aries) Amun held sway as the main deity at Luxor/Karnak. The text of the first division claims, "The god cometh to this court, he passeth through it in the form of a ram and he maketh his transformations therein." Aries is the first sign of the zodiac and is well-known as the best time of the year to begin the process of alchemy, to begin working with the body and mind to purify it and allow the transformation to the astral gold.

The ram figure stands beneath a nous or tabernacle. He is identified by the name Afu, meaning flesh. Some translate Afu as dead body believing that one needs to die to enter the Duat. Mystery School initiates need to experience and prepare for the realm of death while alive. The text claims, "it is useful to him who is on earth." Thus the Book of What is in the Duat is a text to teach us how to rid ourselves of our humanness (flesh) and the duality symbolized by the dual register, to become a scarab and transform into light. The fact that he stands beneath a tabernacle reminds us of the hermetic axiom, that the human body is an earthly temple. As above so below, thus the entire universe is contained in ourselves, so we need to fully "know thyself." By knowing every aspect of what we are, we will know everything in the rest of the cosmos.

No greater tie to the world of duality exists than the physical body, which we believe to be "us." The flesh, and the ways of, must be understood as only a part of this world. We are merely inhabiting this particular body as we inhabit the car we drive. The body is a tool and should be respected, but not given our greatest focus. Afu holds the uas scepter in his left hand. The uas is the symbol of control over Set (the conscious mind) and by having it in the left shows that he is being receptive to the learning that will allow him that control. He does not yet have this control or he would be holding it in his right hand, representing action.

Along with Afu in the boat are the Opener of the Ways, Mind (perception, consciousness), Lady of the Barque (who resembles Hathor), Horus the Praiser (in red letters to show key significance), Bull of Truth, the Watchful One, Will (sometimes translated as word) and She Who Guides the Barque. Some of the texts refer also to Ka-Shu instead of the bull (the ka energy of breath or space). These figures are within the boat thus are important navigators for Afu to go beyond the flesh. Horus is that which we are all aspiring to become. Hathor was the counterpart of Horus, the feminine energy that was needed to reach enlightenment. The Mind is our true mind that we must regain and connect with. The bull is a symbol of sexual energy that must be tamed and controlled to lead us to truth. The will is our direct inner energy, power and focus that we will need to decide that the outcome of the texts (illumination) is what is most important in our life.

Hanging over the front of the boat is what has been described as a rug or carpet. Looking at it more closely it resembles the Veil of Isis from Tarot Card 2. This is the veil that all of us have had placed in front of us, not allowing true sight, symbolized by the eye that appears on the side of the boat. To push forward on this journey one will have to lift the veil from the boat (ourselves) in order to reach the light.

A number of deities lead the barque. Directly in front of the boat are the Double Maat (the power of truth and cosmic order that one needs to live constantly in order to go past the duality of the veil). Next is Sekhemet called in the text "the Great Illuminator." Sekhemet represents the power of Qi/Prana that must be brought into the body and stored to be used later to raise the kundalini to reach enlightenment. Next are four tablets with heads that proclaim them to be the orders of Ra, Atum, Khepera and Osiris. The text is written in red, signifying importance, and it may relate to the four priesthoods teaching the key components for the work to begin the journey. A single serpent stands upright, perhaps to signify that the kundalini fire will need to be raised. The procession is led by He Who Passes Through the Hours and holds a stick or serpent.

The hieroglyphic text of this section begins in mid-section "...the gate. The passing of this god into the form of a man." Starting the text in mid-sentence was done intentionally and signifies that the start of these teachings will take place one day in the middle of our lives. One day we are not interested, then something will occur to make us turn to texts like the Book of What is in the Duat and start the possibility of our transformation.

The lower middle register also has a boat, this one carrying the scarab Khepera. The scarab represents transformation from darkness into light, what all of us will have to do on our journey. A key part is to honestly look at and understand our own personal darkness. Khepera teaches not to be afraid of our faults, but to embrace them for they can be transformed into power. With him are two Osiris figures that are looking behind, a Hermetic symbol that in the beginning of the process we need to turn back and look at our own thoughts. Usually our thoughts are never questioned and for the first time we must examine our conscious mind. The first question that will be asked from such an exercise is 'if I am observing my own thoughts, the thoughts can not be me.' Thus we must be more than our thoughts. Three serpents (the number of the Hermetic process) and a number of beings that carry serpent sticks lead the boat. As explained, the serpent refers to either kundalini, wisdom or the conscious mind. A snake that is on the ground refers to the conscious mind as it hovers close to the earth (below) and is constantly moving like the mind. A snake that represents kundalini or wisdom will be either standing upright or will have wings to show it is in the above and no longer on the ground.

In front of all this are two Neiths. Neith was the goddess of weaving and some say war because of her symbol of crossed arrows. Neith actually represents the web of life, depicted by the weaving. Every strand in a weave can be accessed by every other one, just as all things in life are connected to each other. This is a very important teaching in the initial stages for the initiate, leading to the famous saying of "do unto others as they would unto you." This statement actually means that all are connected, and in fact the same. To harm something else in the universe means you are also harming yourself, as you are all that actually exists. Leading the way is the goddess Nepthys (in red), a horned pole with two serpents, and on top is a god that is called The Divider of the Waters. Nepthys and the pole are both representations of water, the cleansing properties that will have to be brought forth in the journey.

The top register is divided into boxes of nine baboons, twelve goddesses, nine gods and twelve goddesses. The bottom register has nine baboons, twelve serpents, nine gods and twelve goddesses. The number nine is the cycle of Osiris (the cycle of nature) and twelve is the cycle of the zodiac. The baboons (wisdom of Tehuti) open the doors, the serpents (kundalini) illuminate the darkness. The goddesses lead, representing intuitive feminine energy, and the gods sing praises using the power of sound.

The hieroglyphic text also helps to provide some answers. "If copies of these things are made according to the ordinances of the hidden home…they shall act as magical protectors to the man who maketh them."[302] This line is a reference that appears often in the texts, meaning that one is supposed to copy the Duat. How exactly does one copy it? Do you make a copy of the text for your home? Is the area to be built, as some believe the Giza pyramid complex is the copy of the Duat? Is this area supposed to built inside yourself? It may be a combination of all of these possibilities.

When Afu enters the Duat, he asks for light and guidance from the gods and bids them to open doors and others to welcome him. "Illuminate thus the darkness of night." The final text of this section calls for one to "shut your doors by your bolts…come ye to me, advance to me, make ye your way to me and ye shall abide in your place."[303] This text is about the sublimation of sexual energy, a key component of the early part of the path. Actually there is nothing wrong with sex, for if it is done properly the creative energy is what stirs the kundalini and allows for mystical moments of the light. Unfortunately most have no idea how to have sex properly, thus most mystery traditions

---

[302] Budge *Heaven* p.9
[303] Budge *Heaven* pp.19-20

advise to control the sexual energy at the beginning. This concept became understood by the Catholic Church that it is wrong to have sex unless you are making babies. The mystery traditions teach that sex is wonderful, and when one has learned the proper methods, leads to great power and wisdom. Until initiates were taught these techniques they were advised to not lose their precious energy from orgasms. They taught instead to keep it inside and build up inner power and strength. Shutting the doors by the bolts refers to not allowing the sexual energy (in the form of sperm) to be lost but kept inside.

The text in the Tomb of Rameses VI has parts of the diagrams defaced. Egyptologists may say this was a random act of defacement but there were no random acts in Egypt. All of the hieroglyphs and reliefs contained the power and magic of what they depicted. When something was defaced it was in order to stop the power and energy of the drawing being used. In this case what was defaced was the scarab (halting the transformative purpose), Afu (that who is on they journey) and Osiris (the cycles of transformation). This of course could have been done signifying that Rameses VI was no longer on his journey (he was dead) and no longer needed to transform or return in the cycle of rebirth (for he had become enlightened and needed no more lives on earth).

Second Division

This division is divided into three registers that will be common for the rest of the text. The upper two are placed on water and the lower is on sand. The middle register now contains five boats. Afu is still under his tabernacle in the first boat along with his crew. Two cobras are added to the front of the boat, and magic is now at the stern. This register is a division of feminine energy, initially signified by the naming of the cobras Isis and Nepthys.

The fifth boat has two human heads at the end, an eye upon the body and inside is a deity holding a feather of Maat and a disk between horns of the crescent moon. The feather of Maat infers that this is a stage of inner truth, while the moon is another symbol of feminine energy. The third boat has a Hathor symbol (the queen of feminine energy) and a scarab, reminding one of the transformation to come through the work.

The first boat is flanked by cobra heads, three armless deities and two stalks of grain. The registers above and below also has to do with fields, seed and planting. All of these symbols are suggesting the Osirian cycle of growth. It is a message describing that what we sow we will reap. Plant your crops properly and with care, and the result in time will be food. This is a much needed analogy for the initial stages of the initiate. The early stages will be hard work, and it may seem like a waste of time. It is a suggestion that by doing the work, even thought the results can not be seen now, they will bloom and blossom like the growth in the fields if they are tended to properly.

The second boat has a crown of the north and south, two scepters and a head coming out of a crocodile. This picture describes that our conscious mind (head) is what creates the crocodiles in our life. With the division concentrating on feminine energy and Osirian cycles it will be one of being receptive, asking questions, and examining emotions and feelings. The main reflection of this stage will be to look at ourselves and our patterns, routines, negative thoughts and actions. These patterns and beliefs are our past and our history that makes us who we believe we are and what we can achieve. One believes they are a failure because they have failed in the past. The crocodile represents these patterns because the negative thoughts lie unseen in our subconscious mind, just as the crocodile lies unseen in the Nile. In an instant, the unseen crocodile strikes to obtain its prey, just as without warning the patterns strike and lead us to a problem.

The upper register has a number of gods having a penis as a knife, showing they are cutting off their sexual desires. Behind them is a deity called "Overcomer of the Power of the Enemy," the enemy being sexual energy not used properly. There is also information of the battle that will occur. Here is a famous picture of Horus that has Set coming out of a side of Horus. Set is the Neteru of destruction, he who killed Osiris. This important carving shows that the parts we will battling are actually parts of ourselves. The battle is not out there, it is within. Also of note is that all of the figures in the upper level hold their objects in their left (feminine) hand, further showing the focus of the teachings of the division.

The lower register has gods with corn in their hair, and others with ear of wheat in the left hand. Three mummified figures sit on blocks in the classic Egyptian meditative posture signifying the starting of the meditative process at this stage. The first mummy has a knife for a phallus and is called "Eater of the Phallus." The next two have an ankh instead of a knife showing that they have already controlled their sexual life force. Another two headed god called Horus-Set appears in the lower register, symbolizing the same ideas as in the upper. Two gods appear holding the ankh upside down. The ankh is rarely depicted this way, perhaps a further example of the turmoil that one will face when beginning this journey as we must overturn all that we have thought and done. The last figure in the line is one holding the symbol of the year, perhaps meaning that one will be given a full year to complete the work of this stage.

The text of the upper register says, "Their work consists of performing the overthrow of enemies at this hour…that ye may not be destroyed and overcome by your own foul odour, and that ye may not be choked by your own dung." The text also calls for the doors to be open to receive fresh air, fresh food and fresh water. All of these texts are suggestions that purification is needed. Few truly understand just in how bad of shape they are in. Every negative action and thought is stored somewhere in our body. Those who have taken a few workshops or lectures have done little. Purification is a lifetime process, to clean away all the junk we have acquired.

There is also talk of Apop, the serpent that Ra must battle each night and cut to pieces. Apop is the conscious mind that must be battled with in order to allow for the stillness and inner silence. "May ye hack into pieces the enemies of Osiris."[304] This statement coincides with the meditative figures and the need for inner silence that will connect us with our true mind that can lead us towards the Light.

Third Division

In the early version of the text the space for Afu in the boat is empty. The later texts, like appear in Rameses VI, have Afu in his usual place. In the next boat is a mummified figure with ram's horns. This may suggest that Afu has transformed not only boats but also forms. In later divisions of all versions the figure is back in place. Once again there are two sections of water and one of sand, and the Division is called "She Who Cuts Up Souls." The main boat now includes fewer figures. Added is Horus tying loops of rope around the oars. It is possible that Horus here is trying to slow down the ability of the boat (our journey) to be controlled and now it is time to allow the feminine intuition that was gained in the previous division for guidance. A Native shaman would suggest this is the stage of leaning to connect with spirit and the let the forces of the universe be our guide.

Three boats lead the barque. The closest boat is the Boat of Branch with the head of a lion, containing a mummified Osiris with ram horns, another mummified figure and a god. An upright serpent is called Set-em-Maat-f (his Maat of Set). The second boat has an eye, ends in baboon heads and is called the Boat of Rest. It has an Osiris mummified figure, and is steered by two beings one who is "He Whose Face is a Knife." Another upright serpent is here and a headless bent over figure. In the tomb of Rameses VI one figure does not have a head. The last boat "Which Capsizeth" has an eye and seems to end in a lotus. Mummified forms of Horus are staring at each other, holding a uas and ankh while standing on a serpent. There is also a serpent known as "Fiery Face." Meeting the boats are four forms of Osiris without lower arms.

The upraised serpents reflect the upward rise of the kundalini energy that is beginning to flow. The figure without a head is a constant one in the texts. This idea is still practiced in Buddhist traditions where they want you to take a photograph of yourself and cut the head off. You are to then look at the photograph constantly. The idea is to begin to think of yourself as headless, for without a head we lose connection to our conscious mind and move to our heart (our true mind). We will then interact with the world through feeling and love and not the ego and what the 'I' wants. The mummies (with no arms appearing)

---

[304] Budge *Heaven* p.41

and the four beings at the end without arms are an example of not being able to feel things with the senses, thus we are learning how to feel with the heart. The connection one makes in this way helps take us to the feeling of oneness with the All and a connection to our true self.

The upper and lower registers have a number of depictions of Osiris and Anubis. There are many symbolic references here but of note is the male and female who bring the pupil or eye, again reference to the usual senses that must be diminished so we can focus on the heart. Anubis appears standing on top of a pylon, a form repeated in the tomb of Tutankhamun.

The lower register has some interesting figures including a number of seated forms of Osiris, and five goose-headed beings with knives. At the far end are two goddesses who hold the uas in both hands and bend while looking behind. Following them are three figures bent over. The text of this register reads, "… the work which they do is to hack souls in pieces…and to destroy such doomed beings…which blazeth fire. They send forth flames and they cause fires to spring up, and the enemies are these who have their knives on their heads. Whoever knows this will have dominion over his legs."[305] The fire is linked to the alchemic fire that is needed to purify the body, of which the kundalini will also be doing as it rises. As one goes farther in the work of Qi Gong they will experience great heat while doing the exercises, the heat turns the blocks of the body into steam by the moving Qi. The Egyptian text claims by doing so one will have dominion over his legs. This is a bit baffling, but Carlos Castaneda wrote that our memories are actually stored in our legs. If this is true then the purifying fire will help us lead to our deepest memories. Unlocking the memories that are hidden will allow us to unlock everything about ourselves. This is often done through the process of recapitulation, reliving every event of our life. Doing so we can see the repetition of our patterns and routines that can be eliminated, see the parts of events we missed that are causing us to act poorly now, and see the truth in a situation we failed to do at the time. With this done one can then move on in the work without the past holding us back.

Fourth Division

The fourth division of the Book of What is in the Duat is a tremendous change from the previous three. The most noticeable feature is a passageway (or road) called Restau, part of the Kingdom of Sokar. It is also referred in the texts as the "road of the secret things of Restau." It was this and the following division that has led Graham Hancock and Robert Bauval to link the text to the pyramids and sphinx at Giza. Both words, "Restau" and "Sokar", appear in

---

[305] Budge *Heaven* p.60

stela inscriptions at Giza. The passageway, sphinx and pyramid that appear in the fifth division make this connection a real possibility.

Without examining the connection in great detail, the pyramid complex at Giza was one of the earliest centers of initiation in the world. The Book of What is in the Duat was derived from the Pyramid Texts at Sakkara, religious documents to help with the path to enlightenment of the Shem-Shu-Hor (Followers of Horus) who were the initiates of Egypt. Some of that training would have happened in the chambers and passages of the Giza complex. An inscription in the lower part of the road says that one entereth the body of Sokar "who is on his sand, the image which is hidden and is neither seen nor perceived." The terms hidden and mysterious are emphasized.

In the fourth division there are more additions besides the passageway. The first gate or door is called Mates-sma-ta, incorporating the sma sign (union of lungs) along with a knife. The second door is the Metes-mau-at. The third door is upright and called Metes-en-neheh.

In the middle register the boat has a serpent head at each end, thus it is a new and different boat than has appeared in the previous three divisions. Four gods tow the boat. Of the boat, it is said, "The flames which the mouth of his boat emit guide him through these pools, he seeth not their forms, but he crieth to them…and they hear his voice." The fire obviously comes from the serpent heads. The fire comes from the mouth, and the use of the voice is key to make the boat move. An important stage in learning the ancient wisdom is to understand sacred sound and how the human voice can be used to heal, for magic or for manifestation.

On the other side of the middle door are a number of the key Neteru of Egypt. First is a mummified Osiris and a leaning crook. The crook is the process of controlling the wandering sheep of the mind. Tehuti "Raiser" and Horus "Wide of Hands" face each other with outstretched arms with an utchat (eye) above them. Another being appears with no head but with what appears to be snakes/worms coming out. Hotep carries the crook in right hand. The text of the middle register says, "These bodies are hidden, whose secret things are hidden. They are the guardians on the way of the holy."

The middle register is very important. Hotep is the Egyptian word for peace, not peace in the world but peace of mind. Since the entire world is nothing but a projection of our conscious mind, by learning to have the mind at peace will create the world around us to be at peace. The crook is the symbol that to obtain peace of mind, the moving thoughts (symbolized by wandering sheep) must be corralled by the crook. Tehuti (wisdom) and Horus (the power of our inner being) must be used to raise ourselves to a new state or vibration in order to make these changes long lasting.

The upper register is most known for its serpents. One snake has a human head with two pairs of feet and legs. Three serpents move "upon their bellies" and of them it says "those who are in this picture make their passage to every place each day." Next is the scorpion (Ankhet) and a large uraeus serpent who "stand in Restau at the head of the way." Restau may then be place of the true mind, one that must be reached by killing the conscious mind with the poisonous bite of the scorpion. A three-headed serpent with hawk's wings and two sets of human legs and feet is the "warder of the holy way to Restau and lives upon abundance which comes from his wings, his body and heads." Facing is the serpent Nebkau (serpent at creation) with two heads and a head instead of a tail who lives on "abundance that issues forth from his mouth." One god holds the curved (spiral) wand in his right hand. The spiral or labyrinth is a constant symbol of the mystical journey and the need to go inside ourselves, and then come out the same way working on the same material.

The lower register also contains a number of serpents including a three-headed one who is the "hidden image of the Aheth chamber which is illuminated daily at the birth of Khepera..." Appearing in this lower register is Sekhemet, Maat, and a figure performing a Qi Gong or Yoga pose. As well are fourteen stars, heads and the winged disk of Khepera (Horus) appear here. Most importantly many of the figures on the bottom have two right hands, while on the upper have two left hands. The figures with two right hands, shows the lower register is a place of action and doing. Thus the figures of Sekhemet (Qi energy), the Qi Gong posture and Maat appear. All are the way we must be living, with cosmic truth, and movement and understanding of our energy or power. The upper register with the two left hands is about being receptive, in this case to the kundalini serpent power beginning to rise and take wings. The lower register shows what must be done to help this process and the upper is explaining that one will need to allow the experience to occur when it does begin to rise. By doing so one can follow the Path of Horus and open the way.

Fifth Division

The fifth division of the text is perhaps the most examined, and for good reason. It, like the division before it, is totally dissimilar to original three divisions. In the middle register the boat is now called the "Power of Life," and is towed by seven gods and seven goddesses, representing the chakras. The kundalini begins to rise in the previous division and now will begin its ascent through the chakras. It is known to rise along two channels, one male and the other female depicted by the gods and goddesses. The boat is serpent headed, giving a further indication of what exactly is being towed. The tow rope end is a spiral, a further indication that the kundalini is flowing up in its spiraling form. The four gods in front are referred to as "the great sovereign chiefs who provide food in this circle." These are likely the four lower bodies (lower chakras) that must be first controlled and purified to ease our connection to this world, and to allow the potential of being grounded in the further worlds.

The text says, "come to Khepera, O Ra! Come to Khepera! Work ye with the cord, O ye who make Khepera to advance so that he may give the hand to Ra." Another text says, "Let Ra advance on the road in the boat which is in the earth, in his own body, and let his enemies be destroyed."[306] Khepera is the scarab that represents the transformation of darkness to light, and here the initiate is calling for Khepera (representing the kundalini that will make the transformation possible) to continue. The cord referred to in the text may represent the spinal cord of the human body. There can be no doubt now to what the fifth division is referring to. The advance is within the body (spinal cord) and the enemies are the aspects of our person that need to be purified.

The scarab and the head that appears on the mound below is referred to, "when this god (Khepera) standeth on the head of the goddess he speakth words to Sokar every day."[307] This quotation could explain that once the kundalini can reach the head, thus cleaning all the seven chakras, it will flow out above the head and allow connection to the All, including being able to speak to God directly. To obtain Gnosis directly was the key teaching of the Hermetic literature.

In the middle of the scene the ground swells up into something resembling a pyramid with a human head. Beneath it is the oval "Egg of Sokar" which guardeth "the hidden body" or the astral golden body of alchemy. At each end rests a sphinx, "his work is to keep ward over his image." Inside of the oval is a two (sometimes three as in the Tomb of Rameses VI) headed serpent with a human head for a tail. It has two large hawk wings that are held apart by the hawk-headed Sokar. The text says the hawk-headed deity's mission is to "protect his own form." Everything in the oval is said to be in "thick darkness…who is on his own sand, his own image."[308] Many have looked at the imagery and combined the text (sand, pyramid and sphinxes) with similar designs at Giza. It is quite possible that this division is not only telling on the rise of the kundalini to the chakra system, but that perhaps that the main work of this stage took place at the Giza complex.

On the lower register to the left of the egg is a serpent without wings who "lives by the voice of the primeval gods of earth" and is "unseen." This figure is likely Apop, the serpent of the conscious mind that we must battle. Four "Blazing Heads" precede Apop and sit upon boiling water (perhaps the burning water of the alchemic Mexicans). Four seated gods follow a serpent to

---

[306] Budge *Heaven* p.86

[307] Budge *Heaven* p.86

[308] Budge *Heaven* p.90

the right of the oval. The constant reminder of the number four informs us to focus the beginning of our work of the four lower chakras.

In the upper register is Maat with her arm at a 90 degree angle. Nine large Neter symbols appear, followed by five "Guardians of the Net," the net being the snares and traps of the mind that must be overcome. What is said to be a chamber or door above has the sign for darkness or night. On the side of it are two Horus falcons. This depiction may be the doorway to the inner (true) mind that has been kept in darkness by the conscious mind. We need the power of Horus to open this doorway. Next comes a serpent who "is in opposition to the scarab," or transformation. This serpent has two heads and crawls along the ground, thus must be the conscious mind of duality. It would oppose the transformation that would lead to the true mind.

The final figure of the upper register may be the most important, yet is almost overlooked. It is a female goddess standing with her hands outstretched to the top of the head of a man who is clearly just a man and not a god. He is naked and has no apparel of the Neteru. He is placing an axe into his own forehead. This man is the human being who is traveling this path. This is now the stage as the kundalini begins the rise that one must take the hatchet to themselves and attack their conscious mind directly. Only by doing so will one make it to the sixth division.

Sixth Division

The sixth division returns to the more familiar look of the first three. In the middle register the solar barque is back to the form in the first three divisions (with lotus ends and crew of beings). Something has happened in division four and five that changed everything, but things are back to normal here. Why? On the mystical journey there comes a period of total hell. Hell is not something you experience after you die but right here while you are on the path. Divisions four and five were showing that everything one thought was getting wiped away. It is a terrible time, one where it seems there is almost no reason to going on living; all has come apart. But by making it through, one comes to division six where a normalcy seems to return but not without new found power. The Buddhist saying is that before training a mountain is just a mountain. With training it is no longer a mountain. After the first stage of work, it is a mountain again. One now will have to move to the second stage and realize that the mountain is only there because we want it to be so.

Directly in front of the boat is a seated baboon with an ibis on his arm. These are the two forms of Tehuti, which shows that it is wisdom that will now be our guide. Our old ways (that were destroyed in divisions four and five) are going to be of no use to us here. The wisdom we have gained will be our only tool. Facing Tehuti is a goddess called "She Who Hides the Images." She is likely a representation of Isis that hides the veil from our sight as the figure is holding two pupils in her hands. At the end of the middle register is a man on his back "Khepera in his own Flesh" surrounded by a five-headed serpent called "Many Faces." The serpent is swallowing its own tail, the alchemic Ouroborus that represents the cyclic nature of time. Thus the figure is within the confines of endless time, and faced with the understanding that time does not exist. He is thrown off his feet representing the loss of his previous beliefs and limitations. The number five is the number of Horus, the spiral, love and growth which are all aspects that will be happening at this stage.

Of note in the upper register are the eyes of Horus (the origin of the eyes of Buddha and Krishna). The upper level also has Isis of Weaving (the interconnectedness of things), and serpents spiting fire into chests or castles. This is the transformative alchemic fire of the kundalini moving farther up the spine. The bottom register has four heads on the back of the serpent called "He Who Swallows the Forms." These four heads are the four sons of Horus (four lower bodies/elements) that have now been swallowed up by the flow of kundalini. We are now able to move past a totally physical existence and be allowed to move into the higher spiritual realm.

Seventh-Twelfth Divisions

The final six divisions of the Duat represent the very advanced work of the initiate so I will only point out a few key details in the rest of the text.

Showing that by the seventh division the initiate is now at another level, Afu is no longer under a shrine but a winding serpent. So high has the kundalini grown, cleansing as it moves, that the initiate is at a level where teachings will change. Powerful forces and energies will now be able to be personally experienced. At the bottom is Horus on the throne, showing that we are now able to work on crowning ourselves as a Horus (Buddha/Christ). The hard work now begins.

The ninth division is filled with the colour green, especially in the trees. This is a stage of getting by the green of the heart, to be one of living with the heart. In the tenth division the two eyes (male and female) are reborn, as they are ready to be joined as one. The eleventh division has two important symbols. The first is the flying serpent with the person riding its back. The kundalini has finally reached the head and is able to fly to the sky, and we are able to fly with it. The second is a similar symbol to the fifth division with Horus holding the wings of a legged serpent. Here however, the eyes appear again that signify the kundalini has reached the eyes and the male and female energies have been combined, the Eye of Horus has been opened. The other realms are now available to our "sight." The twelfth hour is the culmination of the work, with the final image on the middle register the scarab (transformation) and a head (signifying a new person, one who is transformed). At this stage on could now be deemed a high initiate and one who understands the secret mysteries of the universe.

Conclusion

The Book of What is in the Duat is a magnificent text for the modern spiritual initiate. While no book (*New Testament, Bhagavad-Gita, Popol Vuh*) is better than any other, the fact that the Egyptian texts of the Middle Kingdom include so many pictorial references is of great help. By using texts such as these to help understand what is needed to be done on the spiritual path, one can then go to the above-mentioned texts that contain no pictures. The information in the religious texts of the world is incredibly powerful if you can understand the symbolism properly. They are not to be taken literally. They contain hidden wisdom and it is your job to unlock the esoteric secrets in them. The Egyptian texts are a wonderful starting place because all of the further texts evolve from the Egyptian wisdom. In time one will likely find that all of the great religious texts are telling us the same ideas, that humans have the divine right to be magical and live a life of wonder. They also help to explain what is causing us to not live this magical life, and how to take steps to open ourselves to it.

CHAPTER 23
THE EGYPTIAN BOOK OF THE DEAD

129:Weighing of the Heart, Papyrus of Ani plate 4, British Museum

"O you waxen one, who take by robbery, and live on the inert ones. I will not be inert for you, I will not be weak for you, your poison shall not enter into my members, for my members are the members of Atum." -Chapter 7, Book of the Dead-

This text, usually found on papyrus scrolls left with the mummy in the tomb, is by far the most well known writing from Egypt. The reason for its popularity is likely for the great number of scrolls that have been found and exported to Europe where they could be put on display in museums. The Book of Caverns could not be taken off the walls of the tombs (thankfully) but the papyrus scrolls could easily be moved. Because of their easy access, and belief that because so many were found that they were the key Egyptian text,

European scholars focused much of their learning of Egypt upon it. The most famous papyrus today is the Papyrus of Ani, 78 feet in length. It is so called because the papyrus was written for the scribe Ani. If it had been written for Steve it would be the Papyrus of Steve. No text is the same with close to 200 sections (called chapters) for the scribes to choose from. The chapters chosen are never in the same order, thus may be like a modern reference text where one looks up a particular section when needed. It is interesting to note that much of each papyrus of the Book was pre-made, with space left for the name of deceased, and was done by numerous scribes and artists with their results pasted together. The papyrus of Ani has his name often misspelled, and it is suggested that up to three scribes and two artists made it.[309]

Because of the pre-fab nature of the text, especially in later periods where hieroglyphs are not even used but instead their new quick form of hieratic, that the understanding of the text by those with whom it was found with must be considered. So too by those who made it. Texts on tomb walls, of which the Book of the Dead sometimes appeared, was created specifically in mind for the deceased. The papyrus became a sort of quick get in to heaven free card if you had enough money to buy one. That does not necessarily negate the original information that the text provides, but does give clues at to the state of the actual understanding of these concepts by the Late and Greek periods. From this text came smaller versions such as the Book of Breathings or Book for Outlasting Eternity, which were often short forms written on a single piece of papyrus for the lower middle classes.

The name Book of the Dead was given to the text because they were found in tombs with mummies or might be found close by in hollow figures of Osiris or in boxes. The actual title of the work was Pert-em-Hru, which most now translate as the Book of Coming Forth by Day. What exactly does that mean? A better translation of the title provides more understanding. Hru can be the word for day, but it can also mean the sun, light, or Hours. A title that makes more sense is the Book of Becoming Light or the Book of Becoming Horus. Each of us in our life on earth is striving not only to be Horus (connected to our inner self which is Osiris) but also to be one with the Light. The Book of the Dead is claimed by Egyptologists to describe the journey that our soul will take after our death because it includes pictorials of tombs, mummies and funerary ritual. While this text can help those who are dead, it is more to help those who are still alive. In time the understanding of the text was lost except for a few priests, with most of the population gaining possession of this document believing its literal translation (sound familiar)? This is a text that teaches one how to become a Horus or light. It also teaches how to live life with Maat and the wisdom of Tehuti. Thus the text can be described as a teaching tool for our moral behaviour in this world, and a journey to our own

---

[309] Faulkner p.142; Lamy p.27; Naydler p.297

418

heart where Maat, Tehuti and Horus reside. Some also believe that this text gives information on the dream or astral world that our soul will ascend to after death. In time passages of the book were read during the funeral of an individual, and then buried with them as a talisman or document that could be read by the soul in case they had forgotten something, similar to readings of the Bible today at funerals.

The book is similar to the Tibetan Bardo Thodol (also called the Book of the Dead), as both deal with karma, rebirth, the underworld journey and the need to become light. Without diving into too much detail of its hidden wisdom, that is for future books, the Book of Becoming Light gives us a great clue as to what is hidden. The colour of the hieroglyphs used were black and red, while the border is made of yellow or red, and the papyrus itself was make to appear white. The colours black, white and red were the three main Hermetic symbolic colours, while at times the colour yellow could be added.[310] It is quoted and examined in most books on Egypt, with aspects like the Opening of the Mouth, Field of Hotep (peace in the west) and Iaru (Reeds or Rushes in the east), or the Weighing of the Heart closely detailed.

The Pyramid Texts were the teaching tool for those who had awakened. The tomb texts like the Book of What is In the Duat or the Book of Caverns were about challenges and dealing with the process of awakening itself. The Book of the Dead was the Egyptian version of the modern movie *The Matrix* in 1500BC, and focuses on the battle between Ra and the serpent Apop. Apop is the force that has taken over reality, and cast an illusion over it, that has infested the human mind for centuries. The Book of the Dead has the goal of learning how to be rid of this parasite, for self and world.

PLATE 1-2 (with plate 18-19)
CHAPTER 15

---

[310] Norvill p.64; Lamy p.27

130:Isis and Nepthys with Djej, Ankh and rising sun, Papyrus of Ani, British Museum

The first two plates of the Papyrus of Ani, contain chapter 15 (also known as the Hymns to Ra and Osiris). The vignettes (pictures) are very interesting. Both plates have Ani and his wife, Thutu (Lady of the House) making "offerings." While Ani's hands are empty, his wife holds a sistrum (an instrument similar to a rattle that causes the thoughts of the mind to become jumbled) and the menat (combing the male and female principles). Before both is an offering table for Osiris. Ani has two right hands, so he is fully giving. But what is he giving? It may be offerings, but he may also be giving away his attachment to material things, symbolized by what is on the table.

The right side of the first plate has Isis and Nepthys (representing the two channels of kundalini flow, like the goddesses Ida and Pingala in India) and they sit on the hieroglyph neb (gold). They are the forces of kundalini that will cleanse us of our spiritual impurities, and sit on the astral gold of transformation. Between them is the place where this will occur, the djed pillar of Osiris which represents the spine that the force will rise up. Doing so will lead to the ankh (symbol of life, or an awakened life that combines the male cross and female oval). Two arms reach up from the ankh to hold up a red sun disk, symbolic of inner light raised to our highest chakras. Red is also the colour of our root (first) chakra which is also the end of the process. The beginning is also the end. In some papyrus the ankh and disk are replaced with Horus as a falcon with the sundisk on its head. In a few papyrus, Isis and Nepthys are between the twin lions known as the Aker (past and future) to show that such transformations can only happen when time is no longer present. In the Ani papyrus, Isis and Nepthys sit on a mountain, while above them is the symbol for the sky. The sun, our inner light, is rising at Dawn (represented by Khepera the scarab beetle) bringing the light to dispel the darkness. Between them are six baboons, symbolic of Tehuti and wisdom (in many papyrus there are 7 baboons relating to the seven chakras).

This information of the picture is deepened by the hieroglyphic text, which begins with (1:1-2) the sign tua (translated as worship) but is a sound similar to the Duat (inner place of being). It is not the sun that is going to be worshiped, but our inner light that Ra represents. For the sun to rise and dispel the darkness, then we must currently be in darkness, shadow. That is an important point that the Book of the Dead is making right away. There is no need to have the light rise up, unless there is darkness- thus the text is in its way asking us to turn inward to search for the darkness that we are ignoring. The inner light, of the observer, will illuminate the darkness simply by honestly looking for it. Actually, at the beginning, we are not trying to rid ourself of the darkness, but just to see and acknowledge it. Lines (3-5) thank mother Nut, along with a figure Nini who has wavy lines overtop of her outstretched hands. Most translations have this glyph as worship, but there already is a hieroglyph for that word. This symbol is for energetic healing coming from the hands. Doing this one will receive Mannu, a word similar to the word in the Old Testament for bread. This bread is not physical bread, but the spiritual bread (energy, Qi, life force). Connection with this life force will create healing, hotep (inner peace) and Maat (truth and order). It will then link one with the Khu (shining one) and the uas (the wand that represents control of Set, the thoughts of the mind) that will allow us to reach the ankh (life force), and unite our ba and ka (tonal and nagual) as Horakhety (Horus of the Horizon). This will lead one to Osiris (Absolute). Quite a lot of spiritual information in just five line.

Lines (6-8) produce a prayer similar to that of a native shaman. Ani thanks the spirits (Neteru) of the Het-Ba (Seat of the Soul), Pet (above), Ta (below), and Abtet, Resi, Amentet, Mehat (the four directions). A shaman before starting rituals will also thank the seven (four directions, sky, earth and center). Lines (9-12) call upon Tehuti (wisdom) and Maat (right action, truth). Ani will need these forces because the text begins a discussion of what he is up against, the serpent Apop/Sebau. The need to become Ra and defeat the serpent Apop is the central element of this text. Where the term Apop originated his hard to determine, though when the first Hyksos kings took over Egypt during The First Intermediate Period, (Babylon/Sumeria's first invasion) many of their kings were called Appepi. So it is hard to know whether the word was an old Egyptian word that was added to the invaders, or if the word was adopted by the Egyptians because of the words direct connection to the Hyksos invaders.

What the word Apop is referring to is unmistakable, the serpent/lizard force of the alien (called the Archon to the Gnostics) that have the purpose of energetically enslaving the earth. One key part of this text is chapters 31-39 which are called snake charms, but are really words of power to help keep protection from these alien forces. The text wants Ra (origin of light) to rise to "flood the chamber with light," asking our conscious presence to fill our being and burn up Apop with the "energy of fire." The evil one is shown with its arms and legs bound. This is not a prisoner or slave, these depictions are what each of us must do to our mind, bind it so that it can no longer move, thus resulting in inner silence. Such an act is symbolized as great strength. In the text Ra must travel through the Duat and defeat Apop each night, so that he (sun) can rise each morning. In a sense you don't defeat Apop or the mind just once. The mind has many layers, many tricks- and even to break through one layer will just mean another will arise- sometimes with even stronger force. They must be worked through in order for the energy in the mind to finally dissolve, and this constant night battle with Apop is symbolizing this long process of inner transmutation.

Early Coptics symbolized this same concept in paintings of St George and the dragon. The dragon is a personification of Apop, while St. George is Horus. The dragon is the next obstruction, and is why St. George must ride a horse, for he will not just defeat one dragon, but will ride on to the next dragon, and the next. Lastly the word Apop lives on today, in the Christian word for its leader, pope. The Pope is thus King Apop. The *Book of Caverns* describes how the sun disk passes through the succession of caves into the Duat, and when the sun enters the cave that contains Osiris, the sun gets energized as Osiris's penis gets erect. For Osiris to arise he must uncoil the serpent Nehaher (form of Apop) that binds him (the chains of Plato's cave). When uncoiled (unchained) Osiris can release his stored energy, and rise up just as Ra has.

Lines (14-17) ask for inner peace by smiting the ass, Sebau and Apop (three forms of the parasite). Doing so one can allow Horus (our heart) to man the rudder of our boat (guide our journey) along with Tehuti and Maat. The final lines of this plate (20-27) ask for there to be offerings to the Shemshu-Hor (Followers of Horus), one who is following the path of Horus (living like a warrior, or following that which is human). This is also a call to give offerings to all those Followers of Horus before us, as a Buddhist monk will make offerings to all the Buddhas and Bodhisattvas prior. Horus steering out our boat will allow us to reach Neter (God) and be in the land of Osiris (our Higher Self) with Maa-Xeru (pure speech, or pure sound). Shamans often want us to find our song, the true vibration of our being, and I believe this is what Maa-Xeru is asking for, to again be playing "our song."

PLATE 5/6
Chapter 1

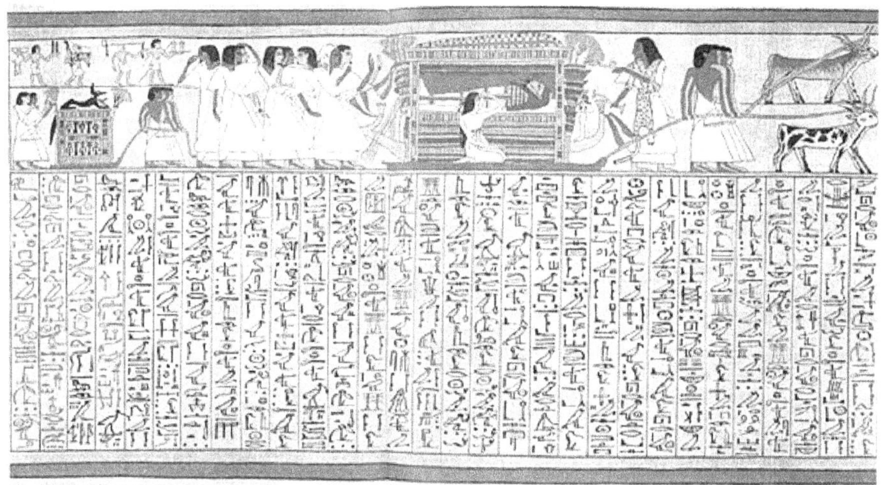

131:Chapter 1, British Museum

Chapter 1 is very famous, and was one of the chapters that would be painted on New Kingdom tomb walls. Along with Chapter 17, it is considered one of the oldest parts of the text. Chapter 1 is considered to be the chapter of the funeral, but the funeral being shown for Ani is not a literal one, but a symbolic one. It shows Ani as a mummy, representing him at the early stages of his training, unable to reach out to the realms of spirit, caught in the illusion of duality. By the Middle and New Kingdoms the Egyptians believed that mummification would provide an eternal afterlife. Few at the time questioned the validity of what was being told to them, as few Christians and Buddhists question the directions of their priests today. In New Kingdom Egypt, mummification was believed to be a need to preserve the body for the afterlife. They also needed to build special houses where the dead could be worshiped, where the name of the deceased could be said over and over, so a person could remain "alive." This of course is not what the symbolic use of a mummy meant in Old Kingdom texts. What became a business scam in the New Kingdom, it evolved out of something older. New Kingdom ideas such as scooping out the brain but keeping the heart, was a corruption of the early texts they had that could no longer be properly understood- similar to how the Aztec sacrifice came from their misunderstanding of the old murals of the Toltec and Maya. In the box Ani is not dead, he is asleep.

Plate 5 begins with the scene divided into two sections, similar to the first division of *The Book of What is in the Duat*. The scene top has four men carrying the material goods of Ani's profession as a scribe (showing he must release his attachments to the physical), while below four men carry his funeral box with Upuat on top. The chest itself has the djed pillar and the tet (knot of Isis) and is similar to the chest found in Tutankhamun's tomb. The funeral box[311] is our enclosed state, while Upuat (opener of the ways) is the Neteru who is our guide from the this confining state. Ani needs to wake up. Next the vignette returns to one single image, and first is eight male mourners with some looking to the front and others looking behind. They are looking at the past and future. They are not mourning the death of a person, but the death of time. Next is the funeral coffin of Ani with his wife beside crying. Again think of Ani as asleep. The coffin itself rests on a sled, symbolizing the vehicle body we use in this life. On the boat's stern are Isis and Nepthys, sometimes represented by two kites, the twin forces of kundalini. Lotus flowers appear on the top (light from darkness), wanting to awaken Ani from the darkness of his mind that keeps him asleep to his true reality.

In front of the coffin is an Egyptian priest wearing the leopard/jaguar skin (as did Maya priests) symbolizing a master of stalking the mind. He offers purification with cleansing oils. The sled itself is pulled by four men (symbolizing the four directions) and four cattle (control of those directions). Continuing on Plate six are men carrying offerings. Next come the group of so-called "wailing women," often depicted in tombs like Ramose (TN 55). These bare-breasted women appear in a pose similar to one taught to me by an Oriental monk to put the energy of sun into our eyes and head. Thus perhaps they are not crying, but energizing. Next comes more cattle, offerings and a man carrying the right leg of one of the cattle. Finally come three priests to perform the "opening of the mouth" ceremony. This ceremony is done with an instrument called an adze, made of iron and shaped like the "thigh" of the big dipper. This ceremony will not only open the "dead man's" mouth, but his eyes as well, thus a suggestion of perhaps opening a deeper state of perception.

Anubis holds the mummy of Ani, while Thutu kneels before him, her breast now bare like the "wailing women." He posture seems to suggest that she is swallowing his penis. Thus the opening of the mouth ceremony may in fact be an oral sex tantric rite that would allow kundalini to flow to the head of the recipient, and open their spiritual eyes and ears. Oral sex has long a taboo in modern religions, likely because original church fathers realized that it has some great power in increasing kundalini flow, so they made it a "sin" to scare people away from practicing it. This Egyptian sexual tradition was kept alive by the original Gnostics, who used tantric sexual energy to produce an energetic egg that would protect them from the advances of the serpent Apop

---

[311] When one finds a coffer or box in a tomb, if it is painted, it is likely a coffin. Not painted means it is a wisdom box.

(archon). The vignettes end with a pyramid on top of a square house that some believe to be a rocket ship. I will leave it up to you to decide.

The text of plate 5-6 is very revealing. It is considered Chapter 1 by the original Egyptologists because of its opening line of text "Pert Em Hru" which they translated as "The Beginning of the Chapter of Coming Forth by Day," but as mentioned is more correctly translated as the "Book of Becoming light," or the "Book of Becoming Horus." Line 2 has hieroglyphs that literally translate as, "coming and going in Neter-Khert Khu Ament Nefer." The normal translation to this is, "coming and going into the underworld shining as the beautiful west." Neter-Khert is God's Domain (oneness), while Nefer means harmony. So the text is asking the reader to "come and go into mystical oneness, shining with the light of our harmonious silence." When added to first line that claims this text is to teach one how to become light, we now have a better understanding of what these papyrus tests were about. The fourth line has prayers to the Bull of Amentet (the control of energy to reach the silence) along with Thoth who is called the King of Eternity. He is in fact the king of "no time." By line seven comes a number of prayers to Osiris (our Higher Self, dreamer) and says "I fought for thee, "I will be victorious over my enemies at the weighting of words" (in the hall of Maat).

Line 18 changes things. Here Ani claims to be with Horus on the day of his clothing Teshtesh (Dismembered One). The clothing is spiritual. He asks to "wash his heart" of the pain and suffering it has felt and doing so will "open the door of the secret things in Restau." Restau can refer here to the place of one's dreamer (usually kept silent by the mind) so the new clothing (new actions, ways of living and thinking) will allow one to reach the place of inner truth. The text now asks to be Horus so that he can protect the left shoulder and arm of Osiris, who is in Sekhem (place of inner power). Doing so Ani comes out of the flames (alchemic fire) to destroy the "Sebau in Sekhem" the egoic mind (Sebau) stealing our inner power (Sekhem). By line 25 Ani now claims to be the Ab-Priest (purifier) in Tettetu (spine). He claims, "I see the hidden things in Restau…I read the ritual book of the soul…I am the Sem Priest at his duties…I am the master carpenter (as Jesus was the master carpenter/builder) on the day of placing the Hennu Boat of Sokar in its sledge." By going through the alchemic fire of transformation he is given a new garment, for he now has reached a new level in understanding and power.

PLATE 3-4, 30-31
Chapter 125

Plate three and four contain the famous weighing of the heart ceremony, but plate 30-31 (which also describes part of the ceremony) must be examined first. This again is another example of how the Book of the Dead is not meant to be read and understood like a normal book. One must piece it together like a puzzle. Plate 30 begins with Ani and Thutu before an offering table (similar to plate 1) and on the far side is Osiris in his shrine (similar to plate four). However Osiris in plate 30 is standing (not seated) and only Isis appears behind him. That Osiris is not seated (in meditative posture) shows that there will be action involved, and Isis is using her right hand to show that her force (wisdom) will be put into action. Osiris is painted green to show that one will be using the wisdom of the heart, and of cyclic existence. All of this is occurring in the Hall of the Double Maat, place of truth and right action. Ani will be tested to see how well he understands this reality. Osiris holds the uas, crook and flail and has a menat around his neck. The crook (to still the wandering sheep of the mind) and the flail (self discipline of mental practice) are two symbolic parts of the process. Doing this one will wear the two crowns (connecting above and below, Horus and Set) that will allow access to the void. In front of him the four sons of Horus (four directions, elements, proteins) appear on top of an open lotus.

The text of plates 30-31 is chapter 125, but only a small portion appears in the Ani papyrus (the full text can be found in Faulkner's appendix). Ani enters and praises Osiris Amentet (the place of the west, thus of stopping internal dialogue and released identity). He declares that this is a place where no trees or plants grow, thus he is in the void where there is only blackness, thus the realm of everything but nothing. In this case Osiris would no longer be green, but would be depicted as All-Black. He then claims to enter the Place of Hidden Things (place of his own inner Gnosis), and to have spoken to his friend Set, which seems strange for on the surface Set is our enemy. Yet by reaching the place of nothingness, Set (the wandering thoughts of the mind) can be seen as part of the whole, thus we come to him in a new way. This new way will cause the "clothing on his face" (veil of Isis) "to fall down and reveal the hidden things." The stillness allows us to go beyond the illusion and see the hidden (Seta) within.

By line (6-7) Anubis (guide) appears saying he knows of a man who has come from Ta-Meri (Egypt) and knows all the roads and towns (material world), then talks of knowing his smell or odour (perhaps the oil or fragrance worn by priests). This smell could also be the reason he was friends with Set, for the lizard group is known to have a terrible smell. It may be the reason for the original creation of perfumes (worn only by the ruling elite), for the reptilian to hide their odour to the human nose.

In line fifteen Ani claims to have come to Restau (Giza) and seen the hidden things there. Again remember that these words are less physical locations, they are locations within ourselves. He then claims, "I was hidden but I found a passage, then clothed myself with what I found there over my nakedness." The clothing means wisdom, and nakedness refers to the state without wisdom. The wisdom is not something he knows, but something he wears (lives by). Line 17 contains one of the most important verses of the entire text, and absolutely vital for understanding the weighing of the heart that will come in plate 3. The line says, "verily Set has spoken to me the things concerning himself. I have told Set, the weighing be within us." Thus the weighing will not be something that happens outside of us, or as some judgment by some deity, we will weigh ourselves in our own heart. And when you know there is only one, as the Mahabharata says, "then who's to judge?"

Line 18 claims he comes to a door and needs to know the name of the door, and all the parts. Knowing the names he can pass through. What follows is the famous 42 Negative Confessions on Plate 31. However, there is an introduction that is omitted in the Ani papyrus. It also has possible connection to lizard creatures and to satanic worship, thus the need to follow the teachings as a pure human. This confession may have been required to tell the difference between the old priests, and the new priests of Amun who represented the parasite. In the Old Kingdom texts Amun is a minor deity but by the New Kingdom he became the chief ruler. Ani claims to come from the Land of Maat (right action) so he can see the "Triple Harmony." He comes to see the 42 gods, always felt by Egyptologists to represent the 42 provinces (nomes) of Egypt and were there to hear a "confession" from the deceased. The text says the 42 "live on those who cherish evil and drank their blood on the day of recovery before Un-Nefer." Now why do the 42 live on evil and blood, unless they are the very force that needs that evil and blood (the alien in human form) to survive in this reality. What is known as Satanic sacrifice is a ritual carried out by the ruling elite that allows them, through the ingestion of human blood (hormones) and ingesting fear in the killing, to keep their "cloak" of seeing human, thus avoid the sight of the multitude.

Next (back on plate 31) Ani says the famous 42 confessions. The are called negative because he claims to "have not done" something. These 42 confessions were later shortened by those who wrote the Hebrew Bible into the Ten Commandments. Some of the confessions seem similar on the surface, so the new writers likely combined things together.[312] All of this must be examined

---

[312]I will list all 42 that Ani has said to have not done: wrong, despoiled, robbed, killed, destroyed food offerings, reduced measures (lied in the market), despoiled the god's property, lied, stolen food, sullen?, fornicated, made anyone cry, not eaten his heart, transgressed, deceived, stolen from the fields, gossiped, brought lawsuits, ragged without cause, had intercourse with a married woman, masturbated, caused terror, transgressed, been angry with rage, neglectful of truthful words, cursed, been violent,

in a couple of ways. By having Ani address each one and saying something he has not done, thus to not be one of them (alien) and not associate with their destructive energy. Ani is in effect saying that he is a true human, living from his human heart and not his alien mind. There is also a number of things Ani says he has not done, things that were not included in the Hebrew Ten Commandments. Ani claims he has also treated the world and nature well. How many today can say they are not polluting the water? How might the earth be today if the need to protect the earth and nature had been included in the Bible? When he says he has not stolen food from children, it does not mean taking from little kids, but to assure that the earth will be in proper healthy order when he dies so that his children will be able to eat of the earth.

The vignette for plate 31 has what appears to be two open doors, which have the 42 "gods" along the top. On the far right are two Maats sitting on a throne of meditation while holding a uas and an ankh. Below is an offering of a lotus to Osiris. Below that is the standard weighing of the heart (examined below), with Tehuti kneeling before a Maat feather of truth. Ani says to the 42, "I know you, I know your names," or I know the truth about you, and what you really are. He claims he "can not be cast down to their knives, or can not be controlled by his mind (their mind)." He claims to have done right and truth in Ta-Meri (Egypt). By line 9 he talks of the need for great compassion and kindness (and for a while will sound like a Buddhist monk). He first claims to not have committed evil. Then claims to have given "bread to the hungry and water to the thirsty, clothes to the needed, and a boat to shipwrecked." He also claims to have "heard what was spoken by the donkey to the cat in the Temple of Hept-R (house of the open mouth)."

By line 21 begins a series of questions coming from various areas of the Hall of the Double Maat. The door starts the questioning by asking, "who are you?" This is the first question that gets picked up on the spiritual search, the recognition that we don't really know who we are, and thus the need to to examine who we are. The door then asks "what is your name?" This questioning continues until the door seems satisfied with all of Ani's answers. He is allowed to pass. To be honest I am not all that clear on the symbolism for this examination by the door. A door in Egypt has the name sba, the same word as for a star. Thus the door could be a code for inner star. Remember, a wall is a barrier but a door is an entrance through that barrier. When the door finally lets him pass, by line 43, he is asked to meet the "recorder of the two lands," Tehuti

---

stirred up strife, been impatient, gossiped again (an important one for Ani I guess), spoke too much (he must have been a chatterbox), done evil, cursed the King, polluted water, made too much noise, cursed a god, theft, given less offerings, stolen offerings, stolen food of the children, slaughtered the sacred animals.

(wisdom). Tehuti asks Ani for his condition, to which he gives a key response of, "I am purified of evil, I have excluded myself from the quarrels of negative acts of those who are living. I am not among them." This does not mean to say that he is dead. That Ani is no longer among the living in this case means he is no longer an average human being, a looping zombie caught in the confines of the parasite. He has let go of his mind, and lives from his true mind. Ani is told that he can now go on to meet Osiris, "who's roof is fire, whose walls living uraei, whose floor is sacred water." Ani has bread as his eyes (life energy) and his voice upon the earth (his speech and actions) are now pure. It is his fate now to meet his Higher Self, Osiris. This is now the time to connect with the positive serpent force, kundalini that will oppose the reptilian alien force.

Returning to Plate 3, Chapter 30B is one of the most famous scenes of the entire text, the Weighing of the Heart Ceremony. In the center is the scale, the heart is being weighed against the feather of Maat. While this is the most common balance depiction, it is not the case in all papyrus versions. Many things can be on the scale. Sometimes the heart is never even shown. At times Maat is on top of the scale, other times a baboon or even the head of Anubis. The balance is equating to one who is following the middle road, always at peace for they are not letting the world around them move them to one extreme- which means they can no longer jump to evil- nor to jumping to complete good. It is also representing the balance of Horus and Set, of our true mind with our conscious mind. Tehuti is beside the balance and is not just writing down the decision of the scales, but also "examining the words." While actions were checked in the 42 Negative Confessions, words and words of the mind (thoughts) are checked here. Thus our heart and mind must be as light as feather, for as Shakespeare said, "a light heart lives long."

The text of Chapter 30B begins by saying "My heart my mother, my coming into being." Thus it is really our heart that birthed us, causing us as form to exist. Two sections of chapter do not appear in the Ani papyrus, such as Chapter 30A, where one gives thanks to their heart so they can meet the Great God of the West (Osiris). The second is a rubric that is very alchemic, which calls for a green scarab stone (to transform the heart) to be placed on the "dead person's neck." It claims that the rubric itself was found at Khemenu (Hermopolis), the place of Tehuti. The famous Emerald Tablet of Hermes/Tehuti comes to mind. This rubric explains where to find this sacred text. To understand it would bring one great strength, and to do so would perform the Ap-Re (opening of the mouth). It is interesting that the opening the mouth ritual, which could include some sort of tantric sex rite, may be connected with a green scarab and perhaps the Emerald Tablet.

To one side of the scale is Anubis, Shai (destiny), Renenet (fortune) and Meshkhenet (karma) thus meaning that all of these concepts are weighed here as well. Of course these forces: destiny, karma and fortune are seen differently upon awakening, than they were prior- and this may be referred to here.. Tehuti claims that Ani is truth (scale is balanced, so mind is balanced) and is also "True of Voice, Amentet can not prevail." Amentet is the "eater of hearts" that is part crocodile, lion and hippo. He stands next to the scale. If the heart is found to be impure, focused on the material illusion of the world, then Ani would have died a "second death." Muata Ashby shows in the Papyrus of Kenna how Ammit is biting above the three lower rings of a seven-ring balance, signifying a bite above the three lower chakras. Thus symbolically Ammit is eating those who only lived in the lower world of the material. Yet this eating is not happening after death, as I will explain shortly.

Should the traveler be found worthy of passing Ammit, then Sennu (cakes) are given. A cake in Egypt is a symbol of the moon, and with a candle atop that leads to inner light. These evolved into our birthday cakes. Ani is now said to be in the presence of Osiris (void, True Self) like a Follower of Horus (Shem-shu-Hor; warrior).

PLATE 4

Now Horus leads Ani to the throne of Osiris. On the throne is a green Osiris with Isis and Nepthys standing behind, holding him upright. Osiris holds the crook, flail and uas. In front of him is a lotus on which stand the four sons of Horus. Outside the throne are offerings and lotus flowers left on a shrine by Ani. Horus, as a falcon, appears above the shine along with a number of upraised cobras. The four sons of Horus are the four lower bodies, or the teachings of the four directions that have been mastered by Ani, thus has become a lotus and transformed darkness into light. Isis and Nepthys symbolize life and death in the material world. To enter the land of Osiris (Amentet in the west) one must leave the realm of birth and death behind. The offerings may be Ani leaving behind all of his worldly goods, for he no longer is attached to the illusion of the world.

The wands Osiris holds says he has controlled all aspects of his lower self. When one comes in front of Osiris they are meant to understand that they are going into the depths of the Abyss, to the Osiris in their heart. It is the reason for calling Ani, "Osiris Ani," for what we have been searching for has really been ourself all along. The same energy that was needed by Isis to resurrect Osiris, will be the same energy we need to resurrect our own Osiris. The only one who can lead us there is Horus, our inner light of the warrior's path, along with Tehuti (Gnosis) and Maat (Dharma, Truth). In the New Kingdom, Osiris was important for it was said he presided over the duat (translated as underworld). In Old Kingdom Egypt, the Duat was not the realm of the dead, but the void- the center that never moves, while Osiris circles it like a wheel. The center point is still while the outer wheel rotates. There is death involved, but not what became the New Kingdom idea (and carried through today) of some realm after physical death. It has nothing to do with physical death, but the breakdown of "me," the death of the self that we have believed to be us all of our life.

Modern writers have always claimed that the state of the deceased in the afterlife hinged on this judgment, because that is how Western religions present death. We die, we have some form of judgment placed on us, then we either spend eternity in heaven or hell. Yet this is a modern idea, not an Ancient Egyptian one. If this was indeed the final event of the whole process, why is it here early in the text? This would be a very easy plate to place at the end, if that is where it is supposed to be? In my understanding, this judgment is not happening at the end of our life, but is happening each and every moment. The weighing of thoughts and actions are going on right now. The judgment happens whenever the "I" wants to prove its existence, when one's "I" is as light as a feather (thus living the truth of Maat), it no longer exists-and you are finally free to see that you are Osiris (void) all along. It is weighing the attachment of "you" to the dream. The more you believe the false self, the less balanced the scale will be. And the realm of Osiris is only reached when all attachments to the illusionary dream have dissolved away. It is called the "Last judgment" because when equal to a feather, time ceases to exist, where there is no before or after.

Chapter 7

Chapter 7 does not appear in the Ani Papyrus, and while short, it is very important for the discussion of this text. Unlike the chapters of the Ani papyrus, I do not have the original hieroglyphic text for Chapter 7, so I must rely on the translation provided by RO Faulkner.

"Chapter for passing the dangerous coils of Apop. O you waxen one, who take by robbery, and live on the inert ones. I will not be inert for you, I will not be weak for you, your poison shall not enter into my members, for my members are the members of Atum. If I am not weak for you, suffering from you shall not enter into these members of mine. I am Atum at the head of the Primordial Water, my protection is from the gods, the lords of eternity. I am He whose name is secret, more holy than those of the chaos gods. I am among them, i have gone forth from Atum, I am one who is not examined. I am hale. I am hale."

This really is a most powerful and insightful chapter. It fully draws into the depth the Archon-Apop presence in the world. To pass or miss the coils of Apop, is to miss the trappings of the reptilian serpent and its parasitic mind, symbolized by the coils of a python. The text calls for Apop to be designated by the term the "waxen one," thus not real- made of wax (hologram). In Egyptian temple ritual, each morning a wax figure of Apop was burned on a fire, and as the wax melted, so too did Apop's power to influence the temple or the people within it also melt away. In the Nag Hammadi Gnostic Texts, the writers revealed that the archons were not directly from Sophia (Isis) but were somehow an abortion, and used the name HAL (simulation). This also might be part of the Egyptian reference to their being waxen.

The chapter claims that Apop "take by robbery" (the gnostic texts claim archons "abduct souls by theft") and that they live on those who are inert (asleep). The chapter calls for the reader not to be inert (asleep) or weak- as often the reptilian is able to infiltrate at time of weakness, especially when one drops into their habits and patterns. By not being asleep or weak the "poison" (the parasite or virus) will have no effect on them (in essence the conscious mind will not function in its energy stealing role). They are again suggesting that awareness is somehow important for deflecting the "poison."

The person in the text next does not compare himself to Atum, but claims to be Atum (first primordial Neter, the creator of everything) thus to say that he is also then the supreme manifestor. Since he is the only thing and the creator of all- what object in creation can possibly harm the creator? It is this knowing that lifts a veil of attack, which will cause "no suffering to enter any of his members." When the reader of the text claims that his name is secret, the best explanation I can give a the line from the Tao Te Ching that says "the Tao you can name, is not the Eternal Tao." Thus What Is, is prior to names, concepts and ideas- thus by saying he has no name, he is fact all names. Everything else is but a shadow appearing from the Absolute's dreaming. Without your armor, defenses, your mask- then Apop can no longer "touch you". You have show the most scary face possible to them, the fact that you have no faces, and all faces. Doing so allows him to claim twice that he is "hale." Hale is an older English term used to signify that one is totally free from illness- in this case- totally free of the alien parasite-virus. I believe that this chapter is a very good addition for anyone who is studying the Nag Hammadi "First Apocalypse of James," or any other text that is focusing on the reptilian influence on the dreamstate.

CHAPTER 24
Shifting the Focus- 2012

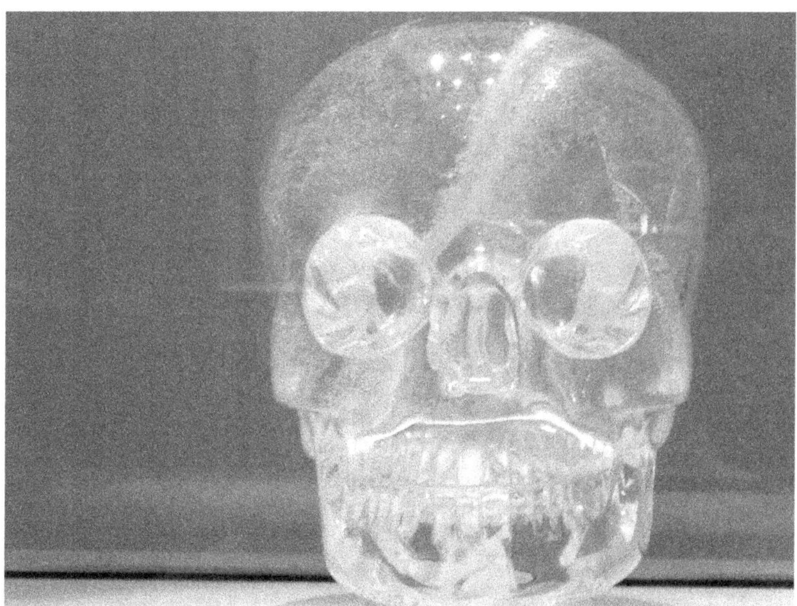

179:Crystal skull of unknown origin, British Museum

This chapter was originally written in 2005, long before 2012 occurred. Now that we are past the famous Mayan date of the ending of their calendar (at least to most researchers calculations) many will say that nothing at all happened. And it is true that on the surface it seemed like not much occurred as we moved from Dec 21 to Dec 22. But now a few years later I believe a change did occur. But the changes are so slight in manifested reality that they are currently unseen by most, and some of those that are seeing it are having a tough time with what they have found. So even though what is written here did not come to pass in 2012, I have left most of it in the revised book simply due to the interesting material that it came from. While reading though, ask yourself- did something change in 2012? Did I change in 2012? With some honest seeing you might be surprised with that you notice.

New Age?

"This is the dawning of the Age of Aquarius…" Hair, the musical

A new age is said to be dawning on human civilization, yet every group has its own interpretation of what might be on the horizon. The New Age Spiritual Movement gets is name from the soon appearing precessional Age of Aquarius. This age is said to usher in a shift of planetary consciousness, a taking over of the earth by humanity, where love and happiness will reign over all, a trend that began to show in the 1960's. Other astrologers see this upcoming age as a time when control elites will take even more power from people and the earth comparing it less to the 1960's and more to the novel 1984 by George Orwell. While many groups cite the supposed end of the Mayan calendar on December 21, 2012 that could bring a wave of cataclysmic apocalypse. In this chapter, The New Age version is that the Age of Aquarius will be .I want to examine what the ancients had to say about the current place that humans and the earth find itself in, and what they may have been attempting to pass along.

Precession

180:Relief from British Museum showing Egyptian version of Hindu "Churning the Milky Ocean"

The planet earth is different than most people realize. The planet is not a perfect sphere, but is wider at the equator. The tropics (Cancer and Capricorn)

are not stationary but shift due to "obliquity of the ecliptic" from 22.1-24.5 degrees every 41,000 years. The earth rotates at 1000 miles per hour, and travels through space at 66,000 miles per hour or 18.5 miles per second.[313] Right not you are moving through the solar system at great speed, in a number of directions without noticing. This is of course if you believe the standard scientific theory of the Earth, there are many today that are starting to share the old idea that the Earth may be flat or concave, and that the planets and solar system just an illusion on a dome shaped sky. No matter, precession ties into either view of reality.

Precession is the most important calendar of the earth and creates what are known as precessional world ages. The earth does not spin on its true axis, as it is more like a wobbling top. This wobble causes the earth's axis to shift a small amount each year. As the earth shifts it appears as though all of the stars have moved slightly. A star's rising point on the horizon will change by one degree every 72 years. The ancients grouped stars into the zodiac constellations. A constellation of stars will remain in the sky to rise at vernal equinox for 2,160 years when the wobble of the earth causes a new constellation to take its place. Each of these 2,160 years is known as a precessional age, when the earth will be influenced by the zodiac constellation rising at the vernal equinox. With twelve zodiac signs, a complete circuit takes 25,920 years and is called a Great World Age when the original zodiac sign will rise again in the sky, completing the cycle. In the comparison of the above to the below, this cycle of precession is mirrored in humanity. The average human will take eighteen breaths per minute, 1080 in an hour, or 25, 920 in a day. The average pulse is claimed to be seventy-two times a minute, or 4, 320 per hour (two precessional cycles).[314] It is said that at the beginning of each Great World Age there will be the need to start again, ridding all that existed in the previous age. Each precessional age does the same restarting, but on a smaller scale.

Today we are nearing the end of the precessional Age of Pisces that began between 100 BC and 100 AD, and we are ready to enter the Age of Aquarius. Each age has its own marker sign based on the sign of the zodiac it represents. Leo is represented by a lion, Taurus by a bull, Aries by a ram, and Pisces by the fish. Today Aquarius is shown as a woman pouring water on the ground, but the ancient symbol was a male. The pouring of water is said to indicate a time of purification or cleansing is in order.[315]

Precession is said to have been discovered by the Greek scholar Hipparchos around 127 BC. Most Western historians still do not believe that

---

[313] Hancock, *Fingerprints* pp. 79, 233, 228

[314] Hancock *Fingerprints* pp.241, 256, 372; Hancock, *Keeper* p.74; West, *Serpent* p.98; Chandler, Wayne B *Ancient Future* (Black Classic Press: 1999) p. 196

[315] West *Serpent* p.98

any of this knowledge could have been available prior to the Greeks, but not only did the cultures before the Greeks understand precession, they also understood its mystical and sacred meanings far better than we do. The Greeks learned it from the Egyptians. Plato, Proclus and Herodotus all wrote that it was the Egyptians who taught the Greeks astronomy and precession. [316] Schwaller de Lubicz believed that all of Egyptian religion, art and way of life were a direct influence of precession. The Egyptian texts claim their country was ruled for thousands of years before the Pharaohs by the Shem-Shu-Hor (Followers of Horus). Herodotus wrote of a time in Egypt when the sun was "rising twice where it now sets and setting twice where it now rises," perhaps some 39,000 years ago.[317]

Due to precession, a date on our calendar must be shifted approximately 20 days per half cycle or 13,000 years. Without such changes in the calendar over a couple of ages (3-4,000 years) a particular date would no longer match the phenomena expected for that day. In 1320 BC a shift of the calendar happened in Egypt because the Summer Solstice (Egyptian New Year) was no longer falling in the first month of the year but began to occur in the previous month (year). They could not have understood the need for the shift unless they were studying precession. [318] Today our Equinox and Solstice have shifted a few days back over the last two thousand years, impacting Christmas. Originally the birth of Jesus (light) was meant to celebrate the Winter Solstice, which 2000 years ago fell on the date of December 25th. With the continuing movement of precession, the solstice has moved to the 21st of December. Following the takeover of the Roman Catholic Church in the 4th century AD and the subsequent literal belief of the texts, the true knowledge of what was being provided was lost. Not understanding that the Hermetic New Testament was a symbol for the initiates and not a literal truth, the priests did not move the celebration of the birth of the New King to coincide with the birth of the New King of Light at the Winter Solstice. Thus December 25 would have only been

---

[316] Hancock *Keeper* p.154, Herodotus *The Histories* Book 2 2-8; "Commentaries of the Timaeus"

[317] During a period of precession a constellation will rise on the eastern horizon on the equinox. Staring at the horizon looking at a sign such as Aquarius, at our back will be the opposite constellation, in this case Leo. A full cycle will take 25, 920 years for the same configuration to happen. However part way through, around 13,000 years, the opposite would happen as Leo would rise to our face and Aquarius would be at our backs. A one and half cycle of precession, or 39,000 years, would have the sun rise twice in Leo (where it now sets) and set twice in Aquarius (where it now rises). Schwaller is claiming that Herodotus was writing of a time in Egypt 39,000 years ago, a time when precession was already understood. Hancock *Fingerprints* pp. 385-88; Hancock *Keeper* p.23; Santilliana, p.59; West *Serpent* p.98

[318] Schwaller de Lubicz, RA Sacred Science (Inner Traditions 1961) p.175

an effective celebration for the birth of light (Jesus) 2,000 years ago. Today our celebrations no longer match the energies of the day the celebration represents.

Precessional Ages

Different astronomers and spiritualists will provide different dates as when one precessional age finished and the next one began. One suggests the previous age start and end dates to be: Leo (10,720-8560 BC), Cancer (8560-6400BC), Gemini (6400-4240 BC), Taurus (4240-2080 BC), and Aries (2080 BC – 80 AD). Under this system our current age, Pisces should end in 2240 AD. Others coincide that the change to Aquarius will be at the exact moment that the Maya calendar runs out in 2012, some that it shifted on February 5, 1962 when the Sun, Mercury, Venus, Jupiter and Saturn were all in the Zodiac sign of Aquarius.

The Egyptians kept a magnificent account of the world ages hidden in their mythology. During different periods in Egypt certain animal deities were worshiped, while others were ignored. Egyptologists have claimed this was an example of different religious cults, who took control of Egypt at differing periods. However there was no animal worship and no warring priesthoods. The new animals were telling something very important: precession. The earliest dynasties of Old Kingdom Egypt worshiped the bull. During this time period the sun rose in the precessional Age of Taurus. Female deities were depicted wearing a moon with bull's horns on their head. Monolithic structures were erected all over Egypt. Around 2,000 BC the bull's worship was followed by the worship of Amun the ram, that Egyptologists confirm as the control of power by the Ram priests of Amun. However 2,000 BC was around the time precession moved from Taurus the bull to Aries the ram. The Egyptian change of focus had nothing to do with warring priesthoods in Egypt but to reflect the new precessional age which brought their own specific energies.[319]

Part of the Osiris myth has Horus ripping the crown off of Isis for letting his arch-enemy Set go free. Tehuti replaces it with a cow head. This could be a piece of precession stored in the myth as Isis wanted to keep the dual principles of Gemini alive by letting Set go free, but Horus (as a high priest) knew Gemini was no longer. Forcefully, he had to rip the crown of Gemini off his mother's head and Tehuti (wisdom) replaced it with the cow to claim the new Age of Taurus had arrived. The Old Testament may be providing similar information with a story of Moses. Moses come down from Mount Sinai as "two horned" and claims, "I am the ram of God," and became angry when he saw his people making and worshiping a golden calf. This has come to be believed that one should not make graven images. Actually Moses was angry that he had come to proclaim that he was the ram, thus the Age of Aries was

---

[319] Tompkins, *Great Pyramid* (Harper and Row 1972) p.172; Lamy, p.5; West *Serpent* p.100

now upon the world, but the people were still making images of the calf representing Taurus.[320]

Around 100 AD came the beginning of a new religion, Christianity. This religion formed at the start of Pisces. Original Christians rarely worshiped a cross but a fish. Jesus came out of Egypt and said "come ye after me and I will make you fishers of men," explaining the new age of Pisces the fish had begun and so too would a new way of thinking. The ram is written of often in the Old Testament (a sign that it was written in the Age of Aries), but rams do not appear in the New Testament.[321]

A key component of a new World Age is that the thinkers of the old age do not want to let go of their grip of power that easily. They do not understand that a new way of living must happen to harmonize with new energies of the age. Schwaller claims the period prior to and just after a change reflect tremendous social disorder and earth disturbances. Prior to the new Age of Pisces, Egypt fell under the reign of the Greeks. This takeover could have been a sign that the old ways of wisdom in Egypt were to be no longer.[322] The surviving priests in Egypt began to depict the gods in human form, perhaps in preparation to let everyone know that the Piscean Age was going to be one of the physical and material world. There can be no doubt that this has been an age marked by humans putting their own needs first, and the needs of the planet and all of its creatures last. The last hundred years has been a time of marked disaster on the planet. Unimagined warfare, starvation, and destruction by earth forces have occurred. The old ways are dying but those in control are attempting to hold on out of fear. Just before an age ends there is a great revival of wisdom in an attempt at spiritual growth. 500 years before the age of Pisces the schools of Pythagoras, Plato, Confucius, Lao Tzu and Buddha appeared, while in 1500 AD the Renaissance attempted to bring forth the ancient wisdom.[323]

Cultures all over the planet differ on the specific number of ages that occurred prior to this one. The Maya, Aztec, Inca, Navajo and Greeks believed there had been four previous suns (Ages), the Hindu's, Tibetans and Hopi three, the Chinese ten.[324] The Maya teachings do not say that one Sun ended and another began, this concept is a Western translation of Maya texts. They actually claim that even though we are in the Fifth Sun, the other four are still happening. They say our entire age is actually rooted in the other four previous

---

[320] Santilliana p.60; West *Serpent* p.100; Noone, Richard 5/5/2000 (Harmony Books 1986) p.8

[321] Hancock Fingerprints p.455; Noone p.10; West *Serpent* p.100

[322] Schwaller pp.117, 124, 180

[323] Schwaller p.18

[324] Sullivan, William *The Secrets of the Incas* (Three Rivers Press 1996) p.29; Gold, p.23; Hancock *Fingerprints* pp.199-204

ages. Maya shaman Martin Prechtel claimed that there were still people alive who could pull up certain rocks to allow one to see the "previous worlds."[325]Every one of these cultures believes that we are nearing the end of a Great World Age. They were very specific about what was to come and what would be needed to be done to survive it. "At the beginning of each new precessional age great structures collapse, pillars topple which supported the great fabric, floods and cataclysms herald the shaping of a new world."[326] If that is true about each of the 2,160 year precessional ages, what kind of cataclysms will be forthcoming when a new Great Age begins?

Hindu and Egypt

To the Hindu there have been 4 great ages, each which were destroyed bringing on a new age: Krita Yuga (golden age of 1,728,000 years); Treta Yuga (1,296,000 years); Davpara Yuga (864,000 years); and our current age of Kali Yuga (432,000 years). Hindus say the last destruction is to be by fire and then there will be 4,320,000 years of peace. Dividing the ages by 432, 000 (a key number of precession) we are left with the ages lasting 4, 3, 2, and 1 years.[327] It seems that this Hindu system may have been written in some sort of binary code.

To Hindus we are in the final age of Kali Yuga, which is believed to be the most morally corrupt of the great cycle. The goddess Dharma in India is the direct counterpart of Maat (truth and cosmic order) from Egypt. Dharma was supposed to walk on four legs during Krita Yuga. With each successive age she lost a leg, or lost some of her moral character. In the age prior to ours she walked on but two legs when "lying and quarreling abounded…mind lessened, Truth declined and there came disease, desire and calamity…it was a decadent age by reason and the prevalence of sin…nevertheless many trod the right path." In our current age, Dharma stands on but one leg referring that only 1¼4 of the original truth and order is still around. "The world is afflicted, all creatures degenerate, men turn to wickedness…they eat voraciously…live in cities filled with thieves…they are oppressed by their kings and by the ravages of nature, famine and wars." According to the Hindus, our decadent age will be ended by Kalki (Fulfiller) who will appear by riding a white horse and holding a sword blazing like a comet. "From the ruins of the earth, a new mankind will arise."[328] The suggestion of a comet may mean that the appearance of Kalki will be noticed by an event in the sky. It is also written that at such times Vishnu will appear to help teach mankind, as he has done in incarnations as Rama and Krishna.

---

[325] Prechtel, Martin *Secrets of the Talking Jaguar* (Tarcher 1999) p. 104
[326] Santilliana p.2
[327] Hancock *Heaven's* pp. 151, 155; Tompkins *Mexican* p. 257
[328] Hancock *Heaven's* p.155

The Rishis (Indian mystics) feel our current age is one overcome by Maya (illusion), whose stupidity, strife and greed exist but would be overcome by a manifestation of Vishnu. This is similar to the Egyptian/Greek Hermetica that explained when Egypt's wisdom fell away and darkness was preferred to light (our present age with the loss of the Egyptian wisdom). The Hermetica says the Creator will come to wash away the evil and return it to the normal world. The Hindus, like the Egyptians, believe that time is not linear as we normally believe, but circular and having no beginning or ending just change. They also see continuous times of creation and destruction of the universe. Vishnu (the Hindu Atum) allows his vitality to "slowly ripen to unfold again in another universe, dispelling the darkness." Vishnu also ejaculated seamen into the cosmic waters, like Atum, and became a golden egg similar to the Egyptian Benben stone. The Hindu myth are thus related to, or Egyptian in origin.

The Egyptian Coffin Texts describe that "you (Osiris) will live more than millions of years, an era of millions, but in the end I (Atum) will destroy everything that I have created, the earth will become again part of the primordial ocean." The Egyptians saw a point when time would cease and all that was created would eventually go back to the Creator. The text says, "All that has been created will return into Nun…Myself alone, I persist, unknown and invisible to all."[329] One can liken this concept to the breath of God. When the Creator breathes out (speaks the Logos) creation will happen. Eventually the breath will end and God will breathe back into itself all that was breathed out. Once finished the complete breath, a new one will begin.

Tibetans

The Tibetans believe we now live in the fourth World Age. The previous worlds were destroyed through cataclysms of floods, fires, earthquakes and violent winds. In each case a few Noah-like survivors would attempt to carry on the spiritual way of life in another potentially perfect world. To Tibetans, a Buddha was the creator of each age. Each world also receives a great teacher who emanates out of the energy of the associated Buddha, and helps lead humans towards enlightenment. As a new 5th world is ready to begin, they are awaiting a dark-green deity (one of the heart) that is said to be the next great teacher. This new deity would help a few to survive by showing them how to live the right way like "the enlightened ones."[330] They fail to mention why everyone did not become enlightened in the previous ages if they too were started by an enlightened Buddha.

---

[329] Laviolette p. 97; Lamy p.19; *Coffin Texts* section 125 and 175

[330] Gold pp.17, 22, 23

Navajo

To the Navajo there were four previous worlds. Each had been pure, but had been destroyed when humans began fighting. In the previous world, men and women had voluntarily separated due to quarrels and sexual infidelities. The women paddled to the opposite shore of a great river on rafts made by the men. The rafts were later burned so they could not come back. Soon the men did not hunt enough and the women's corn crops failed, and they were both starving. After years of separation they were finally reunited, but four days of purification rites were required. This myth describes the destruction that can happen from not being in harmony with the cosmos. To only live with either male or female energy will be headed for destruction. There is a great need for the two forces of the universe to come together and act as one. Today we live in a world mostly made up of male energy.

The fourth world ended when two women tried to swim back to the men. The Water Monster grabbed them and took them to his lair. Talking God and Calling God went to the lair to get the women back. They did retrieve them, but Coyote had gone also and stolen two of Water Monster's babies. When the Water Monster found out, a great flood was created as revenge. The humans escaped through a hole in the sky where a giant reed extended and they climbed to the rocky floor of the fifth world. Only then did they notice the stolen babies. The key part of the myth is that the Navajo realized that the flood would not have happened without their own negative influence. They understood that things around them were influenced by what they themselves did. They placed the babies in a basket of white shell and apologized to the waters. The flow of water immediately ceased.[331] This myth is explaining that the great changes that occur at the end of ages are the direct result of humans. If we live the right way, with each other and the earth, the change will likely be minimal. If we do not live the right way, we will suffer greatly the effects of change.

Inca

Viracocha was the South American Quetzalcoatl, bringer of peace and wisdom. The Inca, as the Mexicans, believed there have been five suns. The first sun was destroyed by water, the second by falling of sky on earth, third by fire and the fourth by air. An age was called pacha, which means place and time simultaneously. In Andean thought "this place" today is not the "same place" tomorrow. Time is a defining condition of space. When one world ends, another begins by what is called a pachakuti (overturning of the world, or turning back). Thus according to the Inca, the end of an age could mean an overturning of space-time.[332]

---

[331] Gold pp. 37-41, 90, 94

Lakota Sioux

Wallace Black Elk comments that the Lakota Sioux believe there have been four whistles (ages) to have sounded. Seven whistles will sound in all. He claims that the final three of these whistles will happen very quickly. Prior to the fifth whistle, the earth will shake, tall buildings will tumble down, and countless people will vanish. On the sixth whistle, the fire will come and all life will cease. When the seventh whistle sounds Tunkashila (Great Spirit) and Grandmother will appear. The whole earth will vibrate. All the star-nation people will come from the sky.[333]

Hopi

To the Hopi of the US Southwest the fourth great age is coming to an end, and the fifth is ready to begin. The Hopi believe they are the chosen Native Indian tribe to hold the wisdom of the true prophecies given to all Native Indian tribes thousands of years ago. They may be right. The ancient prophecy had warned them of the white man's arrival and their attempt to eliminate the Hopi. It also predicted roads in the sky, horseless carriages, moving houses of iron, men speaking through cobwebs (telephone), the atomic bomb and travel to the moon. As each prophecy was fulfilled they began to look more closely at the ones that spoke of great disasters to come. The prophecy claims that only by continuing to live in the right way, connected with the earth, would one survive when the change occurred. Originally they even tried to warn the whitemen of the prophecy, but the whites saw the Indians as savages who needed to be enslaved or killed. As the time of the great change is fast approaching, the Hopi believe they need to share the wisdom and prophecy with the world.[334]

A key part of the prophecy is a petroglyph known as Prophecy Rock, and is interpreted to mean that the way people live will have an effect on when and how the change will happen. They warn that the way of the whites, which they call 'Bahannas,' is a way that forsakes the laws of nature. The Hopi believe that the evil people in the world, called two-hearteds, "simply take advantage of a situation that the Creator has created." The great choice say the Hopi say is the choice of the way of Bahanna (materialism) or the way of the Creator (the Hopi life in connection with Mother Earth). The Hopi see the world as one supported by wheels. The poor choices of modern humans were making the fourth wheel (ours) wobble causing the earth to be in poor health. An enormous effort is needed to stabilize the wheel. If the wheel is not quickly fixed, the wobble will cause the fifth cycle to begin.[335] That they describe a

---

[332] Hancock Heaven's p.275; Sullivan p.29

[333] Black Elk p.145

[334] Mails, Thomas *The Hopi Survival Kit* (Stewart, Tabori and Chang 1997) pp. 5, 30, 78, 88, 95, 106, 110

[335] Mails pp. 37, 69, 83, 110, 154, 164, 173, 175, 182

442

wobble makes it very similar to the way astronomers talk about precession. Could the Hopi prophecy be talking about the great change of the wobble of the earth and how humans must be ready for its effects?

The Hopi claim the prophecy predicts there will be unrest in the world. The desperate people in the world (those without food or goods) will become fed up with the Western people who are not desperate but not willing to share their food and money. The liberators of this world will come from the sky and "they will shake us by the ears, like children who have been bad." They claim a great event, perhaps a war, will cause the earth to shake and turn red signifying the purification has come. This purification will rid the world of those who have disturbed the Native way of living in harmony with the earth. Humans were placed on this earth for a purpose, to protect the earth from harm and love all things. With those who oppose this way gone, Mother Earth will again be in harmony. If the purification did not come, they believe the Creator would simply take the earth back because "if we can not care for it the right way then humans do not deserve to live on it." However the Hopi claim that part of the prophecy is missing, and a white will bring it back. When it returns the exact end of the fourth cycle will be known.

A small group of Hopi, referred to as Traditionalists, and live in a village called Hotevilla, are attempting to keep the old ways alive and ignore the ways of materialism. They still grow all of their own food and have no use for money. Living in this way they say is to be one with the Creator. This is a great challenge in our modern world. The Traditionalist Hopi's way of life is constantly being threatened by the non-traditionalists and the whites who are trying to gain control over them, forcing them to pay for things they do not need, with money they do not use.

The Traditionalists claim the prophecies have made suggestions, called instructions, as to how one should live. To see the complete "Instructions", please read the book *Hopi Survival Kit* by Thomas Mails. One of the instructions is to care for the earth and treat it like the giver of life. Like all shaman they mention the importance of not just spending time in nature, but speaking with plants and animals, to spend time with them as equals. By being more connected with nature we will be calmer, make better choices, be less tempted and enjoy a longer life.[336]

Another key instruction is to become self-sufficient. What happens if the modern world collapses and there are no more supermarkets? How would you eat? If you were dependent on them, you would die. They suggest a simple life is important. Instead of wanting more, we should want less. If something were lost, it would be no big deal. We would have no need for insurance or security, as there would be nothing to steal. Similar to a Buddhist, the Hopi claim the time formerly spent acquiring and wanting things could be now spent

---

[336] Mails pp.198, 208-09, 222, 231, 283, 326-27

with the people and planet we love. The Traditionalist Hopi know that the answers to our problems, or reasons for their occurrence are inside oneself. The ways, thoughts and desires of humans have caused the problems of the world. Without changing this pattern, the world will end. The key is to always put others first, as opposed to how we with our conscious minds put ourselves first. "Don't let the burden of worries trouble you into sickness. Let your hearts be filled with happiness and enjoy your lives to the fullest, for this is the best medicine for sickness. Live long, for there are great and exciting adventures awaiting you."[337]

The Hopi claim that only those who are spiritually strong will survive the passing of the fourth world age and the coming of the fifth. A set of instructions similar to these will need to be followed or we will no longer be upon the earth to be a part of the new world.

Flood Myths

As has been mentioned earlier in this book, mythology is the safest way to keep wisdom and knowledge alive. There are more than five hundred flood stories from around the world, and most include fire, periods of darkness and changing of the heavens. In many cultures it signaled the end of the last great world age. In the myths certain people were warned prior to the flood. They either built a ship and landed on a mountain or climbed a tall tree. The story of Noah is the best known today in the Western World but it is in fact is identical to the older Sumerian tale of Utnapishtim from 3,000 BC. In most of the stories it is God who has decided that mankind has become too wicked and needs to be destroyed. This does not at all sound like the loving and caring Creator we are told to believe. The Sumerian story relates that when the flood happened it "turned into darkness all that was light." Why would a loving Creator turn light into darkness?[338]

The Gnostics claim the God of the Old Testament is not the true Creator, but an evil one. They claim that prior to the flood mankind was on the verge of great wisdom and needed to be stalled. The evil god of the Old Testament was the one who tried to destroy the world. It was the true God that whispered into a few humans' ears (as intuition or Gnosis) of what was to come. In the Inca myth of Peru it was the llama that warned the Noah-like hero after watching the sky at night. Shamans in Peru are known as the llama. In other words it was the wise shamans watching the sky that warned of great upheaval in the world.[339]

The most well known myths usually have common information of a hero who rode out the flood in an ark, which has always been taken literally to

---

[337] Mails pp. 176-77, 197, 237, 342, 368
[338] Hancock *Fingerprints* p. 194; Hancock *Heaven's* p. 211; Santilliana p. 297
[339] Sullivan p.16-17

444

mean a boat. However the word Ark comes from Sanskrit Argha, which means light. The Hopi claim their set of instructions are a spiritual ark. The Egyptian solar boats were representations of the individual. The Sumerian story has the hero tear down his house and dispose of all worldly goods prior to building the ark.[340] To tear down one's house is to completely examine themselves, purify and throw away all that is negative. To dispose of all worldly goods can be taken as meaning to break away from reliance on the physical, material world. To build an ark can be another way to refer to building a personal house of spiritual light. The Ark of the Covenant was never seen as a boat, and perhaps the flood myth is telling us something very specific. When a person of wisdom is able to read the sky and know of coming changes, they are to work hard at purifying themselves. They are then to build themselves as "Light" as this 'spiritual ark' is what will actually save one from the flood. Perhaps the physical body is turned into light and waits in another dimension until the earth settles down again.

Ice Age

Over 12,000 years ago the earth was inundated with massive flooding, the result of the melting of the last ice age. Understanding the effects of the last ice age may help us to prepare for what may be coming. The last ice age, referred to as Wisconsin because the ice pushed as far south as that state, occurred between 115,000 -15,000 BC. Around 15,000 BC something happened that caused the billions of tons of ice to quickly melt. Scientists are unsure exactly what caused the melting to begin. With the melting came devastating earthquakes and volcanoes caused by the earth's crust rebounding from the previous weight of the ice. By 8,000 BC the glacial period had ended and our more moderate climates were established.

A problem with the period is that not everywhere on the planet saw melting during the warming, some saw rapid freezing. Alaska and Siberia were temperate climates containing animals like the mammoth, lion, rhino and specific plants and trees that could not survive in a cold place. This was the first clue something about the earth during that time was odd. The farther north one goes it should be colder, not warmer. The second was that the animals, especially Mammoth, that were found years later had been frozen instantly. Inside the Mammoth stomachs were undigested berries, buttercups and grasses. Thus the Mammoths were living in a temperate climate, able to eat temperate food and then were frozen instantly.[341]

During the height of the ice age the world's sea levels were four hundred feet lower as most of the excess water was in the form of ice at the poles. The lower sea levels created increased land areas such as the now

---

[340] Norville pp.77-78; Hancock *Fingerprints* p.189; Mails p.226
[341] Hancock *Fingerprints* pp. 210-20

submerged Berring Strait land bridge. The melting was very quick and sea levels rose quickly, submerging areas of the world. Modern historians have always claimed that this period was a period when humans were still living as unevolved savages, but were they?

Hapgood

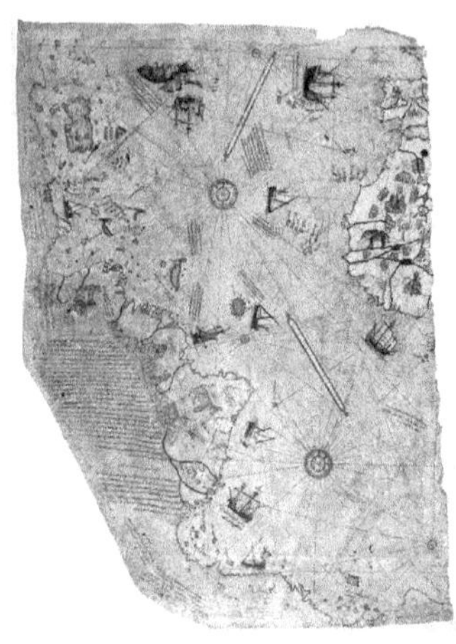

181:The Piri Reis map that began a controversy of how Antarctica could have been mapped in 1513.

A man named Charles Hapgood believed he found the answer to what really happened at the end of the last ice age. He called it a Pole Shift. His research in the 1960's, seconded by Albert Einstein, was controversial geological theory, and was arrived at from discovering and examining some very old maps. He claimed that these maps not only explained the hows and whys of the last ice age, the upcoming similar age, but also that humans were far more advanced in the past than archaeologists and anthropologists believe.

One known as the Piri Reis map of 1513 accurately depicts the coastline of Antarctica. The US airforce in the 1960's had no idea how a map could have been made of an area covered by three miles of ice that can only be mapped today with sophisticated radar. The unknown creator of the map claimed it was a copy from an older map. Hapgood found other maps like one by Finaeus in 1531 that showed not only Antarctica but also its rivers and mountains now covered by ice. The Philippe Buache map of the 18th century shows Antarctica when there was no ice at all. It is depicted as two islands. The air force confirmed that actually Antarctica is two islands, but it is depicted as a solid mass on modern maps as a convenience.

Hapgood found other 14-16th century maps that show accurate depictions of the Caribbean, the St. Lawrence, the land bridge of the Bering Strait (that has not existed for 12,000 years) and islands that would have existed prior to the melting. All the maps claim to be copies of maps made long ago. Hapgood wondered if the voyages by men like Columbus in the 14th and 15th century were actually made in order to prove or disprove some of the ancient maps.[342] Perhaps the reason Columbus was able to 'find' so many places was not that he was lucky, but that he had a perfect map.

It was Antarctica that was the key. Conventional wisdom has said that Antarctica was been covered by ice for millions of years. That is not true. Hapgood established that Antarctica was free of ice in 13,000 BC and slowly began to gain the ice that now exists by 4,000 BC. Science confirms that silt layers caused by running water were deposited as late as 6,000 BC. Further in the past scientists found deciduous trees and tropical flora and fauna. The North Pole has fossilized palm trees and tropical marine creatures. Thus the areas we think were always covered with ice were not. For some areas the change of climate happened less than 10,000 years ago. Thus the 15th century maps were showing the landscape of the world that was not even known to exist, and from a time when it was free of ice.[343]

Accurate mapmaking requires trigonometry and geometry which suggests a highly developed civilization sometime prior to 4,000 BC. The maps prove that there was a time when humans knew and explored Antarctica was not covered with ice, because it was mapped. This led to a couple of conclusions for Hapgood. The first was that someone had to have tremendous knowledge at the time to be able to do the mapping, but something happened to this civilization and became 'lost.' Secondly, something had to cause places like Antarctica and Alaska which were temperate, to get cold very quickly.

Pole Shifts

Hapgood believes that the ending of the last ice age was what caused by what he calls a pole shift. He did not believe that the earth itself moved or rotated, only the crust. Geologists claim that the earth is made up of a number of plates that are in constant motion on top of a molten layer. Along with the pressure of the weight of ice at the poles squeezing down on the earth, Hapgood claimed that the inner core of the earth (which moves faster than the rest of the earth) when under pressure may cause the tectonic plates to slip, and quickly move. He believes the last time a pole shift occurred was around 10, 500 BC, when Antarctica was two thousand miles north of where it is today, and moved south to the Antarctic Circle by the shift. The crust moved in a curve-like manner, which could help to explain how Alaska and Yukon were free of ice while Ontario was covered, when the North Pole was at Hudson Bay. The movement of the earth was so fast that places may have moved hundreds of miles in minutes. This was the reason the animals were frozen so fast. The sky would appear to fall due to the continents moving quickly. No one would think that they could be the ones moving, thus it must be the sky. Chicken Little

---

[342] Hapgood, Charles *Maps of the Ancient Sea Kings* (Dutton 1979) pp. 7-11, 35, 40, 58, 82-83, 93; Hancock *Fingerprints* pp. 3-4, 14, 23-25
[343] Hancock *Fingerprints* pp.4, 476-79

worrying about the sky falling may have well been correct. Glacial zones would quickly begin to melt in the new warm climates. If it happened today, much of our coastal civilization would be flooded, forcing life to move to the mountains until the waters subsided, echoing the Noah Biblical story.[344]

He felt the weight of ice at the poles will eventually cause another shift of the earth's crust. Currently Antarctica is covered by seven million cubic miles of ice weighing ten quadrillion tons (10 followed by 15 zeros). Modern science is now refuting Hapgood's ideas. That does not mean he is wrong. In the 1950's an anthropologist from the Natural Museum of Canada, Thomas Lee, located a site on an island in Lake Huron that could have re-written history. Ancient human remains were discovered at a depth that over one hundred geologists claimed was between 65-125,000 years ago. Unfortunately orthodox dating claimed humans did not arrive in North America until 15,000 years ago across the famous Bering Strait land bridge. No matter what the geologists said, to standard anthropolgists, the site had to be wrong. However instead of investigating, other anthropologists had Lee discredited and fired, with the site covered over to build a resort so no further examination could be made.[345] This is not the only such site where similar things have happened.

Other Earth Theories

182: Pangaea, the geologic time when all land masses were joined in one super continent, about 250 million years ago

Of course this pole shift theory- as it is explained, requires that we agree with science and geology that the earth is made up of moving plates. It is the standard explanation for how mountains are formed, what volcanoes are, large growing rifts in the Pacific and Atlantic Oceans- and attempts to explain the odd occurrence millions of years ago when all of the land on earth was joined in one super-continent called Pangaea. If you take an atlas and cut out all the land masses, you will find that they fit together perfectly. No geologist has ever really explained the "lucky" coincidence that all the moving plates just happened to join together like a glove. That pole shifts and pole reversals seem to have occurred is highly

---

[344] Hancock *Heaven's* p.211,462, 468, 471

[345] Hancock *Fingerprints* p.480; Baigent *Ancient* pp.104-6

likely. However, a recent theory has come along with gives an odd twist to standard geology and pole shifts. A growing earth.

In brief, this new theory holds that the original earth was much smaller than today, and there were no oceans surrounding Pangaea. Pangaea was not a the lucky movement of all the plates of the earth together, there were no plates and no movement. Just one solid land mass, with several interior lakes, no oceans and a uniform tropical climate. Then an event took place that caused the earth's interior to start swelling, like putting pressure from the inside of a tennis ball, began to crack and expand to make room for what was being created in the interior. These cracks became what we now call plates and continents- broken pieces of Pangaea. The "plates" continue to move because the earth is still expanding, growing larger- which can have all sorts of impact on everything from gravity to the speed of the rotation. A smaller earth was said to have a much warmer climate, and less gravity- which could explain how dinosaurs and other ancient creatures could grow so large. It also adds possible answers to how the ancients could move and place such large stones. No one has yet questioned that the effect of gravity might have been different in the past, thus the weight of a stone (comparatively) was less than it would be today. A standard part of most all spiritual teaching is that the earth is a living entity. Thus if the earth is a living entity- like a human, or tree, or grasshopper, then it should grow as time passes. A growing earth is a real possibility.

Another theory held by Brian Desborough is that a planet entered the solar system, and crashed into another planet. The crash created two remnants (modern Jupiter and Venus), while the debris of this collision became the asteroid belt (which no astronomer accurately explains). The appearance of Venus destroyed the atmosphere on Mars which caused it to no longer be habitable. Most of the photos of the recent Mars missions have been altered or classified to not show old civilized structures, the same as happened on original moon landings (not from the fake landing shown to the US public in 1969) where several buildings have been spotted. Thanks to the work of many people who have worked closely on the footage that has been released to the general public, they have found some strange things such as possible Egyptian statues on Mars. Venus continued to where it got caught by the earth's gravitational field for a while (as a moon) before being hurled out again finally settling into its current rotation around the sun. Prior to this event Mars and Earth were closer to the sun (both had warmer climates, and could help explain the climate necessary for the age of dinosaurs on earth, and showing that humans originally habitated Mars).

The earliest cultures on earth have no records for the planet Venus, the planet only appear in later accounts- and when it was finally put in, it was studied very very closely. Desborough says that Venus was an ice-coated comet after the collision, and that ice dissipated when Venus got near the earth and reached a point called the Roche Limit, the ice was projected from Venus to the Earth when it entered the Van Allen Belt (which absorbs most of the sun's radiation). The ice became magnetized, then attracted to the two magnetic poles of earth, and billions of tons of ice fell to the polar regions in an instant (which explained the odd instant freezing of mammoths and tigers). This is the counter argument for a pole shift to explain the quick freezing.

Another theory claims that the earth originally was encircled by a canopy of water vapor (the firmament of the Bible) that was destroyed in a cataclysm. The canopy protected the earth from the dangerous rays of the sun, and at that time the whole planet was moist, humid, and had a mostly constant temperature. According to this theory an alien race destroyed this canopy purposely, symbolized by the 40 days and nights of rain, dooming the climate of the earth where the sun could bake areas that were once totally fertile. At the same time these aliens blocked the natural human telepathic mind link, moved people all over the earth and gave them different languages so they could no longer communicate. Every culture has a Tower of Babel story. The reptiles then interbred with human women to make the race of half-breed blue bloods that they put in key positions of power, a group that rules right to this day.

Another theory to mention is the Hollow Earth theory, that either claims the Earth's interior is either an empty cavern, or an interior space that is habitated. Openings to this inner world are said to be found at the poles and at other locations on the earth (often where sites were built on top such as Giza and Tibet). As amazing as this is, this theory claims that the poles are not solid material at all, but giant openings into the inner earth. One of the scientific phenomena that might support this is the aurora borealis (northern lights, is a similar version in the south). The standard scientific theory for the lights is that energy particles coming from the sun collide with the Earth's magnetic field- and are transported to the poles where they reach the atmosphere and explode in a photon discharge. But many are suggesting that it is actually gas escaping from the interior of the earth through these holes at the poles- and light up when the hit the underside of the atmosphere, not the other way around. This is shown by the fact the aurora makes no sound (while all other electricity events in the atmosphere do) and that there is no effect on compass needles- which there should be if the aurora were an electrical phenomena. Some claim this inner earth has its own central sun, and is "the original Garden of Eden." Some such as Marshall Gardner, Admiral Byrd and Norwegian Olaf Jansen who all claimed to have gone to or seen the world "beyond the poles," one that is not ice cold- but warm and tropical.

Then again there is the possibility that those who study subjects like the Flat Earth might have some validity. We may not be on a planet at all, and such ideas of other planets, solar systems and what not might all be nothing but make believe. The problem is that if you have not been up there, at least over 75,000 feet, we have no direct knowledge of what the Earth actually looks like. All we have are the promises and suggestions of scientists from official organizations. Until we can verify it ourself, which is highly unlikely in our lifetime, we have to stay open. It is easy to manipulate any image so just because we are shown a picture does not make it true unless we can see it as well. Ideas of gravity, curvature, the distance of the sun might all be just a lie. I am writing all this section not to get you to agree with anything, but just examine how little we actually directly know about the very thing we place our feat upon every day, the Earth. It is actually a giant mystery.

The Corpus Hermeticum recalls a time when Egypt fell away and darkness was preferred to light. Researchers like Graham Hancock and John Anthony West believe that a great civilization existed prior to the ice age. In 10,500 BC, during the Age of Leo, a great pole shift (or other great disaster) happened to cause most of the settlements to be totally destroyed. When the flooding ended the survivors wanted to create specific monuments and myths to tell humans in the future of what had happened, what was likely to happen again, and what one needed to look for to signal its return.

To the Egyptians, the hieroglyphs of Tehuti kept alive the wisdom before the flood, as recorded in such Hermetic texts as "The Virgin of the World." This knowledge is said to remain hidden until one is pure enough of heart to be able to find them, "those with true aspiration, honesty and reverence."[346] Places like Giza are said to be markers of the last age, perhaps why a sphinx shaped like a lion appears there, as a warning marker from the Age of Leo.

The Egyptians kept many myths and tales alive about a time before the flood. The Greek ideas of Atlantis are copies of tales related to them by the Egyptians. The tomb of Seti 1 recounts that humanity was destroyed in a great flood. The first Hermes (Tehuti before the flood) used a language the second Hermes could no longer speak. John Greaves wrote of an ancient Egyptian tale whereby the earth turned over, the sky fell and the wise men were warned of a great flood. Pyramids were built to be stored with all of the ancient knowledge and "all may be interpreted by him that knows this character and language."[347] These stories and information were passed on to the numerous flood myths that are kept all over the world.

What this section was to try and not accept any theory of the ancient past or of the earth too quickly- for to possibly predict the future, one must have a good understanding of the past- and has just been demonstrated, for all the

---

[346] Ashby Ausarian p.87
[347] Mead, p.106; Hancock *Fingerprints* p. 197; Hancock *Heaven's* p. 319

scientific knowledge available today, we are really not too sure about anything. It is with that inquiring mind that I would like to take us to a topic that is more coming to everyone's consciousness, the Mayan calendar of 2012.

Akhenaten

171:Statue of the "Heretic Pharaoh" Akhenaten in the Cairo Museum

"A lie told often enough will become the truth" Lenin

One of the most bizarre periods of Egyptian history was that of the Pharaoh Akhenaten, whose son (or brother, depending on the story), Tutankhamun got a lot of press based on his incredible burial. In my view, the "treasures" buried with Tutankhamun are actually unique to Egyptian Pharaohs, the treasures not even "his," and it all links back to Akhenaten. What is more amazing is that even though dead for 3500 years, Akhenaten and Tutankhamun could be playing a big role in the unfolding of events in the last century.

Who or what Akhenaten was is very much up to debate, for he does not fit the mold of any Egyptian Pharaoh before or after. Originally born Amenhotep IV (to father Amenhotep III and mother Queen Tyi) he was second in line for the Pharaoh-ship. After the death (or disappearance- exile) of his older brother Thutmosis- Amenhotep became the successor to his father. What is known is that he ruled through the bloodline woman he married Nefertiti, moved the capital to a previously unused location (modern Tell El Amarna), and began to dismantle the old temple tradition of Egypt changing the religion to Aten- the sun disk. It is possible he was linked to Sumeria, and was attempting "by political means" to take over Egypt.

He did away with all the old gods of Egypt placing first the sun disk, and then himself, as the only thing that could be worshiped. The only blessings that anyone could receive could only come from the Royal Family. No longer could people even have their own personal alters in their homes, only figurines of Akhenaten and his family were allowed. Osiris was no longer the god of the afterlife, Akhenaten now took that role, and as such the old funnery texts such as the *Book of What is in the Duat* or the *Book of the Dead*, were abandoned. His new temples were the opposite of the old ones, where instead of the inner sanctuaries being in dark enclosed spaces (to represent our True Mind) these new temples had the inner chambers without roofs- bathed in sunlight. The artwork of this period is most unique, as now Akhenaten and his family are shown with – full lips, snake eyes, long necks, paunch bellies, swollen hips and thighs, and often as combined two sexes. This period lasted somewhere around ten years when Akhenaten and his reign was ended and he and his followers were forced to flee Egypt. The Moses story that found its way into the Old Testament may be related to the time of Akhenaten. The Moses myth either relates of the Egyptian priesthood forced out of the country by Akhenaten takeover, or the more likely, the escape of the remainder of Akhenaten's followers fleeing back "home" to Sumeria and Babylon. Akhenaten's tomb was found near Tel-El-Amarna, but his mummified body is supposedly still not located, at least that is how the standard historical story goes.

Queen Nefertiti, Akhenaten's famous wife, is also connected to this odd story of history. The famous statue of her is kept in Berlin, and was so captivating to Adolf Hitler that he would go and stare at if for hours claiming his German leadership was somehow connected to the statue. However new evidence seems to indicate that this statue is actually an early 20th century fake, modeled on the wife of the German archaeologist who claimed to have found it I 1912, Ludwig Borchardt. The claim is that it was made by him, not to fool anyone, but to test ancient pigment colours to learn what the Egyptians used. A

Prussian prince saw it and fell in love with the statue, and Borchardt then decided to pretend it was real and keep his important guest happy. . Several art forgers have revealed that the very techniques that they use to create fake statues can be found on this statue.

173:The almost haunting statue of Nefertiti at the Berlin Museum.

Tutankhamun

174:Famous gold mask from tomb of Tutankhamun, Cairo Museum

With Akhenaten gone, Tutankhamun was put on the throne (after short lived Smenkhkare). The treasures that are found in Tut's tomb I do not believe are his, but those of the previous Pharaoh Akhenaten. So the first question is why? Why bury with the body of Tutankhamun the treasures of someone else. And the second question is, why if every other tomb in the valley was robbed, why would this one with such wonderful treasures not be touched? After watching a BBC documentary about the finding of the tomb by Howard Carter a new theory began to come into my mind. Perhaps all of those magnificent objects of Akhenaten were placed into Tutankhamun's tomb not for for the burial- but to lock in it- like a safe. As long as they were magically kept in that tomb, then what those objects contained would be sealed. That would explain why it was basically the only tomb in the Valley of the Kings not robbed. NO ONE, not even tomb robbers, were stupid enough to release Akhenaten back into their world after all they had just gone through in his rule, even for all the gold in there.

The story of Howard Carter's find in 1922 does not stand up to investigation, and when studied closely appears to be an outright lie. The tomb showed signs of forced entry and resealing, something highly unlikely to have

454

been done by the builders. Tomb robbers would have not broke in, stole nothing, and sealed it back up. Supposedly Carter began searching for Tut's tomb in 1914, gridded the valley, and searching grid by grid - only at the last moment, in the last square in 1922 just as money was running out, to find the tomb. That makes for a very romantic story anyway. However canopic jars and objects clearly belonging to the burial of Tutankhamun were found in 1910 very close to where the actual tomb was. If you were looking for a tomb, found burial jars from the person you were looking for- of course you would have looked in that area first. You would not look everywhere else, and saved that final area for ten or twenty years later. That tiny discrepancy in the story was enough to begin to get a better idea of what actually took place.

Likely Carter and his money funder Lord Carnarvon found the tomb right away in 1914, then spent eight years digging in the valley to make it look like they were still searching, while they had the time and solitude to examine and plunder what they wanted. When their plundering was complete in 1922, they pretended to "find" the tomb. Thus it makes you wonder what they may have taken out before and how important and valuable it was. The dates become important to this story as well. Assuming the tomb was found right at the beginning of digging, it would have been found and entered in 1914 (when World War 1 began that set up the chain of modern giant wars, and the financial and commercial changes known as central banks and income tax). The tomb was "opened publicly" on November 4, 1922 and the burial chamber entered on February 16, 1923 (right during Hitler's rise to power in the German Worker's Party). And these events happening at these dates I do not think are simple co-incidence.

Carnarvon died six weeks after the tomb was "opened" in 1922 leading to speculation of a curse. Newspapers continued to report in the 1920's of odd deaths of those involved with the tomb opening. Some have claimed that the deaths were in fact murders to keep people quiet about what Carter and Carnarvon had been doing, and this is also a possibility given that a 1914 finding of such a tomb must have been very hard to keep quiet around Luxor. Perhaps the so called Curse of Tutankhamun was not actually about the people involved in the tomb opening, but was a bigger message. It could be that the Egyptians were not simply burying a pharaoh, they were actually burying objects and energy to try and seal away for eternity. Those objects were safe in the tomb, under a sort of magical spell or controlled energy, but once the tomb was opened- the energy that was held in those objects was free for release.

Please note, that after this book was revised more recent information on King Tut was brought forth. It shows that this tomb is not even a tomb for a male at all, the paint on the walls is the only tomb with fungus growing (due to not enough drying time), and the body is really likely that of crown prince Tuthmose who died several years prior to Tutankhamun. As such the whole story around this is likely a hoax, all created by Carter (see my site egyptian-wisdom-revealed.com for an updated article on the lies of the tomb of Tutankhamun).

The Mayan Calendar

183:Pyramid of Kukulkan (Quetzalcoatl), Chichen Itza

Originally this section appeared with all sorts of detail on the Maya calendar and what many believed would come in 2012. Of course many writers (no double looking to garner book sales with their doom porn) wrote endlessly of the end times in December 2012. When no great cataclysm came, all of this was forgotten. And while I have taken out the information about the calendar and 2012, I do not want to just let it be too quickly. That is because I fully believe that something in fact did happen during that time frame, a great shift did happen- but the shift was not a physical shift. It was an energetic or vibration shift. If everyone really cares to look, almost all I ask do notice that life in some way is quite different now since before 2012. Some talk of how the sun looks different or rises in a different place in the sky, others how they became tired or sick for no reason, others that challenges have come, still others that the world seems more strange and crazy than ever before.

I leave that out to you here, and it is a subject that I will return to in future writings.

Crystal Skulls

185: Picture taken of a worker in what is being called Mexico's "Crystal Cave of Giants"

Another prophecy of Central America has been passed down about this period, and that revolves around the twelve crystal skulls. These objects, claimed to have been made long before the Maya and Toltec, and relate to what will happen in 2012. Twelve skulls were created with the purpose of being sent around the world to be hidden and cared for. At a key moment, the 12 skulls would be brought together, and placed around a larger thirteenth skull. This would cause some sort of power source to open, some sort of storehouse of wisdom to be opened for the entire planet.

If there really are twelve skulls, only a few are publicly known to exist. The most famous is the Mitchell Hedges Skull, said to have been found deep underground a Mayan temple in the 1920's. Others are in the British Museum and in Paris. The scientific community has labeled the skulls of modern origin, due to finding specific modern rotary tool marks upon them. They claim that the ancient people's of Mexico did not have modern tools or technology available to have made the marks, thus the skulls must be modern fakes. But that takes us right back to where this book began, the idea that the ancients were inferior to us, thus anything that shows a hint of something modern means it could not be from the ancient world. In the last decade a most spectacular geologic site called the Cave of the Crystals in Mexico, had its photographs displayed for the world. Here the largest known crystals on earth are found. The photo is not an exaggeration or something on photoshop. If an ancient society also found this cave, or one like it, who is to say that the skulls do not come from this very crystal?

Personally I have only come face to face with the skull in the British Museum. I stared at it for perhaps an hour. Hundreds of museum visitors passed by as my gaze was locked on the skull. It seemed so un-earthly, almost un-human. And within that crystal appears to be something of tremendous power and force. I can not verify for sure of course if the myth of the crystal skulls and their need to come together is true, but I can say after seeing a skull close up, it is a definite possibility for unraveling the 2012 mystery.[348]

------

[348] After a long session at a stone circle in Sweden, my night dream showed me that life on earth might be an experiment of sorts, and that "we" as form really are what shamans call 'shadows.' The experiment is not for some sort of learning or growth for us- in the same way scientists are not injecting rats with cancer cells for the rat's spiritual evolution. They are test subjects to be used as wanted. The dream pointed to the possibility that just like in a dream where there is an artificial "us" sleeping on a bed somewhere, there is a copy projection of our body- mind that goes into the dream world. This world and body and mind that we are deeming to be real may be nothing but a shadow projection of something that is real. Same as a hologram where the image projected is a the hologram, but there is an actual image it was copied from. That could explain Castaneda's cryptic message of a debt in life experiences having to be paid. That the source that created this shadow dream world did it as a test (why so many awful things happen here, for they are testing how the virtual reality characters "us" will respond to the bizarre stimuli). Like rats in a science lab, were are only there for data collection. Just as a the rat could leave when the scientist had collected all the needed data- perhaps by sending our life experiences to the eagle- or moon, that serves the debt to the science experiment- and it can then end, and the holographic shadow image of us can fade away as the original image the hologram copied can awake on its bed free of the sleeping test nightmare of reality. This might be the idea that Castaneda, and Gurdjieff and Ouspensky were symbolically hinting at in their writings.

"Things on earth are like a portrait, the picture has features, but they are false, tricking the sight of the beholders. Those thinking what they see what's true, while what they see is really false...all those who don't see what's false, see truth." Stobias 3:2

Time

186: Aztec Calendar Stone often mistaken to be Mayan or specifically relating to the 2012 end time- Mexico City Museum of Anthropology

The end of the Mayan Calendar is normally interpreted as one of two possibilities. The doomsday side claims it is showing the date of an apocalyptic catastrophe. Those who support this interpretation usually show what they call the Mayan calendar in their books or on their web sites. This calendar, with a figure in the middle supposingly licking up the blood of the dead is not Mayan. This is the Aztec Calendar Stone (found in the Museum of Anthropology in Mexico City). While descended from the Maya, it does not mean that the Aztec calendar were showing things accurately, or that the Aztecs themselves understood the deep mystical explanations of the Maya. The New Age side sees the Maya referring to the 2012 date as a mass awakening, a time of expanding consciousness when all evil in the world will be banished and only good and light will be left. But most importantly, what did the Maya have to say? And interestingly, not that much, The Mayan Calendar (such as found on Stela C at Tres Zapotes) is not indicating there will be an apocalyptic destruction, nor an awakening in consciousness. What they say is that at 13 Baktun (December 21, 2012), time will end, or to be more accurate- there will be no more time.

This ambiguous statement of no more time is one of the things that has been able to cause so much varied interpretation. What does time actually mean? What does no more time mean? On one hand it can sound like a destruction of all, because currently we base ourselves, our experiences and our hopes- on time. Without time it would be easy for the mind to speculate that there is no more life. On the other hand, no more time could be seen as some sort of endless "now" moment where the separation that time creates between past, present and future would be gone. And the now is getting a lot of good press from many authors leading many to speculate the Maya's no time is a utopia.

One thing the Maya claimed about the end of this cycle was that the final 52 year calendar round (1960-2012 AD), was a period they referred to as "No Time," where time go faster and faster, until time ceased to exist. It may be likened to a spinning top, before it stops and falls, it needs to be re-spun- give it another "twist." Have you been paying attention to time the last 10-20 years? Where is time going you might ask. Where did the day go? What you think takes you thirty minutes, takes an hour. This does not seem to be a simple case of relativity but a real case of there actually being fewer real minutes in a day. Activities that I know should take me an hour are still being done three hours later. Something regarding time currently is just not right.

The earth has a pulse called the Schumann Resonance, which has been 7.83 cycles per second for a long time. Since 1980, the pulse has been going up and currently is around 12 cycles per second. What that means is that we now have the equivalent of 16 "old" pre-1980 hours in our current day. Our clock is still marking time as 60 minutes per hour, but in the dimension of actual time there may be only 40. The reason you feel so stressed and time consumed is because we are still trying to fit the same number of activities into our day when "relatively" there is less of it. Time itself only exists in this realm, but when we focus our attention on this world we are subject to it. It is not actually time that is speeding up, but the speed that manifestation is happening. It appears to us as faster time, but that was a warning sign of the Maya.

Time and space are related, why astrophysicists often use the hyphened word space-time. If you refer to one, you are automatically referring to the other. If time speeds it up, space will shrink. If I drive a car at 60 miles per hour, it takes me 1 hour to get from A to B if the distance is 60 miles. But if I drive 120 miles per hour (increase speed) the distance between A and B (still 60 actual miles) is relatively "less," and the drive is now 30 minutes (space has shrunk, as time has increased). This shrinking of space and speeding of time can be noticed through technology. By charting the increase of technology and its effects, say over the last 500 years, we can chart the "speed" of time. For example, the telephone shrank time (a message moves across a city in seconds rather than hours) thus shrank space (two distant cities were now closer for messages). Trains, airplanes, computers, you name it, and the history of technological advancement is really the history of time-space. As technology shrank space, time would speed up, and vice versa. The last decade- with the amazing explosion of new technology is also mirroring the fastest speeding up of time. The Maya calendar's prophecy that time since 3114 BC would be going exponential faster. In 3110 BC the difference in the speed of time since 3114BC would be negligible, while by now the difference in "actual" time must be vast. Could a person who lived 25 "earth years" in 30000 BC, had the equivalent of perhaps 250 "modern years" in length? That could explain why so much could be done in the past with so little "time?"

This last fifty-two year calendar round of this Baktun cycle, ending in 2012, would have begun in 1960. The last calendar round might need to create a wake up call to warn humans to prepare for what is ahead. Isn't that exactly what began in the 1960's? A time of free love, peace, interest in native and Oriental traditions, and of alternate levels of consciousness, drug journeys, an examination of society and civilization, government, war and the commerce system.. Perhaps some type of energy was released to the earth, perhaps by the ancient Maya themselves, to give humans one last chance for personal growth and change before it is too late. The year 2012 seems to be a long way away… but is it?

Time Loops

187: The alchemic ouroborus, serpent eating its own tail- possible reference to the looping nature of time

One of the most interesting things about the Maya, or any ancient civilization, is why they seemed to care so much about a time frame thousands of years in the future. Why were the Hopi willing to pass information orally generation after generation, or the Egyptians construct massive pyramid monuments, or the Hindu record huge passages of history- for a time when they would be long gone? No archaeologist, philosopher or spiritual teacher has answered that question adequately. But perhaps this question helps to unravel what the Mayan Calendar was really pointing to in the year 2012. That time is not linear as we are led to believe.

The Maya may not have been pointing towards some sort destruction/ catastrophe, or a global awakening. The Maya viewed time to watch for repeating patterns, and cyclic events. It is very highly probable that what they were actually marking was something so crazy to modern thinking as to go overlooked. They were marking a time loop, one that began in 3114 BC ending in 2012 AD. Thus the end of time is reaching the end of the circle to start over at the beginning again. If true that would mean that the day following December 21, 2012 would not be December 22, 2012, but August 13, 3114 BC. Thus the end of the Mayan Calendar may be indicating a RESET, back to an earlier point in time, similar to the trials faced by Phil Connors in the movie *Groundhog Day*, or the main characters of the Ken Grimwood novel *Replay*. These two fictional works might be touching more to the way reality actually is than many believe. This idea can be found in ancient mythology in the myth of Sisyphus, who must continually roll a rock up a hill. The rock symbolized the block of the mind, the mountain to reach enlightenment- which never happens. Another myth is that of Prometheus who after stealing fire for humans was punished with having an eagle (there is that symbol again) eating out his liver each day, only to have it regrown and have the cycle continue. This only stops until Hercules (the Greek Horus) could rescue him. This idea also finds its way into philosophy into the works of Schopenhauer and Nietzsche who called it Eternal Return. This concept postulates that the universe has been recurring and will continue to recur in a similar form for an infinite number of times.

This revelation would mean that each of us has lived our life, as it is, millions or perhaps billions of times over. Not necessarily in some sort of reincarnating form (which requires the idea of past and future influenced by each other), but perhaps instead constantly repeating the same period of time, like a movie encoded onto a DVD. 2012 would just be when the DVD skips back to the beginning to play the movie again. However like a mobeus strip, several movies could be on a DVD- looping between them. Recall that to the Inca a new world age was called a pacha-kuti, means and overturning of space-time, which could be a good definition of a loop. In this explanation there could be past lives on the DVD, but unlike the Buddhist idea of karma, they are not related to each other in any way that can effect each other- as the actions of a character in one movie on a DVD can not impact on the character of a different movie.

The standard view of death is that once dead, consciousness of the deceased person leaves this realm either for some eternal resting place, or is reincarnated back into the ongoing linear timeline, or exists in a limbo world where interaction is possible, or simply vanishes. Yet one other possibility gives insights that may help explain this ancient dilemma. The idea that consciousness will loop and return to the very same body, in the very same life. It could help explain why the "spirit" of the dead can still be communicated with (for where does one go in a loop, just remaining in the hologram). Thus ghosts, or visions of past and future- are just ways touching a looping holographic dreamworld where everything is here and not here, at the same moment. It is possible that the ancient shamans began to notice an odd-looping "deja vu" type phenomena and then set up a particular system in order to study it. To keep their consciousness to remain stable after their death, to watch time as it flowed after their death. All that matters is whether one awakes as a baby with the "drink of forgetfulness," as most do- or if consciousness could be kept aware upon their rebirth, remember the previous loop. Perhaps a way to do this was created. To keep their consciousness awake through several of the loops, able to see and remember the circular loop, to see like the main street in the movie Pleasantville, where the end has simply become the beginning.

Knowledge that time and existence was a loop would literally extinguish all attempts at self-development, improvement, spirituality, fixing anything- for what can be fixed in a loop, how can a DVD movie be altered? All the famous spiritual work from being in the now, to meditation, to compassion- would be seen as further entrapments of the loop itself. To have kept consciousness awake through several of these cycles would lead to some conclusions that perhaps only two things could happen. One is to keep looping, living the same life (or lives) exactly as occurred again and again, or attempt to do something to change that loop. Thus much like the teachings of the few modern remaining actual Zen masters, all that matters is awakening, everything else is a game. All is vanity. That leads to questions. Why is there a loop? Was time always a loop? If not when did it begin? Why do I have knowledge of it when others do not? Can it be stopped or altered? And this is where the ancients seemingly great future focus may have arisen. My new book will examine all of this in detail.

It is possible that these shamans saw that the only "time" that change to to the loop could happen would be at the switch point- 2012 AD. Psychics view of the future generally mirror the beliefs most have about the Mayan Calendar- one a future of chaos and destruction (end times, apocalypse) and the other a consciousness raising utopia (vibrational shift). I believe that both could possibly be correct. The standard loop might need a great amount of chaos and destruction to make time jump the record groove and break the forces that hold it in place, but doing so would in fact lead to a new vibrational existence for everything. However the main opposing force- Apop/egoic mind, has as its main job keeping things in place to have the CD skip back to the beginning and start everything all over again. No apocalypse, no vibrational shift- just Phil Connors seeing Ned Ryerson on the street one more time.

This understanding could mean that the only way any individual could be free (even when reaching the supposed highest level of enlightenment) was for the loop to be turned off at the switch point. Everything jumps the loop, or nothing does. No awakening, enlightenment, moral perfection, purification, wisdom- would have any real significance if the loop resets and all starts again. Hence the only thing that could seem of value to someone who will die before the end point was to try and pass on to the next generation what they knew, the secrets of the loop. They could try and display the mathematic-geometric timing of the loop, make future prophecy to make those wonder "how could they know the future," reveal how the loop and illusion is being manifested and created from within and without, or provide the insights of what to do at the end to jump the groove. If they could just escape the loop individually, they would have done so and not focused much on those in the future- but they did focus in great detail on those who would follow (us), which indicates that they must have seen some great need for those in the future to act for them. Everything goes, or nothing goes. The Gnostics, echoed by Carlos Castaneda, set themselves up in groups called cells- made up of 16 or 21 people. They claimed that it was only in group form could any individual make it completely out of bondage to the dreamstate. (Appendix 5 has a dream vision that relates to loops, nature, and human origins).

It may explain the Egyptian practice of mummification, which might have originally been used as a way to preserve the body, not for some eternal happy afterlife in the Field of Rushes (as it became) but could have been a trick to keep conscious awareness after death (perhaps if the body does not rot, consciousness stays to view the rest of the timeline), and could be "brought through" the loop. Thus those properly mummified could bring that knowledge back into their next loop to provide more insights, information and ideas about the nature of reality, the loop and what to try (for they would have seen what was tried the last time didn't work, for they again looped.) Egypt was not the only ones to mummify, and the farther back in time one goes, the more cultures are found to have been mummifying their bodies. Why go to such trouble, if as is currently believed about life-death in modern religion that once done with the body, we are done with this world. If anything, the practices of the ancients, their massive stone building projects and their need to pass on information of large stretches of time, indicates that they were paying great attention to the future- which makes sense if their very own escape from the prison of egoic constraints was linked to the actions of those in the future at the switch point. The idea of a time loop is not something that is a big seller like a fear generating "headline grabbing" apocalypse, or the heart-warming, all is going to be a happy, full of love- consciousness shift. Back in the chapter on mathematics and number I mentioned that instead of this being a dual world like is always thought- there is a third force, a third way, a third understanding. Duality is the illusion, it is the third force, the third viewpoint that can show something else, something beyond duality.

CHAPTER 25

JUST PASS IT ON

188:Presentation of light

"Pleasure puts you to sleep and pain wakes you up. If you don't want to suffer, don't go to sleep." Nisargadatta Maharaj

The ancient world was full of secrets, but those were not secrets simply meant to remain hidden- the secrets were hidden to survive. They tried to understand the universe, and also to discover the best way to pass along what they had discovered. The mythology, temples, pyramids, tombs, texts, statues and everything else was all a part of that plan- their version of a timeless video camera. However the TV-player needed to "watch" the video is not external, but internal. Just knowing that something was left there for "us," and that we have a filter (egoic mind) that is keeping us from reading their messages, is all we really need to know to get started. Each part of the filter that is removed, reveals a bit more of what the ancients were trying to pass through time.

It truly was a message of hope they were leaving, not just for "us," but for themselves as well. It is no surprise that the great ancient explanation of the trap of reality is the cave analogy of Plato- who was trained in the last remaining Egyptian Mystery School temples. Understanding that all is one carries many different layers. One of those layers is- if there is any sort of confinement or delusion, it can not just be for one human, but all humans- all of creation is trapped. To their way of thinking, it was delusion to believe that one individual can escape confinement, while the rest stay behind within it. The trap of consciousness is so vast, ingenious, and yet at the same time simple- it is generally missed. Even someone who thinks they understand, probably doesn't (this author included). While we contain all within, we may need some help without to bring everything together so that creation as a whole can take its next step-whatever that may be. We have a part to play, it may seem small, but viewed from the completed puzzle- no individual part was any greater than the rest "no matter what the corners have to say."

All of the ancient cultures were telling us change is about to happen. Whether an apocalyptic event, a great shift in consciousness, or a re-set of a time loop- astronomical events in the sky would mark the timing of the change. Within each ancient myth was the idea that the only way for a person, group or a civilization as a whole to survive was to learn to live in the right way. To do so was to live in harmony with nature, the opposite of the way our modern world has developed which destroys the natural environment for our own individual gain. Living the right way was said to live from the heart.

The planet that we rely on for our life is in a desperate condition. Pollution, destruction of ecosystems and the loss of plant and animal life jeopardize the fabric and harmony of the earth. Water is unsuitable to drink, air is toxic to breathe and our food is poisonous. This damage is the result of the ways of humans. For two thousand years humans have followed the Judeo-Christian attitude that the earth is ours to use. With the reliance on money, that has meant using the earth in any way possible to get rich.

Worse is the untold devastation by warfare and killing. Even today, the sickening torture of people continues all over the world by others wanting control, power or wealth. Governments have stockpiled nuclear and biological weapons. Mind control and subliminal programming is being used to enslave populations. For two thousand years humans have been finding more and more ways to kill, harm and destroy each other. The light has been turning to darkness. Thankfully a few still exist to help warn us of the uselessness of these ways and to offer hope for the future.

Humanity is at a crossroads, and we as individuals and a species must decide to either live as we have for the last few thousand years, or to regain our true power. Do we really want to be the magical beings we were intended to be? The prophecies warn of untold disasters like glacial melting, nuclear war, meteor collusion and such. That is one scenario for the upcoming change, but the change could be more subtle than those who predict a great catastrophe. In fact it may not seem like much of a catastrophe at all. For example, what happen if all the molecules that made up steel no longer decided to be steel? They just dispersed, a possibility of physics. If steel no longer existed then every building would collapse, cars would not exist, and trucks to transport food and supplies to cities would be no more. Assuming grocery stores survived, the food supply would run out instantly. Think about it, all of your food is likely obtained from a store. If there were no more stores or trucks to bring food to the stores, do you have crops or the knowledge to hunt or fish? Without buildings there would be no water, electricity etc. Cities would turn into armed camps with those who had food and supplies and those who did not. Killing would likely occur on a great scale until handfuls of humans were left, realizing that they could not keep killing each other as they needed each other to survive. This scenario would match many of the visions that I have had over the years.

Instantly the new occupations of the world, real estate or banking would be useless. All that mattered now would be who could provide shelter, food, water, care for the young, creation of supplies, healing and wise people to relate to the earth and spirit. By beginning today to learn to live in a new way with spiritual understanding, and how to live with the earth will provide the ability to survive a new dangerous world. Learning to be self-sufficient would allow one to prepare for potential catastrophe. If you rely on the city for everything, what happens if there are no more cities? Only those who can live the ancient ways will be able to survive. The Hopi for example suggest starting to practice self-sufficiency and learn to depend on the ways of the modern world less. That way if that world no longer exists you will not quickly go with it.

I don't suggest go live in the woods and ignore the world. Simply learn the techniques that would be needed if a situation developed. Can you make a fire without matches, make fishing line from trees or know how to heal yourself without pills from a pharmacy? Don't be worried about what will happen in ten years, only try to live the best you can from where you are right now. Strive for Gnosis and wisdom, just be prepared as well for "what if." Even if the change is something more subtle than a catastrophe, learning to make shelter in the wilderness is never a bad skill to have.

Someone may suggest that if everything is going to go to hell why do anything positive? Become even more ruthless to get what you want because we won't be around long. I believe this attitude is seen lately in the upswing of violence, particularly with youth who instinctively may realize that time is nearly up. However, remember the ancients have said how we live today will affect the future. The world is only what we make it to be. The problems are not out there, they are in each one of us. Don't try to change the world, change yourself. The world is a reflection of our own being, thoughts and actions. By only trying to change the world, very little will change. Change happens one person at a time. Each person must want to change; they can not be forced. By gaining enough spiritual wisdom one can see the true reality and not be bound by this one.

We can learn to treat everything around us, from humans to rocks to the air as not only as equals but as interdependent partners. We need each other, more desperately than many may think. If we let them slip away, we will likely follow. Only through working with the ancient teachings and ways of understanding will one have the knowledge and wisdom available to survive most anything.

Some scientists claim that we are about to complete our circuit around the Pleiades by entering its photon belt. This they claim may create an explosion of particles that will produce vast amounts of light. This increase of high vibrational light could cause everything in our solar system to have to jump vibrations, thus everything on earth could be altered similar to the suggestions of this being a new period of transformation. This higher vibration would cause each of us to access previous unknown states of higher consciousness. For those who believe there will be such a shift, they recommend that what must be done is get our body-mind to a higher state of energetic vibration so that we will be able to match the shift that will come from the earth. Those that do not ready themselves for this, will be left behind in the previous world, or perhaps burnt up.

Then there is the time loop. This takes away all meaning of day to day life that we have come to believe (as mentioned by Zen and Advaita traditions) where all gains or loses in the reality we call real and affected by us, have nothing to do with us, but are scripted parts of a loop. And any gains will just vanish from existence at the end of the loop, recalling the old saying of material possessions and death, "you can't take em with you."

A most important philosophy for Richard Rose's was the concept of "just pass it on." Even if you haven't learned everything, pass along to someone else what you did learn that could be of help. You might say that these three volumes are an effort to do that, "pass on" what I discovered about the ancient world and their wisdom, presented through my own particular viewpoint. To me, the ancient world took one thing very seriously, though shrouded it in great humour and trickster ways: the secrets of reality and the egoic mind. They were clear that the ego was not naturally "human" or originally within this place of creation. Carlos Castaneda would call it, a "foreign installation"- a parasite, whose job was to suck us into a constant energetic stealing time loop. And once you examine the level of horrors that humans beings inflict on each other, between nations, within a community, within a family- the idea that it is being directed by a parasite becomes the only rational explanation for the bizarre behaviour. To the ancients this was the number one topic of investigation.

"This explains why it is so important for the mind vampires to keep their presence unknown, to drain the lifeblood without the person being aware of it. A person who defeats the mind vampires becomes doubly dangerous to them.... In such cases the vampires probably try to destroy him in another way, by trying to influence other people against him." Colin Wilson

The ancients had the goal of understanding the force, its origins, its methods, its effect on time-space- then "just pass it on." Perhaps the greatest text created to explain these topics was the Egyptian inspired Nag Hammadi Gnostic Codexes. Mostly thought of as writings of early Christians prior to the New Testament, in fact these writings are likely the closest link to the wisdom text of Egypt's Tehuti. My next book will use the Nag Hammadi texts as a key guide for unraveling the detail of what I have but touched upon in these three volumes.

They created carefully designed texts, built such structures as pyramids and giant earth works on the outer landscape (created with the building blocks of reality, sacred geometry and sacred mathematics) to combine them with mythological symbol based on timeless human archetypes of the inner landscape. Their hope was to bridge the body-mind of those who looked. If acted upon, the loop could be broken- and the next stage of being human would transpire, and all of humanity and nature, from all time periods, would be free. Or so went their thinking to my eyes. You will have to examine this information and think for yourself as to how much of this you choose to see as correct or not.

This started as a very spiritual book, but it is ending as a very un-spiritual book. When I began this exploration of ancient wisdom in the 1990's I wanted to know what they knew about reality. My perception of what they were pointing to has changed over the years, and the volumes in this book reflect that revision of thought. While some of this information can be unsettling, I want to offer hope, for whatever this upcoming event will be- it is neither a negative nor a positive (as that would be making a judgment based upon our dual world) but simply a challenge. While we are close to the end, its final blow will likely not happen tomorrow. We still have time, though not a great deal for the work each one of us must do. No matter what people like Buddha, Lao Tzu, Jesus or Catherine of Genoa became, they started out as flesh and blood humans just like you or I. Like Jed McKenna wrote, "If they could figure it out, maybe you too can figure it out. Maybe their message is not one about being supermen, but of that you can do it too."

The Maya date of December 21, 2012 is approaching. Even if the specific date is incorrect, all ancient prophecy is pointing to great change sometime in a near future. This entire book was based on one underlying principle- the Ancient Egyptians claimed that the nature of self and of reality could be discovered, and only having been invaded by a non-human parasitic mind has a veil been lifted over us. No longer can we see the wisdom of Isis and Tehuti because of it.

We are closing in on the last years before the prophesized great change. I don't believe that the "end of the world" is coming, but rather the end of time. The moment that the current cycle will be complete, and the loop will kick back, restart over again, exactly as it was. I for one can say that I am not interested to relive the junk of my life again, and I certainly do not want all those tortured and abused for generations to have to suffer through all of that again. The first task is to break free of the egoic mind- first in ourselves- and then perhaps assist those around us. This is not simple task. But to try and be free from it simply for ourselves is very selfish, thus egoistic and separate, thus actually re-enforcing the very thing we are trying to be free from. In a sense while there is only one, we are in that one together (even the very egoic mind we seek escape from), yet we appear to be separate and also need to proceed on that basis. Hard to explain, but just the way it seems to be.

We live in a holographic dream world of three dimensions. Yet there is also a fourth dimension that is of even more importance now. That dimension is time. Our usual experience of time is to view (see) it as it moves away from us, as if we are moving backwards and watching all experiences drift away. Even what we call the now is nothing but a very short seen microsecond of the past. The future is always behind us, unseen as we can only view the past. The great Toltec shift is to turn around and face time as it comes towards us (future) and the past stays behind to remain unseen. This shifting the focus from seeing the past to seeing the future is what our egoic mind fears. This shift is a place the ego can not go. Shift the focus and the future will not be some unknown blur of possibility, but like fast forwarding a DVD, it will easily be seen- making current navigation much easier.

Don Juan Matus said to Carlos Castaneda in *The Active Side of Infinity* "I am most careful about what I do and say with you or anybody else. The difference between you and me is that I don't have any time at all, and I act accordingly. You on the other hand believe you have all the time in the world, and you act accordingly."[349] Time to learn the secrets of personal transformation and understanding is lessening by the day.

Thank you for joining me on this walk through the previous 500 pages. Hopefully something within will have been of value to you in some way. The ancients were experimenters of the highest degree, Phil Connors glorified. Phil succeeded at the end of *Groundhog Day* and awoke to a new day. The question for us today, is can we?

---

[349] Castaneda, Carlos *Active Side of Infinity* (Harper Collins 1998)

APPENDIX

ALCHEMY

"I suppose that the same thing will happen to me, namely that I will suffer great difficulty, grief and weariness at first; but in the end shall come to glimpse pleasantries and easier things." Michael Maier

Nicholas Flamel (1330-1417) found a book with illustrations of a virgin being swallowed by snakes, crucified snakes and a wilderness region with fountains. He searched for years until an alchemist interpreted it for him. He became an alchemist himself- claimed to have been able to make silver, then gold form mercury. It was said that he became very wealthy and used his money to found hospitals, schools, churches and restored cemeteries. Of course, all alchemical stories are symbolic, even the story of the alchemists themselves.

Alchemy was symbolized as a process that involves the transmutation of base metal (lead) into gold. This of course was symbolic for the transmutation of human consciousness from a lead (ego based) to gold (integrated and unified). The different stages together make up what is called the "great work." It is a journey of dying and being reborn to a new identity. The word alchemy itself is subject to discussion about it's origin. The modern root, Al Kimia, is Arabic and is translated as the black art, or the the Egyptian art. Kem in Ancient Egyptian meant the black land, while in Hebrew Chamamun means " mystery, occult". The word alchemy could also come from the Egyptian city name Khemenu, the city of eight that was home to Tehuti, Thoth. Hermes (Mercurius) was the key figure of the Renaissance alchemic works

Alchemy over time became the science of chemistry. The laboratory processes techniques became modified to work with metals, alloys and their properties. Alcohol in its original distillation was seen for its healing qualities (Benedictine) and its ability to extract herbal and plant essences, found in modern flower remedies. Yet chemistry's roots lie in Descartes mechanical ideas of matter which led to taking things apart to understand them (an ego/dualistic view) rather than seeing how parts fit the whole (a unified holographic view). Thus the aim of chemistry is not the perfection of matter but its analysis, while true alchemy was about not understanding matter- but going beyond it.

Alchemy, and its Hermetic symbolism- can be found all over the world. It was alchemy, as much as the Corpus Hermeticum, that fueled the

Renaissance. Some famous alchemists: Albertus Magus, Roger Bacon, Thomas Aquinas, Jakob Boheme, Paracelsus, Michael Maier (author of the famous Atalanta Fugiens), Robert Fludd, Thomas Vaughan, Marsiglio Ficino and HC Aggripa. A famous modern alchemist was Carl Jung who brought alchemy into the psychological realm. He had a 7 year breakdown, his relationship with Toni Wolf (his Sorror Mystica?) who took him to the depths of his own psyche to grasp the "collective unconsciousness" of humanity. His writings and findings come from his direct work of alchemy on himself. In 1925, French chemist Jean-Julien Champagne claimed that the secrets of alchemy were encoded in the carvings found at Notre Dame, Amiens and Chartres. The castle I found to have the most alchemic symbolism in it, especially the ceiling of the great banquet hall, is Frederiksborg Slot in Hillerod Denmark.

The art was mostly passed by word of mouth. When placed into texts, it was always written in symbolic language, that of the laboratory- including fire, cauldrons, puffers and blowers, flasks, metals etc. Many became convinced that this art was indeed a physical laboratory process, and spent years around scientific instruments trying to obtain the changing of metals into gold. Of course, this was all symbolic. The flask that was being worked in was the alchemist himself, and what was happening was a deep examining of each and every layer of consciousness, to be burned in the alchemic fire, until the next layer could be found and also burned. The work was all internal, symbolized to hide the process from those except for the serious. the time period many of the texts were written was a time of religious persecution, and anyone deemed to not be following the direct teachings of Jesus or Mohamed were subject to torture and death- thus the current religion of the area was weaved into a scientific symbolic setting that would keep the alchemist safe from external pressure.

The texts were also written as they were, because of the difficulty the alchemists faced in expressing their understanding in words, and the fact that while the illustrations would give some pointers as to how to proceed- no one could really understand without doing the work themselves. Dream-like, they are images from the unconscious, yet they play on our conscious and the depth of our being. Some key symbology was the seven planets: moon (silver), Mercury (quicksilver), Venus (copper), Sun (gold), Mars (iron), Jupiter (tin), Saturn (lead). Also are the Old King (old state of consciousness), Sol (sun, sulpher, male), Luna (moon, quicksilver, female), mercurius (Mercury, Hermes, agent, androgynous bisexual principle), Lady Alchymia (spirit of alchemy, initiator), Alchemist, Soror Mystica or Frates Mysterium (Mystical sister or Secret Brother, the alchemists companion in the work).

The fundamental aim of alchemy was the production of the Philosopher's Stone, also known as the elixir or tincture- which was said to come from the first thing worked on called the Lesser Stone (or the Prima Materia). It was the formation of the Philosopher's Stone that would turn a base metal into gold. Of course, the stone was not a stone, and the gold was not actually gold. Lastly in this part is advice being given by a famous alchemist to the novice, "In the first place, let him carry on his operations with great secrecy in order that no scornful or scurrilous person may know of them, for nothing discourages the beginner so much as the mockery, taunts and well-meant advice of foolish outsiders. Moreover, if he does not succeed, secrecy will save him from derision; if he does succeed it will safeguard him against the persecution of greedy and cruel tyrants. In the second place, he who would succeed in the study of this Art should be preserving, industrious, learned, gentle, good-tempered, a close student, and neither discouraged or slothful; he may work in co-operation with one friend, not more, but should be able to keep his own counsel. It is also necessary that he should have a little capital to procure the necessary implements and to provide himself with food and clothing while he follows this study, so that his mind may be undistributed by care and anxiety. Above all, let him be honest, God-fearing, prayerful and holy. Being thus equipped, he should study Nature, read the books of the genuine sages who are neither impostors or jealous churls, and study them day and night.."[350]

Emerald Tablet

Every alchemist believes they are a descendant of Hermes Trismegistus, especially his Emerald Tablet, a famous text which is said to come from an inscribed tablet of emerald. The first written translation of the Emerald Tablet is in Arabic in 650 AD The Book of Balinas the Wise on Causes, and based on the writings of Apollonius. It is said to contain the sum of all knowledge, for those able to understand it. A translation is as follows:

1 In truth certainty and without doubt whatever is below is like that which is above, and whatever is above is like that which is below to accomplish the miracles of one thing. 2 First as all things proceed from One above by meditation on One alone, so are they born from this one thing by adaption. 3 It's father is the sun, and mother is the moon. The wind has carried it in its womb. It's nurse is the earth. 4 It is the father of all works of wonder in the world. 5 The power therof is perfect. 6 Separate the earth from the fire and the

---

[350] cherry 64 from Treatises of Philalethes in the Hermetic Museum byAE Waite)

subtle from the gross, softly and with great prudence. 7 It rises from earth to heaven and comes down again from heaven to earth and their acquires the power of the realties above and the realities below, and all obscurity will fly from thee.8 This is the power of all powers for it conquers everything subtle an penetrates everything solid. 9 Thus the little world is created according to the prototype of the great work. 10 From this, and in this way, marvelous applications are made. 11 For this reason I am called Hermes Trismegistus, for I possess the three parts of wisdom of the whole world. 12 Perfect is what I have said of the work of the sun.

Preperation

The preparation for the first process is about earth (first matter) and fire (first agent), the dan tien to the Taoists, and it is what we will throw the layers of self into. There is no physical battle endured by a human that can compare to the struggle that will take place in his own mind, but to try to help symbolize it, the whole mental task has been alegorized as a combat. Some of these examples are a long journey partly on water and land, ascent of a high mountain, combat to the death with a monster (Minataur), journey of maze or labyrinth, Herculean tasks, voyage to a lost island. The preparation begins with the Prima Materia sometimes called the First Matter, literally the material which is to be transformed. All who wrote about it concealed its true nature, but has been commented as, "it has no price or value…whoever comes across it hardly troubles to pick it up, it is thrown away by both poor and rich". The Gloria Mundi said, "it is familiar to young and old. It is found in the country, in the village in the town, in all things created by God; yet it is despised by all. Rich and poor handle it every day. It is cast into the streets by servant maids. Children play with it. No one prizes it, yet next to the human soul, it is the most beautiful thing upon the earth and has the power to pull down kings and princes."

It is often pictured as a journey into a mine (a place that is under the surface and dark). The Prima Materia lies very deep. It is the most physical and mysterious thing there is. At its deepest and purist level it is the original ground, the original state. It is called the "Hidden Stone", a stone that through the process becomes the Philosopher's Stone, transmuting and transforming. Sometimes the Prima Materia is shown as a pair of poisonous serpents or fire-breathing dragons to emphasize its bisexual nature and to warn other alchemists that it could be dangerous for mortals to handle the heavenly earth. In the beginning we must make a real commitment. The size of the choice we make is always related to the size of the purpose involved and always releases energy. We chose, and then the thing begins to move, quicken and flow. Say yes and release the energy. We touch on this experience every time we come into stillness or the need for space to be alone (be it a day or a weak). The secret fire is a hidden fire, and inner heat. It is the invisible energy that sustains matter. The alchemists had many versions of fire to use. Swords or arrows are fire as the symbolic power of thought. The secret fire is a warm nourishing heat, it is the heavenly inspiration that burns steadily within a person, in its highest sense, equivalent of Thoth, who speaks only the true Word. Alchemical figures often show a man turning around, with the motto Solve et Coagula (Solve and Fix) This means to turn the mental powers inwards, and act that will dissolve the thoughts and fix them on stillness.

The Prima Materia was said to be made of the 4 elements, and is mentioned in the Emerald Tablet along with the Sun and Moon. The 4 elements as I have mentioned are the four directions of teaching, which connect in the body as the four proteins of the DNA. The Sun is 0, Moon is 1 (the Yin and Yang that makes up the computer program of reality.) These four elements were called the lower elements (and also can be found in the four lower chakras), but alchemists spoke of the three heavenly elements (which could be perhaps the pineal, pituitary and the thyroid.

Lastly was talk of a strange substance they called Vitarol- an acid that putrefies and kills, and appears as vinegar given to Jesus on the cross. Vitriol comes from the first letters of the phrase, 'Vista Interiora Terrae Rectificando Invenies Occultum Lapidum (Visit the interior of the earth; purifying and rectify the hidden stone). The earth is the conscious mind, the stone is the lesser stone that once transformed will become the philosopher's stone. Thus whenever there is call for destruction, one brings their Vitriol- vising the interior of the earth' purify and rectify the hidden stone.

NIGREDO

Alchemy begins in darkness with the Prima Materia and goes further down into the night, a dark night. It is known as the black earth and becomes Nigurm Nigrius Nigro (a black blacker than black). It is a full-scale descent into the mind. One could say there can be no birth or rebirth, without first death. The essence of Nigredo is a blackening, why it is also referred to as **Calcinatio** (to burn) or **Mortificatio** (to Mortify). It takes place under Saturn (associated with lead -intellect), and is shown in illustration destroying the old king. Other images of Nigredo include **Capet Mortum** (dead head), the green lion (instinctual force of nature who swallows the sun- ego), ravens (birds of death) a desert of human skeletons/coffins. The smell is of decomposition and rotting which has to do with what is literally happening in the flask [body]. The main single image is of Sol Niger, a black sun shining over a lifeless land.

Consciousness descends towards the unconscious (what we can not see, the black). In illustrations, the king is not aware what is about to descend on him.

The Prima Materia is pulverized and rolled like dough, mixed with fire and then moistened with dew (blood, sweat and tears of the work). This compost is then placed in the "philosophic egg' which refers to consciousness, awareness. This egg must be kept warm, but not hot, thus the need for the fire to be restrained from overheating or the work will be lost. At this time also comes the male or female companion (sun/moon). Called the The Sorror or Frater Mystica, they may exist outwardly in the form of another person, or inwardly as part of oneself. Her first gesture is a raising of a finger to her lips (silence). It is a gesture of secrecy, and an invitation not to speak but to feel. The term means mystical sister, and weather inwardly our outwardly is unusually charged and helps bring us to a taboo area because it feels incestuous. What is important is that it taking unconsciousness to a taboo area, even while at the same time seeming uncannily familiar.

Sol meets Luna and they make love (in illustrations they are crowned and making love on water). It is **Conjunctio** (joining of opposites). It is referred to as "opening the matrix." It is uninhibited and lusty. It happens the way it happens and is not neat and tidy. Its function is to open, and is sometimes referred to as the 'gross work' before the 'lesser work'.This love-making confronts the deep pain and regressive trauma, returning to childhood and the deepest level of primal being. From this connection and pain, a new individual is born, Mercurius (Hermes), emerging both innocent and experienced. Often depicted with wings and holding caduceus with a masculine body and a feminine soul. When Sol and Luna made love, they tied the golden thread together, but this is a complete process not a nice stop over point, and soon it begins to fall dark. The gold turns to black, for it was not a pure gold. They begin to fight, and wound each other until they finally kill each other, in order to decompose and arrive at a new better form. This is the reverse of Conjunction, and the shadow side erupts. The male and female are at odds, polarized. Now everything between them point toward death, yet death will lead to a rebirth. They are black fire. Sometimes they are pictured as lion and ass clawing at each other, or a dragon and griffin chasing each other. Just as the metal has to be broken down before it can be transmuted, its original form must be destroyed. Sol and Luna die. This death leads to decay, Negrum Nigris Nigro. We are at the primal level, formless origin, sun in total eclipse, blackness, our minds have gone and it can last for months.

Finally, there is a drying out, an evaporation that leaves a residue of precious ash, out of which the Mercury of the wise appears. This is another Mercury, not the union of opposites, but this is destruction. It is a birth like a calm after a storm, brought forth after depression, breakdown and despair. Thus Nigredo is movement from solid (base metal) to liquid (liquid blackness) to ash (residue) to free the soul from its paralysis, thus free the soul from ego, so it reverts to its original unconditioned state with the ash (soul). The Nigredo is a head-on, ego-shattering experience, and can bring about a fear of continuing while it is going on. There is a fear that this darkness can overtake one. Resistance to continue is understandable. Many report the feeling of "nothing they can do." As hard as you try to get out, it is as if a counterforce is driving you back in. These reactions came from the Old King (or Queen) in us who wants to stay on the throne and rule. This experience keeps us in, and thus is important. There is no way out, only in. Try to hide or distract ourselves from it, but it will just continue much longer and be more painfully than it needs to be.

So we go in, and this is where breakdown, or what feels like breakdown can take place. The unconscious is both light and dark. It holds all we suppress in the name of sanity. If there is no flask to keep it in, it comes out as murder or even suicide. Even a feeling of lead poisoning with the face becoming grey can occur. Often bad dreams are had but on deeper investigation, there is light awaiting from all of this. Nigredo is about the death of the ego, illusion, all the light we have ever known. But it will always lead to the place where new light can shine.

SOLUTIO

"Burn your books and whiten your latten." Alchemic Saying

"Go to the woman who washes her sheets and do the same as she does." Atalanta Fugiens

In solutio we come to whiteness, beyond the blackness. The essence is a whitening called **Ablutio** (washing) and **Baptisma** (Baptism by fire and water). It is here where Luna, the feminine principle comes into its own. For some this was the goal of the whole work, while others went farther. Images here are the King at sea drowning, and calling for help; or in a sauna sweating, or a pelican touching his breast (tugging at his heart). There are images of purity: unicorn, virgins (one who was at one in herself). We see repeated washing (congealing and redissolving of matter inside as the fire intensifies). Watery images: baptism, womb, fountain, pool all come in. Dreams, the realm of Neptune are exceedingly relevant here. Purification is not an easy process. It is pain, tears, grief which have been bottled up for years. Hurt places need to be healed, for only then can our hearts awaken. The white rose is shown blossoming which symbolizes spiritualized romantic love, and white stone. The white stone is opposed to the black sun, where the light becomes solid due to repeated distillation. It is a pure spiritual substance.

The water of wisdom is seen as tears. The whiteness gets stronger with repeated cleansing, and continues until the white is strong and clear. As the heat is turned up from repeated **distillation**, there appears a residue, the stone. As the stone emerges, a beautiful thing happens, colours appear and is referred to as **Cauda Pavonis**, or peacock's tail. It opens out representing whiteness and healing, until the blackness is gone. Some see it as Christ or the heart opening. Now appearing is a new vital residue, the **Red King** signifying rebirth. Sol and Luna, who are dead, get rained on. There is an awakening or healing. They are no longer the same people, even if they outwardly appear so. This is the whitening. For a time, their sexual activity is suppressed. It is the heart that must be opened and this takes time. We see repeated washing (congealing and redissolving of matter inside as the fire intensifies). An often quoted piece of advice is "burn your books and whiten your latten". This is meant that the answer will not be found in any book, but in the seekers own mind. The latten a word play on Latona the woman of revelation and alternate Isis. Thus the stage must be brought to the white stage of the mind.

Luna is key with her softening, communication, listening and feeling. Sol is dissolving as Luna purifies. In terms of alchemy (sulpher and quicksilver), in Nigredo they fight. But now he dissolves in her, so his heart or anger dissolve in her coolness. Solutio is pictured as a woman washing sheets, humbling and grounding work that we might not rather do. It strips us of our defenses and takes on a lot of water. As they alternate, the fire and water change each other. Water becomes more fiery and fire becomes more watery. A blending is taking place. We will come to a new appreciation of love, a quality of loving that is 100% more feeling and alive. Thus we have a **White Queen**, the new woman to go with the Red King.

Be careful, solutio has its shadow side, superbia in Greek, of being too good or special for this world, or stuck in a fantasy or chemical unreality. Don't stay in the womb too long, we must actually be reborn after all.

COAGALATIO

Coagalatio, the beginning of the "great work" is a new kind of dying. Its essence is yellowing, it is also known as **Citrinitas** (where we get the word citrine and citrus fruit which are yellow/orange with a tart taste full of energy). Yellow is a creative energy, vibrant and alive like the day. It is at this stage that the masculine principle re-emerges. After baring the soul in Solutio, there is a reclothing in earth that parallels the Egyptian rites of Osiris, where the initiate is reclothed as he emerges from darkness. And takes place under the signs of Venus (earth, love and embodied woman) and Mars (sword, redness of fire and strength). Venus and Mars are Luna and Sol at a higher, more expanded level. There are eight phases of Coagulation.: four in Venus (**Seperatio, Fermentatio, Illuminatio, Nutrimentum**), and four in Mars (**Fixatio, Multiplicatio, Reunificatio, Sublimatio**).

A constant image of Coagulation is the alchemist scattering what he has gained in Solutio. On the foliate earth in the form of fermenting gold. Foliate means "leaf-covered", suggesting autumn, a time of letting go. There is also the snake, serpens mercurialis again Mercury in his animal guise, twisting around and encircling and piercing the luner egg of Sol in the flask, clawing it until it cracks and re-forms as the sun. There are bird images of ascent that include the swan giving way to the eagle who can fly nearer to the sun. Sometimes, solar rays are shown as birds with small bows and arrows. These solar rays are rays of spirit infusing the body. There may be a rainbow, connecting heaven and earth, of dawn or sunrise…all images of solar return. Sometimes a new earth is shown, emerging like a continent from the waters of sol, at first islands in a stream then a land mass.

Sol and Luna now descend. He lies upon her and begins to fall or wind down. He is sinking to earth, as the snake slides into the flask. While this happens, Luna rises. She is now out of reach. They both are. This is Seperatio. Both are serperating, the key is for man to know it is luna that is going to call on Sol's power as a man. This is the first action of sulpher: corrosive, dissolving, and coming to matter. It clarifies essential male energy. The dying here is to create a richer fertility, similar to grain falling to earth in John 12:23, "but it dies, it bringeth forth much fruit." The earth is fertile which is why we need to enter. Sol is waking up and it is painful and slow. The medicine is the awakening of consciousness that links above and below. Then comes Nutrimentum, "feeding the raw". It is about nourishment. Sol has sunk deeper, the snake continues to break the egg. Sol is becoming black, like Nigredo, but here it is more like depression constrained by physical form. But now is a feeding, Sol feeding from the feminine. It is man awakening to his own feminine as nourishment, and feeding from the earth herself, connecting him to matter. Thus we open our hearts to the earth.

The temperature rises and we come to Fixatio, where Mars allows Sol to come into his own. In this phase mutable silver is said to acquire the consistency of gold, or gold-likeness. Consistency is a key word here, a feeling of standing our ground, literally standing in his own fire. The sense here is the need to go on, to not be held back by dwelling in a negative way on feelings or pain. Then, like a lighting flash, the snake coils, twisting with its tail in its mouth. The contents of the flask catch fire and in the blaze we have the strength of the rising sun, of rising power. Soul and spirit are beginning to come together. The snake's movements have made the egg to a golden globe. The snake now dies, it has done its work. This is Reuificatio (resurrection) phase.

We may still experience ourselves as being alone, but at this point luna comes close, as if magnetized by an invisible force. The magnetism is what Sol has achieved in himself, and she being a woman senses it without the need for speech. The stone is now becoming articulate. Sol and luna meet in blood (often pictured in a bath of blood) , thus the final phase or reddening here as a shared thing. The pelican is shown here pecking at is chest to feed her young, which are gathered at her feet lapping up the fresh blood. The alchemist must nurture its own spiritual child with his own soul by surrendering his old self. Like the blood of Christ it is a redemption through sacrifice, and what is sacrifice is the dearly held emotions and ego centered beliefs. This can be an extremely painful process. Their meeting reveals what all this work has been for, to enable a greater thing to come from them. They were enriched by separation, and now pictured together,the spirit can reach them. They make love now as the two triangles of Salomon, or the yin and yang. They return to the center. They are capable of being alone or together, "it is a special rewarding love, the love that gives and asks for nothing, and whatever comes back is pure gold"

In Coagulation there is movement first of descent, then of rising and return. It is circular in this sense, as the snake is swallowing its own tail. It prepares us for the embodiment of the spirit. The spirit is not yet here, so we are preparing the body (strengthening the flask) to hold the spirit that if not made will would otherwise shatter us. This is the longest stage of the work, as we need to be IN our body. We are trying to reclaim the original purpose of the body, to understand why we are human and do not yet have wings. Coag is about earthing, grounding. A kind of spiritualization of experience. Begin to experience what is all around you. You get a sense of being reclothed, of having everything you need right in your own physical body.)

Coagulation is the longest stage in the process, it is also the longest journey, and we can get tired of it. There is a temptation to give up, to roll over, and go to sleep. There may be a recognition of internal betrayal, which can be painful "I know what I'm supposed to do, and I hevent' been doing it."Another kind of suffering is illness, so common to this phase. For all our apparent earthiness, we are not really in touch with the earth other than to see it as a thing or to be used and abused. We are out of touch with feeling. This is a particular kind of darkness before the dawn. Then true fermentation could occur in which the dead material seems to come alive. This changed the fundamental nature of the material, in which was seen as spiritualization. The signal this is taking place is a display of rainbow colours called the peacock's tail. This rep our first glimpse into the astral realm, seeing of visions ect [psychic ability].

RUBEDO

"white always precede red."

"The work is a spiral, for we are always coming back to things that we have learned. Our experiences never forget us, but we can lose touch with them." Jay Ramsey

Rubedo is the realization of unity. It is a leap in consciousness as it is something we can not grasp with our usual mind; we have to go beyond. Thus Rubedo is the embodiment of spirit that we have come all this way for. rubedo is a reddening (as the name suggests) and it suggests assuming royal purple. Purple is another colour associated with the high spirit [crown chakra].In Rubedo everything comes together, above and below marry. There is a sense of timelessness, of time slowing down or not existing. There is an inner and outer reality. It is a dimension where everything is still alive, and is available to our expanded mind. Being centered on the Sun, Rubedo is very hot like a kiln. The images of this phase are: starry lion, red lion (with stars on pelt linking us to above), the yolk of an egg, gold lions as a symbol of spiritual and literal abundance, a garden of endless fertility, the coffin of eternal life which enacts the mystery of death and resurrection, landscapes and dreamscapes of beautiful cites and the universe. Finally there is **Ouroboros**, the great snake with its tail in its mouth signifying completion and encircling, and of course the recognition of the loop of time.

Sol and Luna again die, eaten by the green lion of Nigredo, so again we have a separation that precedes a wedding. Alchemists claim the key to the rose garden is a soul place and maybe a soul wound, yet in that wound lies the key and the 'rejected stone' that is the cornerstone of the whole building. "your heart is the wound, and your heart is the key."In the flask is a birth out of the egg. This birth is the Philosopher's Son, who is referred to as the child of the work and is the final stone. The alchemist is worried like with any birth, is there too much heat. What is born with this child? A universal or expanded quality of consciousness that is like a threshold or a doorway we need to go through so spirit can enter. Multiplication happens again. Last time it was a yellowing, now it is a reddening. The temperature is raised to the highest level here so it (the stone) can be perfected. Flames fill the whole of the flask with a beautiful light. It is a body-heat too, a complete sense of burning, and sometimes there is a light you can sense or see, showing we are alone with light and fire. The fire makes the redness permanent. This brings us to a state of being that is strangely impervious to mood swings and anything on a human level. We are less self-centered, less solely directed towards ourselves, we discover a fantastic source of energy in the heart. This source of energy is revealed as the "elixir of life."Or you might say know what the universe really is and how it works now, or perhaps can say you are living the realm of the true shaman.

The energy rises, this is where alchemy sees the resurrected body as the Corpus Glorification, the golden body. The flask begins to blaze like the sun, we pass between worlds experiencing the 'little death.' Now the alchemist raises the lid of the coffin containing himself, with soul and spirit purified. They are now meeting and marrying. Now he sees that there is a death and there is no death. He gives birth to himself as the Red King, the King that Sol has been making. Sol and Luna are at a special place: death is the wedding, love is the wedding. They both bring us to the same place. There is integration and wholeness. The longer the marrying goes on, the more awesome it becomes. At this stage one develops skills like: levitation, clairvoyance, telepathy, channeling, distant healing, miracles ect. These are magical abilities, but in alchemy they only really come at the point in which we are designed to handle them. They are gifts that come out of purity, not toys or manipulative games. They are effects of the stone. Not as it is today with people in Nigredo doing and paying anything to try to pick up as many super powers as they can in order to show off or try and manipulate the world and other people. This is true awakening of the latent power of the human being in the dreamstate, in an integrated and unified not a segregated and ego-centric way.

Sol and Luna in this union transcend all opposition. She becomes a man, and he a woman even though they outwardly remain the same. Moon and Sun blend and circulate like a current in the figure 8 that is eternity. Circles of wholeness ripple out from the stone. One is contained in the phrase "the sun and its shadow complete the work". The sun is pictured shining down on the earth, with the moon, and the shadow. The earth here is revealed as the stone and the stone is made up of sun and shadow (light and shadow). The 2nd ripple is known by the phrase squaring the circle. The symbol is a triangle meaning a unity of body/mind/spirit. The square is the 4 elements used in the process. The large circle is the stone's transforming power which changes male to female, thus without male and female there would be no stone. The 3rd ripple is the etheric body, The 4th ripple is detachment and objectivity, The 5th ripple is the Red King and the golden body, The 6th ripple is secrecy. [not only silence, but seeing the need to not speak to much to the people of the world about this.] The 7th ripple is Cosmic Man. Hermes (Mercury in Rome) is present at all stages. Inthis final stage he appears like Asclepius, holding the staff of healing the caduceus.

It is called the most ancient, secret, unknown, heavenly, natural incomprehensible, blessed sacred Stone of the Sages. It is the glorious Phoenix, the most precious of all natures. Life and health flow from the stone in the form of the Elixir. This True Medicine could restore a man of 80 to the youth of a child in 28 days [1 moon cycle]. The elixir perfected any living tissue, and was the vital force of life. There were tales of alchemists living for hundreds of years, and were usually attributed to their discovery of a kind of philosophers stone, which they transmuted from the elements of their own body. Nothing in the universe can top this stone.

The standard answer given in books is that Rubedo is the end of the work and brings us to oneness, completion and unity. And that is true, Rubedo is the awake state, awake within the dream. Yet alchemy was very clear that there was another stage past Rubedo- rarely talked about or written about- which is the state of no self.

NOTE: two interesting alchemic paintings from the middle ages/renaissance that should be examined and looked:- the painting by Daniel Mylius which is said to show the entire work within it, and which many alchemists just stared for hours at to try and soak up its wisdom; and the famous Azoth- a bearded man surrounded by rays that depict alchemy in its 7 stage configuration. Both can be found in Dennis Hauk's book *Emerald Tablet*.

APPENDIX

HERMES MYTH UNVEILED

Hermes was born in a *cave* {dark place where the inner mind is still pure and calm) on *Mount Cyllene* {mountain symbolizing the attainment of knowledge} in *Arcadia* {Greek land of plenty}. Zeus had impregnated *Maia* [Maya, illusion in Hindu] in the dead of *night* {time when the conscious mind and darkness reigns}while all the other gods *slept {inner awareness not alert}*. When *dawn* {light dispelling darkness} broke Hermes was amazingly *born {awakened to his inner being}*. Maia wrapped him in *swaddling bands {new outer garment symbolizing the internal change}*, then she fell back to *sleep*. Hermes however, *squirmed free* {escaped the mind} and ran off to Thessaly. There his *brother* {fellow initiate} Apollo grazed *cattle [power]*.. Hermes *stole* [used trickery] a number of the heard and drove them back to Greece. He kept them in a small *grotto* near the city of Pylos, then *covered his tracks* [kept his internal work secret from the rest of the world.]

Before returning to the cave, he killed a *tortoise* and removed the entrails, using the intestines if a cow stolen from Apollo and the hollow tortoise shell he made the first *lyre*. When he returned to the cave, he *wrapped himself back* in the swaddling clothes. Apollo finally realized that he had been robbed and protested to Maia that it was Hermes, but she saw him sleeping in his bands that she could not believe it was him. All-powerful Zeus however had been watching the whole thing and acknowledged the theft and that Hermes should return the stolen cattle. An agreement was reached, but while it was happening, Hermes played his lyre and the *music enchanted* Apollo, and he offered to let Hermes keep the cattle in exchange for the lyre. Appolo later became the *grandmaster* of the instrument.

Hermes while *watching over his heard* [keeping track of the thoughts of his mind] also invented the pan-pipe and the flute. Apollo also wanted these instruments, so Hermes bartered with him and received a *golden wand* [gold representing transformation and wisdom]which became his famous staff (in some stories it is Zeus who gives him the golden wand.) Later Hermes liberated Io from Hera's servant the hundred-headed *giant* [egoic mind that seems huge and unable to be defeated]Argus. Hermes played his flute and the *giant slept [was occupied on its own self-importance]*, so Hermes *cut off the giant's head* [destroyed and killed the egoic mind] and released Io. Hera was so taken by her former giant servant that she placed his hundred eyes and put them on a *peacock's tail* [alchemic symbol of transformation].

193: The mysteries of reality await your investigation

BIBLIOGRAPHY

Adams, Marsham *The Book of the Master* (Putnam: London 1898)

Agrippa, HC *Three Books of Occult Magic*

Alder, Vera Stanley *Finding the Third Eye* (Samuel Wiser: New York 1970)

Alford, Alan F. *Gods of the New Millennium* (Hodder and Stoughton: London 1996)

Amoran, Hugh and Kelley, David *The Ancient Alphabet and the Ancient Calendar Signs* (Daily Press: California, 1969)

Anderson, Hans Christian *Complete Fairy Tales* (Doubleday: New York 1974)

Andrews, Ted *How to See and Read the Aura* (Llewellyn: St. Paul 1993)

-----*Animal Speak* (Llewellym 2000)

Angelo, Jack *Hands on Healing* (Healing Arts Press: Rochester 1994)

Arewa, Caroline Shula *Opening to Spirit* (Thorsons: London 1998)

Arguelles, Jose *The Mayan Factor* (Bear and Co: Sante Fe 1987)

Arrien Angeles *Four Fold Way* (Harper: San Francisco 1993)

Ashby, Muata *Egyptian Yoga* (Cruzian Mystic Books: Miami 1997)

-----*Egyptian Proverbs* (Cruzian Mystic Books: Miami 1996)

-----*The Ausarian Resurrection* (Cruzian Mystic Books: Miami 1998)

-----*Initiation into Egyptian Yoga* (Cruzian Mystic Books: Miami 2002)

-----*Kemetic Diet* (Cruzian Mystic Books: Miami 2000)

-----*Meditation* (Cruzian Mystic Books: Miami 1998)

-----*Properties of Matter* (Cruzian Mystic Books: Miami 1998)

-----*Yoga of Wisdom* (Cruzian Mystic Books: Miami 1998)

Baigent, Michael *Ancient Traces* (Penguin Press: New York 1998)

Baigent, Michael and Leigh, Richard *The Elixir and the Stone* (Penguin Books: London 1997)

Batchelor, Martine *Way of Zen* (Thorson's 2001)

Bauval, Robert and Gilbert, Adrian *The Orion Mystery* (Doubleday Canada: Toronto 1994)

Berendt, Joachim-Ernst *The World is Sound* (Destiny: Vermont 1987)

Berrin, Kathleen and Pasztory, Ester editors *Teotihuacan: Art from the Valley of the Gods* (Thames and Hudson: London 1993)

Bettelheim, Bruno *The Uses of Enchantment* (Alfred A Knopf: New York 1989)

Bhagavad Gita

Bierhorst, John *The Mythology of Mexico and Central America* (William Morrow and Company: New York 1990)

Black Elk, Wallace and Lyon, William *Black Elk: the Sacred Way of a Lakota* (Harper and Row: San Francisco 1990)

Bly, John *Iron John* (Vintage Books 1992)

Boksabazen, John *Zen Meditation in Plain English* (Wisdom Publications 2002)

Brennan, Barbara Ann *Light Emerging* (Bantam: Toronto 1993)

Brennan, JH *The Astral Projection Workbook* (Sterling Publishing Co: New York 1990)

Brennan, Martin *The Hidden Power* (Bear and Co: Santa Fe 1998)

Brown, Tom Jr *The Vision* (Berkley 1998)

-----*The Quest* (Berkley 1992)

Brunton, Paul *In Search of Ancient Egypt* (Samuel Weiser: Maine 1936)

Budge, EA Wallis *The Egyptian Book of the Dead* (Dover Publications: New York reprint1967)

-----*Osiris and the Egyptian Resurrection* (Putnam and Sons: London 1899)

-----*The Egyptian Heaven and Hell* (Dover Publication: London reprint 1996)

-----*Egyptian Ideas of the Future Life* (Putnam and Sons: London 1899)

-----*Egyptian Magic* (Dover Publications: New York reprint 1970)

-----*An Ancient Egyptian Reading Book* (Dover: New York 1993 reprint)

-----*Egyptian Language: Lessons in Egyptian Hieroglyphs* (Dorsett Press: New York 1993 reprint)

Carnie, LV *Chi Gung* (Llewellyn Press: St. Paul 1997)

Carradine, David *Introduction to Chi Kung* (Owl Books: New York 1997)

Carse, James *Finite and Infinite Games* (Ballantine: NY 1986)

Castaneda, Carlos *The Teachings of Don Juan* (Simon and Schuster: New York 1973)

-----*A Separate Reality* (Simon and Schuster: New York 1971)

-----*Journey to Ixtlan* (Simon and Schuster: New York 1973)

-----*Tales of Power* (Touchstone: New York 1974)

-----*Eagle's Gift* (Simon and Schuster: New York 1981)

-----*Fire From Within* (Simon and Schuster: New York 1984)

-----*The Power of Silence* (Simon and Schuster: New York 1987)

-----*The Art of Dreaming* (Harper Collins: New York 1993)

-----*The Active Side of Infinity* (Harper Collins: New York 1998)

Chandler, Wayne B *Ancient Future* (Black Classic Press: New York 1999)

Chaney, Farlyne and Messick, William *Kundalini and the Third Eye* (Astara: California 1980)

Cheun, Master Lam Kam *Chi Kung* (Broadway Books: NY 1999)

-----*The Way of Energy* (Gaia Books: NY 1991)

Chia, Mantak *Iron Shirt Chi Kung I* (Healing Tao Press: New York 1986)

-----*Awaken the Healing Light of the Tao* (Healing Tao Press: New York 1995)

Christian, Paul *History of Magic* (The Citadel Press: New York 1969)

Clark, Rosemary *Sacred Tradition in Ancient Egypt* (Llewellyn 2000)

Cleary, Thomas (translator) *Further Teachings of Lao-Tzu* (Shambhala: Boston 1991)

Clulee, Nicholas H *John Dee's Natural Philosophy* (Routledge: New York 1988)

Coe, Michael *The Maya* (Thames and Hudson: New York 1993)

Coelho, Paulo *The Alchemist* (Harper: San Francisco 1993)

Copenhaver, Brian (translator) *Hermetica* (Cambridge University Press 1982)

Cousineau, Paul *Art of Pilgrimage* (Conari Press: Berkeley 1998)

Crowley, Brian and Esther *Words of Power* (Llewellyn: St. Paul 1992)

Curl, James *The Egyptian Revival* (George Allen and Unwin: London 1982)

Devereaux, Paul *Revisioning the Earth* (Fireside Books: New York 1996)

Davidovits, Joseph *The Pyramids- An Enigma Solved* (Dorsett Press: New York 1988)

Douglas, Nik *Spiritual Sex* (Pocket Books: New York 1997)

Dunn, Christopher *Giza Power Plant* (Bear and Co: 1998)

Dumas, Alan editor *Cinderella a Casebook* (University of Wisconsin Press 1982)

Edwards, IES *The Pyramids of Egypt* (Pelican 1976)

Faulkner RO *Ancient Egyptian Coffin Texts* (Aris and Phillips: England 1973)

-----*Ancient Egyptian Pyramid Texts* (Aris and Phillips: England 1969)

-----*Book of the Dead* (Chronicle 1998)

Feinstein, David *The Mythic Path* (Putnam Press: New York 1997)

Feuerstein, Georg and Kak, Subbash and Frawley, David *In Search of the Cradle of Civilization* (Quest Books: Illinois 1994)

Ficino, Marsiglio *The Book of Life*

Fielder, Rick and Taylor, Peggy and Weyler, Rex *Chop Wood, Carry Water* (Penguin: New York 1984)

Fix, Wm R *Pyramid Oddysey* (Mayflower Books: NY 1978)

Fowden, Garth *The Egyptian Hermes* (Princeton University Press: New Jersey 1986)

Frantzis, BK *Opening the Energy Gates of Your Body* (New Age Books, Berkeley 1993)

Freke, Timothy and Gandy, Peter *The Hermetica* (Piatkus Press: London 1997)

-----*The Complete Guide to World Mysticism* (Piatkus Press: London 1997)

-----*Jesus Mysteries* (Thorsons: London 1999)

Freke, Timothy *Encyclopedia of Spirituality* (Sterling: London, 1999)

Friedel, David and Schele, Linda and Parker, Joy *Maya Cosmos* (William and Morrow: New York 1993)

Furlong, David *Keys to the Temple* (Judy Piatkus Limited: London 1997)

Gadalla, Moustafa *The Historical Deception* (Bastet Press: Erie 1996)

-----*Egyptian Cosmology* (Bastet Press: Erie 1997)

Gardner-Gordon, Joy *Pocket Guide to the Chakras* (Crossing Press: California 1998)

Gettings, Fred *The Secret Lore of the Cat* (Grafton Books: London 1989)

Gilbert, Adrian *Signs in the Sky* (Bantam: Toronto 2000)

Gilbert, Adrian and Cotterell, Maurice *The Maya Prophecies* (Harper Collins 1996)

Gilchrist, Cherry *The Elements of Alchemy* (Element: New York 1991)

Giles, Cynthia *The Tarot* (Paragon: New York 1992)

Goethe *Faust* (translation by Barker Fairley) (University of Toronto Press 1970)

Gold, Dave *After the Absolute* (1998)

Gold, Peter *Navajo and Tibetan Sacred Wisdom* (Inner Traditions: Vermont 1994)

Goldman, Johnathon *Healing Sounds* (Element Inc: Rockport Mass 1992)

Goodchild, Peter *Raven Tales* (Chicago Review Press: Chicago 1991)

Gray, Eden *The Tarot Revealed* (Signet: New York 1960)

Grimm Brothers *Complete Grimms Fairy Tales* (Partheon Books, New York 1944)

Gyatso, Kelsang *Meaningful to Behold* (Tharpa Books: London 1994)

Haikun, trans Waddell, Norman *Wild Ivy* (Shambalah 1997)

Hall, Manly *Freemasonry of the Ancient Egyptians* (Philosophers Press: Los Angeles 1937)

Hancock, Graham *Fingerprints of the Gods* (Doubleday Canada: Toronto 1995)

-----*Heaven's Mirror* (Doubleday Canada: Toronto 1998)

-----*TLC Videos*

Hancock, Graham and Bauval, Robert *The Message of the Sphinx: Keeper of the Genesis* (Doubleday Canada: Toronto 1996)

Hapgood, Charles *Maps of the Ancient Sea Kings* (Dutton: New York 1979)

Harner, Michael *The Way of the Shaman* (Harper and Row: San Francisco 1990)

Hauck, Dennis William *Emerald Tablet* (Penguin: New York 1999)

Herotodus *The Histories* (Penguin Classics: New York 1978)

Hoffman, William H *Robert Fludd and the End of the Renaissance* (Routledge: New York 1988)

Hope, Murry *The Sirius Connection* (Element: Rockport Mass. 1996)

Hornung, Erik *The Valley of the Kings* (Timker Publishers: NY 1990)

Houston, Jean *The Passion of Osiris and Isis* (Ballentyne: New York 1995)

Hunter, Bruce C *A Guide to Ancient Maya Ruins* (U of Oklahoma Press: 1974)

Imbrie, John *Ice Ages* (Short Hills: New Jersey 1979)

Ingerman, Sandra *Soul Retrieval (*Harper Collins: New York 1991)

Ions, Veronica *Egyptian Mythology* (Peter Bedrick Books: New York 1968)

Ivimy, John *The Sphinx and the Megaliths* (Harper and Row Publishers: New York1975)

James, George *Stolen Legacy* (Julian Richardson Associates: San Francisco 1998, original 1954)

James, Julian *The Origin of the Consciousness in the Breakdown of the Bicameral Mind* (Houghton Miffin: New York 1976)

Jenkins, John Major *Maya Cosmogenesis 2012* (Bear and Co: 1998)

Jochaman, YAA *Abu Simbel to Ghizeh Guidebook* (self published)

Kalakaua *Legends and Myths of Hawaii* (Charles E Tuttle and Co: Vermont 1992)

Kapleau, Phillip *Three Pillars of Zen* (Anchor Books 1980)

King, Serge-Kahili *Urban Shaman* (Simon and Schuster: New York 1990)

Kornfield, Jack *After the Ecstacy, the Laundry* (Bantam: NY 2001

-----*A Path With Heart* (Bantam: NY 1999)

Lamy, Lucy *Egyptian Mysteries* (Crossroad: New York 1981)

Landsberg, Alan *In Search of Ancient Mysteries* (Bantam Books: New York 1974)

Laviolette, Paul *Beyond the Big Bang* (Park St. Press: Rochester, 1995)

Leedom, Tim ed. *The Book Your Church Doesn't Want You to Read* (Kendall Hunt: Iowa 1993)

LeGuin, Ursula Lao *Tzu- Tao Te Ching* (Shambhala Publishing: Boston 1997)

Lewis-Paulson, Genevieve *Kundalini and the Chakras* (Llewellyn Publishing 1995)

Lichteim, Miriam *Ancient Egyptian Literature* (U of California Press: Berkeley 1975)

Lindgren CE and Baltz, Jennifer *Aura Awareness* (Blue Dolphin Publishing: California 1997)

Linn, Denise *Quest: A Guide for Creating Your Vision Quest* (Ballantyne Books: New York 1997)

-----*Past Lives, Present Dreams* (Piatkus: London 1994)

Lucius Apuleius *The Golden Ass* (Noonday Press: New York 1951, translation by Robert Graves)

Macritchie, James *The Chi Kung Way* (Thorsons: London 1997)

Maier, Michael *Atalanta Fugiens* trans J. Goodwin (Phanes Press: Grand Rapids 1989)

Mails, Thomas *The Hopi Survival Kit* (Council Oak Books 1997)

Mares, Theun *Return of the Warriors* (Lionheart: S.Africa 1995)

-----*Cry of the Eagle* (Lionheart: S.Africa 1995)

----*Mists of the Dragon Lore* (Lionheart: S.Africa 1995)

Martin, Fran *Raven* (Harper and Row: New York 1951)

Masters, Robert *The Goddess Sekhmet* (Amity House, New York 1988)

Matos, Eduardo *Teotihuacan: The City of the Gods* (Rizzoli: New York 1990)

Matthews, Andrew *Follow Your Heart* (Penguin Books: New York 1997)

Matthews, Caitlin and John *The Western Way vol 1-2* (Arkana: London 1985-86)

Mcdonald, John *Tomb of Nefertiti* (J Paul Getty Trust: LA 1996)

McGaa, Ed *Rainbow Tribe* (Harper: San Francisco 1992)

McKenna, Jed *Spiritual Enlightenment, The Damndest Thing* (Wisefool Press 2002)

--- *Spiritually Incorrect Enlightenment* (Wisefool Press 2004)

Mead, GRS *Thrice Greatest Hermes* (Harper and Row: San Francisco 1987)

Meadow, Kenneth *The Medicine Way* (Element: Rockport 1990)

Medicine Eagle, Brooke *Buffalo Woman* Comes Singing (Ballantyne Books 1991)

Medicine Hawk, Grey Cat *American Indian Ceremonies* (Inner Light Publications 1990)

Mehler, Steven *Land of Osiris* (Adventures 2000)

Melody *Love is in the Earth* (Earth Love 1991)

Mercati, Maria *The Handbook of Chinese Massage* (Healing Arts Press, Vermont 1997)

Meyer, Marvin *The Sacred Teachings of Jesus* (Random House: New York 1994)

Mickoski, Howard *Twelve Months of Mystical Wisdom* (Tehuti Press: Calgary 2000)

Millman, Dan *No Ordinary Moments* (HJ Kramer Inc: Tiburon Cal, 1992)

-----*Everyday Enlightenment* (Warner Books: New York 1998)

-----*Way of the Peaceful Warrior* (HJ Kramer 1984)

Mindel, Arnold *The Shaman's Body* (Harper: San Francisco 1993)

Mitchell, John *New View Over Atlantis* (Harper and Row: San Francisco 1969)

Moondance, Wolf *Rainbow Medicine* (Sterling Publishing: New York 1994)

-----*Spirit Medicine* (Sterling Publishing: New York 1995)

Morenz, Siegfried *Egyptian Religion* (Cornell University Press: Ithaca 1973)

Moss, Robert *Conscious Dreaming* (Crown Trade Paperbacks: New York 1990)

Naydler, Jeremy *Temple of the Cosmos* (Inner Traditions: Rochester Vermont 1996)

Nelson, Mary *Beyond Fear* (Council Oak Books 1997)

Noone, Richard *5/5/2000* (Harmony Books: New York 1986)

Norville, Roy *Hermes Unveiled* (Ashgrove Press: London 1986)

Ogilvy, James *Living Without a Goal* (Currency: New York 1995)

Osho *Book of Secrets* (St Martins: New York 1974)

Osman, Ahmed *Out of Egypt* (Arrow: London 1998)

Ozaniec, Naomi *The Elements of Egyptian Wisdom* (Element: London 1994)

Palos, Stephen *The Chinese Art of Healing* (Bantam Books: Toronto 1972)

Papus, translated by AP Morton *Tarot of the Bohemians* (Studio Editions: London 1994)

Patrick, Richard *Egyptian Mythology* (Octopus Books: London 1972)

Pennick, Nigel *Mazes and Labyrinths* (Robert Hale: London 1990)

Perl, Lila *Mummies Tombs and Treasures* (Scholastic Inc: New York 1987)

Perrault *Perrault's Classic Fairy Tales* (Meridith Press: New York 1982)

Peterson, Robert *Out of Body Experience* (Hampton Roads: Publishing 1997)

Piankoff, Alexandre *Tomb of Rameses VI* Pantheon Books: New York 1954)

-----*Pyramid Texts of Unas* (Princeton University Press: Princeton 1968)

Pila of Hawaii *The Secrets and Mysteries of Hawaii* (Health Communications 1995)

Plato *Republic* (Translated by Francis MacDonald) (Oxford University Press 1941)

Prechtel, Martin *Secrets of the Talking Jaguar* (Tarcher: NY 1999)

Ramsey, Jay *Alchemy* (Thorsons: San Francisco 1997)

Regula, De Tracy *The Mysteries of Isis* (Llewellyn: St Paul 1999)

Redfield, James *The Celestine Prophecy* (Warner Books: New York 1994)

Reid, Bill *Raven Steals the Light* (Douglas and McIntyre: Vancouver 1984)

Reymond, EAE *The Mythical Origin of the Egyptian Temple* (Manchester U Press: Manchester 1969)

Requena, Yves *Chi Kung: The Chinese Art of Mastering Energy* (Healing Arts Press: Vermont 1995)

Robbins, James *Build a Better Buddha* (Nicolas Hayes 2003)

Robinson, James *Nag Hammadi Library* (Harper: San Francisco 1990)

Rohl, David *A Test of Time* (Century Books: London 1993)

Rola, Stanislas Klossowski De *Alchemy, the Secret Art* (Avon: New York 1973)

Roland, Paul *Revelations: Wisdom of the Ages* (Ulysses Press: Berkley 1995)

Rose, Richard *Psychology of the Observer* (TAT Foundation 1972)

Ruiz, Don Miguel *The Four Agreements* (Amber Allen 1997)

-----*Mastery of Love* (Amber Allen 1999)

Sanchez, Victor *Toltecs of the New Millennium* (Bear and Co: New Mexico 1996)

-----*Teachings of Don Carlos* (Bear and Co: New Mexico 1990)

-----*Toltec Path to Recapitulation* (Bear and Co: New Mexico 1998)

Santillana, Giorgiode, Dechand, Hertha Von *Hamlet's Mill* (Gambit Inc: Boston 1969)

Schneider, Michael *A Beginner's Guide to Constructing the Universe* (Harper Perennial: New York 1995)

Schul, Bill and Pettit, Ed *The Secret Power of Pyramids* (Faucett Publications: Connecticut 1975)

Schuler, Gerald and Betty *Egyptian Magic* (Llewellyn Publications: St. Paul 1994)

Schwaller de Lubicz, Isha *The Opening of the Way* (Inner Traditions International: Rochester 1979)

-----*Her-Bak* (Hodder and Stoughtan: London 1954)

Schwaller de Lubicz, RA *Sacred Science* (Inner Traditions: New York 1961)

Scott, Gini Graham *Shamanism for Everyone* (Whitford Press: Atglen Pa 1988)

Scott, Joseph and Lenore *Egyptian Hieroglyphs for Everyone* (Funk and Wagnall's: New York 1968)

Sejourne, Laurette *Burning Water* (Thames and Hudson: New York 1957)

Shantideva *Guide to the Boddhisattva's Way of Life* (Tharpa Books: London 2002)

Sharmon-Burke, Juliet *Understanding the Tarot* (Stoddart: Toronto 1998)

Sierra, Judy *Cinderella* (Oryx Press: Phoenix 1992)

Siliotti, Alberto *The Valley of the Kings* (Geodia: Italy 2000)

Silverman, David *Ancient Egypt* (DBP: London 1997)

Simon, Sylvie *The Tarot* (Promotional Reprint Company: Toronto 1991)

Sitchin, Zechariah *When Time Began* (Avon Books: New York 1993)

Speeth, Kathleen *The Gurdjieff Work* (Putnam: New York 1989)

Stevens, Jose and Lena *Secrets of Shamanism* (Avon Books: New York 1988)

Sunbear *Dancing With the Wheel* (Simon and Schuster: New York 1971)

Suares, Carlo *Cipher of the Genesis* (Shambhala Publishing: Colorado 1970)

Sullivan, William *The Secrets of the Incas* (Three Rivers Press: New York 1996)

Suzuki, DT *The Zen Koan* (Charles E Tuttle: Boston 1994)

Talbot, Michael *Holographic Universe* (Harper: NY 1991)

Taizan, Maizumi Roshi *Appreciate Your Life* (Shambhala 2002)

Temple, Robert *Cyrstal Sun*

Tompkins, Peter *Mysteries of the Great Pyramid* (Harper and Row Publishing: New York 1972)

-----*Mysteries of the Mexican Pyramids* (Harper and Row Publishing: New York 1976)

Tolle, Eckhart *Power of Now* (Namaste 1998)

Tse, Michael *Qi Gong for Health and Vitality* (Piatkus: London 1995)

Underhill, Evelyn *Mysticism* (EP Dutton: New York 1961)

Unknown, *Egyptian Mysteries* (Samuel Weiser Inc: Maine 1981)

Waite, Arthur Edward *Alchemists Through the Ages* (Kessinger Publishing: Montana)

-----*The Hermetic Museum* (Samuel Weiser: Maine reprint 1999)

Weeks, Kent *The Valley of the Kings* (Friedman: NY 2001)

-----*The Illustrated Guide to Luxor* (American University in Cairo Press: 2005)

Wesselman, Hank *Spiritwalker* (Bantam Books: New York 1995)

West, John Anthony *Serpent in the Sky* (Theosophical Publishing: Wheaton 1993)

-----*Traveler's Key to Ancient Egypt* (Quest Books: Wheaton 1985)

-----*The Case for Astrology* (Arkana, NY 1992)

Whitaker, Kay *Reluctant Shaman* (Harper: SF 1991)

Wilkinson, Richard *Symbol and Magic in Egyptian Art* (Thames and Hudson: London 1994)

Willard, Terry *Encyclopedia of Herbs* (Key Porter Books: Toronto 2002)

Wilson, Colin *From Atlantis to the Sphinx* (Virgin Books: London 1996)

Wilson, Hillary *Understanding Hieroglyphs* (Passport Books, Illinois 1995)

Wong, Eva *Taoism* (Shambhala Press: Boston 1997)

Yates, FA *The Rosicrucian Enlightenment* (Routledge and Paul Keegan: Boston 1972)

Ancient Egypt (National Geographic Society: Washington 1978)

Glory of Ancient Egypt (Kraus Reprint Co: New York 1988)

Monuments of Civilization- the Maya (Madison and Squires Press: New York 1973)

Mysteries of the Ancient Americas (Readers Digest Books: New York 1986)

The New Larousse Encyclopedia of Mythology (Hamlyn Publishing: London 1959)

PHOTO CREDITS

All Photos and illustrations are private photos from the author except for the following credits, all which have been released to the public domain. They are also used in the book as per "fair use" guidelines for scholarly works.

3, 8, 18, 19, 26, 51, 56, 75, 76, 77, 78, 87, 89, 129, 151, 158, 160, 162, 163, 164, 169, 171, 174, 177, 178 (Jon Bodsworth, egyptarchive.co.uk)

20 (Golden Meadows), 49 (820PX), 58 (Kabuto 7), 66 (Jonas S), 69 (Neith Saber), 79 and 107 (A Parrott), 82 (Paul Cowie), 83 (Bryan Dickson), 85 (Josi Fresco), 94 (Gorgo), 96 (Jack Hynes), 99 and 102 (Madman), 111 (MB2), 116 and 118 (George and Audrey Delange), 117 (Elazihu Situ), 124 (Bjorn Christian Torrissen), 130 and 131 (M Mass), 172 (Gerbil) 182 (en.User.Kieff), 183 (B Mamlin)

39, 54, 68, 184 (Are from an unknown source)

185 photo from crystalinks website, likely origin National Geographic

23, 64, 81, 84, 91, 92, 93, 103, 106, 181, 186, 187, 191, 192 (are considered to have no copyright and have no presenter listed)

ABOUT THE AUTHOR

Howdie Mickoski, is an historian who has spent over 20 years studying Egyptian mysticism, comparative world religion, shamanic and hermetic teachings as well as books of a spiritual nature. He began his Egyptian study through standard history and archaeology, but quickly found that the data and conclusions being presented- did not in any way match that stone monuments that still exit on site in the world. He went looking for new ways to explain what these ancient sites are, and why and how they were put there. As he reached out to those who claimed to be in the know- mystics, healers etc. He found more things built for business to sell seminars, retreats, dvds and healing packages. The more he searched, the less he found out there to be of valuable help to anyone. Yet the few honest people he did find, mainly Native Indian Medicine people still living on the reserve, provided the greatest insight and hope. It is an ongoing quest.

Sharing what one has found, in a simple, open and available way has been something he has been striving to do for many years.

Should you be interested on more information, have suggestions to this work, or just want to say hello- please visit and click the contact button:

www.egyptian-wisdom-revealed.com